The Carolina Rhetoric

Edited by LEE BAUKNIGHT
with GERALD JACKSON

As a textbook publisher, we are faced with enormous environmental issues due to the large amount of paper contained in our print products. Since our inception in 2002, we have worked diligently to be as eco-friendly as possible.

Our "green" initiatives include:

Electronic Products
We deliver products in non-paper form whenever possible. This includes pdf downloadables, flash drives, & CD's.

Electronic Samples
We use a new electronic sampling system, called Xample. Instructor samples are sent via a personalized web page that links to pdf downloads.

FSC Certified Printers
All of our Printers are certified by the Forest Service Council which promotes environmentally and socially responsible management of the world's forests. This program allows consumer groups, individual consumers and businesses to work together hand in hand to promote responsible use of the world's forests as a renewable and sustainable resource.

Recycled Paper
Almost all of our products are printed on a minimum of 10-30% post consumer waste recycled paper.

Support of Green Causes
When we do print, we donate a portion of our revenue to Green causes. Listed below are a few of the organizations that have received donations from Fountainhead Press. We welcome your feedback and suggestions for contributions, as we are always searching for worthy initiatives.
    Rainforest 2 Reef
    Environmental Working Group

Cover and text designer: Ellie Moore

Copyright © 2015 Fountainhead Press

All rights reserved. No part of this book may be reproduced or utilized in any form or by any means, electronic or mechanical, including photocopying and recording, or by any informational storage and retrieval system, without written permission from the publisher.
Books may be purchased for educational purposes.

For information, please call or write:
    1-800-586-0330
    Fountainhead Press
    Southlake, TX 76092

Web site: www.fountainheadpress.com
E-mail: customerservice@fountainheadpress.com

ISBN: 978-1-59871-955-0

Printed in the United States of America

Contents

Introduction 1
"National Information Literacy Awareness Month Proclamation," President Barack Obama   4
"Drowning, Surfing and Surviving," James Gleick   5

PART I: PRAXIS: A Brief Rhetoric

Chapter 1: Practicing Rhetoric   1
Through Praxis, Theory Becomes Action   2
Become Part of the Academic Conversation   3
Collaborative Groups Help Students Enter the Academic Conversation   5
Rhetoric and Argument   6
Rhetoric and Power   9
Selected Definitions of Rhetoric   10
Visual Map of Meanings for the Word "Rhetoric"   11
Rhetorical Argument   12
Why Study Rhetoric?   21
Encountering Visual Rhetoric   27
Rhetorical Arguments Stand the Test of Time   28

Chapter 2: Responding Rhetorically   33
Thinking Critically, Reading Rhetorically   34
Rhetoric's Visual Heritage and Impact   38
The Rhetorical Triangle   40
Ways of Reading Rhetorically   47

Close Reading of a Text   56
Responding to Oral and Visual Media   59
Responding to Visual Rhetoric   63
Interaction between Texts and Images   66

Chapter 3: Analyzing Rhetorically   73
Discover the Kairos–The Opening for Argument   74
Aristotle's Persuasive Appeals   82
Arguments from Logos   83
Deductive Reasoning   86
Inductive Reasoning   87
Logical Fallacies   88
Arguments from Pathos   93
Arguments from Ethos   98
Combining Ethos, Pathos, and Logos   102
Photos Heighten Ethos or Pathos   103

Chapter 4: Inventing Rhetorically   109
Aristotle's Classification of Rhetoric   110
The Five Canons of Rhetoric   111
The Modern Writing Process Overview   112
Stasis Theory Identifies Critical Point in Controversy   115
Using Stasis Questions   118
Stasis Theory and Kairos   120
Other Invention Strategies   133
Expand Your Personal Knowledge through Observation   138

Chapter 5: Writing Rhetorically   145
Through Writing, Enter the Conversation   146
Organize Your Essay   146
Write a Thesis Statement   148
Compose an Introduction   149

Combine Your Ideas with Support from Source Materials   155
Support Your Thesis   156
Answer Opposing Arguments   156
Vary Your Strategies or Patterns of Development   157
Write a Conclusion   157
Consider Elements of Page Design   158
Including Images in Your Projects: Copyright Implications   160

Chapter 6: Revising Rhetorically   169
Revision Is Part of the Writing Process   170
Begin Revision by Rereading   170
Qualities of Effective Writing   171
Remember to Proofread   179
Gain Feedback by Peer Editing   185
Independent Reviewing   186
Sample Questions for Peer Review   186

Chapter 7: Researching Rhetorically   197
Research Provides Inartistic Proofs   198
You Do Research Every Day   199
Primary and Secondary Research   200
Secondary Research Sources Expected by Professors   205
Employ Computerized Library Catalogs   208
Utilize Electronic Library Resources   209
Find Internet Information   210
Evaluate Sources   213
Avoid Plagiarism   215

Appendix A: Citing Sources   225
Evolving Formats of Document Citation   226
When You Have a Choice of Electronic Source
    Format, Choose a PDF   227

MLA Style   228
APA Style   234

Praxis Works Cited   243

PART II: The Carolina Rhetoric

Chapter 8: Reading Response   249

"Am I My Brother's Keeper?" Elie Wiesel
   and Richard D. Heffner   250
"Advice to Graduates," George Saunders   259
"Is American Nonviolence Possible?" Todd May   263
"Reclaim Your Mind from Technology," Alex
   Soojung-Kim Pang   249
"Ripping Off Young America: The College-
   Loan Scandal," Matt Taibbi   277
"The Path Forward," Students for
   Educational Debt Reform   286
"The United States of Apathy," Howard
   Steven Friedman   299
"Teaching against Idiocy," Walter C. Parker   301
"Fashioning Justice for Bangladesh," Robert Kuttner   312
"How to Be More than a Mindful
   Consumer," Annie Leonard   319

Chapter 9: Reading Consent   325

"The 'Yes' Means 'Yes' World," Jake New   326
"'Yes' Is Better Than 'No,'" Michael Kimmel
   and Gloria Steinem   330
"What Affirmative Consent Looks
   Like," Charlie Glickman   332

Contents

"Why All Colleges Should Adopt Affirmative Consent," Kelli Gulite 336
"In a Mattress, a Lever for Art and Political Protest," Roberta Smith 340
"A Feminist Says 'No' to Yes-Means-Yes," Roz Galtz 343
"Remarks by the President at 'It's On Us' Campaign Rollout," President Barack Obama 346
"'Yes Means Yes'": A New Approach to Sexual Assault Prevention and Positive Sexuality Promotion," Dawn E. LaFrance, Meika Loe, and Scott C. Brown 350

Chapter 10: Reading.com 365

"The Third Replicator," Susan Blackmore 366
"Trolls," Jaron Lanier 371
"Hooked on Technology, and Paying a Price," Matt Richtel 381
"Is Google Making Us Stupid?" Nicholas Carr 389
"Google Makes Us All Dumber: The Neuroscience of Search Engines," Ian Leslie "Get Smarter," Jamais Cascio 397
"Get Smarter" Jamais Cascio 401
"Liking Is for Cowards. Go for What Hurts." Jonathan Franzen 410
"Even in Real Life, There Were Screens Between Us," Caitlin Dewey 415

Chapter 11: Reading Eating 419

"The Pleasures of Eating," Wendell Berry 420
"The Culinary Seasons of My Childhood," Jessica B. Harris 426
"A Healthy Constitution," Alice Waters 434
Angelica Kitchen Menu 436
"Attention Whole Food Shoppers," Robert Paarlberg 443

"Fear Factories: The Case for Compassionate
   Conservatism—for Animals," Matthew Scully   451

"Organic Foods: Do Eco-Friendly Attitudes Predict
   Eco-Friendly Behaviors?" Molly J. Dahm, Aurelia
   V. Samonte, and Amy R. Shows   463

"Bad Food? Tax It," Mark Bittman   476

"Declare Your Independence," Joel Salatin   483

Chapter 12: Reading Humor   495

"Laughter and the Brain," Richard Restak   496

"The Social Value of Humor," John Morreall   504

"One Professor's Attempt to Explain Every
   Joke Ever," Joel Warner   510

"Review: The Mead Spiral 100 College-Ruled
   Notebook," Zach Miller   516

"Mommie Fearest," Heather Havrilesky   519

"Wake Up Geek Culture. It's Time to Die." Patton Oswald   523

"Chicken in the Henhouse," David Sedaris   529

"Nation Shudders at Large Block of
   Uninterrupted Text," *The Onion*   536

Appendix B: English 102   539

The Carolina Rhetoric Credits   559

 Introduction

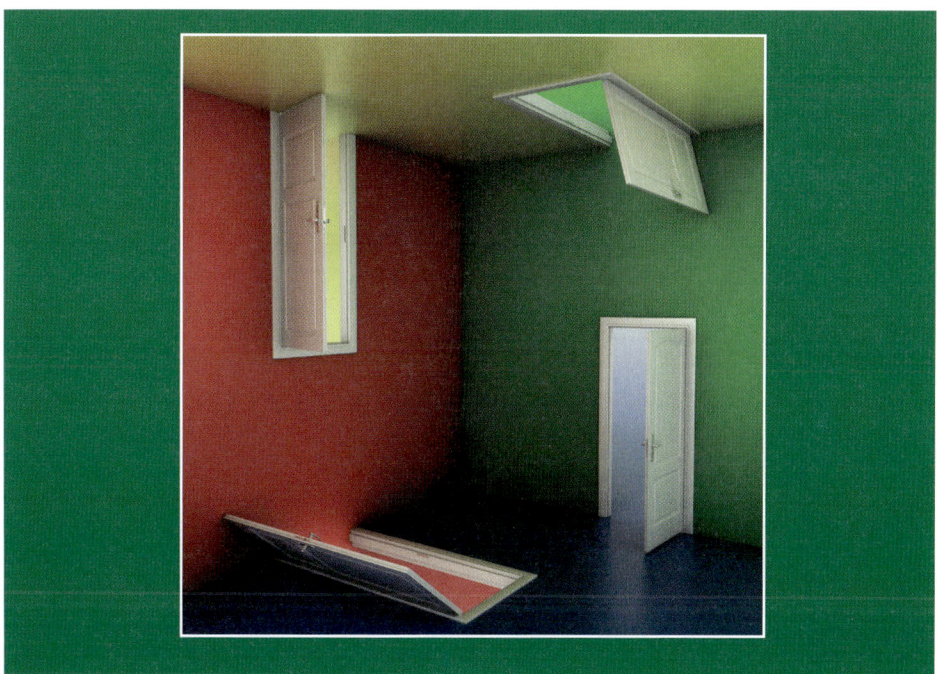

You live in an information age. No news there, right? You've probably been hearing this for several years, in a variety of ways—as part of the wave of information that supposedly washes over you each day, every day—and it would be hard to find someone to argue the point. You'll find far less agreement, however, about the nature of this age of information—about what exactly all of this information is and where it comes from; about how to best find information and assess its value; and about what you do with the information you encounter (or that encounters you) and what it does to you. These concerns, long at the heart of the English 102 curriculum at USC, are part of what has come to be called "information literacy."

You've probably heard the term "information literacy," or something like it, before. The Association of College and Research Libraries (ACRL) defines it as the ability to find, manage, critically evaluate, and make use of information. For years in USC's English 101 and 102 classes (and probably in your high school), these have been called "research skills." And as the name has evolved along with the astronomical growth of available information, the central message has become even more important. To use President Obama's words, from his proclamation below: "Rather than merely possessing data, we must also learn the skills necessary to acquire, collate, and evaluate information for any situation." Journalist and author James Gleick, in the essay "Drowning, Surfing and Surviving," puts it this way:

"Choosing the genuine information requires work." And The Carolina Rhetoric—as part of the English 102 curriculum—is designed to help you manage that work as you develop your writing skills.

With that in mind, we hope that you'll take a close look at the image above and think about the implications of those four doors leading ... well, anywhere (or nowhere). We like this image as a metaphor for the possibilities of the information age: It seems like there's always somewhere else to go or something else to come. And, of course, there's no promise that whatever comes next will be worth the effort. This might seem overwhelming, but it needn't be that way. And that's the point of information literacy. Just as writing seems daunting to many people, because it is a recursive act, until they develop some confidence and skill, the creative and effective use of information is something that can be learned through diligence and practice. To that end, we have included a variety of thinking, research, and writing prompts in the Rhetoric to help you engage with the texts you'll be asked to read and—more importantly, perhaps—to help you develop your ability to efficiently and responsibly wade through the flood of information that you'll encounter so that you can find the "genuine information" you need.

As you browse through the book, you'll see that The Carolina Rhetoric consists of two parts: The first eight chapters are from a textbook titled Praxis: A Brief Rhetoric (Fountainhead Press) and are meant to provide you with a foundation of basic rhetorical concepts and terminology that will help you with the writing you'll have to do in English 102 and beyond. The second half of the book is made up of readings and writing prompts designed specifically for English 102 at the University of South Carolina. We begin, here in the Introduction, with two short texts and a few writing exercises that we hope will get you thinking about reading, writing, research, and information. The first reading is a proclamation that President Obama issued in 2009 declaring October to be National Information Literacy Awareness Month. The second is an essay by James Gleick published in April 2011 in New Scientist and based on his latest book, The Information: A History, a Theory, a Flood. Together they offer a brief but pointed introduction to information literacy as a topic and a tool. A variety of writing prompts accompany these readings (setting the pattern for the rest of the book): Some will give you a few things to think and write about before you read; others will ask you to complete specific research and writing tasks after you've completed your reading. Your teacher may ask you to complete these for homework or in class, on your own or with some of your classmates.

Good luck!

—Lee Bauknight and the English 102 team

Chapter i | **Introduction**

BEFORE YOU READ

In a paragraph or two, craft a detailed definition of "information literacy," including examples of what it means to be "information literate" and "information illiterate." Then, based on your definition, explain whether you are information literate or not. Use other sources if you need to, but make sure you credit them in your response.

NATIONAL INFORMATION LITERACY AWARENESS MONTH: A PROCLAMATION
President Barack Obama

Every day, we are inundated with vast amounts of information. A 24-hour news cycle and thousands of global television and radio networks, coupled with an immense array of online resources, have challenged our long-held perceptions of information management. Rather than merely possessing data, we must also learn the skills necessary to acquire, collate, and evaluate information for any situation. This new type of literacy also requires competency with communication technologies, including computers and mobile devices that can help in our day-to-day decision-making. National Information Literacy Awareness Month highlights the need for all Americans to be adept in the skills necessary to effectively navigate the Information Age.

Though we may know how to find the information we need, we must also know how to evaluate it. Over the past decade, we have seen a crisis of authenticity emerge. We now live in a world where anyone can publish an opinion or perspective, whether true or not, and have that opinion amplified within the information marketplace. At the same time, Americans have unprecedented access to the diverse and independent sources of information, as well as institutions such as libraries and universities, that can help separate truth from fiction and signal from noise.

Our Nation's educators and institutions of learning must be aware of—and adjust to—these new realities. In addition to the basic skills of reading, writing, and arithmetic, it is equally important that our students are given the tools required to take advantage of the information available to them. The ability to seek, find, and decipher information can be applied to countless life decisions, whether financial, medical, educational, or technical.

This month, we dedicate ourselves to increasing information literacy awareness so that all citizens understand its vital importance. An informed and educated citizenry is essential to the functioning of our modern democratic society, and I encourage educational and community institutions across the country to help Americans find and evaluate the information they seek, in all its forms.

NOW, THEREFORE, I, BARACK OBAMA, President of the United States of America, by virtue of the authority vested in me by the Constitution and the laws of the United States, do hereby proclaim October 2009 as National Information Literacy Awareness Month. I call upon the people of the United States to recognize the important role information plays in our daily lives, and appreciate the need for a greater understanding of its impact.

IN WITNESS WHEREOF, I have hereunto set my hand this first day of October, in the year of our Lord two thousand nine, and of the Independence of the United States of America the two hundred and thirty-fourth.

DROWNING, SURFING AND SURVIVING
James Gleick

A half-century ago Marshall McLuhan wrote: "We are today as far into the electric age as the Elizabethans had advanced into the typographical and mechanical age. And we are experiencing the same confusions and indecisions which they had felt when living simultaneously in two contrasted forms of society and experience." His electric age had no email, no web-surfing, no cellphones, much less Facebook and Twitter. McLuhan was mainly watching television.

We don't call it the electric age any more. We know perfectly well that we are living in the information age. But McLuhan was right: we are still experiencing "confusions and indecisions," more than ever before. There is a universally recognized metaphor for our predicament: flood. There is a sensation of drowning, of information as a rising, churning deluge. Data washes over us from above and below. One may lose the ability to impose order on the chaos of sensations. Truth seems hard to find amid a multitude of plausible fictions.

Our world is built on the science of information theory, created by engineers and mathematicians in the 1940s, but hard on the heels of information theory have come "information overload," "information glut," "information anxiety," and "information fatigue." This last was recognized by the *Oxford English Dictionary* in 2009 as a syndrome for our times: "apathy, indifference, or mental exhaustion arising from exposure to too much information, especially (in later use) stress induced by the attempt to assimilate excessive amounts of information from the media, the internet, or at work."

In 2007, the writer David Foster Wallace coined a more ominous name for this modern condition: "total noise," created by "the tsunami of available fact, context, and perspective." He talked about the sensation of drowning and also of a loss of autonomy, of personal responsibility for being informed.

Another way to speak of the anxiety is in terms of the gap between information and knowledge. A barrage of data so often fails to tell us what we need to know. Knowledge, in turn, does not guarantee enlightenment or wisdom. As T. S. Eliot asked in his pageant play *The Rock*: "Where is the wisdom we have lost in knowledge? Where is the knowledge we have lost in information?" It is an ancient observation, but it seems to bear restating as information becomes ubiquitous—and we live in a world where all bits are created equal and information is divorced from meaning.

What do you do when you have everything at last? The philosopher Daniel Dennett imagined in 1990, just before the internet made this possible, that electronic networks could upend the economics of publishing poetry. Instead of slim books, elegant specialty

Chapter i | Introduction

items marketed to connoisseurs, what if poets could publish online, instantly reaching not hundreds but millions of readers, not for tens of dollars but fractions of pennies?

That same year, the publisher Charles Chadwyck-Healey conceived of The English Poetry Full-Text Database as he walked through the British Library one day. Four years later, he had produced it, and it represented not the present or future of poetry, but the past, and not, at first, online but in four compact discs: 165,000 poems by 1250 poets spanning 13 centuries, priced at $51,000.

Readers and critics had to work out what to make of this. Not read it, surely, the way they would read a book. Delve into it, perhaps. Search it, for a word, an epigraph, a half-remember fragment. His CD-ROMs are already obsolete. All English poetry is on the network now—or if not all, some approximation thereof, and if not now, then soon.

The past folds accordion-like into the present. Different media have different event horizons: for the written word, three millennia, for recorded sound, a century and a half—and within their time frames the old become as accessible as the new. Yellowed newspapers come back to life. Under headings of "50 Years Ago" and "100 Years Ago," veteran publications recycle their archives: recipes, card-playing techniques, science, gossip, once out of print and now ready for use. Record companies rummage through their attics to release, or re-release, every scrap of music, rarities, B-sides and bootlegs. For a certain time, collectors, scholars or fans possessed their books and their records. There was a line between what they had and what they did not. For some, the music they owned (or the books, or the videos) became part of who they were.

That line fades away. Most of Sophocles's plays are lost, but those that survive are available at the touch of a button. Most of Bach's music was unknown to Beethoven; we have it all—partitas, cantatas and ringtones. It comes to us instantly, or at light speed. It is a variety of omniscience. It is what the *New Yorker* music critic Alex Ross calls the Infinite Playlist, and he sees that as a mixed blessing: "anxiety in place of fulfillment, an addictive cycle of craving and malaise. No sooner has one experience begun than the thought of what else is out there intrudes." Another reminder that information is not knowledge, and knowledge is not wisdom.

Strategies emerge for coping. There are many, but they boil down to two: filter and search. The harassed consumer of information turns to filters to separate the metal from the dross. Filters include blogs and aggregators—the choice raises issues of trust and taste. The need for filters intrudes on any thought experiment about the wonders of abundant information. When Dennett imagined his Complete Poetry Network, he saw that filters would be needed in the shape of editors and critics. When information is cheap, attention becomes expensive.

A "file" was originally a wire on which slips of paper, bills, notes and letters could be strung for preservation and reference. Then came file folders, file drawers, file cabinets, and then their electronic namesakes. The irony, in all these cases, was the same: once a piece of information is filed, it is statistically unlikely ever to be seen again by human eyes. The British mathematician and logician Augustus de Morgan knew this even in 1847. For any random book, he said, a library was no better than a waste-paper warehouse. "Take the library of the British Museum ... valuable and useful and accessible as it is: what chance has a work of being known to be there, merely because it is there? If it be wanted, it can be asked for; but to be wanted it must be known. Nobody can rummage the library."

When new information technologies alter the landscape, they bring disruption: new channels and new dams rerouting the flow of irrigation and transport. The balance between creators and consumers is upset: writers and readers, speakers and listeners. Market forces are confused; information can seem too cheap and too expensive at the same time. The old ways of organizing knowledge no longer work. Who will search, who will filter?

We will learn new ways. No deus ex machina waits in the wings; no man behind the curtain. We have no Maxwell's demon to help with our sorting. "We want the Demon, you see," wrote Stanislaw Lem in *The Cyberiad*, "to extract from the dance of atoms only information that is genuine, like mathematical theorems, fashion magazines, blueprints, historical chronicles, or a recipe for ion crumpets, or how to clean and iron a suit of asbestos, and poetry too, and scientific advice, and almanacs, and calendars, and secret documents, and everything that ever appeared in any newspaper in the Universe, and telephone books of the future."

Because omniscience is a curse. The answer to any question may arrive at the fingertips—via Google or Wikipedia or IMDb or YouTube or Epicurious or the National DNA Database or any of their natural heirs and successors—and still we wonder what we know. Choosing the genuine information requires work. Then forgetting takes even more work.

Chapter i | **Introduction**

■ WHAT?

1. Write two 250-word summaries of the Obama and Gleick texts. In the first, explain the readings to a friend in a composition class at another college. In the second, write your summary for a grandparent or another older relative. Be prepared to discuss the differences in the two summaries with your classmates and teacher.

■ WHAT ELSE? WHAT'S NEXT?

2. What else do you wish you knew about information literacy?
3. While President Obama's proclamation presents the "vast amounts of information" that inundate us every day as a challenge, James Gleick's essay takes a more ominous tone. Point to specific places in the text where Gleick expresses his concerns, either directly or through his choice of language. Then, find at least two sources that discuss information consumption and the effects the Internet is having on us in a more positive manner. Summarize these sources in a couple of paragraphs. Conclude your response by answering this question: Which of the positions you have read do you find most compelling? Why?
4. How do you think schools—from K-12 to college—should respond to Obama's and Gleick's calls for a more informed approach to information consumption?
5. Gleick ends his essay by writing: "Choosing the genuine information requires work. Then forgetting takes even more work." What do you think he means by that final sentence? What is Gleick asking us to do?

■ WHO CARES?

6. What is *New Scientist* (the journal that published Gleick's essay)? After studying its website, explain who you think reads *New Scientist*. Why do you think this?

-Part I-
PRAXIS: A Brief Rhetoric

1
PRACTICING RHETORIC

Praxis in Action

Why Rhetoric Is Important in My Writing by Elizabeth Jimenez

Rhetoric is an intangible power that has the ability to motivate and manipulate. If I master rhetoric, I know I possess the ability to move my audience toward my goal.

I communicate effectively when I gain the confidence of the audience. Influencing my class and professor is my number one goal and is done so by my ethos. My use of rhetoric is validated by my credibility in the subject I disseminate. I must possess credibility if I am to be a reputable source of information.

Once I have gained the attention of the audience, I obtain logos when I clearly and logically disseminate my thoughts. I accomplish my purpose when I prove my statements. This is done by substantiating my thoughts with supporting evidence. Many contributing factors that come into play have an influence on my argument, such as bias. If my argument is biased, this can strongly detract from my goal.

Persuasive rhetoric is not necessarily accomplished when I use too much emotion. I find if I overuse pathos, the general idea gets lost. If I want my idea to be well received, it is important for me to communicate with levelheadedness.

These elements help me to establish effective rhetoric, which is crucial as I write for different audiences in college. Rhetoric will open doors throughout my college career as I discover new ways of conveying information and opinions.

Elizabeth Jimenez writes that understanding rhetoric gives her the power to persuade an audience.

Through *Praxis*, Theory Becomes Action

The word **praxis** can be translated as "process" or "practice." Aristotle, the great Greek rhetorician, employed the term in a special way to mean practical reasoning, for which the goal was action. To be practical in the Aristotelian sense is a little different from what being practical means today. It indicates the ability to apply abstract theory to concrete situations and thus, to move from theory to action. Moreover, praxis embodies a creative element that raises it above the mundane or merely pragmatic. Therefore, "practicing rhetoric" is not practice in the sense of rehearsal. Rather, it is performing, or applying, or acting out rhetoric—taking theory and turning it into action.

So, if we understand praxis or the "practicing" part of "practicing rhetoric," what does the "rhetoric" part of the chapter title mean? In common usage, the word *argument* has a narrow definition that emphasizes heated or angry exchanges of clashing and often irreconcilable viewpoints. Moreover, sides in such arguments are limited to black and white opposites and include no shades of gray. If one person is right, then the other must be wrong.

In academia, in contrast, we argue because it causes us to examine critically our own as well as others' ideas. Argument compels us to consider conflicting claims, to evaluate evidence, and to clarify our thoughts. We know that even wise, well-intentioned people don't always agree, so we consider others' ideas respectfully. After one person presents an argument, either orally or in writing, others respond with arguments that support, modify, or contradict the original one. Then, in turn, more individuals counter with their own versions, and thus, the interchange becomes a conversation.

Academic arguments can be divided into several different categories, depending upon the extent of the writer's desire to persuade and the scope of the conversational exchange.

1. **One type of argument simply makes a point about the topic.** For example, later in this chapter you will read an article titled, "San Ysidro Shooting Survivor Lives His Dream of Being a Cop." In the article, the author describes the wounds inflicted on a young man during the McDonald's Massacre in San Ysidro in 1984 and then explains how and why this young man later became a cop. No one is likely to disagree with the writer's line of reasoning, at least not if the author offers sufficient evidence to back up the original statement that, for this man, being a cop is his dream. This article is a profile, a type of argument more often seen in magazines and newspapers than in journals.

2. **A second type of argument involves a controversial issue, and the writer's aim is to persuade the audience to change its stance on the matter.** The ideal result, for the writer, would be that members of the audience alter their positions to coincide with the writer's viewpoint. In this second type of argument, it is essential that the writer offer the complete structure of thesis, evidence, possible opposition viewpoints which are discussed and countered, and a conclusion. "The Sleepover Question," another reading in this chapter, presents this kind of argument. The author, who has conducted research in both America and Holland, argues the controversial position that if American parents would adopt more liberal attitudes toward their children's sexuality, like the parents in Holland, "the transition into adulthood need not be so painful for parents or children." A reading in Chapter 3, "Why Executions Should Be Televised," offers a more extreme version of this type of argument. Either executions are televised or they aren't, and the writer advocates that they should be.

3. **A third type of argument emphasizes multiple perspectives and viewpoints and tries to find common ground that participants can agree upon.** In Chapter 4, several readings are collected in a casebook called "The $300 House." The *Harvard Business Review* initiated a design competition intended to spark inclusive argument with the aim of gathering ideas about how to build inexpensive but adequate homes for the poor in the world's slums. "Hands Off Our Houses," one response to the competition that appears in the casebook, argues, for example, that bringing $300 houses into the slums of Mumbai is not the answer to the housing problem. In contrast, other responses posted on a website associated with the competition suggest ways the idea of the $300 house might work, while admitting enormous difficulties.

These three types of arguments represent points in a spectrum, and all persuasive texts may not neatly fit into one of the three categories. A crucial thing to remember, though, is that all arguments involve the presentation of a line of reasoning about a topic or an issue—a thesis, hypothesis, or claim—and the support of that reasoning with evidence.

Become Part of the Academic Conversation

As a student, you are expected to join academic conversations that are already in progress. How do you do that? How do you know what kind of response is appropriate? Have you ever entered a party where everyone is talking excitedly? Most likely, you paused near the doorway to get a sense of who was there and what they were discussing before you decided who to talk to and what to say. Or, have you become part of a Facebook group or a listserv discussion group? If so, you know it is a good idea to "lurk" for a while before asking questions or contributing a remark. Writing an academic paper involves a similar process. You read about a subject until you have a good grasp of the points authorities are debating. Then you find a way to integrate your own ideas about that subject with the ideas of others and create an informed contribution to the conversation.

For example, the following students' introductions to movie reviews demonstrate they not only understand the films and have interesting things to say about them; their writing also displays knowledge of what others have written about the films, whether the students agree with those evaluations or not.

- Roger Ebert claims that audience members who haven't seen the first two *Lord of the Rings* films (Peter Jackson, 2001, 2002) will likely "be adrift during the early passages of [the third] film's 200 minutes." But then again, Ebert continues, "to be adrift occasionally during this nine hour saga comes with the territory" (par. 3). Ebert, though, misses one crucial fact regarding *Lord of the Rings: The Return of the King* (2003). This third installment opens with a flashback intended to familiarize new spectators about what happened in the previous two films. Within these five minutes, the audience discovers how Gollum (Andy Serkis) came to be corrupt through the destructive power of the Ring. The viewer, therefore, will not necessarily be "adrift," as Ebert claims, since the lighting, setting, and sound in the opening of *The Return of the King* show the lighter, more peaceful world before Gollum finds the ring, compared to the darker, more sinister world thereafter.

- "It's hard to resist a satire, even when it wobbles, that insists the most unbelievable parts are the most true" (*Rolling Stone* par. 1). This is Peter Travers's overarching view of Grant Heslov's satire, *The Men Who Stare at Goats* (2009). Travers is correct here; after all, Goats's opening title card, which reads, "More of this is real than you would believe," humorously teases the viewer that some of the film's most "unbelievable parts" will, in fact, offer the most truth. We experience this via Bill Wilson's (Ewan McGregor) interview of an ex "psy-ops" soldier, when Wilson's life spirals out of control, and all the other farfetched actions presenting "reality." But again, it is the film's opening—specifically, its setting, camera

Chapter 1 | **Practicing Rhetoric**

movements and angles, dialogue, effects, and ambient noise—that sets the foundation for an unbelievably realistic satire.*

In both of these introductions, the students quote reviews by professional film critics and respond to the critics' opinions. Moreover, the students continue their arguments by using the critics' ideas as springboards for their own arguments. These two short examples indicate these students have learned how to counter positions advocated by authorities without losing their own voices. If the rest of their essays continue as they have begun, the students will have written essays to which others can reply, thus continuing the conversation. Later in this textbook, you will have your own chance to enter the conversation of film reviews by reviewing a favorite movie of your own.

Collaborative Groups Help Students Enter the Academic Conversation

Likely, your writing class will include collaborative group work as part of the mix of activities, along with lecture, class discussion, and in-class writing. You may wonder why there is so much talk in a writing class, which is a good question. Use of collaborative groups is based on extensive research, which shows that students who work in small groups as part of their courses tend to learn more and retain the knowledge longer than students who are not asked to work in groups. Also, research shows students who participate in collaborative group work generally are more satisfied with the course. Groups give students a chance to apply knowledge they have learned and provide a change of pace from lectures or other class activities. There are several types of groups, and your class may include one or all of them:

- Informal, one-time pairs or groups. After presenting some material, your instructor may ask you to turn to the person next to you and discuss the topic or answer a question.

- Ongoing small classroom groups. Usually, these groups work together for a significant part of the semester, and your instructor may assign roles to members of the group such as recorder, facilitator, editor, and spokesperson. Often, the roles will rotate, so that everyone has a chance to try out each job. Your instructor may give you a job description for each role or train the class in the tasks for each role.

---

* Kelli Marshall. "Entering a Conversation, Teaching the Academic Essay," *Unmuzzled Thoughts about Teaching and Pop Culture*, October 23, 2010, http://kellimarshall.net/unmuzzledthoughts/teaching/academic-essay/. Accessed August 30, 2011.

- **Task groups.** These groups are formed to write a report, complete a project, or do some other task together. These groups meet several times, often outside of class. The products of these groups are usually graded, and your instructor will often require members to rate each other on their performance.

- **Peer editing groups.** When you have completed a draft of an essay or other text, your instructor may ask you to exchange papers in pairs or within small groups. You will be asked to read your classmate's paper carefully and make comments, either on a peer editing form or on the paper itself. Likewise, your classmate will read and make comments on your paper. Then, when you receive your paper back, you can make revisions based on your classmate's comments.

An added benefit to the use of collaborative groups in writing classes is that students can help each other figure out what the ongoing conversation is for a particular topic or issue before writing about it. Also, groups provide a forum where students can practice making comments that are part of that conversation.

Rhetoric and Argument

The structure of an argument—introduction (including a thesis), supporting evidence, counterarguments, and conclusion—will be familiar to you from previous English classes. What you may not realize is that ancient Greeks developed this argumentative structure out of necessity. Their democratic system of government required that citizens be able to speak persuasively in public, as there were no attorneys or professional politicians. Ancient Greeks called their persuasive strategies rhetoric, and rhetoric became the primary means of education of the elite youth in Athens.

Rhetoric, like argument, is a word that has both a popular meaning and an academic meaning. You have probably heard someone say of a politician's speech, "Oh, that's just rhetoric," meaning the politician's words are empty verbiage or hot air. The politician is attempting to sound impressive while saying nothing that has real meaning. Or perhaps the politician is making promises that listeners believe he or she has no intention of keeping. Politicians who engage in verbal deception often succeed only in acquiring the reputation of dishonesty.

In the field of rhetoric and composition today, rhetoric has a much different meaning. Though definitions vary somewhat from one practitioner to another, rhetoric generally means the study and use of persuasive communication (or argument), a meaning that traces its roots back to the original use of the term by ancient Greeks. Rhetoric, in the form of oratory, was essential to the Greeks, as they used it to resolve disputes in the law courts and to promote political action in the Assembly.

Are We All Greeks?

As Americans, we owe an immense debt to ancient Greek civilization. Our laws, our democratic form of government, our literature, and our art have their roots in ancient Athens. Earlier generations of Americans and Western Europeans, who often studied Latin and Greek, may have had a clearer understanding of the direct connections of our culture to Athens of the 4th and 5th centuries BCE. Indeed, the English poet Percy Bysshe Shelley famously said, "We are all Greeks" because of the essential influence of ancient Greek culture upon Western civilization. However, even translated into 21st century American English, the linkage is still there.

Something quite amazing happened in Athens, around 500 BCE. Instead of being invaded by a foreign country who appointed a puppet ruler or experiencing a coup in which a strong man seized power, the people peaceably chose to put in place a direct democracy. Attica was not the only city-state to have a democracy, but it was the most successful. During the golden age of Greece, from roughly 500 BCE to 300 BCE, art, architecture, and literature thrived.

Direct or radical democracy meant all male citizens of Attica over the age of 20 could vote in the Assembly, the policy-making body of the city-state. They did not elect senators or representatives as we do today. Each of these men *voted directly*. Moreover, they could settle differences with fellow citizens by suing in the law courts. Out of 250,000 to 300,000 residents in Attica, some 30,000 were citizens. Amazingly, it was not unusual for 10,000 of these eligible men to vote in the Assembly. The law courts had juries of 500 or more. Imagine trying to speak to an audience of 10,000 people without modern loudspeakers. Even with the wonderful acoustics in Greek theatres, it would have been a challenge.

Ordinary citizens were required to speak in the Assembly or the courts to promote laws or defend themselves from lawsuits, as there were no attorneys or professional politicians. Certainly, speaking before such large audiences necessitated special skills acquired only through extensive training and practice. Many sought out teachers to help them learn how to speak persuasively, and, indeed, training in rhetoric became the primary method of education for the elite young men of Athens. A few women were also educated in rhetoric, but they were in the minority.

The earliest teachers of verbal persuasive skills we now call rhetoric were Sophists who migrated from Sicily and other Greek states. Some of their viewpoints were curiously modern—for example, that knowledge is relative and that pure truth does not exist. However, they became known for teaching their pupils to persuade an audience to think whatever they wanted them to believe. Sophists such as Gorgias themselves often presented entertainment speeches during which they would argue, on the spur of the moment, on any topic raised by the audience, just to show they were able to construct effective arguments on any subject.

The term rhetoric comes from the Greek word *rhetorike*, which Plato coined as a criticism of the Sophists, claiming the Sophists' rhetoric could be employed to manipulate the masses for good or ill, and that rhetoricians used it irresponsibly. Ironically, Plato demonstrates excellent rhetorical techniques himself when he condemns rhetoric and argues that only the elite who are educated in philosophy are suited to rule, not the rhetoricians. Aristotle, Plato's student, took a more moderate viewpoint toward rhetoric. Indeed, he was the first philosopher to classify rhetoric as a tool for practical debate with general audiences. His book *On Rhetoric* (though it was probably lecture notes possibly combined with student responses, rather than a manuscript intended for publication) is the single most important text that establishes rhetoric as a system of persuasive communication.

Athens, even in its glory days, seethed with controversy and bickering over the many inefficiencies of democracy. Men trained in rhetoric executed two coups, the Tyranny of the Four Hundred in 411 BCE and the Tyranny of the Thirty in 404 BCE, neither of which was an improvement; after each coup, democracy returned. Moreover, Athenians fought wars with Persia (the Battle of Marathon in 490 BCE and the Battle of Thermopylae in 480 BCE) and Sparta (the Peloponnesian War in 431–404 BCE and the Corinthian War of 395–387 BCE). Finally, the armies of Philip II of Macedonia defeated Athens at the Battle of Chaeronea in 338 BCE, ending Athenian independence. Despite coups and wars, democracy remained in place in Athens for nearly 200 years.

If Americans might be called Greeks because our country is based on Greek traditions, this is not to say that rhetoric appears in all cultures. True, one might say that all civilizations have some sort of persuasive negotiation process; but profound differences exist between cultures in terms of what verbal strategies are persuasive. Indeed, disparity in expectations and the actions of individuals and groups from different traditions can be a cause of strife.

Rhetoric and Power

Aristotle defined rhetoric as "the faculty of discovering, in a given instance, the available means of persuasion," which we might paraphrase as the power to see the means of persuasion available in any given situation. Each part of this definition is important. Rhetoric is power; the person who is able to speak eloquently, choosing the most suitable arguments about a topic for a specific audience in a particular situation, is the person most likely to persuade. In both Greece and Rome, the primary use of rhetoric was oratory—persuasion through public speaking. However, the texts of many famous speeches were recorded and studied as models by students, and prominent rhetoricians wrote treatises and handbooks for teaching rhetoric. To Greeks and Romans, a person who could use rhetoric effectively was a person of influence and power because he could persuade his audience to action. The effective orator could win court cases; the effective orator could influence the passage or failure of laws; the effective orator could send a nation to war or negotiate peace.

Skill with rhetoric has conveyed power through the ages, though in our contemporary world, rhetoric is often displayed in written text such as a book, newspaper or magazine article, or scientific report, rather than presented as a speech. Persuasive communication also can be expressed visually, as an illustration that accompanies a text or a cartoon that conveys its own message. Indeed, in our highly visual society, with television, movies, video games, and the Internet, images can often persuade more powerfully than words alone.

Using rhetoric effectively means being able to interpret the rhetoric we are presented with in our everyday lives. Knowledge of persuasive communication or rhetoric empowers us to present our views and persuade others to modify their ideas. Through changes in ideas, rhetoric leads to action. Through changes in actions, rhetoric affects society.

Selected Definitions of Rhetoric

Aristotle, 350 BCE—*Rhetoric is "the faculty of discovering, in a given instance, the available means of persuasion."*

Cicero, 90 BCE—*Rhetoric is "speech designed to persuade" and "eloquence based on the rules of art."*

Quintilian, 95 CE—*Rhetoric is "the science of speaking well."*

Augustine of Hippo, ca. 426 CE—*Rhetoric is "the art of persuading people to accept something, whether it is true or false."*

Anonymous, ca. 1490–1495—*Rhetoric is "the science which refreshes the hungry, renders the mute articulate, makes the blind see, and teaches one to avoid every lingual ineptitude."*

Heinrich Cornelius Agrippa, 1531—*"To confess the truth, it is generally granted that the entire discipline of rhetoric from start to finish is nothing other than an art of flattery, adulation, and, as some say more audaciously, lying, in that, if it cannot persuade others through the truth of the case, it does so by means of deceitful speech."*

Hoyt Hudson, 1923—*"In this sense, plainly, the man who speaks most persuasively uses the most, or certainly the best, rhetoric; and the man whom we censure for inflation of style and strained effects is suffering not from too much rhetoric, but from a lack of it."*

I. A. Richards, 1936—*"Rhetoric, I shall urge, should be a study of misunderstanding and its remedies."*

Sister Miriam Joseph, 1937—*Rhetoric is "the art of communicating thought from one mind to another, the adaptation of language to circumstance."*

Kenneth Burke, 1950—*"[T]he basic function of rhetoric [is] the use of words by human agents to form attitudes or to induce actions in other human agents."*

Gerard A. Hauser, 2002—*"Rhetoric, as an area of study, is concerned with how humans use symbols, especially language, to reach agreement that permits coordinated effort of some sort."*

Chapter 1 | **Practicing Rhetoric**

Activity 1.1 Historical Usage of the Word "Rhetoric"

Read through the list of historical definitions of the word "rhetoric" on the previous page, and choose one that you find interesting. In a discussion, compare your chosen definition with those of your classmates.

Activity 1.2 Contemporary Usage of the Word "Rhetoric"

Find at least two recent but different examples involving use of the word "rhetoric." For example, search your local newspaper for an example of how the word "rhetoric" is being used. A search of the *Dallas Morning News* for the word "rhetoric" led to a story about citizen efforts to clean up a neglected area of town: "He now hopes for help to finally fill the gap between rhetoric and reality." Or ask a friend, fellow employee, or a family member to tell you what the word "rhetoric" means and write down what they say. Discuss your examples in your small group and present the best ones to the class.

Visual Map of Meanings for the Word "Rhetoric"

The word map for the word "rhetoric" shown in figure 1.1 has branches for different meanings of the word, with some branches splitting again to display subtle subsets of connotation. It was created by a website, Visual Thesaurus (www.visualthesaurus.com), which computes visual word maps for any word inputted in its search box. The idea is that words lead to branches that lead to more words, inspiring users to think of language in new ways.

At the Visual Thesaurus site, if you place your cursor over one of the circles connecting the branches, a small box will pop up that defines that connection. One of these connection boxes is visible. Notice it says, "using language effectively to please or persuade." This is the branch of the visual map that is closest to the meaning of "rhetoric" as used in this book. The other branches illustrate other contemporary uses of the word.

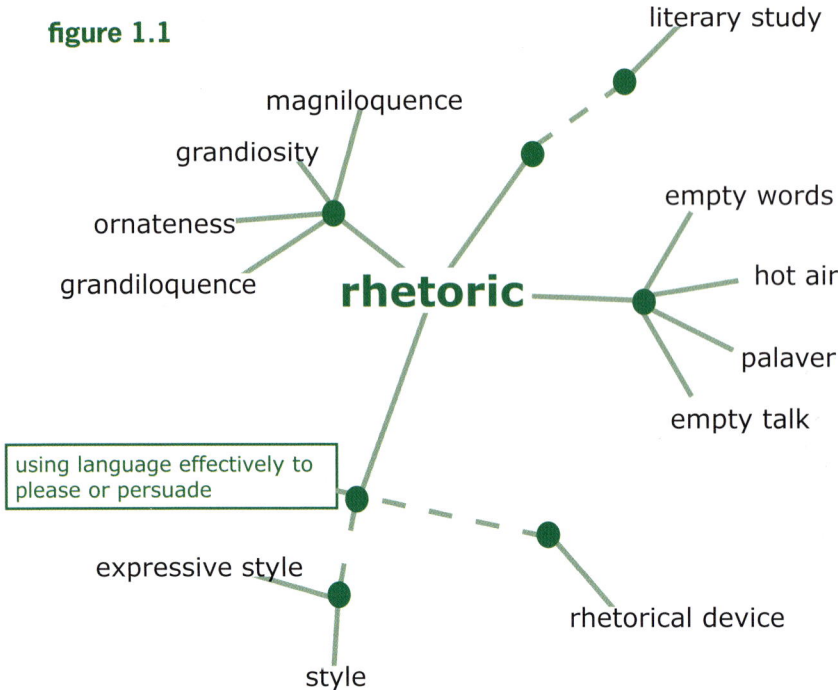

figure 1.1

Activity 1.3 Explore the Visual Map of the Word "Rhetoric"

In your small group, choose one of the five branches of words in the visual map of the word "rhetoric." Go to one or more good dictionaries and explore the meanings of the words in that branch. A good place to start would be the *Oxford English Dictionary*, which your college library may offer online. The *OED* offers intricate analyses of the histories of word meanings. Report to the class what you find out about the words on your particular branch.

Rhetorical Argument

Often, in our culture, the word "argument" is taken to mean a disagreement or even a fight, with raised voices, rash words, and hurt feelings. We have the perception of an argument as something that has victory and defeat, winners and losers. Argument, in the sense of a **rhetorical argument**, however, means the carefully crafted presentation of a viewpoint or position on a topic and the giving of thoughts, ideas, and opinions along with reasons for their support. The persuasive strength of an argument rests upon the rhetorical skills of the rhetor (the speaker or the writer) in utilizing the tools of language to persuade a particular audience.

Aristotle identified three appeals (see figure 1.2) or three ways to persuade an audience, and we are still using these today, though often without using the Greek terms to identify the means of persuasion:

Ethos—The rhetor convinces an audience by means of his character or credibility. In oratory, the speaker projects an air of confidence and authority. In writing, ethos is conveyed by the qualifications of the writer or the authorities that are cited and also by the quality of the writing.

Pathos—The rhetor persuades by playing upon the listener's (or reader's) emotions. He or she may refer to children, death, disaster, injustice, or other topics that arouse pity, fear, or other emotions.

Logos—The rhetor persuades by the use of reasoning and evidence. Arguments based on logos employ deductive or inductive reasoning.

figure 1.2

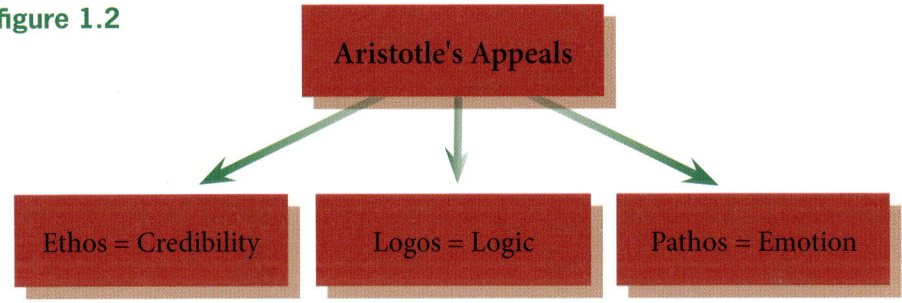

Although a good argument will contain at least traces of all three appeals, skilled rhetors analyze their audiences to determine which of the three would be most persuasive to that particular audience. Then, they construct arguments that emphasize that particular appeal.

In addition, a knowledgeable rhetor considers the time, place, audience, topic, and other aspects of the occasion for writing or speaking to determine the **kairos**, or opportune moment of the composition (see figure 1.3). This factor or critical moment both provides and limits opportunities for appeals suitable to that moment. For example, someone giving a commencement address has certain opportunities and constraints. Likewise, an attorney writing a last-minute appeal for someone on death row has a very different set of options.

figure 1.3

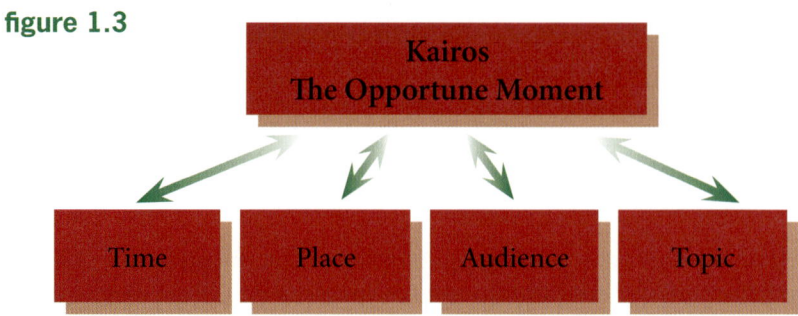

The editorial below addresses the shooting attack on Arizona Congresswoman Gabrielle Giffords that killed six and left Giffords and others seriously wounded. The text, published on *Time* magazine's website shortly after the attack, addresses the kairos of the situation—a United States Congresswoman has been shot, certainly an exceptional moment in many ways. The editorial demonstrates several important things to remember in understanding rhetoric and its use in American society. The author, Nathan Thornburgh, addresses the controversy about whether "overheated rhetoric" (exaggerated pathos) had inspired the shooting, an important question considering the often-inflammatory language of political rhetoric in the United States. However, his text is not filled with rash or harsh words that could further inflame the controversy. Though the text is an opinion piece, taking a position regarding this controversy and offering evidence to support his opinion, it is not itself "overheated rhetoric." As you read the text, think about whether he emphasizes ethos, pathos, or logos. You may or may not agree with his position. Rhetorical language is never neutral; its purpose is to persuade an audience to share the author's opinion. Good arguments, though, do not use "overheated rhetoric," false evidence, or logical fallacies to win over an audience.

Reading 1.1

Violent Rhetoric and Arizona Politics
by Nathan Thornburgh

This editorial by Nathan Thornburgh was originally printed in *Time* shortly after the shooting of Arizona Congresswoman Gabrielle Giffords.

Sometimes, rumors of violence beget actual violence. Saturday's mass shooting at a Safeway on North Oracle Road in Tucson, which killed six and left Democratic Congresswoman Gabrielle Giffords and others gravely wounded, may well be one of those occasions.

It's impossible to know this early what the motivations for the attack were. Was the alleged shooter—who has been identified as 22-year-old Tucsonan

Jared Loughner—angry about immigration? Or perhaps another hot-button issue? YouTube videos ascribed to him bore the mark of mental illness—they were conspiratorial, unintelligible, espousing no particular cause—but no matter his mental state, his crime took place in an overheated political environment. Last March, at the height of the health care reform battle, Giffords's office was vandalized. She mentioned in an MSNBC interview that a Sarah Palin graphic had depicted her district in the crosshairs of a gun sight. "They've got to realize there are consequences to that," she said. "The rhetoric is incredibly heated." The corner next to her office had also become, she said, a popular spot for Tea Party protests.

As Pima County Sheriff Clarence Dupnik put it in an extraordinary and melancholic press conference after the shooting, "we have become the Mecca for prejudice and bigotry." He added that he's "not aware of any public officials who are not receiving threats."

Another shooting victim, a federal judge named John Roll, had been placed under 24-hour security in 2009 after ruling in favor of illegal immigrants in a high-profile case. It's unclear why he was at the supermarket event. But for almost a year now, Arizona's leaders have been grappling with anti-immigration sentiments, inflamed by reports of crossborder violence. National media attention, with its attendant voices of hysteria, only added to the churn. Pundits spoke gravely about a wave of violence, born in Mexico and now flooding Arizona. Arizona's two most famous politicians fueled the fury. Republican Senator John McCain, facing an unexpected reelection challenge from the right, ran a campaign obsessed with crossborder crime. And GOP Governor Jan Brewer, who invited the national spotlight by championing strict anti-illegal immigrant legislation, talked of beheadings in the desert.

The only problem with all this talk about a massive crossborder crime wave is that it wasn't true. Phoenix had not become one of the world's kidnapping capitals. Crime rates in Arizona had been steady or even fallen in some areas. There had been no beheadings in the desert. There were plenty of deaths there, but they were pathetic and meek tragedies: impoverished border-crossers, abandoned by their heartless guides, dying of exposure and dehydration.

But the idea of a state under siege took hold. When I was on the border last year reporting on the murder of rancher Rob Krentz, I talked to many who sincerely believed that they were under attack. Krentz's murder was a terrible event, but it was an isolated event. The relatively small number of home invasions, holdups and other crimes deeply disturbed border communities, but only because they had been living in such calm for so long. Their crime rates still don't match most cities in the states.

The supermarket meet-and-greet where Giffords was shot was actually a testimony to just how safe southern Arizona is. As a press release from her office last week put it, "'Congress on Your Corner' allows residents of Arizona's 8th Congressional District to meet their congresswoman one-on-one and discuss with her any issue, concern or problem involving the federal government." Not exactly the kind of event a politician would hold in a war zone.

It's true that Giffords was not a fan of the state's anti-immigration bill SB1070, but there were higher-profile opponents, such as her fellow Congressional Representative in Tucson, Raul Grijalva. Yet the idea that Arizona is under attack has been pushed hard enough that it's very possible that the coward who shot her (in the head, according to a Tucson paper) believed that the 40-year-old Democrat, who had been tarred by some as soft on immigration because she didn't support SB1070, was contributing to larger-scale violence against Arizonans.

If that is the case, it would only add to the tragedy. The fact is, that among all the overwrought promises and all the panic I heard last summer in Arizona, I found that Giffords was one of the few politicians offering concrete law enforcement steps that would actually work against the drug cartels and other smugglers. It's not just that she fought for more money and police for border protection, although she did that. She co-sponsored legislation last year with a California Republican that aimed to give law enforcement important new tools in cracking down on the cash cards that were a favored method of money-laundering. It was one of the many sensible, pragmatic ideas she had for cracking down on crime.

Whatever dark fantasies drove someone to try to take her life, Giffords is a sensible politician who was likely shot because she dealt with Arizona's reality, not its rumors.

Activity 1.4 Write a Summary of "Violent Rhetoric and Arizona Politics"

Summarizing is an excellent technique to use when preparing for an exam or doing research for an essay. It allows you to discern the main points of a text and how they fit together. With a classmate, review the editorial by Thornburgh. Read the article together carefully, and list the main points individually. After you've listed the main points, put them into paragraph form.

Caution: Beware of the temptation to add your own analysis of what the text is saying. For example, if you are summarizing a scientist's article on global warming, you need to be careful not to reveal your personal opinion about whether or not global warming is occurring or whether or not human actions are to blame. In this assignment, you summarize only. You do not argue or analyze.

When you're finished, compare your summary with that of your partner.

Activity 1.5 Analyzing "Violent Rhetoric and Arizona Politics"

1. What does Nathan Thornburgh mean when he uses the term "overheated rhetoric"?

2. What is the argument that Thornburgh is making about the cause of the attack on Representative Giffords?

3. What evidence does Thornburgh offer to support his argument?

4. Does Thornburgh make his case? Is he convincing? Why or why not?

Reading 1.2

The Sleepover Question

by Amy Schalet

This text by Amy Schalet was first published in *The New York Times*. "The Sleepover Question" hazards an argument that many Americans—or at least American parents—may find controversial. Backed by her credentials as a professor of sociology, she cites research from 130 interviews, both in the United States and the Netherlands, and tackles the issue of whether or not American parents should allow their adolescent children to have sex in the family home. Pay particular attention, for she shows how to argue a subject that is not only controversial but often ignored.

NOT under my roof. That's the attitude most American parents have toward teenagers and their sex lives. Squeamishness and concern describe most parents' approach to their offspring's carnality. We don't want them doing it—whatever "it" is!—in our homes. Not surprisingly, teenage sex is a source of conflict in many American families.

Would Americans increase peace in family life and strengthen family bonds if they adopted more accepting attitudes about sex and what's allowable under the family roof? I've interviewed 130 people, all white, middle class and not particularly religious, as part of a study of teenage sex and family life here and in the Netherlands. My look into cultural differences suggests family life might be much improved, for all, if Americans had more open ideas about teenage sex. The question of who sleeps where when a teenager brings a boyfriend or girlfriend home for the night fits within the larger world of culturally divergent ideas about teenage sex, lust and capacity for love.

Kimberly and Natalie dramatize the cultural differences in the way young women experience their sexuality. (I have changed their names to protect confidentiality.) Kimberly, a 16-year-old American, never received sex education at home. "God, no! No, no! That's not going to happen," she told me. She'd like to tell her parents that she and her boyfriend are having sex, but she believes it is easier for her parents not to know because the truth would "shatter" their image of her as their "little princess."

Natalie, who is also 16 but Dutch, didn't tell her parents immediately when she first had intercourse with her boyfriend of three months. But, soon after, she says, she was so happy, she wanted to share the good news. Initially her father was upset and worried about his daughter and his honor. "Talk to him," his wife advised Natalie; after she did, her father made peace with the change. Essentially Natalie and her family negotiated a life change together and figured out, as a family, how to adjust to changed circumstance.

Respecting what she understood as her family's "don't ask, don't tell" policy, Kimberly only slept with her boyfriend at his house, when no one was home. She enjoyed being close to her boyfriend but did not like having to keep an important part of her life secret from her parents. In contrast, Natalie and her boyfriend enjoyed time and a new closeness with her family; the fact that her parents knew and approved of her boyfriend seemed a source of pleasure.

The difference in their experiences stems from divergent cultural ideas about sex and what responsible parents ought to do about it. Here, we see teenagers as helpless victims beset by raging hormones and believe parents should protect them from urges they cannot control. Matters aren't helped by the stereotype that all boys want the same thing, and all girls want love and cuddling. This compounds the burden on parents to steer teenage children away from relationships that will do more harm than good.

The Dutch parents I interviewed regard teenagers, girls and boys, as capable of falling in love, and of reasonably assessing their own readiness for sex. Dutch parents like Natalie's talk to their children about sex and its unintended consequences and urge them to use contraceptives and practice safe sex.

Cultural differences about teenage sex are more complicated than clichéd images of puritanical Americans and permissive Europeans. Normalizing ideas about teenage sex in fact allows the Dutch to exert *more* control over their children. Most of the parents I interviewed actively discouraged promiscuous behavior. And Dutch teenagers often reinforced what we see as 1950s-style mores: eager to win approval, they bring up their partners in conversation, introduce them to their parents and help them make favorable impressions.

Some Dutch teenagers went so far as to express their ideas about sex and love in self-consciously traditional terms; one Dutch boy said the advantage of spending the night with a partner was that it was "Like Mom and Dad, like when you're married, you also wake up next to the person you love."

Normalizing teenage sex under the family roof opens the way for more responsible sex education. In a national survey, 7 of 10 Dutch girls reported that by the time they were 16, their parents had talked to them about pregnancy and contraception. It seems these conversations helped teenagers prepare, responsibly, for active sex lives: 6 of 10 Dutch girls said they were on the pill when they first had intercourse. Widespread use of oral contraceptives contributes to low teenage pregnancy rates — more than 4 times lower in the Netherlands than in the United States.

Obviously sleepovers aren't a direct route to family happiness. But even the most traditional parents can appreciate the virtue of having their children be comfortable bringing a girlfriend or boyfriend home, rather than have them sneak around.

Unlike the American teenagers I interviewed, who said they felt they had to split their burgeoning sexual selves from their family roles, the Dutch teens had a chance to integrate different parts of themselves into their family life. When children feel safe enough to tell parents what they are doing and feeling, presumably it's that much easier for them to ask for help. This allows parents to have more influence, to control through connection.

Sexual maturation is awkward and difficult. The Dutch experience suggests that it is possible for families to stay connected when teenagers start having sex, and that if they do, the transition into adulthood need not be so painful for parents or children.

Activity 1.6 Analyze "The Sleepover Question"

1. What do you think about the "not under my roof" approach to a parent controlling a teen's sexuality versus the Dutch approach of allowing a teen's partner to sleep over? Discuss in your small group.

2. How do stereotypes play against the argument for a more open approach to teen sex in America? How much of parents' discomfort with their teen potentially having sex is guided by how their parents treated the subject when they were teens?

3. "The Sleepover Question" emphasizes logos. Can you paraphrase the logic of the argument? How does emotion (pathos) play a role in resistance to this argument?

4. In the article, the writer discusses the link between the use of oral contraceptives and lower teen pregnancy rates but does not mention the risk of STDs or condom use. Is it irresponsible of the author not to discuss the risk of STDs and sex, especially when she is willing to discuss teen pregnancy? Does it feel like an incomplete argument without discussing STDs?

5. If you were going to write a letter to the editor about this article, what would you say?

Chapter 1 | **Practicing Rhetoric**

Why Study Rhetoric?

Rhetoric, or persuasive communication, happens all around us every day, in conversation at the grocery store, in blogs, on television, and in the classroom. We Americans constantly air our opinions about almost everything. Sometimes it is to convince others to share our opinions, sometimes the reason is to engage in a dialogue that will help us understand the world around us, and sometimes it is to persuade others to action.

Argument is essential to human interaction and to society, for it is through the interplay of ideas in argument that we discover answers to problems, try out new ideas, shape scientific experiments, communicate with family members, recruit others to join a team, and work out any of the multitude of human interactions essential for society to function. When issues are complex, arguments do not result in immediate persuasion of the audience; rather, argument is part of an ongoing conversation between concerned parties who seek resolution, rather than speedy answers.

Rhetoric provides a useful framework for looking at the world, as well as for evaluating and initiating communications. In the modern world, writing and communicating persuasively is a necessary skill. Those who can present effective arguments in writing are, in the business world, often the ones who are promoted. In addition, those who are able to evaluate the arguments presented to them, whether by politicians, advertisers, or even family members, are less likely to be swayed by logical fallacies or ill-supported research.

Also, writing rhetorically is a tool with sometimes surprising uses. Research shows that, as students, we are more likely to remember material we have written about rather than simply memorized. Also, through the process of writing, writers often find that they initiate ideas and connections between ideas that they might not otherwise have found. Thus, writing may lead to new discoveries.

Rhetoric is a part of our everyday lives. When we're in a conversation with someone, we use rhetoric on a conscious or subconscious level. If you go to class wearing the T-shirt of your favorite musician or band, you're ultimately sending a rhetorical message identifying you as a fan of that artist or group.

If you've ever written a profile on a dating site, you've used rhetorical principles to convince an audience of potential partners to contact you or to write you back if you have chosen to make the first contact. You build ethos by talking about yourself in order to build credibility among potential partners, and you establish pathos when you talk about an interest that is shared by a potential mate.

Being able to use the tools of rhetoric effectively gives you the power to control your communication—both incoming and outgoing—and to affect your environment in a positive way.

Reading 1.3

San Ysidro Shooting Survivor Lives His Dream of Being a Cop

by Janine Zuniga

In this feature story from the San Diego Union-Tribune, *Janine Zuniga describes vividly how Alberto Leos, then a 17-year-old cook and high school football star, was shot and left for dead during James Oliver Huberty's rampage at a San Ysidro McDonald's in 1984. The 21 dead and 19 wounded made the massacre the worst one-day shooting by a single individual in United States history at the time. But Leos's story did not end there. The young man underwent surgeries and completed rehabilitation, going on to become a policeman. Notice how the author makes use of both ethos and pathos in writing this profile.*

The shots fired at point-blank range pierced both arms, his right leg, stomach and chest, and Alberto Leos crumpled to the kitchen floor next to three co-workers at a San Ysidro McDonald's. Even with his injuries, the 17-year-old cook, three weeks into his first job, knew the others were dead. He could tell by the lifeless positions of their bodies.

During a harrowing 77 minutes 20 years ago today, Leos, a high school football star, watched in helpless horror as a heavily armed James Oliver Huberty "executed, killed families, babies, my manager."

In all, 21 people were killed and 19 wounded in what was, up to that time, the worst one-day massacre by a single gunman in U.S. history. "All I remember is saying a prayer," Leos said. "I prayed to see my family one more time . . . before I died."

The McDonald's Massacre, as it came to be called, has faded for many San Diegans during the past two decades, but for those such as Leos who survived, it became the defining moment of their lives.

Leos's recovery included three months in the hospital, where he underwent five surgeries to remove the bullets and repair damage. He spent two years in therapy, for both physical and emotional injuries.

Despite painful rehabilitation, scars and memories, Leos became even more determined to fulfill his childhood dream of becoming a police officer. He has been a cop for 17 years.

After stints with the National City and Chula Vista police departments, Leos is now a San Diego police sergeant working the Southern Division, which includes routine patrols of San Ysidro.

"I was born to do this work," said Leos, who is married and lives in Chula Vista. "I was born to be in this profession. That's how I feel."

Leos said that while growing up in Cudahy, a city southeast of Los Angeles, the only time he saw deputies was when they were taking someone to jail. But that image changed one day when an L.A. County sheriff's deputy visited his third-grade classroom.

"To see him in the school setting, I was in awe—his uniform, his nice, shiny badge," Leos said. "He told us they were there to help people, to help those who can't help themselves. I told myself that when I was older, I wanted to do that."

But Leos's parents quickly and, for a decade, successfully discouraged him from pursuing the dream, saying it was too dangerous a career for their only son. Their opposition vanished on the day he almost lost his life.

"When I was shot and my friends and co-workers were killed, my parents were very, very supportive of me doing whatever I wanted," Leos said. "I guess they felt I had a second chance."

Photo by Howard Lipin / Union-Tribune

San Diego police sergeant, Alberto Leos, preparing to go out on patrol recently, overcame five surgeries and two years of painful therapy after the McDonald's Massacre to fulfill his childhood dream of becoming a police officer.

The short sleeves of Leos's dark-blue uniform can't hide the scars on his arms, but he doesn't often share the details of that day. The 5-foot-8, clean-shaven officer is soft-spoken and somewhat formal.

"Even as a young, young man, I could tell he was a serious kind of person, not in a sober sense, but in that he had a job and wanted to help his folks, that he was a good kid," said Andrea Skorepa, who as an employee of the local social-services agency Casa Familiar helped administer a $1.4 million fund for survivors and those injured in the McDonald's Massacre.

Skorepa, who has remained friends with the officer, said some who lived through it, such as Leos, have accomplished their goals, while others have succumbed to the tragedy.

"For the people who survived, that day was the beginning of a new life for them," Skorepa said. "What they have done with their lives becomes the important story. He doesn't live as a victim. He's not gone that way."

He tries to get assigned to San Ysidro when he can, because he wants to give back to the community and to Casa Familiar. The agency not only helped with the fund but helped get his family through a very tough time.

"That's when I learned about community service and how much it's needed," Leos said.

Said Skorepa, now executive director of Casa Familiar, "I think it gives you a different perspective, if you've come that close to losing your life and are somehow spared, on how to live your life."

In all his years in law enforcement, Leos has never fired his weapon at anyone. He's sure he will if he has to, but his instincts, which he has learned to trust, help guide him more calmly through tense situations.

Now, if a situation doesn't feel right, he will take a few steps back and think it through. Back on that unforgettable day, Leos said something told him not to go to work, but he didn't listen to his gut.

"I woke up with this feeling that I shouldn't go in," said Leos, who will turn 38 next month. "My friends were going to the beach and invited me to go. But it was the first job I ever had, and I talked myself out of it."

Activity 1.7 Consider a Profile

1. In your small group, decide what argument Janine Zuniga is making in this profile of the San Ysidro massacre survivor.

2. Describe what you think are the best specific details the writer includes, either of the shooting or of Leos's subsequent recovery and career as a policeman. How do these details contribute to the story?

3. A profile generally emphasizes the ethos of the subject. In this profile, how does the author do that? How does the author also make use of pathos?

Chapter 1 | **Practicing Rhetoric**

4. As the readers, what conclusion are you left with after you read the article? Is this the impression that the writer wanted you to have, do you think?

Reading 1.4

Memories of McDonald's Rhetorical Actions 20 Years Later

Shortly after the shooting that injured Alberto Leos, wounded 18 others, and killed 21 people (see the reading on page 22), a committee in San Ysidro, California, collected 1,400 signatures asking that the McDonald's be razed and a memorial park built. Although McDonald's was in no way responsible for the attack, it responded to the committee's rhetorical appeal. Bob Kaiser, director of media relations for McDonald's, said, "The concern is for the people, not simply business" and reported that the company's decision whether to reopen the restaurant was being held in abeyance. Later, the company tore down the restaurant and donated the land to the city. After debating what to do with the land, the city used it to build a community college.

In 2004, twenty years after the massacre, a memorial service was held at the site, and the media ran stories about the anniversary. Many people contributed to a blog associated with the anniversary story in the local newspaper:

> Jennifer wrote: "I live in La Jolla, exactly twenty five miles north of the former McDonald's where this tragedy took place some twenty plus years ago. The site is now the home of Southwestern College, but I have seen the memorial and am always filled with sadness when I go there. They have done a wonderful job on the memorial which is just in front of the former McDonald's building which you can tell was once the eatery, but has been painted grey, though the general shape of the building is still there. I am especially touched by the comments in this story and it is great that the memory of what happened not so long ago in our city is kept alive. ALL those that survived or not on that very sad day, were heroes, but their memories will never be in vain and we, as the citizens of this beautiful city will always be proud of their bravery and courage."

Leonor wrote: "I was seven at the time and I lived half a block from McDonald's. I saw bullets flying in the air and I remember police officers not letting us go to our house. They told us to get down in our car and not move. It was scary because we did not know what was going on. We were going to eat at McDonald's but my grandma invited us to her house. I still live in San Ysidro and I graduated from Southwestern College and I see the area everyday. It's not easy to forget what I do remember."

Armida wrote: "I remember that day. I was there. I had just turned 17. This was my first job. I lost my cousin and two friends because they threw a coffee pot at him to save this guy who became a cop. I saved a co-worker. I never told anybody or wrote about this day till now."

Sergio wrote: "I still remember this event. I'm now 33 years old and I was 9 years old. I still remember the gun shots, many of them. I grew up about 3 blocks away. I remember the countless police officers blocking the streets of Sunset Lane, which was my street. Two of my friends were murdered. I could have been there. My best friend died that day. This has been a funeral I will always remember. I just like to share a tiny bit on that day in the summer of July."

Joe Bloggs wrote: "I remember this happening. I was only about 12 years old at the time and living in Australia, but it is something I never forget about. Why America is so obsessed with guns I will never understand. Nobody except the police and army should have access to firearms. The private ownership of guns should be illegal and there should be gun amnesty days where guns can be handed in to be crushed. This is going to happen time and time again, people, unless you stand up and say no to gun ownership."

The blog entries show the impact of the event, even 20 years later. Notice that there are no negative comments about the McDonald's, nor about what the community decided to do with the land. Nothing McDonald's could have done would have erased the pain of the event, but its rhetorical actions, in both word and deed, did not add to the trauma of the event. McDonald's response to the citizens' request to tear down the building and donate the land to the city continues to be praised 20 years later.

Activity 1.8 Blogging and Responding to Blogging

In your group, discuss the blog entries above about the San Ysidro shooting. Which blog entry attracts your attention the most? What do you think was the author's rhetorical purpose?

Chapter 1 | **Practicing Rhetoric**

Write your own blog entry in response to the McDonald's story. What would you say to the citizens who remember the event? What would you say to the people at McDonald's who made the decision to tear down the building and donate the land to the city?

Do you blog? Why? Do you check your blog frequently? How do you feel if there are responses to your comments? How do you feel if there are no responses to your comments? Does it matter if the response is positive or negative?

Activity 1.9 Write about Everyday Arguments

Read your local newspaper or magazines such as *Time* or *Fortune* or search the Internet and bring to class a copy of a recent text or visual image that makes an argument about an issue. You might find, for example, an editorial in your local newspaper about recycling efforts in your community or a blog entry about parenting practices. Be sure, however, that the text or image takes a position on the issue. Write a paragraph of approximately 100 to 150 words describing the argument to your classmates and your reaction to it.

Encountering Visual Rhetoric

Why is a visual so powerful? Colors, shapes, and symbols impact viewers in ways text alone cannot. Many images present arguments and, because they are visual, they communicate more quickly and, sometimes, more powerfully than words.

The images on the next page are covers from *GQ* magazine. On the left, Sacha Baron Cohen, in the Bruno character, graces the humor edition of the magazine in a pose echoing that of Jennifer Aniston, on the right, which was printed on a cover a few months previously. What do you think when you see a man positioned in a way that is typical for a scantily dressed (or nude) female? Is it funny? Many think so, but not everyone. A posting on a blog called thesocietypages.org says of Cohen, "The contrast between the meaning of the pose (sexy and feminine) with the fact that he's male draws attention to how powerfully gendered the pose is… women look sexy when they pose like this, men look stupid when they do."

A photo's ability to persuade can be significant, whether it is a news photo or an advertisement. However, not everyone interprets images the same way, especially when they evoke stereotypes of gender, race, or religion.

© GQ Magazine

Compare these two cover photos from GQ magazine. Though the poses are similar, because the figure on the left is a man and the one on the right is a woman, they evoke very different responses from readers. Some see the photo on the left as paying humorous tribute to the one on the right. Others interpret both images as exploiting feminine gender stereotypes.

Activity 1.10 Write a Caption for a Photo or a Pair of Photos

Choose a news photo or advertisement from a newspaper, magazine, or the Internet that presents an argument. Alternatively, compare two news photos or advertisements. Copy or paste the photo or photos on a piece of paper and write a caption that expresses the argument(s) you see in the photo.

Rhetorical Arguments Stand the Test of Time

Abraham Lincoln's Gettysburg Address is the short speech that the president delivered at the site of the battle of Gettysburg where, four months previously, the Union Army defeated Confederate forces. His was not the only talk that day at the dedication of the Soldiers' National Cemetery, but it is the only one remembered. In just over two minutes, he was able to reframe the Civil War not just as a victory for the North but as a "new birth of freedom" for all

Americans. Now, during the 150th anniversary of the Civil War, is a good time to remember Lincoln's rhetoric—in terms of both the content and the style of his speech.

Reading 1.5

Text of the Gettysburg Address

Four score and seven years ago our fathers brought forth on this continent, a new nation, conceived in Liberty, and dedicated to the proposition that all men are created equal.

Now we are engaged in a great civil war, testing whether that nation, or any nation so conceived and so dedicated, can long endure. We are met on a great battlefield of that war. We have come to dedicate a portion of that field, as a final resting place for those who here gave their lives that that nation might live. It is altogether fitting and proper that we should do this.

But, in a larger sense, we cannot dedicate—we cannot consecrate—we cannot hallow—this ground. The brave men, living and dead, who struggled here, have consecrated it, far above our poor power to add or detract. The world will little note, nor long remember what we say here, but it can never forget what they did here. It is for us the living, rather, to be dedicated here to the unfinished work which they who fought here have thus far so nobly advanced. It is rather for us to be here dedicated to the great task remaining before us—that from these honored dead we take increased devotion to that cause for which they gave the last full measure of devotion—that we here highly resolve that these dead shall not have died in vain—that this nation, under God, shall have a new birth of freedom—and that government of the people, by the people, for the people, shall not perish from the earth.

Though no actual recording exists of Lincoln giving the speech, you can listen to it if you search on the Internet for "recording of Gettysburg Address." Listen to the speech, noting the phrase "Four score and seven years ago," which is so famous that Americans know instantly, when it is quoted by orators or writers, that it is a reference to Lincoln. Consider what arguments the president makes in his speech. Think about their relevance today.

Activity 1.11 Paraphrase the Gettysburg Address

Rephrase each sentence of the Gettysburg Address, one by one, in your own words, putting it in 21st century wording rather than Lincoln's ceremonial, 19th century phrasing. In a paraphrase, the text does not become shorter; it is recreated in different words. This is a useful technique in helping you understand a text. It is also helpful when you are writing an analysis of a text because you can use your paraphrase rather than long, block quotes. Remember, though, when you are writing an essay, you must cite a paraphrase in the text and also include it in your list of references.

Activity 1.12 Keep a Commonplace Book

Ancient rhetoricians performed speeches with little warning, often to advertise their services as teachers of rhetoric. Thus, they frequently memorized arguments about specific topics that could be adapted to the audience and situation on a moment's notice. They called these memorized arguments "commonplaces." Commonplace books are an outgrowth of the Greek concept of commonplaces, but they are a little different. They became popular in the Middle Ages as notebooks in which individuals would write down quotes or ideas about a particular topic.

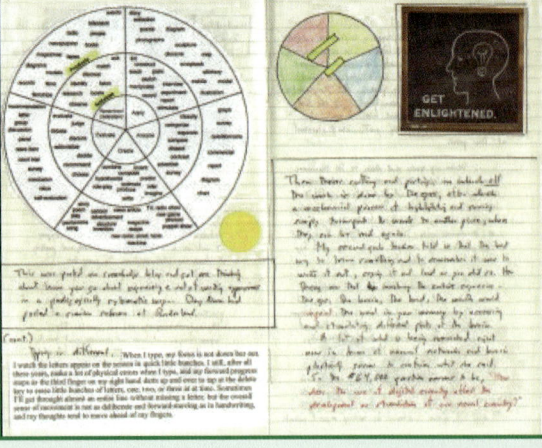

For thousands of years, people have been keeping commonplace books, a kind of journal or diary in which the author includes quotes, drawings, and images.

These notations might later be used to generate an idea for a composition. In more modern times, people have created commonplace books in the form of scrapbooks in which they collect quotes as well as drawings and clippings. Thus, they become a record of a person's intellectual life and can be saved for later reference.

For this class, take a notebook, perhaps one with a colorful or interesting cover, and keep notes, quotes, vocabulary words, and clippings related to the topics discussed in class. As your instructor directs, this commonplace book may be graded as evidence of class participation or it may be a private journal. Take a look at the commonplace books shown here for ideas. Be creative and enjoy adapting this ancient journal form to record ideas that interest you.

Activity 1.13 Create Your Own Blog

Create a home page for a professional blog using a site like Blogger, WordPress, or Live Journal. Blogger is the easiest to use, but the others have more flexible options. Read the help screens for instructions on how to create your blog. Your design choices should reflect your personality. Keep in mind, though, that you are building an "academic self," so all the topics you write about should be of an academic nature and in an academic tone. Some students decide to have two blogs, one for their friends and one for professional networking, so you may want to do this, especially if you already have a blog.

During this class, you'll use the blog to explore different aspects of each chapter in the textbook (and other topics that your instructor directs). You can also blog about other topics related to your writing this semester, and you can link to other blogs that you think your readers would find of interest.

After you have created the look of your blog, write a first entry that introduces you to your readers. You might include your major, your college, and something interesting that might attract readers to your blog.

2
RESPONDING RHETORICALLY

Praxis in Action

Why I Annotate Readings by Lauren Connolly

Annotating a reading gives me the ability to participate in a conversation with the author of the text in order to develop my ideas for writing and understanding the information presented. My annotation style uses two methods: one is with a pencil and the other is with a highlighter.

As with a conversation, my side comments may be to protest the author's ideas or to make connections with other things in my life, other readings for the class, or my other classes. By making notes, I am actively participating in the conversation, opposed to passively taking in the information presented, and it gives me an opportunity to create something meaningful from the text. Using the highlighter sparingly, I only mark a word or phrase, in order to point out specific ideas or words that I want to reference, understand, or quote in my writing at a later point in time. The meaningful interaction is when, using a pencil, I write comments in the margins in response to these highlights. These comments are frequently a part of my prewriting stage, as I use my marginal comments directly in my early written drafts. Annotating allows me to respond, clarify, and develop my ideas about what I have learned, enabling me to use the ideas later in both my writing and research.

Lauren Connolly likes to annotate readings because it allows her to have a conversation with the writer.

Thinking Critically, Reading Rhetorically

In contemporary times we study texts to encourage students to develop critical thinking, a skill which is essential for understanding the scientific method and for making effective judgments in the workplace and in civil life. This student-centered emphasis would have seemed strange to ancient Greek and Roman rhetoricians and their students. They believed that a rhetor's skill was best developed by honoring the skills of those who excelled in the past. Therefore, a large part of the educational process involved having students study the texts of well-regarded speeches, memorize and recite them, and model new compositions based on their approaches to topics and language style. As Isocrates explained:

> Since language is of such a nature that it is possible to discourse on the same subject matter in many different ways—to represent the great as lowly or invest the little with grandeur, to recount the things of old in a new manner or set forth events of recent date in an old fashion—it follows that one must not shun the subjects upon which others have composed before, but must try to compose better than they . . . (Panegyricus).

Thus, students in ancient Greece or Rome would have been presented with a text, often read aloud by a teacher, and they would be asked to transcribe or copy it down with the idea that they would internalize the skills of the master rhetor who had originally given the speech. Then, they would be asked to write about the same subject in a way that built upon what they had learned from the master text but incorporated their own personal attitudes or perspectives.

Today, rather than being asked to model new compositions based upon the techniques of classic texts, students are asked to read texts carefully and then to engage in critical thinking and discussion about those texts.

Critical thinking involves considering issues thoughtfully and independently. Critical thinkers do not believe facts or opinions just because they are published—whether it is in newspapers, textbooks, on television, or on the Internet. Nor do they focus upon just understanding or memorizing information, as in facts and figures. Critical thinkers examine the reasoning of the information in front of them, looking for premises and considering the inferences drawn from those premises. They are able to think for themselves, making logical connections between ideas, seeing cause and effect relationships, and using information to solve problems.

Chapter 2 | **Responding Rhetorically**

Reading rhetorically makes use of critical thinking skills, but it also involves looking at texts as arguments and evaluating them for validity, adequacy of evidence, and presence of bias. Moreover, reading rhetorically involves having a knowledge of rhetoric and specialized Greek terms such as logos, pathos, ethos, and kairos—words that were defined briefly in Chapter 1 and will be discussed more extensively in Chapter 3. Practice reading rhetorically as you read the following article on the Strauss-Kahn sexual assault case.

Reading 2.1

In Sex-Crime Cases, Credibility a Thorny Issue

by Paul Duggan

In 2011, Dominique Strauss-Kahn, the head of the International Monetary Fund (IMF), was accused of sexual assault by a housekeeper at the Sofitel New York hotel. He pled not guilty. During the case, the victim's credibility was called into question, as she had reportedly lied to the police in her first statement about the case. The following article, by Paul Duggan, published in *The Washington Post*, talks about the credibility of alleged victims in sex-crime cases, and how, in the Strauss-Kahn case, it could affect the outcome. To begin a critical reading of an article, you want to read the entire piece first for content. Then, reread the introduction. How does the author attempt to capture the audience's attention? How does the author use the Lanigan case as a frame of reference?

A wealthy public figure accused of sexual misconduct in a swanky hotel says that the charge is trumped up, that his alleged victim lacks credibility.

In their eagerness to bag a famous name, the defendant says, investigators have rushed to judgment. He says they have failed to carefully consider whether the woman who reported being accosted had a motive to lie.

That's what Dominque Strauss-Kahn says, through his attorneys.

And that's what lawyer A. Scott Bolden says. He represents Washington Redskins lineman Albert Haynesworth, awaiting trial on a misdemeanor charge that he indecently groped a waitress at the posh W Hotel in Washington.

"Let me tell you something about sex-crimes prosecutors," said Bolden, a former sex-crimes prosecutor. "They tend to be true believers. I mean, they've never met a victim they don't want to save or who they don't believe. . . . And when credibility issues arise, they tend to just want to explain them away."

As authorities Friday acknowledged doubts about the credibility of Strauss-Kahn's accuser in New York, and the rape case against the former head of the International Monetary Fund seemed in jeopardy, Bolden and other lawyers said the news highlights one of the thorniest issues in sex-crimes prosecutions:

Will jurors believe the alleged victim?

Sometimes the believability issue has nothing to do with the allegation itself. The witness may have a troubled past that could cast doubt on her testimony.

Harry O'Reilly, a retired New York City police detective who helped create the department's Special Victims Unit in the early 1970s—the unit that handled the Strauss-Kahn case—said investigators often deal with accusers who have less-than-savory backgrounds and who offer changing accounts of alleged assaults.

"It's quite common for there to be credibility issues," he said. He said detectives initially should focus only on whether the alleged crime occurred, and not be deterred by the woman's personal history, even if it involves dishonesty.

"If someone makes an allegation, we listen," he said. "And then we look for chinks in the story. And if the story begins to dissipate, then we go from there. But at the onset, we're not looking at things in her past that aren't relevant to the allegation."

Attorney Peter Greenspun, who defended Fairfax County teacher Sean Lanigan, acquitted this year of sexually molesting a 12-year-old female student, said authorities have to proceed in such cases with caution.

"These are the kinds of cases where the most care has to be exercised before anyone is charged, because of what allegations like this do to people," Greenspun said.

Jurors in the Fairfax trial later voiced outrage at the dearth of evidence against Lanigan, a married father of three whose life was shattered by the allegations.

"These are devastating charges," Greenspun said. "There's an assumption of guilt by the public, and reputations and life trajectories are destroyed."

In New York, prosecutors acknowledged that the hotel maid who accused Strauss-Kahn of raping her in his luxury suite May 14 later lied to investigators about her personal history and gave them inconsistent accounts of the moments after the alleged assault.

Strauss-Kahn, 62, who was arrested hours after the allegation and resigned from the IMF, was ordered released from home confinement in Manhattan on Friday. But the district attorney's office has not moved to dismiss the rape case.

"She said it happened, and he's sort of a pompous guy with a reputation … for grabbing women, so they thought, well, of course, it must have happened," Greenspun said. He said police generally spend too little time investigating such cases before making arrests, especially when the suspects are prominent men.

Even if Strauss-Kahn's attorneys have information about his accuser that they could use in court to cast doubt on her veracity, prosecutors have a "moral obligation" to proceed with the case if they believe that the woman is being truthful, said lawyer Mai Fernandez, director of the National Center for Victims of Crime.

"You could have Attila the Hun come to you and say he's a victim, and the truth of the matter is, in this particular case, he may be," Fernandez said.

"You have to look first at the evidence that's directly related to the case at hand," she added. "The victim? Well, everybody has a past. None of us is without sin. There's always something that a defense lawyer can use to tarnish your reputation."

Kristina Korobov, a former prosecutor, agreed with Fernandez, but only to an extent.

"It's true that you can't just say to a victim, 'Well, you have a credibility problem, so too bad,' and then, based on that, you don't proceed with the case," Korobov said. "Because that just rewards offenders who choose victims with credibility problems."

In a case like Strauss-Kahn's, she said, prosecutors are probably weighing whether the woman's credibility is so badly damaged that a conviction would be highly unlikely.

"There were a number of victims in my lifetime who I legitimately believed had been victimized, but I didn't file a charge," said Korobov, now a senior attorney with the National Center for the Prosecution of Violence Against Women. "You've got to be very selective about what cases you bring, based on what you think you can prove."

Activity 2.1 Analyze a Text

In your small group, discuss the following questions and then report your group's opinion(s) to the class.

1. What is the problem that the author is concerned about in regard to prosecuting sex crimes?

2. What court cases does he mention? How was the victim's ethos involved?

3. How does the writer appeal to logos? To pathos?

4. If your group were writing a letter to the editor of the *Washington Post* commenting about this article, what might you say about the controversy the writer presents?

Rhetoric's Visual Heritage and Impact

The first televised presidential debate in September 1960 is a famous example of the power of visual rhetoric and a vivid illustration of the fact that visual elements must be considered when "reading" rhetorical situations. Radio listeners who could hear but not see the debate rated Vice President Richard Nixon as the winner over Senator John F. Kennedy—Nixon's arguments sounded more logical and were more clearly expressed. However, the television audience experienced a new element in the history of presidential debates: They could see the performances of the handsome and tan Senator Kennedy and the pasty-white and ill-looking Vice President Nixon, and they clearly preferred Kennedy. He *looked and acted presidential*, which overcame the drawbacks that had troubled his campaign previously—that he was relatively unknown, young, and Catholic. It overcame any advantage that Nixon may have had in presenting logical arguments and also by being an incumbent vice president. And unfortunately for Nixon, by 1960, 88 percent of Americans had televisions. "It's one of those unusual points on the timeline of history where you can say things changed very dramatically—in this case, in a single night," says Alan Schroeder, a media historian who authored the book, *Presidential Debates: Forty Years of High-Risk TV*.* Indeed, after the unexpected impact of the Kennedy-Nixon debates, presidential candidates were so apprehensive about competing on television that it was 16 years before candidates (President Gerald R. Ford and former Governor Jimmy

---

* Kayla Webley, "How the Nixon-Kennedy Debate Changed the World" *Breaking News, Analysis, Politics, Blogs, News Photos, Video, Tech Reviews,* September 23, 2010. http://www.time.com/time/nation/article/0,8599,2021078,00.html. Accessed July 30, 2011.

Carter) were again willing to risk presenting themselves side by side on television.

Why did the experience of seeing the two candidates, rather than hearing them or reading their speeches, make such a difference? The ancient Greeks and Romans who developed rhetoric would have understood the reason: It was what they called ethos, which can be translated only imperfectly as credibility. A person's ethos is determined partially by his or her reputation, but as Richard Nixon learned the hard way, it is conveyed even more powerfully by appearance, gestures, tone, and cadence of speech. It is important to remember that the standards and perceptions of Americans are heavily influenced by rhetoric as it was defined and implemented by the Greeks and Romans—first in oral presentations. Many of the attributes of rhetoric translate to written texts, but not all. Thus, when considering a text that was originally presented as a speech, reading rhetorically means thinking about visual rhetoric—the impact the speech would have had on an audience that was *watching and listening to the presentation.*

The first presidential debate between Vice President Richard Nixon and Senator John F. Kennedy illustrated the power of visual rhetoric.

Moreover, the impact of visual rhetoric involves more than speeches: It concerns television shows, films, photographs, paintings, advertisements, and even the typesetting layout of a text that has no illustrations. We will consider these types of visual rhetoric in more detail later in this chapter.

On page 41, we reprint President Barack Obama's speech announcing the death of Osama bin Laden. This speech is available widely on the Internet at such sites as AmericanRhetoric.com, NYTimes.com, and YouTube.com. If possible, watch the speech before you read the text, and as you do so think about the impact of the speech, including the president's verbal presentation and the setting at the White House, as well as the content of the speech. Think about the various audiences President Obama was speaking to—Americans and people around the world who might be watching at that moment, as well as a historic audience of people such as yourself who would be viewing the speech months or years later.

The Rhetorical Triangle

When reading a text or listening to a speech, keep in mind the three parts of the rhetorical triangle—writer, audience, and subject (see figure 2.1). Each of these can be framed as a question:

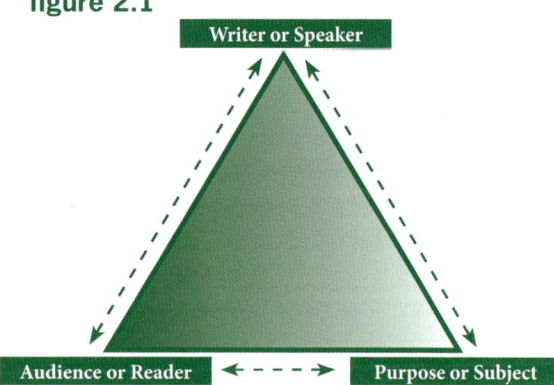

figure 2.1

- Who is the writer? What is the impression the writer wants to make on the audience? What does the writer do to establish credibility (ethos)? How does the writer create common ground with the audience?

- Who is the intended audience? How would a logical appeal influence the audience? An ethical appeal? An emotional appeal? What does the audience anticipate in terms of organization and format of the presentation or paper? What is the extent of their knowledge about the subject, and do they have prejudices or preferences?

- What is the purpose of the communication? In the case of an argument, the purpose would be to persuade. Is that the case with this reading? Is it clear what the writer wants to persuade the audience to believe or to do? Is the request phrased in a logical manner?

Activity 2.2 Apply the Rhetorical Triangle

For each of the readings presented thus far in the textbook, identify the speaker, the audience, and the purpose. Then analyze how each of those elements affects the content of the reading.

1. "Violent Rhetoric and Arizona Politics" (Chapter 1, p. 14)
2. "The Sleepover Question" (Chapter 1, p. 18)
3. "San Ysidro Shooting Survivor Lives His Dream of Being a Cop" (Chapter 1, p. 22)
4. "In Sex-Crime Cases, Credibility a Thorny Issue" (Chapter 2, p. 35)

Reading 2.2

President Barack Obama on the Death of Osama bin Laden

Good evening. Tonight, I can report to the American people and to the world that the United States has conducted an operation that killed Osama bin Laden, the leader of al Qaeda, and a terrorist who's responsible for the murder of thousands of innocent men, women, and children.

It was nearly 10 years ago that a bright September day was darkened by the worst attack on the American people in our history. The images of 9/11 are seared into our national memory—hijacked planes cutting through a cloudless September sky; the Twin Towers collapsing to the ground; black smoke billowing up from the Pentagon; the wreckage of Flight 93 in Shanksville, Pennsylvania, where the actions of heroic citizens saved even more heartbreak and destruction.

President Barack Obama announced the death of Osama bin Laden.

And yet we know that the worst images are those that were unseen to the world. The empty seat at the dinner table. Children who were forced to grow up without their mother or their father. Parents who would never know the feeling of their child's embrace. Nearly 3,000 citizens taken from us, leaving a gaping hole in our hearts.

On September 11, 2001, in our time of grief, the American people came together. We offered our neighbors a hand, and we offered the wounded our blood. We reaffirmed our ties to each other, and our love of community and country. On that day, no matter where we came from, what God we prayed to, or what race or ethnicity we were, we were united as one American family.

We were also united in our resolve to protect our nation and to bring those who committed this vicious attack to justice. We quickly learned that the 9/11 attacks were carried out by al Qaeda—an organization headed by Osama bin Laden, which had openly declared war on the United States and was committed to killing innocents in our country and around the globe. And so we went to war against al Qaeda to protect our citizens, our friends, and our allies.

Over the last 10 years, thanks to the tireless and heroic work of our military and our counterterrorism professionals, we've made great strides in that effort. We've disrupted terrorist attacks and strengthened our homeland defense. In Afghanistan, we removed the Taliban government, which had given Bin Laden and al Qaeda safe haven and support. And around the globe, we worked with our friends and allies to capture or kill scores of al Qaeda terrorists, including several who were a part of the 9/11 plot.

Yet Osama bin Laden avoided capture and escaped across the Afghan border into Pakistan. Meanwhile, al Qaeda continued to operate from along that border and operate through its affiliates across the world. And so shortly after taking office, I directed Leon Panetta, the director of the CIA, to make the killing or capture of Bin Laden the top priority of our war against al Qaeda, even as we continued our broader efforts to disrupt, dismantle, and defeat his network.

Then, last August, after years of painstaking work by our intelligence community, I was briefed on a possible lead to Bin Laden. It was far from certain, and it took many months to run this thread to ground. I met repeatedly with my national security team as we developed more information about the possibility that we had located Bin Laden hiding within a compound deep inside of Pakistan. And finally, last week, I determined that we had enough intelligence to take action, and authorized an operation to get Osama bin Laden and bring him to justice.

Chapter 2 | **Responding Rhetorically**

Today, at my direction, the United States launched a targeted operation against that compound in Abbottabad, Pakistan. A small team of Americans carried out the operation with extraordinary courage and capability. No Americans were harmed. They took care to avoid civilian casualties. After a firefight, they killed Osama bin Laden and took custody of his body.

For over two decades, Bin Laden has been al Qaeda's leader and symbol, and has continued to plot attacks against our country and our friends and allies. The death of Bin Laden marks the most significant achievement to date in our nation's effort to defeat al Qaeda.

Yet his death does not mark the end of our effort. There's no doubt that al Qaeda will continue to pursue attacks against us. We must—and we will—remain vigilant at home and abroad.

As we do, we must also reaffirm that the United States is not—and never will be—at war with Islam. I've made clear, just as President Bush did shortly after 9/11, that our war is not against Islam. Bin Laden was not a Muslim leader; he was a mass murderer of Muslims. Indeed, al Qaeda has slaughtered scores of Muslims in many countries, including our own. So his demise should be welcomed by all who believe in peace and human dignity.

Over the years, I've repeatedly made clear that we would take action within Pakistan if we knew where Bin Laden was. That is what we've done. But it's important to note that our counterterrorism cooperation with Pakistan helped lead us to Bin Laden and the compound where he was hiding. Indeed, Bin Laden had declared war against Pakistan as well, and ordered attacks against the Pakistani people.

Tonight, I called President Zardari, and my team has also spoken with their Pakistani counterparts. They agree that this is a good and historic day for both of our nations. And going forward, it is essential that Pakistan continue to join us in the fight against al Qaeda and its affiliates.

The American people did not choose this fight. It came to our shores, and started with the senseless slaughter of our citizens. After nearly 10 years of service, struggle, and sacrifice, we know well the costs of war. These efforts weigh on me every time I, as Commander-in-Chief, have to sign a letter to a family that has lost a loved one, or look into the eyes of a service member who's been gravely wounded.

So Americans understand the costs of war. Yet as a country, we will never tolerate our security being threatened, nor stand idly by when our people have been killed. We will be relentless in defense of our citizens and our friends and allies. We will be true to the values that make us who we are. And on nights like this one, we can say to those families who have lost loved ones to al Qaeda's terror: Justice has been done.

Tonight, we give thanks to the countless intelligence and counterterrorism professionals who've worked tirelessly to achieve this outcome. The American people do not see their work, nor know their names. But tonight, they feel the satisfaction of their work and the result of their pursuit of justice.

We give thanks for the men who carried out this operation, for they exemplify the professionalism, patriotism, and unparalleled courage of those who serve our country. And they are part of a generation that has borne the heaviest share of the burden since that September day.

Finally, let me say to the families who lost loved ones on 9/11 that we have never forgotten your loss, nor wavered in our commitment to see that we do whatever it takes to prevent another attack on our shores.

And tonight, let us think back to the sense of unity that prevailed on 9/11. I know that it has, at times, frayed. Yet today's achievement is a testament to the greatness of our country and the determination of the American people.

The cause of securing our country is not complete. But tonight, we are once again reminded that America can do whatever we set our mind to. That is the story of our history, whether it's the pursuit of prosperity for our people, or the struggle for equality for all our citizens; our commitment to stand up for our values abroad, and our sacrifices to make the world a safer place.

Let us remember that we can do these things not just because of wealth or power, but because of who we are: one nation, under God, indivisible, with liberty and justice for all.

Thank you.
May God bless you.
And may God bless the United States of America.

Chapter 2 | **Responding Rhetorically**

Activity 2.3 Evaluate the President's Speech

After you have both watched President Obama's speech on the Internet and read the text, discuss these questions in your small group and then present the consensus of your group's answers to the class.

1. Discuss the president's presentation of the speech. Do you think the speech had a different impact on those who watched it on television versus those who heard it on the radio? What about those who neither saw nor heard it but rather read the speech?

2. How would you describe the president's tone, appearance, and mannerisms (all part of his ethos)? What about the location he chose for the speech and the timing just after news agencies had announced Bin Laden's death (the kairos)?

3. Summarize what the president says about the government's reasons for seeking Osama bin Laden and killing him. Does the president make a good argument for the necessity and importance of this act?

4. Notice that the president uses visual imagery in his speech. For example, in paragraph two, immediately after he announces his news, he refers to 9/11—"a bright September day was darkened by the worst attack on the American people in our history." What is the purpose of the visual descriptions in his speech?

5. Do you agree or disagree with what the president has to say? How so?

Activity 2.4 Research Reactions to President Obama's Speech

Using Google or another search engine, research the reactions to the president's speech announcing the death of Bin Laden.

1. In the days after the speech, what did the media report about the attack on Bin Laden's compound?

2. What were some American reactions to the speech and to the killing of Bin Laden?

3. What was the reaction around the world, both in Muslim and non-Muslim countries?

4. Did you learn anything during your research that surprised you? How so?

As your instructor directs, either discuss these questions in class or turn in written answers to the questions.

Reading 2.3

The Lexicon
by Charles McGrath

A *lexicon* is a synonym for dictionary, thesaurus, and wordlist. Charles McGrath, in his *New York Times* essay, "The Lexicon," examines the changes that 9/11 wrought in the English language. The attack on the World Trade Center, unlike other world-changing violent events, hasn't yet created many new words, he decides. Rather, it has brought already-existing words to our everyday vocabulary—such as jihad, T.S.A. shoe bomber, and sleeper cell. These not-so-pretty words are the lexicon of 9/11.

Ground zero, sleeper cells, progressive vertical collapse: The most resonant phrases of 9/11 are imbued with what might be called antipoetry, a resistance to prettification.

Unlike some other momentous events in our history—World War II, say, or the Vietnam War—the attacks that took place on Sept. 11, 2001, have not particularly changed or enriched our vocabulary. Sometimes these things take a while. It wasn't until the 1960s, for example, that the term "holocaust," which used to mean any large-scale massacre, took on the specific connotations it has today. For now, though, you could argue that the events of 9/11 still seem so unfathomable that they have actually impoverished the language a little, leaving us with a vacuous phrase like **war on terror**, which manages to empty both "war" and "terror" of much their meaning, or the creepy, Nazi-sounding **homeland**, which seems a far less pleasant place to live than just plain America.

We do know a lot of words now that we probably should have known before, like **jihad, Taliban, mujahedeen** and **Al Qaeda**. And some that we'd just as soon forget, like **T.S.A., security checkpoint, shoe bomber** and **progressive vertical collapse**. A term like **sleeper cell** probably sticks in our heads because it contains a tiny hint of embedded poetry, and for the same reason it's hard to forget those **72 black-eyed virgins** whom the terrorists believed they were on their way to meet. The "black-eyed" bit is a brilliant touch, even if it's probably a mistranslation.

But the most resonant phrases that have taken residence in our consciousness since that September morning are ones imbued with what might be called antipoetry, a resistance to metaphor or to prettification. **Ground zero**, for example—a term that originated with the Manhattan Project and was originally used in connection with nuclear explosions—seems particularly

Chapter 2 | **Responding Rhetorically**

apt in this new context, with its sense of absolute finality, of a point that is both an end and a beginning and to which everything else refers.

And even **9/11** itself has a kind of rightness. No one says "September 11th" anymore as shorthand for that awful day. (To do so, a friend once joked, would be "so September 10th.") There's a pleasing, no-nonsense simplicity and precision to the expression—the same effect created by "24/7," only starker, and with none of the exaggeration. These four syllables are right at the end of language, where words turn into abstraction. Individually, they're just random, empty numbers, but yoked by that fateful slash they contain volumes. 9/11—everyone knows what that means, and to say any more would be pointless. Sometimes words fail.

Activity 2.5 Develop a Lexicon

Choose one of the following activities and create a lexicon as a group or individually:

1. Reread President Obama's speech about the death of Osama bin Laden. What words have become a more frequent part of the nation's vocabulary as a result of Bin Laden's actions? Al Qaeda and Taliban are two. Can you find others? Do an Internet search for Osama bin Laden, until you have five to seven words. Then write a 250 to 300 word essay, similar to McGrath's, in which you consider how Bin Laden's life and death have affected our country's vocabulary.

2. Do a search on the Internet for "new words." You will find lists of words and phrases that have been added to new editions of dictionaries. Examples may include such words as "aquascape," "soul patch," and "sandwich generation." Choose five to seven new words that are related to each other in some way. Create a lexicon of your own with a paragraph about each word that emphasizes the invention or recent history of the word. Give examples of each word's usage in blogs or other publications.

Ways of Reading Rhetorically

Reading theorist Louise Rosenblatt suggests a technique for analyzing written texts—particularly those with few visual cues other than words on paper or a computer screen. She says that we take the pattern of verbal signs left by the author and use them to recreate the text, not in the exact way the author perceived the text, but guided by it.

So, as we read, there is a constant stream of response to the text. However, Rosenblatt says that even as the reader is recreating the text, he or she is also reacting to it. Thus, there are two interacting streams of response involved as the person moves through the text. The reader, rather than being a passive receptor for the author's text, actually participates in the creative process during reading.

However, we read differently depending on the text and the occasion. For example, if you take a paperback novel on an airplane trip, you probably read simply for entertainment and to pass the time in the air. If you read *King Lear* for a literature class, you read for the plot, characterization, and other elements that you know will be discussed in class. If you read a chapter in your chemistry textbook before an exam, you are focusing on remembering concepts and details that might be on the test. Reading as a writer is another type of reading. You examine the text with an eye for the choices the writer made when crafting the text, such as whether the writer begins with a narrative introduction, a quote from a noted authority, or a startling statement. You notice, for example, what people are mentioned in the text, either as authorities or participants in activities.

Rosenblatt also makes a useful distinction between two main kinds of reading—aesthetic reading and efferent reading. In **aesthetic reading**, the reader is most interested in what happens "during the reading event, as he fixes his attention on the actual experience he is living through," according to Rosenblatt. Readers focus upon the ideas, images, and story of the text that evoke an aesthetic experience in the moment of reading. **Efferent readers**, in contrast, read to learn from the text, and, thus, according to Rosenblatt, "concentrate on the information, the concepts, the guides to action, that will be left with him when the reading is over."

Reading rhetorically is efferent reading, focusing not on the experience of reading but on the information the text conveys and upon the way an argument is established and supported in a text. Some arguments are written in an engaging style that is a pleasure to read, while others are written in a highly emotional tone that arouses a visceral response in the reader. A text that inspires aesthetic reading must sometimes be read several times in order for the reader to focus on the structure of the argument beneath the creative language.

Some theorists say that critical thinking is "thinking about thinking" or "reasoning about reasoning," and that is exactly what reading rhetorically involves—reasoning about whether or not a text presents a reasoned argument. A good way to begin reading rhetorically is to be aware of the essential elements of an argument and identify these elements in the text you are evaluating. See the Checklist of Essential Elements in an Argument presented below.

Checklist of Essential Elements in an Argument

☑ *A debatable issue.* By definition, for a text to be an argument, there must be at least two sides that can be asserted and supported.

☑ *A clearly stated position, claim statement, or thesis.* Arguments assert different kinds of claims, such as taking a position on an issue of fact, asserting a cause and effect relationship, declaring the value of some entity, or advocating a solution to a problem; but, in each case, after you read the argument, you should be able to restate or summarize the position, claim, or thesis in one or two sentences.

☑ *An audience.* To evaluate an argument, you need to know the original intended audience or place of publication, so that you can decide if the argument takes into account the audience's attitudes, background, and other factors. Ask yourself, for example, if the writer is assuming too much or too little background knowledge on the part of the audience or if the writer is using language that assumes the reader's agreement on the issue when that assumption is not warranted.

☑ *Evidence from reliable sources.* Quotes, statistics, and other evidence should be credited to reputable sources, even if your text is not a document that offers academic-style citations. The evidence should be sufficient to support the author's position or thesis.

☑ *Acknowledgment of the opposing argument.* A good rhetorician does not ignore any potential weaknesses in the argument. It is better to acknowledge points in favor of the opposing argument and then, if possible, refute the opposition's strong points than it is to allow an audience to poke holes in an argument.

☑ *A conclusion and/or call to action.* An argument can be concluded in a variety of effective ways, but it is important to note that it does, indeed, conclude. The conclusion can be a call to action on the part of the audience, but it should not be the beginning of an additional argument that is not supported by the evidence presented.

Reading 2.4

The Web Means the End of Forgetting
by Jeffrey Rosen

Several years ago, Stacy Snyder was a fairly typical 25-year-old college student training to be a teacher. That all changed forever when she did something that she probably thought was harmless fun—she posted a photo of herself on a social network site. In this article published in *The New York Times*, Jeffrey Rosen uses Snyder's case to illustrate how notions of privacy are changing because of the ever-growing presence and popularity of social networking sites. What is even more alarming, according to Rosen, is that photos and information, once posted on the web, are there forever. The web does not forget, and this lack of forgetting is changing society's ability to forgive and forget.

You may enjoy posting status updates about your life on a MySpace, Facebook, or Twitter account; however, with employers increasingly conducting background checks on such sites, it's very important to be careful about what you choose to post. This includes status updates, photographs, and videos. If you read the following article carefully, you may never look at social networking sites quite the same again.

Four years ago, Stacy Snyder, then a 25-year-old teacher in training at Conestoga Valley High School in Lancaster, Pa., posted a photo on her MySpace page that showed her at a party wearing a pirate hat and drinking from a plastic cup, with the caption "Drunken Pirate." After discovering the page, her supervisor at the high school told her the photo was "unprofessional," and the dean of Millersville University School of Education, where Snyder was enrolled, said she was promoting drinking in virtual view of her underage students. As a result, days before Snyder's scheduled graduation, the university denied her a teaching degree. Snyder sued, arguing that the university had violated her First Amendment rights by penalizing her for her (perfectly legal) after-hours behavior. But in 2008, a federal district judge rejected the claim, saying that because Snyder was a public employee whose photo didn't relate to matters of public concern, her "Drunken Pirate" post was not protected speech.

When historians of the future look back on the perils of the early digital age, Stacy Snyder may well be an icon. The problem she faced is only one example of a challenge that, in big and small ways, is confronting millions of people around the globe: how best to live our lives in a world where the Internet records everything and forgets nothing—where every online photo, status update, Twitter post and blog entry by and about us can be stored forever. With websites like LOL Facebook Moments, which collects and shares embarrassing personal revelations from Facebook users, ill-advised photos and online chatter are coming back to haunt people months or years after the fact.

Examples are proliferating daily: there was the 16-year-old British girl who was fired from her office job for complaining on Facebook, "I'm so totally bored!!"; there was the 66-year-old Canadian psychotherapist who tried to enter the United States but was turned away at the border—and barred permanently from visiting the country—after a border guard's Internet search found that the therapist had written an article in a philosophy journal describing his experiments 30 years ago with LSD. According to a recent survey by Microsoft, 75 percent of U.S. recruiters and human-resource professionals report that their companies require them to do online research about candidates, and many use a range of sites when scrutinizing applicants—including search engines, social networking sites, photo- and video-sharing sites, personal websites and blogs, Twitter and online gaming sites. Seventy percent of U.S. recruiters report that they have rejected candidates because of information found online, like photos and discussion-board conversations and membership in controversial groups.

Technological advances, of course, have often presented new threats to privacy. In 1890, in perhaps the most famous article on privacy ever written, Samuel Warren and Louis Brandeis complained that because of new technology—like the Kodak camera and the tabloid press—"gossip is no longer the resource of the idle and of the vicious but has become a trade." But the mild society gossip of the Gilded Age pales before the volume of revelations contained in the photos, video and chatter on social media sites and elsewhere across the Internet. Facebook, which surpassed MySpace in 2008 as the largest social-networking site, now has nearly 500 million members, or 22 percent of all Internet users, who spend more than 500 billion minutes a month on the site. Facebook users share more than 25 billion pieces of content each month (including news stories, blog posts and photos), and the average user creates 70 pieces of content a month. There are more than 100 million registered Twitter users, and the Library of Congress recently announced that it will be acquiring—and permanently storing—the entire archive of public Twitter posts since 2006.

In Brandeis's day—and until recently, in ours—you had to be a celebrity to be gossiped about in public: today all of us are learning to expect the scrutiny that used to be reserved for the famous and the infamous. A 26-year-old Manhattan woman told *The New York Times* that she was afraid of being tagged in online photos because it might reveal that she wears only two outfits when out on the town—a Lynyrd Skynyrd T-shirt or a basic black dress. "You have movie-star issues," she said, "and you're just a person."

We've known for years that the web allows for unprecedented voyeurism, exhibitionism and inadvertent indiscretion, but we are only beginning to understand the costs of an age in which so much of what we say, and of what others say about us, goes into our permanent—and public—digital files.

The fact that the Internet never seems to forget is threatening, at an almost existential level, our ability to control our identities; to preserve the option of reinventing ourselves and starting anew; to overcome our checkered pasts.

In a recent book, "Delete: The Virtue of Forgetting in the Digital Age," the cyberscholar Viktor Mayer-Schönberger cites Stacy Snyder's case as a reminder of the importance of "societal forgetting." By "erasing external memories," he says in the book, "our society accepts that human beings evolve over time, that we have the capacity to learn from past experiences and adjust our behavior." In traditional societies, where missteps are observed but not necessarily recorded, the limits of human memory ensure that people's sins are eventually forgotten. By contrast, Mayer-Schönberger notes, a society in which everything is recorded "will forever tether us to all our past actions, making it impossible, in practice, to escape them." He concludes that "without some form of forgetting, forgiving becomes a difficult undertaking."

It's often said that we live in a permissive era, one with infinite second chances. But the truth is that for a great many people, the permanent memory bank of the web increasingly means there are no second chances—no opportunities to escape a scarlet letter in your digital past. Now the worst thing you've done is often the first thing everyone knows about you.

THE CRISIS—AND THE SOLUTION?

Concern about these developments has intensified this year, as Facebook took steps to make the digital profiles of its users generally more public than private. Last December, the company announced that parts of user profiles that had previously been private—including every user's friends, relationship status and family relations—would become public and accessible to other users. Then in April, Facebook introduced an interactive system called Open Graph that can share your profile information and friends with the Facebook partner sites you visit.

What followed was an avalanche of criticism from users, privacy regulators and advocates around the world. Four Democratic senators—Charles Schumer of New York, Michael Bennet of Colorado, Mark Begich of Alaska and Al Franken of Minnesota—wrote to the chief executive of Facebook, Mark Zuckerberg, expressing concern about the "instant personalization" feature and the new privacy settings. In May, Facebook responded to all the criticism by introducing a new set of privacy controls that the company said would make it easier for users to understand what kind of information they were sharing in various contexts.

Facebook's partial retreat has not quieted the desire to do something about an urgent problem. All around the world, political leaders, scholars and citizens are searching for responses to the challenge of preserving control of our identities in a digital world that never forgets. Are the most promising solutions going to be technological? Legislative? Judicial? Ethical? A result of shifting social norms and cultural expectations? Or some mix of the above? Alex Türk, the French data protection commissioner, has called for a "constitutional right to oblivion" that would allow citizens to maintain a greater degree of anonymity online and in public places. In Argentina, the writers Alejandro Tortolini and Enrique Quagliano have started a campaign to "reinvent forgetting on the Internet," exploring a range of political and technological ways of making data disappear. In February, the European Union helped finance a campaign called "Think B4 U post!" that urges young people to consider the "potential consequences" of publishing photos of themselves or their friends without "thinking carefully" and asking permission. And in the United States, a group of technologists, legal scholars and cyberthinkers are exploring ways of recreating the possibility of digital forgetting. These approaches share the common goal of reconstructing a form of control over our identities: the ability to reinvent ourselves, to escape our pasts and to improve the selves that we present to the world. [. . .]

[. . .] In the near future, Internet searches for images are likely to be combined with social-network aggregator search engines, like today's Spokeo and Pipl, which combine data from online sources—including political contributions, blog posts, YouTube videos, web comments, real estate listings and photo albums. Increasingly these aggregator sites will rank people's public and private reputations, like the new website Unvarnished, a reputation marketplace where people can write anonymous reviews about anyone. In the Web 3.0 world, Michael Fertik, a Harvard Law School graduate, predicts people will be rated, assessed and scored based not on their creditworthiness but on their trustworthiness as good parents, good dates, good employees, good baby sitters or good insurance risks.

One legal option for responding to online setbacks to your reputation is to sue under current law. There's already a sharp rise in lawsuits known as Twittergation—that is, suits to force websites to remove slanderous or false posts. Last year, Courtney Love was sued for libel by the fashion designer Boudoir Queen for supposedly slanderous comments posted on Twitter, on Love's MySpace page and on the designer's online marketplace-feedback page. But even if you win a U.S. libel lawsuit, the website doesn't have to take the offending material down any more than a newspaper that has lost a libel suit has to remove the offending content from its archive.

Some scholars, therefore, have proposed creating new legal rights to force websites to remove false or slanderous statements. Cass Sunstein, the Obama administration's regulatory czar, suggests in his new book, "On Rumors," that there might be "a general right to demand retraction after a clear demonstration that a statement is both false and damaging." (If a newspaper or blogger refuses to post a retraction, they might be liable for damages.) Sunstein adds that websites might be required to take down false postings after receiving notice that they are false—an approach modeled on the Digital Millennium Copyright Act, which requires websites to remove content that supposedly infringes intellectual property rights after receiving a complaint.

As Stacy Snyder's "Drunken Pirate" photo suggests, however, many people aren't worried about false information posted by others—they're worried about true information they've posted about themselves when it is taken out of context or given undue weight. And defamation law doesn't apply to true information or statements of opinion. Some legal scholars want to expand the ability to sue over true but embarrassing violations of privacy—although it appears to be a quixotic goal.

Daniel Solove, a George Washington University law professor and author of the book, *The Future of Reputation*, says that laws forbidding people to breach confidences could be expanded to allow you to sue your Facebook friends if they share your embarrassing photos or posts in violation of your privacy settings. Expanding legal rights in this way, however, would run up against the First Amendment rights of others. Invoking the right to free speech, the U.S. Supreme Court has already held that the media can't be prohibited from publishing the name of a rape victim that they obtained from public records. Generally, American judges hold that if you disclose something to a few people, you can't stop them from sharing the information with the rest of the world.

That's one reason that the most promising solutions to the problem of embarrassing but true information online may be not legal but technological ones. Instead of suing after the damage is done (or hiring a firm to clean up our messes), we need to explore ways of preemptively making the offending words or pictures disappear.

Zuckerberg said in January to the founder of the publication TechCrunch that Facebook had an obligation to reflect "current social norms" that favored exposure over privacy. "People have really gotten comfortable not only sharing more information and different kinds but more openly and with more people, and that social norm is just something that has evolved over time," he said.

However, norms are already developing to recreate off-the-record spaces in public, with no photos, Twitter posts or blogging allowed. Milk and Honey, an exclusive bar on Manhattan's Lower East Side, requires potential members to sign an agreement promising not to blog about the bar's goings on or to post photos on social-networking sites, and other bars and nightclubs are adopting similar policies. I've been at dinners recently where someone has requested, in all seriousness, "Please don't tweet this"—a custom that is likely to spread.

But what happens when people transgress those norms, using Twitter or tagging photos in ways that cause us serious embarrassment? Can we imagine a world in which new norms develop that make it easier for people to forgive and forget one another's digital sins? [. . .]

[. . .] Perhaps society will become more forgiving of drunken Facebook pictures in the way Samuel Gosling, the University of Texas, Austin, psychology professor says he expects it might. And some may welcome the end of the segmented self, on the grounds that it will discourage bad behavior and hypocrisy: it's harder to have clandestine affairs when you're broadcasting your every move on Facebook, Twitter and Foursquare. But a humane society values privacy, because it allows people to cultivate different aspects of their personalities in different contexts; and at the moment, the enforced merging of identities that used to be separate is leaving many casualties in its wake. Stacy Snyder couldn't reconcile her "aspiring-teacher self" with her "having-a-few-drinks self": even the impression, correct or not, that she had a drink in a pirate hat at an off-campus party was enough to derail her teaching career.

That doesn't mean, however, that it had to derail her life. After taking down her MySpace profile, Snyder is understandably trying to maintain her privacy: her lawyer told me in a recent interview that she is now working in human resources; she did not respond to a request for comment. But her success as a human being who can change and evolve, learning from her mistakes and growing in wisdom, has nothing to do with the digital file she can never entirely escape. Our character, ultimately, can't be judged by strangers on the basis of our Facebook or Google profiles; it can be judged by only those who know us and have time to evaluate our strengths and weaknesses, face to face and in context, with insight and understanding. In the meantime, as all of us stumble over the challenges of living in a world without forgetting, we need to learn new forms of empathy, new ways of defining ourselves without reference to what others say about us and new ways of forgiving one another for the digital trails that will follow us forever.

Activity 2.6 Discuss "The Web Means the End of Forgetting"

1. What is the significance of the title, "The Web Means the End of Forgetting"?
2. What does Jeffrey Rosen mean when he suggests that in the future Stacy Snyder may be an icon?
3. What is the main point in Jeffrey Rosen's main essay? What is he arguing?
4. Does Rosen offer sufficient evidence to make you take his argument seriously? Why or why not?
5. Are you a member of any social networking sites? What can you do in order to protect your reputation?
6. A woman interviewed in the article said, in regard to being tagged in online photos, "you have movie-star issues—and you're just a person." If you are a member of any social networking sites, do you tag friends in photos? Is it important to be careful about this? Why or why not?

Activity 2.7 What Is the Current State of Identity Protection in Social Networking Sites?

In your group, explore news, watchdog, and government sites to see if any new laws or other protections have been implemented to safeguard individuals posting personal information on the web. Report what you learn to the class.

Close Reading of a Text

Rhetorical reading involves careful and patient attention to the text, even reading the text several times. Following are several strategies for reading critically. You do not need to use all of the reading strategies suggested for each essay you read, but as you begin to read critically, you should try all of the strategies at least once to see which ones supplement your natural reading and learning style.

1. **Learn about the author.** Knowing whether an author is a biologist, a professional writer, or a politician can guide your expectations of the essay. If you are reading in a magazine or journal, you can often discover information in the contributor's notes at the beginning or end of the essay or at the beginning or end of the magazine. Many books have a dust jacket or a page giving a short biography of the author. As you learn about the author, jot down any impressions you may have about the author's purpose in writing the essay. Does the author have an obvious agenda in promoting a certain viewpoint on the topic?

2. **Skim the text.** Once you've gotten to know the author a little, it is helpful to read the essay quickly and superficially by reading the introduction, the first sentence in every paragraph, and the conclusion. Read quickly. When you skim a text, you are not trying to understand it. You are preparing for the more careful read that will follow. If the essay tells a story, skimming will give you a good sense of the chronology of the story. When is the story taking place? How much time seems to pass? If the essay is argumentative, skimming will provide knowledge of the basic structure of the argument and will introduce you to the main points of support. If the essay is primarily informative, you will learn some of the important distinctions and classifications the author uses to organize the information.

   It may be interesting to note whether you can get the gist of the reading by skimming. Has the writer provided topic sentences for paragraphs or sections? If so, the writer is trying to make his or her message easily accessible.

3. **Explore your own knowledge and beliefs on the subject.** Make a list of what you already know about the topic of the text. Then make a list of what you believe about this topic. Finally, make a note beside each entry that marks where that information or belief came from.

4. **Reflect on the topic.** The final step before reading is reflecting on what you expect from the essay before you begin a careful reading. What does the title lead you to expect from the essay? Does your quick glance at the essay seem to support the title? How do you feel about the essay so far? Does it anger you, interest you, bore you? Do you think you have any experience that relates to the essay? Will your experience and the

author's experience lead you to the same conclusions? One effective way to reflect is to freewrite on the topic of the essay. Exploring what you know before you embark on a careful reading of the essay can deepen your responses.

5. Annotate. Read the essay slowly, thinking about what meaning the author is trying to convey. It is a good idea to annotate as you read, particularly points that seem important and/or raise questions in your mind. If you don't want to write in your text, try photocopying assigned essays so you can annotate them. You'll probably develop your own system of annotation as you begin to use this technique more often, but here are some basic guidelines to help you begin your annotations:

- Underline sentences, phrases, and words that seem important to the essay.
- Circle words you don't know but think you understand from the context. Then you can look them up later to see if the dictionary definition matches the definition you assumed from the context.
- Write questions in the margins. If the margins aren't large enough to write a complete question, a couple of words to remind you of what you were thinking and a question mark will do. You can also write brief comments in the margins, again just a few words to remind you of your thoughts.
- Number or put check marks in the margin by major points. Careful annotation of each point in the margin will help you later if you choose to outline.
- Use arrows, lines, and symbols in the margins to connect ideas in the essay that seem related or depend on each other.
- Note transitions, sentence structures, examples, topic sentences, and other rhetorical moves that seem particularly effective in the essay by writing a brief comment or an exclamation mark in the margin next to the underlined text.

See figure 2.2 on page 60 for an example of an annotated article.

6. Outline. An excellent way to distill the meaning of a text is to create an informal outline of the argument. If, as part of annotating the essay, you jot down the main subject of each paragraph in the margin, this will allow you to see the organization of the essay and outline it easily. An outline should list the focus of the essay and track how that focus unfolds paragraph by paragraph. If you are outlining a narrative essay, the outline will probably follow the chronology of the events. Outlining an informative essay, you might find that the outline tracks the steps of a process or reveals divisions and classifications. Outlining an argumentative essay, you'll probably find your outline works to prove a thesis by making statements which support that thesis, raising objections and refuting them, or, perhaps, proposing solutions to solve a problem.

7. **Freewrite about the text.** Another way to distill the meaning of a text after you have read it carefully is to lay the essay aside and freewrite for a few minutes about the content and purpose of the essay. If you have not tried freewriting before, it is easy. You simply put your pen to the paper, focus the topic in your mind, and write whatever comes to mind about the topic for a set period of time, perhaps five minutes. If you cannot think of anything to write, you write, "I can't think of anything to write," and then you continue writing what is in your mind. You may find it helpful to begin your freewriting by writing, "This essay is about . . ." and continue writing, explaining to yourself what you think the essay is about.

8. **Summarize the text.** Write a summary of what you consider to be the primary meaning of the text. Your summary should answer these questions about claims, support, purpose, and audience:

- What is the author of the essay trying to show or prove (claim)?

- What does the writer use to convince me that he or she is well informed or right (support)?

- Why did the writer choose to write this essay (purpose)?

- Who is the author addressing or writing for (audience)?

To write a clear summary, you have to understand the essay. You might test your understanding by reading the essay again and deciding whether your summary is accurate. Writing summaries helps you understand your assignments and prepares you for the numerous summaries you will complete.

Responding to Oral and Visual Media

Increasingly, young "politically minded viewers" are plugging into YouTube, Facebook, and comedy shows like "The Daily Show" and other alternative media instead of traditional news outlets. According to a *New York Times*

figure 2.2

Reading 2.2

President Barack Obama on the Death of Osama bin Laden

One man affected so many

Good evening. Tonight, I can report to the American people and to the world that the United States has conducted an operation that killed Osama bin Laden, the leader of al Qaeda, and a terrorist who's responsible for the murder of thousands of innocent men, women, and children.

Where was I when it happened?

visual image— good technique

It was nearly 10 years ago that a bright September day was darkened by the worst attack on the American people in our history. The images of 9/11 are seared into our national memory—hijacked planes cutting through a cloudless September sky; the Twin Towers collapsing to the ground; black smoke billowing up from the Pentagon; the wreckage of Flight 93 in Shanksville, Pennsylvania, where the actions of heroic citizens saved even more heartbreak and destruction.

strong verbs

Presidential seal— ethos

President Barack Obama announced the death of Osama bin Laden.

And yet we know that the worst images are those that were unseen to the world. The empty seat at the dinner table. Children who were forced to grow up without their mother or their father. Parents who would never know the

refers to children— Pathos

article, surveys and interviews during the 2008 presidential election indicate that "younger voters tend to be not just consumers of news and current events but conduits as well—sending out e-mailed links and videos to friends and their social networks. And in turn, they rely on friends and online connections for news to come to them." **Word of mouth** (via e-mail) is replacing traditional media as the major news filter, at least for young viewers. In this new process, moreover, "viewers" or "writers of e-mail" move seamlessly back and forth between e-mail, text-messaging, television viewing, and Internet surfing, appreciating and sharing the choicest rhetorical pieces with others. "We're talking about a generation that doesn't just like seeing the video in addition to the story—they expect it," said Danny Shea, 23, the associate

Chapter 2 | **Responding Rhetorically**

media editor for *The Huffington Post* (huffingtonpost.com). "And they'll find it elsewhere if you don't give it to them, and then that's the link that's going to be passed around over e-mail and instant message." This multistream, cross-platform method of communication among younger viewers/readers is a fertile forum for rhetorical analysis.

Actually, the lines between oral, written, and visual "texts" have always been somewhat blurred. Speeches delivered orally in person or on television have a visual component, as the audience sees the speaker present the text. A written text is also, in a sense, visual because the audience's mind must process the little squiggles of ink on paper or on the computer screen into words. A visual text such as an advertisement or cartoon often includes written text, and, even if it does not, the image will inspire thoughts that are often distilled into language for expression. Reasonably, many of the same techniques used to analyze written and oral texts also can be applied to visual media (cartoons, advertisements, television, etc.).

Reading 2.5

I know I said I love you,

I know you know it's true,
I've got to put the phone down,
and do what we got to do.

One's standing in the aisleway,
Two more at the door,
We've got to get inside there,
Before they kill some more.

Time is runnin' out,
Let's roll.
Time is runnin' out,
Let's roll.

No time for indecision,
We've got to make a move,
I hope that we're forgiven,
For what we got to do

Let's Roll
by Neil Young

Music lyrics are performance texts, just as are speeches. They are written to be heard, not written to be read. However, you can analyze the argument in song lyrics, such as "Let's Roll," reprinted here, which was written by Neil Young. The song was inspired by the last words of a passenger named Todd Beamer, who died in the hijacking of Flight 93 on September 11, 2001. To analyze the song's lyrics rhetorically, you can consider whether the lyrics have a debatable issue, a clear thesis or claim, evidence to support that claim, a particular audience, and a conclusion. With a song, moreover, you can also consider the impact of the lyrics as they are presented by a vocalist accompanied by musical instruments. How does the musical presentation of the lyrics affect their impact as an argument?

How this all got started,
I'll never understand,
I hope someone can fly this thing,
And get us back to land.

Time is runnin' out,
Let's roll.
Time is runnin' out,
Let's roll.

No one has the answer,
But one thing is true,
You've got to turn on evil,
When it's coming after you,
You've gotta face it down,
And when it tries to hide,
You've gotta go in after it,
And never be denied,

Time is runnin' out,
Let's roll.

Let's roll for freedom,
Let's roll for love,
We're going after Satan,
On the wings of a dove,
Let's roll for justice,
Let's roll for truth,
Let's not let our children,
Grow up fearful in their youth.

Time is runnin' out,
Let's roll.
Time is runnin' out,
Let's roll.
Time is runnin' out,
Let's roll.

Activity 2.8 Respond to Song Lyrics

1. Reflect on what you know about the September 11 attacks. At the end of the first stanza, Young writes, "I've got to put the phone down, and do what we got to do." What is the call to action he is making here? What rhetorical significance does it have in this historical context?

2. Who is Young referring to when he says, "We're going after Satan"? What action is he advocating?

Activity 2.9 Consider a Song as an Argument

In your small group, explore the Internet for a song that seems to make an argument, and answer the following questions. Share your findings with the class.

1. What message is the artist/group trying to transmit with the song?

2. What are some lyrics that help to support this message?

3. How would you describe the musical style of the song? In what ways does the style of singing and instrumentation help the rhetorical message?

Responding to Visual Rhetoric

Methods of analyzing visual rhetoric draw upon several theoretical traditions. In art criticism, viewers may look for symbolism in an image or consider what meaning the artist was trying to convey. Semiotics views images as having intertextuality, as similar images come to have similar meanings, and those meanings may create similar emotions in the viewer. Rhetoricians, as you might expect, consider the argument that an image may present to a viewer. They think about how the subject of the image is presented in relation to other elements in the visual, how the image is cropped, and what types of lighting and colors are present. Rhetoricians also pay particular attention to the interplay between the visual image and any text that may appear with the image and how the two together construct an argument.

Courtesy BMW premium advertising.

In the BMW advertisement shown above, for example, a beautiful blonde-haired young woman is presented without clothes and lying down with her hair artfully arranged in waves. *Salon* magazine reprinted a copy of the BMW advertisement, pointing out that, "in small print scrawled across her bare shoulder, it reads: 'You know you're not the first.' As your eyes drift to the bottom of the advertisement—and the top of her chest—you learn that it's an advertisement for BMW's premium selection of used cars."

Of course, sexual appeal has been used for decades to sell a whole range of products. However, what do you think is BMW's argument here? *Salon* thinks the ad is implying, "Used cars, used women" and that the ad gives a "whole new meaning" to BMW's slogan, printed in the ad: "Sheer Driving Pleasure."

The image that appears below, surprisingly, isn't advertising a car. No, it is selling a community college, West Hills College, capitalizing on the idea that with all the money you would save by going to a community college, you could buy a nice car.

Courtesy West Hills College

Activity 2.10 Interpret Advertisements

1. What is the symbolism of the beautiful young woman (presumably naked) posed as she is in the BMW advertisement?

2. What meaning do you think the tag line, "You know you're not the first," adds to the image? Then, when you realize that the image is an ad for BMW used cars, does your interpretation of this tag line's meaning change?

3. What are the creators of the West Hills College advertisement trying to say by showing the image of the student sitting on the car?

4. The use of fonts is another important element in transmitting a message in an advertisement. In the West Hills College ad, why are the words "and save" written in a different font and inserted with the caret?

5. As a college student, would you be convinced by the West Hills advertisement? Why or why not? What elements exist in the ad that would or would not convince you to attend the college mentioned?

6. Do you find the BMW advertisement amusing, objectionable, or appealing? Does it make you want to buy a used BMW?

Activity 2.11 Find Advertisements with Effective Arguments

Bring to class an advertisement that you think makes an effective argument. It can be torn from a magazine or downloaded from the Internet. In your small group, evaluate each advertisement for its effectiveness in selling something, and choose the one with the most effective argument. Present your choice to the class along with an explanation of why you think it is effective.

Interaction between Texts and Images

Many of the texts we encounter in everyday life—in newspapers, magazines, and on the Internet—are not texts in isolation but texts combined with images. Indeed, when readers first glance at one of these media, likely their attention is caught first by photos, then by headlines. Only after being engaged by these attention-getting visual elements (for headlines are visual elements as well as written) are readers likely to focus on the written text. Student writers today, like professionals, have access to the use of visual elements in their compositions, and adding photos can not only catch the reader's attention but also emphasize particular points of an argument or create an overall mood.

Chapter 2 | **Responding Rhetorically**

All-Star Rockers Salute Buddy Holly

by Andy Greene

R&R

All-Star Rockers Salute Buddy Holly

McCartney, Cee Lo, the Black Keys, Kid Rock and more cut killer covers disc

When Buddy Holly died in a plane crash in 1959, he was just 22 years old and had been writing and recording songs for only about two years. But that music—including immortal hits like "Not Fade Away" and "Peggy Sue"—has had an incalculable impact on rock history. "He was a major influence on the Beatles," Paul McCartney told Rolling Stone recently. "John and I spent hours trying to work out how to play the opening riff to "That'll Be the Day," and we were truly blessed by the heavens the day we figured it out. It was the first song John, George and I ever recorded."

A half-century later, McCartney has returned to Holly's catalog, cutting a smoking rendition of "It's So Easy." It's one of 19 newly recorded Holly covers—by an all-star lineup including the Black Keys, My Morning Jacket, Kid Rock Fiona Apple, Patti Smith, and Lou Reed—for the tribute

NOT FADE AWAY
Holly in 1950. McCartney and Cee Lo recorded new songs commemorating Holly's 75th birthday.

disc *Rave on Buddy Holly*, spearheaded by Randall Poster, music supervisor of movies such as *The Royal Tenenbaums* and *I'm Not There*. "We wanted to commemorate Buddy's 75th birthday," Poster says. "I've used a lot of his songs in movies, and they're so powerful and so ripe for interpretation."

Florence and the Machine cut a New Orleans-flavored version of "Not Fade Away" while on tour in the Big Easy last year. "My grandmother took me to the musical *Buddy: The Buddy Holly Story* when I was a kid, and it changed my life," says singer Florence Welch. "When we were in New Orleans, we decided it would be good to use the environment around us, so we brought in local Cajun musicians." Cee Lo Green tackled the relatively obscure "You're So Square (Baby, I Don't Care)." "We wanted to keep the rockabilly intact," he says. "But we broadened it and gave it a bit of something unique to me. There's something Americana about it, something country and something African." Smith selected "Words of Love." "During the song she talks in Spanish and is sort of channeling [Holly's widow] Maria Elena Holly," says Poster. "It's so romantic and so novel. More times than not, we were just overwhelmed by the power of the renditions that we received." Despite Holly's extremely brief career, Poster thinks the set could have been even longer: "There's probably a half-dozen more songs we could have done. If I had more time and more of a budget, I would have kept on going." ANDY GREENE

Activity 2.12 Analyze Interaction between Texts and Images

Read the article, "All-Star Rockers Salute Buddy Holly," by Andy Greene, published in *Rolling Stone* magazine. Look at how the images and layout work together and answer the questions:

1. What rhetorical purpose do the photos of these musicians achieve in relation to the article? Hint: think about the ethos (credibility, reputation, power) of these particular musicians, especially when they appear together on the page.

2. Consider the way the text is wrapped around the pictures. In particular, notice how this layout suggests a close relationship between Buddy Holly, Paul McCartney, and Cee Lo Green. What does this layout signify?

Activity 2.13 Write a Summary

Summarizing is an excellent technique to use when preparing for an exam or researching for an essay. It allows you to discern the main points of a text to see what is beneficial for you to know for the exam or paper. With a classmate, search for an article from a newspaper or magazine that presents a strong argument. Read the article, and list the main points individually. After you've listed the main points, put them into paragraph form. Caution: Beware of the temptation to add your own analysis of what the text is saying. For example, if you are summarizing a scientist's article on global warming, you need to be careful not to reveal your personal opinion about whether or not global warming is occurring or whether or not human actions are to blame. In this assignment, you summarize only. You do not argue or analyze.

When you're finished, compare your summary with that of your partner.

Kindle users love reading. But let's face it—a book is in your hands.

Sure, Amazon's Kindle makes it possible to read more books, clears up a lot of shelf space, fits snugly in anyone's baggage and can actually be cheaper in the long run. But each reading feels the same. The only difference is the words you read and your reaction to them. You begin to miss that sometimes rough feel of a hardback book, along with the slick, almost slippery design

of a paperback. Each book seems to have a smell of its own, something unique. And getting your hands dirty with ink from the finely written words was half the journey.

The Kindle erases that part of your reading experience. It feels the same, smells the same and even looks the same. Instead of turning pages, which is different sizes, thicknesses and colors from book to book, you're pressing the same button over and over again. In some ways, reading a classic on your Kindle actually devalues its adventure. But the eBook reader is convenient, practically weightless and serves up immediate literature consumption.

So where's the compromise?

Well, you can have the best of both worlds—sort of . . .

Reading 2.7

How to Make a Kindle Cover from a Hollowed Out Hardback Book

by Justin Meyers

The author of the following article explains why you would want to make a Kindle cover out of an old book instead of buying a new Kindle cover. What does the article say are the drawbacks of the Kindle? Think about it. These instructions are an argument, saying in text and photos that as wonderful as the Kindle is, it does not satisfy the needs of a reader to touch and smell a book. The author attempts to rectify the Kindle's shortcomings through these instructions for making a cover out of a book.

Notice also how the author uses photos to illustrate his text. If you had just the text and no photos, following the instructions would be much more difficult.

ebonical has crafted the perfect Kindle case—out of a hardcover book. Kindle cases can be expensive, so making a homemade Kindle cover is the perfect weekend project. And chances are you already have the perfect book for your Kindle collecting dust on your bookshelf. If not, you'll need to shop the local bookstores.

"I decided to carve out the pages of a printed book and thus complete the poetic circle of digital book readers destroying the printed word.

"Getting the right book turned out to be harder than I thought as most hardcover books are designed to be a particular size and variance is slight. Too small and the edges would be brittle. Too large and it would just become a hassle and ruin the point of having the small digital reader in the first place. With some time spent scouring thrift shops and second hand book stalls I managed, with some luck, to find what seemed to be the right book."

So, then how do you actually make the Kindle book cover?

STEP 1 Gather the Materials

- Your perfectly-sized hardcover book
- Hobby PVA glue (polyvinyl acetate) or Elmer's white glue
- Paintbrush
- Scalpel, box cutter or other sharp utility knife
- Ruler
- Pencil
- More books (for use as weights)

STEP 2 Crafting Your Kindle Case

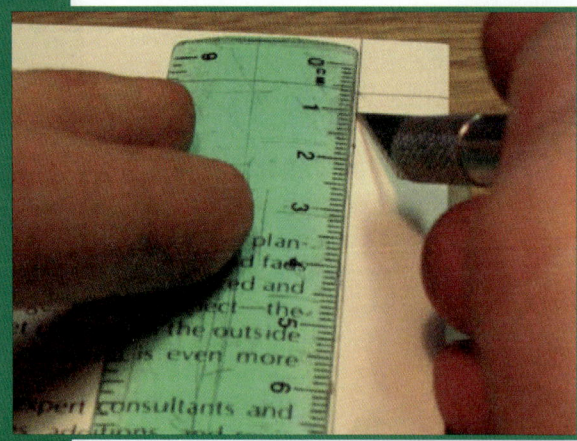

Getting your book ready for your Kindle is an easy process, though a lengthy one.

You begin by choosing where you want your hole to start. Once you have your spot picked, you use the paintbrush to spread the glue onto the edges of the pages where the hole will be cut. Use your extra books to weigh it down during the drying process.

Chapter 2 | **Responding Rhetorically**

When dry, open the book back up to your chosen starting point. Use the ruler and pencil to mark your hole the size of the Kindle. Once all marked, use your utility knife to start cutting on the outline. It's probably best to use your ruler as a straight edge to help guide the blade along, for a better, straighter cut. This is the longest step, because you have a lot to cut through. The time will vary depending on how deep your book is. I wouldn't recommend *War and Peace*.

Once you've gotten all the way to the back cover, the rest is easy. Just clean up the edges of your cuts as best you can, then use your paintbrush again to spread some glue along the cut edges.

TIP: When choosing your first page to cut, it's good to actually save it for later. Don't cut with the rest of them. When you have your hole fully cut open and have applied the glue, apply another thin line on the top border of your actual first page cut (essentially, the second page). Then close the book and add the weights to the top and let dry. Saving the first page helps reduce the chance of you accidentally gluing unwanted pages to cut ones, causing you to have to cut the pages you didn't want to cut to open the hole back up. Saving your first page makes it premeditated.

After fully dried, open it up and cut the final page (first page) to open the hole up. Then, you'll need to let it dry again, with the book open. After dried, that's it. You're done!

Activity 2.14 Write and Illustrate Instructions

Write and illustrate your own set of instructions for an activity that includes an argument. For example, during a lawn party at the White House, First Lady Michelle Obama served Carrot Lemonade to children who gave the drink rave reviews. Such a recipe could include an introduction explaining that creating healthy adaptations of popular foods and drinks for children only works if they taste good. Or, you might write instructions for how to remove geotags from photos before posting them on Facebook or other social networking sites. In your instructions you could explain that this process prevents people that you don't know from learning where you took the picture—and possibly learning where you live if you took it at home. Your argument would be that it is important to protect your privacy when you post photos on the Internet.

Try out your instructions on a friend, so you are sure you have included all the necessary steps and illustrated them adequately. Don't forget to include a brief statement of your argument, as does the writer of the Kindle cover article.

Activity 2.15 Create Your Own Blog

Read an article on the Internet related to a topic in which you're interested. Make sure the article has a substantial amount of text, as well as related images. In your blog, discuss how the text and the images both contribute to the article's rhetorical message. Include the title of the article, the author, the name of the publication or web page, and a link to the article.

Activity 2.16 Write in Your Commonplace Book

What do you read for fun? Magazines, blogs, books? Do you engage in what Louise Rosenblatt calls "aesthetic reading"? (See the section titled, "Ways of Reading Rhetorically") Write down a quote in your commonplace book from something that you have read for fun. First, reflect about what the quote means to you. Then, comment about why it is important to read things for fun and how that experience is different than reading to learn.

3
ANALYZING RHETORICALLY

Praxis in Action

Analyzing Arguments Improves My Writing by Eurydice Saucedo

Reading enables my creative mind to soar to undreamed-of worlds, to visit the deepest of memories, and to laugh as words describe a child's joy. Yes, reading enables me to be a bigger dreamer, but it also opens my eyes to better understand this world we live in.

Reading essays teaches me definitions and meanings, and, with practice, allows me to discern the validity and reliability of arguments. I can distinguish between fair representation of an issue, embellishment of truth, and bitter sarcasm. Every sentence has more than just simple grammar and punctuation. Every text, just like everything else in life, needs to be taken with a grain of salt, slowly simmered, and thought about before the final evaluation can be made. If I know rhetorical concepts, I can recognize when a text is trying to persuade me of something, and I can decide if the writer presents a good argument and sufficient evidence to merit serious consideration.

Reading and analyzing texts helps me learn how to structure my own argument. I may find a flaw in an argument, for example, a lack of acknowledgement of a counterargument that causes me to distrust a text. This causes me to be more careful to include the counterargument in my own text. And when I read and reread a classic argument such as Martin Luther King's "I Have a Dream" speech, I may make note of a strategy that I can use later. For example, Dr. King's adapting of President Lincoln's memorable language, saying, "five score years ago" instead of Lincoln's "four score and seven years ago" is highly effective. Perhaps I will try adapting a highly memorable quote when it fits in my argument.

One of the best ways to become a better writer is to read good writing.

Eurydice Saucedo writes, "Every text, just like everything else in life, needs to be taken with a grain of salt, slowly simmered, and thought about before the final evaluation can be made."

Discover the Kairos—The Opening for Argument

Kairos is a Greek word often translated as the right or opportune moment to do something, though it has no exact English translation. The first recorded use of the word kairos is in Homer's *Iliad*, where it appears as an adjective referring to an arrow striking the "deadliest spot" on the human body. When the word appears again later in Greek writing as a noun—a kairos—it retains this essential meaning as an opening or aperture. Twelve bronze axes with ring openings for wooden shanks are positioned in a line, so archers can practice by aiming at the kairos or ring opening, with the arrow passing down the line, through each ax. Clearly, launching an arrow through the kairos of twelve axes placed a yard apart required strength, training, practice, and a precise visual and muscle awareness of place. When people today say, "I saw my opening, and I took it, " they are conveying this meaning of kairos as an opening, combined with the idea of kairos as an opportunity.[1]

Ancient Greek archer

Ancient bronze ax with a ring hole for a wooden shank

Each time a rhetor (a speaker or writer) constructs an argument, he or she is working within a context of a certain moment, a particular time and place, that come together in a unique opportunity or opening for action—a kairos. A kairos both constrains and enables what a rhetor can say or write effectively in a particular situation. So, to compose the most effective text, a rhetor must do more than develop a thesis or statement of the main idea that takes a position about the subject—he or she must discover the kairos of the argument and its ramifications. What opportunities does the kairos present for making a persuasive argument, and what restrictions may be wise in consideration of the audience or occasion?

Use Kairos to Make Your Own Argument

Consider the following suggestions for determining the kairotic moment for your argument—the opening of sensitivity where you can shoot your metaphoric arrow:

- *Consider timeliness.* What is going on right now with the issue and how can you emphasize that in an argument? For example, if you are writing

[1] Thomas Rickert, "Invention in the Wild: On Locating Kairos in Space-Time," in *The Locations of Composition*. eds. Christopher J. Keller and Christian R. Weisser (Albany: SUNY Press, 2007) pp. 72–73.

Chapter 3 | **Analyzing Rhetorically**

about the death penalty, choose to write about the current cases on death row or the most recent person to be executed. Or, if your topic is about the unemployed exhausting their government benefits and you have, yourself, recently become unemployed, you can use your own experience as an illustration of the problem.

- *Know your audience.* What are the characteristics of the audience? Do they agree with your position on the issue or not? What is their educational level and the extent of their knowledge about the subject? For example, if you are writing about immigration policy reform, does your audience believe there is a need for reform? Do they have personal experience with illegal or legal immigrants? You can judge the amount of background information you need to provide based upon the characteristics of your audience. Also, the most important members of the audience, so far as an argument is concerned, are not those who already agree with you but those who are neutral or even slightly opposed to your position but willing to listen. Be careful not to phrase your argument in ways that are insulting to people who do not agree with you, for if you do so, they will stop listening to you.

- *Find a place to stand.* In the reading that follows, Martin Luther King, Jr., stood in front of the Lincoln Memorial as he gave his famous speech, "I Have a Dream." This location greatly impacts the speech and increases King's ethos, which we discuss in more detail below. You can make a similar rhetorical move, for example, if you live in a border community because you stand, metaphorically and physically, at an important juncture for issues such as immigration, free trade, and national security.

When Martin Luther King, Jr., gave his "I Have a Dream" speech, his words were carefully crafted to take into consideration the setting in front of the Lincoln Memorial. He said, "Five score years ago, a great American, in whose symbolic shadow we stand today, signed the Emancipation Proclamation." The words "five score" recall the "four score and seven years ago" of Lincoln's words in the Gettysburg Address. And King also pointed out that he and his audience that day stood in the "symbolic shadow" of the president who signed the Emancipation Proclamation. In these ways, he made use of Lincoln's shadow to legitimize what he was saying about civil rights.

In other ways, however, the kairos of the moment limited what he could say. His audience included both the thousands of people in front of him who were dedicated to the cause of racial equality and also the audience of those millions watching on television who may or may not have agreed with his message. Thus, the tone of his message needed to be subtly measured not to antagonize those among his audience, particularly the television audience, who may have opposed aspects of the civil rights movement such as school integration. However, he spoke to let both his supporters and his opponents know, "The whirlwinds of revolt will continue to shake the foundations of our nation until the bright day of justice emerges." Yes, King advocated nonviolent demonstrations, but they were demonstrations nonetheless; he was putting opponents on notice that the disruptions caused by demonstrations would continue "until justice emerges." King consistently took the high road, while maintaining the power of the kairotic moment when he spoke. This is one reason why his words continue to be studied decades after his death.

Reading 3.1

I Have a Dream
by Martin Luther King, Jr.

Martin Luther King, Jr., delivered this speech on August 28, 1963, at the Lincoln Memorial in Washington, D.C., as part of the March on Washington for Jobs and Freedom. A Baptist minister, King received the Nobel Peace Prize in 1964 for his efforts to end racial discrimination through nonviolent means. He was assassinated in 1968.

I am happy to join with you today in what will go down in history as the greatest demonstration for freedom in the history of our nation.

Five score years ago, a great American, in whose symbolic shadow we stand today, signed the Emancipation Proclamation. This momentous decree came as a great beacon light of hope to millions of Negro slaves who had been seared in the flames of withering injustice. It came as a joyous daybreak to end the long night of their captivity.

But one hundred years later, the Negro still is not free. One hundred years later, the life of the Negro is still sadly crippled by the manacles of segregation and the chains of discrimination. One hundred years later, the Negro lives on a lonely island of poverty in the midst of a vast ocean of material prosperity. One hundred years later, the Negro is still languished in the corners of American society and finds himself an exile in his own land. And so we've come here today to dramatize a shameful condition.

In a sense we've come to our nation's capital to cash a check. When the architects of our republic wrote the magnificent words of the Constitution and the Declaration of Independence, they were signing a promissory note to which every American was to fall heir. This note was a promise that all men, yes, black men as well as white men, would be guaranteed the "unalienable Rights" of "Life, Liberty and the pursuit of Happiness." It is obvious today that America has defaulted on this promissory note, insofar as her citizens of color are concerned. Instead of honoring this sacred obligation, America has given the Negro people a bad check, a check which has come back marked "insufficient funds."

But we refuse to believe that the bank of justice is bankrupt. We refuse to believe that there are insufficient funds in the great vaults of opportunity of this nation. And so, we've come to cash this check, a check that will give us upon demand the riches of freedom and the security of justice.

We have also come to this hallowed spot to remind America of the fierce urgency of Now. This is no time to engage in the luxury of cooling off or to take the tranquilizing drug of gradualism. Now is the time to make real the promises of democracy. Now is the time to rise from the dark and desolate valley of segregation to the sunlit path of racial justice. Now is the time to lift our nation from the quicksands of racial injustice to the solid rock of brotherhood. Now is the time to make justice a reality for all of God's children.

It would be fatal for the nation to overlook the urgency of the moment. This sweltering summer of the Negro's legitimate discontent will not pass until there is an invigorating autumn of freedom and equality. Nineteen sixty-three is not an end, but a beginning. And those who hope that the Negro needed to blow off steam and will now be content will have a rude awakening if the nation returns to business as usual. And there will be neither rest nor tranquility in America until the Negro is granted his citizenship rights. The whirlwinds of revolt will continue to shake the foundations of our nation until the bright day of justice emerges.

But there is something that I must say to my people, who stand on the warm threshold which leads into the palace of justice: In the process of gaining our rightful place, we must not be guilty of wrongful deeds. Let us not seek to satisfy our thirst for freedom by drinking from the cup of bitterness and hatred. We must forever conduct our struggle on the high plane of dignity and discipline. We must not allow our creative protest to degenerate into physical violence. Again and again, we must rise to the majestic heights of meeting physical force with soul force.

The marvelous new militancy which has engulfed the Negro community must not lead us to a distrust of all white people, for many of our white brothers, as evidenced by their presence here today, have come to realize that their destiny is tied up with our destiny. And they have come to realize that their freedom is inextricably bound to our freedom.

We cannot walk alone.

And as we walk, we must make the pledge that we shall always march ahead.

We cannot turn back.

There are those who are asking the devotees of civil rights, "When will you be satisfied?" We can never be satisfied as long as the Negro is the victim of the unspeakable horrors of police brutality. We can never be satisfied as long as our bodies, heavy with the fatigue of travel, cannot gain lodging in the motels of the highways and the hotels of the cities. We cannot be satisfied as long as the negro's basic mobility is from a smaller ghetto to a larger one. We can never be satisfied as long as our children are stripped of their selfhood and robbed of their dignity by a sign stating: "For Whites Only." We cannot be satisfied as long as a Negro in Mississippi cannot vote and a Negro in New York believes he has nothing for which to vote. No, no, we are not satisfied, and we will not be satisfied until "justice rolls down like waters, and righteousness like a mighty stream."[2]

I am not unmindful that some of you have come here out of great trials and tribulations. Some of you have come fresh from narrow jail cells. And some of you have come from areas where your quest—quest for freedom left you battered by the storms of persecution and staggered by the winds of police brutality. You have been the veterans of creative suffering. Continue to work with the faith that unearned suffering is redemptive. Go back to Mississippi, go back to Alabama, go back to South Carolina, go back to Georgia, go back to Louisiana, go back to the slums and ghettos of our northern cities, knowing that somehow this situation can and will be changed.

Let us not wallow in the valley of despair, I say to you today, my friends.

And so even though we face the difficulties of today and tomorrow, I still have a dream. It is a dream deeply rooted in the American dream.

I have a dream that one day this nation will rise up and live out the true meaning of its creed: "We hold these truths to be self-evident, that all men are created equal."

I have a dream that one day on the red hills of Georgia, the sons of former slaves and the sons of former slave owners will be able to sit down together at the table of brotherhood.

I have a dream that one day even the state of Mississippi, a state sweltering with the heat of injustice, sweltering with the heat of oppression, will be transformed into an oasis of freedom and justice.

I have a dream that my four little children will one day live in a nation where they will not be judged by the color of their skin but by the content of their character.

I have a dream today!

I have a dream that one day, down in Alabama, with its vicious racists, with its governor having his lips dripping with the words of "interposition" and "nullification"—one day right there in Alabama little black boys and black girls will be able to join hands with little white boys and white girls as sisters and brothers.

I have a dream today!

I have a dream that one day every valley shall be exalted, and every hill and mountain shall be made low, the rough places will be made plain, and the crooked places will be made straight; "and the glory of the Lord shall be revealed and all flesh shall see it together."[3]

This is our hope, and this is the faith that I go back to the South with.

With this faith, we will be able to hew out of the mountain of despair a stone of hope. With this faith, we will be able to transform the jangling discords of our nation into a beautiful symphony of brotherhood. With this faith, we will be able to work together, to pray together, to struggle together, to go to jail together, to stand up for freedom together, knowing that we will be free one day.

And this will be the day—this will be the day when all of God's children will be able to sing with new meaning:

> My country 'tis of thee, sweet land of liberty, of thee I sing.
> Land where my fathers died, land of the Pilgrim's pride,
> From every mountainside, let freedom <u>ring</u>!

> And if America is to be a great nation, this must become true.

> And so let freedom ring from the prodigious hilltops of New Hampshire.
> Let freedom ring from the mighty mountains of New York.
> Let freedom ring from the heightening Alleghenies of Pennsylvania.
> Let freedom ring from the snow-capped Rockies of Colorado.
> Let freedom ring from the curvaceous slopes of California.

But not only that:
Let freedom ring from Stone Mountain of Georgia.
Let freedom ring from Lookout Mountain of Tennessee.
Let freedom ring from every hill and molehill of Mississippi.
From every mountainside, let freedom ring.

And when this happens, when we allow freedom to ring, when we let it ring from every village and every hamlet, from every state and every city, we will be able to speed up that day when all of God's children, black men and white men, Jews and Gentiles, Protestants and Catholics, will be able to join hands and sing in the words of the old Negro spiritual:

> Free at last! Free at last!
>
> Thank God Almighty, we are free at last![4]

[2] Amos 5:24 (rendered precisely in The American Standard Version of the Holy Bible)

[3] Isaiah 40:4–5 (King James Version of the Holy Bible). Quotation marks are excluded from part of this moment in the text because King's rendering of Isaiah 40:4 does not precisely follow the KJV version from which he quotes (e.g., "hill" and "mountain" are reversed in the KJV). King's rendering of Isaiah 40:5, however, is precisely quoted from the KJV.

[4] "Free at Last" from *American Negro Songs* by J. W. Work.

Activity 3.1 Use Microsoft's Comment Feature to Annotate a Text

If you download Dr. Martin Luther King's speech from AmericanRhetoric.com, you can make use of Microsoft's Comment feature to annotate the speech with your comments, as is done in the example below. In Microsoft Word, highlight the text you want to annotate, go to the "Insert" pull-down menu, and select "Comment." A box will appear where you can enter your comment.

> I am happy to join with you today in what will go down in history as the greatest demonstration for freedom in the history of our nation.
>
> Five score years ago, a great American, in whose symbolic shadow we stand today, signed the Emancipation Proclamation. This momentous decree came as a great beacon light of hope to millions of Negro slaves who had been seared in the flames of withering injustice. It came as a joyous daybreak to end the long night of their captivity.
>
> But one hundred years later, the Negro still is not free. One hundred years later, the life of the Negro is still sadly crippled by the manacles of segregation and the chains of discrimination. One hundred years later, the Negro lives on a lonely island of poverty in the midst of a vast ocean of material prosperity. One hundred years later, the Negro is

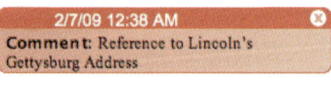

2/7/09 12:38 AM
Comment: Reference to Lincoln's Gettysburg Address

Chapter 3 | **Analyzing Rhetorically**

Activity 3.2 Discuss "I Have a Dream"

Read the "I Have a Dream" speech by Rev. Martin Luther King, Jr., and, if possible, watch the speech. It is archived at http://www.americanrhetoric.com, where it is listed as the most requested speech and #1 in its list of the top 100 American speeches.

1. Discuss the kairos of Dr. King's speech. What was the occasion? Who was his audience, both present and absent? What were the issues he spoke about?

2. How did Dr. King take advantage of the kairos of the situation in the wording of his speech?

3. Why do you think the speech continues to be so popular and influential?

Activity 3.3 Identify the Kairos

Identifying the kairos in Martin Luther King's speech in front of the Lincoln Memorial is easy. In some speeches, however, identifying the kairos is more difficult. Every speech and every text has a kairos, but some rhetors are better at identifying it and utilizing it than others. Identify the kairos in the following readings that have appeared thus far in the text. Then discuss in your group how the writer or speaker does or does not utilize kairos to maximum effect.

1. "Violent Rhetoric and Arizona Politics" (Chapter 1, p. 14)
2. "The Sleepover Question" (Chapter 1, p. 18)
3. "San Ysidro Shooting Survivor Lives His Dream of Being a Cop" (Chapter 1, p. 22)
4. "President Barack Obama on the Death of Osama bin Laden" (Chapter 2, p. 41)
5. "The Web Means the End of Forgetting" (Chapter 2, p. 50)

Activity 3.4 Analyze an Audience

Select a group that you do not belong to and analyze it as a potential audience. As one method, you might locate a blog on the Internet that advocates a point of view different from your own. For example, if you believe in global warming, read a blog frequented by those who do not share that belief. If you are a Democrat, look for a Tea Party or Republican blog. Find a yoga blog if you are a football fan. Read blog entries for a week and write a one-page analysis. Answer these questions:

1. What are the two or three issues of primary interest to the group? What is the general position on each issue?
2. Who are these people? Where do they live? What is their educational level?
3. What is the extent of their knowledge about the issues of primary interest? Are they familiar with the evidence, or do they just repeat opinions?
4. What types of appeals would make a difference to the readers of this blog: ethos, pathos, or logos? How so?

Aristotle's Persuasive Appeals

Some theorists associate the rhetorical triangle directly with Aristotle's **appeals** (or proofs): ethos, pathos, and logos. **Ethos** refers to the writer's (or speaker's) credibility; **pathos** refers to emotion used to sway the audience; and, finally, **logos** refers to the writer's purpose (or subject), for an effective argument will include evidence and other supporting details to back up the author's claims.

Aristotle wrote:

> Of those proofs that are furnished through the speech there are three kinds. Some reside in the character [*ethos*] of the speaker, some in a certain disposition [*pathos*] of the audience and some in the speech itself, through its demonstrating or seeming to demonstrate [*logos*].

Contemporary theorist Wayne C. Booth said something similar:

> The common ingredient that I find in all writing that I admire—excluding for now novels, plays, and poems—is something that I shall reluctantly call the rhetorical stance, a stance which depends upon discovering and maintaining in any writing situation a

Chapter 3 | **Analyzing Rhetorically**

proper balance among the three elements that are at work in any communicative effort: the available arguments about the subject itself [*logos*], the interests and peculiarities of the audience [*pathos*], and the voice, the implied character of the speaker [*ethos*].

Arguments from Logos

Logos or reason was Aristotle's favorite of the three persuasive appeals, and he bemoaned the fact that humans could not be persuaded through reason alone, indeed that they sometimes chose emotion over reason. Aristotle also used the term *logos* to mean rational discourse. To appeal to logos means to organize an argument with a clear claim or thesis, supported by logical reasons that are presented in a well-organized manner that is internally consistent. It can also mean the use of facts and statistics as evidence. However, logos without elements of pathos and ethos can be dry, hard to understand, and boring.

Consider the following logical argument that advocates the televising of executions.

Reading 3.2

Earlier this month, Georgia conducted its third execution this year. This would have passed relatively unnoticed if not for a controversy surrounding its videotaping. Lawyers for the condemned inmate, Andrew Grant DeYoung, had persuaded a judge to allow the recording of his last moments as part of an effort to obtain evidence on whether lethal injection caused unnecessary suffering.

Though he argued for videotaping, one of Mr. DeYoung's defense lawyers, Brian Kammer, spoke out against releasing the footage to the public. "It's a horrible thing that Andrew DeYoung had to go through," Mr. Kammer said, "and it's not for the public to see that."

We respectfully disagree. Executions in the United States ought to be made public.

Executions Should Be Televised
by Zachary B. Shemtob and David Lat

In this opinion piece published in *The New York Times*, Zachary B. Shemtob and David Lat argue what they know is going to be an unpopular position in the United States— that executions should be televised. Shemtob is an assistant professor of criminal justice at Connecticut State University and Lat is a former federal prosecutor who also founded a legal blog, *Above the Law*. They reason, "democracy demands maximum accountability and transparency." Knowing that their position contradicts present policy, they carefully address possible objections to their position, such as the idea that executions are too gruesome to put on television.

Right now, executions are generally open only to the press and a few select witnesses. For the rest of us, the vague contours are provided in the morning paper. Yet a functioning democracy demands maximum accountability and transparency. As long as executions remain behind closed doors, those are impossible. The people should have the right to see what is being done in their name and with their tax dollars.

This is particularly relevant given the current debate on whether specific methods of lethal injection constitute cruel and unusual punishment and therefore violate the Constitution.

There is a dramatic difference between reading or hearing of such an event and observing it through image and sound. (This is obvious to those who saw the footage of Saddam Hussein's hanging in 2006 or the death of Neda Agha-Soltan during the protests in Iran in 2009.) We are not calling for opening executions completely to the public—conducting them before a live crowd—but rather for broadcasting them live or recording them for future release, on the Web or TV.

When another Georgia inmate, Roy Blankenship, was executed in June, the prisoner jerked his head, grimaced, gasped and lurched, according to a medical expert's affidavit. The *Atlanta Journal-Constitution* reported that Mr. DeYoung, executed in the same manner, "showed no violent signs in death." Voters should not have to rely on media accounts to understand what takes place when a man is put to death.

Cameras record legislative sessions and presidential debates, and courtrooms are allowing greater television access. When he was an Illinois state senator, President Obama successfully pressed for the videotaping of homicide interrogations and confessions. The most serious penalty of all surely demands equal if not greater scrutiny.

Opponents of our proposal offer many objections. State lawyers argued that making Mr. DeYoung's execution public raised safety concerns. While rioting and pickpocketing occasionally marred executions in the public square in the 18th and 19th centuries, modern security and technology obviate this concern. Little would change in the death chamber; the faces of witnesses and executioners could be edited out, for privacy reasons, before a video was released.

Of greater concern is the possibility that broadcasting executions could have a numbing effect. Douglas A. Berman, a law professor, fears that people might come to equate human executions with putting pets to sleep. Yet this seems overstated. While public indifference might result over time, the initial broadcasts would undoubtedly get attention and stir debate.

Still others say that broadcasting an execution would offer an unbalanced picture—making the condemned seem helpless and sympathetic, while keeping the victims of the crime out of the picture. But this is beside the point: the defendant is being executed precisely because a jury found that his crimes were so heinous that he deserved to die.

Ultimately the main opposition to our idea seems to flow from an unthinking disgust—a sense that public executions are archaic, noxious, even barbarous. Albert Camus related in his essay "Reflections on the Guillotine" that viewing executions turned him against capital punishment. The legal scholar John D. Bessler suggests that public executions might have the same effect on the public today; Sister Helen Prejean, the death penalty abolitionist, has urged just such a strategy.

That is not our view. We leave open the possibility that making executions public could strengthen support for them; undecided viewers might find them less disturbing than anticipated.

Like many of our fellow citizens, we are deeply conflicted about the death penalty and how it has been administered. Our focus is on accountability and openness. As Justice John Paul Stevens wrote in *Baze v. Rees*, a 2008 case involving a challenge to lethal injection, capital punishment is too often "the product of habit and inattention rather than an acceptable deliberative process that weighs the costs and risks of administering that penalty against its identifiable benefits."

A democracy demands a citizenry as informed as possible about the costs and benefits of society's ultimate punishment.

Activity 3.5 Analyze an Argument from Logos

1. In your small group, go over the Checklist of Essential Elements in an Argument (Chapter 2), and decide if the authors of this article fulfill each one. Be prepared to defend your decisions to the class.

2. Shemtob and Lat present a logical argument about why executions should be televised. Ignoring your own reaction to their editorial, outline the main points.

3. How do the authors handle their audience's possible emotional objections to their argument? Give an example.

4. What is your reaction to the argument that executions should be televised? Did reading and evaluating the article cause you to see the issue differently? If so, in what way?

Deductive Reasoning

Aristotle was the first person in Western culture to write systematically about logic, and he is credited with developing and promoting syllogistic or **deductive reasoning** in which statements are combined to draw a **conclusion**. He wrote that "a statement is persuasive and credible either because it is directly self-evident or because it appears to be proved from other statements that are so." This logical structure is called a **syllogism**, in which premises lead to a conclusion. The following is perhaps the most famous syllogism:

Major premise: All humans are mortal.

Minor premise: Socrates is human.

Conclusion: Socrates is mortal.

The **major premise** is a general statement accepted by everyone that makes an observation about all people. The second statement of the syllogism is the **minor premise**, which makes a statement about a particular case within the class of all people. Comparison of the two premises, the general class of "all humans" and the particular case of "Socrates" within the class of "all humans" leads to the conclusion that Socrates also fits in the class "mortal," and thus his death is unavoidable. Thus, the logic moves from the general to the particular.

Chapter 3 | **Analyzing Rhetorically**

Similarly, if you try the pumpkin bread at one Starbucks and like it, you may infer that you will like the pumpkin bread at another Starbucks. The argument would look like this:

> Major premise: Food products at Starbucks are standardized from one Starbucks to another.
>
> Minor premise: You like the pumpkin bread at one Starbucks.
>
> Conclusion: You will like the pumpkin bread at another Starbucks.

However, if your major premise is wrong, and the owner of one Starbucks substitutes an inferior stock of pumpkin bread, then your conclusion is wrong. Deductive reasoning is dependent upon the validity of each premise; otherwise the syllogism does not hold true. If the major premise that food products are standardized at all Starbucks franchises does not hold true, then the argument is not valid. A good deductive argument is known as a valid argument and is such that if all its premises are true, then its conclusion must be true. Indeed, for a deductive argument to be valid, it must be absolutely impossible for both its premises to be true and its conclusion to be false.

Inductive Reasoning

Aristotle identified another way to move logically between premises, which he called "the progress from particulars to universals." Later logicians labeled this type of logic as **inductive reasoning**. Inductive arguments are based on probability. Even if an inductive argument's premises are true, that doesn't establish with 100 percent certainty that its conclusions are true. Even the best inductive argument falls short of deductive validity.

Consider the following examples of inductive reasoning:

> Particular statement: Milk does not spoil as quickly if kept cold.
>
> General statement: All perishable foods do not spoil as quickly if kept cold.
>
> Particular statement: Microwaves cook popcorn more quickly than conventional heat.
>
> General statement: All foods cook more quickly in a microwave.

In the first example, inductive reasoning works well because cold tends to prolong the useable life of most perishable foods. The second example is more problematic. While it is true that popcorn cooks more quickly in a microwave oven, the peculiarities of microwave interaction with food molecules does not produce a uniform effect on all food stuffs. Rice, for example, does not cook much, if any, faster in a microwave than it does on a stovetop. Also, whole eggs may explode if cooked in their shells.

A good inductive argument is known as a strong (or "cogent") inductive argument. It is such that if the premises are true, the conclusion is likely to be true.

Activity 3.6 Identify Deductive and Inductive Reasoning

In your small group, identify an example of a deductive argument and list the premises and conclusion. Then identify an inductive argument and identify the particular statement and the general statement. Report to the class.

Logical Fallacies

Generally speaking, a **logical fallacy** is an error in reasoning, as opposed to a factual error, which is simply being wrong about the facts. A **deductive fallacy** (sometimes called a *formal fallacy*) is a deductive argument that has premises that are all true, but they lead to a false conclusion, making it an invalid argument. An **inductive fallacy** (sometimes called an *informal fallacy*) appears to be an inductive argument, but the premises do not provide enough support for the conclusion to be probable. Some logical fallacies are more common than others and, thus, have been labeled and defined. Following are a few of the most well-known types:

Ad hominem (to the man) are arguments that attempt to discredit a point of view through personal attacks upon the person who has that point of view. These arguments are not relevant to the actual issue because the character of the person that holds a view says nothing about the truth of that viewpoint.

Example: Noam Chomsky is a liberal activist who opposes American intervention in other countries. Noam Chomsky's theory of transformational grammar, which suggests that humans have an innate ability to learn language, is ridiculous.

Non sequitur (Latin for "it does not follow") arguments have conclusions that do not follow from the premises. Usually, the author has left out a step in the logic, expecting the reader to make the leap over the gap.

Example: "Well, look at the size of this administration building; it is obvious this university does not need more funding."

Either/or or **false dichotomy** arguments force an either/or choice when, in reality, more options are available. Issues are presented as being either black or white.

Example: With all the budget cuts, "we either raise tuition or massively increase class size."

Red herring arguments avoid the issue and attempt to distract with a side issue.

Example: "Why do you question my private life issues, when we have social problems with which to deal?"

Ad populum (Latin for "appeal to the people") arguments appeal to popularity. If a lot of people believe it, it must be true.

Example: "Why shouldn't I cheat on this exam? Everyone else cheats."

Ad verecundium (Latin for "argument from that which is improper") arguments appeal to an irrelevant authority.

Example: "If the President of Harvard says it is a good idea, then we should follow suit." Or, "That is how we have always done it."

Begging the question arguments simply assume that a point of view is true because the truth of the premise is assumed. Simply assuming a premise is true does not amount to evidence that it *is* true.

Example: A woman's place is in the home; therefore, women should not work.

Confusing cause and effect is a common problem with scientific studies in which the fact that two events are correlated implies that one causes the other.

Example: Obese people drink a lot of diet soda; therefore, diet soda causes obesity.

Post hoc (from the Latin phrase "Post hoc, ergo proper hoc," or after this, therefore because of this) is a fallacy that concludes that one event caused another just because one occurred before the other.

Example: The Great Depression caused World War II.

In a **straw man** fallacy, a position of an opponent is exaggerated or weakened, so that it is easier for the opponent to argue against it.

Example: Pro-choice advocates believe in murdering unborn children.

A **slippery slope** argument asserts that one event will inevitably lead to another event.

Example: the Dilbert cartoon below:

DILBERT: © Scott Adams/Dist. by United Feature Syndicate, Inc.

These logical fallacies are summarized in table 3.1.

Chart of Fallacies and Examples		
Fallacy	**The Error in Reasoning**	**Example**
Ad hominem	When speakers attack the person making the argument and not the argument itself.	"We can't believe anything he says; he is a convicted felon."

table 3.1

Chapter 3 | Analyzing Rhetorically

Fallacy	The Error in Reasoning	Example
Ad populum	When we attempt to persuade people by arguing our position is reasonable because so many other people are doing it or agree with it.	"Why shouldn't I cheat on this exam? Everyone else cheats."
Ad verecundium	An appeal to persuasion based on higher authority or tradition.	"If the president of Harvard says it is a good idea, then we should follow suit." Or, "That is how we have always done it."
Begging the question	When a speaker presumes certain things are facts when they have not yet been proven to be truthful.	"Oh, everyone knows that we are all Christians."
Confusing cause and effect	A common problem with scientific studies in which the fact that two events are correlated implies that one causes the other.	"Obese people drink a lot of diet soda; therefore, diet soda causes obesity."
Either/or	Presents two options and declares that one of them must be correct while the other must be incorrect.	"We either raise tuition or massively increase class size."
Non sequitur	When you make an unwarranted move from one idea to the next.	"Well, look at the size of this administration building; it is obvious this university does not need more funding."
Post hoc	Assumes that because one event happened after another, then the preceding event caused the event that followed.	"Every time Sheila goes to a game with us, our team loses. She is bad luck."
Red herring	When a speaker introduces an irrelevant issue or piece of evidence to divert attention from the subject of the speech.	"Why do you question my private life issues, when we have social problems with which to deal?"
Slippery slope	Assumes that once an action begins it will follow, undeterred, to an eventual and inevitable conclusion.	"If we let the government dictate where we can pray, soon the government will tell us we cannot pray."

Fallacy	The Error in Reasoning	Example
Straw man	When a speaker ignores the actual position of an opponent and substitutes a distorted and exaggerated position.	"Oh, you think we should agree to a cut in our salaries. Why do you want to bleed us dry?"

Activity 3.7 Identify Logical Fallacies

Match the following types of logical fallacies with the examples below:

Types:
Ad hominem
Begging the question
Confusing cause and effect

Post hoc
Straw man
Slippery slope

Examples:

1. Legalization of medical marijuana will lead to increased marijuana use by the general population.

2. Twenty-one is the best age limit for drinking because people do not mature until they are 21.

3. If you teach birth control methods, more teenage girls will get pregnant.

4. The culture wars of the 1960s were a result of parents being unable to control their children after the post–World War II baby boom.

5. Al Gore claims that global warming is a dangerous trend. Al Gore is a liberal. Therefore, there is no global warming.

6. Immigration reform advocates want to separate families and children.

Activity 3.8 Create Examples of Logical Fallacies

In your small group, work through the chart of logical fallacies above and create a new example for each type of fallacy. Then report to the class, one fallacy at a time, with the instructor making a list of each group's examples on the chalk board. Discuss any examples that are not clear cases of a particular fallacy.

Chapter 3 | **Analyzing Rhetorically**

Arguments from Pathos

Pathos makes use of emotion to persuade an audience.

Aristotle wrote:

> Proofs from the disposition of the audience are produced whenever they are induced by the speech into an emotional state. We do not give judgment in the same way when aggrieved and when pleased, in sympathy and in revulsion.

Effective rhetors know their audiences, particularly what emotions they hold that are relevant to the issue under consideration. What motivates them? What are their fears, their hopes, their desires, and their doubts? If the audience has the same emotions as you do, fine. However, if they do not already hold those emotions, you need to bring them to share the hurt, the anger, or the joy that will persuade them to share your viewpoint—through the stories you tell, the statistics you cite, and the reasoning you offer.

For example, when Martin Luther King, Jr., in his "I Have a Dream" speech (reprinted earlier in this chapter) referred to the "hallowed spot" of the Lincoln Memorial, he was appealing to his audience's feelings of patriotism and reverence for the accomplishments of President Lincoln. Subtly, he was also garnering this emotion toward Lincoln in contemporary support of civil rights. Lincoln had issued the Emancipation Proclamation that declared all slaves to be free, yet, according to King, America had not lived up to Lincoln's promise.

Reading 3.3

People for Sale
by E. Benjamin Skinner

E. Benjamin Skinner has written on a wide range of topics. His articles have appeared in *Newsweek International, Travel and Leisure*, and other magazines. This essay was adapted from *A Crime So Monstrous: Face-to-Face with Modern-Day Slavery* and appeared in *Foreign Policy*.

Most people imagine that slavery died in the 19th century. Since 1810, more than a dozen international conventions banning the slave trade have been signed. Yet today there are more slaves than at any time in human history.

And if you're going to buy one in five hours, you'd better get a move on. First, hail a taxi to JFK International Airport and hop on a direct flight to Port-au-Prince, Haiti. The flight takes three hours. After landing, take a tap-tap, a flatbed pickup retrofitted with benches and a canopy, three-quarters of the way up Route de Delmas, the capital's main street. There, on a side street, you will find a group of men standing in front of Le Réseau (the Network) barbershop. As you approach, a man steps forward: "Are you looking to get a person?"

Meet Benavil Lebhom. He smiles easily. He has a trim mustache and wears a multicolored striped golf shirt, a gold chain, and Doc Martens knockoffs. Benavil is a courtier, or broker. He holds an official real estate license and calls himself an employment agent. Two-thirds of the employees he places are child slaves. The total number of Haitian children in bondage in their own country stands at 300,000. They are restavèks, the "stay-withs," as they are euphemistically known in Creole. Forced, unpaid, they work in captivity from before dawn until night. Benavil and thousands of other formal and informal traffickers lure these children from desperately impoverished rural parents with promises of free schooling and a better life.

The negotiation to buy a child slave might sound a bit like this:

"How quickly do you think it would be possible to bring a child in? Somebody who could clean and cook?" you ask. "I don't have a very big place; I have a small apartment. But I'm wondering how much that would cost? And how quickly?"

"Three days," Benavil responds.

"And you could bring the child here?" you inquire. "Or are there children here already?"

"I don't have any here in Port-au-Prince right now," says Benavil, his eyes widening at the thought of a foreign client. "I would go out to the countryside."

You ask about additional expenses. "Would I have to pay for transportation?"

"Bon," says Benavil. "A hundred U.S."

Smelling a rip-off, you press him, "And that's just for transportation?"

"Transportation would be about 100 Haitian," says Benavil, "because you'd have to get out there. Plus, [hotel and] food on the trip. Five hundred gourdes"—around $13.

"OK, 500 Haitian," you say.

Now you ask the big question: "And what would your fee be?" Benavil's eyes narrow as he determines how much he can take you for.

"A hundred. American."

"That seems like a lot," you say, with a smile so as not to kill the deal. "Could you bring down your fee to 50 U.S.?"

Benavil pauses. But only for effect. He knows he's still got you for much more than a Haitian would pay. "Oui," he says with a smile.

But the deal isn't done. Benavil leans in close. "This is a rather delicate question. Is this someone you want as just a worker? Or also someone who will be a 'partner'? You understand what I mean?"

You don't blink at being asked if you want the child for sex. "Is it possible to have someone who could be both?"

"Oui!" Benavil responds enthusiastically.

If you're interested in taking your purchase back to the United States, Benavil tells you that he can "arrange" the proper papers to make it look as though you've adopted the child.

He offers you a 13-year-old girl.

"That's a little bit old," you say.

"I know of another girl who's 12. Then ones that are 10, 11," he responds.

The negotiation is finished, and you tell Benavil not to make any moves without further word from you. You have successfully arranged to buy a human being for 50 bucks.

It would be nice if that conversation were fictional. It is not. I recorded it in October 2005 as part of four years of research into slavery on five continents. In the popular consciousness, "slavery" has come to be little more than just a metaphor for undue hardship. Investment bankers routinely refer to themselves as "high-paid wage slaves." Human rights activists may call $1-an-hour sweatshop laborers slaves, regardless of the fact that they are paid and can often walk away from the job.

The reality of slavery is far different. Slavery exists today on an unprecedented scale. In Africa, tens of thousands are chattel slaves, seized in war or tucked away for generations. Across Europe, Asia, and the Americas, traffickers have forced as many as 2 million into prostitution or labor. In South Asia, which has the highest concentration of slaves on the planet, nearly 10 million languish in bondage, unable to leave their captors until they pay off "debts," legal fictions that in many cases are generations old.

Few in the developed world have a grasp of the enormity of modern-day slavery. Fewer still are doing anything to combat it. . . . Between 2000 and 2006, the U.S. Justice Department increased human trafficking prosecutions from 3 to 32, and convictions from 10 to 98. By the end of 2006, 27 states had passed anti-trafficking laws. Yet, during the same period, the United States liberated only about 2 percent of its own modern-day slaves. As many as 17,500 new slaves continue to enter bondage in the United States every year . . . Many feel that sex slavery is particularly revolting—and it is. I saw it firsthand. In a Bucharest brothel, I was offered a mentally handicapped suicidal girl in exchange for a used car. But for every woman or child enslaved in commercial sex, there are some 15 men, women, and children enslaved in other fields, such as domestic work or agricultural labor.

Save for the fact that he is male, Gonoo Lal Kol typifies the average slave of our modern age. (At his request, I have changed his name.) Like a majority of the world's slaves, Gonoo is in debt bondage in South Asia. In his case, in an Indian quarry. Like most slaves, Gonoo is illiterate and unaware of the Indian laws that ban his bondage and provide for sanctions against his master. His story, told to me near his four-foot-high stone and grass hutch, represents the other side of the "Indian Miracle."

Gonoo lives in Lohagara Dhal, a forgotten corner of Uttar Pradesh, a north Indian state that contains 8 percent of the world's poor. I met him one evening in December 2005 as he walked with two dozen other laborers in tattered and filthy clothes. Behind them was the quarry. In that pit, Gonoo, a member of the historically outcast Kol tribe, worked with his family 14 hours a day. His tools were a hammer and a pike. His hands were covered in calluses, his fingertips worn away.

Gonoo's master is a tall, stout, surly contractor named Ramesh Garg. He makes his money by enslaving entire families forced to work for no pay beyond alcohol, grain, and subsistence expenses. Slavery scholar Kevin Bales estimates that a slave in the 19th-century American South had to work 20 years to recoup his or her purchase price. Gonoo and the other slaves earn a profit for Garg in two years.

Every single man, woman, and child in Lohagara Dhal is a slave. But, in theory at least, Garg neither bought nor owns them. The seed of Gonoo's slavery, for instance, was a loan of 62 cents. In 1958 his grandfather borrowed that amount from the owner of a farm where he worked. Three generations and three slave masters later, Gonoo's family remains in bondage.

Recently, many bold, underfunded groups have taken up the challenge of tearing out the roots of slavery. Some gained fame through dramatic slave rescues. Most learned that freeing slaves is impossible unless the slaves themselves choose to be free. Among the Kol of Uttar Pradesh, for instance, an organization called Pragati Gramodyog Sansthan (PGS)—the Progressive Institute for Village Enterprises—has helped hundreds of families break the grip of the quarry contractors.

The psychological, social, and economic bonds of slavery run deep, and for governments to be truly effective in eradicating slavery, they must partner with groups that can offer slaves a way to pull themselves up from bondage. One way to do that is to replicate the work of grassroots organizations such as the India-based MSEMVS (Society for Human Development and Women's Empowerment). In 1996 the group launched free transitional schools where children who had been enslaved learned skills and acquired enough literacy to move on to formal schooling. The group also targeted mothers, providing them with training and start-up materials for microenterprises. . . . In recent years, the United States has shown an increasing willingness to help fund these kinds of organizations, one encouraging sign that the message may be getting through.

For four years, I encountered dozens of enslaved people, several of whom traffickers like Benavil actually offered to sell to me. I did not pay for a human life anywhere. And, with one exception, I always withheld action to save any one person, in the hope that my research would later help to save many more. At times, that still feels like an excuse for cowardice. But the hard work of real emancipation can't be the burden of a select few. For thousands of slaves, grassroots groups like PGS and MSEMVS can help bring freedom. Until governments define slavery in appropriately concise terms, prosecute the crime aggressively in all its forms, and encourage groups that empower slaves to free themselves, however, millions more will remain in bondage. And our collective promise of abolition will continue to mean nothing at all.

Activity 3.9 · Analyze an Argument from Pathos

After reading Skinner's essay on slavery, reread the passage in which he negotiated to buy a child slave. Then freewrite for five minutes about how that negotiation made you feel.

Most people feel emotional when they read about a child in distress, and Skinner further highlights that emotional effect by putting this particular episode in dialogue, always a point of emphasis in an essay. Do you think Skinner deliberately appealed to pathos in this part of his essay? Discuss in your group.

List other areas where the essay evokes an emotional response. Consider why, and freewrite on the feelings and beliefs that are brought into play. How did the author know that you would probably react this way?

Although much of Skinner's argument relies on pathos, he also provides statistics and references to authorities to bolster his argument. Identify the paragraphs which provide statistics or other evidence that would qualify as logos.

Arguments from Ethos

No exact translation exists in English for the word *ethos*, but it can be loosely translated as the credibility of the speaker. This credibility generates good will which colors all the arguments, examples, and quotes the rhetor utilizes in his text. Rhetors can enhance their credibility by evidence of intelligence, virtue, and goodwill and diminish it by seeming petty, dishonest, and mean-spirited. In addition, a speaker or writer can enhance his or her own credibility by references to quotes or the actions of authorities or leaders.

Aristotle wrote:

> Proofs from character [ethos] are produced, whenever the speech is given in such a way as to render the speaker worthy of credence—we more readily and sooner believe reasonable men on all matters in general and absolutely on questions where precision is impossible and two views can be maintained.

For example, Martin Luther King, Jr., pointed out in his "I Have a Dream" speech, that, according to the framers of the Constitution and the Declaration of Independence, "unalienable Rights" of "Life, Liberty and the pursuit of Happiness" apply equally to black men and white men. He was, in effect,

Chapter 3 | **Analyzing Rhetorically**

borrowing the ethos of Thomas Jefferson and the framers of the Constitution in support of the unalienable rights of blacks.

Consider the following article and how the author's credibility or ethos enhances the appeal of his arguments.

Reading 3.4

I remember the first time the concept of another world entered my mind. It was during a walk with my father in our garden in Sri Lanka. He pointed to the Moon and told me that people had walked on it. I was astonished: Suddenly that bright light became a place that one could visit.

Schoolchildren may feel a similar sense of wonder when they see pictures of a Martian landscape or Saturn's rings. And soon their views of alien worlds may not be confined to the planets in our own solar system.

Alien Life Coming Slowly into View
by Ray Jayawardhana

Ray Jayawardhana, the author of "Alien Life Coming Slowly into View," which was originally published in *The New York Times*, is a professor of astronomy and astrophysics at the University of Toronto. He is also the author of *Strange New Worlds: The Search for Alien Planets and Life Beyond Our Solar System*.

After millenniums of musings and a century of failed attempts, astronomers first detected an exoplanet, a planet orbiting a normal star other than the Sun, in 1995. Now they are finding hundreds of such worlds each year. Last month, NASA announced that 1,235 new possible planets had been observed by Kepler, a telescope on a space satellite. Six of the planets that Kepler found circle one star, and the orbits of five of them would fit within that of Mercury, the closest planet to our Sun.

By timing the passages of these five planets across their sun's visage—which provides confirmation of their planetary nature—we can witness their graceful dance with one another, choreographed by gravity. These discoveries remind us that nature is often richer and more wondrous than our imagination. The diversity of alien worlds has surprised us and challenged our preconceptions many times over.

It is quite a change from merely 20 years ago, when we knew for sure of just one planetary system: ours. The pace of discovery, supported by new instruments and missions and innovative strategies by planet seekers, has been astounding.

What's more, from measurements of their masses and sizes, we can infer what some of these worlds are made of: gases, ice or rocks. Astronomers have been able to take the temperature of planets around other stars, first with telescopes in space but more recently with ground-based instruments, as my collaborators and I have done.

Two and a half years ago, we even managed to capture the first direct pictures of alien worlds. There is something about a photo of an alien planet—even if it only appears as a faint dot next to a bright, overexposed star—that makes it "real." Given that stars shine like floodlights next to the planetary embers huddled around them, success required painstaking efforts and clever innovations. One essential tool is adaptive optics technology, which, in effect, takes the twinkle out of the stars, thus providing sharper images from telescopes on the ground than would otherwise be possible.

At the crux of this grand pursuit is one basic question: Is our warm, wet, rocky world, teeming with life, the exception or the norm? It is an important question for every one of us, not just for scientists. It seems absurd, if not arrogant, to think that ours is the only life-bearing world in the galaxy, given hundreds of billions of other suns, the apparent ubiquity of planets, and the cosmic abundance of life's ingredients. It may be that life is fairly common, but that "intelligent" life is rare.

Of course, the vast majority of the extra-solar worlds discovered to date are quite unlike our own: many are gas giants, and some are boiling hot while others endure everlasting chills. Just a handful are close in size to our planet, and only a few of those may be rocky like the Earth, rather than gaseous like Jupiter or icy like Neptune.

But within the next few years, astronomers expect to find dozens of alien earths that are roughly the size of our planet. Some of them will likely be in the so-called habitable zone, where the temperatures are just right for liquid water. The discovery of "Earth twins," with conditions similar to what we find here, will inevitably bring questions about alien life to the forefront.

Detecting signs of life elsewhere will not be easy, but it may well occur in my lifetime, if not during the next decade. Given the daunting distances between the stars, the real-life version will almost certainly be a lot less sensational than the movies depicting alien invasions or crash-landing spaceships.

The evidence may be circumstantial at first—say, spectral bar codes of interesting molecules like oxygen, ozone, methane and water—and leave room for alternative interpretations. It may take years of additional data-gathering, and perhaps the construction of new telescopes, to satisfy our doubts. Besides, we won't know whether such "biosignatures" are an indication of slime or civilization. Most people will likely move on to other, more immediate concerns of life here on Earth while scientists get down to work.

If, on the other hand, an alien radio signal were to be detected, that would constitute a more clear-cut and exciting moment. Even if the contents of the message remained elusive for decades, we would know that there was someone "intelligent" at the other end. The search for extraterrestrial intelligence with radio telescopes has come of age recently, 50 years after the first feeble attempt. The construction of the Allen Telescope Array on an arid plateau in northern California greatly expands the number of star systems from which astronomers could detect signals.

However it arrives, the first definitive evidence of life elsewhere will mark a turning point in our intellectual history, perhaps only rivaled by Copernicus's heliocentric theory or Darwin's theory of evolution. If life can spring up on two planets independently, why not on a thousand or even a billion others? The ramifications of finding out for sure that ours isn't the only inhabited world are likely to be felt, over time, in many areas of human thought and endeavor—from biology and philosophy to religion and art.

Some people worry that discovering life elsewhere, especially if it turns out to be in possession of incredible technology, will make us feel small and insignificant. They seem concerned that it will constitute a horrific blow to our collective ego.

I happen to be an optimist. It may take decades after the initial indications of alien life for scientists to gather enough evidence to be certain or to decipher a signal of artificial origin. The full ramifications of the discovery may not be felt for generations, giving us plenty of time to get used to the presence of our galactic neighbors. Besides, knowing that we are not alone just might be the kick in the pants we need to grow up as a species.

Activity 3.10 Analyzing an Argument from Ethos

1. In the above article, Ray Jayawardhana draws upon the ethos of his position as a professor of astronomy and astrophysics to formulate a convincing argument for the strong possibility of the existence of alien life. In your group, discuss how Jayawardhana's profession increases the credibility of his argument.

2. How do you think this essay would compare to essays by people of more credentials who argue that no alien life exists? What kinds of other evidence could Jayawardhana have offered that would strengthen his argument?

3. Is Jayawardhana appealing to pathos with his opening narrative? What effect does he want to have on his audience by describing this childhood memory?

Combining Ethos, Pathos, and Logos

The ethos, pathos, and logos appeals are equally important and merit equal attention in the writing process. No text is purely based on one of the three appeals, though more of the argument in a particular text may be based on one appeal rather than another. In each writing situation, however, an effective rhetor will think about how each plays into the structure of the argument.

In today's world, for example, a public speaker's effectiveness is affected by the ability to use a teleprompter, or, if one is not available, to memorize a speech well enough so he or she can speak without frequently referring to notes. If a speaker's eyes flit from left to right across the text of a teleprompter, it shows on television. This reduces the credibility, or ethos, of the speaker, no matter how well the other appeals are executed in the speech. The equivalent of presentation for a written text would be to produce a document that is essentially free from grammatical errors, spell-checked, and printed on good paper stock with the correct margins and type size. If the document does not look professional, it will lose credibility or ethos no matter what it says.

To give another example, E. Benjamin Skinner's essay, "People for Sale," relies on the highly emotional image of a child being sold into slavery for its major appeal. However, if you read back through the essay, you will see that it has a clear thesis, which could be stated as the following: Slavery exists in the present time, even in the United States, and it is not even that difficult to buy a slave. The essay is well organized and offers a variety of evidence, including statistics and first-person observation. Logos may not stand out as the primary appeal in Skinner's essay, but it is nevertheless strong in its appeal to logos.

If you want to develop your writing skills, it is essential that you pay attention to each of Aristotle's appeals—ethos, pathos, and logos.

Chapter 3 | **Analyzing Rhetorically**

Activity 3.11 Writing about Ethos, Pathos, and Logos

Choose one of the texts in Chapters 1, 2, or 3 and write an essay that identifies the ethos, pathos, and logos of the particular text. Then discuss how the three appeals together are used by the author to produce an effective essay. Alternatively, discuss which of the appeals is weak in the particular essay and how that affects the effectiveness of the essay.

Photos Heighten Ethos or Pathos

When Steve Jobs was in the process of turning over the reins of Apple to Tim Cook, the two appeared in a series of photos in a variety of publications. For example, see the photo below (from wired.com). Notice the "twinning effect," as both Jobs and Cook wear blue jeans and black pullover sweaters. In a not-so-subtle way, Apple was using ethos to visually state that since Jobs and Cook look alike, they must be alike. Thus, Cook would be successful in running Apple.

Photos can be equally effective in presenting pathos, though logos is more problematic.

Meet Tim Cook: The Man in Charge of Apple

For millions of Apple fans, Steve Jobs is irreplaceable. But if there's one man Jobs himself trusts to stand in his shoes it is his second in command Apple Chief Operating Officer Tim Cook.

Activity 3.12 Logos Activity: Write a Letter to the Editor

In the following letter, originally published on the blog, *The Frisky* (www.thefrisky.com), the author uses both humor and logic to argue that *The New Yorker* reviews shouldn't give away the ending of movies.

An Open Letter To The New Yorker
via The Frisky on 4/25/11

Dear *New Yorker*,

Obviously, you are an awesome magazine. However, I have one small, teensy weensy beef. Could you please—possibly—stop ruining the ending of movies for me? Last night, on a 10-hour flight from Buenos Aires to New York, I sat down determined to catch up on your last three issues. In one, I read a review of Jake Gyllenhaal's newish movie, "Source Code." I had been planning to see it. Emphasis on the *had*. While you didn't go into details, you told me how it unfolds in the end. Which sort of takes the wind out of a movie's sail, doesn't it? But even worse, in a fantastic article about Anna Faris and her specific brand of girl humor, you let me know the surprise twist ending of her upcoming click, "What's Your Number?" Which. Doesn't. Even. Come. Out. Until. SEPTEMBER. Reading this reminded me of the collective sigh of 100 students in my Intro to Film Studies class in college when our professor told us the secret to "Chinatown" before we watched.

Choose one of your favorite magazines and write a letter to the editor. You can protest something the magazine has done recently that bothered you, or you can praise something that it has done well. Your letter does not need to be long, but you need to make your argument clear and support it with specific examples. If appropriate for your target publication, use humor as does the author of the letter to the editor of *The New Yorker*.

After you have written your letter to the editor, write a paragraph describing your target publication, what you have written in your letter, and why your letter is an illustration of logos.

Activity 3.13 Pathos Activity: Portray an Emotion in a Collage

Think of an emotion that you've been feeling lately and that you are willing to explore. Create a collage to express that emotion. Use these criteria.

- You can create your collage with cut and paste paper or you can create it through a computer program.

- Have little white space. Use colors with emotional connotations (blue for calm, for example).

- Have at least three images. You can find these on the Internet or in magazines, or take your own photos.

- Before you begin your collage, write down the emotion you are trying to explore and describe how you plan to represent it. In other words, make a plan, even though you will likely deviate from it.

- When you finish, write a paragraph describing the experience of creating the collage. Turn your paragraph in with your collage.

Activity 3.14 Ethos Activity: Create a Professional Facebook Page

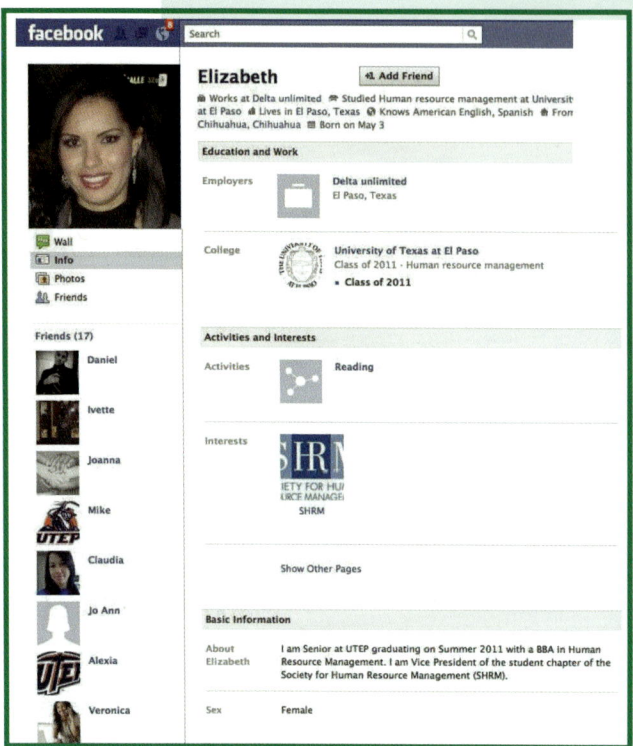

Facebook is not just used to tell your friends about what you did over the weekend. Corporations use it as a networking tool. As you learned in the reading in Chapter 2, "The Web Means the End of Forgetting," it is a good idea to be cautious about what you post about yourself on Facebook because information and photos may be seen by unintended audiences, including future employers. Some individuals choose to have two Facebook pages, one for their personal friends and one for networking.

For this assignment, create a professional Facebook page similar to the one shown here. Consider in your small group what information and photos you want to post on a page you will use for networking. In effect, you are creating an ethos for yourself by these choices.

After you have completed your Facebook page, write a paragraph that explains the ethos you wanted to project in your page and how your content choices project that ethos.

Activity 3.15 Write a Rhetorical Analysis

In this essay you will make use of rhetorical vocabulary to analyze a text or combined text and images. The sample student essay in Chapter 7 (see page 190) analyzes a speech archived on the American Rhetoric website (http://www.americanrhetoric.com), which features many presidential and other prominent speeches. Alternatively, you can write a rhetorical analysis of a Facebook page, a newspaper or magazine article, or website.

In your analysis, apply several of the rhetorical concepts you have studied this semester:

- Speaker or writer—Does the speaker's identity affect the text?
- Purpose—What was the speaker or writer trying to achieve?
- Audience—Who was the speech/text directed to? Are there multiple audiences?
- Rhetorical appeals—How does the speaker or writer use ethos, pathos, and logos?
- Kairos—What is special about the rhetorical moment of the text/speech in terms of place and time?

Activity 3.16 Write on Your Blog

In your blog, do a freewrite exercise in which you argue for some type of policy change related to a topic you are interested in writing about. What is the kairos of your topic? Where can you use the three rhetorical appeals (pathos, ethos, and logos)?

Activity 3.17 Write in Your Commonplace Book

Do a search on the Internet for kairos, ethos, pathos, and logos. Print out and paste a short section about each from the Internet. Then comment briefly about each section.

4
INVENTING RHETORICALLY

Praxis in Action

How I Do Invention by Adam Webb

Before I start a research and writing project, I like to explore as many perspectives, arguments, or interpretations of a topic as possible. After I have chosen my topic, I write down everything I know about it. Next, I read broadly about my topic. I call this early stage of the research process "reading around," similar to information gathering.

Then, I usually ask myself a series of questions, such as: (1) Why is this topic important to me? (2) What has been said or written on this topic? (3) Who has already written on this topic? (4) How do these perspectives or arguments relate to my own perspective on this topic? and (5) How has media, such as television or the Internet, portrayed this topic? If I don't know the answers, either from my personal knowledge or my "reading around," I ask individuals who are knowledgeable about my topic. By answering these questions, I usually develop a larger contextual framework in which I can better understand and situate myself within the various perspectives on my topic. This is all before I start to integrate specific material from research sources.

Next, I start locating any recurring terms, themes, symbols, connections, or references as well as listing other ideas, beliefs, or values that might be relevant to my topic. In order to keep track of my ideas and information, I like to use Dragon Dictation, a note-taking and voice recording program application on my smartphone. I sometimes use this application to start writing an outline of my ideas.

By this time, I know what I want to argue and the general framework of my project. Then I can begin adding in specific paraphrases and quotes from my research.

Adam Webb has developed his own process for doing research that he applies to different projects.

Aristotle's Classification of Rhetoric

Aristotle, in *The Art of Rhetoric* (or *On Rhetoric*), laid the groundwork for today's persuasive writing by being the first to write systemically about how to teach rhetoric. His teacher Plato, in contrast, had distrusted rhetoric. Plato deplored the way rhetoricians (or politicians) of his era skillfully manipulated the people of Athens, particularly the masses of up to 10,000 voters in the Assembly or 500 in the juries of the law courts. Aristotle, on the other hand, perceived great potential in rhetoric, when taught properly. Rhetoric, as he envisioned it, could be both persuasive and ethical, and in *The Art of Rhetoric* he laid out an organization and classification of rhetoric as he believed it should be taught.

Aristotle divided the process of writing and delivering a composition into five parts. The first of these was **invention**, during which the writer or speaker expanded a topic into ideas that were later arranged into a text or speech. According to the ancient Greeks, the rhetor *invented* these ideas, though they may have mirrored or adapted thoughts presented by previous rhetors. Today, we call this the **prewriting stage** of the writing process, an adaptation of Aristotle's invention stage.

In the previous chapter, we discussed the three appeals or means that a rhetor can use to persuade an audience: ethos, pathos, and logos. In *The Art of Rhetoric*, Aristotle divides these appeals or means of persuasion into two types of proofs: artistic and inartistic. Today, these proofs are still part of the writing process though we call them by different names.

Artistic Proofs

Artistic proofs are logical arguments constructed by rhetors from ideas plucked from their minds. An individual then develops these thoughts into a line of reasoning and, in the process, explores and narrows the topic, creates a thesis, and determines the ideas that need to be conveyed to the audience. These proofs are the ones that Aristotle and other ancient rhetoricians believed were critically important, for they are the ones developed from the *rhetor's own mind* and, thus, *invented*. These ideas can be shaped into two types of arguments—deductive and inductive—which we will discuss in the next few pages.

Inartistic Proofs

Inartistic proofs are direct evidence that the speaker might use to support the argument, such as testimony, documents, and anything else that rhetors do not invent through their own thinking. Today, we would call these proofs research. They, also, are essential to writing, but they should *support* the writer's ideas, rather than lead them.

For Aristotle's students, the use of artistic and inartistic proofs might not have been a two-step process—first one and then the other, though the proofs are arranged that way in *The Art of Rhetoric*, as they are in this book. Rather, similar to the process used by Adam Webb (see the *Praxis in Action* at the beginning of this chapter), they might have developed both proofs in an alternating or recursive process. After developing basic ideas for a composition through invention, these students would then collect information from authorities (testimony), what Webb refers to as "reading around." Then they would return to inventing artistic proofs about the project, followed by more references to inartistic proofs. Today, we have more resources for research than did the ancient Greeks, but this does not make artistic proofs any less important. The differences between artistic and inartistic proofs are summarized in table 4.1 below.

table 4.1

Aristotle's Artistic and Inartistic Proofs	
Artistic	**Inartistic**
Ideas from the rhetor's own mind, thus *invented*	Information gained from external sources
Personal knowledge	Authorities
Observation	Testimony
Patterns of reasoning	Documents

The Five Canons of Rhetoric

Greek and Roman teachers of rhetoric divided rhetoric into five parts or canons. These canons corresponded to the order of activities in creating a speech, as they perceived the process: Invention, arrangement, style, memory, and delivery. These five parts are described in many handbooks of rhetorical instruction, including the *Rhetorica ad Herennium*, which was composed by an unknown author between 86 and 82 CE:

> The speaker . . . should possess the faculties of Invention, Arrangement, Style, Memory, and Delivery. Invention is the

devising of matter, true or plausible, that would make the case convincing. Arrangement is the ordering and distribution of the matter, making clear the place to which each thing is to be assigned. Style is the adaptation of suitable words and sentences to the matter devised. Memory is the firm retention in the mind of the matter, words, and arrangement. Delivery is the graceful regulation of voice, countenance, and gesture.

Today, classes in composition or writing studies still emphasize the necessity of **invention**, now interpreted as prewriting activities that enable writers to develop the logic and words needed for effective arguments. **Arrangement** involves organizing an argument into a logical format that leads the reader easily from the thesis to the conclusion. **Style** has to do with the author's voice and tone and the structure of sentences and paragraphs. **Memory** is used somewhat differently today, as students are no longer required to memorize compositions for oral presentation. Instead, memory is utilized in ways such as remembering how and where to retrieve information from the Internet, books, and other reference materials. Finally, **delivery**, which once involved gestures and tone of voice in an oral presentation, today has to do with document design, so that the final product is presented in a professional manner according to Modern Language Association (MLA) or American Psychological Association (APA) style. Delivery also involves grammatical accuracy because surface errors detract from the effective impact of a document. See table 4.2 below for a summary of the five parts of rhetoric.

The Five Parts (or Canons) of Rhetoric		
English	**Greek**	**Latin**
invention	*heuresis*	*inventio*
arrangement	*taxis*	*dispositio*
style	*lesis*	*elocutio*
memory	*mneme*	*memoria*
delivery	*hypocrisis*	*actin*

table 4.2

The Modern Writing Process Overview

Prewriting (Inventing)

Writing is not only about putting the pen to paper. As did rhetors in ancient Greece and Rome, you have to think deeply and critically about a subject before you begin a composition. The "invention" step of the writer's process is designed to help you find a worthwhile topic and develop your ideas about that topic before you start to write a draft. It includes writing, discussion, and research, as well as informal writing to help you explore your thoughts and feelings about a subject. Whatever method you choose, keep a record of your thoughts and discoveries as you spend this time in close examination of your subject.

Drafting

It may seem odd that writing a draft should come in the middle of the writer's process. However, research has shown that students and professionals alike write more effective essays when they don't reach for the pen too quickly. If you have spent enough time in the invention stage, the actual drafting stage may go more quickly. After writing the first draft, in succeeding drafts you can add details, observations, illustrations, examples, expert testimony, and other support to help your essay entertain, illuminate, or convince your audience.

Revising

Today, we talk more about the revision stage of writing than did ancient rhetoricians. If you are a student who tends to write assigned essays at the last minute, you may have missed this step entirely, yet many writers claim this is the longest and most rewarding step in the writing process. To revise, you must, in a sense, learn to let go of your writing. Some students think their first drafts should stay exactly the way they are written because they are true to their feelings and experience. Many writers find, however, that first drafts assume too much about the reader's knowledge and reactions. Sometimes readers, reading a first draft essay, are left scratching their heads and wondering what it is the writer is trying to convey. Writers who revise try to read their writing as readers would, taking note of gaps in logic, the absence of clear examples, the need for reordering information, and so on. Then they can revise their content with the reader in mind.

Editing and Polishing

Once writers have clarified their messages and the methods by which they will present those messages, one more step must be taken. Particularly because their compositions are written, rather than presented orally, they must go over their work again to check for correct spelling, grammar, and punctuation, as well as the use of Standard Written English. Some students finish with an essay, print it, and turn it in without ever examining the final copy. This is a critical mistake, because misspelled words and typographical and formatting errors can make an otherwise well-written essay lose its credibility. The five canons of rhetoric and the modern writing process are summarized in table 4.3 below.

table 4.3

The Five Canons of Rhetoric and the Modern Writing Process

Five Canons of Rhetoric	Modern Writing Process
Invention—Devising the arguments that will make the case convincing, often basing them on models of famous speeches.	Prewriting—Determining the thesis, points of argument, counterargument, and rebuttal. Researching evidence to support the argument.
Arrangement—Ordering the argument into a logical format. Style—Finding suitable words and figures of speech. [Note: This may have been a recursive process, but the ancients did not consider that aspect important.]	Drafting, revising, and editing—Putting ideas and prewriting into a useable form through a recursive process of drafting, revising, and editing.
Memory—Retaining the argument in the mind, including its content and arrangement.	Remembering how and where to retrieve information from the Internet, books, and other reference materials.
Delivery—Effective use of voice and gestures to present argument.	Publication—Putting text, images, and other elements in a suitable format and releasing the document to an audience.

Activity 4.1 Compare the Five Canons of Rhetoric and the Modern Writing Process

In your group, reread the discussions in this chapter on the five canons of rhetoric and the modern writing process and review the table above. What parts of the five canons correspond to the modern writing process?

Chapter 4 | **Inventing Rhetorically**

> What step in the five canons is not included in the contemporary writing process? If the similarities and differences are not clear to you, consult the Internet. If you search for either "Five Canons of Rhetoric" or "Writing Process" you will find resources. What explanations can you offer for the differences? The similarities?

Stasis Theory Identifies Critical Point in Controversy

Stasis theory presents a series of four questions that were developed by Greek and Roman rhetoricians, primarily Aristotle, Quintilian, and Hermagoras. Answering these questions for an issue enabled rhetors to determine the critical (or stasis) point in a disagreement. This was a technique the ancients developed for the law courts to enable advocates to focus their arguments on the crux of the case. Quintilian, the great Roman teacher of rhetoric, explained in regard to a defendant:

> By far the strongest mode of defense is if the charge which is made can be denied; the next, if an act of the kind charged against the accused can be said not to have been done; the third, and most honorable, if what is done is proved to have been justly done. If we cannot command these methods, the last and only mode of defense is that of eluding an accusation, which can neither be denied nor combated, by the aid of some point of law, so as to make it appear that the action has not been brought in due legal form.

In other words, Quintilian is saying that in law cases, advocates have four choices in developing a focus for their arguments. You have probably watched a courtroom drama on television or film and can recall various defenses made on behalf of defendants. The strongest and most obvious defense is that the defendant is not guilty, that is, he or she did not do the deed in question. The same was true in Quintilian's day. However, sometimes an argument of innocence is not possible, perhaps because it seems obvious that the defendant did perform the deed in question. Thus, the advocate must develop a different strategy. For example, in defense of one accused of murder, the attorney may argue self-defense or mitigating circumstances (such as that the killing was an act of war). In rare cases, other defenses are offered; for example, if the supposed victim's body has not been found, the advocate can argue that the victim

Marcus Fabius Quintilianus (Quintilian) was a Roman orator from Spain who taught stasis theory.

may still be alive. An attorney can discover these possible defenses by using stasis theory to analyze the situation.

Another great advantage of stasis theory is that, if pursued diligently, it prevents the rhetor from making the mistake of organizing an argument by simply forwarding reasons why he or she is correct and the opposition is wrong. That approach may please people who agree with the rhetor, but it will not likely gain any support from the opposition. Answering the stasis questions carefully forces the writer to consider aspects of the issue that may have been overlooked but are crucial to an effective argument.

The wording of the four questions has varied somewhat over time, but essentially they are questions of fact, definition, quality, and policy. The same questions can be applied to any issue, not only issues of law. The four stasis questions are as follows:

1. What are the facts? (conjecture)
2. What is the meaning or nature of the issue? (definition)
3. What is the seriousness of the issue? (quality)
4. What is the best plan of action or procedure? (policy)

Many writers prefer stasis theory to other prewriting techniques because answering the questions determines whether or not the different sides of an argument are at stasis. Being at **stasis** means that the opponents are in agreement about their disagreement—the stasis point—which can be identified by one of the four stasis questions. If the sides are at stasis, they have common ground to build upon, for they are arguing the same issue. There is, thus, a greater chance the sides can reach a workable consensus or compromise. If opponents are not at stasis, there is much more work to be done to reach consensus.

> *The point where the opposing sides agree upon their disagreement is the stasis point.*

For example, in the argument about the teaching of evolution and/or intelligent design in schools, the two sides are not in agreement about how to discuss the issue. Those in favor of teaching evolution claim intelligent design should not be called science, which is an issue of definition. Those who propose teaching intelligent design along with (or instead of) evolution tend to focus on "proving" evidence, an issue of fact. Until the two sides can agree upon what is the stasis point, or crux of the issue, they cannot debate effectively. They are not presenting arguments about the same question.

Chapter 4 | **Inventing Rhetorically**

The four stasis questions can be broken into the subquestions listed in table 4.4. If you want to find the stasis point, work through the list for your issue, answering all of the subquestions. However, for each question, you must identify not only how *you* would answer the question but also how the opposing side or sides would answer. For example, if you are considering the issue of global warming, people with different positions will not agree on the facts. Thus, you must identify the basic facts of global warming represented by your side, and then identify the facts that might be presented by the opposing side.

table 4.4

Stasis Questions

Fact

- Did something happen?
- What are the facts?
- Is there a problem/issue?
- How did it begin and what are its causes?
- What changed to create the problem/issue?
- Can it be changed?

It also may be useful to ask the following critical questions of your own research and conclusions:

- Where did I obtain my data and are these sources reliable?
- How do I know they're reliable?

Definition

- What is the nature of the problem/issue?
- What exactly is the problem/issue?
- What kind of a problem/issue is it?
- To what larger class of things or events does it belong?
- What are its parts, and how are they related?

It also may be useful to ask the following critical questions of your own research and conclusions:

- Who/what is influencing my definition of this problem/issue?
- How/why are these sources/beliefs influencing my definition of the issue?

Quality
• Is it a good thing or a bad thing? • How serious is the problem/issue? • Who might be affected by this problem/issue (stakeholders)? • What happens if we don't do anything? • What are the costs of solving the problem/issue? It also may be useful to ask the following critical questions of your own research and conclusions: • Who/what is influencing my determination of the seriousness of this problem/issue? • How/why are these sources/beliefs influencing my determination of the issue's seriousness?
Policy
• Should action be taken? • Who should be involved in helping to solve the problem/address the issue? • What should be done about this problem? • What needs to happen to solve this problem/address this issue? It also may be useful to ask the following critical questions of your own research and conclusions: • Who/what is influencing my determination of what to do about this problem/issue? • How/why are these sources/beliefs influencing my determination of what to do about this issue?
Source: Adapted from Purdue Owl Resource on Stasis Theory, http://owl.english.purdue.edu/owl/resource/736/1.

Using Stasis Questions

To illustrate the use of stasis questions, a team of writers working together to compose a report on racism in America might use the stasis questions to talk through information they will later use in their report. In the following sample dialogue, team members disagree about what actions are racist.

Chapter 4 | **Inventing Rhetorically**

> "Flying the Confederate battle flag is racist."
>
> "Flying the Confederate battle flag is *not* racist."
>
> "Yes, it is, because it represents the Confederate states that supported slavery, and it's generally accepted that slavery in America was racist."
>
> "Flying the Confederate battle flag is not racist, because it's a part of American history and Southern heritage."

These two team members disagree about whether or not flying the Confederate battle flag is a racist act. This sort of disagreement might lead to a complete breakdown of group work if common ground cannot be found.

In this example, the team members go on to agree that some people still exhibit the Confederate battle flag (*fact*) on their vehicles and on their clothes, but that the flag is also displayed in museums (*fact*). They go on to agree that the issue is still very important to some people since a number of American states have recently debated the flag in legislatures and assemblies (*quality*). Moreover, group members note that a number of legal suits have been filed for and against the display of the flag in public places, so it's clear the issue still matters to a lot of people (*quality*).

In this sense, the team members have achieved stasis on two of the four stases—*fact* (people still display the flag, though in different places) and *quality* (it's a very important issue). Where the team members disagree, however, is in the stases of *definition* (is the display of the flag "racist"?) and *policy* (what should we do about this?).

Thinking about this disagreement using stasis theory allows people to build common ground so that parties who disagree can move toward resolution and action even if they can't agree on all levels. For example, team members who disagree about whether or not flying the Confederate battle flag is racist might still be able to agree on what to do about it.

> "Ok, we disagree about whether flying the flag is racist, but we can agree that flying the flag is probably protected under the First Amendment to the United States Constitution—that flying the flag is protected by our freedom of speech."
>
> "Yeah."
>
> "So, people are free to display the flag on their vehicles, on their clothes, and on their property, as well as in museums. But,

state legislatures and assemblies will have to debate and vote on whether or not the flag can be displayed on publicly funded property or in public symbols, such as state flags and seals."

"That sounds pretty democratic. Sure."

Not every team situation is going to end this amicably; however, by using the stasis questions to help keep the dialogue going—on a reasonable course—team members can find common ground and work toward action that is acceptable to most, if not all, of the group members.*

Stasis Theory and Kairos

As you will remember from Chapter 3, the *kairos* of an argument is the context, opportune moment, or point in time in which the rhetor, the audience, the issue, and the current situation provide opportunities and constraints for an argument. If you keep kairos in mind as you analyze an issue, you take advantage of timeliness. For example, if you want to write an argument about the death penalty, you might consider that United States courts are increasingly questioning the validity of eyewitness testimony, evidence which has been the deciding factor in many death penalty cases.

As part of your use of stasis theory, consider the four questions in relation to kairos:

1. How do recent developments (new facts) or the local situation affect the issue? Will it change your audience's perception of the facts?

2. Does the current situation affect your audience's definition of the issue? Is it defined differently by an audience in this location than elsewhere?

3. Have recent events made the issue more or less important to your audience? Is it more or less important in your location than elsewhere?

4. Do recent events, locally or widely, affect the need or lack of need for action, in your audience's perception?

As a rhetorician, it is important for you to be aware of the history of a controversy. But it is equally important to have an awareness of the kairos of the argument. Such an awareness enables you to adopt a "ready stance" and adjust your argument, so that it reflects an awareness of your audience's position and interests, as well as contemporary developments in the issue.

---

* Allen Brizee, "Stasis Theory for Teamwork," *Purdue Owl,* April 17, 2010, http://owl.english.purdue.edu/owl/ (Accessed October 3, 2011).

Chapter 4 | **Inventing Rhetorically**

Such a flexible stance may afford you an opportunity to be persuasive that you might otherwise miss.

Activity 4.2 Identify the Defense in a Television or Film Courtroom Drama

As your instructor directs, watch a courtroom drama on television or film and decide what defense the defendant's attorney is offering. Report your conclusion to your small group or the class. Then, after you have discussed the stasis questions, identify which of the four questions the attorney in the drama is focusing upon as the crux of the defense. Discuss with your group or the class.

Activity 4.3 Use Stasis Theory to Explore Your Topic

Choose an issue that interests you and answer all the stasis questions in the table on pages 117-118, both for your position and for the opposing argument. Elaborate with three or four sentences for each subquestion that is particularly relevant to your topic. Is your issue at stasis for any of the questions? Report to your group or to the class.

Activity 4.4 Evaluate a Public Debate

Locate a public debate that has been reported recently in newspaper editorials, television programs, or other media that can be analyzed by using stasis theory. In a paper of 350 to 500 words, do the following:

- Describe the context (kairos).
- Identify the sides of the argument and their principal points.
- Decide which stasis question each side is primarily addressing.
- Determine whether or not the issue is at stasis and explain your answer.
- Include a citation in MLA or APA format for your source or sources.

Activity 4.5: Use Stasis Theory to Analyze a Case

Professors Vijay Govindarajan and Christian Sarkar launched a competition on the *Harvard Business Network* blog for designs to build $300 houses for the poor. Word of the competition spread quickly, and a wide variety of people began to write about the competition—in editorials in *The New York Times*, the *Economist*, and in a companion blog, http://www.300house.com/blog.

Your Task: Read the four articles written about the $300 house competition that appear on the following pages. Discuss them in class and in small groups. In particular, note that Matias Echanove and Rahul Srivastava write in their *New York Times* op-ed essay, "Hands Off Our Houses," that the idea of a $300 house is impractical and will fail in places such as Mumbai, India. In contrast, "A $300 Idea that Is Priceless," the editorial from the *Economist*, praises the design competition for initiating an "explosion of creativity." Work through the stasis questions, with one side of the controversy being those who support this design initiative. The other side would be those who foresee problems in applying this idealistic initiative in the real world, a viewpoint that is expressed in "Hands Off Our Houses."

Write a paper of approximately 750 words in which you do the following:

- Briefly present the idea of the design competition.
- Summarize the arguments of those in favor of the initiative.
- Explain the reservations expressed in "Hands Off Our Houses."
- Identify a stasis point, if one exists, and explain why you think the sides have common ground on that particular stasis question.
- Discuss whether the discovery of common ground might allow individuals involved in this debate to talk to one another and work toward solutions for the problem of substandard housing in slums worldwide.
- As your instructor directs, cite your sources in APA or MLA style.

Chapter 4 | **Inventing Rhetorically**

Reading 4.1

David A. Smith, the founder of the Affordable Housing Institute (AHI) tells us that "markets alone will never satisfactorily house a nation's poorest citizens... whether people buy or rent, housing is typically affordable to only half of the population."

The $300 House: A Hands-On Lab for Reverse Innovation?
by Vijay Govindarajan

Published in the *HBR Blog Network*.

The result? Smith points to a "spontaneous community of self-built or informally built homes—the shanty towns, settlements, and ever-expanding slums that sprout like mushrooms on the outskirts of cities in the developing world."

We started discussing the issue, examining the subject through the lens of reverse innovation.

Here are five questions Christian and I asked ourselves:

1. How can organic, self-built slums be turned into livable housing?
2. What might a house-for-the-poor look like?
3. How can world-class engineering and design capabilities be utilized to solve the problem?
4. What reverse-innovation lessons might be learned by the participants in such a project?
5. How could the poor afford to buy this house?

Livable Housing. Our first thought was that self-built houses are usually built from materials that are available—cardboard, plastic, mud or clay, metal scraps and whatever else is nearby. Built on dirt floors, these structures are prone to collapse and catching fire. Solution: replace these unsafe structures with a mass-produced, standard, affordable, and sustainable solution. We want to create the $300-House-for-the-Poor.

Look and Feel. To designers, our sketch of this house might be a bit of a joke, but it's useful nonetheless to illustrate the concept, to get started. We wanted the house to be an ecosystem of products and solutions designed around the real needs of the inhabitants. Of course it would have to be made out of sustainable, green materials, but more crucially, it would have to be durable enough to withstand torrential rains, earthquakes, and the stress of children playing. The house might be a single room structure with drop-down partitions for privacy. Furniture—sleeping hammocks and fold-down chairs would be built in. The roof would boast an inexpensive solar panel and battery to light the house and charge the mobile phone and tablet computer. An inexpensive water filter would be built in as well.

In effect, the house is really a one-room shed designed around the family ecosystem, a lego-like aggregation of useful products that "bring good things to life" for the poor.

World-Class Design. Our next question was: "Who will do this?" We decided that it would have to be a collaboration between global design and engineering companies and non-profits with experience solving problems for the poor. The usual suspects ran through our minds—IDEO, GE, TATA, Siemens, Habitat-for-Humanity, Partners In Health, the Solar Electric Light Fund, the Clinton Global Initiative, the Gates Foundation, Grameen. Governments may play an important part in setting the stage for these types of cross-country innovation projects.

The Reverse Innovation Payoff. Participating companies will reap two rewards. First, they will be able to serve the unserved, the 2.5 billion who make up the bottom of the pyramid. Second, they create new competencies which can help transform lives in rich countries by creating breakthrough innovations to solve several problems (scaled housing for hurricane victims, refugees, and even the armed forces).

A House of One's Own: Affordability. To move beyond charity, the poor must become owners of their homes, responsible for their care and upkeep. The model of social business introduced by Muhammad Yunus resonates strongly with us. Micro-finance must surely play a role in making the $300 House-for-the-Poor a viable and self-sustaining solution.

Of course, the idea we present here is an experiment. Nevertheless, we feel it deserves to be explored. From the one-room shacks in Haiti's Central Plateau to the jhuggi clusters in and around Delhi, to the favelas in São Paulo, the problem of housing-for-the-poor is truly global.

We ask CEOs, governments, NGOs, foundations: Are there any takers?

Reading 4.2

Hands Off Our Houses
by Matias Echanove and Rahul Srivastava

Published in *The New York Times*.

Mumbai, India

Last summer, a business professor and a marketing consultant wrote on The Harvard Business Review's website about their idea for a $300 house. According to the writers, and the many people who have enthusiastically responded since, such a house could improve the lives of millions of urban poor around the world. And with a $424 billion market for cheap homes that is largely untapped, it could also make significant profits.

The writers created a competition, asking students, architects and businesses to compete to design the best prototype for a $300 house (their original sketch was of a one-room prefabricated shed, equipped with solar panels, water filters and a tablet computer). The winner will be announced this month. But one expert has been left out of the competition, even though her input would have saved much time and effort for those involved in conceiving the house: the person who is supposed to live in it.

We work in Dharavi, a neighborhood in Mumbai that has become a one-stop shop for anyone interested in "slums" (that catchall term for areas lived in by the urban poor). We recently showed around a group of Dartmouth students involved in the project who are hoping to get a better grasp of their market. They had imagined a ready-made constituency of slum-dwellers eager to buy a cheap house that would necessarily be better than the shacks they'd built themselves. But the students found that the reality here is far more complex than their business plan suggested.

To start with, space is scarce. There is almost no room for new construction or ready-made houses. Most residents are renters, paying $20 to $100 a month for small apartments.

Those who own houses have far more equity in them than $300—a typical home is worth at least $3,000. Many families have owned their houses for two or three generations, upgrading them as their incomes increase. With additions, these homes become what we call "tool houses," acting as workshops, manufacturing units, warehouses and shops. They facilitate trade and production, and allow homeowners to improve their living standards over time.

None of this would be possible with a $300 house, which would have to be as standardized as possible to keep costs low. No number of add-ons would be able to match the flexibility of need-based construction.

In addition, construction is an important industry in neighborhoods like Dharavi. Much of the economy consists of hardware shops, carpenters, plumbers, concrete makers, masons, even real-estate agents. Importing prefabricated homes would put many people out of business, undercutting the very population the $300 house is intended to help.

Worst of all, companies involved in producing the house may end up supporting the clearance and demolition of well-established neighborhoods to make room for it. The resulting resettlement colonies, which are multiplying at the edges of cities like Delhi and Bangalore, may at first glance look like ideal markets for the new houses, but the dislocation destroys businesses and communities.

The $300 house could potentially be a success story, if it was understood as a straightforward business proposal instead of a social solution. Places like refugee camps, where many people need shelter for short periods, could use such cheap, well-built units. A market for them could perhaps be created in rural-urban fringes that are less built up.

The $300 house responds to our misconceptions more than to real needs. Of course problems do exist in urban India. Many people live without toilets or running water. Hot and unhealthy asbestos-cement sheets cover millions of roofs. Makeshift homes often flood during monsoons. But replacing individual, incrementally built houses with a ready-made solution would do more harm than good.

Chapter 4 | **Inventing Rhetorically**

A better approach would be to help residents build better, safer homes for themselves. The New Delhi–based Micro Homes Solutions, for example, provides architectural and engineering assistance to homeowners in low-income neighborhoods.

The $300 house will fail as a social initiative because the dynamic needs, interests and aspirations of the millions of people who live in places like Dharavi have been overlooked. This kind of mistake is all too common in the trendy field of social entrepreneurship. While businessmen and professors applaud the $300 house, the urban poor are silent, busy building a future for themselves.

Reading 4.3

The $300 House: A Hands-On Approach to a Wicked Problem
by Vijay Govindarajan with Christian Sarkar

Published in the *HBR Blog Network*

When *The New York Times* printed "Hands Off Our Houses," an op-ed about our idea for a $300 House for the poor, we were both delighted and dismayed—delighted because the $300 House was being discussed, and dismayed because authors Matias Echanove and Rahul Srivastava, co-founders of the Institute of Urbanology, didn't seem to have read the series of blog posts about our idea.

Nearly every criticism the authors levy in their op-ed is answered in 12 blog posts, a magazine article from January/February 2011, a video interview, and a slideshow that integrated community and commentary, which were published between last October and this May.

In critiquing our vision, the authors cite Micro Homes Solutions as "a better approach." In fact, the leaders of that venture were invited several months ago to contribute a blog post to our series as a way of joining the discussion and helping us understand what they've seen on the ground there. They declined to be part of the conversation.

The authors also write that students who tried to write a business plan to serve the poor and who visited poor urban areas of India found "the reality here is far more complex than their business plan suggested."

Yet a fundamental tenet of our project and the blog series about it is that slums present complex challenges that can't be fixed with a clever shack alone. Rather than creating an echo chamber of rah-rah rhetoric, we told blog authors to focus on one of the many knotty issues that Echanove and Srivastava cite in their critique. From the start we asked: What are the complexities of financing these homes? How do you get energy and infrastructure into such dwellings? How do you get corporations to invest in a significant way? We acknowledged that we didn't have the answers. "Just because it is going to take longer than it should doesn't mean we should walk away," wrote Seth Godin in one of the posts. "It's going to take some time, but it's worth it."

The op-ed suggests that the $300 House doesn't acknowledge that "space is scarce" in urban poor areas. Yet, Sunil Suri wrote in a post on the urban challenge that "slums by their nature are located where land and space are limited." Suri proposed potential solutions, including innovative materials, new ways of thinking of the construction process, and building up.

The authors also say that "one expert has been left out of the challenge . . . the person who is supposed to live in it." But a post in the series on the co-creation challenge from Gaurav Bhalla addressed this squarely. "It will be unfortunate if the house were to be designed by those who will never live in it," wrote Bhalla. "Investments need to be made understanding the daily habits and practices of people for whom the house is being designed." Bhalla used the case study of the chulha stove, co-created by businesses, NGOs, and slum dwellers, to make his point. We are also bringing students to India and Haiti to do ethnographic research that will inform development of a $300 House, and when prototypes are developed, they will be deployed and tested with those who will live in them.

Echanove and Srivastava also state that a $300 House "would have to be as standardized as possible to keep costs low. No number of add-ons would be able to match the flexibility of need-based construction." While we agree that a one-size-fits-all approach will not work, we disagree that a $300 House would be inflexible. Core tenets from a blog post about the overall design challenge of creating a $300 House by Bill Gross include "give your customers options" and "make it aspirational." And David Smith's entry on the financial challenge shows that flexibility can be born out of financing options as well. A need-based approach alone also ignores the scale of the problem we are facing. "Triple the U.S. population by three. That's how many people around the world live on about a dollar a day," Godin writes. "Triple it again and now you have the number that lives on $2. About 40% of the world lives on $2 or less a day." In any situation where scale is required, so is some level of standardization.

Chapter 4 | Inventing Rhetorically

The most puzzling critique in the op-ed was that "construction is an important industry in neighborhoods like Dharavi. Much of the economy consists of hardware shops, carpenters, plumbers, concrete makers, masons, even real-estate agents. Importing prefabricated homes would put many people out of business, undercutting the very population the $300 house is intended to help."

In fact, our contest's design briefing said these dwellings should be "self built and/or self-improvable." It also stated that the design should rely as much as possible on local materials, which of course would be harvested and crafted by local workers. Our goal is to increase demand for local trades, not drive them away. And the idea that jobs would disappear belies the fact that with progress comes new jobs; teachers for the kids who can now go to school; health care professionals for the families that can now afford check-ups; technology professionals who could service solar panels or internet access devices; farmers who could manage shared crop spaces in the neighborhoods. The $300 House project is a housing ecosystem project.

Finally, Echanove and Srivastava state that "The $300 house could potentially be a success story, if it was understood as a straightforward business proposal instead of a social solution."

We disagree completely. We do support other applications for low-cost housing—bringing these dwellings back to the industrialized world for hurricane relief, for example, would be a reverse innovation success story. However, trying to pigeonhole ideas as either "for good" or "for profit" is an outmoded way of thinking.

The authors have an implicit negative view on business. For them, profit seems to be a dirty word. For us, good business and social innovation are one and the same. The rising tide of New Capitalism, what Michael Porter calls "shared value" and what Umair Haque calls "thick value," is perhaps the most important reaction to the corruption and greed that spurred the most recent global economic crisis. The *Economist* was right when it suggested that this is a "can do" moment in history.

Our goal is neither to start yet another charity—one of our advisers, Paul Polak, tells us that "you can't donate your way out of poverty"—nor to start just another business. Rather we must encourage existing businesses to find ways to create new, scalable markets; to get NGOs to share their on-the-ground expertise; and to force governments to make it as simple as possible to work across the hybrid value chain in order to make such a project a reality and begin the process of instilling dignity in and creating options for individuals who now don't have either.

We are happy that Echanove and Srivastava share our passion for the problem of affordable housing, which is a wicked problem. We simply disagree with the idea that if it's a market, it can't also be a socially progressive solution. Trying to categorize the regeneration of slums as either a business problem or social problem is like trying to categorize a flame as either heat or light. It is both, always.

Reading 4.4

A $300 Idea that Is Priceless

from Schumpeter, a column in the *Economist*

Applying the world's business brains to housing the poor.

Friedrich Engels said in "The Condition of the Working Class in England," in 1844, that the onward march of Manchester's slums meant that the city's Angel Meadow district might better be described as "Hell upon Earth." Today, similar earthly infernos can be found all over the emerging world: from Brazil's favelas to Africa's shanties. In 2010 the United Nations calculated that there were about 827m people living in slums—almost as many people as were living on the planet in Engels's time—and predicted that the number might double by 2030.

Last year Vijay Govindarajan, of Dartmouth College's Tuck School of Business, along with Christian Sarkar, a marketing expert, issued a challenge in a *Harvard Business Review* blog: why not apply the world's best business thinking to housing the poor? Why not replace the shacks that blight the lives of so many poor people, thrown together out of cardboard and mud, and prone to collapsing or catching fire, with more durable structures? They laid down a few simple guidelines. The houses should be built of mass-produced materials tough enough to protect their inhabitants from a hostile world. They should be equipped with the basics of civilized life, including water filters and solar panels. They should be "improvable," so that families can adapt them to their needs. And they should cost no more than $300.

Mr. Govindarajan admits that the $300 figure was partly an attention-grabbing device. But he also argues that it has a certain logic. Muhammad Yunus, the founder of Grameen Bank, has calculated that the average value of the houses of people who have just escaped from poverty is $370. Tata Motors has also demonstrated the value of having a fixed figure to aim at: the company would have found it more difficult to produce the Tata Nano if it

Chapter 4 | Inventing Rhetorically

had simply been trying to produce a "cheap" car rather than a "one lakh" car (about $2,200).

The attention-grabbing certainly worked. The blog was so inundated with positive responses that a dedicated website, 300house.com, was set up, which has attracted more than 900 enthusiasts and advisers from all over the world. On April 20th Mr. Govindarajan launched a competition inviting people to submit designs for a prototype of the house.

Why has a simple blog post led to such an explosion of creativity? The obvious reason is that "frugal innovation"—the art of radically reducing the cost of products while also delivering first-class value—is all the rage at the moment. General Electric has reduced the cost of an electrocardiogram machine from $2,000 to $400. Tata Chemicals has produced a $24 purifier that can provide a family with pure water for a year. Girish Bharadwaj, an engineer, has perfected a technique for producing cheap footbridges that are transforming life in rural India.

Another reason is that houses can be such effective anti-poverty tools. Poorly constructed ones contribute to a nexus of problems: the spread of disease (because they have no proper sanitation or ventilation), the perpetuation of poverty (because children have no proper lights to study by) and the general sense of insecurity (because they are so flimsy and flammable). Mr. Govindarajan's idea is so powerful because he treats houses as ecosystems that provide light, ventilation and sanitation.

Numerous innovators are also worrying away at this nexus of problems. Habitat for Humanity, an NGO, is building durable houses of bamboo in Nepal. Idealab, a consultancy, is on the verge of unveiling a $2,500 house that will be mass-produced in factories, sold in kits and feature breakthroughs in ventilation, lighting and sanitation. Philips has produced a cheap cooking stove, the Chulha, that cuts out the soot that kills 1.6m people a year worldwide. The Solar Electric Light Fund is demonstrating that you can provide poor families with solar power for roughly the same cost as old standbys such as kerosene and candles.

Profits and other problems

These thinkers, like the advocates of the $300 house, must solve three huge problems to succeed. They must persuade big companies that they can make money out of cheap homes, because only they can achieve the economies of scale needed to hit the target price. They need to ensure sufficient access to microloans: $300 is a huge investment for a family of squatters living on a couple of dollars a day. And they need to overcome the obstacle that most slum-dwellers have weak or non-existent property rights. There is no point in offering people the chance to buy a cleverly designed house if they have no title to the land they occupy. Solving these problems will in turn demand a high degree of co-operation between people who do not always get on: companies and NGOs, designers and emerging-world governments.

However, the exciting thing about the emerging world at the moment is a prevailing belief that even the toughest problems can be solved. And a similar can-do moment, in the late 1940s, offers a striking historical precedent for the application of mass-production techniques to housing: as American servicemen flooded home after the second world war to start families, Levitt & Sons built Levittowns at the rate of 30 houses a day by mass-producing the components in factories, delivering them on lorries and using teams of specialists to assemble them.

Some emerging-world governments are beginning to realize that providing security of tenure is the only way to deal with the problem of ever-proliferating slums. And big companies that face stagnant markets in the West are increasingly fascinated by the "fortune at the bottom of the pyramid." Bill Gross of Idealab reckons the market for cheap houses could be worth at least $424 billion. But in reality it is worth far more than that: preventing the Earth from becoming what Mike Davis, a particularly gloomy follower of Marx and Engels, has termed a "planet of slums."

Chapter 4 | Inventing Rhetorically

Other Invention Strategies

Great myths have grown up around writers who can supposedly sit down, put pen to paper, and write a masterpiece. If these myths had developed about any other type of artist—a musician or a painter—we would scoff about them and ask about the years of study and practice those artists had spent before they created their masterpieces. Since all of us can write to some degree, perhaps it seems more feasible that great authors simply appear magically amongst us. Alas, it is not so; like all talented artists, good writers must learn their craft through consistent and continuous practice. Similar to how the ancient Greeks used **topoi** (a strategy or heuristic made up of questions about a topic which allows a rhetor to construe an argument) to generate raw material for their compositions, many writers today use the following invention strategies as prewriting activities.

Freewriting

One practice method developed in the 1970s and often attributed to Peter Elbow, author of *Writing without Teachers*, is called freewriting. This method is just what it sounds like—writing that is free of any content restrictions. You simply write what is on your mind. This method is freeform, but there is some structure—you must set a time limit before you begin, and once you begin, you must not stop. The time period is usually 10 to 20 minutes, and you must keep your pen or pencil moving on the page—no hesitations, no corrections, no rereading. Don't worry about spelling, or punctuation, or grammar—just download onto the paper whatever comes to mind. It will seem awkward at best; some have said it is downright painful. But after a few weeks practice, you will realize it is effective and a wonderful individual method of getting at your thoughts on a subject.

Invisible Freewriting

If you just cannot stop paying attention to your spelling and grammar, or if you find yourself always stopping to read what you have written, you can freewrite invisibly. To do this, you will need carbon paper and a pen that is retracted or out of ink. You sandwich the carbon paper, carbon side down, between two sheets of paper and write on the top sheet with your empty pen. You cannot see what you are writing, but it will be recorded on the bottom sheet of paper. If you prefer to work on the computer, you can easily modify this technique by taping a blank sheet of paper over the monitor while you type.

Focused Freewriting

When freewriting, you are writing without sticking to any particular topic. You are exploring many ideas and your sentences may roam from your day at work, the letter you just got from your sister, or a story you read in the paper about a man who tracks the nighttime migrations of songbirds. With focused freewriting, you are trying to concentrate on one particular subject. You can write the name of that subject at the top of the page to remind you of your topic as you write. The rules are the same as the other types of freewriting, but you are focusing on one question or idea and exploring it in depth.

One drawback of focused freewriting is that students sometimes confuse it with a different step in the writing process, drafting. Remember that freewriting is "invention" work, intended only to help you explore ideas on paper. Drafting takes place only after you have explored, analyzed, and organized those ideas. Freewriting helps you think and write critically about a topic while drafting occurs once you have done the critical thinking necessary to come up with a unified, cohesive, and organized plan for an essay.

Listing/Brainstorming

This method of mapping is the least visual and the most straightforward. Unlike freewriting, where you write continuously, with listing you write down words and/or phrases that provide a shorthand for the ideas you might use in your essay, much as you would a grocery or "to-do" list. Brainstorming is a bit looser. Lists usually follow line after line on the page; brainstorming consists of words and phrases placed anywhere you want to write them on the page.

Clustering

When you think of a cluster, you think of several like things grouped together, often with something holding them together. Peanut clusters, a type of candy, are peanuts joined together with milk chocolate. Star clusters are groupings of stars, like the Pleiades or the Big Dipper, connected by their relative positions to each other in space. You can create clusters of like ideas by grouping your ideas around a central topic on a blank sheet of paper.

Organizing or Arranging

The "invention" process is intended to get our ideas out of our heads and onto a piece of paper, but rarely do these ideas arrive in the most logical or effective order. Take some time (an hour or so for a short essay) to analyze your inventions. Place all the ideas in a logical order, and join similar ideas. Next, look for your most significant point, the most important thing you want to say about your subject. This may become your tentative thesis. Then identify which of the other items on your list will help you communicate your point and delete items that are irrelevant to your thesis.

Reading 4.5

Take a Leap into Writing
by Craig Wynne

When I was working at Berkeley's College Academic Support Center, I often tutored second-language learners who struggled with sentences that had awkward constructions. Sometimes, I would say to a student, "What is it you're trying to say here?" The student inevitably could state the point orally with accuracy and clarity. I would then say to the student, "Write down what you just said." The student would write it down with pen and paper. Then I'd say, "Okay, pretend you're the professor. Which do you think is the easier sentence to understand: what you wrote or what you typed?" The student would say, "What I wrote. Whenever I type, I'm always afraid of what the professor will say."

Craig Wynne says, "When jumping out of an airplane, you don't have time to think about consequences. You just have to do it….The same principle applies to writing."

Around that time, I read an article in *Writer* magazine entitled "Forget the Rules and Take a Leap," by an author named Deanna Roy. In this article, Roy had been suffering from writer's block, and she found that skydiving was a way for her to release her thoughts without fear of saying the "wrong thing." So I decided to put this idea into practice myself for the purposes of teaching my students about overcoming their inhibitions when it came to writing.

When jumping out of an airplane, you don't have time to think about consequences. You just have to do it. You can see from the photo, jumping wasn't an easy thing for me to do, but afterwards I was glad I had gone through with taking that leap.

The same principle applies to writing. You need to find a way to write without thinking about whether your words are spelled correctly or whether the professor won't like the idea. Those thoughts get in the way with your writing process. Some students can write with that kind of freedom on a computer, but others find that with the computer comes an uninvited editor who looks over their shoulder and criticizes. Yet, they can escape that editor by talking out their thoughts and then writing with pen and paper. Whatever works. This doesn't mean that writing is ever going to be easy. It's just easier if you can get your thoughts down on a piece of paper before that internal editor starts looking for errors.

A professor named Peter Elbow developed a process called freewriting, which helps writers take that leap from thoughts into words. To freewrite, you put your pen to paper and just write. You don't want to think about whether something is spelled incorrectly or whether the professor will like an idea. Freewriting is the chance for you to get your ideas down on paper (or on the computer). When you freewrite, you don't stop. You just write. Even if you have an idea you think sounds completely stupid or off-the-wall, just write it down. You never know. Sometimes, those "silly" ideas could contain something you might be able to use for your assignment. When I start a project, I begin by letting all my ideas out in words in a row, even if they don't sound quite right. Professor Elbow remarked that freewriting results in a lot of words that are garbage. That's true. However, eventually, I come to words that express an idea I like. In order to get to the point of liking my words, I have to take that leap onto the page. Eventually, I have to worry about grammar, structure, and the end product, but not while I'm freewriting.

Activity 4.6 Consider "Take a Leap into Writing"

1. How do you write most easily? On a computer? With pen and paper? Share your experience getting words onto a page.

2. What do you think of Wynne's comparison of writing to skydiving? What do the two things have in common?

3. Do you have an internal editor that keeps you from writing freely? Can you describe your editor? What does it do?

Activity 4.7 Focused Freewriting

1. Write your topic at the top of a blank sheet of paper.

2. Write a list of at least 10 aspects or characteristics of your topic.

3. Choose two or three items from your list and do a focused freewriting on each item for five to eight minutes.

4. Add more items to your list if you have discovered new ideas during your freewriting.

Activity 4.8 Begin with What You Know

In your small group, make a list of controversial topics that you already have some knowledge about because of personal experience or course work. For example, one of you may be among the millions of Americans without health insurance or you may know someone else in this position. If so, you probably know about some of the failings of the American health care system. Alternatively, you may have lost a job during the 2009 recession or been unable to find a job when you needed one. If so, you probably have some thoughts about the efforts of the federal government to deal with the economic crisis. These personal connections with controversial issues give you a starting point for research on a topic. Share your group's list with the class.

Expand Your Personal Knowledge through Observation

Close observation for descriptive detail can enhance almost any topic. If you are writing a paper on the effectiveness of recycling in your community, you might take a trip to your community's processing area for recycled glass. There you could gather information through observing the glass recycling process. You also might be able to conduct short, informal interviews with the employees about the process.

You may need to call to get permission to visit certain places. You'll need to identify yourself and your topic. Usually you can get permission to visit and observe. However, if you cannot get permission to visit an area, you can ask your contact if there is a similar area nearby. Again, look at your research questions before you visit to decide which questions might be answered by your observations. For example, if you have read about recycling centers in other communities, during your visit to the local center, you could observe the similarities and differences in their procedures. Good writers always gather more detail than they actually use so they have choices about what to include.

The key to successful observation is tuning the senses. Can you remember what your room smelled like when you woke up this morning, the first thing you saw when you opened your eyes, the way your sheets or blanket felt against your skin, the sounds in the room after you turned off your alarm, or the taste of the orange juice or coffee you had with breakfast? Our minds are trained to ignore seemingly unimportant information, so if you can't remember any sensory details from your morning, you're not alone. When conducting an observation, however, those sensory responses are an important part of your research. Sitting in the place you're observing, freewrite for at least five minutes on each of the senses: touch, taste, smell, sight, and sound. You might even freewrite on each of the senses from several different vantage points, depending on the size of the place or the event you're observing. Take notes on the responses given by those you speak with.

Within fifteen minutes of leaving the place you have been observing, take a few minutes to read over your notes and write a few overall impressions or add details you missed in your description. Look again at your research questions and decide which ones have been answered by your visit.

Chapter 4 | **Inventing Rhetorically**

Activity 4.9 Observation Exercise

In this exercise, describe your classroom. Alternatively, go to another setting such as a museum, restaurant, or library and describe that space and the people in it.

- How large is the space, approximately? Describe the shape of the room, and the color and texture of the walls, the ceiling, and the floor.
- How is the space furnished? Describe the color, shape, and style of the furnishings.
- What about representing the other senses? Is the room silent or noisy? Does it have a characteristic smell? Describe.
- How many people are in the room? What are they doing? Describe their ages, general style of dress, and possessions such as computers, backpacks, or purses.
- Pick two or three people that stand out in some way from the other occupants and write a sentence or two about each, describing what it is about each person that caught your attention.

Reading 4.6

BMW 1M: Miniature, Mighty and Miles of Fun
by Dan Neil

Dan Neil, auto columnist for *The Wall Street Journal*, reviewed the new BMW Coupe in his weekly column "Rumble Seat."

As you read the article that follows, pay attention to how the author uses details from both personal knowledge and close observation to enrich his writing.

Typically, car makers will choose a special color for the introduction of a special vehicle, known in the biz as the "launch color." In the case of the 1M Coupe—the Motorsports division variant of BMW's beastly looking 135i—the launch color is a sort of burnt tangerine, a phrase that also describes my own mental citrus after a weekend behind the wheel.

A bratty little barrel-racer of a car, with a spirit that seems to want to bite through the bit, the 1M Coupe is quick, playful, aggressive and laugh-out-loud fun to drive; indeed, it's as much fun as the law will allow. For BMW fanboys, I gather, that's just the problem.

A little history is in order: The M division began in the 1970s building highly tuned versions of the Werks' production cars, with more powerful engines, bigger brakes, more athletic legs and edgier electronics. Some of these cars have been, simply, epic. The M3 that I imprinted on was a '96 Euro-spec yellow coupe. That car is, to this day, the best handling five-seater I've ever driven.

Bratty Little Barrel Racer

(Note to Bavaria: Bring back the narrow-section steering wheel. And stop hogging all the good scenery.)

To describe the pleasures of that M3—known to the geek squad as the E36 model—is to define a kind of atavism that the Bimmerphiles pine for. Those cars were relatively simple (in-line six, manual transmission and spare amenities), with beautifully quick and sensitive steering and an easy progressiveness that meant you could let the rear end slide around without fear of losing it, catching the car with a dab of throttle and counter-steer. It wasn't the fastest car in the world but it was such a sheer limbic pleasure to drive, to wheel, to wield, to control. That's it: a sense of mastery. You got out of that car wearing a cape and a big S on your chest.

Most of all, that car was lightweight. That E36 coupe weighed about 3,200 pounds. By contrast, the current model-year M3 (E92) weighs fully 500 pounds more on a 2.4-inch-longer wheelbase. And while the current M3 has vastly more go-fast hardware—including a 414-horsepower V8, optional dual-clutch gearbox, cybernetic brakes and the M Variable Differential Lock (sounds like an outlawed wrestling hold, doesn't it?)—a certain something, call it a dynamic lucidity, has been lost.

And the fanboys feel betrayed. They whine, they fume, they wear black. You'd think Rudolph Valentino had just died or something. Why does the M3 have to be so heavy? What part of Ultimate Driving Machine does BMW itself not understand?

But everyone's favorite M3 of yore didn't have to have a monster stereo, navi, power seats, umpteen airbags or five-star crash structure. The M3 so fondly remembered has been essentially optioned up and regulated out of existence. Unless BMW discovers the formula for Flubber, that car isn't coming back.

And the bloat isn't confined to the weight scales. The current M3 is also punitively pricey, starting at $61,075 (with gas-guzzler tax) and luxed-out to nearly $70,000. More fanboy despair. Oh, Rudy!

To these disconsolate few, the news last year that the M division was going to hot up the 135i coupe (the E82 platform, in nerd-speak) must have sounded like salvation. The numbers were there. Not quite 3,400 pounds, with a twin-turbo 3.0-liter in-line six delivering 335 hp and 332 pound-feet of torque—with brief computer-summoned overboost of 369 pound-feet—and the sole choice of a six-speed manual transmission, the 1M Coupe sounded like more than just a cool car. It promised a return to form, an end to a kind of despised lavishness, a cure for what ails the BMW brand.

2012 BMW 1M Coupe

Base price: $47,010

Price as tested: $49,000 (est.)

Powertrain: Twin-turbo 3.0-liter in-line six cylinder with variable valve timing; six-speed manual transmission; rear wheel drive with variable differential lock

Horsepower/torque: 335 hp at 5,900 rpm/332 pound-feet at 1,500–4,500 rpm (369 pound-feet at overboost)

Length/weight: 172.4 inches/3,362 pounds

Wheelbase: 104.7 inches

EPA fuel economy: 19/26 mpg, city/highway

Cargo capacity: 8 cubic feet

Now that the car is here, is it? You know, it is, sort of.

To boil it down a bit, the 1M Coupe is the smaller car with the mighty M3's dirty bits, less 400 pounds. The same highly evolved suspension componentry, the same massive brakes behind the same stick-with-a-grip 35-series, 19-inch tires and wheels, the same electronically controlled rear differential, and the same M-tuned dynamics control, which allows drivers to color outside the lines safely at the track. And yes, you can turn the electronic interventions off. But once the nannies are dismissed, be advised, the car has a measure of the old-school, free-gimbaling character of the early M's. In other words, it can get away from you. Me? Oh, please. You'd like that, wouldn't you?

The 1M is certainly track-day ready, with a dry-sump engine-lubrication system with its own heat exchanger as well as a radiator for the heavy-duty six-speed transmission. The car I drove had a brake warning light come on—I think the 14-inch cross-drilled brakes got a little too warm after being lapped at Laguna Seca for a half-hour or so—but they never failed to haul the car down with a precise and determined yank rearward.

Here, at last, is a man's clutch—heavily weighted, with a smooth, precise uptake—and slick-shifting gearshift to go with it. Pedal position is just about perfect for heel-and-toe footwork.

Serene and smooth at low speeds, but with an increasingly impatient growl from the quad exhaust as the revs build, the 1M does several dynamic things particularly well. First, at corner exits, it pulls like hell, like it has deployed some magical torque spinnaker. BMW gives the 0–60 acceleration at 4.7 seconds, but the way this thing gets on the cam in second and third gear will bring a tear to your eye. Like my favorite M3 of olden days, the car is not unnervingly fast but it's hugely willing. This thing hits redline faster than one of the Real Housewives of Atlanta.

Second, it has splendid cornering grip, and the corner-to-corner transitions happen without a lot of heaving, rolling or rebound to unsettle the car or

Chapter 4 | Inventing Rhetorically

cause you to correct your line. The 1M Coupe has impeccable cornering manners, and the M Sport Seats lock you in driving position.

Third, it trail-brakes like a dream. Turn in to a corner with the brakes on and ease off the binders. The car's rear end slides gracefully to the outside, the world swivels and now you're looking at corner exit. Dig in the spurs, up come the revs. Hi-yo, Silbern, away!

So what could possibly be wrong? Well, for one thing, the 1M Coupe is a total buttaface, one of the ugliest, most disturbingly wrong car designs in modern history. The addition of all the massive wheel arches, lip spoilers, aero mods and the so-called Air Curtain front spoiler helps not at all. This car is the last revenge of former BMW styling head Chris Bangle. Jeez, put a flag over its head and drive for glory.

Second—at least to the fanboys—it's still too heavy, despite the fact it's actually 77 pounds lighter than the standard 135i. But I checked the trunk for lead bars and found none, and I found very little in the way of depleted uranium in the cabin.

I can only conclude that, for some old-schoolers, nothing BMW makes will ever be light enough again. That's too bad. This thing's a tangerine dream.

Activity 4.10 Find Artistic and Inartistic Proofs in a Reading

Much of Dan Neil's column, "BMW 1M: Miniature, Mighty and Miles of Fun," comes from his own personal experience and observation. For example, his description of the car as a, "bratty little barrel-racer of a car, with a spirit that seems to want to bite through the bit," is his own evaluation or thought and, thus, an artistic proof. So is the first sentence, "Typically, car makers will choose a special color for the introduction of a special vehicle, known in the biz as the 'launch color.'" That information comes from his long experience with reviewing cars. Also, his remark that the brake light came on in the car he drove is his observation.

However, the information that the car has "a dry-sump engine-lubrication system with its own heat exchanger as well as a radiator for the heavy-duty six-speed transmission" may have come from the manufacturer's promotional literature.

For this activity, go through the reading and highlight (or underline) the parts that you think come from Dan Neil's own knowledge or observation. These are the artistic proofs. Information he has obtained from other sources (such as the car company) would be inartistic proofs. If you aren't sure whether or not a sentence is his own knowledge or observation, make a note of that in the margin. Discuss this as a class.

Activity 4.11 Write a Product Review

Choose a new product in a category you know well, such as a computer or an MP3 player, and write a review as if you were a columnist for a newspaper, magazine, or blog. Using the techniques explained in this chapter, do prewriting to elicit what you know about the product and the product category. Then, observe the product and try it out, so that you can review its positives and negatives. If you need specific information that you do not know, consult the product advertising, packaging, or instruction manual.

Like Dan Neil's auto product review, you can use vivid language and insider slang in order to provide an enjoyable experience for your reader. Remember, however, that this is an argument. You need to evaluate whether the product is a good or bad selection for its target audience and why.

Activity 4.12 Write on Your Blog

Choose a controversial topic and speculate in your blog whether or not that topic is at a stasis point for any of the stasis questions.

Activity 4.13 Write in Your Commonplace Book

In your commonplace book, freewrite about how you do invention. What methods do you use to extract from your mind what you already know about a subject (what Aristotle would call artistic proofs)?

5
WRITING RHETORICALLY

Praxis in Action

How I Write by Matthew Harding

Writing can seem very daunting at times, especially when you have a major writing assignment that's worth as much as a test. It should be easy since you know about the assignment way ahead of time, but somehow the time ends up getting away from you because it's hard to get started. You end up both stressing about the paper and trying to write it at the last minute. One way that I reduce the pressure of a writing assignment is to start writing long before the paper is due, giving myself enough time to work on it.

If I tell myself that I am only going to write a certain amount at a time, say a page a day, it is less intimidating to write. While this method may seem drawn out, it works. Whenever I come back to the paper the next day, I always review what I have already written, so I can be sure I keep the topic in mind. This way, I avoid burning myself out, getting my ideas confused, or losing track of the topic and, ultimately, rushing to finish by the end. This allows me to come to my paper with a fresh perspective and new ideas with every installment I write. Once I finish that day's work I feel good because I am getting the paper done while also giving it my best effort, which also greatly reduces the stress of having to write it.

Matthew Harding points out that writing can be daunting even for experienced writers.

Through Writing, Enter the Conversation

Cicero's famous work, *On the Ideal Orator*, is not a treatise or handbook about how to be an effective rhetorician. Instead, it is a dialogue, a conversation. The setting is a villa outside Rome belonging to Lucius Licinius Crassus, and the time is 91 CE, an era of dangerous unrest in the Roman Empire. Prominent and respected citizens gather with Crassus to escape, for a while, the political crisis developing in the city. Crassus and his guests settle at leisure under a wide, spreading plane tree, not only to enjoy its shade but also to pay homage to Plato's *Phaedrus*, which similarly took place under a plane tree, though in Greece. They take time this day to dialogue about the attributes of an ideal orator. The purpose of the arguments they present to each other is not to win out over the others but, conversing together, to come to knowledge. It is not a trivial pursuit. Cicero reveals what his characters do not know—soon they will all die horribly as part of the civil unrest in Rome, violence traceable to the failure of leaders to resolve their differences in nonviolent dialogue.

Throughout ancient times, dialogue appears alongside rhetoric. It was through dialogue that rhetoricians such as Aristotle, Isocrates, and Cicero taught their students rhetorical skills. Today, in the writing classroom, group discussion or pairs dialogue is also part of the teaching process. A rhetorical text, too, is a conversation with previous texts, responding to ideas they have presented. In addition, arguments include paraphrases and quotes from others' compositions, making them part of the conversation. Moreover, writers composing texts must anticipate their audiences' reactions—questions they might ask or objections they might raise—so responses to these questions and objects can be included in the argument. This process of responding to audiences in advance continues the conversation.

Organize Your Essay

All texts are conversational, a characteristic reflected in the format or organization. In ancient times, orators began a speech by attracting the audience's attention in what was called the *exordium*, which we would call the opening or introduction. Next, they provided background information in a *narratio* (narration), followed by an *explication* in which they defined terms and enumerated the issues. During the *partition* they would express the thesis or main issue to be discussed, and in the *confirmation* they would provide evidence to support the thesis. Opposition arguments would be addressed in the *refutatio,* and the composition would be wrapped up with a *peroratio* or conclusion. The order of these different elements was not rigid in ancient times, nor is it today. Sometimes one or more sections were eliminated if they were not needed, but then, as now, an effective text included most of these elements. For example, if your audience is very familiar with a particular subject, you may not need to define terms, as you would with an audience who was unfamiliar with the material.

As did the ancient Greeks and Romans, when you write an argument, you begin with an introduction that gains your audience's attention and presents your thesis; likewise, you end with a conclusion that ties together what you have said or presents a call to action. However, you have a choice of several formats for what happens between that introduction and conclusion. Following are three prominent alternatives; your choice of which to use depends on your purpose and the type of evidence you have.

- Created by Stephen Toulmin, the **Toulmin model** for persuasion grew out of the 20th century emphasis upon empirical evidence and is *most effective for arguments that rely on evidence from scientific studies, surveys, or other data.* His model requires six elements. First, rhetors present a claim or statement that they want the audience to accept. Then, they back up the claim with data and facts, what Aristotle would have called inartistic proofs. A warrant links these data to the claim, explaining why the data make the claim valid. Backing provides additional support for the argument, while a counterclaim acknowledges any objections or weaknesses in the argument. And, finally, the rebuttal responds to any counterclaims, removing possible objections to the argument.

- The **Rogerian** (or common ground) **argument** is named for psychologist Carl Rogers. It is *most effective for arguments that attempt to establish common ground between opponents* on an issue. Rogerian argument begins with an introduction that states the problem to be considered. Second, in a much different move than the Toulmin pattern, the rhetor states the opposing argument in neutral language to demonstrate that he or she understands the other side's position, as well as instances when it may be valid. The assumption is that, since the rhetor has been willing to pay attention to the other side's position, they will, in fairness, listen as the rhetor states his or her own position, as well as discusses the instances when it is preferable. The Rogerian argument ends on a positive note, describing how the rhetor's position could, at least in some instances, benefit the opposition.

- The **general modern format** for argument is one that will probably be familiar to you from previous English classes. It is a *format that you can use when your argument does not fit neatly into either the Toulmin or Rogerian patterns.* Moreover, you can adapt it to serve the needs of your argument. It is the standard five-paragraph essay modified for presenting an argument, and, like that pattern, it can be expanded to accommodate longer essays. Similar to the five-paragraph essay, you begin with an introduction that attracts your audience's attention and states your thesis. Then two or three sections each present major points that support your thesis. The next section presents a counterargument, which anticipates audience questions or objections and is followed by a rebuttal of the counterargument. Finally, a conclusion ties the argument together, perhaps by reflecting back to the introduction or issuing a call for action.

Notice that all of these formats include an attempt to dialogue with the audience. In the Toulmin model, the warrant, in particular, is designed to help the audience make the logical link between the claim and the data offered as evidence. In a Rogerian argument, the rhetor carefully and in emotionally-neutral language demonstrates that he or she has been listening to the opposition and can even restate their argument fairly. The arguments produced via these models, even if they do not immediately convince, will not worsen the situation. The aim of well-intentioned rhetors is not to convince at any cost but to continue the conversation until reasonable solutions can be found. For a comparison of the different argument formats, see table 5.1 presented on page 150–151.

Like the ancient Greeks, you will begin with an opening and end with a conclusion. However, in between the bookends of your essay, you have more flexibility to adapt the basic format than did the Romans.

Write a Thesis Statement

A **thesis** may be a sentence or a series of sentences, or in a few cases it may be implied rather than stated explicitly; but a thesis is at the heart of any piece of writing. If a reader cannot identify your thesis, the meaning of your text is not clear. How do you develop a thesis? First, you determine your occasion for writing—who is your audience, what is your purpose, and what special circumstances are there (if any)? Then you write a working thesis that makes an assertion or claim about your topic, something that will be affected by

Chapter 5 | **Writing Rhetorically**

your audience and purpose. For example, if you are writing a research paper about the advantages and disadvantages of biodiesel fuel, your claim may be stated differently depending on whether your audience is an English class or a chemistry class. In the latter, you might need to use technical language that would be unfamiliar to your English professor.

Working theses are statements that develop and change as essays are written; they are basic frameworks that provide a connection for the ideas you have decided to convey to your reader. Later, after you have completed a draft of your text, examine your working thesis. If needed, rewrite your thesis so that it states the main idea of your essay in a clear and engaging fashion. Consider the following examples of thesis statements.

> The United States should implement a guest worker program as a way of reforming the illegal immigration problem.

> Nuclear power should be considered as part of a program to reduce the United States's dependence on foreign oil.

Compose an Introduction

Experienced writers have different methods of creating a good introduction. One writer who tends to discover his paper as he goes along swears the best way to write an introduction is to write the entire paper and then move the conclusion to the beginning of the essay and rewrite it as the introduction. Another writer lets the paper sit around for a few days before she writes her introduction. A third always writes two or three different introductions and tries them out on friends before deciding which to use. However you choose to write the introduction, make sure it is interesting enough to make your reader want to read on.

The introduction to your essay is an invitation to your reader. If you invite readers to come along with you on a boring journey, they won't want to follow. In magazine and

Essay Starters

If, after you have done extensive invention (prewriting and research), you still find it intimidating to face the blank computer screen, try one of the essay starters below. These are phrases to get the words flowing. Then, later, after you have written a rough draft, go back and revise the beginning. Delete the essay starter and, in its place, write a real introduction. As you probably know, you do not need to say, "In my opinion," because what you write in your essay, unless you attribute it to someone else, is your opinion. See the section in this chapter on writing introductions.

In my opinion . . .

I agree . . .

I disagree . . .

Studies show . . .

Experts say . . .

My paper is about . . .

I am writing this essay because . . .

In the beginning . . .

Argument Formats: A Comparison

Ancient Roman	General Modern Format
Standard pattern the ancients modified to suit the argument.	Good all-purpose format that can be adapted for the needs of the argument.
Introduction—Exordium Attracts the interest of the audience and identifies the argument.	**Introduction** Attracts the interest of the audience through its opening strategy and states the thesis.
Background or narration—Narratio Details the history or facts of the issue.	**First main point** Supports the thesis.
Definition—Explication Defines terms and outlines issues.	**Second main point** Supports the thesis.
Thesis—Partition States the particular issue that is to be argued.	**Third main point** Supports the thesis.
Proof—Confirmation Develops the thesis and provides supporting evidence.	**Counterargument** Acknowledges the opposing argument or arguments.
Refutation or opposition—Refutatio Addresses the arguments opposing the thesis.	**Rebuttal of counterargument** Refutes the opposing argument or arguments.
Conclusion—Peroratio Reiterates the thesis and may urge the audience to action.	**Conclusion** Ties together the elements of the composition and gives the reader closure. May summarize the essay and include a call to action.

Chapter 5 | Writing Rhetorically

table 5.1

Toulmin Model	Rogerian Argument
Good for an argument that relies on empirical evidence such as scientific studies or data collection.	Good when the object is consensus or compromise, so that opponents can work together while retaining their positions.
Claim Presents the overall thesis the writer will argue.	**Introduction** States the problem to be solved or the question to be answered. Often opponents will also agree there is a problem.
Data Supports the claim with evidence.	**Summary of opposing views** Describes the opposing side's arguments in a neutral and fair manner.
Warrant (also known as a bridge) Explains why or how the data support the claim. Connects the data to the claim.	**Statement of understanding** Concedes occasions when the opposing position might be valid.
Counterclaim Presents a claim that negates or disagrees with the thesis/claim.	**Statement of position** Avoids emotionally charged language, and identifies position.
Rebuttal Presents evidence that negates or disagrees with the counterclaim.	**Statement of contexts** Describes the specific contexts in which the rhetor's position applies/works well.
Conclusion Ties together the elements of the composition (if not included with the rebuttal).	**Statement of benefits** Presents benefits that may appeal to the self-interest of readers who may not yet agree with you; shows how your position benefits them. Ends on a positive note.
	Conclusion Ties together the elements of the composition (if not included in the statement of benefits).

newspaper writing, the introduction is sometimes called a *hook* because it hooks the reader into reading the text. If a magazine writer does not capture the reader's attention right away, the reader is not likely to continue. After all, there are other and possibly more interesting articles in the magazine. Why should readers suffer through a boring introduction? Depending on the topic and pattern of your essay, you might employ one of the following techniques to hook your readers and make them want to keep reading:

- An intriguing or provocative quotation
- A narrative or anecdote
- A question or series of questions
- A vivid sensory description
- A strongly stated opinion

Your introductory paragraph makes a commitment to your readers. This is where you identify the topic, state your thesis (implicitly or explicitly), and give your readers clues about the journey that will follow in the succeeding paragraphs. Be careful not to mislead the reader. Do not ask questions you will not answer in your paper (unless they are rhetorical questions). Do not introduce a topic in your introduction and then switch to another one in your paper.

Although the introduction is the first paragraph or so of the paper, it may not be the first paragraph the writer composes. If you have problems beginning your essay because you cannot immediately think of a good introduction, begin with the first point in your essay and come back to the introduction later.

If you have problems writing anything at all, consider the suggestions offered in the following essay.

Reading 5.1

The Truth about Writer's Block
by Judith Johnson

Judith Johnson suggests in this essay, first published in *Huffington Post Books*, that there is no such thing as writer's block. She suggests what writers experience is the ebb and flow of the writing process.

I don't choose to experience "writer's block" which I see as simply a matter of faulty perception. It is a mislabeling of a very natural part of the ebb and flow of the writing process. To say "I have writer's block" is to judge a temporary or permanent absence of writing momentum and productivity as wrong and therefore to see oneself as a failure in some way. The process of writing is an intricate interplay of conscious and unconscious dynamics and what actually lands on the page is a small part of it all. When we label and judge that process, we interfere with its natural flow and take a position of againstness with ourselves. It's all in how you look at it.

When a writer declares that he or she is experiencing writer's block, it is like grabbing hold of a fear (Fantasy Expectation Appearing Real) and fueling it with emotional distress. A way to reframe this is to simply trust that what appears to be a dry spell is a normal part of the process of being a writer and that either you need time to be away from the writing focus or that the process is largely unconscious at that time. Each writer has to make peace with this by finding their own particular rhythm and honoring that. For example, what works for me is not to have any rigid writing schedule, but rather to let the words come to me—and they always do—sooner or later. When working on a deadline, whether self-imposed or not, I never lose sight of the deadline, it is always there, but I don't beat myself up with it if time keeps passing and nothing is getting on paper. I'll notice that the topic is alive in me—turning this way and that finding its way to the paper. It takes a lot of trust to let this be. So far, it has never failed me.

I have lots of books and articles and projects on the back burner and no fear of running out of things to write about. I know that each piece of writing has a life of its own. For example, I have a poem that I started at the age of 16 that rumbles around in my head from time to time looking for its ending. I know it will end someday, but hasn't so far. That's not a problem to me—just a reality. I also keep what I call a "dump" file for each project and whether I am actively working on it or not, I capture ideas and information there.

In addition to building a strong bond of trust with yourself, here are some other keys to maintaining a good relationship with yourself as a writer:

Just Do It: There is a point at which every writer just has to sit down and write. Whether you write for five minutes or five hours straight doesn't matter, but if you are going to be a writer, you have to sit down and write.

Write with Freedom and Abandon, Then Edit Ruthlessly: It is important to give yourself permission to write whatever comes up without any judgment. Just focus on capturing your thoughts and ideas—forget about grammar, structure and eloquence. Just get a hold of whatever comes up. Then, just as Michelangelo described the sculpting process as discovering a statue inside every block of stone, each writer must ruthlessly revise and refine a piece of work until pleased with it.

Get Out of Your Own Way: If you get into a pattern of negativity and beating up on yourself when writing, find a way to be more loving with yourself and do not feed the negativity.

Patience: Writing takes enormous patience. As with any other art form, you are constantly revising and refining your work. For an artist the equation is never time is money, but rather "do I feel complete with this piece? Is it my best effort given the time I have available?"

Flexibility, Cooperation and Balance: There is always some level of agitation just under the surface that propels a writer forward giving momentum to the working process. But there are always other forces at work and writing is only one of many activities in an individual's life. Finding your own rhythm and being willing to cooperate with the other elements of life that often seem to intrude on the writer's solitary endeavor are like moving between shooting the rapids and gliding along on calm waters, never quite knowing which is going to present itself and when. Experience teaches us all to go with the flow and somehow that seems to yield maximum inner peace and outward productivity.

Keeping a Sense of Humor and Humility: I've learned never to take myself too seriously as a writer. I do my best and need to laugh at myself from time to time when I give too much importance to what I write. If people get value from what I write, that's great and positive feedback is extremely gratifying. However, while writing is ultimately about communication, I find it very funny that I don't write to communicate, but rather because I simply need to write—I am compelled to do so. If the end product of my endeavors is of value to others, that's great, but the solitary process of engaging in the art form itself is entirely for me and I think that is pretty funny.

Letting Go of the Illusion of Control: A really good writer is never in control of the writing process. You may find that having a rigid schedule works well for you or you might be someone who writes when the spirit moves you to do so. Either way, a good writer taps into the wellspring of human consciousness and like love, you can't make that happen on demand.

Is writing challenging? Absolutely! However, it is a great way to learn some profound lessons in life and to be of service to others.

Chapter 5 | **Writing Rhetorically**

Activity 5.1 Discuss "The Truth about Writer's Block"

1. How does Judith Johnson choose to reframe the concept of writer's block?

2. Johnson makes recommendations to deal with the "absence of writing momentum." Which of her suggestions makes the most sense to you? Which makes the least sense to you?

3. What do you think? Is there such a thing as "writer's block"?

Combine Your Ideas with Support from Source Materials

A research paper, by definition, makes use of source materials to make an argument. It is important to remember, however, that it is *your* paper, *not* what some professors may call a "research dump," meaning that it is constructed by stringing together research information with a few transitions. Rather, you, as the author of the paper, carry the argument in your own words and use quotes and paraphrases from source materials to support your argument. How do you do that? Here are some suggestions:

- After you think you have completed enough research to construct a working thesis and begin writing your paper, collect all your materials in front of you (photocopies of articles, printouts of electronic sources, and books) and spend a few hours reading through the materials and making notes. Then, put all the notes and materials to the side and freewrite for a few minutes about what you can remember from your research that is important. Take this freewriting and make a rough outline of the main points you want to cover in your essay. Then you can go back to your notes and source materials to flesh out your outline.

- Use quotes for the following three reasons:
  1. You want to "borrow" the ethos or credibility of the source. For example, if you are writing about stem cell research, you may want to quote from an authority such as Dr. James A. Thomson, whose ground-breaking research led to the first use of stem cells for research. Alternatively, if your source materials include the *New England Journal of Medicine* or another prestigious publication, it may be worth crediting a quote to that source.

2. The material is so beautifully or succinctly written that it would lose its effectiveness if you reworded the material in your own words.

3. You want to create a point of emphasis by quoting rather than paraphrasing. Otherwise, you probably want to paraphrase material from your sources, as quotes should be used sparingly. Often, writers quote source material in a first draft and then rewrite some of the quotes into paraphrases during the revision process.

- Introduce quotes. You should never have a sentence or sentences in quotation marks just sitting in the middle of a paragraph, as it would puzzle a reader. If you quote, you should always introduce the quote by saying something like this: According to Dr. James A. Thomson, "Stem cell research. . . . "

- Avoid plagiarism by clearly indicating material that is quoted or paraphrased. See the appendix (at the end of the book) for more information about citing source material.

Support Your Thesis

After you have attracted the interest of your audience, established your thesis, and given any background information and definitions, you will next begin to give reasons for your position, which further develops your argument. These reasons are, in turn, supported by statistics, analogies, anecdotes, and quotes from authorities which you have discovered in your research or know from personal knowledge. Ideally, arrange your reasons so that the strongest ones come either at the beginning or at the end of this portion of the paper (points of emphasis) and the weaker ones fall in the middle.

Answer Opposing Arguments

If you are aware of a contradicting statistic or other possible objection to your argument, it may be tempting to ignore that complication, hoping your audience will not notice. However, that is exactly the worst thing you can do. It is much better to anticipate your audience's possible questions or objections and address them in your discussion. Doing so prevents you from losing credibility by either appearing to deceive your audience or being unaware of all the facts. Also, acknowledging possible refutations of your position actually strengthens your position by making you seem knowledgeable and fair-minded.

Vary Your Strategies or Patterns of Development

When composing your essay, you have many different strategies or **patterns of development** available to you. You may write entire essays whose sole strategy is argumentation or comparison and contrast, but more often, you will combine many of these different modes while writing a single essay. Consider the following strategies or patterns of development:

- *Analysis* entails a close examination of an issue, book, film, or other object, separating it into elements and examining each of the elements separately through other writing modes such as classification or comparison and contrast.
- *Argumentation* involves taking a strong stand on an issue supported by logical reasons and evidence intended to change a reader's mind on an issue or open a reader's eyes to a problem.
- *Cause and effect* is an explanation of the cause and subsequent effects or consequences of a specific action.
- *Classification* entails dividing and grouping things into logical categories.
- *Comparison and contrast* examines the similarities and differences between two or more things.
- *Definition* employs an explanation of the specific meaning of a word, phrase, or idea.
- *Description* uses vivid sensory details to present a picture or an image to the reader.
- *Exemplification* makes use of specific examples to explain, define, or analyze something.
- *Narration* uses a story or vignette to illustrate a specific point or examine an issue.

Write a Conclusion

After they have read the last paragraph of your essay, your readers should feel satisfied that you have covered everything you needed to and you have shared an insight. You may have heard the basic rules: A conclusion cannot address any new issues, and it should summarize the main points of the essay. Although these are valid and reliable rules, a summary is not always the best way to end an essay. The prohibition against new ideas in the final paragraph also might limit certain effective closures like a call to action or a question for the reader to ponder.

One effective technique for writing a conclusion is to refer back to your introduction. If you began with a narrative anecdote, a sensory description, or a question, you can tie a mention of it to your ending point. Or, if you are composing an argumentative essay, you might choose to summarize by using an expert quote to restate your thesis, giving the reader a final firm sense of ethos or credibility. You might also end with a single-sentence summary followed by a suggestion or a call to action for the reader. Another effective way to end an argument can be a paragraph that suggests further research.

A conclusion doesn't have to be long. As a matter of fact, it does not even need to be a separate paragraph, especially if your essay is short. If your closing comments are related to the final paragraph of the essay, one or two sentences can easily be added to the final body paragraph of the essay.

Consider Elements of Page Design

Professors now take it for granted that you word-process your paper using a professional looking typeface such as Times Roman. However, producing your text on a computer with Internet access gives you the option to do much more—including adding one or more images and other page design elements. Several of the assignments in this chapter offer you the opportunity to be creative with your project presentation. Even if you are required to submit your project in standard MLA or APA essay formats, however, you can still include one or more images, and it is important to consider where you place the images.

Some simple guidelines will help you design effective documents:

- Use space as a design element. Do not overcrowd your pages. Place material so that important parts are emphasized by the space around them.
- Rarely (if ever) use all capital letters. Words in all caps are hard to read, and on the Internet all caps is considered shouting.
- Use headings to group your information and make your pages easy to skim. Readers often like to skim pages before deciding what to read.

Indeed, many people will skim all the headlines, headings, and photo captions first, before reading the body text of any section.

- Put important elements in the top left and lower right parts of the screen. English readers are trained to read from left to right, so our eyes naturally start at the upper left-hand corner of the screen. Our eyes, when skimming, don't flow line by line, but move in a Z pattern, as illustrated in the following diagram (see figure 5.1).

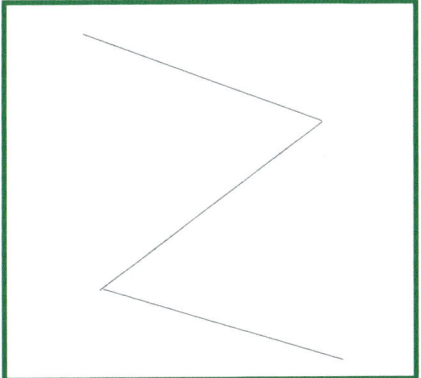

figure 5.1

Eye movement when skimming a page

If you want to include a photo in your research paper, for example, you should put it either in the top left or the bottom right corner of the page, points of emphasis in the Z pattern. Today, with a sophisticated word processing program such as Microsoft Word, it is easy to import an image, size it, and move it to the desired place on a page. Once you have imported an image, you can click on it, hold your cursor at a corner, and enlarge or shrink the image by dragging the cursor. Also, by clicking on the image, you can activate the dialogue box that allows you to specify having the text run tightly around the image. Then you can easily move the image around on the page until you have placed it in a pleasing spot. Alternatively, Microsoft Word provides document templates that you can use for newsletters, brochures, and other types of projects.

If you look closely at figure 5.2 on the next page, you may notice that the text surrounding the image does not seem to make any sense (though it is actually Latin). That's because the text is Lorem ipsum text, sometimes called placeholder or dummy text, which designers use to create page layouts before they have the real text from writers. If you want to try using Lorem ipsum yourself, just do a search on the Internet for that name, and you will find sites that provide paragraphs of the nonsense words that you can utilize as placeholder text.

figure 5.2

The image in this article has been effectively placed in the lower right corner, which is a point of emphasis.

Including Images in Your Projects: Copyright Implications

United States copyright law includes a provision called "fair use" that allows copyrighted images to be used for educational projects. However, copyright laws are complicated, and the implications of using digital images is still being determined in the courts. Clearly, if you take the photo yourself, you own the copyright. Many photographers post photos on websites such as Flikr.com and give permission for "fair use" of the images on the Internet, so long as their work is credited. Others, however, post their work for viewers to enjoy but do not allow it to be copied. Scanning a photo from a published work and using it once for a class project falls more clearly under the spirit of the "fair use" law than does putting such an image up on the Internet. If you are doing a web page or blog project that includes images, be sure to contact the copyright owner to obtain permission.

Chapter 5 | **Writing Rhetorically**

Activity 5.2 Write a Research-Based Argument Paper

The Purpose of the Assignment

Writing a research paper gives you the opportunity to practice key academic writing skills, including locating and utilizing research materials, prewriting, drafting, and revision. It also requires you to take a position on a topic, create an argument, and support it with quotes and paraphrases from authoritative sources.

Purpose as a Writer

Your purpose as a writer is to convince readers to consider your argument carefully, and, if possible, to persuade them to agree with your point of view. To do this, include appropriate background material and definitions, as well as a consideration of opposing arguments.

Topic

Your topic should address a current issue about which you can take and support a position in the paper length your instructor specifies. Choose your topic carefully, as it should be one that engages your interest and enthusiasm.

Audience

Unless your instructor specifies otherwise, you can assume that your audience has general awareness of your issue but is unfamiliar with scholarly sources on the topic.

Sources

To do your research, you will need to utilize recent and credible sources that include a mix of recent books, scholarly articles, public speeches, and news articles. You may also use interviews, observation, and personal experience, if they are relevant to your topic. Sources will need to be cited in the text and in a works cited page or references page, according to MLA or APA style.

Information that you gather from your sources should support the argument you have created. A research paper is not an assignment in which you take information from sources and simply reorganize it into a paper. The expectation for this course is that you will use your sources to create an argument that is distinctly your own.

Thesis

Your essay should have a clear thesis that takes a position on an issue that can be supported within the word limitations of the assignment.

Rough Draft

As directed by your instructor, bring two copies of your rough draft essay to class for peer editing. The draft should have your sources credited in the text and should have a works cited page or references page.

Final Draft

Submit your final draft in MLA or APA format in a folder with your rough draft and copies of all of your source materials with the location of quotes or paraphrased material highlighted. If you are using material from a book or books, copy enough of the text before and after your quotes or paraphrases so that your instructor can determine the context of the material being quoted.

Reading 5.2

Film Review: *The Hangover* (2009)
by Owen Gleiberman

This film review by Owen Gleiberman appeared in EW.com. As you read the review, decide what you think is the author's position. How does he support his argument?

Going to Las Vegas for a "wild" bachelor party is now the ultimate middle-class hedonist cliché. It's not just that the jaunt has been done so often, in the movies as well as in life. It's that there's a contradiction embedded in the lure of the Vegas bacchanal. Men—and women too, of course—go there to be as reckless as humanly possible. But the naughtiness is so *organized* that there's not much recklessness left in it. Sure, you can craps-table your way to financial ruin, but the lap dances, the glorified college drinking binges, the ritualized ordering of hookers: It's all about as spontaneous as a shuffleboard tournament on a cruise ship.

The fun of *The Hangover*—what makes it more than just one what-happens-in-Vegas romp too many—is that the film completely understands all this. The four comrades who drive from Los Angeles to the Nevada desert to prepare for the wedding of Doug (Justin Bartha) aren't daring or cool; they aren't born swingers. They're an unglamorous Everyguy quartet, doing what they all think they're supposed to do. They're probably imitating Vegas movies as much as those films imitated reality.

Phil (Bradley Cooper), the one who's good-looking enough to strut into a casino like he owns it, is a junior-high teacher devoted to his wife and kid; Stu (Ed Helms), the group dweeb, is an anxious-eyed dentist who's like the 21st-century version of *American Graffiti*'s Terry the Toad, with a fascist girlfriend (Rachael Harris) who treats him like a slave; and Alan (Zach Galifianakis), so brick-stupid he qualifies as more nutzoid than dorkish, is a pudgy, bearded runt who stands up in the group's cruising convertible and shouts "Road trip!" That's an inside nod to the fact that Todd Phillips, the movie's director, made *Road Trip* as well, though it also indicates that these four think they're living inside a stupid teen comedy.

They arrive at their hotel, and the film then cuts to the next day, when they wake up in their trashed villa. There's a tiger in the bathroom, and a baby in the cabinet. Stu is missing his top right incisor; the groom is nowhere to be seen. And the thing is, none of them remembers . . . anything. *The Hangover* is structured, basically, as one long morning-after *OMG what have I done?*, and the kick of the film is that the discovery of what the characters have, in fact, done becomes the perfect comeuppance to their tidy fantasy of Vegas bliss. A light-buttered comic nightmare, like Martin Scorsese's *After Hours* (or Peter Berg's scandalous, overlooked *Very Bad Things* with things not nearly so bad), *The Hangover* is a riff on what the stuff you do when you're *really* out of control says about you.

The surprises in this movie are everything, so without giving much away, I'll just say that a Vegas chapel figures into the mix. So does a crowbar-wielding Asian gangster (Ken Jeong) who might be the epicene brother of Long Duk Dong in *Sixteen Candles*. There's also a juicy run-in with Mike Tyson. *The Hangover* has scattered laughs (many in the cathartically funny end-credit montage), but overall it's more amusing than hilarious. The most deftly acted character is Stu, played by Helms with a realistic alternating current of horror and liberation. As Alan, Zach Galifianakis makes blinkered idiocy a cartoon rush, though a little of him goes a long way. I wish Phillips, working from a script by the knockabout team of Jon Lucas and Scott Moore (*Ghosts of Girlfriends Past*), had nudged the characters closer to being a true shaggy-dog Apatow-style ensemble. You're always a little too aware that they're types. But it's fun seeing each of them have the "fun" they deserve.

Activity 5.3 Discuss Review of *The Hangover*

1. Owen Gleiberman says that the "wild" bachelor party in Las Vegas has become a cliché. Is this true? What other films portray bachelor parties in Las Vegas?

2. What is different about the Vegas bachelor party in *The Hangover*, according to the review?

3. What is Gleiberman's thesis? What evidence does he offer to support his thesis?

4. Does the review make you want to see the movie, if you haven't? How so?

Activity 5.4 Write a Film Review

In this assignment, you are a film critic. Write a review that could appear in a newspaper, magazine, or blog. Your style and tone will be dictated by your audience, so identify the publication just under the title of your review by saying something like this: "Written for Undergroundfilms.com." Be sure to read several reviews published in your chosen media outlet.

1. Select a film you would like to review. Films that are social commentaries are particularly good for reviewing. It does not have to be a serious movie, but it should be one that makes you think about some social trend or historical event.

2. After you decide on a film, learn about its context. Who are the director, producer, and primary actors? What films have these individuals worked on before? Have they won awards? Are they known for a certain style? Read and annotate other reviews of the film, marking sections that you might paraphrase or quote to support your opinions.

3. What about the historical event or social context? Can you learn more about it to see if the film presents a reasonably accurate picture of that time and place (a kairos)? Is it based on a book? If so, what kind of a job does it do creating the world of the book?

4. Is the film persuasive? Does the film appeal to ethos, pathos, or logos? In what way?

5. Create a working thesis that makes an argument about the film. You can modify this thesis later, but it helps to identify early on what you want to argue.

6. Use some of the invention strategies in Chapter 4 to help you articulate what proofs you can use to support your argument.

7. Near the beginning of your draft, briefly summarize enough of the film that your review will be interesting to those who have not seen it. However, don't be a "spoiler." Don't ruin the film for potential viewers by giving away the ending.

8. Organize your essay into three main points that support your thesis and at least one counterargument that complicates or disagrees with your argument.

9. Write a compelling introduction that uses one of the approaches discussed in this chapter. You want your reader to be interested in what you have to say. For example, you might begin with a startling quote from the film or a vivid description of a pivotal scene.

10. Be sure to include specific examples and colorful details. These are essential to make your review interesting to the reader.

Activity 5.5 Write an Op-Ed Argument

The Op-Ed Project (www.theop-edproject.org) is an online initiative to "expand the range of voices" submitting op-ed essays to media outlets. According to its statistics, 80 to 90 percent of op-ed pieces are currently written by men, which is something it endeavors to change by helping women and members of other underrepresented groups develop the skills to get published in top media markets. Whether you are male or female, you may belong to an underrepresented group that is not having its voice heard as part of the national conversation about issues.

An op-ed is an opinion piece printed in a newspaper, magazine, blog, or other media outlet. The name derives from earlier times in print journalism when these opinion pieces would be printed on a page opposite the editorial page. Op-eds are written by individuals not affiliated with the publication, as opposed to editorials that are written by the publication's staff.

Tips for Op-Ed Writing from the Op-Ed Project

1. Own your expertise
Know what you are an expert in and why—but don't limit yourself. Consider the metaphors that your experience and knowledge suggest.

2. Stay current
Follow the news—both general and specific to your areas of specialty. If you write about Haiti, read the Haitian press. If you write about pop culture, read the media that cover it.

3. The perfect is the enemy of the good
In other words: write fast. You may have only a few hours to get your piece in before the moment is gone. But also . . .

4. Cultivate a flexible mind
Remember that a good idea may have more than one news hook; indeed, if the idea is important enough it can have many. So keep an eye out for surprising connections and new news hooks—the opportunity may come around again.

5. Use plain language
Jargon serves a purpose, but it is rarely useful in public debate, and can obfuscate—sorry, I mean cloud—your argument. Speak to your reader in straight talk.

6. Respect your reader
Never underestimate your reader's intelligence or overestimate her level of information. Recognize that your average reader is not an expert in your topic and that the onus is on you to capture her attention—and make the argument compel.

This assignment asks you to write an op-ed piece suitable for submission to a major newspaper or other media outlet. It does not require you to submit your text. That is up to you.

For this assignment, you need to do the following:

1. Read op-eds that appear in the major regional newspaper or other media outlet for your city, such as the *Chicago Tribune*, the *Washington Post*, or the *Arizona Republic*. The Op-Ed Project provides a list of the top 100 U.S. media outlets on its website. Read several op-eds to get a sense of the topics and style of the articles that the newspaper or other media outlet prints.

2. Notice that op-eds are not academic writing. They must be well-researched, but they also generally are written in a more casual and engaging style than traditional academic writing. You must first attract your audience's attention in order to present your case. Analyze how each op-ed you read captures the reader's interest.

3. Choose a topic that is timely and of interest to the readers of the publication that you choose. Research that topic using some of the tools in the research chapter of this textbook.

4. The length and structure of your op-ed should follow the pattern of pieces recently published in your publication.

5. Keep your audience in mind—the readers of the publication.

6. Follow the basic op-ed structure recommended by the Op-Ed Project, reprinted below.

7. Read the "Tips for Op-Ed Writing from the Op-Ed Project," in the sidebar.

(*Note*: A *lede* (or lead) is a journalism term that means the beginning of your article that catches your reader's attention and establishes your topic.)

Basic Op-Ed Structure from the Op-Ed Project

(*Note*: This is not a rule—just one way of approaching it.)

Lede (around a news hook)

Thesis (statement of argument—either explicit or implied)

Argument (based on evidence, such as stats, news, reports from credible organizations, expert quotes, scholarship, history, and first-hand experience)

- 1st Point
  - Evidence
  - Evidence
  - Conclusion
- 2nd Point
  - Evidence
  - Evidence
  - Conclusion
- 3rd Point
  - Evidence
  - Evidence
  - Conclusion

Note: In a simple, declarative op-ed ("policy X is bad; here's why"), this may be straightforward. In a more complex commentary, the 3rd point may expand on the bigger picture (historical context, global/geographic picture, mythological underpinnings, etc.) or may offer an explanation for a mystery that underpins the argument (e.g., why a bad policy continues, in spite of its failures).

"To Be Sure" paragraph (in which you preempt your potential critics by acknowledging any flaws in your argument and address any obvious counterarguments)

Conclusion (often circling back to your lede)

Activity 5.6 Write on Your Blog

Write an informal review of a film you have seen recently. What did you like and what did you dislike? Would you recommend the film to a friend?

Activity 5.7 Write in Your Commonplace Book

Find a piece from the Opinion/Editorial section of your local newspaper that interests you. If you were going to write a letter to the editor in response, what might you say?

The Casebook: In 2011, two professors launched a competition on the *Harvard Business Network* blog for designs to build $300 houses for the poor. Word of the competition spread quickly, and a wide variety of people began to write about the competition—in editorials in *The New York Times* and the *Economist* and in a companion blog, http://www.300house.com/blog.

Your Task: In Chapter 4 you read four articles about the $300 house competition. Read and discuss them in class and in small groups. Make a list of the different positions being argued in these texts and what evidence the writers offer to support their opinions. Then construct your own short research-based argument about the design competition or an op-ed essay (as your instructor specifies) agreeing with one of the positions or developing your own.

6
REVISING RHETORICALLY

Praxis in Action
How I Revise by Amber Lea Clark

Revising is an essential part of the writing process. One of the first things I do when I revise a paper is read with organization in mind. How is my introduction? Does my argument make sense? Did I transition well between points? Next, I look for words and phrases I have repeated too many times and look for other ways to say what I'm trying to say.

For me, a very necessary part of the revision process is reading the paper out loud to see how it flows. I look for any awkwardly worded sentences. It also helps me find typos and misused words. If I'm in a lab setting, I read very quietly, just mouthing the words. I might get a couple of funny looks but I don't care, it is a must when it comes to the revising process for me.

One of the best things to do in the revising process is set your paper aside and come back to it several hours or a day later. This requires some planning and an attempt not to procrastinate too much. Doing this allows me to look at my paper again with fresh eyes and see what I might have left out or want to say differently.

My mother always told me to have someone else give me feedback on my papers before I turn them in. This is valuable advice. I always have someone look over my papers and try to help others when they need someone to look at their papers. I ask the person who is proofing my paper to look for typos but also any sentences that do not make sense as they are worded. Is my argument coming through clearly?

Also, I always run my paper through the computer's spell check and grammar check. The computer will flag things as grammatically wrong that aren't, so I don't follow everything it says; but the computer also finds errors I haven't. Oh, be sure to spell the proper names right!

Amber Lea Clark says that one important part of her revision is setting her paper aside for a few hours or overnight and then looking at it with fresh eyes.

Revision Is Part of the Writing Process

In ancient times, the focus of the rhetor was upon the presentation of oral arguments in the form of speeches and students trained to perform in pressured situations before a law court or assembly. Though a speaker might spend time in preparation, most speeches were one-time opportunities. If the words were not well-chosen and well-spoken the first time, there was no second chance to influence an audience.

With modern written documents, a composition does not have to be perfect when the words first appear on the page. A document is not truly finished until it is transmitted to an audience, and, even then, important documents are often circulated in draft stages to colleagues for comments before they are presented to an audience.

Many writers claim that revising is the most rewarding step in writing, the time when they have words on a page to work with and can manipulate them to create a composition that communicates effectively. Yet, many students feel that their first drafts should stay exactly the way they've written them because these writings are truest to their feelings and experience. They are sure they have made their point clearly. In reality, a first draft often leaves the reader scratching his or her head and wondering what it was the writer meant to say. To communicate effectively, a writer must learn to interact with his reader to ensure he has communicated his message clearly.

Begin Revision by Rereading

The first step of revising is rereading. This step can be simple, if you are reading something written by someone else. When it is your own writing, it becomes infinitely more difficult. After all, you know what you meant to say—you know the research behind the writing and why you chose certain words or phrases. You even know how every sentence is supposed to read—even though you may have left out a word or two or three—and your mind can trick you into seeing the missing words right where they belong. Unfortunately, the reader does not have your understanding, and communication can break down. You need to learn to read your own work critically, as if it were written by a stranger. One of the first aids in this process is to read your work aloud. You can often hear stumbling blocks quicker than you can see them.

You can also learn to read your own work more objectively by reading and commenting on other writers' work. Look at the structure of essays, at the

Chapter 6 | **Revising Rhetorically**

way the writers use transitions and topic sentences, and at the sentence structure and choice of words. As you learn to see how good writers put ideas and words together, you will begin to think about the readings in a more thorough manner—thinking of alternative, perhaps even better, ways to express the message of each essay. You will also learn to read your own work with a more critical eye.

Qualities of Effective Writing

Reading the work of some professional writers, you may have developed the idea that the best writing is writing that is difficult to understand, writing that sends the reader to the dictionary with every sentence, or writing that uses many technical or specialized terms. Often, we think something difficult to read must be well written. Although it is sometimes difficult to read about topics that are new to us because we're learning new vocabulary and struggling with complex ideas, it simply is not true that the best writing is hard to read. Indeed, the most effective writing, the kind of writing you want to produce in your classes, is simple, concise, and direct.

Keep It Simple

Simple means "unadorned" or "not ornate." *Writing simply* means saying something in common, concrete

William Safire's Rules for Writing

William Safire, long-time language enthusiast, political columnist, and contributor to "On Language" in the *New York Times Magazine*, has a little fun with grammar rules and myths.

- Remember to never split an infinitive.
- The passive voice should never be used.
- Do not put statements in the negative form.
- Verbs has to agree with their subjects.
- Proofread carefully to see if you words out.
- If you reread your work, you will find on rereading a great deal of repetition can be avoided by rereading and editing.
- A writer must not shift your point of view.
- And don't start a sentence with a conjunction. (Remember, too, a preposition is a terrible word to end a sentence with.)
- Don't overuse exclamation marks!!
- Place pronouns as close as possible, especially in long sentences, as of 10 or more words, to their antecedents.
- Writing carefully, dangling participles must be avoided.
- If any word is improper at the end of a sentence, a linking verb is.
- Take the bull by the hand and avoid mixing metaphors.
- Avoid trendy locutions that sound flaky.
- Everyone should be careful to use a singular pronoun with singular nouns in their writing.
- Always pick on the correct idiom.
- The adverb always follows the verb.
- Last but not least, avoid clichés like the plague; seek viable alternatives.

language without too much complication in the sentence structure. Writing simply doesn't mean you have to use only short or easy words. It doesn't mean that all your sentences will be simple sentences. It doesn't mean that you can't use figures of speech or intricate details. Simple writing means that you try to get your point across in a direct and interesting way. You aren't trying to hide your ideas. Instead, you are trying to amplify those ideas and begin an intelligible conversation with your reader.

Rely on Everyday Words

When writing about computers or other technical subjects, it's tempting to use **jargon** or specialized words you might use when talking to others with the same knowledge, interest, and background. When writing for a limited audience whose members are familiar with technical terms, a bit of jargon might be acceptable. However, most of the writing you will do in college and later in the workplace will address a larger audience. You will want to avoid the use of highly technical terms, acronyms, and abbreviations.

If it seems that the writers in this text use many big words or technical terms, stop for a minute to consider the original audience for each of the essays. Consider how your vocabulary grows each year as you read, discuss, and consider new ideas. The everyday words of a tenth grade student will probably be fewer in number than the everyday words of a junior in college. Similarly, the everyday words of a college freshman will be different from the everyday words of a computer professional with three years of work experience. Use words that are comfortable and familiar to you and your readers when you write, and you will write clear, effective essays.

Use Precise Words

We sometimes assume that the reader will know what we mean when we use adjectives like "beautiful," "quiet," or "slow." However, the reader has only his or her own ideas of those adjectives. You can make your writing more interesting and effective by adding concrete details to give the reader an image that uses at least two of the five senses.

You can use details from all of the senses to make your writing even more concrete and precise. What are some of the sensual qualities of the experience or thing? Can you compare it to another thing that your readers may be familiar with to help them understand it better? Can you compare it to something totally unlike it? Can you compare it to a different sense to surprise readers and help them understand the image you are trying to create?

A good way to practice your ability to write original concrete images is to expand on a cliché. A **cliché** is an overused saying or expression. Often, clichés begin as similes that help make images more concrete. They become clichéd or overused because they lose their originality or they don't contain enough detail to give us the entire picture. Choose a cliché and write a sentence that expands the cliché and uses the senses to create a clear picture of the thing described. You might try some of the following clichés:

> She is as pretty as a picture.
>
> It smelled heavenly.
>
> It was as soft as a baby's bottom.
>
> His heart is as hard as stone.
>
> It tastes as sour as a pickle.
>
> We stared at the roaring campfire.
>
> We listened to the babbling brook.

Precise details allow us to experience the world of the writer. We leave our own views and perceptions and learn how someone else sees the world. We learn what "quiet" is like for one writer and what "beautiful" means to another. Fill in the gaps between your words and ideas with vivid images and your writing will become more interesting and more effective.

Be Concise

Rid your writing of excess words and leave only that which makes your meaning clear and concrete. Becoming aware of several common problems can help you make your writing more concise. When you begin a sentence with either "it is" or "there is," you transfer all the meaning of the sentence to the end of the sentence. This is known as a **delayed construction**. You have delayed the meaning. The reader must read on to find out what "it" or "there" refer to. They don't get anything important from the beginning of the sentence.

> Examine the following sentences:
>
> > It is important to change the oil in older gasoline engines.
> >
> > There is an apple on the table.
> >
> > There isn't anything we need to fear except our own fear.

We can rewrite these sentences, making them more concise, by deleting the "there is" or the "it is" and restructuring the sentence.

> Changing the oil in older gasoline engines is important.

> An apple is on the table.

> We have nothing to fear but fear itself.

Notice that the second group of sentences is shorter and the important information is no longer buried in the middle. Revising this type of sentence can make your writing more concise and get information to the reader more effectively.

If you think you may be guilty of using "it is" and "there is" (or "it's" and "there's") too often, you can use most word processing programs to seek these constructions out. Use the "search" or "find and replace" tool that's found in the Edit portion of your pull-down menu. Type "it is" and ask your computer to find every place you use this construction in your document. When you find a sentence that begins with "it is," revise the sentence to make it more concise. Do the same with "there is," "it's," and "there's." After you become more aware of these errors by correcting them, you'll find that you notice the errors before or as you make them. You will begin to write more concisely, and you'll have fewer delayed constructions to revise.

You can also make your writing more concise by avoiding common wordy expressions. Sometimes when we're nervous about writing or insecure about our knowledge of a topic, we try to hide that insecurity behind a wall of meaningless words, such as in the following sentence:

> At this point in time, you may not have the ability to create a web page due to the fact that you've avoided using computers for anything other than playing Solitaire.

This sentence is full of deadwood phrases that add no meaning to the sentence. If we take out the unneeded words, we have this sentence:

> You may not be able to create a web page because you've only used your computer to play Solitaire.

Your computer may have a grammar checker that will identify some commonly used wordy expressions. If your computer doesn't have a grammar checker, or if your instructor has asked you not to use the grammar checker in your computer, you can still learn to revise the wordiness out of your paragraphs. Use the computer to separate a paragraph of your writing into sentences. As you scroll through the paragraph, hit the hard return or "Enter" key on your keyboard twice every time you find a period. Once you have separated the sentences, look at each sentence. What is the important idea in the sentence? What words are used to convey that idea? What words don't add any meaning to the sentence? Delete words that don't convey meaning, and revise the sentence to make it more concise.

Use Action Verbs

Action verbs are words that convey the action of a sentence. They carry much of our language's nuance and meaning. Many inexperienced writers use only "to be" verbs: *am, is, are, was, were, be, been,* and *being*. If you use too many of these verbs, you risk losing much of the power of language. If I say someone is coming through the door, I've created a picture of a body and a doorway. If I say someone marches or slinks through the door, I've added information not only about movement but also about the quality of that movement. I've given my subject the attitude of a soldier or a cat. For example, consider this sentence written by Howard Rheingold:

> Thirty thousand years ago, outside a deceptively small hole in a limestone formation in the area now known as southern France, several adolescents shivered in the dark, awaiting initiation into the cult of toolmakers.

By using the verb "shivered," especially when accompanied by the words "in the dark," Rheingold paints a word picture much more vivid than he would have conveyed with the use of a "to be" verb. Using interesting verbs can enliven your writing.

If you want to focus upon using more action verbs, skim through your essay and circle all the "to be" verbs. Read the sentences with circled "to be" verbs more closely, and choose several to rewrite using active verbs in place of the "to be" verbs. You won't be able to do this for every sentence, but replace them where you can and your writing will become more lively, more concise, and more effective.

Fill in the Gaps

When we write, we sometimes forget that we are writing to an audience other than ourselves. We expect that our readers are people just like us, with our experiences, memories, and tastes. Because we have assumed they're so much like us, we expect our readers to be able to read more than what we've written on the page. We expect them to read our minds. We may leave large gaps in our essays, hoping the reader will fill in exactly the information we would have included.

If I'm writing an essay about my childhood in the South and I say it was always so hot in the summer that I hated to go outside, I might think my reader knows what I mean by hot. However, there are many different ways to be "hot." In east Texas where I grew up, the hot was a sticky hot. Eighty degrees made me long for a big glass of sweetened iced tea with lots of ice. The heat made my clothes cling. Sweating didn't help because the sweat didn't dry. I spent the day feeling as if I'd never dried off after my morning shower. In New Mexico, I never really felt hot unless the temperature got above 110 degrees. At that point, the heat would rush at me, making it difficult to breathe. I would open the door to leave the house, and it felt as if I had opened the oven door to check on a cake. If I say I was hot in the summer without describing how heat felt to me, my reader may not get the message I'm trying to convey. Don't expect your reader to know what you mean by "hot" or by any other general description. Instead, take a minute to add details that will fill in the gaps for the reader.

Speak Directly

To *speak directly* is to say, up front, who is doing what. Sometimes we don't tell the reader who is completing the action or we tell them too late. Let's look at the following sentences:

> The steak was stolen from the grill.
>
> The decisive battle was fought between the Confederate and the Union armies in Vicksburg, Mississippi.
>
> The red truck has been driven into the side of the green car.

Although we might be able to guess who the actors are in each of the sentences, the first and last sentences don't tell us directly. Even if the reader can guess that it was a dog who stole the steak from the grill or my neighbor who drove the red truck into the side of the green car, the reader has to stop and figure out who is doing what before he or she can read on. This slows the reader down and diminishes the effectiveness of your writing.

Chapter 6 | **Revising Rhetorically**

Language professionals call this **passive voice**. The action comes before the actor. Note that sometimes, as in the first and last sentences above, the writer doesn't mention the actor at all. To identify passive verbs in your writing, look for verbs coupled with another action word that ends in "-ed" or "-en" such as "was stolen" or "was forgotten."

Find the action and the actor in the sentence to make sure that they are in the most effective order. The most effective sentence order is actor first, then action. If the sentence does not specify the actor but leaves it implied, chances are that it is a passive sentence. For example, read this sentence: "The red truck was driven into the green car." It does not say who the driver was, and thus it is a passive sentence.

Rewriting some of your sentences to eliminate use of the passive voice will make your writing stronger and more interesting.

President Barack Obama has won high marks for his verbal eloquence, as illustrated by this cartoon published in the *International Herald Tribune*. His 2004 Keynote Speech at the Democratic National Convention and his best-selling book, *The Audacity of Hope*, helped propel him to national prominence.

Activity 6.1 When You Reeeaaallly Want to Describe Something

This activity requires a thesaurus or access to the Visual Thesaurus website (http://www.visualthesaurus.com).

1. Strunk and White's *The Elements of Style,* in an entry on "Misused Words and Expressions," says,

   "*Very*. Use this word sparingly. Where emphasis is necessary, use words strong in themselves."

   With a partner, paraphrase and discuss this Strunk and White writing tip.

2. To demonstrate Strunk and White's advice in (1) above, revise the following sentence, getting rid of the adverb "very."

   Julie is very pretty.

   No, don't say, "Julie is beautiful." Make a list of more precise and vivid words that could be used instead. Refer to a thesaurus (or the Visual Thesaurus website) to find words such as "stunning" and so on.

3. As a class, brainstorm other intensifying adverbs such as "awfully" or "extremely" that you tend to use as words of emphasis (in writing or in everyday speech) and list those words on the board.

4. In pairs again, compose a short paragraph of two or three sentences about a subject or event (e.g., a tornado, a celebrity sighting, a sports event, a news event, a concert, etc.) and intentionally use as many common or trite intensifying words as possible.

5. Exchange the short paragraph you composed in (4) above with another pair of classmates. Revise the other partnership's dialogue with the use of a thesaurus. The revised dialogue should not contain any "intensifiers" or trite words of emphasis. Replace such words and phrases with more powerful and concise language. For example, "I was really happy to see the Hornets win. They totally beat the Giants," could be revised to read (with the help of more concise and powerful words): "I was euphoric to see the Hornets thrash the Giants."

Chapter 6 | **Revising Rhetorically**

6. Read your "before" and "after" dialogues to the class. Afterward, discuss which words were eliminated and how the words that replaced those intensifiers changed the tone and/or meaning of the dialogue.

Source: Adapted from a lesson plan, "When You Reeeaaallly Want to Say Something," from the Visual Thesaurus website, http://www.visualthesaurus.com/cm/lessons/1450.

Remember to Proofread

It is understandably difficult to find the errors in an essay you have been working on for days. A few tricks used by professional writers might help you see errors in your essay more clearly.

1. With pencil in hand, read the essay aloud, slowly—and preferably to an audience. When you are reading aloud, it is more difficult to add or change words, so you tend to catch errors you would not see reading silently to yourself. Plus the reactions of your audience may point out areas where future readers may become confused or lose interest.

2. Another trick is to read the essay backwards, sentence by sentence. This forces you to look at sentence structure and not at the overall content of the essay. If you are working on a computer, another way to accomplish this is to create a final edit file in which you hit the hard return twice at the end of every question or statement. You might even go so far as to number the sentences so they look more like grammar exercises. Then look at each sentence individually.

10. **A run-on sentence is a really long sentence.** Wrong! They can actually be quite short. In a run-on sentence, independent clauses are squished together without the help of punctuation or a conjunction. If you write "I am short he is tall," as one sentence without a semicolon, colon, or dash between the two independent clauses, it's a run-on sentence even though it only has six words.

Reading 6.1

Grammar Girl's Top Ten Grammar Myths
by Mignon Fogarty, quickanddirtytips.com

In this blog entry by Mignon Fogarty, she offers her top-ten list of grammar mistakes and misunderstandings.

9. **You shouldn't start a sentence with the word "however."** Wrong! It's fine to start a sentence with "however" so long as you use a comma after it when it means "nevertheless."

8. **"Irregardless" is not a word. Wrong!** "Irregardless" is a bad word and a word you shouldn't use, but it is a word. "Floogetyflop" isn't a word—I just made it up and you have no idea what it means. "Irregardless," on the other hand, is in almost every dictionary labeled as nonstandard. You shouldn't use it if you want to be taken seriously, but it has gained wide enough use to qualify as a word.

7. **There is only one way to write the possessive form of a word that ends in "s." Wrong!** It's a style choice. For example, in the phrase "Kansas's statute," you can put just an apostrophe at the end of "Kansas" or you can put an apostrophe "s" at the end of "Kansas." Both ways are acceptable.

6. **Passive voice is always wrong. Wrong!** Passive voice is when you don't name the person who's responsible for the action. An example is the sentence "Mistakes were made," because it doesn't say who made the mistakes. If you don't know who is responsible for an action, passive voice can be the best choice.

5. **"i.e." and "e.g." mean the same thing. Wrong!** "e.g." means "for example," and "i.e." means roughly "in other words." You use "e.g." to provide a list of incomplete examples, and you use "i.e." to provide a complete clarifying list or statement.

4. **You use "a" before words that start with consonants and "an" before words that start with vowels. Wrong!** You use "a" before words that start with consonant sounds and "an" before words that start with vowel sounds. So, you'd write that someone has an MBA instead of a MBA, because even though "MBA" starts with "m," which is a consonant, it starts with the sound of the vowel "e"—MBA.

3. **It's incorrect to answer the question "How are you?" with the statement "I'm good." Wrong!** "Am" is a linking verb and linking verbs should be modified by adjectives such as "good." Because "well" can also act as an adjective, it's also fine to answer "I'm well," but some grammarians believe "I'm well" should be used to talk about your health and not your general disposition.

Chapter 6 | **Revising Rhetorically**

2. **You shouldn't split infinitives. Wrong!** Nearly all grammarians want to boldly tell you it's OK to split infinitives. An infinitive is a two-word form of a verb. An example is "to tell." In a split infinitive, another word separates the two parts of the verb. "To boldly tell" is a split infinitive because "boldly" separates "to" from "tell."

1. **You shouldn't end a sentence with a preposition. Wrong!** You shouldn't end a sentence with a preposition when the sentence would mean the same thing if you left off the preposition. That means "Where are you at?" is wrong because "Where are you?" means the same thing. But there are many sentences where the final preposition is part of a phrasal verb or is necessary to keep from making stuffy, stilted sentences: "I'm going to throw up," "Let's kiss and make up," and "What are you waiting for" are just a few examples.

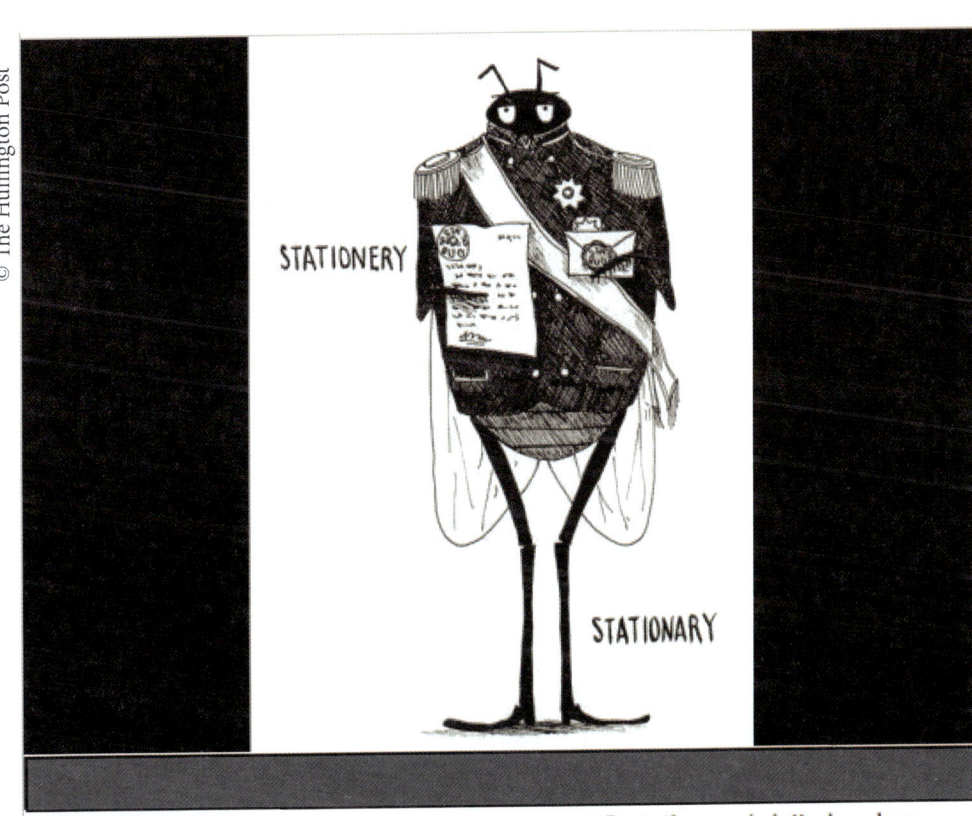

© The Huffington Post

Stationary means "fixed in place, unable to move;" *stationery* is letterhead or other special writing paper. (Hint: *Station<u>e</u>ry* with an *e* comes with an <u>e</u>nvelope.) Examples: Evan worked out on his *stationary* bike. The duke's initials and crest appeared atop his personal *stationery*.

© The Huffington Post

Eminent means "distinguished or superior"; *imminent* means "impending, sure to happen." Also, *eminent* domain is the right of a government to take over private property for public use. Examples: The rain was *imminent*; it would arrive soon, soaking the *eminent* dignitaries on the stage. (Think of *imminent* and *impending*, which both begin with the same letters.)

Reading 6.2

Top Ten Distractions for Writers, or Any Job Really

by Sam Scham

The following list, "Top Ten Distractions for Writers, or Any Job Really," by Sam Scham, was published in the Yahoo Contributor Network.

When you have a set goal in mind, whether it is for personal or work reasons, so many other things can become easy distractions. For writers in particular, life seems to get in the way. There are other pressing matters that we have to worry about.

1. The Internet

The Internet is a very huge distraction these days. For writers who do research online for their great idea, it is easy to stumble upon different links and steer

Chapter 6 | **Revising Rhetorically**

away from the main point in focus. If you find yourself doing this, try to limit the time you do research therefore getting off the Internet earlier and allow more time for writing.

2. The Radio

Music can help a writer generate ideas and feelings. Listening to the radio can be a distraction if you leave it on for too long. If you are like me, you are able to write the best in silence. You need to be able to hear yourself think. If you are listening to the radio and it is hard to turn away from it, listen to it in segments. Listen to some music and when a commercial comes on, mute the radio and start writing. Maybe, before you know it, you will forget that you were ever listening to the radio.

3. The Television

The television and the radio are similar in many ways. For one, it is hard to turn off, especially if you are in the middle of a show that you want to finish. But then, you see a commercial for what is coming up next and you are intrigued to watch it. At the end of the current show, turn off the TV and get writing. Soon, you will not notice the absence of the picture box.

4. Own Procrastination

You want to sit down and write, but at the same time you don't, you have no motivation. The solution is to take a day off, do not think of it at all. Work on any other pressing matters like home chores or calling up an old friend that you've been meaning to catch up with. On the next day, wake up and get writing. Just jump right into it and it will be like you never took a break.

5. Other People

Especially if you live with family or friends other people always being around can be a huge distraction. In order to solve this, find out when everyone will be out and fit in time to write while they are gone. If that just doesn't work with your everyday schedule, find a nice place outside or at the local library where you can work in peace without other people bugging you.

6. Other Responsibilities

Work, chores, walking the dog; these everyday responsibilities are tiring and at the end of the day you just cannot get the energy to write. Try writing in the morning, even if it is just for a few minutes. Get the best out of what you got and do not get discouraged.

7. Telephones

With cell phones these days, you can be getting texts at every minute either from friends or social networks. When you are writing, the best way to refrain from your cell phone is by turning it completely off and leaving it somewhere out of sight so that you are not tempted to check it.

8. Outdoor Activities

Especially on a really nice day, you may want to forget the writing and spend some time outdoors. That is completely fine. Enjoy life to the fullest. If you end up not writing for the day, remember that there is always tomorrow. But be careful not to put it off for too long and too often. If you really want to spend time outside, take the writing with you and kill two birds with one stone.

9. Everyday Needs

You need to eat sometime and when you work and do everything else, cooking can really tire you out and make you not want to write. On those days, try to make simple meals if you absolutely do not want to order out. There is nothing wrong with having a bowl of cereal for dinner.

10. Being Bored

We all get bored sometimes, even of our own writing. Take a break. Do not work on writing your big project, but work on something else. A day or two later go back to that big project and start working on writing it again and if you are still bored, put it to the side again. At least you cannot say that you did not try.

Activity 6.2 Write a List of Your Writing Habits

As you write an essay assigned by your instructor, keep notes about your writing process. What distracts or keeps you from writing? What works well when you write? What kind of prewriting do you do? What are the best (or worst) conditions for you when you write?

Organize your notes about your writing process into a theme such as "Best Places to Write" or "Ways to Avoid Procrastinating." As Sam Scham does, write two or three sentences about each of your writing habits.

Chapter 6 | **Revising Rhetorically**

Gain Feedback by Peer Editing

Your instructor may schedule class periods for peer workshops. These workshops are opportunities for you to get responses from your readers. Often, you will be divided into groups of three or four students and you will be given a list of questions to answer about your peers' essays. Your peers will get copies of your essay, and they will give you comments as well. The first peer workshop can be a difficult experience. It is never easy to take criticism, constructive or not. Taking criticism in a small group is even more difficult. There are several things you can do to make your peer groups more productive.

When Your Essay Is Being Reviewed

1. Write down everything the reviewers say. You think you will remember it later, but often you will forget just that piece of advice you need. More importantly, writing while the reviewers speak is an effective way to keep the channels of communication open. It is hard to come up with a defense for your paper if you are busy writing.

2. Save your comments until all the reviewers are done. If you have specific questions, write them in the margins of your notes. If they ask you questions, make a note to answer them when everyone is done. If you allow yourself to speak, you will be tempted to start defending your essay. Once you start defending your essay, two things happen. First, you stop listening to the comments. Second, you offend your reviewers, making it less likely that they will give you honest criticism in the future.

3. The first comment you should make to your reviewers is "Thank you." The second comment can be anything but a defense. Your readers are only telling you how they have interpreted your essay. They are giving you their opinions; you do not have to make the changes they suggest.

4. Save all the comments you get on your essay. Set them aside for a day or so. Then make the changes that you think will make your essay better.

When You Are the Reviewer

1. Read an essay through, at least one time, just to browse the content of the essay. Appreciate the essay for what it does well. Try to ignore any problems for now. You will get back to them the second time you read

and begin your comments in the margins. Every essay will have at least one thing about it that is good.

2. Always begin your comments with a sincere discussion of what you like about the essay.

3. Be specific in your comments. Your peers will probably understand you better if you say, "The topic sentence in paragraph four really sets the reader up for what the essay accomplishes in paragraph four. But I can't really find a topic sentence for paragraph six, and the topic sentences in paragraphs two and three could be improved." Note how this statement gives a positive response and then identifies specific places where the author can improve the essay. This works much better than a generalized statement like, "Topic sentences need work."

4. Be descriptive in your comments. It is often helpful for students to hear how you are reading their essays. "Paragraph five seems to be telling me . . ." or "I got the feeling the essay's overall message is . . ." are good ways to start descriptive sentences.

5. Realize that you are analyzing a paper and not a person. Directing your comments toward the essay, "Paragraph nine doesn't really have anything new to add, does the paper need it?" sounds better to the listener than "You repeat yourself in paragraph nine. Do you really need it?"

Independent Reviewing

If your instructor does not require peer editing, you can ask someone to review your essay. Choose someone you trust to give you an honest opinion. It might not be effective to ask a parent, spouse, or girlfriend/boyfriend to give you a critique if you know they are going to like anything you write, just because you wrote it. It might be better to ask another student who has recently had an English class or one of your current classmates. In exchange, you might offer to look over their work. Remember, you learn to read your own essays better by reading other peoples' essays more critically.

Sample Questions for Peer Review

When you have revised your paper several times, have someone answer these questions regarding its overall content, paragraph development, and word choice and sentence structure.

Overall Content

1. What is the thesis or main point of the essay? Where does the writer state this main point? If the main point is implied rather than stated, express it in a sentence. Does the main point give a subject and an opinion about the subject? How might the writer improve his/her thesis?

2. What is the purpose of this essay? What are the characteristics of the audience the writer seems to be addressing (formal, fun-loving, serious, cynical, laid-back, etc.)?

Paragraph Development

1. Do each of the paragraphs in the essay work to support the main point of the essay? Which paragraphs seem to wander from that main point? What other information needs to be added to develop the main point?

2. List two places in the essay where the writer uses vivid sensory details. How effective are those details? Are they used to support the thesis of the essay? Identify two places in the essay where the writer needs more effective details. What kind of details might he or she include?

3. What grade would you give the introduction? How does it draw the reader into the essay? What specific things can the writer do to make the introduction more inviting?

4. Which paragraph do you like the best? Why? Which paragraph in the essay do you like the least? Why? What can the writer do to improve his/her paragraphs?

5. What grade would you give the conclusion? How does it provide closure for the essay? What specific things can the writer do to make the conclusion more effective?

Word Choice and Sentence Structure

1. Are adequate transitions used between the paragraphs? Find an effective paragraph transition and identify it. Why does it work? Find two places between paragraphs that need more or better transitions. What can the writer do to improve these transitions?

2. Are a variety of sentences used? Where might the writer vary the sentence structure for better effect? What two sentences in the essay did you find most effective? Why?

3. Are there any words that seem misused or out of place? What positive or negative trigger words are used? Do they enhance the message of the essay or detract from it?

Activity 6.3 Peer Editing of Sample Student Essay

As your instructor directs, either individually or in groups, peer edit one of the following sample student papers and then answer the questions regarding overall content, paragraph development, and word choice and sentence structure listed in the above section, Sample Questions for Peer Review. Then discuss your peer editing in your small groups, comparing your answers to those of others in your group.

Sample Student Essay for Peer Editing, Profile Assignment

Longing for Better Days

As she sits in her cramped room in Amman, Jordan, watching the recent news, Aysha Mustafa, 92, is saddened by the world she lives in today. As she places her wrinkled hands on her lap and begins to recall a time when things were pleasant, tears begin to flow down her cheeks. Those times are long gone she says. Aysha moved from Palestine to Jordan after the sudden death of her husband in 1995. Moving here was tough she says, "It was hard to leave my country." Aysha's story goes back 60 years ago, where she lived in her homeland Palestine. She recalls her childhood as being peaceful and joyous. She smiles as she describes memories of her and her brother riding in the back of her father's wagon. "Life was good," she says. Although her family had very little to live on, she was still happy.

Like many Palestinians, Aysha still dreams to one day return back and live in her homeland Palestine, where she longs to rekindle sweet memories there. "Jordan is fine she says but I rather live on the land that is mine." As we sit in the living room watching the crisis in Gaza in January 2009, Aysha begins to wipe the tears from her sad yet hopeful eyes, and reiterates with a sigh in her voice, "May God be with them." The appalling images of young children being killed by Israeli rockets leave 92 year old Aysha in distress. How many more men, women and children will die before both sides reach an agreement she questions? As her grandson flips through the channels, he crosses upon the Al-Jazeera news that announces that the number killed in Gaza has reached the disturbing number of 781. She suddenly lowers her head and gazes into space. . "It kills me to see my people getting killed like this," she stutters trying to hold back tears. The Israeli and Palestinian conflict has been going on for more than 60 years now. Many innocent civilians of both sides have been killed due to this grotesque war.

Despite all of this, it is people like Aysha that still carry hope that one day they will return back to their homeland and live in peace and harmony. Aysha's wish like many others is for all Palestinians to live a life of security and freedom, freedom to make their own choices and decisions on their own land. Aysha struggles to explain how as a child she used to run around in the fields freely, fearing no one or anything. "The feeling of freedom is indescribable," she says. "I was free to walk and go as I pleased, with no blockades to hold me back."

Today however, boys and girls in Palestine do not share the same luxury that Aysha experienced before the occupation. It is heart breaking watching this old yet strong willed woman recalling her childhood memories. Suddenly, Aysha begins to hold her chest and breathe heavily; her grandson approaches her and gives her her heart medicine. He explains that talking about such a personal and stressful topic leaves his grandmother feeling tired and overwhelmed. She has a weak heart, "My days are getting shorter," she says. Aysha is an inspiration, throughout this interview she kept calm and never wavered or seemed weak. One would think she would be vulnerable to everything surrounding her, but on the contrary she was full of wisdom. When asked what she hoped for, she said with a confident tone, "My people will see better days than this; I know this for a fact. They will be happy again; mothers will no longer be forced to bury their children. The day of justice and freedom is near, I can feel it." As she said this, Aysha seemed certain that this war will not last very long. Many Palestinians have the same hopes as Aysha, they too are confident that the day will come when their people will believe in security again.

Aysha is one of many Palestinians who shares the same dream as millions, which is a liberated and a prosperous Palestine. As she stands up and leans on her cane she says, "We want our rights, we want justice, we want freedom on our land, and we want Palestine."

Aysha's final words were that she prays that once her soul rests, she hopes to be buried next to her husband's grave on the holy land of Palestine.

Sample Student Essay for Peer Editing, Rhetorical Analysis Assignment

Rhetorical Analysis of President Reagan's "Challenger Speech"

FIVE, FOUR, THREE, TWO, ONE, WE HAVE LIFT OFF! THE SPACE SHUTTLE CHALLENGER HAS CLEARED THE LAUNCH PAD. This was supposed to be a glorious day in American history, a mile stone in the United States Space Program. Instead this day quickly turned into one of the most horrific scenes witnessed live by the American public, which included thousands of school children, who watched from the comfort and safety of their classrooms.

On January 28, 1986, the space shuttle Challenger was scheduled for launch in Florida. It would mark the second flight by the United States Space program and it was the first educational launch program. On this particular flight there was to be a teacher on board, she was the first teacher on a space shuttle as a result of a special program from NASA. Although there were some clear concerns regarding whether the shuttle should launch, NASA officials gave the green light and the mission moved forward. Within seconds of lift off, the space shuttle Challenger burst into flames and disintegrated in mid flight, instantly killing all seven passengers aboard. The nation was shocked, especially thousands of young children who eagerly watched the live coverage on television. Within hours of the explosion President Ronald Reagan went on live television and addressed the nation from the White House. President Reagan was scheduled to address the nation on that particular day to report on the state of the Union, instead he went on television and paid tribute to the Challenger Seven. President Reagan delivered one of the most inspirational, and motivational speeches of his tenure as the President of the United States. It is a speech, like all great speeches, that would out live his presidency, and be regarded as one of the great speeches of our time.

The nation stood still, not knowing what to make of the days events. In such times of sorrow people tend to need support, guidance, and reassurance. The American people needed someone to follow, a shoulder to lean on, a vision of the future, a leader. President Reagan went on live television and paid tribute to the "Challenger Seven" in a speech from the White House. President Reagan sat alone behind a large desk surrounded in the background by family pictures. President Reagan used his ethos as a credible individual; he was the leader of the free Nation. He gave the speech from the White House, which is clearly recognized by the American public

Chapter 6 | Revising Rhetorically

as a symbol of power and security. The image of him sitting behind a great desk flanked by pictures of family and loved ones borrowing once again from their ethos. This was a not only the President of the United States delivering this speech, this was a husband, a father, and a son too.

The occasion for the speech was obvious: The Nation had just witnessed seven brave individuals perish before their very eyes. These brave souls were, husbands, sons, daughters, fathers, and they had paid the ultimate sacrifice for mankind. President Reagan portrayed all of these different roles played by each of the "Challenger Seven" from behind that desk. As the speech proceeded, President Reagan was careful to not down play the Challenger incident, but he appealed to logos, or logic, by saying "But we have never lost an astronaut in flight. We've never had a tragedy like this one." Here he used pathos to emphasize the severity of the incident while at the same time letting the nation know that there have been other brave astronauts who have also paid the ultimate price for the visions and progress of mankind. President Reagan throughout his speech used his words very carefully and with great insight. His words and the double meaning or relation to the events of the day made a huge impact on the delivery and acceptance of his speech by the American public. As he stated "Your loved ones were daring and brave, and they had that special grace, that spirit that says, Give me a challenge, and I'll meet it with joy." As one can see, President Reagan is using the word challenge here, this is a direct reference to the space shuttle Challenger.

President Reagan goes on to address the thousands of children who also witnessed the event, addressing the emotion or pathos of the occasion. He states, "And I want to say something to the schoolchildren of America who were watching the live coverage of the shuttle's take-off. I know it's hard to understand, but sometimes painful things like this happen. It's all part of the process of exploration and discovery. It is all part of taking a chance and expanding man's horizons. The future doesn't belong to the fainthearted; it belongs to the brave. The Challenger crew was pulling us into the future, and we'll continue to follow them." Here President Reagan's audience is the children, who in turn are the future of the nation. By saying that the Challenger was taking them towards the future, he is saying what everybody already knows. The children are the future of the nation and he is telling them that they must continue to move forward, for one day they will be the leaders of the country.

President Reagan's message is very clear: This was a tragedy, yet we as a nation must continue to move forward in order to honor the memory of the "Challenger Seven." President Reagan, utilizing logos, then mentions the

NASA employees in his speech. Here he does not blame or degrade the space program or its employees. Instead he praises there hard work and dedication to the American people and the space program. He does not speculate on the cause of the explosion nor does he address any issues related to who is to blame. He completely omits any negative or accusatory comments in his speech. This was a very tactful and extremely intelligent move by Reagan. He knew the American public had many questions regarding the explosion. He also knew that those questions needed to be answered and that it was his responsibility to provide those answers to the nation. Yet on this day, and in this speech, it was not the right time to do so.

President Reagan in closing his speech borrows from the ethos of the past when he stated "There's a coincidence today. On this day three hundred and ninety years ago, the great explorer Sir Francis Drake died aboard ship off the coast of Panama… a historian later said, He lived by the sea, died on it, and was buried in it. Well, today, we can say of the Challenger crew: their dedication was, like Drake's complete."

President Reagan's speech on the space shuttle Challenger served several purposes. First, it paid tribute to the seven astronauts who lost their lives in the explosion. Second, it provided the nation with a much needed reassurance that everything was going to be all right. And although this was terrible accident and set back for our country, he also left no doubt that the Nations commitment to NASA and the space program would not only survive, but continue to advance forward into the future.

Sample Student Essay for Peer Editing, Short Op-Ed Argument

Women in Combat

It is without a doubt that most of us have seen, read, or even heard about women in foreign countries, specifically the Middle East, being victims of sexual discrimination in male dominated work. But, would anyone possibly imagine, that even at a smaller scale, it occurs right here right now. This op-ed piece focuses on women in combat. While some countries do allow women to fight in combat, it seems archaic that the leader of the free world and by many referred as the #1 nation in the world, that we still bar women from certain roles in the military.

The most common fallacies believed by many include, women's enervated strength. Or, there psychological structure is so that they are considered nurturers not murderers. The most archaic mentality yet is that women are a distraction to men. The list can go on, but the above seems to be the most common misconceptions.

The case against the strength of a woman seems irrefutable. No one can argue that in general men are stronger than women. But there are many factors to be considered in arguing the rebuttal. For instance, the double standards set by our military. The annual Physical fitness test clearly subordinates the female's potential physical ability. A study conducted in Great Britain by the Ministry of Defense concluded that "women can be built to the same levels of physical fitness as men of the same size and build" (Shepard, 2007). How can we expect a woman to perform closer to a man's standards when we delude her understanding of what it really takes to achieve physical fitness? Would it be any different if we took a male chef and only taught him how to cook appetizers, then graded him for the entire meal including entre and desert?

Psychological structure is also a hot topic. Women are nurturers, not murderers. Kingsley Browne, author of Co-Ed Combat, The New Evidence Why Women shouldn't Fight the Nation's Wars, made a diluted attempt to answer this question by stating "There are large differences in men and women and willingness to take Physical risks. For example something like 93% of work place deaths are men" (Traders Nation, 2007). While men seem quite capable to murdering, Browne failed to cite that women are also capable of committing heinous crimes, as evidenced by the 2.1 million women serving sentences in American Prisons for violent crimes (Shepard, 2007).

Psychological Structure is an important factor in wars, as Browne reiterates. "Women's greater fear of death and injury and greater aversion to physical risks are likely to affect their combat performance negatively" (Arron, 2007). Clearly not all women are cut out for combat. But if we use this formula, it is also evidenced that not all men are cut out for combat. It is said that over 100,000 men panicked at the thought of going to the Vietnam War and fled the country to avoid the draft (Shepard, 2007). Surely any veteran of any War would consider this a perfect paradigm of a coward?

Another myth is that, women are a distraction to men. While the idea may rain ring true one could also conclude that any soldier, male or female, that is so easily distracted may be a danger not only to themselves but also to the unit they serve. While this conclusion does not rectify that argument, it does show the weak rationales that women face. Furthermore this mentality sends society the message that it's acceptable to punish/exclude women from full participation due to men's personal failings. Since World War One female nurses have served on the front line, and it has never been documented that women distract men (Jericho, 2008, p. 8).

This topic clearly incites emotions from opponents and proponents of women in combat. Women deserve attention to the matter starting with the Pentagon ensuring our women are properly trained and given the tools to succeed. But the story doesn't begin there, it begins at home. If we cannot treat a boy and a girl the same when growing up, why should we expect anyone to treat them any different as adults. How many times do we see a girl with a dole while the father teaches the son to hunt? Or watch a father rough house with his son, while the mother teaches her daughter how to apply makeup? Give your sister the tools and she will build you a bridge.

References

Arron. (2007) The Clock Stopped. Retrieved from: http://thestoppedclock.blogspot.com/2007/12/cowardly-untrustworthy-women.html

Jericho, J. (2008) Effectiveness of the Sex Discrimination Act. Retrieved from: http://www.aph.gov.au/Senate/committee/legcon_ctte/sex_discrim/submissions/sub02.pdf

Sheppard, c. (2007) Women in Combat. Strategy Research Project. Retreived from: http://www.carlisle.army.mil/usawc/Registar/policies.cfm

Traders Nation. (2007) Retrieved from: http://www.youtube.com/watch?v=1VgAd3WdaD0

Activity 6.4 Write on Your Blog

Choose one of your previous blog postings, and revise it using the suggestions provided in this chapter.

Activity 6.5 Write in Your Commonplace Book

Choose one of the readings in this chapter that you think could be improved, and write in your commonplace book about how it could be changed. Give specific examples.

7
RESEARCHING RHETORICALLY

Praxis in Action

How I Do Research by Jane Concha

You have your topic and you're ready to go. But now you think, "Where do I go from here?" I have definitely been there. Sometimes, I am so nervous that I don't even research until the last minute, thinking that the Internet would grant me some great sources. Unfortunately, that *never* works.

What I have now realized is that research takes time; with patience and a clear path, I have always managed to find sources that are geared to my topic and add depth to my paper.

To start, I brainstorm ideas of where I want to go with my research. Sometimes, a quick search on Google can help give me some hints on where to start. For example, if I choose to write on the desert in El Paso, a quick search can help me find the name of the desert, the type of climate, and the habitat. From there, I could easily go on the library database and search the keywords I have based on my online search.

I like to use online databases from my library website like Jstor and Academic Search Complete (EBSCO) because I can access print articles from my computer, and that satisfies professors who require that you have a certain number of print sources.

However, I'd recommend to fellow students that it's a good idea to get over their fear of actually going to the library in person except to use the computers or have study dates. Yes, you may be able to access articles and even books (Google Books, etc.) from your computer, but the library does have one great advantage—the research ninjas called librarians. These are people to cultivate, not once but throughout your academic career. They can help you find sources you wouldn't have thought of and can be invaluable when you can't find that essential bit of information.

Jane Concha uses the Internet, online databases, and librarians when conducting research for a paper.

> Even when websites look useful, I'm careful with a *.com* website because those sites usually get their information from research that is easily accessible on a database or information that is slanted toward a certain point of view. However, I do like *.gov* websites because they usually have great statistics I can add to my paper.
>
> Once I find my sources, I pick out the ones that I don't want and discard them. I usually don't look at anything over five years old. I also reject information that pertains to my topic, but is too boring to be interesting to my reader.
>
> Once I'm done finding great sources, it is a lot easier to write my paper.

Research Provides Inartistic Proofs

As discussed in Chapter 4, ancient Greeks began the writing process with invention, a stage in which they searched their memories for data related to the topic at hand. This information constituted artistic proofs, knowledge that rhetors invented from their own minds, emotions, and observation. However, rhetors also supplemented their invented proofs with information that was gleaned from other sources such as the testimony of witnesses, evidence given under torture, and written contracts. Yes, evidence given under torture was considered a legitimate proof. None of these inartistic proofs were generated from the rhetor's mind or "invented." As such, the Greeks considered these sources of information to be inartistic proofs.

Today, the range of inartistic proofs available to writers and speakers is vastly expanded—scientific studies, opinions from authorities, videotapes of events, government documents, and so on. You can locate these in the traditional way—library books and print periodicals—but more likely you will begin your search with the Internet, a resource the ancients could not have imagined. However, as in ancient times, it is still the task of today's rhetor to locate available resources, sift through them to locate those that are relevant, evaluate their reliability and validity, and incorporate them into a text to support an argument.

Researching rhetorically, the title of this chapter, refers to making use of your ethos or credibility as a writer by incorporating your expert knowledge because of everyday experiences and the subjects you have studied. It also involves maximizing as well as "borrowing" the credibility of source materials you quote or paraphrase in your text. When you quote or paraphrase an expert, your paper gains authority that it would not otherwise have. For example, if you are the parent of a child with attention deficit hyperactivity disorder (ADHD), your experiences caring for that child and interacting with the health care and educational systems, as well as the reading you have done to seek out effective treatment, qualifies you to speak with authority about what it is like to raise such as child. If you are writing a paper about educational options for children with ADHD, you can cite some of your own experiences, but you will also want to quote or paraphrase opinions of authorities about the best ways to provide a quality educational environment for these children. These opinions of experts can be found in books, periodicals, and possibly government documents, and including them will increase your power to convince an audience.

You Do Research Every Day

Although the words "research paper" sound imposing to many students, research is really a natural part of your experience. You do research every day, often without being aware of the process, whether it is determining the calorie count of a serving of sugar-free ice cream or calculating the dollar amount you will spend on gasoline for a weekend trip. The information-gathering you do for a research paper builds on the informal research skills you already have by adding additional places to look for information and additional tools to use in that search.

How do you go about finding the best reference sources to support your general knowledge? A key factor to keep in mind is the credibility of each of the sources you choose. Citing information from a source written in the last three years is generally more credible than a source published ten years ago because the information is obviously more current. Peer-reviewed journals and books published by reputable publishers are probably the most credible sources. Information from a news magazine such as *Time* has more credence than material found in popular magazines such as *Glamour* or *People,* which are designed for entertainment rather than covering the news. Indeed, many instructors will forbid the use of Wikipedia as a source, not because all the information is inaccurate (because it is not) but because the reader has no way of evaluating whether information is correct or not since the entries were written by volunteers and the content has not been vetted by a reputable publisher or other authoritative organization.

Don't be reluctant to ask for help. Your instructor may be willing to suggest resources on your topic, as will librarians. Instructors may refer you to specific books or authors. Others may demonstrate a journal search for you, in the process finding you valuable sources. As noted by Concha in the chapter opener, librarians can be valuable allies in your search, as their job is to serve your needs as a library patron. If you ask for help, a librarian will often run a search for you in the online catalog or may even walk with you into the stacks to find appropriate source materials.

Primary and Secondary Research

If you've ever purchased a major consumer product, say a computer, chances are you already knew quite a bit about what was available before you took out your charge card. For example, many of your friends probably have computers as well as definite opinions about what brands and models are preferable. Perhaps you already own a computer and like it so much that you want to upgrade to the next model or maybe you have complaints about its performance. Still, before you made your purchase, you probably did some research on the Internet, reading product specifications and reviews. Maybe you tried out a computer or two at the local Apple Store or another retailer. If you went through this sort of process before buying a computer or another consumer product, you already know the basics about primary and secondary research.

Primary research involves personal interaction with your subject. Interviews with people on the scene of an event and questionnaires are all primary sources. Novels, poems, diaries, and fictional films are also primary sources because they stand alone and are not interpreting anything else. To return to the computer purchase analogy, when you visited the Apple Store or other retailers to examine computers, you were doing primary research. When you looked at product reviews in magazines, you were doing secondary research. Similarly, when you read a *Time* magazine article that analyzes climate change and quotes prominent experts in the field, you are conducting secondary research.

A little later in this chapter, Activity 7.1 asks you to interview someone who has had an unusual life experience and write a profile of that person. You may be able to gather all the information you need for this assignment by doing an interview, though it might be a good idea to revisit the observation exercise (Activity 4.10) in Chapter 4. If you know the person personally, you can also utilize that prior knowledge.

Other writing assignments ask you to combine your own experience or primary research with information gained from secondary research in books or periodicals. For example, you might be asked to write an essay about recycling. You can include your own experience with recycling or visit a recycling center in your community and report what you see. You can also support this primary research with secondary research in books or periodicals in which authorities offer facts and opinions about the effectiveness of recycling. In addition, you can interview an authority on recycling, perhaps a professor or chairperson of a community committee, as an additional secondary source.

You may notice that many magazine articles or books refer to other books, statistical studies, or additional evidence but do not document sources in the text or give a bibliography. In this course, however, your instructor will probably ask you to document outside references following the Modern Language Association (MLA) or American Psychological Association (APA) format. The purpose is to train you in academic writing, which differs from journalism or popular writing in that all sources are credited both in the text and in a works cited page. Documentation also benefits those who read your essays and might want to use the same sources for additional research of their own. It is, therefore, not a check against plagiarism but an important tool for other researchers.

Reading 7.1

Bringing History to Life with Primary Sources

by Alexander A. Aimes

In this article, Alexander A. Aimes argues that primary sources add depth and help bring a research topic to life.

History sometimes bores because of the way it is taught. Often, educators merely present students with information they are supposed to remember, rather than encourage students to explore historic documents and draw conclusions. As a Museum Studies intern at Mystic Seaport, a maritime history museum in Mystic, Connecticut, I worked with other interns to create history education programs targeted at high school audiences. We presented students with primary sources and asked them to think critically about the documents, to develop their own ideas about history.

My favorite program we developed related to the Temperance Movement, a mid-nineteenth century social reform movement that aimed to put an end to alcohol consumption. Members of the Greenman family, prominent shipbuilders and storeowners who lived in Mystic, became involved in Temperance as the movement gained national momentum. We traced the development of their beliefs through historic documents relating to their business and civic activities. For example, we showed students pages from the 1840s account books of the family-owned Greenman General Store that had frequent references to the sale of alcohol. By the 1850s, those references had vanished. Also, we gave students newspaper articles from the 1870s in which the Greenmans publicly stated their support of Temperance, indicating the passion with which the Greenmans advocated against alcohol. The text of the education program encouraged students to discover the Greenmans apparently stopped selling alcohol, a decision that affected the company's profits, *before* their public announcement of their change in attitude toward alcohol.

Students going through the educational program realized they would not know this fascinating detail, which hints the Greenmans were willing to lose company revenue in support of their beliefs, if they had not scrutinized account books from the 19th century. Moreover, we asked students to think about whether they could cite negative evidence—that is, the *absence* of liquor sales in the 1850s account books—as sufficient grounds for assuming the Greenmans changed their business practices by that decade? What other evidence would help support this conclusion—an open ended question students can answer in a variety of ways.

Focusing on historical evidence allows us to ask deeper questions about our conclusions. The questions we encouraged the students at Mystic Seaport to think about show the debatable nature of historical conclusions based on primary sources. While applied here to a museum activity, this strategy of poring over primary sources can be used in almost any research context. Original documents get us as close as possible to whatever subject we are studying. They also add depth to our interpretations by encouraging critical analysis of sources.

Interviews

Depending on your topic, your community probably has some excellent sources sitting behind desks at the nearest college, city hall, or federal office building. If you are looking into the environment, you could contact the Environmental Protection Agency, an attorney who specializes in environmental law, a professional employee of the park system or the Bureau of Land Management, a college professor who works in the natural sciences, or a group in your area dedicated to beautification and restoration efforts.

If you don't know anyone connected with these organizations, a look in the yellow pages or blue government pages of the phone book should give you the information you need.

When you contact the person you'd like to interview, identify yourself and your reason for wanting to speak with him or her. Most people are happy to assist college students in their research, and almost everyone is flattered by the attention. If your first choice refuses, ask him or her if they know anyone who might be knowledgeable about your topic and available for an interview. When you get a positive response, arrange an hour and a location convenient for both of you. If the interview is scheduled more than a week from the initial contact, you can write a letter confirming your appointment, or you can call the day before the scheduled interview to confirm the time and location.

Once you've scheduled the interview, make a list of questions you will ask your interview subject. There are two types of questions you can ask your subject: open and closed. **Open questions** such as the following leave room for extended discussion because they don't have a yes, no, or specific answer:

> Could you tell me about the most positive experience you've had with [topic]?
>
> When did you decide to study [topic]?
>
> What's the most negative experience you've had with [topic]?

Questions like these allow for extended discussions. Even if it seems your subject has finished his or her response to the question, let a few moments of silence pass before you ask another question. Silence can be uncomfortable for some people, and he or she might feel compelled to expand on the response to your question in interesting ways.

Closed questions are useful for gathering specific information. Questions such as "When did you graduate?" and "How long have you been involved in [topic]?" are closed questions. Although closed questions are important to an interview, be sure they're balanced by questions that allow your subject room to talk and expand on his or her ideas.

Before the interview, confirm the exact location of your appointment. If you are unfamiliar with the planned meeting place, go by the day before to make sure you can find it. Take several pens or pencils with you to the interview in addition to a writing tablet with a stiff back. If possible, use a recorder to record the interview, but be sure to ask your subject if it is okay. Most people will allow recording, if you assure them that the recording is only for your use in collecting information for your research paper. If you are using a recorder, test its operation before you get to the interview location so you won't have any surprises when you're with your subject or discover later that the machine was not working.

Although you've prepared a list of questions to follow, don't be afraid to ask a question that isn't on your list. If your subject mentions briefly an experience that seems relevant to your topic, you might want to ask him or her more about that experience, even though it isn't on your list of questions. Indeed, the best way to interview may be to read over your questions just before you meet your subject, then not refer to them during the interview. Before you leave, however, look over your list to see if you have missed any questions of importance.

Remember to let lulls in the conversation work for you by drawing your interview subject into further explanations or illustrations of previous comments. If you interview a talkative person who strays from the topic, try to steer him or her back to the questions you've prepared, but if you can't, don't worry. You'll probably get useful information anyway. Be courteous and attentive. Even if you're recording the interview, take notes. It makes both the subject and the interviewer feel more comfortable and serves as a backup, should your recording not work.

Within 15 minutes after leaving the interview, jot down some notes about your subject's appearance; the sights, sounds, and smells of the place where you conducted the interview; and any overall impressions of the meeting. Make sure you have the date and location of the interview in your notes because you will need it for documentation on your works cited page.

Activity 7.1 Write a Profile of a Person

> Write a profile of a person that is unusual in some way. Your profile should include description, quotes, and whatever background explanations are needed to provide a context, so that the story flows logically from one element to another. The length should be approximately 750 to 1,000 words. Answering the following questions will help you elicit information you need to write your profile.

1. **History**—What is the history of the person? Does the history affect the present?
2. **Qualities**—What qualities make this person worth writing about? Can you give examples that *show* the qualities?
3. **Values and standards**—What does the subject believe in most strongly? How does this shape his/her actions? Can you give specific examples?
4. **Impact**—How does the subject affect those around him or her? This may include both positives and negatives. Give examples.
5. **Description**—Write a physical description of the person, including any unusual aspects that make the person stand out in a crowd. Describe the setting where you interviewed the person or where the person works or lives.

Secondary Research Sources Expected by Professors

You have been assigned a research paper or project. What does your professor expect? First of all, you need to understand the assignment: What specifically does your professor want you to research? Do you have instructions about what kinds of sources your professor wants? Are restrictions put on what Internet or database sources you can use? Possibly, your instructor has specified that you need to use books, journals, major magazines and newspapers, and certain web-based information. This means that you are to use reputable sources to obtain a balanced, impartial viewpoint about your topic. So, how do you find these sources?

Neither you nor your professor should be surprised that you can find enough material for your research paper through the Internet, even if your professor says you can use only print sources. Your library has full-text databases such as Jstor and Academic Search Complete (EBSCO) that will provide you with PDF images of actual journal pages, not web pages. Moreover, Google and other online libraries have the full-text versions of many book chapters or entire books.

However, in many cases the latest books in a field are not online, so you need to venture into the actual library building to find some of the best sources for your research. This is also true of primary sources such as letters and maps. Moreover, librarians can aid you in finding the research materials you need.

Consider the following secondary research sources:

Books: In these days of easy-to-find resources on the Internet, students may wonder why they should bother with books at all. However, scholarly books treat academic topics with in-depth discussion and careful documentation of evidence. College libraries collect scholarly books that are carefully researched and reviewed by authorities in the book's field. Look for recently published books rather than older books, even if they are on your topic. Academic books or well-researched popular books often have bibliographies or lists of additional references at the end of the book. These lists are useful for two reasons: First, if such lists of books are present, it is a good clue this is a well-researched book, and, second, it gives you a ready list of other possible resources you can consult for your research project.

Scholarly journals: Just having the word "journal" in the title does not mean it is a journal. *Ladies Home Journal,* or *The Wall Street Journal,* for example, are not journals. Your instructor means peer-reviewed journals in which the authors have documented their sources. Peer-reviewed means that articles have been reviewed by experts in the field for reliability and relevance before being published. Your library should have print indexes to journals in which you can look up your topic. You may also be able to find journal articles—sometimes in full text—through the online databases offered by your college library.

Major magazines and newspapers: These publications report the news based on the actual observation of events and interviews with experts and also present informed editorial opinions. Examples are magazines such as *Time* and *Fortune* and newspapers such as *The New York Times,* the *Boston Globe, The Wall Street Journal,* and the *Washington Post.* You can locate full-text articles directly from the online versions of major print magazines and newspapers. Often, these publications charge a fee for articles not published recently. However, you can often find the same articles free through one of your library databases.

Special interest publications: These are periodicals that focus on a specific topic but are written for a wider audience than scholarly journals. Authors of articles base their articles on interviews with experts, recent scholarly books and journals, and other reputable sources. Examples include *Psychology Today* and *Scientific American*.

Government documents: Government documents present a wealth of information for many contemporary events and issues. Your library may be a federal depository, which means that users can locate many federal documents onsite. If so, you can look up government sources in the online library catalog. Government documents are also available through online databases.

Encyclopedias: Encyclopedias can be useful to browse when you are looking for topics. They are also helpful for providing background information such as dates when events occurred. However, most instructors prefer that you do not use encyclopedias as sources in your paper. This is particularly true for Wikipedia, the online encyclopedia that is assembled by volunteers who have specialized knowledge on topics and, thus, has no systematic vetting of the contents. However, Wikipedia entries often include bibliographies which can be useful in pointing you to books, articles, or other websites that can be used as references.

Web pages: The problem with web-based information is that anyone with some knowledge of computers can put up a website on the Internet. Thus, information from websites must be carefully evaluated as to author, publishing organization, etc. One way to deal with this problem is to find web information through librarian-generated indexes and search engines that are designed to screen websites for credibility (see the section titled "Find Internet Information," which appears later in this chapter).

As you use the categories above to find secondary sources for your paper or project, realize that your topic influences your choice of reference materials. If you are writing about a literary topic such as Shakespeare's *Othello*, you will find a number of relevant books and journal articles. If your topic is more contemporary, such as the current status of the country's housing market, you may be able to find some books or journal articles for background information, but you will need to use recent magazine and newspaper articles to find the latest information.

As you examine your sources, remember that gathering the information should help you discover what you think about your topic, not just what others think. This will enable you to create a paper based on *your* ideas and opinions, with source materials supporting your position.

Employ Computerized Library Catalogs

Public Access Catalogs (PACs) or computerized catalogs, accessed through the Internet, have replaced card catalogs. A library computerized catalog provides bibliographical information about the library's collection, including thousands of books, photos, videos, journals, and other items. Generally, catalogs can be accessed by any of the following methods: keyword, subject, author, title, or call number. You may also find books that are available in digital form through the catalog. In addition, on the library home page, you will find links to other information and services such as database searches, interlibrary loans, and course reserves.

Types of Computerized Searches

Conducting a computerized search involves accessing the library's catalog using one of the following search methods:

- *Keyword*—Unless you know the author or title of a book, keyword is the best type of search because it finds the search word or words anywhere in the bibliographical citation.

    Example: water quality

- *Title*—Type the exact order of words in the title.

    Example: History of the United Kingdom

- *Author*—Type the author's name, putting the last name first. You don't need to include a comma.

    Example: Miller Henry J.

- *Subject*—Type the exact Library of Congress subject heading.

    Example: Spanish language—Grammar, Historical

- *Call Number*—Type the exact call number.

    Example: B851.P49 2004

If you have a general topic, you probably want to use the keyword search, for subject search actually refers to the exact Library of Congress subject-search designations, and, unless you use the precise search terms specified by that classification system, you may not get the results you want. The use of keywords, however, will lead you to hits on your topic. Then, once you have found one book that is in your topic area, you can examine the screen for Library of Congress subject headings and click on those to browse for more books.

An invaluable resource of any library is the Interlibrary Loan department. Here you can request books your library does not own, as well as journal articles from periodicals not in the library's collection or obtainable through the library's databases. Books and articles are obtained for you by the staff on a minimal or no-fee basis. This is extremely helpful because you can request books you find in bibliographies. However, it generally takes seven to ten days to obtain books through an interlibrary loan, so you need to plan well in advance. To request an item, you simply go to the Interlibrary Loan department in your library or fill out a form on the library's website.

Activity 7.2 Locate Books on Your Topic

Using the online card catalog at the library, locate three books about your topic. Write down the titles, authors, publishers, dates of publication, and catalog numbers. Now, go to the stacks and find the books. While you are there, find two other books nearby on the same topic. Check the table of contents and index to see if they contain information you can use.

Utilize Electronic Library Resources

College and university libraries increasingly rely on databases to provide digital versions of articles published in journals, magazines, newspapers, and government documents, as well as other publications and materials. Generally, the databases are available to students and faculty through the Internet via the library home page, though a library card and a password may be required for off-campus access.

Library databases make use of online forms similar to those of a library computerized catalog. Searches are by subject, title, author, and name of publication. Advanced search features are available. Some databases provide the full-text versions of articles published in newspapers, journals, and magazines. Others give publication information only, such as title, author, publication, date of publication, and an abstract of the article. Popular databases include Lexis-Nexis, Academic Search Complete (see figure 7.1), Periodical Archive Online (ProQuest), Project Muse, and JSTOR.

figure 7.1

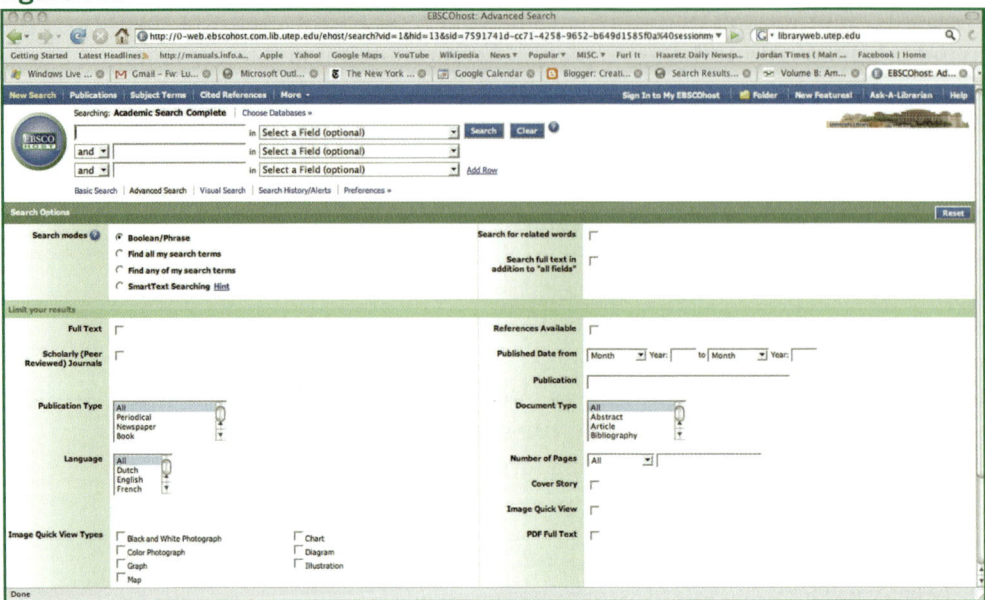

Academic Search Complete is one of EBSCO's popular online databases that can be accessed by students through their library's website. The database indexes full-text articles on a wide variety of topics.

Activity 7.3 Locate Newspaper and Magazine Articles

> Go to your library's online databases and choose one that relates to your topic. Then access it and type in your topic. Try using various key words. Jot down titles, authors, and publication information concerning any articles that look interesting. If full-text versions are available, save them to your computer or disk drive or e-mail them to yourself. If not, find out if your library has a hard copy version or microfilm of the articles.

Find Internet Information

The World Wide Web is an incredible resource for research. Through it, you can find full texts of pending legislation, searchable online editions of Shakespeare's plays, environmental impact statements, stock quotes, and much, much more. Finding credible research sources is not always easy. Anyone with an Internet connection and a little knowledge can put up a web page and claim to be an expert on a chosen topic. Therefore, information from the Internet must be scrutinized with even more diligence than print sources. For example, if you enter the word "environment" in one of the keyword search engines, you may receive thousands of "hits," or sites that relate to that topic from all over the world. How do you sift through all of that feedback in order to find information relevant to your topic? It is a problem that has not been completely solved on the Internet.

However, the search engine Google now provides Google Books, http://books.google.com, which offers the full-text versions of millions of books, though usually not the full text of the entire book unless the book is no longer copyrighted. Also, Google Scholar, http://scholar.google.com, provides access to scholarly papers, though if your library has computerized databases (see figure 7.2), it will likely have a more extensive collection available to you. Also, the Directory of Online Open Access Journals, http://www.doaj.org, enables you to search online journals that offer free access.

figure 7.2

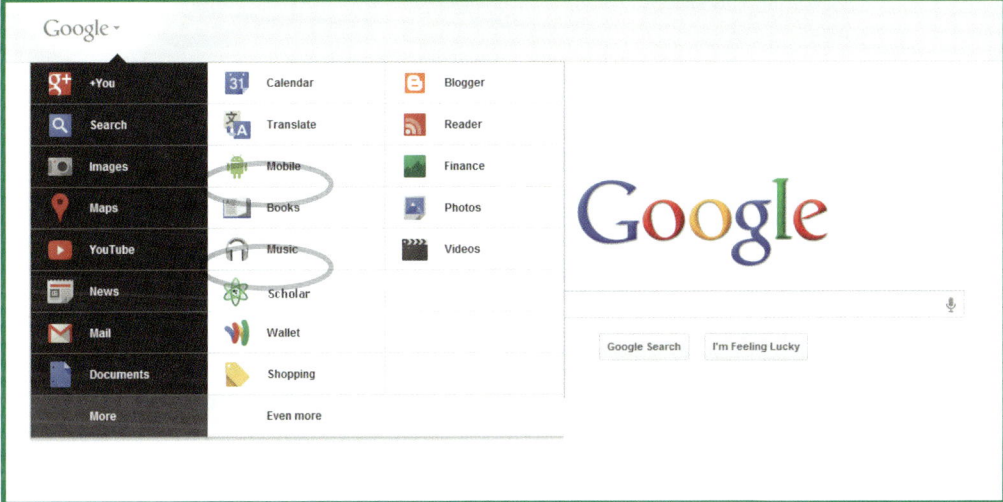

Click on the menu bar on the left side of the Google.com search page to find links to Google Books and Google Scholar. Google Books offers the full-text versions of millions of books, though usually not the full text of the entire book unless the book is no longer copyrighted. Also, Google Scholar, at http://scholar.google.com, provides access to scholarly papers, though not always full text.

One of the best ways for students to find Internet resources is through indexing projects sponsored by major libraries. In the case of each directory/search tool, librarians have personally reviewed and selected websites that are of value to academic researchers, including both students and faculty. These indexing websites may be organized by subject area, in addition to having keyword search engines. Thus, you might quickly locate the most authoritative websites without having to wade through masses of sites looking for the reliable ones. The following websites offer links to a variety of reputable sources:

IPL2: Information You Can Trust, http://www.ipl.org (see figure 7.3)

Infomine, http://infomine.ucr.edu

figure 7.3

IPL2: Information You Can Trust is a public library on the Internet. It offers links to resources by subject, newspapers and magazines, and special collections created by the Internet Public Library.

Government documents also can be found easily through the Internet and are indexed at a variety of sites, including these:

    FirstGov, http://www.firstgov.gov

    Thomas Legislative Information, http://thomas.loc.gov

    Federal Citizen Information Center, http://www.pueblo.gsa.gov/

    FedWorld.Gov, http://www.fedworld.gov/

Activity 7.4 Find a Journal Article in Google Scholar

Go to Google Scholar either through Google.com or directly at http://scholar.google.com and search for a journal article on your chosen topic. If the Google link does not offer you full text, then go to the index of electronic journals on your college library website and search for the journal. Likely, your library will offer a database that provides full text for the article. Note: The advantage of this method of finding journal articles is that Google Scholar indexes articles from journals available in many different databases.

Evaluate Sources

Many people tend to believe what they see in print. They may think that if information is in a book or a news magazine, it must be true. If you read critically, however, you know that all sources must be evaluated. With the Internet, perhaps even more than with print texts, it is important to evaluate your sources. Here are some guidelines to consider when evaluating sources.

- **Who is the author?** This question is equally important, whether the source in question is a book, a magazine, or a website. If you have the dust jacket of the book, the back flap will quickly provide you with essential information to screen the author. In the short biographical sketch, usually included along with a photo, you can learn the author's academic credentials and university affiliation, what previous books the author has published, and other qualifications that the publisher thinks qualifies the author to write this particular book. If there is no dust jacket (as is often true with library books), you can try to find information about the author through an Internet search engine or a reference text such as *Contemporary Authors*. A magazine or journal will often provide brief biographical information at the end of the article or on a separate authors' page. If the text is on a website, determining the authorship is more complex, as authors often are not named. In that case, you are forced to rely on the credibility of the entity publishing the website. Many websites have a link called something like "About Us" or "Mission Statement," and that page will give you some idea about the motivations of the entity sponsoring the site. Is it selling something? Is it part of an organization that has a political agenda? These are things to keep in mind when considering the bias of the site's content.

- **For what audience is the text written?** Determining this may require some detective work. In the case of a book, the preface or introduction may give you some clues. With magazines and journals, consider the demographics of the readership. With a website, a little clicking around in the site and a look at the kind of texts, graphics, and advertising used (if any) should tell you what readers the site is designed for.

- **What sources does the author rely upon?** If you are working with an academic text, the sources should be clearly cited in the text by author and page number, footnotes, or endnotes. If it is a more popular book or article, sources are acknowledged less formally; however, a credible author will still make an effort to credit sources. For example, an article might say, "According to the March issue of the *New England Journal of Medicine*...."

- **Does the text have an obvious bias?** Ask yourself if the argument is logical and if sources are mentioned for any statistics or other evidence. Are any opposing viewpoints discussed fairly? Does the author engage in name calling (a clear sign of bias)? Are there obvious holes or contradictions in the argument? For most purposes, you are looking for texts which do not appear to have been written with a biased agenda. However, in some cases, the opposite is true. If you are looking for a political candidate's position on a certain issue, then reading the candidate's book or going to the candidate's website will provide you with a biased viewpoint but one which you can analyze for the purposes of your paper. When dealing with information from sources with an obvious agenda, though, you must be careful not to represent the material as unbiased in your text.

- **What do others think of the text?** For a book, you can look for a review in *Book Review Digest* or *Book Review Index*, two publications you can find in the reference section of the library. Also, *The New York Times* and other newspapers review prominent popular books. Most magazines and newspapers print letters to the editor, which may offer comments on controversial articles. The Scout Report, which can be found at the *Scout Project*, http://scout.wisc.edu, reviews selected websites. If you locate a review of your text, you can cite the review in your research paper to provide additional evidence of the text's credibility.

Activity 7.5 Locate and Evaluate a Source

Locate one source (book, magazine or newspaper article, or website page) which you think would be a credible source for a research paper. For that source, answer the questions in the Evaluate Sources section above.

Activity 7.6 Evaluate a Website

Go to the Internet and look up a website related to a topic you are researching. Answer these questions as fully as you can.

1. Who is the author of this source? Is the author credible on this topic? Why or why not?
2. What does the text focus on? Is it thoughtful and balanced, or does it seem one-sided? What gives you that impression?
3. When was the website last updated?

4. What is the purpose of this site? Is it to provide information? Or is it trying to persuade readers to accept a particular point of view?

5. How professional is the tone, and how well-designed is the site? How carefully has it been edited and proofread? Are there any grammatical and spelling errors that compromise its credibility?

6. What kinds of links does the site provide? Do they add to the website's credibility or detract from it?

Avoid Plagiarism

Plagiarism is defined as follows by the Writing Program Administrators (WPA), a group of English professors who direct college composition programs: "In an instructional setting, plagiarism occurs when a writer deliberately uses someone else's language, ideas, or other original (not common-knowledge) material without acknowledging its source." A keyword here is "deliberately." Instructors, however, may have difficulty distinguishing between accidental and deliberate plagiarism. The burden is upon you as the writer to give credit where credit is due. These are some examples of plagiarism:

- Turning in a paper that was written by someone else as your own. This includes obtaining a paper from an Internet term paper mill.
- Copying a paper or any part of a paper from a source without acknowledging the source in the proper format.
- Paraphrasing materials from a source without documentation.
- Copying materials from a text but treating it as your own, leaving out quotation marks and acknowledgement.

The guidelines provided in table 7.1 can help you identify when it is appropriate to give credit to others in your writing.

Table 7.1 Choosing When to Give Credit

Need to Document	No Need to Document
• When you are using or referring to somebody else's words or ideas from a magazine, book, newpaper, song, TV program, movie, web page, computer program, letter, advertisement, or any other medium. • When you use information gained through interviewing another person. • When you copy the exact words or a "unique phrase" from somewhere. • When you reprint any diagrams, illustrations, charts, and pictures. • When you use ideas given to you by others, whether in conversation or through e-mail.	• When you are writing your own experiences, your own observations, your own insights, your own thoughts, or your own conclusions about a subject. • When you are using "common knowledge"—folklore, common-sense observations, or shared information within your field of study or cultural group. • When you are compiling generally accepted facts. • When you are writing up your own experimental results.

The Online Writing Lab (OWL) at Purdue University provides an excellent handout on avoiding plagiarism, including the information about when to give credit to sources in the table above. See http://owl.english.purdue.edu.

Activity 7.7 Plagiarism Exercise

In this exercise you will intentionally plagiarize a text. Then you will collaborate with a partner to produce a text that paraphrases and cites sources.

1. With a partner, choose a public figure currently in the news. On your own, write a brief bio of the individual you have both chosen, intentionally quoting extensively from one source without using quotation marks or citing the source.

2. Exchange your text with your partner by e-mail. Now, paste into Google or another search engine a sentence or long phrase copied in your partner's text, putting the copied text in quotation marks. Search. Repeat until you are able to identify the source of the text that your partner has intentionally plagiarized. Your partner should follow the same exercise using your text.

3. Finally, back in class, work with your partner to compose a brief bio of the individual that paraphrases these texts (and others, if needed).

4. Turn in the final version, along with the plagiarized versions. Describe your experience in trying to locate the source of your partner's plagiarized text.

Reading 7.2

Anatomy of a Fake Quotation
by Megan McArdle

In this article, originally published in *The Atlantic*, Megan McArdle tells the story of how a fake Martin Luther King, Jr. quote was created and posted on the Internet.

Yesterday, I saw a quote from Martin Luther King Jr. fly across my Twitter feed: "I mourn the loss of thousands of precious lives, but I will not rejoice in the death of one, not even an enemy."—Martin Luther King, Jr. I was about to retweet it, but I hesitated. It didn't sound right. After some Googling, I determined that it was probably fake, which I blogged about last night.

Here's the story of how that quote was created.

It turns out I was far too uncharitable in my search for a motive behind the fake quote. I assumed that someone had made it up on purpose. I was wrong.

Had I seen the quote on Facebook, rather than Twitter, I might have guessed at the truth. On the other hand, had I seen it on Facebook, I might not have realized it was fake, because it was appended to a long string of genuine speech from MLK Jr. Here's the quote as most people on Facebook saw it:

> I will mourn the loss of thousands of precious lives, but I will not rejoice in the death of one, not even an enemy. Returning hate for hate multiplies hate, adding deeper darkness to a night already devoid of stars. Darkness cannot drive out darkness; only light can do that. Hate cannot drive out hate, only love can do that.

Everything except the first sentence is found in King's book, *Strength to Love*, and seems to have been said originally in a 1957 sermon he gave on loving your enemies. Unlike the first quotation, it does sound like King, and it was easy to assume that the whole thing came from him.

So how did they get mixed together?

Thanks to Jessica Dovey, a Facebook user, that's how. And contrary to my initial assumption, it wasn't malicious. Ms. Dovey, a 24-year-old Penn State graduate who now teaches English to middle schoolers in Kobe, Japan, posted a very timely and moving thought on her Facebook status, and then followed it up with the Martin Luther King, Jr., quote.

> I will mourn the loss of thousands of precious lives, but I will not rejoice in the death of one, not even an enemy. "Returning hate for hate multiplies hate, adding deeper darkness to a night already devoid of stars. Darkness cannot drive out darkness; only light can do that. Hate cannot drive out hate, only love can do that." MLK Jr.

At some point, someone cut and pasted the quote, and—for reasons that I, appropriately chastened, will not speculate on—stripped out the quotation marks. Eventually, the mangled quotation somehow came to the attention of Penn Jillette, of Penn and Teller fame. He tweeted it to his 1.6 million Facebook followers, and the rest was Internet history. Twenty-four hours later, the quote brought back over 9,000 hits on Google.

The quote also went viral on Twitter, and since the 140-character limit precluded quoting the whole thing, people stripped it down to the most timely and appropriate part: the fake quote. That's where I saw it.

The speed of dissemination is breathtaking: mangled to meme in less than two days. Also remarkable is how defensive people got about the quote—though admirably, not Penn Jillette, who posted an update as soon as it was called to his attention. The thread for my post now has over 600 comments, and by my rough estimate, at least a third of them are people posting that I need to print a retraction, because of the nonfake part of the quotation. But I didn't quote that part; I was only interested in the too-timely bit I'd seen twittered.

Even more bizarrely, several of these readers, who clearly hadn't read too closely, started claiming that I had retroactively edited the post to make them look like idiots, even going so far as to scrub all the versions in RSS readers so that they, too, showed that I was talking about the truncated version. Even if you think I am the sort of low scoundrel who would do such a thing, this seems like a lot of work for not much reward. I'm not sure whether it's even possible to completely scrub an RSS feed, but even if it were, I'd have had to notify my bosses, who tend to frown on retroactive editing.

Meanwhile, several other people began confabulating a provenance for it. *Obviously*, he was talking about Vietnam, and what sort of moral midget couldn't understand that? This even though the latest citation for the true part of the quote was a book published in 1967, which would have been written earlier than that, when U.S. casualties in Vietnam were still relatively low. Moreover, the ambiguity with which the antiwar movement viewed the North Vietnamese makes "enemy" a hard fit.

It is, of course, not strange that people might look for possible confirming facts. What's strange is that they were sure enough of themselves to make fun of anyone who disagreed. Yet several other people on the comment thread had linked to a version of the quotation from 1957. I am second to no one in my admiration for Dr. King. But I do not think that he prefigured Vietnam by seven years.

Which only illustrates why fake quotes are so widely dispersed. Though one commenter accused me of trying to make people feel stupid for having propagated the quote, that was hardly my intention—we've all probably repeated more fake quotations than real ones. Fake quotations are pithier, more dramatic, more on point, than the things people usually say in real life. It's not surprising that they are often the survivors of the evolutionary battle for mindshare. One person actually posted a passage which integrated the fake quotation into the larger section of the book from which the original MLK words were drawn.

We become invested in these quotes because they say something important about us—and they let us feel that those emotions were shared by great figures in history. We naturally search for reasons that they could have said it—that they could have felt like us—rather than looking for reasons to disbelieve. If we'd put the same moving words in Hitler's mouth, everyone would have been a lot more skeptical. But while this might be a lesson about the need to be skeptical, I don't think there's anything stupid about wanting to be more like Dr. King.

Ms. Dovey's status now reads: "has apparently gone back in time and put her words into one of MLK's sermons. I'm somewhere between nervous and embarrassed and honored . . . I really hope I haven't said anything he wouldn't agree with . . . Only what I feel in my heart."

A lot of us were feeling the same thing—and I think it's clear from his writings that MLK would have too. There's no reason to be embarrassed about that.

Activity 7.8 Discuss "Anatomy of a Fake Quotation"

1. How was the fake quotation created? How did it spread on the Internet?

2. Note the speed and the reach of the fake quote. What does Megan McArdle suggest the story of this fake quote says about why fake quotes can become so widely disbursed?

3. What is your reaction to this story of the fake quotation?

Activity 7.9 Prepare an Annotated Bibliography

An annotated bibliography is a list of bibliographical citations with a few sentences or a paragraph for each entry that offers explanatory information or critical commentary about the source. Many instructors request an annotated bibliography as a step in writing a research paper because it is an indication of the scope and direction of your research.

1. Select 10 quality sources about your topic. These should be, as your instructor directs, a mix of books, scholarly journal and magazine articles, government documents, and selected texts from websites.

2. Skim the text of each source and read portions more closely that seem relevant to your topic.

3. Write a bibliographical citation for each source in MLA style. (See the appendix that follows this chapter for MLA style samples.)

4. Write a few sentences for each source in which you do the following:
   (a) Summarize the content and purpose of the source.
   (b) Explain how you might use the source in your research paper.

Sample Annotated Bibliography on the Federal Aviation Administration User Fees

Horne, T. A. (2007, February). User Fee Debate. *AOPA Pilot Magazine, 50,* 27.

The author of this article is an experienced, commercial rated pilot that has flown for over 30 years. He also sits on the Aircraft Owners and Pilots Association (AOPA) board. This article explains what the Federal Aviation

Administration (FAA) has proposed and what it means to pilots. Congress is cutting the budget for the FAA and in turn wants to impose fees for anyone who flies into a controlled airspace. This would have a very tragic effect on general aviation. This is huge because if anyone is flying anywhere around a decent-sized city, they are going to fly through these airspaces. Also, the FAA wants to charge for approaches into airports and landing on airport runways. This is bad because all of these charges would add up to more than $200. This would discourage people from flying, making them sell their aircraft. This would slowly dissolve the general aviation industry. I can use this article to explain what is going on and why the government wants to charge these fees.

Boyer, P. (Director) (2007, October 6). AOPA's Reasonable Analysis of User Fee Issues at AOPA Expo. *AOPA Expo 2007*. Lecture conducted from AOPA, Hartford, CT.

This lecture was given by the president of AOPA, Phil Boyer. He spoke of the fees that the FAA is trying to impose and what they would mean for general aviation pilots. He explains that the fees that the FAA wants are directed toward general aviation and not toward the airlines. He also gave some examples of what would be better for everyone, if the FAA really is in a crisis. This source is important because it provides an explanation and breakdown of these user fees and gives some examples of what could be put in place of these proposed fees.

Fact Sheet—Impact of Administration's Financing Proposal on General Aviation. (2007, April 23). *FAA: Home*. Retrieved March 2, 2011, from http://www.faa.gov/news/fact_sheets/news_story.cfm?newsid=8747.

This website is the official FAA website that has all of its information. This one fact sheet lists all the facts and myths related to this issue. It goes over what the FAA wants to put into place and where and when it will happen. It brings up all of the more important issues regarding the topic, but leaves some out as well. For example, nowhere in the sheet does it say anything about controlled airspace fees, which is one of the biggest fees it would implement. It does mention another, which is the fuel tax hike. This would weaken general aviation because a lot of pilots cannot afford higher fuel prices. This will be important to have a government agency's point of view on the topic.

AOPA Online: What's the FAA's user fee proposal? (2006, November 30). *AOPA Online: Aircraft Owners and Pilots Association.* Retrieved March 2, 2011, from http://www.aopa.org/whatsnew/newsitems/2006/061130userfees.html.

This website is the official website for AOPA, which is a foundation that protects flying and everything related to aviation. This article goes over what the user fees would be, but it goes into greater detail about what the fuel prices would be after the legislation is put into place. Fuel is needed for all flights and is already expensive. What the government wants to do in addition to implementing user fees is to put more tax on fuel. This would make it much harder for the average pilot to afford flying his/her aircraft. This is beneficial to the argument because it focuses on one of the major fees that the FAA would implement: the fuel hikes.

User Fees—NBAA Calls Proposed FAA Budget a 'Sweetheart Deal' For the Airlines. (2006, November 30). *California Pilots Association.* Retrieved March 2, 2011, from http://www.calpilots.org/index.php?option=com_content&view=article&id=1141&catid=45: pre-2008-archived-articles&Itemid=81.

Cal Pilots is an organization similar to the AOPA, but it has a defined area. It is also very concerned with this issue. The article is from the NBAA which is the National Business Aviation Association. The article explains that the airline industry is getting it easy with this proposal. It says that the government is trying to move fees from the airlines to general aviation. The problem with this is that the airline industry can handle it, general aviation cannot. General aviation includes every aspect of aviation excluding the airlines and the military. The majority of general aviation pilots are your everyday, fly-for-fun kinds of people. These people cannot afford all the fees that would be put into place. This would destroy the industry. This is important because it ties the airline industry into the argument.

Network, A. (2009, October 12). Aero-TV: AirVenture Meet the Boss—Randy Babbitt Tackles User Fees. Retrieved from http://www.youtube.com/watch?v=J14ut3O_j3M.

This video is from AirVenture, which is a fly-in expo. Randy Babbitt is one of the head officials for the FAA and he explains that the FAA needs money to meet the needs of the industry. He says that the planes now are more efficient, making them use less fuel which means that the fuel tax in effect now is less effective. He goes on to explain that the FAA needs to make up this deficit, but it does not know exactly where it is going to come from.

Chapter 7 | Researching Rhetorically

> This is important because it is a government official who is explaining the situation the FAA is in and what he thinks will happen.
>
> Wald, M. L. (2006, March 7). F.A.A. Seeks New Source of Revenue in User Fees. *The New York Times*. Retrieved March 2, 2011, from http://query.nytimes.com/gst/fullpage.html?res=9507E0D91531F934A35750.
>
> Matthew L. Wald is a journalist for *The New York Times*. In the article, he interviews some very influential people in the aviation industry. Another important fact about him is that he is also a general aviation pilot. This article explains that because of the drop of airline tickets that the FAA needs to find new ways to make money because the tax implemented on tickets is not getting the job done. It says that the FAA is going to tax the users of the air traffic control system. This article is important because it gives specific numbers on how much the FAA is in debt and what the budget proposal is.

Activity 7.10 Compare and Contrast Media

> Your instructor will select an article on a topic or event that is currently in the news. Find another article on the same subject either from the same news outlet or another major news source (*The New York Times, The Wall Street Journal, CNN, Time*, etc.). Compare and contrast how the reporting of the event is similar or different in the two texts. Note: You are not to write a report on the content of the articles themselves; instead, identify the author's perspective in each text and how it influences how the news is portrayed to readers.
>
> Look for opinions, adjectives with positive or negative connotations, facts or evidence presented, the tone of the headline, and the text itself. Also consider the target audience.
>
> Organize your observations in a one- to two-page report with a clear thesis that presents your evaluation of the two texts.

Activity 7.11 Write on Your Blog

> In your blog, write a summary and a response to a source you might use to research your topic. Is it useful for your research? Why or why not?

Activity 7.12 Write in Your Commonplace Book

Copy a quote from a source that you think makes a critical point about the argument paper you are writing. Then comment about the quote—what does it mean and why is it important?

APPENDIX A
CITING SOURCES

Praxis in Action

How I Cite by Craig Wynne

Make no mistake about it: Doing the citations can be an annoying part of the writing process. I don't know of anyone who enjoys doing citations because it is not easy to get the information in the right order, as well as put periods and commas where they are required; but citations are necessary, so your instructor knows from where you obtained your sources. If your instructor doesn't specify a format, ask if you should use MLA or APA. Also, if you are lucky enough to have an instructor who will take a look at a rough draft of your Works Cited page or bibliography, be sure to take advantage of that opportunity!

I find it can be stressful trying to put together citations at the end of a paper, as it can take a few hours trying to remember where you got your sources. I prefer to do them as I write, as it actually saves time to do that. Whenever I insert a quote or a paraphrase, I cite it immediately after I've written it. I do the internal citation, and I add the reference to my Works Cited page. I find it helps me to complete this part of the process, and it saves me time at the end having to go back through sources.

I'm also careful about using citation generators such as EasyBib and RefWorks. Many students find they can be effective time-savers, but I don't recommend relying on them entirely. Generators do a good job in setting up the order of a citation, but citations have to look a certain way, and the generators don't always get the periods and the capitals in the right places. They also won't cite inside the text. Personally, I find it easier and faster just to do the citations myself without using a citation generator. If you decide to try out EasyBib, RefWorks, or another citation generator, remember to allow yourself enough time to double-check all your citations against a handbook or handout that gives you the correct formats.

To save time and avoid undue stress, Craig Wynne prepares citations as he writes.

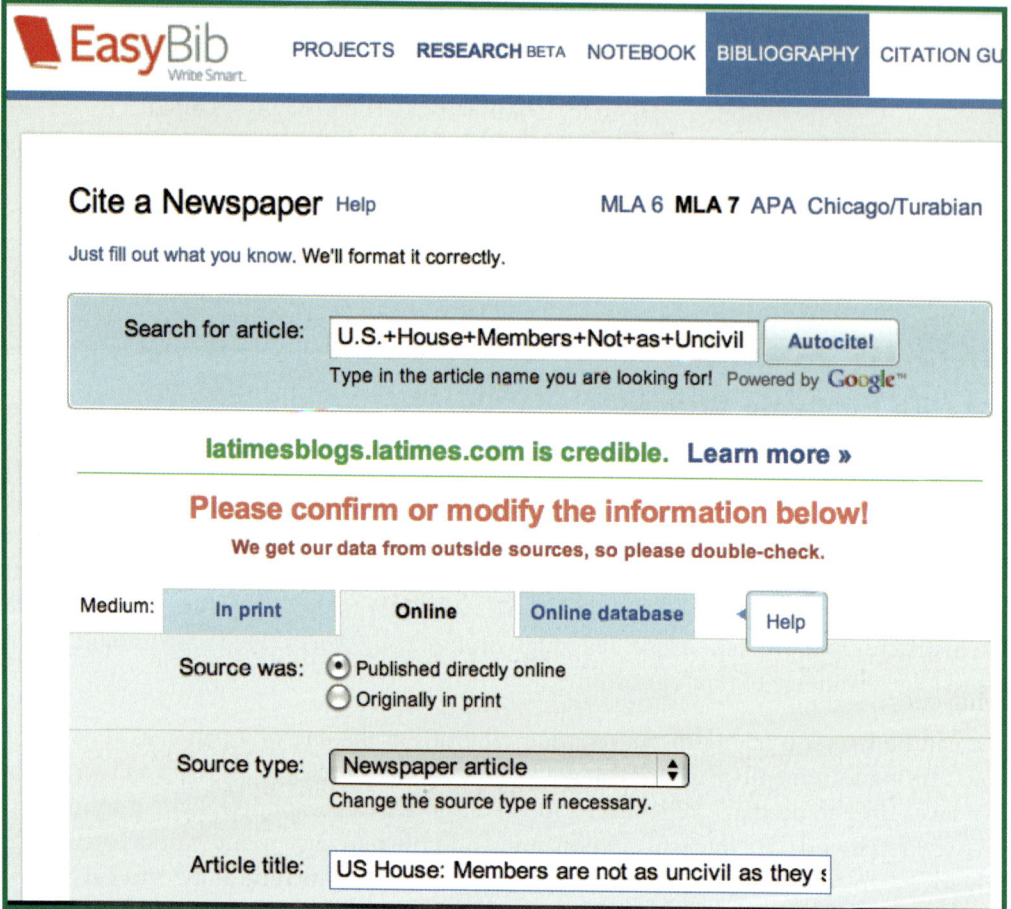

EasyBib is one of the citation generators available on the Internet through a keyword search. Most offer a free version, with upgraded features for a subscription fee. Note that EasyBib encourages users to double-check their entries both for content and form. Citation generators assist with documentation format, but they cannot eliminate errors.

Evolving Formats of Document Citation

The widespread use of the Internet for research is changing the way sources are cited in documents. This is certainly true of electronic sources because of the ephemeral nature of web pages. Although documents may look like print sources (often with title, author, and publication information), they also share a characteristic of live performances in that you can access them after they have occurred only if you can find a recorded version. Once web pages are removed from a website, you cannot view them unless they have been archived. Also, web pages can be updated or changed, while retaining the same appearance, which makes systematic documentation difficult.

In the past, Modern Language Association (MLA) style recommended including the URL (web address) of web page documents in the Works Cited list. However, more recently MLA has taken the position that including that information has limited value because URLs are prone to change and are cumbersome in any case. The current recommendation is that students include URLs only when the material would otherwise be difficult to locate or if the instructor requires it. If you do include a URL, enclose it with an angle bracket and follow with a period. For example, the web page for *The New York Times* would be <http://nytimes.com>.

APA style suggests including the elements of a citation in the same order as you would for a print source, adding information about electronic retrieval after the standard information. However, APA also recognizes that information such as author, publication date, publisher, or even title may be missing in an electronic source. APA suggests giving the DOI (Digital Object Identifier) a unique alphanumeric string that is a persistent link, whenever possible. If it is not available, APA recommends giving the URL of the item being cited.

Interestingly, the prevalence of Internet sources is changing the way print sources are cited. MLA style recommends adding the word "print" after printed source citation information, as you would add "web" after a source accessed on the Internet.

When You Have a Choice of Electronic Source Format, Choose a PDF

When searching for articles in online databases or web pages, you may be offered a choice of formats: HTML or PDF. If you have that choice, select the PDF because it will have page numbers. Essentially, a PDF document reproduces print documents exactly, so that reading one is just like reading the original article except that it is not surrounded by the other content of the original publication.

If you are utilizing electronic documents as sources and they are not PDFs, you may be missing several of the usual elements of document citation, such as author name, publisher or sponsoring organization, page numbers, and even a title. In this case, give as much information about these traditional elements of citation as you can, and review the examples that follow for help with format. As an easy rule of thumb, though, keep this in mind: The more of the traditional elements used to classify and place a document within the scholarly world that are missing, the less likely the text is to be credible and reliable. If readers cannot tell where the information originated, how are they to trust it?

> *Note that MLA and APA both specify that documents should be double-spaced. The following examples are single-spaced to save space.*

MLA Style

For MLA style, you may refer to the *MLA Handbook for Writers of Research Papers* and the MLA website, http://www.mla.org. The Purdue Owl, http://owl.purdue.english.edu, is also an excellent reference.

A paper written in MLA style should be double-spaced, with margins set at one inch on all sides. Choose a standard typeface such as Times Roman in 12 pt. type.

Beginning on the first page, generate a heading on the upper right-hand side of the page that gives the page number.

Do not create a cover page unless your instructor specifies one. Instead, on the upper left-hand side of the first page, give your name, your instructor's name, the course, and the date. These items should all be flush left, double-spaced, and set on separate lines.

Double-space again and center the title. Follow the title with another double-space and indent the first line of text. Indent each paragraph.

Bibliographical Documentation

In MLA style, this is called either the Works Cited page or an Annotated Bibliography. The title, either Works Cited or Annotated Bibliography, should appear centered on the top margin of the last page of a researched essay. The Works Cited page should be double-spaced with no extra line spacing between entries. The first line of each entry begins at the margin, and all subsequent lines of a particular entry are indented 5 spaces on the left margin. All entries should be in alphabetical order. The Annotated Bibliography is formatted like the Works Cited page with the addition of an annotation or description of the source in a paragraph following the citation. The following entries are typical citations prepared according to MLA style.

Examples are offered for both print, online, and database versions, when applicable.

Book

Egan, Jennifer. *A Visit from the Goon Squad*. New York: Alfred A. Knopf, 2010. Print.

Book with Two Authors

Friedman, Thomas L. and Michael Mandelbaum. *That Used to Be Us: How America Fell behind in the World It Invented and How We Can Come Back*. New York: Farrar, Straus and Giroux, 2011. Print.

Two or More Selections from the Same Print Collection or Anthology

Note: To avoid repetition on the list of works cited, cite an anthology or reader as a separate entry. Then cross-reference entries to the anthology as in the example below.

Burns, Gary. "Marilyn Manson and the Apt Pupils of Littleton." Petracca and Sorapure 284–90. Print.

Fox, Roy. "Salespeak." Petracca and Sorapure 56–72. Print.

Petracca, Michael and Madeleine Sorapure, eds. *Common Culture: Reading and Writing About American Popular Culture*. 5th ed. Upper Saddle River: Pearson, 2007. Print.

Note: Alphabetize each entry among other entries on the Works Cited page. Do not group the entries from the anthology together unless they fall next to one another alphabetically. Also, remember that you will have no parenthetical citation referencing the editors Petracca and Sorapure. You should cite Burns and Fox in the parenthetical citations in your paper.

Book with Multiple Editors

Mennuti, Rosemary B., Arthur Freeman, and Ray W. Christner, eds. *Cognitive-Behavioral Interventions: A Handbook for Practice*. New York: Routledge, 2006. Print.

Online Edition of Book or Novel

James, Henry. *The American*. 1877. Fiction: *The Eserver Collection*. Web. 15 June 2008.

(This book was published before 1900, so the name and city of the publisher are not needed. For more recent books, give the print information first, then the information about web publication.)

Macfie, A. L. *Orientalism: a Reader*. New York: New York UP, 2000. *Google Books*. Web. 26 Sept. 2011.

Scholarly Article in Print Journal

Thompson, Jason. "Magic for a People Trained in Pragmatism: Kenneth Burke, and the Early 9/11 Oratory of George W. Bush." *Rhetoric Review* 30.4 (2011): 350–71. Print.

Scholarly Article Found in Online Database

Angel, R. J. "Immigrants and Welfare: The Impact of Welfare Reform on America's Newcomers." *Contemporary Sociology: A Journal of Reviews* 39.5 (2010): 568–69. Academic Search Complete. Web. 10 September 2011.

Scholarly Article from Journal Published Online

Gustafsson, Amanda. "Beware the Invisible." *Papers from the Institute of Archeology* 20 (2010): n. pag. Web. 29 Sept. 2011.

Note: MLA specifies including page numbers for scholarly publications, so if the online journal does not provide page numbers, include n. pag. (no page).

Book Review

Schneider, Robert J. Rev. of *Modern Physics and Ancient Faith*, by Stephen M. Barr. *Anglican Theological Review* 86 (2004): 506–07. Print.

Book Review Published Online

Garner, Dwight. "An Unearthed Treasure That Changed Things." Rev. of *The Swerve: How the World Became Modern*. *The New York Times*, 27 Sept. 2011. Web. 28 Sept. 2011.

An Editorial

Wolfe, Gregory. "The Operation of Grace." Editorial. *Image: A Journal of the Arts and Religion* 70 (Summer 2011): 3–4 Print.

An Editorial Published Online

"U.S. House: Members Are Not as Uncivil as They Seem." Editorial. *Nation Now. Los Angeles Times*, 28 Sept. 2011. Web. 29 Sept. 2011.

> **Note**: This editorial was published in a blog called *Nation Now* that is published by the *Los Angeles Times*.

Magazine Article

Perry, Alex. "Epidemic on the Run." *Time* 26 Sept. 2011: 46–49. Print.

Magazine Article from Online Database

Neuwirth, Robert. "Global Bazaar: Shantytowns, Favelas and Jhopadpattis Turn Out to Be Places of Surprising Innovation." *Scientific American* Sept. 2011: 56–63. *Academic Search Complete*. Web. 29 Sept. 2011.

Online Magazine Article

Leonard, Andrew. "Inside the Shadow Economy: The Growing Underwater Bazaar." *Salon*. Salon Media Group, 29 September 2011. Web. 29 September 2011.

> **Note**: The title of the magazine is followed by the publisher or sponsor of the site, a comma, and the date of publication. MLA uses this format because it does not consider online-only magazines to be periodicals. If no publisher is given, add n.p., and if no date is given, add n.d.

Interview

"Samantha Stosur, U.S. Open Champion." Interview by Cassandra Murnieks. *Time*. Time Inc., 23 Sept. 2011. Web. 29 Sept. 2011.

Online Speech

King, Jr., Martin Luther. "I Have a Dream." Speech. March on Washington for Jobs and Freedom. Lincoln Memorial, Washington, D.C. 28 Aug. 1963. *Americanrhetoric.com*. Michael E. Eidenmuller. n.d. Web. 29 Sept. 2011.

> **Note**: The citation includes n.d. (no date) because the date when the speech was posted on the site is not given.

Page on a Website

Coe, Jennifer. "How to Refinish a Dresser." *How To*. SheKnows LLC, 3 Aug. 2011. Web. 29 Sept. 2011.

> **Note**: The blog *How To* lists its publisher as SheKnows LLC. If the publisher were not given, then you would use n.p. (no publisher).

Image from a Website

Gogh, Vincent Van. *Cypresses*. 1889. Oil on canvas. *The Metropolitan Museum of Art*, New York. The Metropolitan Museum of Art. Web. 29 Sept. 2011.

Blog Posting

"Respect Your Audience." Web log post. *Writer's Block*. NIVA Inc., 2009. Web. 15 Sept. 2011.

> **Note**: The blog does not list an author for the posting, so the citation begins with the title.

Government Document

"El Chamizal Dispute: Compliance with Convention of the Chamizal." 1964. *U.S. Senate Hearing*. Cleofas Calleros Papers. University of Texas at El Paso Library Special Collections. 33–9. Print.

Government Document Online

Travis, William Barret. "Letter from the Alamo, 1836." Texas State Library & Archives Commission. Web. 15 Apr. 2011.

Government Document from Online Database

"United Nations Resolutions on Operation Desert Storm." Aug–Nov 1990. *Essential Documents in American History: 1492–Present.* 1–17 *Academic Search Premier.* Web. 8 May 2011.

A Film on DVD

The Lord of the Rings: The Return of the King. Dir. Peter Jackson. New Line, 2003. DVD-ROM.

Television Program

Martin, David. "The Pentagon's Ray Gun." *60 Minutes.* CBS. New York, New York, 2 Mar. 2008. Television.

MLA Parenthetical or (In-Text) Documentation

Parenthetical documentation refers to the process of citing sources within the text. Citing sources within the text is necessary for students to indicate when they are using the words, thoughts, or ideas that are not their own and borrowed from an outside source. Whether students use a direct quote, a paraphrase, or a summary of the information, they must properly provide credit to the original author(s) of that source. Using appropriate sources for support and documenting these sources accurately adds to the credibility and value of a student's essay. The following examples provide a guideline to proper parenthetical documentation.

Direct Quote (three lines or less)

"Scientists estimate that the rangewide population of the San Joaquin kit fox prior to 1930 was 8,000 . . . " (Conover 44).

Direct Quote (more than three lines)

Conover's 2001 study of the San Joaquin kit fox found the following:

> For the most part, in the "real" world, kit foxes escape their predators and the high temperatures of their desert environment by spending the day underground in a den. In Bakersfield, they follow suit. Kit foxes move every couple of weeks to a new den.

> Moving to different dens may be one reason why they have persisted; the constantly changing abodes provided new places to hide. (199)

Note: For a direct quote that is more than three lines, the passage should be indented 10 spaces and set as a block, as shown here.

Direct Quote When the Author Is Named in the Text

Hildebrand states that "generals of Alexander the Great brought news to Europe of vegetable wool which grew in tufts of trees in India" (144).

Information from Printed Source (but not a direct quote)

It is common to see an Osprey make its nest on an electric power pole (Askew 34).

Electronic Sources

Many electronic sources are not numbered with pages unless they are presented in a PDF file. If paragraphs are numbered, use numbers following the abbreviation, par. Most often the source will not have page, paragraph, section, or screen numbers. In this case, include no numbers in the parentheses. Instead, include the words that come first in the bibliographic citation.

(Coe, Jennifer. "How To")

APA Style

For APA style, you will want to refer to the *Publication Manual of the American Psychological Association* and the website provided by the American Psychological Association, http://www.apastyle.org, which offers free tutorials for APA style. The Purdue Owl also offers excellent information at http://owl.english.purdue.edu.

APA specifies that your essay should be typed in 12 pt. Times Roman type and double-spaced, with one-inch margins. In addition, APA style specifies the following general rules for formatting a paper or essay:

- Running heads—Create running heads for your page numbers, flush left, beginning on the title page. Also, on the title page, you should have a running head that reads like this:

Running head: Title of Your Paper

with the title actually being your paper title. On succeeding pages, the flush left header should include only the title of your paper, not the words "Running Head."

- Title page—In addition to the running heads, your title page will contain the title of the paper (one- or two-line title), followed by your name on the second line, and then the name of your college on the third line, all centered.

- Unless your instructor specifies otherwise, the second page of your paper is a 150- to 200-word abstract that summarizes the major aspects of your paper.

- Begin your essay on the third page, after the running head, which is the title of your paper and the centered title. Indent each paragraph and double-space.

- At the end of your paper, include your References, which lists your sources according to APA citation style.

Bibliographical Documentation

In APA style, this is called either the References or the Annotated Bibliography. The title, either References or Annotated Bibliography, should appear centered on the top margin of the last page of a researched essay. The References or Annotated Bibliography page should be double-spaced with no extra line spacing between entries. The first line of each entry begins at the margin, and all subsequent lines of a particular entry are indented on the left margin 5 spaces for a References Page. All entries should be in alphabetical order. The Annotated Bibliography is formatted like the References page with the addition of an annotation or description of the source in a paragraph following each citation.

> **Note**: APA suggests that when you are citing a source from the web or an online database you should give the DOI (Digital Object Identifier) of the source in the References List. If the DOI is not available, you can give the URL (web address) for the

text. APA does not require that you give the date you access a source on the Internet unless you have reason to believe that the text may change or disappear from the Internet. Also note that if you cite an entire website, simply include the website address in parentheses in the text with no entry in the References page. The following entries are typical citations for APA style. Examples are offered for both print, online, and database versions, when applicable.

Book

Egan, J. (2010). *A visit from the Goon Squad*. New York: Alfred A. Knopf.

Book with Two Authors

Friedman, T. L., & Mandelbaum, M. (2011). *That used to be us: how America fell behind in the world it invented and how we can come back*. New York: Farrar, Straus & Giroux.

Book with Multiple Editors

Mennuti, R.B., Freeman, A., & Christner, R.W. (Eds.). (2006). *Cognitive-behavioral interventions in educational settings: A handbook for practice*. New York: Routledge.

Book Online Edition

James, H. (1960). The American. Retrieved from http://eserver.org/fiction/novel.html

(If the book has a DOI, then give that instead of the URL).

Online Edition of Book

Macfie, A. L. (2000). *Orientalism: a reader*. New York: New York University Press. Retrieved September 26, 2011, from Google Books.

Scholarly Article in Print Journal

Thompson, J. (2011). Magic for a people trained in pragmatism: Kenneth Burke, and the early 9/11 Oratory of George W. Bush. *Rhetoric Review, 30* (4), 350–371.

Scholarly Article Found in Online Database

Angel, R. J. (2010). Immigrants and welfare: the impact of welfare reform on America's newcomers. *Contemporary Sociology: A Journal of Reviews*, 39(5), 568–569.

> **Note:** APA does not require that you list the database where you obtained an article unless the article would be difficult to locate. Instead, use the citation format you would if it were a print source.

Scholarly Article from Journal Published Online

Gustafsson, A. (2010). Beware the invisible. *Papers from the Institute of Archeology*, 20. Retrieved September 29, 2011, doi:10.5334/pia.343.

> **Note**: This citation includes a doi (digital object identifier), which provides a permanent way to locate an article, even if databases or websites change.

Book Review

Schneider, R. J. (2004). [Review of the book *Modern physics and ancient faith*]. *Anglican Theological Review, 86*, 506–07.

Book Review Published Online

Garner, D. (2011, September 27). An unearthed treasure that changed things [Review of *The Swerve: How the world became modern*]. *The New York Times*.

An Editorial

Wolfe, G. (2011). The operation of grace [Editorial]. *Image: A Journal of the Arts and Religion*, 70, 3–4.

An Editorial Published Online

U.S. House: Members are not as uncivil as they seem [Editorial]. (2011, September 28). *Nation Now*. Retrieved September 29, 2011, from http://latimesblogs.latimes.com/nationnow/2011/09/us-house-more-civil-than-the-mid-90s-but-trouble-could-lay-ahead-.html.

Note: This editorial was published in a blog called *Nation Now* that is published by the *Los Angeles Times*.

Magazine Article

Perry, A. (2011, September 26). Epidemic on the run. *Time*, 46–49.

Magazine Article from Online Database

Neuwirth, R. (2011, September). Global bazaar: Shantytowns, favelas and jhopadpattis turn out to be places of surprising innovation. *Scientific American*, 56–63.

Note: APA does not require you to cite the database where you obtained the article unless you think the article would be difficult to find.

Online Magazine Article

Leonard, A. (2011, September 29). A growing underworld bazaar. *Salon*. Retrieved September 29, 2011, from http://www.salon.com/news/inside_the_shadow_economy/?story=/politics/feature/2011/09/29/shadowintro.

Interview

Samantha Stosur, U.S. Open Champion [Interview by C. Murnieks]. (2011, September 23). In *Time*. Retrieved September 29, 2011, from http://www.time.com/time/arts/article/0,8599,2094349,00.html.

Online Speech

King, Jr., M. L. (1963, August 28). *I have a dream*. Speech presented at March on Washington for Jobs and Freedom at the Lincoln Memorial, Washington, D.C. Retrieved September 29, 2011.

Page on a Website

Coe, J. (2011, August 3). How to refinish a dresser. *How To*. Retrieved September 29, 2011.

Image from a Website

Van Gogh, V. (1889). *Cypresses* [Painting found in The Metropolitan Museum of Art, New York]. Retrieved September 29, 2011.

Blog Posting

Respect your audience [Web log post]. (2009). Retrieved September 15, 2011, from http://www.writersblock.ca/tips/monthtip/tipjan98.htm.

Government Document

El Chamizal dispute: Compliance with convention of the Chamizal. (1964). *U.S. Senate Hearing*. Cleofas Calleros Papers. University of Texas at El Paso Library Special Collections (#33–9).

Government Document Online

Travis, W. B. (2005). Letter from the Alamo, 1836. Retrieved from Texas State Library & Archives Commission, http//www.tslstate.tx.us/treasures/republic/Alamo/travis01.gov.

A Film or DVD

Coen, E. & Coen, J. (Producers and directors). (2007). *No country for old men* [Motion picture]. United States: Paramount Vantage.

Television Program

Martin, D. (Reporter). (2008, March 2). The Pentagon's ray gun [Television series episode]. In M. Walsh (Producer) *60 Minutes*. New York, New York: CBS.

APA Parenthetical or (In-Text) Documentation

Direct Quote (three lines or less)

"Scientists estimate that the rangewide population of the San Joaquin kit fox prior to 1930 was 8,000 . . . " (Conover, 2001, p. 44).

Direct Quote (more than three lines)

Conover's 2001 study of the San Joaquin kit fox found the following:

> For the most part, in the "real" world kit foxes escape their predators and the high temperatures of their desert environment by spending the day underground in a den. In Bakersfield, they follow suit. Kit foxes move every couple of weeks to a new den. Moving to different dens may be one reason why they have persisted; the constantly changing abodes provided new places to hide. (p. 199)

> **Note**: For a direct quote that exceeds three lines, indent the passage 5 spaces and set as a block, as shown here.

Direct Quote When the Author Is Named in the Text

Hildebrand (2004) stated that "generals of Alexander the Great brought news to Europe of vegetable wool which grew in tufts of trees in India" (p. 144).

Information from Printed Source (but not a direct quote)

It is common to see an Osprey make its nest on an electric power pole (Askew, year, p. 34).

Naming the Author of a Reference in Your Text, but Not Using a Direct Quote

Thompson (2002) maintained that . . .

In 2002, Thompson discovered . . .

Electronic or Other Sources Missing Author, Date, or Page Numbers

If your source provides section notations or paragraph numbers, indicate those. Use the paragraph ¶ symbol or the abbreviation para. and number.

(Bussell, 2000, ¶ 9)

If you include a quote from a text that has neither page numbers nor paragraph or section numbers, then simply give the author and the date:

(Bussell, 2000).

If there is no author, as in an editorial, then give part of the name of the text and the date:

("Respect your audience," 2009).

If there is no date, then use n.d. If you have no date, no page number, and no author, your in-text citation will look as follows:

("The future of space," n.d.)

Praxis Works Cited

"20 Years Later, San Ysidro McDonald's Massacre Remembered." Web log post. *North County Times.* Lee Enterprises Inc., 2004. Web. 17 July 2004.

"A $300 Idea that Is Priceless." *The Economist* 28 Apr. 2011. Print.

Adams, Scott. "Dilbert." Comic Strip. *United Feature Syndicate.* Print.

Aimes, Alexander. "Bringing History to Life with Primary Sources." Student essay. Used by permission.

"Choosing When to Give Credit." *The Purdue Online Writing Lab.* Purdue University. 9 June 2009. Web. 12 Nov. 2011.

Davey, Monica M. "Meet Tim Cook." 12 August 2007. Photograph. European Pressphoto Agency, Frankfurt.

Duggan, Paul. "In Sex-Crime Cases, Credibility a Thorny Issue." *The Washington Post* 1 July 2011. Print.

Echanove, Matias, and Rahul Srivastava. "Hands Off Our Houses." *The New York Times* 1 June 2011: A27. Print.

Fogarty, Mignon. *Grammar Girl: Quick and Dirty Tips for Better Writing.* New York: St. Martin's Press, 2008. Print.

Gleiberman, Owen. "Film Review: The Hangover." Rev. of *The Hangover*, by Dir. Todd Phillips. *EW.com* 2 June 2009. Web. 15 Nov. 2010.

Govindarajan, Vijay. "The $300 House: A Hands-On Lab for Reverse Innovation?" Web log post. *HBR Blog Network*, Harvard Business School Publishing, 26 Aug. 2010. Web. 22 Oct. 2011.

Govindarajan, Vijay. "The $300 House: A Hands-On Approach to a Wicked Problem." Web log post. *HBR Blog* Network, Harvard Business School Publishing, 7 June 2011. Web. 22 Oct. 2011.

Greene, Andy. "All Star Rockers Salute Buddy Holly." *Rolling Stone.* Straight Arrow Publishers, 7 July 2011. Print.

Jayawardhana, Ray. "Alien Life, Coming Slowly into View." *The New York Times.* 27 March 2011: WK10. Print.

Johnson, Judith. "The Truth about Writer's Block." *The Huffington Post.* HuffPost News, 25 July 2011. Web. 11 Nov. 2011.

King, Jr., Martin Luther. "I Have a Dream." Speech. March on Washington for Jobs and Freedom. Lincoln Memorial, Washington, D.C. 28 Aug. 1963. *Americanrhetoric.com.* Michael E. Eidenmuller. n.d. Web. 12 Nov. 2011.

Lincoln, Abraham. "Gettysburg Address." Speech. Dedication of the Soldiers' National Cemetary. Gettysburg, Pennsylvania 19 Nov. 1863. *Ourdocuments.gov.* n.d. Web. 15 Nov. 2011.

McArdle, Megan. "Anatomy of a Fake Quotation." *The Atlantic* 2 May 2011. Print.

McGrath, Charles. "The Lexicon." *NYTimes.com* 8 Sept. 2011. Web. 9 Sept. 2011.

Meyers, Justin. "How to Make a Kindle Cover from a Hollowed Out Hardback Book." *Wonder How To*. n.p., March 2011. Web. 12 Nov. 2011.

Neil, Dan. "BMW 1M: Miniature, Mighty and Miles of Fun." *The Wall Street Journal* 3 Sept. 2011. Print.

Obama, Barack. "Remarks by the President on Osama bin Laden." Speech. Address to the Nation that Osama bin Laden is dead. The White House, Washington, D.C. 1 May 2011. *The White House Blog*. Macon Phillips. 2 May 2011. Web. 29 Sept. 2011.

Rosen, Jeffrey. "The Web Means the End of Forgetting." *The New York Times* 25 July 2010: MM30. Print.

Schalet, Amy. "The Sleepover Question." *The New York Times* 23 July 2011: SR9. Print.

Scham, Sam. "Top Ten Distractions for Writers, or Any Job Really." *Yahoo*.com 12 Aug. 2008. Web. 12 Nov. 2011.

Shemtob, Zachary, and David Lat. "Executions Should Be Televised." *The New York Times* 31 July 2011: SR4. Print.

Skinner, E. Benjamin. "People for Sale." *Foreign Policy*. March–April 2008. Print.

Thornburgh, Nathan. "Violent Rhetoric and Arizona Politics." Editorial. *Time* 9 Jan. 2011. Print.

Wright, Don. "Obama Grammarian Cartoon." *International Herald Tribune* 20 January 2009. Print.

Wynn, Craig. "Take a Leap Into Writing." Student essay. Used by permission.

Young, Neil. "Let's Roll." *Are You Passionate?* Reprise Records, 2002. CD.

Zuniga, Janine. "San Ysidro Shooting Survivor Lives His Dream of Being a Cop." *San Diego Union-Tribune* 18 July 2004. Print.

-Part II-
The Carolina Rhetoric

CHAPTER 8

Reading Response

IMAGE 8.1
"I would not want to live in a world today in which a person or a community, because of color, because of religion, because of ethnic origin, or because of social conditions, would feel totally neglected or abandoned," Elie Wiesel writes in the piece that opens this chapter. "There must be someone who speaks to and for that group, every group."

This chapter is about problems and responses to those problems. Notice that we didn't say problems and solutions. Why? Because the latter implies a finality that rarely occurs in the maze-like world of public policy debate. In other words, few public problems are ever solved, once and for all, even if we are able to agree on what to do about them. Many of these readings are similar to the researched policy essay you will be asked to write in English 102 in that they clearly define a public problem, attempt to make readers care about that problem, and then propose a course of action for dealing with the problem. In this sense, they are meant to serve as models as well as sources for ideas.

> *Holocaust survivor and Nobel laureate Elie Wiesel is a teacher, a writer, and one of the world's most persistent and eloquent voices for peace and moral responsibility. His best-known book is* Night, *a memoir about his time in a Nazi death camp as a child, though he has written scores of other books, speeches, and essays. Richard D. Heffner is a professor of communications and public policy at Rutgers University and the producer and longtime host of the radio program* The Open Mind. *The text that follows is from the 2001 book* Conversations with Elie Wiesel.

BEFORE YOU READ
Write a paragraph or two in which you explain your thinking about the difference between information and knowledge and the responsibilities that each carries with it.

AM I MY BROTHER'S KEEPER?
Elie Wiesel and Richard D. Heffner

Elie, this is a question that perhaps is not understood too well by a good many people in our time. What does it mean to you?

> It is a question that Cain asked of God, having killed Abel: "Am I my brother's keeper?" And the answer, of course, is, we are all our brothers' keepers. Why? Either we see in each other brothers, or we live in a world of strangers. I believe that there are no strangers in God's creation. There are no strangers in a world that becomes smaller and smaller. Today I know right away when something happens, whatever happens, anywhere in the world. So there is no excuse for us not to be involved in these problems. A century ago, by the time the news of a war reached another place, the war was over. Now people die and the pictures of their dying are offered to you and to me while we are having dinner. Since I know, how can I not transform that knowledge into responsibility? So the key word is "responsibility." That means I must keep my brother.

Yet it seems that despite the fact that we live in an age of rapid, immediate communications, we know so little about what is happening to our brothers.

> We are careless. Somehow life has been cheapened in our own eyes. The sanctity of life, the sacred dimension of every minute of human existence, is gone. The main problem is that there are so many situations that demand our attention. There are so many tragedies that need our involvement. Where do you begin? We know *too* much. No, let me correct myself. We are *informed* about too many things. Whether information is transformed into knowledge is a different story, a different question.
>
> But we are in the world of communication. Nothing has caught the fantasy, the imagination, of the world these last years as communication has. So many

radio stations, so many television stations, so many publications, so many talk shows. It's always more and more information that is being fed. And I'm glad that these things are happening, because I think people should be informed.

However, let us say that on a given day a tragedy has taken place. For a day we are all glued to the television. Three days later, we are still glued. A week later, another tragedy occurs and then the first tragedy is overshadowed by the next one. I remember when I saw the hungry children of Biafra for the first time. I didn't sleep. I tried everything I could to address the problem—to write articles and call up people and organize activities to send food to those children. But if you had shown those pictures for a whole month, by the second month people would not have been moved by them. What happened to the information there? It is still stored, but yet we don't act upon it, because we are summoned by the current event.

There seems to be almost an inevitability about what you are describing, because extending and perfecting the means of communication is certainly a major thrust of our times.

I would like to be able to say to my students that there are so many things in the world that solicit your attention and your involvement that you can choose any one. I really don't mind where that particular event is taking place. But I would like my students to be fully involved in *some* event. Today, for instance, they will say, "I go to zone A, and then I go to zone B." But as long as zone A has not been covered fully, as long as it is a human problem, I don't think we can abandon it. All the areas must be covered. I would not want to live in a world today in which a person or a community, because of color, because of religion, because of ethnic origin, or because of social conditions, would feel totally neglected or abandoned. There must be someone who speaks to and for that group, every group.

Is there any question but that we have seen the faces of those who suffer and yet we are not moved sufficiently?

I plead your case: In 1945, all the newspapers and magazines in the United States showed the pictures of the concentration camps. And yet for another five years, displaced persons remained in those camps. How many were allowed to come to America? They were told, "Those who want to go to Palestine, good. All the others, come and we shall give you what you really need most—human warmth?" Furthermore, look at what happened in South Africa. Apartheid was a blasphemy. We saw these white racists killing. I remember images that moved me to anger—images of funeral processions. Whites had killed blacks because they were black. And then the whites disrupted the funerals, killing more black people. That is the limit of endurance, the limit of any tolerance. We should have protested louder. And yet we didn't.

We talk about a world that is, perhaps, too much with us, so much so that there is no time to focus. How do you help your students deal with that?

I mentioned Cain and Abel. Why did Cain kill Abel? It is not because he was jealous. According to the text that we read and comment upon, it was because Cain spoke to Abel, his younger brother, and he told him of his pain, of his abandonment, of his solitude—that God didn't want to accept his offering. In the Bible it's said, "And Cain spoke to Abel." And we don't even know whether Abel listened. There was no dialogue. So the first act, really, among brothers, was a lack of communication.

So what I would teach my students is communication. I believe in dialogue. I believe if people talk, and they talk sincerely, with the same respect that one owes to a close friend or to God, something will come out of that, something good. I would call it presence. I would like my students to be present whenever people need a human presence. I urge very little upon my students, but that is one thing I do. To people I love, I wish I could say, "I will suffer in your place." But I cannot. Nobody can. Nobody should. I can be present, though. And when you suffer, you need a presence.

When you say "communicate," you mean to accept communication, don't you?

To be able to give and to receive at the same time.

Does it seem to you that we're not listening to the world around us, that we're so much involved in our individual pursuits?

Absolutely. I think the noise around us has become deafening. People talk but nobody listens. People aren't afraid of that silence. Have you seen those youngsters and not-so-young people go around in the street with a Walkman on their ears? They don't want to hear anything. They want to hear only their own music. Which is the same music, by the way, that they heard yesterday. It's a kind of repetition which is deafening. People don't want to hear the world. The world is, I think, in need of being heard.

Elie, I find that as I get older and older still, I so often find that I want to shut things out, because I can't focus on what needs to be focused on if I'm listening to everything. That seems to me to be where we began, in a sense.

To me too, of course. So often I want to turn off everything and say, "Look, it's easier to talk about *Romeo and Juliet* than to talk about what's happening today anywhere in the world." Naturally. Because in that play, there is a text and there is a story. It's a story I can turn in any direction I want, really. You think that *Romeo and Juliet* is a story of love. It's a story of hate. So whatever subject I discuss, I can always turn it one way or another. It's familiar, graspable. I prefer to discuss Plato, naturally. But we must open our eyes, and—

I don't want to be a devil's advocate here. I understand the subjective need not to feel that I am my brother's keeper, the subjective need to shut out the pain—

Sure. You couldn't take it. There is a need to remember, and it may last only a day or a week at a time. We cannot remember all the time. That would be impossible;

Chapter 8 | **Reading Response**

we would be numb. If I were to remember all the time, I wouldn't be able to function. A person who is sensitive, always responding, always listening, always ready to receive someone else's pain ... how can one live? One must forget that we die; if not, we wouldn't live.

So what do we do? Can we both attend to our own needs and to the various needs of our family and friends and still extend the notion of "Am I my brother's keeper?" way beyond Abel to the far points of the world?

Perhaps we cannot, but we must try. Because we cannot, we must, even though Kant used to say, "We can, therefore we must." There is so much forgetfulness, so much indifference today, that we must **fight** it. We must fight for the sake of our own future. Is this the nature of human beings? Yes, it's part of our nature.

I know it all seems like too much—even in our own city, New York. There is so much hate and so much mistrust and distrust that you wonder what can reach these people who live together, who can live together, who after all must live together. Where do you begin? Now, I always feel very strongly about the person who needs me. I don't know who that person is, but if the person needs me, I somehow must think of that person more than about myself. Why? Because I see my own life in him or her. I remember there were times when I needed people, and they were not there. If there is a governing precept in my life, it is that: If somebody needs me, I must be there.

When I ask the question that we began with—"Am I my brother's keeper?"—I most often receive a blank stare. Obviously that stare comes from people for whom the concept is, if not anathema, at least terribly foreign. More so now, don't you think?

More so, because it involves us more deeply, because it goes further. If I say yes, then I have to do something about it. Then it really goes further than that: What does it mean? Who is my brother? It's a definition. Who is my brother? Is any person in the street my brother? Is a person in Somalia my brother? Is a person in Armenia my brother? Come on. If I say, "My brother," what do I mean? Have I seen them? Have I met them? So of course it could be a poetic expression, which means very little. But if you say that there are people in the world who need a brother, I will say, "Then I would like to be that brother." I don't always succeed, of course. I cannot. I am only an individual. I am alone, as you are alone. What can we do? We can be the brother to one person and then another person, to ten people, a hundred people in our whole life. Does it mean that we are brothers to everybody in the world? No, we cannot be. So even if we say that at least we can tell a story about a brother who is looking for a brother and finds one, I think that's quite enough.

Yes, but aren't we experiencing a new kind of isolationism today? "Please, I can't solve these problems. Don't burden me with them. I'm not my brother's keeper!"

Today brothers become strangers. How do you expect strangers to become brothers? People who live in the same country today are strangers to one another.

Take what's happened in Eastern Europe when the reactionary, exclusionary forces rule. They are neighbors, close to one another, but they see in each other a threat, a source of suspicion, a conqueror, not a brother. I think it's an historical phenomenon, which is worrisome.

Elie, what's the scriptural response to the question "Am I my brother's keeper?"

It is actually written as a dialogue, a scenario. Cain kills Abel. And God says to him, "Hi, good morning, how are you?" "All right," says Cain. Then God says, "By the way, where is your brother?" "I don't know," is the answer. "What do you mean, you don't know?" asks God. The answer: "I don't know. Am I my brother's keeper?" And then God says, "Come on, you know. I hear the voice of your brother's blood coming from the bowels of the earth. And you want to cheat me." The whole thing is a little bit silly. Does it mean that God didn't know where Abel was? God is playing a game. It's simply a story which I like to interpret as meaning that it is possible, unfortunately, throughout history, for two brothers to be brothers and yet to become the victim and/or the assassin of the other. However, I go one step further and I try to teach my students that we learn another lesson: Whoever kills, kills his brother.

Kills his brother or kills some part of himself?

It's possible, as I interpret it, that Cain and Abel were only one person. Cain killed Abel in Cain.

The Darwinian response to "Am I my brother's keeper?" is: "Of course not. If you pretend to be, you are interfering with natural selection." How do we build again upon the more ancient notion that indeed we are our brothers' keepers in many, many, ways?

But remember again, Cain was *not* his brother's keeper. He killed him.

But the question asked by God—

The question is good.

I know that's your specialty—questions.

I love questions, true. Because there is "quest" in "question." I love that. But today, I would like to put a face on words. When I see words, I see a face. When you speak about, let's say, "my brother's keeper," I see faces of people I knew or know, or people I've just seen this morning. Crossing the street, there is an old man with his hand outstretched. Now, am I his keeper?

Are you?

I must tell you that when I see that, I always feel strange. Because on the one hand, reason tells me that if I give him a dollar, he will go and buy alcohol. But then I say to myself, So what? Who am I to decide what he will do with the money that I give him? I cannot see an outstretched hand and not put something there. It's impossible. I know sometimes it's a weakness. I want to feel better, not to feel bad about it. But in fact I cannot.

You talked about communications before. If we don't "listen" by providing, presumably our brother will rise up and strike us down.

> Or we would strike him down. Who are we? Children of Cain or children of Abel?

What's your answer?

> You know, in my tradition, there is a marvelous way out. We are neither the children of Cain nor the children of Abel. There was a third son that Adam and Eve had afterward called Seth. And we are children of Seth. Which means you can be both.

Is that a cop-out?

> No, not really. I think we are always oscillating between the temptation for evil and an attraction to goodness. It's enough for me to close my eyes and remember what men are capable of doing, to become terribly, profoundly, totally pessimistic, because they haven't changed. But then again, I open my eyes and close them again and say, "It would be absurd not to absorb some images and turn them into good consciousness." And it's up to us to choose. We are free to choose.

Don't you think that in our country at this time we're less concerned with, have less compassion for, those who suffer?

> Absolutely. But it's really about what you are doing all your life. Can we really help more than the people around us? I go around the world, I travel, and whenever I hear about someone suffering, I try to go there and bear witness. That's my role, at least to bear witness. To say, "I've seen, I was there." Sometimes it inspires others to do what I am doing. More often than not, it doesn't.

If the moral imperative that you pose is one that seemingly is rejected in our time, why do you maintain this posture: "We must be caring, rather than careless?"

> Because I don't have a position of power. Maybe that's the reason. You and I can afford to speak on moral issues. We don't have to make a decision on them. I am sure that if you had someone facing you here who had power, a senator or a member of the Cabinet, he or she would say, "We cannot do this or that." Why? "Because so much money would be needed. We don't have the money. Housing would be required. We don't have the housing." So I can afford, really, only to pose questions, and I know that.

Yes, but I'm convinced that you raise questions because you know what the right moral answers are.

> That's true.

And you believe that by raising those questions, we will come to those answers.

> I would like to think that. But even if I knew that I would not succeed, I would still raise those questions.

Why?

> Otherwise, why am I here? I have the feeling, honestly, that my life is an offering. I could have died every minute between '44 and '45. So once I have received this gift, I must justify it. And the only way to justify life is by affirming the right to life of anyone who needs such affirmation.

Aren't you affirming, too, a conviction that something will be done in response to your question?

> Here and there one person might listen and do something. Another person might listen and not do something. But I prefer to think, that here and there, there are small miracles. And there are: a good student, a good reader, a friend. I think we spoke about it years ago: Once upon a time, I was convinced I could change the whole world. Now I'm satisfied with small measures of grace. If we could open the door of one jail and free one innocent person … if I could save one child from starvation, believe me, to me it would be worth as much as, if not more than, all the work that I am doing and all the recognition that I may get for it.

You've spoken about those who put people in the death camps and brought about their deaths directly. You also speak about others who stood around indifferently. Do you feel that that is increasingly a theme in our own times?

> Oh, more and more. I have the feeling that everything I do is a variation on the same theme. I'm simply trying to pull the alarm and say, "Don't be indifferent." Simply because I feel that indifference now is equal to evil. Evil, we know more or less what it is. But indifference to disease, indifference to famine, indifference to dictators, somehow it's here and we accept it. And I have always felt that the opposite of culture is not ignorance; it is indifference. And the opposite of morality is not immorality; it's again indifference. And we don't realize how indifferent we are simply because we cannot *not* be a little indifferent. We cannot think all the time of all the people who die. If, while I sit with you, I could see the children who are dying now while we talk, we wouldn't be able to talk, you and I. We would have to take a plane, go there and do something. We wouldn't be able to continue to try to be logical and rational.

Chapter 8 | Reading Response

You've said that if we ignore suffering, we become accomplices, as so many did during the Holocaust. Where is it written that we are not moral accomplices?

> But we are.

But what can you expect of us?

> Learning. After all, I don't compare situations. I don't compare any period to the period of the Second World War. But we have learned something. I have the feeling that sometimes it takes a generation for an event to awaken our awareness. But if now, so many years after that event, we are still behaving as though it did not occur, then what is the purpose of our work as teachers, as writers, as men and women who are concerned with one another's lives?

We have a tradition in this country of extending ourselves through our wealth, our material well-being. That tradition was set aside somewhat for some time. Do you think we will recapture it more fully?

> I hope so. I hope that there will be enough students and teachers and writers and poets and communicators to bring back certain values. If a father cannot feed his children, then his human rights are violated. We are such a wealthy society. I think of the United States and am overtaken by gratitude. This nation has gone to war twice in its history to fight for other people's freedoms. Then, after the wars, consider the economic help, the billions of dollars that we have given to those poor countries ravaged, destroyed by the enemy. And even now, what would the free world do without us? We have always been ready to help.
>
> So why not? It would show that we still have compassion. Now, those are nice words, I know. But what else do we have? We have words, and sometimes we try to act upon them.

■ WHAT?

1. Definitions play an important role in Wiesel's comments. What does he mean when he distinguishes between information and knowledge? How does he define responsibility? How does he link knowledge and responsibility? How does he define presence?
2. What role does listening play in Wiesel's world view?
3. How does Wiesel use references to God, religion, and religious texts in argument? Think especially about his audience and his ethos.
4. Weisel's comments about our responsibilities, and our desensitization to those responsibilities, implicate technology and the media. Technology allows us to know more than ever before about the sufferings of our "brothers and sisters" throughout the world, he argues, but it also can overwhelm us to the point that a kind of numbness sets in. How, according to Wiesel, can we deal with this conundrum?

■ WHAT ELSE? WHAT'S NEXT?

5. Wiesel sets the bar pretty high when he says that "we are all our brothers' keepers." How do you think this belief can play out in day-to-day life? As a starting point for your answer, research Wiesel's responses to specific events—wars, natural disasters, terrorist attacks—but also think about your responses.

■ WHO CARES?

6. Do you feel like Wiesel is speaking to you in his responses to Heffner's questions? Explain your answer.

Chapter 8 | **Reading Response**

> *George Saunders, who teaches creative writing at Syracuse University, has published several collections of stories, including* In Persuasion Nation, Pastoralia, *and* CivilWarLand in Bad Decline; *a children's story,* The Very Persistent Gappers of Frip; *and a collection of essays,* The Braindead Megaphone. *This speech, delivered to the Class of 2013 at Syracuse University, addresses "the need for kindness and all the things working against our actually achieving it," according to Joel Lovell, who published the speech at his* New York Times *blog titled "The 6th Floor".*

BEFORE YOU READ

Make a list of what Saunders calls the periods of "High Kindness" and "Low Kindness" you have experienced in your life—times when you were exceptionally kind or the beneficiary of such kindness, and other times when you were less than kind or treated unkindly.

ADVICE TO GRADUATES
George Saunders

Down through the ages, a traditional form has evolved for this type of speech, which is: Some old fart, his best years behind him, who, over the course of his life, has made a series of dreadful mistakes (that would be me), gives heartfelt advice to a group of shining, energetic young people, with all of their best years ahead of them (that would be you).

And I intend to respect that tradition.

Now, one useful thing you can do with an old person, in addition to borrowing money from them, or asking them to do one of their old-time "dances," so you can watch, while laughing, is ask: "Looking back, what do you regret?" And they'll tell you. Sometimes, as you know, they'll tell you even if you haven't asked. Sometimes, even when you've specifically requested they not tell you, they'll tell you.

So: What do I regret? Being poor from time to time? Not really. Working terrible jobs, like "knuckle-puller in a slaughterhouse?" (And don't even ASK what that entails.) No. I don't regret that. Skinny-dipping in a river in Sumatra, a little buzzed, and looking up and seeing like 300 monkeys sitting on a pipeline, pooping down into the river, the river in which I was swimming, with my mouth open, naked? And getting deathly ill afterwards, and staying sick for the next seven months? Not so much. Do I regret the occasional humiliation? Like once, playing hockey in front of a big crowd, including this girl I really liked, I somehow managed, while falling and emitting this weird whooping noise, to score on my own goalie, while also sending my stick flying into the crowd, nearly hitting that girl? No. I don't even regret that.

But here's something I do regret:

In seventh grade, this new kid joined our class. In the interest of confidentiality, her Convocation Speech name will be "ELLEN." ELLEN was small, shy. She wore these blue cat's-eye glasses that, at the time, only old ladies wore. When nervous, which was pretty much always, she had a habit of taking a strand of hair into her mouth and chewing on it.

So she came to our school and our neighborhood, and was mostly ignored, occasionally teased ("Your hair taste good?"—that sort of thing). I could see this hurt her. I still remember the way she'd look after such an insult: eyes cast down, a little gut-kicked, as if, having just been reminded of her place in things, she was trying, as much as possible, to disappear. After awhile she'd drift away, hair-strand still in her mouth. At home, I imagined, after school, her mother would say, you know: "How was your day, sweetie?" and she'd say, "Oh, fine." And her mother would say, "Making any friends?" and she'd go, "Sure, lots."

Sometimes I'd see her hanging around alone in her front yard, as if afraid to leave it.

And then—they moved. That was it. No tragedy, no big final hazing.

One day she was there, next day she wasn't.

End of story.

Now, why do I regret that? Why, forty-two years later, am I still thinking about it? Relative to most of the other kids, I was actually pretty nice to her. I never said an unkind word to her. In fact, I sometimes even (mildly) defended her.

But still. It bothers me. So here's something I know to be true, although it's a little corny, and I don't quite know what to do with it:

What I regret most in my life are failures of kindness.

Those moments when another human being was there, in front of me, suffering, and I responded … sensibly. Reservedly. Mildly.

Or, to look at it from the other end of the telescope: Who, in your life, do you remember most fondly, with the most undeniable feelings of warmth?

Those who were kindest to you, I bet.

It's a little facile, maybe, and certainly hard to implement, but I'd say, as a goal in life, you could do worse than: Try to be kinder.

Now, the million-dollar question: What's our problem? Why aren't we kinder?

Here's what I think:

Each of us is born with a series of built-in confusions that are probably somehow Darwinian. These are: (1) we're central to the universe (that is, our personal story is the main and most interesting story, the only story, really); (2) we're separate from the universe (there's US and then, out there, all that other junk—dogs and swing-sets, and the State of Nebraska and low-hanging clouds and, you know, other people), and (3) we're permanent (death is real, o.k., sure—for you, but not for me).

Now, we don't really believe these things—intellectually we know better—but we believe them viscerally, and live by them, and they cause us to prioritize our own needs over the needs of others, even though what we really want, in our hearts, is to be less selfish, more aware of what's actually happening in the present moment, more open, and more loving.

So, the second million-dollar question: How might we DO this? How might we become more loving, more open, less selfish, more present, less delusional, etc., etc?

Well, yes, good question.

Unfortunately, I only have three minutes left.

So let me just say this. There are ways. You already know that because, in your life, there have been High Kindness periods and Low Kindness periods, and you know what inclined you toward the former and away from the latter. Education is good; immersing

Chapter 8 | Reading Response

ourselves in a work of art: good; prayer is good; meditation's good; a frank talk with a dear friend; establishing ourselves in some kind of spiritual tradition—recognizing that there have been countless really smart people before us who have asked these same questions and left behind answers for us.

Because kindness, it turns out, is hard—it starts out all rainbows and puppy dogs, and expands to include ... well, everything.

One thing in our favor: Some of this "becoming kinder" happens naturally, with age. It might be a simple matter of attrition: As we get older, we come to see how useless it is to be selfish—how illogical, really. We come to love other people and are thereby counter-instructed in our own centrality. We get our butts kicked by real life, and people come to our defense, and help us, and we learn that we're not separate, and don't want to be. We see people near and dear to us dropping away, and are gradually convinced that maybe we too will drop away (someday, a long time from now). Most people, as they age, become less selfish and more loving. I think this is true. The great Syracuse poet, Hayden Carruth, said, in a poem written near the end of his life, that he was "mostly Love, now."

And so, a prediction, and my heartfelt wish for you: As you get older, your self will diminish and you will grow in love. YOU will gradually be replaced by LOVE. If you have kids, that will be a huge moment in your process of self-diminishment. You really won't care what happens to YOU, as long as they benefit. That's one reason your parents are so proud and happy today. One of their fondest dreams has come true: You have accomplished something difficult and tangible that has enlarged you as a person and will make your life better, from here on in, forever.

Congratulations, by the way.

When young, we're anxious—understandably—to find out if we've got what it takes. Can we succeed? Can we build a viable life for ourselves? But you—in particular you, of this generation—may have noticed a certain cyclical quality to ambition. You do well in high-school, in hopes of getting into a good college, so you can do well in the good college, in the hopes of getting a good job, so you can do well in the good job so you can. ...

And this is actually O.K. If we're going to become kinder, that process has to include taking ourselves seriously—as doers, as accomplishers, as dreamers. We have to do that, to be our best selves.

Still, accomplishment is unreliable. "Succeeding," whatever that might mean to you, is hard, and the need to do so constantly renews itself (success is like a mountain that keeps growing ahead of you as you hike it), and there's the very real danger that "succeeding" will take up your whole life, while the big questions go untended.

So, quick, end-of-speech advice: Since, according to me, your life is going to be a gradual process of becoming kinder and more loving: Hurry up. Speed it along. Start right now. There's a confusion in each of us, a sickness, really: selfishness. But there's also a cure. So be a good and proactive and even somewhat desperate patient on your own behalf—seek out the most efficacious anti-selfishness medicines, energetically, for the rest of your life.

Do all the other things, the ambitious things—travel, get rich, get famous, innovate, lead, fall in love, make and lose fortunes, swim naked in wild jungle rivers (after first having it tested for monkey poop)—but as you do, to the extent that you can, err in the direction of kindness. Do those things that incline you toward the big questions, and avoid the things that would reduce you and make you trivial. That luminous part of you that exists beyond personality—your soul, if you will—is as bright and shining as any that has ever been. Bright as Shakespeare's, bright as Gandhi's, bright as Mother Teresa's. Clear away everything that keeps you separate from this secret luminous place. Believe it exists, come to know it better, nurture it, share its fruits tirelessly.

And someday, in 80 years, when you're 100, and I'm 134, and we're both so kind and loving we're nearly unbearable, drop me a line, let me know how your life has been. I hope you will say: It has been so wonderful.

Congratulations, Class of 2013.

I wish you great happiness, all the luck in the world, and a beautiful summer.

■ WHAT?

1. Why is kindness so important to Saunders?
2. Why, according to Saunders, aren't we as kind as we might wish to be? And what does he say happens to make us kinder?

■ WHAT ELSE? WHAT'S NEXT?

3. How does the concept of kindness echo through the rest of the readings in this chapter? Select at least one other reading from the chapter and explain how kindness either explicitly or implicitly informs the argument that the author of that reading is trying to make.
4. Do you think kindness can be an institutional imperative? Should it be? Explain your response by using at least two examples.

■ WHO CARES?

5. Do you think Saunders' speech could change someone's life? If your answer is yes, explain what, rhetorically, gives the speech that power. If your answer is no, explain why the speech failed in that regard.

Chapter 8 | **Reading Response**

THE PROBLEM: America's Culture of Violence

> Todd May is Class of 1941 Memorial Professor of the Humanities at Clemson University, and the author of, most recently, Friendship in the Age of Economics. *He is currently working on a book on the philosophy of nonviolence. This essay was published on the* New York Times' *philosophy blog called The Stone on April 21, 2013, less than a week after a terror attack killed three people and injured more than 250 others during the Boston Marathon.*

BEFORE YOU READ

Early in his essay, Todd May writes, "Now is as good a time as any to reflect on our responses to the many recent horrors that seem to have engulfed us." You no doubt remember the Boston Marathon bombing and the Sandy Hook Elementary School shooting that he mentions, but you might not be familiar with the Constitution Project report on torture. Research the Constitution Project's Report on Detainee Treatment, write a brief summary of its conclusions, and explain why the report is important to May's argument.

IS AMERICAN NONVIOLENCE POSSIBLE?
Todd May

> The choice is not between violence and nonviolence but between nonviolence and nonexistence.
>
> — Martin Luther King Jr.

We are steeped in violence.

This past week was of course a searing reminder: Monday's bombing at the Boston Marathon and the ensuing manhunt that ended on Friday with the death of one suspect and the capture of another, his brother, dominated the news. But there were other troubling, if less traumatic reminders, too. On Tuesday, a 577-page report by the Constitution Project concluded that the United States had engaged in torture after the Sept. 11 attacks. On Wednesday, a turning point in the heated national debate on gun control was reached when the United States Senate dropped consideration of some minimal restrictions on the sale and distribution of guns. Looming above all this is the painful memory of the mass killing at Sandy Hook Elementary School.

Now is as good a time as any to reflect on our responses to the many recent horrors that seem to have engulfed us, and to consider whether we can hope to move from an ethos of violence to one nonviolence. Facing ourselves squarely at this difficult moment might provide a better lesson for the future than allowing ourselves to once again give in to blind fury.

We might begin by asking the question, Who are we now?

IMAGE 8.2
"Are we capable at this moment of taking on the mantle of nonviolence?" Todd May asks in his essay "Is American Nonviolence Possible?" How does he answer that question?

Clearly, we are a violent country. Our murder rate is three to five times that of most other industrialized countries. The massacres that regularly take place here are predictable in their occurrence, if not in their time and place. Moreover, and more telling, our response to violence is typically more violence. We display our might—or what is left of it—abroad in order to address perceived injustices or a threat to our interests. We still have not rid ourselves of the death penalty, a fact that fills those in other countries with disbelief. Many of us, in response to the mindless gun violence around us, prescribe more guns as the solution, as the Republicans sought to do during the gun debate. And we torture people. It is as though, in thinking that the world responds only to violence, we reveal ourselves rather than the world.

Why is this? How has the United States become so saturated in slaughter?

There are, of course, many reasons, but three stand out, one of which is deep and longstanding and the others of more recent vintage. The deep reason lies in our competitive individualism. Americans are proud of our individualism, and indeed it is not entirely a curse. To believe that one has a responsibility to create oneself rather than relying on others for sustenance has its virtues. No doubt many of the advances—scientific, technological and artistic—that have emerged from the United States have their roots in the striving of individuals whose belief in themselves bolstered their commitment to their work. However, the dark side of this individualism is a wariness of others and a rejection of the social solidarity characteristic of countries like Denmark, Sweden, New Zealand and, at least to some extent, France. We make it, if we do make it, but we do so alone. Our neighboring citizens are not so much our fellows as our competitors.

The second reason is the decline of our ability to control events in the world. We might date this decline from our military failure in Vietnam, or, if we prefer, more recently to the debacle in Iraq. In any event, it is clear that the United State cannot impose its will as it did during much of the 20th century. We live in a different world now, and this makes many of us insecure. We long for a world more cooperative with our wishes than the one we now live in. Our insecurity, in turn, reinforces our desire to control, which reinforces violence. If we cannot control events in the world, this must be a result not of our impotence or the complexity of the world's problems but of our unwillingness to "man up." And so we tell ourselves fairy tales about what would have happened if we had committed to victory in Vietnam or bombed one or another country back to the Stone Age.

The third reason is economic. The welfare state has been in decline for more than 30 years now. The embrace of classical liberalism or neoliberalism erodes social solidarity. Each of us is an investor, seeking the best return on our money, our energies, our relationships, indeed our lives. We no longer count on government, which is often perceived as the enemy. And we no longer have obligations to those with whom we share the country, or the planet. It is up to each of us to take our freedom and use it wisely. Those who do not are not unlucky or impoverished. They are simply imprudent.

Competitive individualism, insecurity, neoliberalism: the triad undergirding our penchant for violence. This, as much as anything else, is the current exceptionalism of America. Others are not our partners, nor even our colleagues. They are our competitors or our enemies. They are hardly to be recognized, much less embraced. They are to be vanquished.

What would the alternative, nonviolence, look like? And what does it require of us?

We must understand first that nonviolence is not passivity. It is instead creative activity. That activity takes place within particular limits. To put the point a bit simply, those limits are the recognition of others as fellow human beings, even when they are our adversaries. That recognition does not require that we acquiesce to the demands of others when we disagree. Rather, it requires that our action, even when it coerces the other (as boycotts, strikes, sit-ins and human blockades often do), does not aim to destroy that other in his or her humanity. It requires that we recognize others as fellow human beings, even when they are on the other side of the barricades.

This recognition limits what we can do, but at the same time it forces us to be inventive. No longer is it a matter of bringing superior firepower to bear. Now we must think more rigorously about how to respond, how to make our voices heard and our aims prevail. In a way it is like writing a Shakespearean sonnet, where the 14-line structure and iambic pentameter require thoughtful and creative work rather than immediate and overwhelming response.

To recognize someone's humanity is, in perhaps the most important way, to recognize him or her as an equal. Each of us, nonviolence teaches, carries our humanity within us. That humanity cannot always be appealed to. In some cases, as with the tragedy at Sandy Hook, it can even become nearly irrelevant. However, in all but the most extreme cases nonviolence summons us to recognize that humanity even when it cannot serve as the basis for negotiation or resolution. It demands that we who act do so with a firm gaze upon the face of the other. It demands the acknowledgment that we are all fragile beings, nexuses of hope and fear, children of some mother and perhaps parents to others: that is, no more and no less than fellow human beings in a world fraught with imponderables.

Can we do this? Are we capable at this moment of taking on the mantle of nonviolence?

The lessons are already there in our history. The civil rights movement is perhaps the most shining example of nonviolence in our human legacy. After 9/11, after Hurricane Katrina and Hurricane Sandy, and now, in the immediate on-the-ground responses to the Boston bombing, Americans pulled together with those they did not know in order to restore the web of our common existence. We are indeed violent, but we have shown flashes of nonviolence, that is to say moments where our competitive individualism, our insecurity, our desire for the highest return on our investment of time and money, has been trumped by the vividness of the likeness of others. Granted, these are only moments. They have not lasted. But they teach us that when it comes to nonviolent relations with others, we are not entirely bereft.

What would it require for these lessons to be become sedimented in our collective soul? There is much work to be done. We must begin to see our fellow human beings as precisely that. fellows. They need not be friends, but they must be counted as worthy of our respect, bearers of dignity in their own right. Those who struggle must no longer be seen as failures, but more often as unlucky, and perhaps worthy of our extending a hand. Those who come to our shores, whatever our policy toward them, must be seen as human beings seeking to stitch together a decent life rather than as mere parasites upon our riches. Those who are unhealthy must be seen as more than drains upon our taxes but instead as peers that, but for good fortune, might have been us.

None of this requires that we allow others to abdicate responsibility for their lives. Nor does it require that we refuse, when no other means are available, to defend ourselves with force. Instead it calls upon us to recognize that we, too, have a responsibility to more than our own security and contentment. It commands us to look to ourselves and at others before we start casting stones.

Would this end all senseless killing? No, it would not. Would it substitute for the limits on guns that are so urgently needed? Of course not. While the recently rejected limits on guns, however timid, might have provided a first public step toward the recognition of the requirements of our situation, our task would remain: to create a culture where violence is seen not as the first option but as the last, one that would allow us to gaze upon the breadth of space that lies between an unjust act and a violent response.

The philosopher Immanuel Kant said that the core of morality lay in treating others not simply as means but also as ends in themselves. Nonviolence teaches us nothing more than this. It is a simple lesson, if difficult to practice—especially so at a moment like this when our rage and grief are still raw. But it is a lesson that has become buried under our ideology and our circumstances. We need to learn it anew.

Learning this lesson will not bring back the life of the Martin Richard, Krystle Campbell or the other murdered victims in Boston. It will not return to health those who were injured on that day. It won't bring back Trayvon Martin or the children of Sandy Hook. But it will, perhaps, point the way toward a future where, instead of recalling yet more victims of violence in anger and with vows of retribution, we find ourselves with fewer victims to recall.

Chapter 8 | Reading Response

■ WHAT?

1. Explain the problem that May addresses in his essay. How does he make the problem relevant? Does he make you care about it? Explain your response.
2. What are the three causes of the problem that May is addressing? Write a sentence or two explaining each of these.
3. What course of action does May advocate for dealing with the problem that he addresses? What does he say needs to be done?

■ WHAT ELSE? WHAT'S NEXT?

4. Develop a definition of "nonviolence" that reflects the various ways May uses the term in his essay.
5. Look online and find other recent responses to America's violence problem. What do others say we should do to address this issue?

■ WHO CARES?

6. How did readers respond to May's argument? (You will find about 400 reader comments at the end of the essay online.) Are you persuaded by May's ideas? Explain why or why not.

THE PROBLEM: Tech Obsession

> *Alex Soojung-Kim Pang, according to his online biography, "studies people, technology and the worlds they create" and writes for a variety of national publications (this essay was published in August 2013 at* Salon.com). *His latest book, from which this piece is excerpted, is titled* The Distraction Addiction.

BEFORE YOU READ

Research the concept of "contemplative computing" online. How are people talking about this idea? Is anyone trying to enact the concept? Do you think you could unplug from the internet for an hour or two while you read this article and respond to the prompts at the end?

RECLAIM YOUR MIND FROM TECHNOLOGY
Alex Soojung-Kim Pang

On the western edge of the ancient city of Kyoto, Japan, on the slope of Mount Arashiyama (literally "Stormy Mountain"), stands the Iwatayama Monkey Park. The park has winding paths and fine views of Kyoto, but the main attraction is the tribe of about a hundred and forty macaques who live there. The monkeys of Iwatayama are famously gregarious, playful, and, occasionally, crafty. Like all members of the Macaca genus, they combine sociability and intelligence. They play with their kin, watch one another's young, learn new skills from one another, and even have distinctive group habits.

Some develop a mania for bathing, snowball-making, washing food, fishing, or using seawater as a seasoning. Iwatayama macaques are known for flossing and for playing with stones. This has led some scientists to argue that macaques have a culture, something we've traditionally thought of as distinctly human. They're also humanlike in their natural curiosity and cunning: one second, you're watching one do something cute, and the next second, his friends are making off with the bag of food you bought at the park's entrance.

They're like humans in one other way. For all their smarts, nothing keeps their attention for very long. The mountainside gives them a fantastic view of one of the world's most historic cities, but it doesn't impress them. They keep up a constant chatter, a running monologue of inconsequence. The macaques are living examples of the Buddhist concept of the monkey mind, one of my favorite metaphors for the everyday, undisciplined, jittery mind. As Tibetan Buddhist teacher Chögyam Trungpa explains, the monkey mind is crazy: it "leaps about and never stays in one place. It is completely restless."

The monkey mind's constant activity reflects a deep restlessness: monkeys can't sit still because their minds never stop. Likewise, most of the time, the human mind delivers up a constant stream of consciousness. Even in quiet moments, minds are prone to wandering. Add a constant buzz of electronics, the flash of a new message landing in your in-box, the ping of voicemail, and your mind is as manic as a monkey after a triple espresso.

Chapter 8 | Reading Response

The monkey mind is attracted to today's infinite and ever-changing buffet of information choices and devices. It thrives on overload, is drawn to shiny and blinky things, and doesn't distinguish between good and bad technologies or choices.

The concept of the monkey mind appears throughout Buddhist teachings—one small indicator of the fact that the mind and its relationship to the world have been studied deeply for thousands of years. Every religion has contemplative practices, calls to use silence and solitude to quiet the mind. In John Drury's introductory note to the Anglican Matins and Evensong, he exhorts worshippers "to be patient and relaxed enough to allow a long tradition to have its say" and "allow our own thoughts and feelings to become closer to us than life outside admits." Only then can one fully enter "the cool and ancient order of the services which gives a space and a frame, as well as cues, for reflections on our regrets and hopes and gratitudes." Catholic monastics treat meditation as preparing the mind to receive God's wisdom; the busy mind cannot hear the divine. In Buddhism, though, mental discipline is more an end in itself, rather than just a means to an end. The everyday mind is like churning water; learn to make it still, like the mirror-flat surface of a calm lake, Buddhists say, and its reflection will show you everything.

A few miles away from Iwatayama, a robotics laboratory at Kyoto University houses a robot controlled by another monkey, a rhesus named Idoya. Incredibly, Idoya isn't in Japan; she lives in North Carolina, in a neuroscience laboratory at Duke University, and her brain is connected to the robot via the Internet. The laboratory is run by neuroscientist Miguel Nicolelis, who, to make things just a bit more global, was born and educated in Brazil. Nicolelis has been studying the brain and how the brain changes as it learns executive functions; he's also developed a specialty in what scientists call brain-computer interface (BCi) technologies. Today you can buy primitive brain-wave readers that can control video games, and scientists are mapping brain functions and testing the brain's ability to control complex objects through BCis. Eventually, they hope, BCis will be used to route brain signals around damaged nerves, restoring body control to people with spinal-cord injuries or neurodegenerative disorders.

Idoya is the latest in a series of monkeys Nicolelis has worked with. Over the previous decade, he and his team demonstrated that a monkey with electrodes implanted in its brain could operate joysticks or robotic arms with its mind. Brain scans showed something remarkable: the neurons in the monkey's frontoparietal lobe—the section that controlled the animal's arms—fired when the monkey operated a robot arm. In other words, the monkey's brain stopped treating the robot arm as a tool, as something that it used but that was clearly separate from itself. The brain remapped its picture of the monkey's body to incorporate the robot arm. At the neural level, the distinction between the monkey's arms and the robot arm blurred. As far as the monkey's brain was concerned, monkey arms and robot arm were all part of the same body. Nicolelis and his colleagues in Japan implanted electrodes in the section of Idoya's brain that regulated walking; they then taught her to walk on a treadmill and studied how her brain's neurons fired as she walked. When she obeyed commands to speed up or slow down, she was rewarded with food. They then put a video monitor in front of the treadmill. Instead of showing The View or CNBC, however, the screen showed Idoya a live video feed of CB-1, the human-size robot in Kyoto. (CB-1 itself is a prodigy, equipped with four video cameras, gyroscopic stabilizers, and hands that can grasp objects. It can hold a bat, swing at baseballs, and learn manual tasks by imitating humans.)

When Idoya started walking while looking at the Kyoto robot on the monitor, the electrodes in her brain picked up the signals generated by the neurons that control locomotion. The signals were transmitted over the Internet to CB-1, which, following those same signals, stepped with her. The better she controlled the robot, the more treats she got. After an hour of Idoya walking and munching Cheerios, the scientists switched off her treadmill. Still focused on the screen, the monkey stopped walking—but she kept CB-1 on course, and for the next several minutes, she continued to make it walk. Once again, Nicolelis's team had shown that a primate brain could learn to directly control robots—and, in the process, that brain would start to treat the robot as an extension of its own body. Brain scans showed that Idoya's brain performed exactly the same way whether she was using her own flesh-and-fur legs or the electronic-and-plastic ones. As far as her brain was concerned, there was no longer any difference between the two.

Idoya and the monkeys of Iwatayama represent two different sides of the human mind, two contrasting relationships with information technology, and two futures. The chattering monkey is the untutored, undisciplined reactive mind, the mind that loves stimulation but doesn't hold a thought. The cyborg monkey represents a mind that isn't overwhelmed by technology, because it no longer experiences the technologies it uses as separate from itself, as requiring conscious effort and attention. A mix of deliberate practice, tinkering and experimenting, and neural rewiring have created an extended mind in which brain, body, and tools are entangled and work together effortlessly.

For too long, we've left the chattering monkey in charge of our technologies, and then we wonder why things go bad. We want to be like the cyborg monkey (albeit not as hairy and without the electrodes). We want that same capability to use complicated technologies without thinking about them, without experiencing them as burdens and distractions. We want our technologies to extend our minds and augment our abilities, not break up our minds.

Such control is within our reach. Rather than being forced into a state of perpetual distraction, with all the unhappiness and discontent such a state creates, we can approach information technologies in a way that is mindful and nearly effortless and that contributes to our ability to focus, be creative, and be happy.

It's an approach I call contemplative computing.

The term sounds oxymoronic. What could be less contemplative than today's technology-intensive environment? What could possibly be less conducive to a clear, meditative state than interactions with computers, cell phones, Facebook, and Twitter?

Contemplative computing isn't enabled by a technological breakthrough or scientific discovery. You don't buy it. You do it. It's based on a blend of new science and philosophy, some very old techniques for managing your attention and mind, and a lot of experience with how people use (or are used by) information technologies. It shows you how your mind and body interact with computers and how your attention and creativity are influenced by technology. It gives you the tools to redesign your relationships with devices and the Internet, to make them work better for you. It's a promise that you can construct a healthier, more balanced relationship with information technology.

To get a sense of how that can happen, let's look at what digital life is like for many of us—and then at what it could be like.

Chapter 8 | Reading Response

Imagine a Monday morning. You reach over to the nightstand, grab your smartphone, and switch off the alarm. You rub your eyes with one hand and open the phone's e-mail program with the other. You're not really awake; you do it automatically. You watch the icon spin as the phone connects to your e-mail server.

Nineteen messages in your in-box. Most are automatically generated newsletters, coupons, daily deals, or social-media updates; six are from colleagues up even earlier than you. You answer one, start another, and realize you're not sure what to say, so you flip over to the Web browser and check the news. You'll finish the message later. European bankers arguing over the terms of the latest bailout ... another NASDAQ flash crash ... roundup of blog posts commenting on the suicide of a cast member of a reality-TV show ... Suddenly you realize it's been twenty minutes. Gotta get up.

On the train to work, you look out the window and see a driver holding his phone and steering wheel in the same hand as he uses the phone to navigate, and another person steering with one hand and texting with the other. It makes driving while talking on your cell phone seem downright cautious. The police should give out more tickets to distracted drivers, you think, but as more cruisers are equipped with laptops, more police are getting distracted too.

Work turns out to be one of those days: these coworkers need numbers, those colleagues need your feedback; can you help with this problem, explain these options, talk to this person? It's one thing when there's lots of input directed toward one goal, but this multitasking is something else entirely. You're used to dealing with a constant stream of interruptions, but today, even your interruptions get interrupted. It's hard to say no, and it's hard to get back on task. After each interruption, you need a couple minutes to remember what you were doing, to gather your thoughts and start again.

By late afternoon, you're finally ready to print out your work. You hit print, and an error message appears: you need to update your printer driver. When you click okay, a minute goes by, and then there's another message: The latest driver isn't compatible with the old version of your operating system. You or your IT department need to update that too. Half an hour later, you restart your computer and finally print out your work. The experience is frustrating, but it's not at all unusual. According to a 2010 Harris interactive poll (sponsored by tech giant Intel), computer users spend an average of forty-three minutes every day—five hours a week, or eleven days a year—waiting for computers to start up, shut down, load software, open files, connect to the Internet.

On your way to meet a friend for a drink after work, you pass by people who are focused on their cell phones and have trouble tearing their attention away from their screens. You feel your phone buzzing in your pants pocket, but when you reach to answer it, there's no phone there. You check your other pockets, worried that you've lost it. The last time it happened, you felt like part of your brain had been shut off. But it's a false alarm: it's in your jacket.

During drinks, you and your friend each get the occasional text. Conversation flows and trails off as you each look at your phone, nearly finish a thought as you start typing. One message from an old ex is especially weird: it's all garbled, and it's the middle of the night in that time zone. "I've heard of that happening," your friend says, not looking up from her phone. "She's probably sleep-texting." Really? "It's like sleepwalking"— type-type-type—"except you"—type-type-type—"you know, text people."

It makes sense that some of us would start texting in our sleep. After all, information technologies and the Internet have thoroughly insinuated themselves into our everyday lives. Worldwide in 2010, according to the International Telecommunications Union, 640 million homes, housing 1.4 billion people, had at least one computer in the house; 525 million of those households and 900 million people were connected to the Internet. In the United States, about 90 million American households (80 percent of the U.S. total) had PCs and Internet access, and nearly half of those had two or more computers at home; 70 million had a game platform like Wii, PlayStation, or Xbox; 45 million households shared some 96 million smartphones; 7 million had tablet computers. Sixty percent of households had three Internet-enabled devices; a quarter had five.

Over the course of a typical day, you send and receive an average of 110 messages. You check your phone thirty-four times, visit Facebook five times, spend at least half an hour liking things and messaging friends. Like most people, your smartphone is more smart than phone: for every hour you spend talking to someone, you spend five hours surfing the Web, checking e-mail, texting, tweeting, and social networking. Nielsen and the Pew Research Center have found that Americans spend an average of 60 hours a month online, or 720 hours a year. That's the equivalent of 90 eight-hour days per year. Twenty of those days are spent in social networking sites, 38 viewing content on news sites, YouTube, blogs, and so on, and 32 doing e-mail. If maintaining your online life feels like a job, maybe that's because it is.

The increase in the number of digital devices we own and the amount of time we spend with them doesn't mark just a quantitative shift. It's a qualitative one too. Digital technologies and services are entwined with our everyday lives, whether we like it or not. As one Silicon Valley engineer put it, "Computers used to be part of my daily life. Now they're part of my daily minute." A veteran of Google and Facebook, even she feels the change; like many of us, she's aware of information technology playing a larger role in the casual and necessary things we do to maintain our homes and family and social lives. People who spend all day with computers used to be called hackers. Today, that's all of us.

Digital life can be great, but it also has a price. Keeping up with everything that everyone's sharing can become overwhelming—not just the sheer volume of material, but also the obligation to stay on top of it. These are your friends (or "friends"), and if you don't keep checking in on what they share, you might miss something. The little buzz from a new text message or e-mail is nice, but it's also disappointing when you hit refresh and nothing's there.

Sometimes the problem feels bigger. Having to stay focused when everyone wants your attention and the world—as well as your friends—throws a constant stream of distractions at you is hard. It's easy to get sidetracked at work by one thing, then another, and then have real trouble finishing the task you started. Recent surveys and field studies have found that a majority of workers have only three to fifteen minutes of uninterrupted working time in a day, and they spend at least an hour a day—five full weeks a year—dealing with distractions and then getting back on task. Each little thing you respond to feels urgent and gives you that sense of being busy, although you have the sneaking suspicion that all the interference and overlaps make you less productive. But when everyone looks perpetually busy, being overloaded is a badge of honor; working too hard is the new normal. Multitasking makes you feel like you're working even when it's counterproductive.

Organizations pay a price for their employees' chronic distraction. In a 1996 global survey of managers, two-thirds thought that constant distraction and information overload affected their quality of life. More recent studies estimated that in 2010, information overload cost U.S. businesses about 28 billion hours of wasted time and $1 trillion, and this was a year when the nation's gross domestic product was $14.6 trillion. The average worker spends half an hour a day troubleshooting devices or dealing with network problems. Over the course of a year, that's fifteen workdays lost to computer problems.

The constant buzz, the need to keep up with the never-ending rush of information, and the efforts to divide and spread one's time and attention ever thinner are starting to take their toll. It's getting harder to concentrate when you really need to. You reach the bottom of a page and can't always remember what you just read. Not only do you have trouble getting back to that task you started an hour ago, but you have to struggle to remember what that task was. You forget things on your mental shopping list. At home, sometimes you head to a room to do something and forget what you meant to do by the time you get there.

Now let's imagine a different Monday.

Monday morning. You reach over to the nightstand, grab your smartphone, and switch off the alarm. You don't check your mail or the online news just yet. After a few months of evaluating your mood when you check your mail first thing, you know you'll have a better day if you wait. Besides, you want just a little more time offline. Late Saturday night, after setting up your coffeemaker, you put your phone on silent and stowed the laptop and tablet in a desk drawer. Six days of the week you're connected; now you and some friends spend Sundays doing intensely analog things. Sometimes you head for hiking trails or cook; a couple of them have rediscovered knitting and painting. This Sunday was taken up by baking and reading. After a few hours at the market and some measuring and mixing, you had enough coffee cake to get you through the rest of the eight-hundred-page novel penned by the latest writer to burst from Brooklyn's literary scene.

When you do check your mail on your phone, you open the program, then put the phone screen-down on the table while you get coffee. It's a little act of resistance: I'll get to you, you're saying, when I choose. There's not much in your in-box, even after thirty-six hours away: you've turned off every notification, unsubscribed from all but the most useful newsletters, and have an aggressive set of filters that shunt nonessential mail out of your in-box before you see it.

At work, you need to be heads down, regardless of your colleagues' immediate needs. Yes, it's important to be responsive, but a frantic request isn't the same as a high-priority one, and you have work to do. So you switch off your phone and fire up a program that blocks your Internet access. For two hours, you've got no external distractions and no opportunity for self-distraction: e-mail, Facebook, Pinterest, Amazon, your colleagues—they all have to wait. if coworkers need something, they know where you are, but by making people invest a little effort to get your attention, you filter out the ones who want your time but don't really need it.

Now you have a single task, which you think of as kind of like a game: produce this many words, or write this much code, or get through this many accounts. After a while, your mind settles into a groove. You feel a bit like a jazz drummer: totally engaged but on beat, not a movement wasted.

After two hours, you switch everything back on. It's amazing how much you can get done when you focus on one goal. It often still involves multitasking, but it's the sort of multitasking that converges on a single point, not the kind that pulls you in different directions.

In the evening, you give yourself half an hour to see what your friends are doing on Facebook and Twitter. Occasionally, you pare down your list of friends. Your timeline is less cluttered, because you're more careful about whom you give your attention to. In real life, your circle of friends contracts and expands, and the amount of time you can devote to people is constantly changing. You write fewer messages and check in less frequently, and you try to post things that are well composed and thoughtful. Your aim isn't to get noticed or to accumulate lots of followers. Being online is about connecting meaningfully with people, about conserving your attention and respecting your friends' minds, not about killing time or engaging with media for its own sake. More generally, you try to use information technologies as mindfully as possible. You observe what you do, see how different practices affect your productivity and mood, then take up better practices and discard obsolete ones. But when things go well, you can turn off that mental camera, feel a device go from a tool to an extension of yourself, and become completely absorbed in the moment.

Relating to and using technologies this way—practicing contemplative computing, in other words—requires understanding and applying four principles.

The first is our relationships with information technologies are incredibly deep and express unique human capacities. It sometimes seems that technology threatens to reduce us all to scary, soulless man-machine cyborgs like the Borg and the terminator. But as Andy Clark, a philosopher and cognitive scientist at Edinburgh University, argues, we're really "natural-born cyborgs," forever seeking to extend our bodies and cognitive abilities through technology. In fact, it's best not to see the mind as something confined to the brain or even the body; it's useful to think of oneself as having an "extended mind" (to use Clark and David Chalmers's term) made up of overlapping parts that link brain, senses, body, and objects. Today's information technologies, I contend, cause us pain not because they're supplanting our normal cognitive abilities, which have always been flexible and mobile, but because they are often poorly designed and thoughtlessly used; they're like limbs that we can't bring under control.

The second big idea is the world has become a more distracting place—and there are solutions for bringing the extended mind back under control. Contemplative spaces are disappearing as quickly as tropical forests, work and life are becoming more frenetic, and modern technologies present challenges to one's ability to concentrate that may be unique. But humans have always had to deal with distraction and lack of focus—and for thousands of years, they have been cultivating techniques that effectively address them. In Asia, Buddhist and Tantric meditation, Japanese Zen, and Korean Son and yoga have all evolved to tame the distractible, chattering, undisciplined monkey mind. Neuroscientists, psychologists, and therapists have all observed that meditation practices can have a powerful effect on the brain; they can sharpen physical abilities and help deal with a host of psychological problems. Contemplative practices offer more than just a way to control the monkey mind or curb compulsive multitasking. They can also be adapted to allow you to regain control of your extended mind.

The third big idea is it's necessary to be contemplative about technology. You have to look closely at how you interact with information technologies and how you think about those interactions in order to understand how your extended mind develops and works. Our interactions with information technologies—with the outer reaches of our extended minds—are shaped by a variety of factors: the designs of devices and interfaces, the ways and contexts in which we use devices, and our mental models about the interactions and ourselves. Those models often carry unexamined assumptions about how information technologies work and how we work that are detrimental to us.

The fourth big idea is you can redesign your extended mind. Understanding the extended mind, having a better grasp of how to choose and use technology, and being familiar with contemplative practices let you find ways to be calmer and more purposeful when using information technology. It helps you be more powerful in exercising your extended mind and more deliberate in strengthening it. By understanding how all these pieces fit together, you can be contemplative through technology—and, in the process, regain your ability to deal with challenges, think deeply, and be creative.

Contemplative computing isn't just a philosophical argument. It's theory and practice. It's a thousand little methods, mindful habits informed by the four principles. Guidelines for checking e-mail in non-distracting ways. Rules for using Twitter and Facebook that encourage thoughtfulness and kindness. Ways of holding—literally holding—a smartphone so it commands less of your attention. Techniques for observing and experimenting with your technology practices. Methods for restoring your capacity to focus.

Information technologies are so pervasive, so much a part of work and home, so thoroughly embedded in modern life, it can be hard to know where to push back first. A good choice is to begin where many contemplative practices start. With breathing.

■ WHAT?

1. Explain the problem that Pang addresses in his essay. How does he make the problem relevant? Does he make you care about it? Explain your response.
2. What is the "monkey mind"? How does Pang use this concept in his explanation of contemplative computing?
3. "[P]racticing contemplative computing," Pang writes, "requires understanding and applying four principles." List and explain each of these four principles.

■ WHAT ELSE? WHAT'S NEXT?

4. Find other authors who address the ever-evolving ways that technology is permeating our lives. What benefits do they talk about? What problems do they foresee? Do you see any kind of consensus building about how we should deal with this issue?

■ WHO CARES?

5. In the middle of his article, as he outlines his two Monday morning scenarios, Pang begins writing in the second person. What is the rhetorical effect of this change in perspective? How does it feel to have the author speaking directly to you?

Chapter 8 | **Reading Response**

THE PROBLEM: Student Debt

Did you know that tuition at public and private colleges is rising faster than just about anything else in the United States—health care, energy, even housing? And that to cover these costs, many students and their families are going deep into debt? The two pieces that follow address this issue in very different ways: Matt Taibbi argues in a Rolling Stone *article published in August 2013 that the federal government has made it easier than ever to borrow money for higher education, which is saddling more and more students with crushing, life-altering debt. And in the report that follows Taibbi's, a student advocacy group in Oregon called Students for Educational Debt Reform proposes what it calls "a dramatically different approach" to the student debt problem, "one that demonstrates shared responsibility, a commitment to future generations, and a seriousness about the value of higher education."*

BEFORE YOU READ

Look online and/or use resources available on campus to answer the following questions: What percentage of USC students (or their families) take out student loans? What is the average amount of student loan debt held by USC graduates who took out loans? What kinds of loan and debt counseling does USC provide to students? Was this information difficult to find?

RIPPING OFF YOUNG AMERICA: THE COLLEGE-LOAN SCANDAL   Matt Taibbi

On May 31st, president Barack Obama strolled into the bright sunlight of the Rose Garden, covered from head to toe in the slime and ooze of the Benghazi and IRS scandals. In a Karl Rove-ian masterstroke, he simply pretended they weren't there and changed the subject.

The topic? Student loans. Unless Congress took action soon, he warned, the relatively low 3.4 percent interest rates on key federal student loans would double. Obama knew the Republicans would make a scene over extending the subsidized loan program, and that he could corner them into looking like obstructionist meanies out to snatch the lollipop of higher education from America's youth. "We cannot price the middle class or folks who are willing to work hard to get into the middle class," he said sternly, "out of a college education."

Flash-forward through a few months of brinkmanship and name-calling, and not only is nobody talking about the IRS anymore, but the Republicans and Democrats are snuggled in bed together on the student-loan thing, having hatched a quick-fix plan on July 31st to peg interest rates to Treasury rates, ensuring the rate for undergrads would only rise to 3.86 percent for the coming year.

Though this was just the thinnest of temporary solutions—Congressional Budget Office projections predicted interest rates on undergraduate loans under the new plan would still rise as high as 7.25 percent within five years, while graduate loans could reach an even more ridiculous 8.8 percent—the jobholders on Capitol Hill couldn't stop congratulating themselves for their "rare" "feat" of bipartisan cooperation. "This proves Washington can work," clucked House Republican Luke Messer of Indiana, in a typically autoerotic assessment of the work done by Beltway pols like himself who were now freed up for their August vacations.

Not only had the president succeeded in moving the goal posts on his spring scandals, he'd teamed up with the Republicans to perpetuate a long-standing deception about the education issue: that the student-loan controversy is now entirely about interest rates and/or access to school loans.

Obama had already set himself up as a great champion of student rights by taking on banks and greedy lenders like Sallie Mae. Three years earlier, he'd scored what at the time looked like a major victory over the Republicans with a transformative plan to revamp the student-loan industry. The 2010 bill mostly eliminated private banks and lenders from the federal student-loan business. Henceforth, the government would lend college money directly to students, with no middlemen taking a cut. The president insisted the plan would eliminate waste and promised to pass the savings along to students in the form of more college and university loans, including $36 billion in new Pell grants over 10 years for low-income students. Republican senator and former Secretary of Education Lamar Alexander bashed the move as "another Washington takeover."

The thing is, none of it—not last month's deal, not Obama's 2010 reforms—mattered that much. No doubt, seeing rates double permanently would genuinely have sucked for many students, so it was nice to avoid that. And yes, it was theoretically beneficial when Obama took banks and middlemen out of the federal student-loan game. But the dirty secret of American higher education is that student-loan interest rates are almost irrelevant. It's not the cost of the loan that's the problem, it's the principal—the appallingly high tuition costs that have been soaring at two to three times the rate of inflation, an irrational upward trajectory eerily reminiscent of skyrocketing housing prices in the years before 2008.

How is this happening? It's complicated. But throw off the mystery and what you'll uncover is a shameful and oppressive outrage that for years now has been systematically perpetrated against a generation of young adults. For this story, I interviewed people who developed crippling mental and physical conditions, who considered suicide, who had to give up hope of having children, who were forced to leave the country, or who even entered a life of crime because of their student debts.

They all take responsibility for their own mistakes. They know they didn't arrive at gorgeous campuses for four golden years of boozing, balling and bong hits by way of anybody's cattle car. But they're angry, too, and they should be. Because the underlying cause of all that later-life distress and heartache—the reason they carry such crushing, life-alteringly huge college debt—is that our university-tuition system really is exploitative and unfair, designed primarily to benefit two major actors.

First in line are the colleges and universities, and the contractors who build their extravagant athletic complexes, hotel-like dormitories and God knows what other campus embellishments. For these little regional economic empires, the federal student-loan system is essentially a massive and ongoing government subsidy, once funded mostly by emotionally vulnerable parents, but now increasingly paid for in the form of federally backed loans to a political constituency—low- and middle-income students—that has virtually no lobby in Washington.

Next up is the government itself. While it's not commonly discussed on the Hill, the government actually stands to make an enormous profit on the president's new federal student-loan system, an estimated $184 billion over 10 years, a boondoggle paid for by hyperinflated tuition costs and fueled by a government-sponsored predatory-lending program that makes even the most ruthless private credit-card company seem like a "Save the Panda" charity. Why is this happening? The answer lies in a sociopathic marriage of private-sector greed and government force that will make you shake your head in wonder at the way modern America sucks blood out of its young.

In the early 2000s, a thirtysomething scientist named Alan Collinge seemed to be going places. He had graduated from USC in 1999 with a degree in aerospace engineering and landed a research job at Caltech. Then he made a mistake: He asked for a raise, didn't get it, lost his job and soon found himself underemployed and with no way to repay the roughly $38,000 in loans he'd taken out to get his degree.

Collinge's creditor, Sallie Mae, which originally had been a quasi-public institution but, in the late Nineties, had begun transforming into a wholly private lender, didn't answer his requests for a forbearance or a restructuring. So in 2001, he went into default. Soon enough, his original $38,000 loan had ballooned to more than $100,000 in debt, thanks to fees, penalties and accrued interest. He had a job as a military contractor, but he lost it when his employer ran a credit check on him. His whole life was now about his student debt.

Collinge became so upset that, while sitting on a buddy's couch in Tacoma, Washington, one night in 2005 and nursing a bottle of Jack Daniel's, he swore that he'd see Sallie Mae on 60 Minutes if it was the last thing he did. In what has to be a first in the history of drunken bullshitting, it actually happened. "Lo and behold, I ended up being featured on 60 Minutes within about a year," he says. In 2006, he got to tell his debt story to Lesley Stahl for a piece on Sallie Mae's draconian lending tactics that, curiously enough, Sallie Mae itself refused to be interviewed for.

From that point forward, Collinge—who founded the website StudentLoanJustice. org—became what he calls "a complaint box for the industry." He heard thousands of horror stories from people like himself, and over the course of many years began to wonder more and more about one particular recurring theme, what he calls "the really significant thing—the sticker price." Why was college so expensive?

Tuition costs at public and private colleges were, are and have been rising faster than just about anything in American society—health care, energy, even housing. Between 1950 and 1970, sending a kid to a public university cost about four percent of an American family's annual income. Forty years later, in 2010, it accounted for 11 percent. Moody's released statistics showing tuition and fees rising 300 percent versus the Consumer Price Index between 1990 and 2011.

After the mortgage crash of 2008, for instance, many states pushed through deep cuts to their higher-education systems, but all that did was motivate schools to raise tuition prices and seek to recoup lost state subsidies in the form of more federal-loan money. The one thing they didn't do was cut costs. "College spending has been going up at the same time as prices have been going up," says Kevin Carey of the nonpartisan New America Foundation.

This is why the issue of student-loan interest rates pales in comparison with the larger problem of how anyone can repay such a huge debt—the average student now leaves school owing $27,000—by entering an economy sluggishly jogging uphill at a fraction of the speed of climbing education costs. "It's the unending, gratuitous, punitive increase in prices that is driving all of this," says Carey.

As Collinge worked to figure out the cause of those cost increases, he became focused on several highly disturbing, little-discussed quirks in the student-lending industry. For instance: A 2005 Wall Street Journal story by John Hechinger showed that the Department of Education was projecting it would actually make money on students who defaulted on loans, and would collect on average 100 percent of the principal, plus an additional 20 percent in fees and payments.

Hechinger's reporting would continue over the years to be borne out in official documents. In 2010, for instance, the Obama White House projected the default recovery rate for all forms of federal Stafford loans (one of the most common federally backed loans for undergraduates and graduates) to be above 122 percent. The most recent White House projection was slightly less aggressive, predicting a recovery rate of between 104 percent and 109 percent for Stafford loans.

When Rolling Stone reached out to the DOE to ask for an explanation of those numbers, we got no answer. In the past, however, the federal government has responded to such criticisms by insisting that it doesn't make a profit on defaults, arguing that the government incurs costs farming out negligent accounts to collectors, and also loses even more thanks to the opportunity cost of lost time. For instance, the government claimed its projected recovery rate for one type of defaulted Stafford loans in 2013 to be 109.8 percent, but after factoring in collection costs, that number drops to 95.7 percent. Factor in the additional cost of lost time, and the "net" projected recovery rate for these Stafford loans is 81.8 percent.

Still, those recovery numbers are extremely high, compared with, say, credit-card debt, where recovery rates of 15 percent are not uncommon. Whether the recovery rate is 110 percent or 80 percent, it seems doubtful that losses from defaults come close to impacting the government's bottom line, since the state continues to project massive earnings from its student-loan program. After the latest compromise, the 10-year revenue projection for the DOE's lending programs is $184,715,000,000, or $715 million higher than the old projection—underscoring the fact that the latest deal, while perhaps rescuing students this coming year from high rates, still expects to ding them hard down the road.

But the main question is, how is the idea that the government might make profits on defaulted loans even up for debate? The answer lies in the uniquely blood-draining legal framework in which federal student loans are issued. First of all, a high percentage of student borrowers enter into their loans having no idea that they're signing up for a relationship as unbreakable as herpes. Not only has Congress almost completely stripped students of their right to disgorge their debts through bankruptcy (amazing, when one considers that even gamblers can declare bankruptcy!), it has also restricted the students' ability to refinance loans. Even Truth in Lending Act requirements—which normally require lenders to fully disclose future costs to would-be customers—don't cover certain student loans. That student lenders can escape from such requirements is especially pernicious, given that their pool of borrowers are typically one step removed from being children, but the law goes further than that and tacitly permits lenders to deceive their teenage clients.

Not all student borrowers have access to the same information. A 2008 federal education law forced private lenders to disclose the Annual Percentage Rate (APR) to prospective borrowers; APR is a more complex number that often includes fees and other charges. But lenders of federally backed student loans do not have to make the same disclosures.

"Only a small minority of those who've been to college have been told very simple things, like what their interest rate was," says Collinge. "A lot of straight-up lies have been foisted on students."

Talk to any of the 38 million Americans who have outstanding student-loan debt, and he or she is likely to tell you a story about how a single moment in a financial-aid office at the age of 18 or 19—an age when most people can barely do a load of laundry without help—ended up ruining his or her life. "I was 19 years old," says 24-year-old Lyndsay Green, a graduate of the University of Alabama, in a typical story. "I didn't understand what was going on, but my mother was there. She had signed, and now it was my turn. So I did." Six years later, she says, "I am nearly $45,000 in debt. … If I had known what I was doing, I would never have gone to college."

"Nobody sits down and explains to you what it all means," says 24-year-old Andrew Geliebter, who took out loans to get what he calls "a degree in bullshit"; he entered a public-relations program at Temple University. His loan payments are now 50 percent of his gross income, leaving only about $100 a week for groceries for his family of four.

Another debtor, a 38-year-old attorney who suffered a pulmonary embolism and went into default as a result, is now more than $100,000 in debt. Bedridden and fully disabled, he accepts he will likely be in debt until his death. He asked that his name be withheld because he doesn't want to incur the wrath of the government by disclosing the awful punch line to his story: After he qualified for federal disability payments in 2009, the Department of Education quickly began garnishing $170 a month from his disability check.

"Student-loan debt collectors have power that would make a mobster envious" is how Sen. Elizabeth Warren put it. Collectors can garnish everything from wages to tax returns to Social Security payments to, yes, disability checks. Debtors can also be barred from the military, lose professional licenses and suffer other consequences no private lender could possibly throw at a borrower.

The upshot of all this is that the government can essentially lend without fear, because its strong-arm collection powers dictate that one way or another, the money will come back. Even a very high default rate may not dissuade the government from continuing to make mountains of credit available to naive young people.

"If the DOE had any skin in the game," says Collinge, "if they actually saw significant loss from defaulted loans, they would years ago have said, 'Whoa, we need to freeze lending,' or, 'We need to kick 100 schools out of the lending program.'"

Turning down the credit spigot would force schools to compete by bringing prices down. It would help to weed out crappy schools that hawked worthless "degrees in bullshit." It would also force prospective students to meet higher standards—not just anyone would get student loans, which is maybe the way it should be.

But that's not how it is. For one thing, the check on crappy schools and sleazy "diploma mill" institutions is essentially broken thanks to a corrupt dynamic similar to the way credit-rating agencies have failed in the finance world. Schools must be accredited institutions to receive tuition via federal student loans, but the accrediting agencies are nongovernmental captives of the education industry. "The government has outsourced its responsibilities for ensuring quality to weak, nonprofit organizations that are essentially owned and run by existing colleges," says Carey.

Fly-by-night, for-profit schools can be some of the most aggressive in lobbying for the raising of federal-loan limits. The reason is simple—some of them subsist almost entirely on federal loans. There's actually a law prohibiting these schools from having more than 90 percent of their tuition income come from federally backed loans. It would seem to amaze that any school would come even close to depending that much on taxpayers, but Carey notes with disdain that some schools use loopholes to go beyond the limit (for instance, loans to servicemen are technically issued through the Department of Defense, so they don't count toward the 90 percent figure).

Bottomless credit equals inflated prices equals more money for colleges and universities, more hidden taxes for the government to collect and, perhaps most important, a bigger and more dangerous debt bomb on the backs of the adult working population.

The stats on the latter are now undeniable. Having passed credit cards to became the largest pile of owed money in America outside of the real-estate market, outstanding student debt topped $1 trillion by the end of 2011. Last November, the New York Fed reported an amazing statistic: During just the third quarter of 2012, non-real-estate household debt rose nationally by 2.3 percent, or a staggering $62 billion. And an equally staggering $42 billion of that was student-loan debt.

The exploding-debt scenario is such a conspicuous problem that the Federal Advisory Council—a group of bankers who advise the Federal Reserve Board of Governors—has compared it to the mortgage crash, warning that "recent growth in student-loan debt...has parallels to the housing crisis." Agreeing with activists like Collinge, it cited a "significant growth of subsidized lending" as a major factor in the student-debt mess.

One final, eerie similarity to the mortgage crisis is that while analysts on both the left and the right agree that the ballooning student-debt mess can be blamed on too much easy credit, there is sharp disagreement about the reason for the existence of that easy credit. Many finance-sector analysts see the problem as being founded in ill-considered social engineering, an unrealistic desire to put as many kids into college as possible that mirrors the state's home-ownership goals that many conservatives still believe fueled the mortgage crisis. "These problems are the result of government officials pushing a social good—i.e., broader college attendance" is how libertarian writer Steven Greenhut put it.

Others, however, view the easy money as the massive subsidy for an education industry, which spent between $88 million and $110 million lobbying government in each of the past six years, and historically has spent recklessly no matter who happened to be footing the bill—parents, states, the federal government, young people, whomever.

Carey talks about how colleges spend a lot of energy on what he calls "gilding"—pouring money into superficial symbols of prestige, everything from new buildings to celebrity professors, as part of a "never-ending race for positional status."

"What you see is that spending on education hasn't really gone up all that much," he says. "It's spending on things like buildings and administration.... Lots and lots of people getting paid $200,000, $300,000 a year to do...something."

Once upon a time, when the economy was healthier, it was parents who paid for these excesses. "But eventually those people ran out of money," Carey says, "so they had to start borrowing."

If federal loan programs aren't being swallowed up by greedy schools for expensive and useless gilding, they're being manipulated by the federal government itself. The massive earnings the government gets on student-loan programs amount to a crude backdoor tax increase disguised by cynical legislators (who hesitate to ask constituents with more powerful lobbies to help cut the deficit) as an investment in America's youth.

"It's basically a $185 billion tax hike on middle-income and low-income citizens and their families," says Warren Gunnels, senior policy adviser for Vermont's Sen. Bernie Sanders, one of the few legislators critical of the recent congressional student-loan compromise.

Gunnels notes with irony that a few years ago, when Obama moved to eliminate private-lender middlemen from the servicing of federally backed loans, much hay was made out of the enormous profits private industry had long earned on the backs of students. The Congressional Budget Office issued a report estimating that Obama's program would save $86.8 billion over a 10-year period by eliminating private profits from the system. Obama said taxpayers were "paying banks a premium to act as middlemen," adding that it was a "premium we cannot afford."

The outrage over profits, however, was short-lived.

"It was wrong when banks were making an $86 billion profit on students, but somehow it's OK when the government makes a $185 billion profit on them," says Gunnels.

One of the reasons the money has kept flying out the government's door over the years is that data about student-loan-default rates has been carefully concealed from the public and from Congress. For years, when it reported statistics about student defaults, the DOE relied upon a preposterous arbitrary calculation called the "cohort default rate," which essentially measured the rate of default only within the first two years of graduation. In 2008, Congress passed a law forcing the DOE to switch to a theoretically more accurate three-year measurement, which it sent to Congress for the first time last year. Overnight, the picture looked a good bit grimmer. The 2009 number, based on the old two-year 2009 "cohort" rate, was 8.8 percent. When the new three-year number came out, the rate had jumped to 13.4 percent.

The Department of Education refuses to release more accurate default numbers. But outsiders think the DOE is lowballing it. The Chronicle of Higher Education charges that the government "vastly undercounts defaults." In 2010, it estimated that one in five had defaulted on their loans since 1995, that 31 percent of community-college students default and that an astonishing 40 percent of students attending for-profit schools end up defaulting. A report by the Inspector General of the Department of Education has come to similar conclusions about the reliability of the absurd and arbitrary "cohort" figure.

However high that default number really is, what's clear is that the state is still able to turn billions in profit on its lending, and expects to continue to do so for the next 10 years. The reason for that, again, lies in something everyone who has a student loan understands implicitly—the state and its collectors are not squeamish collecting the money they're owed. The government is in the pain business, and business is good.

"They called me at work, sometimes two to three times a day, doing all the stuff they aren't supposed to do: threats, et cetera," says 41-year-old Shawn FitzGerald, who owes $300 a month and says he expects to be paying off education loans into his sixties. "They told the receptionist at my job that I was in legal trouble. ..."

"Sallie Mae has started sending letters to my deceased mother," says Thomas Daggett of Chesterfield, Massachusetts, who left school in the Nineties and owes $35,000.

"I have been told I made the wrong decision going to college, as well as being told I was a failure, an idiot and a mooch," says Larissa, a young woman from a blue-collar town outside Chicago. "I've had ex-boyfriends that I never even lived with contacted by collection agents, my childhood friend's distant relatives contacted by them, as well as distant relatives of my own. ..."

"I try not to look at the balances because the prospect of paying them off with my shit salary is so goddamn depressing it makes me want to chug vodka until I pass out," says Robert Boardman, a proud but underemployed owner of a doctorate from the University of Michigan.

There's a particularly dark twist to the education story, which is tied to the collapse of the middle class and the overall shittening of our economic landscape: College degrees are actually considered to be more essential than ever. The New York Times did a story earlier this year declaring the college degree to be the "new high school diploma," describing it as essentially a minimum job requirement. They found an Atlanta law firm that requires even clerks, secretaries and runners to have four-year degrees and cited research that everyone from hygienists to cargo agents needs to have graduated from college to get hired.

You can look at this development in one of two ways. One way is to see a college degree as a better investment than ever, which was the conclusion of the Organization for Economic Cooperation and Development, which noted that the difference in earnings between the poorly and well-educated has risen in recent years with the worsening economy.

But another way to look at this new truth is that, because of the poor job market, young people may have less of a chance than ever to actually get a good job commensurate with their education. If they don't have the degree, then they have no chance at all. So if they even want a clerking job, they must dive face-first into the debt muck and take their chances that they won't end up watching the federal government take bites out of disability checks while their law degree gathers dust downstairs somewhere. So, yes, a college education is a great thing, and you probably need one now more than ever—the problem is that it may very well be mandatory, may have less of a chance of ever getting you a job, and you may still be paying for it on your deathbed no matter what.

There are powerful reasons for both the left and the right to be willfully blind to the root problem. Democrats—who, incidentally, receive at least twice as much money from the education lobby as Republicans—like to see the raging river of free-flowing student loans as a triumph of educational access. Any suggestion that saddling befuddled youngsters with tens of thousands of dollars in school debts is somehow harmful or counterproductive to society is often swiftly shot down by politicians or industry insiders as an anti-student position. The idea that limitless government credit might be at least enabling high education costs tends to be derisively described as the "Bennett hypothesis," since right-wing moralist and notorious gambler/dick/hypocrite Bill Bennett once touted the same idea.

"It is wrong to suggest that student aid is a cause for growing college costs, in any sector," David Warren, president of the National Association of Independent Colleges and Universities, wrote in The Washington Post last year, bemoaning the "re-emergence" of the Bennett theory. "To argue so is counterproductive to the goal of making higher education accessible and affordable."

Conservatives, meanwhile, with their usual "Fuck everybody who complains about anything unless it's us" mentality, tend to portray the student-loan "problem" as a bunch of spoiled, irresponsible losers who are simply whining about having to pay back money they borrowed with their eyes wide open. When Yale and Penn recently began suing students who were defaulting on their federal Perkins loans, a Cato Institute analyst named Neal McCluskey pretty much summed up the conservative take. "You could take a job at Subway or wherever to pay the bills," he said. "It seems like basic responsibility to me."

But conservatives most of all should hate the current system for any number of reasons—for being a massive hidden tax, for being a market-defying subsidy artificially keeping ineffective and poor-performing institutions in business, and for being an example of arbitrary government power seizing not just money borrowed plus interest, but billions in additional fees and penalties from ordinary people.

Progressives should hate the predatory tactics of lenders and the sleazy way universities rely upon loan-shark collection methods to keep themselves in fancy new waterfalls, swimming pools and tenure-track jobs.

But nobody hates it enough, except for the people actually trying to pay the bills with increasingly worthless degrees. Instead, the credit keeps flowing and the debt bubble keeps expanding, thanks to leaders like John Boehner (whose daughter reportedly works at Sallie Mae's student-collections firm, General Revenue Corp.) and Dianne Feinstein (who introduced legislation to increase limits on Pell grants while her husband was heavily invested in for-profit colleges).

In a way, America itself is violating the Truth in Lending Act. It's cheering millions of high school graduates toward college every year, feeding them into the debt grinder under the banner of increased opportunity, when full disclosure would require admitting that there isn't a hell of a lot waiting for them on the other side, where the middle class has nearly vanished and full employment is going the way of the dodo.

We're doing the worst thing people can do: lying to our young. Nobody, not even this president, who was swept to victory in large part by the raw enthusiasm of college kids, has the stones to tell the truth: that a lot of them will end up being pawns in a predatory con game designed to extract the equivalent of home-mortgage commitment from 17-year-olds dreaming of impossible careers as nautical archaeologists or orchestra conductors. One former law student I contacted for this story had a nervous breakdown while struggling to pay off six-figure debt. It wasn't until he tapped into one of the few growth industries open to young Americans that his outlook brightened. "I got my life back on track by working for a marijuana delivery service in Manhattan," he says. "I've had to compromise who I am...because I started down a path that I couldn't turn away from. Student loans aren't hope. They're despair."

THE PATH FORWARD   Students for Educational Debt Reform

Introduction

In a personal story posted on www.studentloanjustice.org, one distraught Oregonian stated, "I truly believed that if I got an education, I would be able to get out of poverty. With the student loan debt I will never get out of poverty." This person was the only individual from their family to graduate from high school, and desperately wanted to obtain a master's degree. Now, with a debt exceeding $80,000, they are struggling to avoid homelessness.

Another Oregonian, Gail, shared her son's heartbreaking battle with student loan debt, expressing that "… it was one of the factors that drove him to his suicide." Gail's son had student debt that exceeded $200,000, and he was unable to reconsolidate his debt, causing him to become increasingly hopeless. Gail continued to receive billing statements long after she had informed lenders that her son was deceased.

The National Context

Higher education has become an essential step to achieving the American Dream. Unfortunately, many young people are forced to finance their education using student loans. This problem is steadily growing; with $864 billion in federal loans and $150 billion in private loans, student debt in America now exceeds $1 trillion (Brown, 2012). Student debt increased nearly 50% in just four years from 2007 to 2011 (Desrochers, Lenihan and Wellman, 2010). This is an issue that poses serious consequences, both economic and social, that we cannot afford to overlook any longer.

The effects of student debt can be felt all over the country. According to data from 2011, two-thirds of students who earn four-year Bachelor's degrees are graduating with an average student loan debt of more than $25,000, and 1 in 10 borrowers now owe more than $54,000 in loans (Ellis, 2012). That is a tremendous financial burden to have on one's back upon completing college. Particularly now, with the economy in a very slow recovery from The Great Recession, it is very hard for college graduates to find a job that allows one to earn enough to live even modestly while paying back these loans. Many graduates are taking low-paying, part time jobs and far fewer are starting their own businesses.

Exacerbating Economic Trends in the National Economy

There are a number of national factors that have complicated the lives of those living with student debt. Low wages, high unemployment, high housing costs and lack of health insurance and effective family policy add to the challenge of skyrocketing student debt faced by young Americans today.

According to *The State of Young America* (Draut et al, 2011), the cost of higher education has tripled since 1980, yet it is ever more necessary to earn a decent living. Young men without a college degree today are earning 21% less than they did in 1980.

Chapter 8 | Reading Response

Earnings for African Americans are only 75% of the average wage for white high school graduates, and for Latinos, only 68%. Low wages are due in part to the decline in union membership, which has fallen steadily every year since 1983. Twenty percent of workers under the age of 35 were members of unions in 1980, as compared to 10% in 2010.

Young people have been the hardest hit by the Great Recession (Draut et al, 2011). The 2010 unemployment rate for ages 18–24 was 17.3% and 10.1% for those 25–34. The unemployment rate of Latinos aged 18–24 was 20%, and nearly 30% for African Americans. Of those under 25 who are working, 25% are underemployed, employed part-time, but would prefer to be working full-time.

According to *The State of Young America* (Draut et al, 2011) workers who are under or unemployed are less likely to have health insurance. During the last 10 years uninsurance levels have risen for those under 35. The number of employees with Employer sponsored health insurance fell 12.8% for workers under 24 and 8.5% for workers 25–34 between 2000 and 2010. According to Draut et al (2011), young people without health insurance are more likely to put off seeking medical care. Emergency room usage is highest among adults 19–29. And those with medical debt have 79% higher credit card debt than those without medical debt. Recent health care reforms under President Obama have helped reduce the rolls of the uninsured by allowing young people under 26 to stay on their parents' health plan but uninsured rates are still far higher for this age bracket than they were 20 years ago.

The cost of living has also negatively affected young Americans. As reported by Draut et al (2011), more than half of adults ages 18–24 live with their parents. More than 41% of those between 25 and 34 spend 30% of their income on housing. This is an increase between 1980 and 2010 of 21% for 25–34 year olds and 35% for those under 24. Lower wages and increased costs of living have led to greater reliance on credit. Credit card debt held by those under 35 is also on the rise, increasing 81% since 1989.

Factors in addition to these have made raising a family even harder for this generation. Childcare costs are higher than for any other generation. Center-based childcare fees for two children cost more than annual home rental payments for every US state. According to *The State of Young America*, only 11% of workers had paid family leave benefits in 2010, and only 5% of those earners in the bottom quarter. Only 35% in this bracket had paid sick leave. Without family protections these workers are at risk of losing their jobs if they are ill, or if they stay home to care for a sick family member. Lack of access to paid leave disproportionately affects women and was cited as the reason for 25% of working mothers quitting their job.

In summary, as shown by Draut et al (2011), workers with higher education are the only group whose wages have increased over the previous generation. While the cost of higher education has tripled from 1980 to 2010, a number of additional factors have put workers under 35 at an economic disadvantage as compared with their parents' generation, including low wages, high rates of underemployment and unemployment, high housing costs and lack of health insurance and strong family policies.

Individual and Social Returns to Investment in Higher Education

Economists understand investment in education—and the creation of "human capital"—to have been a substantial contributor to U.S. economic growth over the last century, and to be closely tied to other key sources of growth, "technological progress" and induced investment in physical capital to take advantage of new possibilities. The "returns" [on] education are both individual—especially in the form of higher earnings, better benefits and lower unemployment rates for more educated people—and social, accruing to the larger society.

Individual returns [on investment] in higher education are well known, and can be thought of as approximating the lifetime accumulation of earnings differentials between the high school and college educated, so markedly demonstrated on an annual basis in Table 1. Indeed, the "wage premium" being earned by college graduates relative to high school graduates in the U.S. is higher now than it has been for nearly 100 years, due in no small part to the decline in the earning power of the high school educated (Goldin and Katz, 2007). Of course, the individual benefits of higher education are not merely pecuniary, as people with college degrees report greater levels of life satisfaction and many people value learning for its own sake.

TABLE 1 EDUCATION AND EARNINGS: YEAR-ROUND, FULL-TIME WORKERS, MEDIAN EARNINGS, AGED 25 AND OVER, 2011

	< 9th Grade	H.S. Grad*	BA/BS
Latin Women	$19,200	$26,539	$42,418
Black Women	na	27,037	45,228
Asian Women	na	26,609	50,075
Non-Hisp. White Women	24,618	31,107	50,374
Latin Men	24,436	32,203	52,334
Black Men	25,449	35,482	51,131
Asian Men	25,029	32,336	62,039
Non-Hisp. White Men	30,570	42,434	70,149

Note: Latins are of all races; Blacks, Asians and Whites are that group only, not including mixed-race people
*Includes people with a GED
Source: CPS Annual Social and Economic Supplement. www.census.gov/hhes/www/cpstables/032012/perinc/pinc03_000.htm

The social returns […] are much less discussed, but sizable. Enrico Moretti (2005), the preeminent U.S. economist working on this topic, describes the social returns [on] investment in education as resulting from

 a. increased productivity and higher wages of people without higher education in labor markets that include a relatively high proportion of people with higher education,
 b. reductions in the social costs of crime when a higher proportion of men, especially, gain more education,
 c. the better health of more educated people, and improvements in the health of their children, which both increase well-being and reduce medical costs, and
 d. the greater likelihood of voting, and of being more informed as a voter of the college educated.

Increased investment in higher education is a particularly powerful form of short-term economic stimulus, as well as the foundation for long-run public returns, according to a report (Ash and Palacio, 2012) discussed this spring in the Massachusetts legislature (State House News Service, 2012). Locally, Joe Cortright (2010) of Impreza Economics has calculated the significant "fiscal returns" to the state of Oregon of increased educational attainment of the state's population, resulting from increased tax revenues and lower state expenditures on health care, incarceration and the social safety net.

However, the pace of gains in the educational level of the U.S. workforce has slowed markedly since 1980, coincident with the timing of the disinvestment in higher education by the federal and state governments, and the shift of the cost of higher education to students (Elwell, 2006).

The Genesis of the Student Debt Crisis

Increased Demand for Higher Education

The demand for a college degree has never been higher. Oregon's universities are already at record enrollment, and this level of enrollment is projected to keep growing (OUS Factbook 2010, p. 10). The state's community colleges reported similar growth in the 2009-2010 school year (Oregon Community Colleges, 2011). Students go through K-12 education being told that they need to go to college to be competitive and that they can't get a good job without a degree. A high school diploma simply will not suffice anymore. This oft-repeated advice is increasingly grounded in fact.

People are increasingly finding that not only do they need a Bachelor's degree, but a Master's as well. A 2011 report from The Commission on Pathways Through Graduate School and Into Careers (Wendler, C. et al, 2012) indicates a 22% growth in jobs requiring a Master's degree. As shown in Table 1, above, having a degree increases earning potential across for all demographic groups.

Demand for higher education exists beyond individual students' needs as well. Growing healthcare and technology industries require degrees and certifications, and employers are more and more frequently looking for employees with degrees. Oregon attracts tech companies like Google, Apple and Intel, as well as new green energy prospects, but in order to make full use of these opportunities, the state needs a better educated workforce. The job outlook for STEM (science, technology, engineering and mathematics) majors in particular is glowingly positive, and there seems to be a nationwide dearth of STEM workers (Schiavelli, 2011).

Despite needing the education, students are finding that they simply can't afford it. After hitting its highest recorded enrollment, Oregon's community college system lost almost 12,000 students in 2010–2011, which many attribute to financial difficulties.

Disinvestment in Public Higher Education by State Governments

In 2001, U.S. states provided public universities an average of $8,974 per full-time student, which dropped to an average of $6,380 in 2011. That's a 42% decrease in real funding, adjusting for inflation. As a consequence of this significant disinvestment in public higher education by state governments, tuition and fees have been rising fast. From 2001–2010, average tuition for public universities in the U.S. increased by 47%.

The shift of the costs of public higher education to students has set off an explosion of student borrowing. Private lenders have vastly expanded their presence in the student loan market, on increasingly harsh terms. Private student loans offer no government protections to stop creditors from taking advantage of the student, leaving students at the mercy of the creditors. Defaulted private loans alone currently total more than $8.1 billion, representing 850,000 individual loans.

Rise of Predatory For-Profit Schools and Lending Agencies

Students from across the nation increasingly rely on private banks and loan companies to obtain funding to accommodate the students' desire for a chance at higher education. For-profit colleges and lending agencies that prey on students lead to lower graduation rates and add to a growing student debt, all while making a large profit.

[Those who attend] for-profit schools will need highly-paid jobs to pay off their student loans, but are defaulting in large numbers. The U.S. Senate Health, Education, Labor and Pensions Committee produced a report titled *Emerging Risk? An Overview of Growth, Spending, Student Debt and Unanswered Questions in For-Profit Higher Education* (U.S. Senate, 2010) that examines how student loans are spread amongst the varied types of schools. In a span of 10 years from 1998 to 2008, enrollment into for-profit schools […] jumped noticeably from about 500,000 to 1,800,000. Comparatively, as student enrollment increased, student loans increased as well. The percentage of federal dollars (Pell grants and federal loans) that go to for-profit schools nearly doubled to about 23% between 1999 and 2008 (U.S. Senate, 2010).

However, the amount of their revenues that for-profit schools spend on education is low, ranging from 32–63% of their overall budgets, and that percentage is shrinking (U.S. Senate, 2010). The rest of the money goes towards administrative staff and marketing; marketing alone averaged 31% of the total budgets of for-profit schools.

According to a very recent Consumer Financial Protection Bureau report (2012), student loan debt reached the one trillion dollar mark in 2012 and is now the largest source of American consumer debt other than mortgages. In a study analyzing approximately 2,900 participants, common complaints by many graduates that borrowed from private lenders were a lack of clarity regarding how much money they owe, difficulty in contacting loan servicers or even determining who their servicer was. The result is that holders of student debt are too often caught off guard and ill informed come payment time (Consumer Financial Protection Bureau, 2012).

According to Alan Collinge (2009), student loan agencies like Sallie Mae prey on borrowers. Corporations like Sallie Mae have found that they can profit off defaults. Sallie Mae's tactics pay off; between 1995 and 2000 its stock price showed an enormous 1,700% increase (Collinge, 2009). Sallie Mae CEO Albert Lord bragged about the company's large profit growth in their 2003 annual report citing in part their collection of defaulted loans (Collinge, 2009).

Student loan agencies like Sallie Mae have little interest in the borrower paying off the loans on time. For these lenders, a defaulted loan is much more profitable as fees and interest rates simply increase; wages, unemployment payments, disability payments, and even Social Security payments can be garnished to meet these payments, and the borrower has no recourse in bankruptcy.

Federal Policy

Policy Evolution in Recent Years

Federal and state governments share responsibility for public higher education to some degree; the state government provides operating costs for institutions while the federal government provides financial aid through Pell grants, and a variety of federal direct loans. Some states have also chosen to offer aid programs (for example, Oregon's Opportunity Grant), but only after it is determined federal aid is insufficient to overcome the cost barriers. The primary source for financial aid is the federal government.

Many consider Pell Grants to be the basis of public higher education in this nation. For many students from lower socio-economic backgrounds, post-secondary education would not be accessible if the Pell Grant were not available. When the Pell Grant started in 1973 it covered the entire cost of tuition and then some. Today the maximum Pell Grant is about $5,000, while average tuition has skyrocketed to about $8,000. Pell Grant recipients are therefore twice as likely to need to take loans to complete their education as those that do not receive the Pell Grant.

In 2011, when Congress was facing yet another budget crisis, cutting funding for the Pell Grant along with doubling the interest rate on federal loans was an option for deficit reduction that was seriously pursued by some members of Congress. Fortunately students around the country rallied and saved the Pell Grant from serious cuts. This isn't the end of the fight to keep the Pell Grant; as we go into the next Congressional session, more cuts will be on the table and higher education is likely to be targeted.

Since the mid 1980s, the federal government has been drastically shifting financial aid from grants to loans. Currently Congress provides about six times as many loans as they do grants. There are two major drivers of this shift. Since the 1980s both federal and state governments have reduced taxes. At the Federal level, this shift was accompanied by increased expenditures that would make future cuts even more draconian. President Reagan led the way in reducing tax rates and increasing the military budget, and beginning the War on Drugs and every president since has followed his lead, sustaining or increasing military spending, sustaining the War on Drugs and cutting taxes. These policies have meant that something had to be cut.

When it comes to budgets the old adage "the squeaky wheel gets the oil" is especially true. Educational costs have been slowly shifted to students. The easiest explanation: low voting turnout, and little communication with representatives. Youth voter turnout has been low for decades but has started to rise, some of that rise attributable to increasing tuition and growing concern about high levels of student debt.

Over time the rules around discharging student debt in bankruptcy have changed drastically. Before 1984, only private student loans made by a "nonprofit institution of higher education" were exempted from discharge. The rationale was to protect the National Defense Student Loan Program, the predecessor to the Perkins Loan Program. Those loans were made by colleges using a revolving loan fund created using matching federal contributions. The Bankruptcy Amendments of 1984 made private student loans from all nonprofit lenders exempt from discharge. The Bankruptcy Abuse Prevention and Consumer

Protection Act of 2005 expanded this exemption to include all "qualified education loans," regardless of whether a nonprofit institution was involved in making the loans. This small change in wording, making it impossible to discharge even the most predatory private student loans in bankruptcy, has had a huge negative impact on students' lives.

While this is a direct example of how students have been hurt by policy, an indirect example comes from food stamp policies. An unemployed person that is not a student can receive food stamps, but if the person is a student they must work 20 or more hours to receive the food stamps. This change in food stamps policy is part of the idea that students are takers, that this generation demands everything but does not want to contribute anything.

The picture has changed fundamentally for students, [and is] well expressed in a conversation with a recently elected member of Congress from Oregon: "When I graduated law school, I had less debt than the current debt average for an undergraduate degree, and I could pay it off in a few short years with the job I got right after graduation."

Some people in Congress and our State Legislature think that students still can do this. Right now we can't, but our great hope is to restore this possibility to the next generation and to make post-secondary education accessible to all Oregonians.

Recommendations for Immediate Federal Action

Students for Educational Debt Reform is calling for reinstatement of consumer protections for student borrowers, and easing the burden of student debt by means of income based repayments. Of the current bills introduced in the U.S. House of Representatives, we recommend the passage of the Student Loan Simplification and Opportunity Act of 2011, the Private Student Loan Bankruptcy Fairness Act of 2011 and the Student Loan Forgiveness Act of 2012. The provisions of these bills would provide tremendous, immediate, positive impact for current and future student debt holders. […]

The Student Loan Simplification and Opportunity Act of 2011, introduced by Senator Sherrod Brown (D) of Ohio and cosponsored by Senator Al Franken (D) of Minnesota, would allow students to convert their existing loans obtained through the Federal Family Education Loan Program (FFELP) to Direct Loans. The conversion would not be mandatory; however those who choose to convert their FFELP loans to Direct Loans would maintain the terms and conditions of their original loan, and additionally receive up to two percent off of the loan's principal. By eliminating FFEL lender subsidies, Senator Brown's bill would save an estimated $1.8 billion over ten years, according to the Congressional Budget Office, which would then be reinvested into the Pell Grant program. According to the Congressional Budget Office, there are 21 million loans that would be eligible for conversion, with an estimated $887 million dollars of potential savings for borrowers. For these reasons, Students for Educational Debt Reform endorses the Student Loan Simplification and Opportunity Act of 2011.

The Private Student Loan Bankruptcy Fairness Act of 2011 introduced by Representative Steve Cohen (D) of Tennessee and the Fairness for Struggling Students Act of 2011 introduced by Senator Richard J. Durbin (D) of Illinois—one for the lower house, one for the upper house, respectively—have the same intent: to restore bankruptcy relief for students with private student loans. Currently, student loans are the only private loans that are non-dischargeable through bankruptcy. Non-dischargeability may make sense with respect to federal student loans that have limits to protect the student from borrowing too much. However, private student loans are *not* subject to limits, but *are* subject to non-dischargeability, incentivizing private lenders to encourage over-borrowing; in other words, the lender is protected, but the borrower is not. Furthermore, the absence of bankruptcy protections inflates the price of the commodity that the loan is used to purchase, in this case, tuition. For these reasons, Students for Educational Debt Reform endorses these two bills.

The Student Loan Forgiveness Act of 2012 introduced by Representative Hansen Clarke (D) of Michigan provides many provisions to help borrowers. First, Representative Clarke's act caps federal loan repayments at ten percent of a borrower's discretionary income and provides forgiveness after 120 payments, or 60 payments if a borrower is a qualifying public service employee, such as a teacher, nurse, or law enforcement official. The act caps the interest rate at 3.4% for federal student loans, which would prevent the interest rate for federal Stafford loans jumping as high as 6.8% in July 2013. Finally, the Student Loan Forgiveness Act allows for borrowers with private student loans to discharge them and obtain a Federal Consolidation Loan, with monthly payment protections, fixed interest rate, etc. For these reasons, Students for Educational Debt Reform endorses the Student Loan Forgiveness Act of 2012.

SEDR Proposal—Pay It Forward

Another Way

There is another way that college can be made more affordable to Oregon students on every rung of the economic ladder and simultaneously maximize the likelihood that a college degree delivers on the promise of a better life. The program is called Pay It Forward.

Pay It Forward is a program that will greatly reduce and possibly eliminate the necessity for students and families to take on debt in order to secure post-secondary education. It achieves this goal through the establishment of a fund that pays the tuition and fees of all students enrolled in Oregon public community colleges and universities. In return, students make a binding commitment to pay into this fund a small fixed percentage of their income for a set number of years after leaving school. Based on an analysis by Jason Gettel, Policy Analyst at the Oregon Center for Public Policy, graduates would pay 1.5% of their adjusted gross income for two-year Associate's degrees, 3% for Bachelor's degrees and 4% for Master's degrees. In other words, graduates would pay 0.75% of their annual adjusted gross income (AGI) for every full-time, academic year attended, based on the current level of tuition and fees in Oregon's public institutions. These payments would continue for 24 years. In this way, students who obtain a bachelor's degree would pay, on average, $39,653 into the Pay It Forward fund, which would include $7,417 on top of the value of tuition and fees that they would otherwise have paid.

Pay It Forward is not a loan program but a system of income-based payment that operates under an economic principle akin to Social Security. Unlike Social Security, costs are incurred prior to payment into the system so the challenge lies in startup funding. In time, however, as graduates pay into the program, the Pay It Forward Fund would build a large enough surplus to pay for future students' tuition and fees without any additional money provided by the State of Oregon. The program assumes, however, that the State appropriations for higher education do not sink below their current level, adjusted for inflation. In other words, this is a program of shared responsibility.

A Sustainable, Solvent Solution

Implementing the Pay It Forward program will require a substantial start up fund, but would lead to solvency for students and the Oregon higher educational system. At a payment rate of 3% of graduates' adjusted gross income for 24 years, the program will take in more than it spends in the 25th year, and begin to build a positive balance that will grow annually thereafter. [M]eanwhile, the gap would be filled either by bonding or philanthropic contributions or both. [...]

A more aggressive payment plan, requiring payment of 1.25% of adjusted gross income for 24 years (i.e. 5% for a four year degree) would allow the state to recuperate costs much more quickly. Annual payments into the Pay It Forward Fund are estimated by the Oregon Center for Public Policy to exceed costs in the 18th year of this program.

A Paradigm Shift

We anticipate that switching to a Pay It Forward program would encourage more people to enroll in Oregon's state universities and community colleges. Research shows that educational costs and fear of debt keeps many people out of college, particularly among low-income and minority populations. Young people in our primary and secondary schools will see their family members go to college and know that path is open to them. Many working adults who want to return to school but cannot afford to will have an opportunity to get the education and skills that lead to careers offering living wages. Parents can save for their children's education and have confidence that it will make a significant impact on college expenses.

Upon enactment of Pay It Forward earning a college degree with low or no debt will no longer be reserved only to the fortunate sons and daughters of the well-heeled. A clear path to higher education will be made available to everyone. In Oregon we will be able to say, "Here, the path to adulthood includes college education."

Potential Challenges and Solutions

Students for Educational Debt Reform propose that Pay It Forward should be the means by which the tuition and fees portion of college expense is paid by the entire full time, in-state student body within Oregon's community colleges and universities. However, several challenges may arise.

Part-time Students

Not everyone is a full-time student in pursuit of a degree. Students who are taking a handful of classes at the behest of an employer or for personal enjoyment could pay at the same rate as full-time students on a Pay It Forward system. Students must earn a minimum of 180 credits to obtain a bachelor's degree at Portland State, or 45 credits a year if they were to study full-time for 4 years—and then would owe 0.75% of their adjusted gross income to the Pay It Forward fund for that year. All students could pay 1/45th of 0.75% of their income per year for each credit in which they enroll. Or it may be more practical to allow students who are enrolled with course loads below some threshold to pay tuition and fees as they do currently.

Chapter 8 | Reading Response

The Potential to "Freeze" Oregon's Higher Educational System at its Current Level
The reputation of our state community colleges and universities depends on providing great facilities, gathering top faculty, and attracting high quality students. Unless the state is committed to increasing its contribution to public higher education, and moving back toward per-student funding levels available 20 years ago, the quality of Oregon's institutions of higher education is at risk of falling further behind those elsewhere.

Would Pay It Forward Incentivize Low Work Effort?
Objections may be raised based on the possibility that some graduates may choose to earn relatively little, thus minimizing their payments. However, few people go to college in preparation for future unemployment. Certainly, unwanted unemployment is its own punishment. One possibility is that people be expected to pay for 288 months (24 years), which ideally would be consecutive but could be deferred on the basis of unemployment. As clearly seen in Figure 7, the risk of unemployment is much greater for those with less education.

If graduates decide to take some time out of the labor force to care for young children, or elderly parents, society as a whole is benefited. And the analysis of the costs and structure of Pay It Forward are based on the earnings histories of college graduates on average in the U.S., which incorporate the fact that a certain proportion of people work part-time or not at all for periods of their lives, for a variety of reasons. If people return to full-time work after a period of part-time or no paid work, they are likely to earn more with more education.

We see no reason to expect that a payment as low as 3% of income would reduce work effort, given the much greater gains available in terms of promotion and career development to those who obtain more education and build on it in the work force, as is clear in Figure 1. [...]

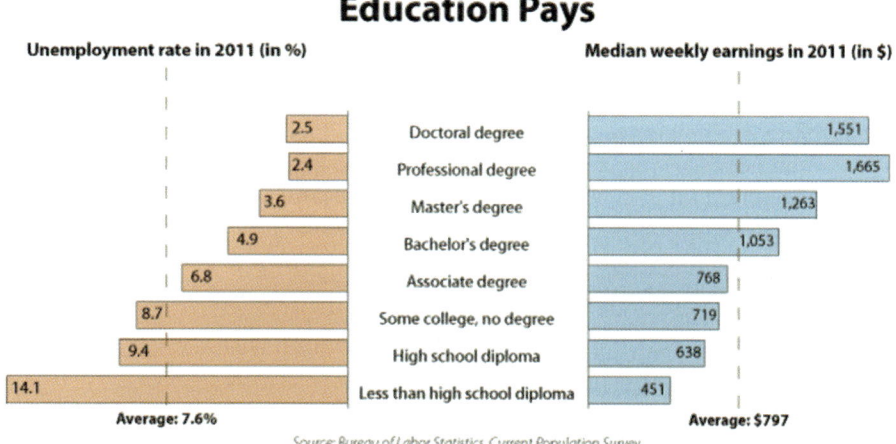

FIGURE 1 UNEMPLOYMENT AND WEEKLY EARNINGS BY EDUCATIONAL LEVEL, 2011

Is a shift to Pay It Forward too ambitious?
Perhaps the most obvious criticism likely to be leveled at Pay It Forward will be that it is simply too ambitious and the money cannot be made available. To this we say that the current level of student debt is at a crisis level and must be addressed.

Second, a Pay It Forward program could be launched on a partial or pilot basis that is less daunting than immediate statewide implementation. One possibility for partial implementation is through designation of pilot institutions, perhaps one university and one community college. If begun on a pilot basis, we anticipate that the Pay It Forward program will be highly sought after by the majority of Oregon's college students.

Conclusion

Student debt is a heavy burden on Oregon's younger generations and a drain on Oregon's economy. Students are being told by parents, guidance counselors, and the State's elected leaders that they need a college education to succeed in today's economy, and yet the State's commitment to funding higher education has been lagging for decades. Thus tuition keeps rising, leaving students with no choice but to borrow significant sums of money before they even know what their future employment prospects will be. The result is that students graduate from Oregon's public colleges and universities into an uncertain job market burdened with high levels of debt. This is not a recipe for success either for the individual or for our state.

There are a number of proposals being considered on a federal level that would alleviate the burden of already existing student debt, through Income Based Repayment plans, loan forgiveness after a certain number of years, a cap on interest rates, and reinstatement of the ability to discharge student debt in bankruptcy. All of these are worthy of support, and our elected leaders should work actively toward their passage.

But for future students, Students for Educational Debt Reform (SEDR) proposes a dramatically different approach, one that demonstrates shared responsibility, a commitment to future generations, and a seriousness about the value of higher education. Pay It Forward represents a social commitment, not a debt. The State will maintain at least its current level funding of higher education, and the students will contribute a small fixed percentage of their actual earnings for a set number of years after graduation.

We have the opportunity to make a dramatic impact on one of society's most urgent and pressing problems and to fulfill a promise to those students who work hard, graduate from high school and look to our public colleges and universities as a pathway to a better future. We owe them nothing less.

REFERENCES

Ash, Michael, and Shantel Palacio. 2012. "Economic Impact of Investment in Public Higher Education in Massachusetts: Short-Run Employment Stimulus, Long-Run Public Returns." <http://umassmsp.org/sites/umassmsp.org/files/Ash%20&%20Palacio%20Report%205-4-12.pdf>.

Brown, Meta. 2012. "Grading Student Loans" (Federal Reserve Bank of New York), March 5, 2012.

Chapter 8 | Reading Response

Collinge, Alan. 2009. *The Student Loan Scam: The Most Oppressive Debt in U.S. History, and How We Can Fight Back*. Boston, MA: Beacon.

Consumer Financial Protection Bureau. "Consumer Financial Protection Bureau Report Finds Private Student Loan Borrowers Face Roadblocks to Repayment." *Consumer Financial Protection Bureau*. Consumer Financial Protection Bureau, 16 Oct. 2012. Web. 25 Nov. 2012. <http://www.consumerfinance.gov/pressreleases/consumer-financial-protection-bureau-report-finds-private-student-loan-borrowers-face-roadblocks-to-repayment/>.

Cortright, Joe. 2010. "The Fiscal Return on Education: How Educational Attainment Drives Public Finance in Oregon." Report to OBC/E[3].

Desrochers, Donna M., Colleen M. Lenihan and Jane V. Wellman. 2010. *Trends In College Spending, 1998-2008: Where does the money come from? Where does it go? What does it buy?* Delta Project on Postsecondary Education Costs, Productivity and Accountability. <http://www.deltacostproject.org/.../Trends-in-College-Spending-98-08.pdf>.

Draut, Tamara, Robert Hiltonsmith, Catherine Ruetschlin, Aaron Smith, Rory O'Sullivan, and Jennifer Mishory. 2011. *The State of Young America: Economic Barriers to the American Dream—The DataBook*. Demos and The Young Invincibles. <http://www.demos.org/sites/default/files/publications/SOYA_TheDatabook_2.pdf>.

Ellis, Blake. "Private student loan debt reaches $150 billion." CNN. 20 Jul. 2012.

Elwell, Craig K. 2006. "Long-Term Growth of the U.S. Economy: Significance, Determinants, and Policy." *Congressional Research Service Report for Congress*, RL 32987. <http://fpc.state.gov/documents/organization/68789.pdf>

Goldin, Claudia and Lawrence Katz. 2007. "Long-run Changes in the Wage Structure: Narrowing, Widening, Polarizing." *Brookings Papers on Economic Activity*, Issue 2, pp 135–165. <http://www.brookings.edu/~/media/Projects/BPEA/Fall%202007/2007b_bpea_goldin.pdf>.

Institute of International Education. 2012. *Open Doors*. <http://www.iie.org/Research-and-Publications/Open-Doors/Data/International-Students/Leading-Places-of-Origin/2010-12>.

Moretti, Enrico J. 2005. "Social Returns to Human Capital." *NBER Reporter: Research Summary*. National Bureau of Economic Research: Boston, MA. <http://www.nber.org/reporter/spring05/moretti.html>.

Oregon Community Colleges (OCC). 2011. <http://www.oregon.gov/ccwd/pdf/Enrollment/2010-2011FinalAuditedTotalFTE.pdf>.

Oregon State Treasury. 2012. "The Opportunity Initiative." <http://buyoregonbonds.com/treasury/AboutTreasury/Pages/Opportunity-Initiative.aspx>.

Oregon University System (OUS) Factbook 2010. <http://www.ous.edu/factreport/factbook/2010>.

Oregon University System. 2011a. "A Report on Strategies to Meet Oregon's 40-40-20 Education Goals." <http://www.oregon.gov/gov/oeib/docs/nnousreport.pdf>.

Oregon University System. 2011b. "Legislative Brief Higher Education." <http://www.ous.edu/sites/default/files/dept/govrel/files/2011IB40-40-20.pdf>.

Oregon University System. 2011c. *OUS 2011 Facts and Figures*. <http://www.ous.edu/factreport/factbook/2011>.

Quinterno, John. 2012. *The Great Cost Shift: How Higher Education Cuts Undermine the Future Middle Class*. Demos. Apr. 3. <http://www.demos.org/publication/great-cost-shift-how-higher-education-cuts-undermine-future-middle-class>.

Sabatier, Julie. 2011. "Restructuring Higher Education." Oregon Public Broadcasting, Jan. 3. <http://www.opb.org/thinkoutloud/shows/restructuring-higher-education>.

Schiavelli, Mel. 2011. "STEM Jobs Outlook Strong, But Collaboration Needed to Fill Jobs." *U.S. News & World Report*, Nov. 3. <http://www.usnews.com/news/blogs/stem-education/2011/11/03/stem-jobs-outlook-strong-but-collaboration-needed-to-fill-jobs>.

State House News Service. 2012. "Study: Higher Ed Investment Returns Exceed Casinos, Tax Cuts." *Worcester Business Journal Online*. <http://www.wbjournal.com/apps/pbcs.dll/article?AID=/20120511/NEWS01/120519991/1040>.

U.S. Bureau of Labor Statistics. 2012. Employment Projections. <http://www.bls.gov/emp/ep_chart_001.htm>

U.S. Dept. of Education. 2012. "Many Non-U.S. Citizens Qualify for Student Aid." <http://studentaid.ed.gov/eligibility/non-us-citizens>.

U.S. Senate Health, Education, Labor and Pensions Committee. 2010. "Emerging Risk? An Overview of Growth, Spending, Student Debt and Unanswered Questions in For-Profit Higher Education." June 24. <http://www.help.senate.gov/newsroom/press/release/?id=2s870217-b476-492b-aace-d015d22bd13d&groups=Chair>.

Wendler, C., Bridgeman, B., Markle, R., Cline, F., Bell, N., McAllister, P., and Kent, J. 2012. *Pathways Through Graduate School and Into Careers*. Princeton, NJ: Educational Testing Service. <http://www.pathwaysreport.org/>.

■ WHAT?

1. In 150-200 words, using information from both articles, summarize the problem that Taibbi and Students for Educational Debt Reform write about, as well as the things they say could be done to address that problem.
2. Explain how the Pay It Forward plan would work.

■ WHAT ELSE? WHAT'S NEXT?

3. What does South Carolina's congressional delegation have to say about the student debt crisis? Do they have any proposals for addressing this problem?
4. The SEDR report was written in late 2012. What is the status of the Pay It Forward plan now? Is it in place in Oregon? Are any other states considering similar plans?

■ WHO CARES?

5. Compare the language and tone of these two pieces. What rhetorical considerations might lead these articles to take such different approaches to the same subject? Explain your response, pointing to specific examples from each text to support your claims.

Chapter 8 | Reading Response

THE PROBLEM: Citizen Apathy

> "Americans don't care," Howard Steven Friedman writes in "The United States of Apathy." Walter C. Parker, in "Teaching against Idiocy," puts it another way: "Idiocy [or self-centeredness] is the scourge of our time and place." Both authors are worried about the fate of America's participatory democracy. Friedman, who works for the United Nations and teaches at Columbia University, sums the problem up in a short piece published in 2010, while Parker, a professor at the University of Washington, argues in an essay published in Phi Delta Kappan in 2005 that schools are the key to reversing this trend.

BEFORE YOU READ

Search online for "Dave Meslin: The Antidote to Apathy" and watch the video sponsored by TED.com. How do Meslin's ideas compare with those presented by Friedman and Parker, in the two readings that follow?

THE UNITED STATES OF APATHY
Howard Steven Friedman

Americans don't care.

We don't care about voting unless we're convinced it's a "once in a lifetime" candidate.

We don't care about our outrageously expensive and often ineffective health care unless we are uninsured and sick.

We don't care that the economic crisis robbed us and future generations of "untraceable" billions unless we're unemployed.

We don't care that tax cuts for the wealthy are provided under the thin guise of "stimulating the economy" unless we are rich.

We don't care that the future of the middle class is being choked by declining support for education unless our children are illiterate.

We don't care about the homeless and the poor unless they are dying on our doorstep.

We don't care that our crime and incarceration rates are vastly higher than other wealthy countries unless we are a victim.

We don't care about America's weak internal security unless we get attacked.

We don't care about the lives lost in Iraq and Afghanistan unless we have a relative or close friend there.

We don't care about religion unless a mosque is being proposed near Ground Zero.

America is truly exceptional in its ability to not care, although Americans do care about some things.

We care about having vast amounts of inexpensive food.

We care about having low gas prices so we can drive our trucks and SUV's.

We care about shopping malls filled with unnecessary imported junk that advertisers convince us we "need" to have.

We care about having cheap labor to build our houses, mow our lawns, clean our apartments, wash our clothes and pick our fruit.

We care about Snooki, Britney, Brad, Angelina, Lebron and A-Rod.

We care about entertainment, not meaningful creation.

We care about comfort, not achieving greatness.

We care about style, not substance.

Our cares are local and ephemeral, not global or impactful.

Is our apathy is another example of American Exceptionalism or is apathy a global phenomenon?

IMAGE 8.3

"Our cares are local and ephemeral, not global or impactful," Howard Steven Friedman writes in "The United States of Apathy." Why do he and Walter C. Parker, in "Teaching Against Idiocy," see this as a problem?

Chapter 8 | Reading Response

TEACHING AGAINST IDIOCY Walter C. Parker

Idiocy is the scourge of our time and place. Idiocy was a problem for the ancient Greeks, too, for they coined the term. "Idiocy" in its original sense is not what it means to us today—stupid or mentally deficient. The recent meaning is deservedly and entirely out of usage by educators, but the original meaning needs to be revived as a conceptual tool for clarifying a pivotal social problem and for understanding the central goal of education.

Idiocy shares with idiom and idiosyncratic the root *idios*, which means private, separate, self-centered—selfish. "Idiotic" was in the Greek context a term of reproach. When a person's behavior became idiotic—concerned myopically with private things and unmindful of common things—then the person was believed to be like a rudderless ship, without consequence save for the danger it posed to others. This meaning of idiocy achieves its force when contrasted with *polites* (citizen) or public. Here we have a powerful opposition: the private individual versus the public citizen.

Schools in societies that are trying in various ways to be democracies, such as the United States, Mexico, and Canada, are obliged to develop public citizens. I argue here that schools are well positioned for the task, and I suggest how they can improve their efforts and achieve greater success.

■ Dodging Puberty

An idiot is one whose self-centeredness undermines his or her citizen identity, causing it to wither or never to take root in the first place. Private gain is the goal, and the community had better not get in the way. An idiot is suicidal in a certain way, definitely self-defeating, for the idiot does not know that privacy and individual autonomy are entirely dependent on the community. As Aristotle wrote, "Individuals are so many parts all equally depending on the whole which alone can bring self-sufficiency."[1] Idiots do not take part in public life; they do not have a public life. In this sense, idiots are immature in the most fundamental way. Their lives are out of balance, disoriented, untethered, and unrealized. Tragically, idiots have not yet met the challenge of "puberty," which is the transition to public life.

The former mayor of Missoula, Montana, Daniel Kemmis, writes of the idiocy/citizenship opposition, though he uses a different term, in his delightful meditation on democratic politics, *The Good City and the Good Life*:

> People who customarily refer to themselves as taxpayers are not even remotely related to democratic citizens. Yet this is precisely the word that now regularly holds the place which in a true democracy would be occupied by "citizens." Taxpayers bear a dual relationship to government, neither half of which has anything at all to do with democracy. Taxpayers pay tribute to the government, and they receive services from it. So does every subject of a totalitarian regime. What taxpayers do not do, and what people who call themselves taxpayers have long since stopped even imagining themselves doing, is governing. In a democracy, by the very meaning of the word, the people govern.[2]

Alexis de Tocqueville, writing 150 years before Mayor Kemmis, also described idiocy. All democratic peoples face a "dangerous passage" in their history, he wrote, when they "are carried away and lose all self-restraint at the sight of the new possessions they are about to obtain."[3] De Tocqueville's principal concern was that getting "carried away" causes citizens to lose the very freedom they are wanting so much to enjoy. "These people think they are following the principle of self-interest," he continues, "but the idea they entertain of that principle is a very crude one; and the more they look after what they call their own business, they neglect their chief business, which is to remain their own masters."

Just how do people remain their own masters? By maintaining the kind of community that secures their liberty. De Tocqueville's singular contribution to our understanding of idiocy and citizenship is the notion that idiots are idiotic precisely because they are indifferent to the conditions and contexts of their own freedom. They fail to grasp the interdependence of liberty and community, privacy and puberty.

Similarly, Jane Addams argued in 1909 that, if a woman was planning to "keep on with her old business of caring for her house and rearing her children," then it was necessary that she expand her consciousness to include "public affairs lying quite outside her immediate household." The individualistic consciousness was "no longer effective":

> Women who live in the country sweep their own dooryards and may either feed the refuse of the table to a flock of chickens or allow it innocently to decay in the open air and sunshine. In a crowded city quarter, however, if the street is not cleaned by the city authorities, no amount of private sweeping will keep the tenement free from grime; if the garbage is not properly collected and destroyed a tenement house mother may see her children sicken and die of diseases from which she alone is powerless to shield them, although her tenderness and devotion are unbounded.[4]

Addams concluded that for women to tend only to their "own" households was "idiotic," for to do only that would prevent women, ironically, from doing just that at all. One cannot maintain the familial nest without maintaining the public, shared space in which the familial nest is itself nested. "As society grows more complicated," she continued, "it is necessary that woman shall extend her sense of responsibility to many things outside of her own home if she would continue to preserve the home in its entirety."

Leaving aside individuals, families can be idiotic, too. The paradigm case is the Mafia—a family that looks inward intensely and solely. A thick moral code glues the insiders together, but in dealing with outsiders who are beyond the galaxy of one's obligations and duties, anything goes. There is no organized cooperation across families to tackle shared problems (health, education, welfare), no shared games, not even communication save the occasional "treaty." There are no bridging associations. Edward Banfield called this amoral familism and articulated its ethos as "maximize the material, short-run advantage of the nuclear family; assume that all others will do likewise."[5]

Amoral familism is certainly not restricted to the Mafia. Social scientists who examine popular culture find no shortage of it today. Perhaps the best contemporary example in the U.S., because it is both so mundane and so pervasive, is the SUV craze. Here, the suburban family provides for its own safety and self-esteem during such mobile tasks as commuting to work and running household errands, but it does so at others' expense. When criticized for putting other drivers and passengers at risk, for widening the ozone hole, and for squandering nonrenewable resources, SUV drivers often justify their behavior by speaking of their "rights" or the advantage of "sitting up higher than others." But they focus especially on "family safety."[6] It is my right to do whatever I choose, goes the argument, with the added and supposedly selfless rationalization of protecting "my" family from dangers real and imagined. To draw the line of obligation so close to the nuclear family is idiotic because it undermines, as Addams and De Tocqueville argued, that family's own safety along with everyone else's.

We could continue this survey of idiocy from its individual and familial forms to its large-scale enactments in ethnocentrism, racism, or the nationalistic variety, wherein a nation secures its own needs and wants in such a way that the world environment—every human's nest—is fouled, whether by conquest or by dumping poisons into the air and water. But let me instead conclude this section with a puzzle: How did idiocy grow from an exception in the Greek polis to a commonplace in contemporary, economically developed societies? Numerous social scientists have asked just this question. Karl Marx saw idiocy ("alienation," he called it) as the inevitable by-product of capitalism, wherein accumulating profit becomes an end in itself and nearly everything—from labor to love—is commodified toward that end. Robert Bellah and his colleagues located idiocy in a deeply pervasive culture of rugged individualism. John Kenneth Galbraith focused on the mass affluence of contemporary North American society, in which, for example, beef cattle are consumed at such a rate as to flood the environment with their waste, while farmland is misdirected to their feed. As Galbraith wrote, "Few people at the beginning of the nineteenth century needed an adman to tell them what they wanted."[7]

■ Schools and Idiocy

Capitalism, individualism, and affluence are a powerful brew. But what about the education sector of society? Do schools marshal their human and material resources to produce idiots or citizens? Does the school curriculum cultivate private vices or public virtues? Can schools tame the rugged individualism and amoral familism that undermine puberty and foul the common nest?

Actually, schools already educate for citizenship to some extent, and therein lies our hope. By identifying how schools accomplish at least some of this work now, educators can direct and fine-tune the effort. The wheel doesn't need to be reinvented; it is at hand and only needs to be rolled more intentionally, explicitly, and directly toward citizenship. There are three assumptions that propel this work and three keys to its success.

The first assumption is that democracy (rule by the people) is morally superior to autocracy (rule by one person), theocracy (rule by clerics), aristocracy (rule by a permanent upper class), plutocracy (rule by the rich), and the other alternatives, mainly because it better secures liberty, justice, and equality than the others do. Among actually attainable ways of living together and making decisions about common problems and projects, democracy (that is, a republic, a constitutional democracy) is, as Winston Churchill said, the worst form of government except for all the others.[8] Democracy is better than the alternatives because it aspires to and, to varying degrees, is held accountable for securing civil liberties, equality before the law, limited government, competitive elections, and solidarity around a common project (a civic unum) that exists alongside individual and cultural manyness (pluribus).

That democracies fall short of achieving these aspirations is obvious, and it is the chief impetus of social movements that seek to close the gap between the actual and the ideal. Thus Martin Luther King, Jr., demanded in his 1963 March on Washington address not an alternative to democracy but its fulfillment:

> We have come to our nation's capital to cash a check. When the architects of our republic wrote the magnificent words of the Constitution and the Declaration of Independence, they were signing a promissory note to which every American was to fall heir. ... We have come to cash this check, a check that will give us upon demand the riches of freedom and the security of justice.[9]

The purpose of the civil rights movement was not to alter the American Dream but to realize it. When a democracy excludes its own members for whatever reason (slavery, patriarchy, Jim Crow, etc.), it is "actively and purposefully false to its own vaunted principles," wrote Judith Shklar.[10] Here is democracy's built-in progressive impulse: to live up to itself.

The second assumption required if schools are to educate for citizenship is that there can be no democracy without democrats. Democratic ways of living together, with the people's differences intact and recognized, are not given by nature; they are created. And much of the creative work must be undertaken by engaged citizens who share some understanding of what it is they are trying to build together. Often, it is the unjustly treated members of a community who are democracy's vanguard, pushing it toward its principles. "We know through painful experience that freedom is never voluntarily given by the oppressor; it must be demanded by the oppressed," King wrote in the "Letter from Birmingham Jail."[11] The Framers of the U.S. Constitution may have been the birth parents of democracy, American style, but those who were excluded, then and now, became the adoptive, nurturing parents.

The third assumption is that engaged citizens do not materialize out of thin air. They do not naturally grasp such knotty principles as tolerance, impartial justice, the separation of church and state, the need for limits on majority power, or the difference between liberty and license. They are not born already capable of deliberating about public policy issues with other citizens whose beliefs and cultures they may abhor. These things are not, as the historical record makes all too clear, hard-wired into our genes. (Just ask any school principal!) Rather, they are social, moral, and intellectual achievements, and they are hard won. This third assumption makes clear the enormous importance of educating children for democracy.

On the foundation of these three assumptions, taken together, educators are justified in shaping curriculum and instruction toward the development of democratic citizens. In poll after poll, the American public makes clear its expectation that schools do precisely this.[12]

Chapter 8 | **Reading Response**

■ Schools Are Public Places

As it turns out, schools are ideal sites for democratic citizenship education. The main reason is that a school is not a private place, like our homes, but a public, civic place with a congregation of diverse students. Some schools are more diverse than others, of course, but all schools are diverse to some meaningful extent. Former kindergarten teacher Vivian Gussin Paley put it plainly: "The children I teach are just emerging from life's deep wells of private perspective: babyhood and family. Then, along comes school. It is the first real exposure to the public arena."[13] Boys and girls are both there. Jews, Protestants, Catholics, Muslims, Buddhists, and atheists are there together. There are African Americans, European Americans, Mexican Americans, Asian Americans, and many more. Immigrants from the world over are there in school.

This buzzing variety does not exist at home, or in churches, temples, or mosques either. It exists in public places where diverse people are thrown together, places where people who come from numerous private worlds and social positions congregate on common ground. These are places where multiple social perspectives and personal values are brought into face-to-face contact around matters that "are relevant to the problems of living together," as John Dewey put it.[14] Such matters are mutual, collective concerns, not mine or yours, but ours.

Compared to home life, schools are like village squares, cities, crossroads, meeting places, community centers, marketplaces. When aimed at democratic ends and supported by the proper democratic conditions, the interaction in schools can help children enter the social consciousness of puberty and develop the habits of thinking and caring necessary for public life. They can learn the tolerance, the respect, the sense of justice, and the knack for forging public policy with others whether one likes them or not. If the right social and psychological conditions are present and are mobilized, students might even give birth to critical consciousness. This is the kind of thinking that enables them to cut through conventional wisdom and see a better way.

This, then, is the great democratic potential of the public places we call schools. As Dewey observed, "The notion that the essentials of elementary education are the three R's mechanically treated, is based upon ignorance of the essentials needed for realization of democratic ideals."[15] Used well, schools can nurture these "essentials," which are the very qualities needed for the hard work of living together freely but cooperatively and with justice, equality, and dignity. Schools can do this because of the collective problems and the diversity contained within them. Problems and diversity are the essential assets for cultivating democratic citizens.

■ Three Keys

But how actually to accomplish this? Three actions are key.

First, increase the variety and frequency of interaction among students who are culturally, linguistically, and racially different from one another. Classrooms sometimes do this naturally. But if the school itself is homogeneous or if the school is diverse but curriculum tracks keep groups of students apart, then this first key will be all the more difficult to turn. It is not helping that resegregation has intensified in recent years, despite an increasingly diverse society. White students today are the most segregated from all other races in their schools.[16] (On this criterion, they may be at the greatest risk of idiocy.) Still, race is not the only source of diversity among students. School leaders must capitalize on whatever diversity is present among students—be it race, religion, language, gender, or social class—and increase the variety and frequency of opportunities for interaction.

Second, orchestrate these contacts so as to foster competent public talk—deliberation about common problems. In schools, this is talk about two kinds of problems: social and academic. Social problems arise inevitably from the friction of interaction itself (Dewey's "problems of living together"). Academic problems are at the core of each subject area.

Third, clarify the distinction between deliberation and blather and between open (i.e., inclusive) and closed (i.e., exclusive) deliberation. In other words, expect, teach, and model competent, inclusive deliberation.

I lay out the pedagogical details of teaching deliberation in elementary and secondary schools in *Teaching Democracy* (Teachers College Press, 2003). In it, I feature numerous successful programs already under way. Here are some highlights.

Deliberation exploits the assets afforded by schools: problems and a diverse student body. Deliberation is discussion aimed at making a decision across these differences about a problem that the participants face in common. The main action during a deliberation is weighing alternatives with others in order to decide on the best course of action. In schools, deliberation is not only a means of instruction (teaching with deliberation) but also a curricular goal (teaching for deliberation), because it generates a particular kind of social good: a democratic community, a public culture. The norms of this culture include, first, engagement in cooperative problem solving. This is in contrast to avoiding engagement either by being idiotically consumed by private affairs or by electing others to do the deliberation and then relapsing into idiocy for the four years between elections. Other norms include listening as well as talking, perspective taking, arguing with evidence, sharing resources, and forging a decision together rather than merely advocating positions taken before the deliberation begins.

Deliberation is ideally done with persons who are more or less different from one another; for pedagogical purposes, therefore, deliberative groups—schools and classrooms—should be as diverse as possible. Teachers and administrators can expand the opportunities for interaction by increasing the number and kind of mixed student groups. These groups should be temporary, because separating students permanently, for whatever reason, undermines both individual and civic health. What the participants have in common in these mixed groups is not culture, race, or opinion but the problems they face together and must work out together in ways that strike everyone as fair.[17]

■ The Social Curriculum

Probably the best-known example of young children deliberating their shared social problems comes from the kindergarten classroom of Vivian Gussin Paley. In a number of books, Paley has captured the look and feel of actual classroom-based deliberation, and she shows how entirely possible it is to do such work in everyday classroom settings, even with the youngest children. In *You Can't Say You Can't Play*, she tells how she facilitated a lengthy deliberation about whether to establish the classroom rule of the book's title. She

Chapter 8 | Reading Response

engages the kindergartners in an ongoing discussion about the desirability and practicability of having such a rule. She tells them, "I just can't get the question out of my mind. Is it fair for children in school to keep another child out of play? After all, this classroom belongs to all of us. It is not a private place, like our homes."[18] The children find this a compelling question, and they have lots to say. Paley brings them to the discussion circle again and again to weigh the alternatives. "Will the rule work? Is it fair?" she asks. Memories and opinions flow. "If you cry, people should let you in," Ben says. "But then what's the whole point of playing?" Lisa complains.

Paley sometimes interviews older children to ascertain their views and brings them back to her kindergartners. Trading classes with a second-grade teacher, Paley tells those children: "I've come to ask your opinions about a new rule we're considering in the kindergarten. ... We call it, 'You can't say you can't play.'" These older children know the issue well. Vivid accounts of rejection are shared. Some children believe the rule is fair but just won't work: "It would be impossible to have any fun," offers one boy. In a fourth-grade class, students conclude that it is "too late" to give them such a rule. "If you want a rule like that to work, start at a very early age," declares one 9-year-old.[19]

Paley takes these views back to the discussion circle in her own classroom. Her children are enthralled as she shares the older children's views. The deliberation is enlarged; the alternatives become more complex. In the Socratic spirit, she gently encourages them to support their views with reasons, to listen carefully, and to respond to the reasoning of other children, both classmates and older children.

High school deliberative projects exist, too. Perhaps the most widely documented are the Just Community schools conducted by Lawrence Kohlberg and his associates.[20] In these projects, democratic governance becomes a way of life in high schools. These projects aim to transform the school culture—its hidden or implicit curriculum—and in this way to systematically cultivate democratic citizenship. Even if the values of justice, liberty, and equality are well explored in the academic curriculum, the students are quick to perceive whether the school itself runs on a different set of values. They will learn the latter as the real rules of the game.

Students in Just Community schools participate in the basic governance of the school. They deliberate on everything from attendance policy to the consequences for stealing and cheating. Today, students might consider whether, as a move against resegregation, cafeteria seating should be assigned randomly.

The Just Community high schools and the kindergarten deliberations of Vivian Paley together suggest five conditions of ideal deliberation.
- Students are engaged in integrated decision-making discussions that involve genuine value conflicts that arise in the course of relating to one another at school. These value conflicts may concern play and name-calling in an elementary school, cliques and taunting in a middle school, and cheating, attendance, and segregation in a high school.
- The discussion group is diverse enough that students have the benefit of exposure to reasoning and social perspectives different from their own.
- The discussion group is free of domination—gross or subtle—by participants who were born into privileged social positions or by those who mature physically before others.

- The discussion leader is skilled at comprehending and presenting reasoning and perspectives that are missing, countering conventional ideas with critical thinking, and advocating positions that are inarticulate or being drummed out of consideration.
- Discussions are dialogic. Discussants engage in conversation about their viewpoints, claims, and arguments, not in alternating monologues.

■ The Academic Curriculum

Citizens need disciplinary knowledge just as much as they need deliberative experience and skill. The suggestion to engage students in dialogues on the shared problems of school life is not an argument for "process" without "content." It is not an argument for lessening emphasis on subject-matter learning. To the contrary, making decisions without knowledge—whether immediate knowledge of the alternatives under consideration or background knowledge—is no cause for celebration. Action without understanding is not wise action except by accident. The Klan acted; the Nazis acted; bullies act every day.

Consequently, a rigorous liberal arts curriculum that deals in powerful ideas, important issues, and core values is essential alongside deliberations of controversial public issues. Moreover, if deliberation is left to the school's social curriculum only—that is, to the nonacademic areas of student relations and school governance—then students are likely to develop the misconception that the academic disciplines are settled and devoid of controversy. Nothing could be further from the truth. The disciplines are loaded with arguments and debates, and expertise in a discipline is measured by one's involvement in these discussions. A good teacher, on this view, is able to engage students, in developmentally appropriate ways, in the core problems of the subject matter.

Historians, for example, argue about everything they study: about why Rome fell, why slavery lasted so long in the U.S., and what forces contributed to the fall of the Soviet Union. What historians do is develop theses—warranted assertions—about such matters. They defend their claims with their interpretations of the evidentiary record. Political scientists likewise don't know with certainty why in the past few years the U.S. has abandoned the UN Charter and embarked on rugged unilateralism, nor do they "know" a host of other things: whether nation states will survive their contest with globalization or why the current cohort of 18- to 25-year-olds has proven so unengaged in politics.

Engaging students in deliberations of academic controversies is arguably the most rigorous approach to disciplinary education available. Its advantage over drill-and-cover curricula, whether of the middle-track pedestrian variety or the Advanced Placement version, is that it involves students in both the substantive (facts and theories) and syntactical (methods of inquiry) dimensions of the disciplines.[21] At the same time, such engagement prepares them for the reasoned argumentation of democratic living.

Fortunately, some resources are readily available that help teachers and curriculum leaders decide which issues are appropriate for study and then lay out several alternatives for students to consider. Two of the best low-cost resources for the high school social studies classroom, especially history and government courses, are published by the National Issues Forum and by Choices for the 21st Century.[22] Each organization produces a series of booklets containing background information on a pressing problem (contemporary or historical) and three to four policy alternatives. Both engage students in the kind of deliberation that develops their understanding of one another, of the array of alternatives, of the problem itself, and of its historical context.[23]

The authors of these materials have developed the policy alternatives. Consequently, students are given (and don't have to generate) grist for the analytic mill. Students can evaluate the authors' diagnosis of the problem and judge their representation of stakeholders on the issue. Then they can deliberate about the options presented. The provision of alternatives by the authors scaffolds the task in a helpful way, modeling for students what an array of alternatives looks like and allowing them to work at understanding these and at listening to one another. After such experience, students are ready to have the scaffold removed and to investigate an issue of their own choosing and create their own briefing booklet.

■ The Three R's?

I would like to see a national campaign against idiocy, and I believe schools are ideal sites for it. Put differently, schools are fitting places to lead young people through puberty and into citizenship. Schools are the sites of choice because they have, to some extent, the two most important resources for this work: diversity and problems.

I realize that this view is apt to be too optimistic for some readers. After all, schools are products of society and are embedded in it. They are not autonomous places where massive social forces can be stopped with a lesson plan. Still, schools are not insignificant sources of social progress. At some level, everyone seems to believe this. It is the reason that curriculum debates are often the most impassioned to be found anywhere in society. My view is that the three R's—mechanically treated and, now, tested with Puritanical fervor—are not the only essentials needed for the realization of democratic ideals. A proper curriculum for democracy requires both the study and the practice of democracy.

Notes

1. Aristotle, *The Politics of Aristotle*, trans. Ernest Barker (New York: Oxford University Press, 1958), p. 6. See also Christopher Berry, *The Idea of a Democratic Community* (New York: St. Martin's Press, 1989).

2. Daniel Kemmis, *The Good City and the Good Life* (Boston: Houghton Mifflin, 1995), p. 9.

3. Alexis de Tocqueville, *Democracy in America*, trans. George Lawrence, ed. J. P. Mayer (Garden City, N.J.: Doubleday, 1969), p. 540.

4. Jane Addams, "Why Women Should Vote," in Aileen S. Kraditor, ed., *The Ideas of the Woman Suffrage Movement, 1880-1920* (1909; reprint, New York: Norton, 1981), p. 69.

5. Edward C. Banfield, *The Moral Basis of a Backward Society* (New York: Free Press, 1958); see also Robert D. Putnam, *Making Democracy Work: Civic Traditions in Modern Italy* (Princeton, N.J.: Princeton University Press, 1994).

6. Sarah Jain, "Urban Errands: The Means of Mobility," *Journal of Consumer Culture*, vol. 2, 2002, pp. 419-38; and Keith Bradsher, *High and Mighty: SUVs* (New York: Public Affairs, 2002).

7. Karl Marx, *Capital*, trans. Ben Fowkes, 3 vols. (1867; reprint, New York: Penguin Classics, 1990), vol. 1; Robert N. Bellah et al., *Habits of the Heart: Individualism and Commitment in American Life* (Berkeley:

University of California Press, 1985); and John Kenneth Galbraith, *The Affluent Society, 40th anniversary ed.* (Boston: Houghton Mifflin, 1998).

8. See Amy Gutmann's treatment of Churchill's statement in "Democracy, Philosophy, and Justification," in Seyla Benhabib, ed., *Democracy and Difference* (Princeton, N.J.: Princeton University Press, 1996), pp. 340-47.

9. Martin Luther King, Jr., "I Have a Dream," in Clayborne Carson and Kris Shepard, eds., *A Call to Conscience* (New York: Warner Books, 2001), pp. 81-82.

10. Judith N. Shklar, *American Citizenship: The Quest for Inclusion* (Cambridge, Mass.: Harvard University Press, 1991), p. 12.

11. Martin Luther King, Jr., *Why We Can't Wait* (New York: Mentor, 1963), chap. 5, p. 80; see also Gary Y. Okihiro, *Margins and Mainstream: Asians in American History and Culture* (Seattle: University of Washington Press, 1994).

12. Jennifer L. Hochschild and Nathan Scovronick, "Democratic Education and the American Dream: One, Some, and All," in Walter C. Parker, ed., *Education for Democracy: Contexts, Curricula, and Assessments* (Greenwich, Conn.: Information Age, 2002), pp. 3-26.

13. Vivian Gussin Paley, *You Can't Say You Can't Play* (Cambridge, Mass.: Harvard University Press, 1992), p. 21.

14. John Dewey, *Democracy and Education*, in Jo Ann Boydston, ed., *The Middle Works of John Dewey*, 1899-1924, vol. 9 (1916; reprint, Carbondale: Southern Illinois University Press, 1985), p. 200.

15. Ibid.

16. Gary Orfield, "Schools More Separate: Consequences of a Decade of Resegregation," Harvard Civil Rights Project, 2001, available on the website of the Harvard Civil Rights Project. For access, simply Google the title. Orfield found, "Whites on average attend schools where less than 20% of the students are from all of the other racial and ethnic groups combined. On average, Blacks and Latinos attend schools with 53% to 55% students of their own group. Latinos attend schools with far higher average Black populations than Whites do, and Blacks attend schools with much higher average Latino enrollments. American Indian students attend schools in which about a third (31%) of the students are from Indian backgrounds."

17. See Thomas F. Pettigrew, "Intergroup Contact: Theory, Research, and New Perspectives," in James A. Banks and Cherry A. McGee Banks, eds., *Handbook of Research on Multicultural Education* (San Francisco: Jossey-Bass, 2004), pp. 770-81; see also Elliot Aronson et al., *The Jigsaw Classroom* (Beverly Hills, Calif.: Sage, 1978).

18. Paley, p. 16.

19. Ibid., p. 63.

20. F. Clark Power, Ann Higgins, and Lawrence Kohlberg, *Lawrence Kohlberg's Approach to Moral Education* (New York: Columbia University Press, 1989); and Ralph Mosher, Robert A. Kenny, Jr., and Andrew Garrod, *Preparing for Citizenship: Teaching Youth to Live Democratically* (Westport, Conn.: Praeger, 1994).

21. Joseph J. Schwab, "Structure of the Disciplines: Meanings and Significances," in G. W. Ford and Lawrence Pugno, eds., *The Structure of Knowledge and the Curriculum* (Chicago: Rand McNally, 1964), pp. 6-30.

22. Information about the National Issues Forum is available at www.nifi.org; information about Choices for the 21st Century is available at www.choices.edu.

23. John Doble, *The Story of NIF: The Effects of Deliberation* (Dayton, Ohio: Kettering Foundation, 1996).

Chapter 8 | **Reading Response**

■ WHAT?

1. In 100-150 words, using information from both articles, summarize the problem that Friedman and Parker are addressing.
2. Explain Parker's use of the term "idiot."
3. While Friedman uses his brief piece only to dramatize a problem, Parker focuses on a specific course of action for dealing with that problem. Explain Parker's proposal for reviving citizenship in the United States.

■ WHAT ELSE? WHAT'S NEXT?

4. Do some research—talk to friends, look online—and find arguments that contradict the notion that America has become a nation of apathetic idiots (in the sense that Friedman and Parker use those terms). Summarize your findings, and be prepared to share them with your classmates.

■ WHO CARES?

5. Who is the "we" to whom Friedman repeatedly refers in his column? Do you see yourself in this group of people? To whom is Friedman speaking in his piece? Why do you think this?
6. Compare the tone of these two pieces. How does each author establish his tone? Which do you think is more effective? Why?

THE PROBLEM: The Human Cost of Consumption

> The year 2013 was especially troubling—even horrifying—for workers in the global garment industry, most significantly because of the Rana Plaza factory collapse that killed 1,129 people in Bangladesh. While those deaths received massive media coverage and prompted impassioned calls for action, the vast majority of those who make the clothes sold in well-known stores in the United States and Europe still toil in dangerous conditions for pennies a day. In the two articles that follow, Robert Kuttner, co-founder and editor of *The American Prospect*, and Annie Leonard, an author and advocate for sustainability, examine the toll that our addiction to inexpensive clothes takes on the people who make those clothes. Kuttner, whose article was published in August 2013 in *The American Prospect*, focuses on the need for aggressive government intervention and enforcement, while Leonard, writing in the Fall 2013 issue of *YES! Magazine*, calls for individual action that moves beyond "mindful consumption."

BEFORE YOU READ

Examine some of the news coverage—video and print—of the Rana Plaza factory collapse in April 2013. What is the focus of the coverage—the victims, factory safety, something else?

FASHIONING JUSTICE FOR BANGLADESH
Robert Kuttner

On April 24, 2013, the Rana Plaza garment factory in Bangladesh collapsed, killing 1,129 workers and injuring at least 1,500 more. Most were young women earning about $37 a month, or a bit more than a dollar a day. The collapse was the worst disaster in the history of the global garment industry, evoking the 1911 Triangle Shirtwaist factory fire in New York City. The Rana Plaza factory made apparel for more than a dozen major international fashion brands, including Benetton, J.C. Penney, and Wal-Mart. This was the third major industrial accident in Bangladesh since November, 2012, when 112 people were killed in a fire at a garment factory producing mainly for Wal-Mart. At Rana Plaza, cracks appeared in the eight-story building the day before it collapsed. Police ordered an evacuation of the building. But survivors say they were told that their pay would be docked if they did not return to the factory floor, and most did.

Bangladesh, a nation of more than 160 million, has some 4 million garment-industry workers and 40 building inspectors. After China, it is the world's second-largest apparel producer: a destination of choice for the fashion industry because workers effectively have no rights and are among the world's most desperately poor people. These tragedies underscored not just the brutality of the global garment industry but also the bankruptcy of a voluntary system of industry-sponsored factory certification by nonprofits funded by the big fashion brands.

In August 2012, one of the most prestigious monitoring groups, Social Accountability International, gave a factory owned by Ali Enterprises in Karachi, Pakistan, a clean bill of health. A month later, the factory burned, killing some 300 workers who were trapped behind locked doors.

In January 2012, Apple selected the monitoring group Fair Labor Association (FLA) to review conditions in the factories of Foxconn, its contractor in China. Two weeks later, The New York Times published an exposé of grim conditions, including 70-hour workweeks and a spate of worker suicides. In February, the head of the FLA toured Foxconn and pronounced the facilities "first class."

Thanks to the notoriety of the Rana Plaza collapse and the persistence of the global labor movement, anti-sweatshop activists in the U.S. and Europe, and an independent, labor-affiliated advocacy group, the Worker Rights Consortium (WRC), the tragedy in Bangladesh could open the door to more robust corporate accountability. A legally binding contract, signed May 15 by some 40 fashion brands, commits the big retailers and apparel producers to take responsibility for what happens in the factories that make the clothing they sell.

Under the Accord on Building and Fire Safety in Bangladesh, the Western fashion companies will invest millions of dollars in factory improvements and provide longer-term supply contracts so that factory owners have the cash flow and confidence to invest in upgrades. The brands agree to independent safety inspections whose results are made public, with binding arbitration in the event of disputes and an enforceable commitment by the brands to terminate business with factories that do not meet safety standards. A seven-person committee enforces the agreement, with three members from labor groups, three from the fashion brands, and a representative of the International Labor Organization (ILO) in Geneva, a U.N.–affiliated watchdog body founded in 1919 to promote worker rights, as chair and tiebreaker. The agreement, however, is about safety. It does not address wages per se, but it does commit the fashion brands to require the large factories they purchase from to allow union representatives to help train factory workers in safety monitoring. Sponsors hope that a union presence will lead to better wages.

By July, some 70 major European fashion brands and retailers with production in Bangladesh had signed the accord. Only a handful of U.S. companies joined, including PVH (the parent company of Calvin Klein and Tommy Hilfiger), Sean John, and Abercrombie & Fitch. Although Europe purchases more than double the volume of clothes from Bangladesh than the United States does, the deal would be more significant if the bigger American retailers such as Wal-Mart and the Gap joined, since both have resisted codes of conduct with independent monitoring and enforcement. Instead, Wal-Mart, the Gap, and 15 other North American brands have created a rival, purely voluntary agreement. Their plan for better factory safety, announced in early July with the Bipartisan Policy Center providing the window dressing, has no arm's-length monitoring, no penalties, no enforceable rights, and no role for unions.

Depending on how well it is enforced, the European accord could be a turning point that could lead to a new wave of rights for workers in Third World manufacturing. "The business model of the apparel industry logically leads to sweatshops," says Scott Nova, executive director of the WRC. "The Bangladesh accord holds the promise of altering the model. But we expect that there will be extensive battles ahead."

The $1.5 trillion garment industry is structured in a way that almost guarantees a race to the bottom for its workers and a convenient distancing of the global fashion brands from the conditions of work. Typically, the fashion brand outsources not just the production but the organization of the entire supply chain. A $20 billion Hong Kong–based firm that most people have never heard of, Li & Fung, dominates the intermediary business. According to Robert Ross of Clark University, author of Slaves to Fashion and an expert on the global apparel industry, "The fashion brands and retailers go to Li & Fung with a design, a price point, and projected volume, and they say, 'Find me a factory.'" Li & Fung, with more than 7,700 clients and 15,000 suppliers, invariably finds several competing factories to keep the pressure on for low prices and wages. So, when a disaster occurs, the retailer is at two levels of remove. It doesn't own the factory, and it didn't organize the production chain.

After the factory collapse in Bangladesh, for instance, Wal-Mart insisted that the Fame Jeans sold in its stores had been produced at Rana Plaza by a subcontractor without its knowledge. Fame Jeans in turn blamed "a rogue employee." But the entire production system is designed to promote this denial of accountability. Large factories in Bangladesh, Pakistan, Vietnam, or Cambodia might produce for 10 or 20 different brands. The brands and their intermediaries keep the factory owners on contracts of just a few months, so that if a rival factory offers a cheaper price, it will get the business.

In the negotiations for the Bangladesh deal, the breakthrough came when H&M agreed to sign. The largest purchaser of clothing made in Bangladesh and the world's second-largest apparel retailer with some 2,900 stores in 43 countries, H&M happens to be a Swedish multinational. Sweden has a long history of powerful trade unions and widely accepted collaboration between management and labor. Unlike every major U.S. fashion company, H&M is a union shop at home. When the Rana Plaza catastrophe occurred, it was a major embarrassment to H&M management. Inditex, the world's largest apparel retailer, quickly agreed to the accord. Based in Galicia, Spain, Inditex has 5,500 stores worldwide under several different brand names such as Zara.

The accord is a welcome change, but it is just a first step. With the Bangladeshi government allied with factory owners, the government could well undermine the agreement. Bangladesh has pursued the strategy of gaining market share by having the world's lowest wages for garment workers. The current minimum wage translates to about 18 cents an hour, up from 10 cents in 2010. Labor activists say a living wage is more like $1.20 an hour—probably the world's widest gap between the legal minimum wage and a minimally decent standard of living. Although new union rights are promised in the accord, there could well be a proliferation of company unions and protracted wrangling over which entities are bona fide unions. The plan could lead to extensive jockeying between companies and factory owners over who is responsible for investing in upgraded safety conditions, as well as conflicts among the brands over which must invest how much in improved standards. The crunch will come when a factory fails to live up to the accord and the brands are pressured to drop it as a supplier. Since other apparel producers such as Vietnam and Pakistan are eager to displace Bangladesh, the race to the bottom is likely to continue until higher standards are mandated worldwide.

The modern anti-sweatshop movement, based on naming and shaming brands through consumer pressure, began in the mid-1990s. As global production chains were created by the industry, Third World factory conditions proliferated both globally and in the United States. In 1995, in El Monte, California, police found 72 Thai workers locked inside a factory producing clothes for major U.S. retailers, working 18 hours a day for less than a dollar an hour. With exposés of near-slave labor conditions in global factories of such brands as Reebok, Levi Strauss, and Kathie Lee Gifford's line of clothing, the companies moved to devise corporate codes of conduct. This led to a strategy of using voluntary organizations like Social Accountability International to monitor and certify labor conditions, which the big brands hoped would satisfy consumer concerns without raising their costs.

During the same period, college students began demanding that their universities set minimum labor standards as a condition of approving licenses to manufacture products with college logos. President Bill Clinton was instrumental in helping universities, corporations, and unions create the Fair Labor Association in 1999. But the FLA was compromised by its need to win the cooperation of the big brands. The unions soon quit, in favor of the more independent Worker Rights Consortium. Unlike the FLA, the consortium promotes union organizing and issues detailed and scathing reports on sweatshop conditions. Each organization has about 200 university members that pledge to hold garment producers accountable to codes of conduct. Today, many universities are affiliated with both groups.

The limitation of the FLA approach is that fashion brands affiliate voluntarily. They agree to create their own codes, and the FLA hires monitors to certify whether factories that produce for the brands are in compliance. But because the whole program is voluntary, the FLA has proceeded gingerly.

Even so, the reputational concerns of the brands and the existence of the FLA have given more aggressive groups such as the WRC and the labor movement useful leverage. For example, in 2008 a member company of the FLA, Russell Athletic/Fruit of the Loom, closed a factory in Honduras rather than recognize the workers' decision to unionize. The FLA resisted taking any action against Russell. Eventually, some 100 universities, mobilized by the WRC and United Students Against Sweatshops, denied Russell licenses to make products with their logos, and the company finally agreed not only to reopen the factory but to allow others in Honduras to unionize.

Despite occasional breakthroughs, the Russell agreement and the Bangladesh accord are fragile exceptions. They still depend heavily on consumer pressure on the reputational concerns of large multinational corporations. In the absence of direct government legal standards, the strategy requires endless investigation and publicity—and the big brands have far deeper pockets than the nongovernmental organizations (NGOs) and more staying power than cohorts of college students that turn over every four years.

One key complement, which the WRC and the unions strongly support, is far greater government involvement in the regulation of working conditions both domestically and globally. A potential but seldom used lever is trade law. Corporations, after all, have invested massively in changing trade law to increase their global freedom of movement.

Trade law might also cover workers' rights, but for the most part it doesn't except at the level of platitude.

Member nations of the World Trade Organization benefit from what used to be called "most favored nation" treatment—they get the same tariffs as those imposed on the most favored nation. The list of tariffs is known as the Generalized System of Preferences (GSP). In 2007, the AFL-CIO filed a petition requesting that Bangladesh be removed from the list of GSP countries because of its repeated violation of even the most minimal labor rights. The Bush administration rejected the petition. This June, the Obama administration acted to suspend GSP status for Bangladesh, but the action is largely symbolic because exports admitted under the GSP affect only about 1 percent of Bangladesh's overall exports to the U.S. and do not include clothing. Still, the move is a diplomatic slap and adds some (minimal) government pressure on the Bangladeshi government, but the U.S. could do more.

Government-to-government pressure would reinforce accords like the Bangladesh safety deal. The European Union is also reviewing whether Bangladesh qualifies for favorable tariff treatment. Activists hope that the combination of bad publicity, the risk of losing favorable tariffs, the new contract with the big fashion brands, and increased worker pressure on the ground will alter Bangladesh's export strategy. Enforceable rights to organize or join unions, a stronger health and safety code, and a higher minimum wage would put more teeth in what is still a private accord that deals primarily with safety and relies on the highly fickle concerns of consumers, most of whom are more interested in price and fashion than in labor rights.

The U.S. government, architect of trade deals that mainly serve industry and finance, could add labor rights to the mix. But then the U.S. has failed to enforce labor rights at home—including the fundamental right to organize or join a union, supposedly guaranteed by the 1935 Wagner Act.

To get a glimmer of the progress that might be made if governments got involved, consider a brief interlude when the United States intervened on behalf of labor rights in one poor country, Cambodia. The story begins with the Clinton administration's embrace of the North American Free Trade Agreement (NAFTA), a deal conceived by industry and negotiated by the outgoing administration of George H.W. Bush. NAFTA was advertised as a trade agreement, but its most important provisions opened Mexico to massive direct investment by U.S. corporations and defined many health, safety, and environmental regulations as obstacles to trade. As a candidate in 1992, Clinton called for meaningful labor provisions as part of NAFTA, but the eventual "side agreement" on labor rights had no teeth. Most Mexican unions are pawns of the government, and the independent ones are subject to persecution. Napoleón Gómez Urrutia, president of the Mexican mining and metalworking union, one of the few legitimate ones, has been in exile in Canada for seven years, fearing arrest.

NAFTA was approved by Congress in 1993, over the fierce objection of the unions and with about two-thirds of House Democrats voting no. Clinton got it through mainly with the support of Republicans. When Clinton came back for new authority in 1997 to negotiate more trade deals, the House rejected his request. So the administration began discussions with the unions to see what kind of labor provisions might win their support. The administration was particularly eager to make a trade agreement with Cambodia, which was just emerging from the Killing Fields years under the Khmer Rouge and desperately needed access to U.S. consumer markets. In those years, textile and apparel imports were allocated according to a national quota system, known as the Multi-Fiber Arrangement. In yearlong discussions with Clinton officials, leaders of the apparel and textile union UNITE proposed a novel approach. As part of the trade deal, the Cambodian government would enforce workers' rights to organize and join unions. If Cambodia kept its word, it would benefit from a significant increase in its import quotas. "The administration didn't exactly take our version," recalls Mark Levinson, one of the union's architects of the plan. "We proposed more power for unions and workers in Cambodia. They accepted the broad idea of trading a quota increase for labor rights but brought in the ILO to oversee it."

Thus did the U.S.-Cambodia free-trade deal come to include the world's only enforceable labor rights as part of a trade agreement. Under the U.S.-Cambodia Bilateral Textile Agreement, signed in January 1999, Cambodia received a bonus export quota to the U.S. if its labor practices were found to be in compliance. Thanks to the agreement, Cambodia's clothing exports increased from $26 million in 1995 to $1.9 billion in 2004, representing 80 percent of its industrial exports. Wages increased, and unions not only gained a foothold in the apparel industry but also were able to negotiate contracts with major hotels such as Raffles. But under another trade pact, the entire multi-fiber quota system was gradually phased out over a ten-year period ending in 2004, and fashion brands were now able to look for the cheapest producer worldwide. Freed from quota constraints, China quickly became the world's largest exporter of clothing, other nations cut costs to match China's price, and the United States gave up its leverage to reward Cambodia for respecting labor rights.

By 2004, Cambodia's factory owners were repressing trade unions, hauling union leaders into court and holding them financially responsible for losses due to strikes. Government, fearing a loss of Cambodia's global market share and no longer having any reward for enforcing workers' rights, was siding with the industry. The popular leader of Cambodia's largest union, Chea Vichea, was assassinated. Between 2001 and 2011, wages in Cambodia's garment industry fell 17 percent. The ILO's monitoring program continues, but cooperation with it has evaporated. Factories have shifted more workers to short-term employment contracts. Trade union members are routinely fired. Illegal overtime has increased, as has child labor. This deterioration has intensified even though the purchasers of garments made in Cambodia are international brands such as Nike, Disney, and H&M, all of which have corporate codes of conduct.

After two major strikes, in 1909 and 1910, and the Triangle Shirtwaist fire in 1911, organizers rode the wave of worker militancy and public outrage to increase union membership of New York's garment factories. With the period of full employment during World War I, unionization in the garment trades peaked at 129,000, despite having little protection from government. But in the 1920s, the industry managed to weaken the unions with a technique identical to the one used by the big fashion brands today. Instead of producing in their own factories, they contracted with "jobbers" and subcontractors, both to disperse the workforce and to diffuse responsibility for the appalling conditions. The economic collapse of the Great Depression reduced union membership even further.

The garment unions recovered only when the Franklin Roosevelt administration first guaranteed the right to unionize in 1933 and 1935, complemented by wage and hours laws in 1938, and then applied strict enforcement of union rights in war production contracts. Sidney Hillman, president of the Amalgamated Clothing Workers of America and FDR's top labor adviser, served as associate director of the Office of Production Management, which was responsible for all war production. It took both union militancy and the help of the government to win organized labor a tenuous foothold in America's implicit social contract. For a couple of generations, unions were part of the industrial landscape in America, and sweatshops vanished, until the progress was reversed by globalization. Between 1989 and 2010, as the Multi-Fiber Arrangement was replaced by a global free-for-all, productivity in global apparel production steadily rose, and the price of garments imported into the U.S. dropped by 48 percent. Wages continued to decline.

Defenders of Third World sweatshops often argue that they benefit American consumers by providing low-priced products. Yet the factory worker receives only a pittance of the retail price. You could double the wage, and the final price would only rise by a percentage point or two. Meanwhile, Americans are under pressure to lower their own wages to be competitive globally. The truth is that workers in the U.S. and in Bangladesh are common victims of the larger production system.

Our own history in the mid-20th century suggests what it will take to rid the world of sweatshops—enforceable rights and effective unions. Yet in the past several decades, that progress has been reversed. Sweatshops have returned to the United States as well as to Bangladesh. In the best case, the Bangladesh accord will open up the possibility for modest improvements in wages and working conditions and for organizing unions. It represents a rare instance of corporations agreeing to binding constraints on their behavior and that of their contractors. With sufficient consumer and union pressure, it could become a template for agreements in other countries.

Accords like this one may be the best available for now, given the failure of the U.S. government to tie labor conditions to trade deals. Still, one has to wonder what might happen if the millions of volunteer and NGO hours devoted to monitoring and publicizing corporate behavior were spent instead on organizing unions—and organizing to elect American progressives, so that our government insisted on labor rights in trade agreements and defended rights at home.

Chapter 8 | Reading Response

HOW TO BE MORE THAN A MINDFUL CONSUMER   Annie Leonard

Since I released "The Story of Stuff" six years ago, the most frequent snarky remark I get from people trying to take me down a notch is about my own stuff: Don't you drive a car? What about your computer and your cellphone? What about your books? (To the last one, I answer that the book was printed on paper made from trash, not trees, but that doesn't stop them from smiling smugly at having exposed me as a materialistic hypocrite. Gotcha!)

Let me say it clearly: I'm neither for nor against stuff. I like stuff if it's well-made, honestly marketed, used for a long time, and at the end of its life recycled in a way that doesn't trash the planet, poison people, or exploit workers. Our stuff should not be artifacts of indulgence and disposability, like toys that are forgotten 15 minutes after the wrapping comes off, but things that are both practical and meaningful. British philosopher William Morris said it best: "Have nothing in your house that you do not know to be useful or believe to be beautiful."

■ Too Many T-shirts

The life cycle of a simple cotton T-shirt—worldwide, 4 billion are made, sold, and discarded each year—knits together a chain of seemingly intractable problems, from the elusive definition of sustainable agriculture to the greed and classism of fashion marketing.

The story of a T-shirt not only gives us insight into the complexity of our relationship with even the simplest stuff; it also demonstrates why consumer activism—boycotting or avoiding products that don't meet our personal standards for sustainability and fairness—will never be enough to bring about real and lasting change. Like a vast Venn diagram covering the entire planet, the environmental and social impacts of cheap T-shirts overlap and intersect on many layers, making it impossible to fix one without addressing the others.

I confess that my T-shirt drawer is so full it's hard to close. That's partly because when I speak at colleges or conferences, I'm often given one with a logo of the institution or event. They're nice souvenirs of my travels, but the simple fact is: I've already got more T-shirts than I need. And of all the T-shirts I have accumulated over the years, there are only a few that I honestly care about, mostly because of the stories attached to them.

My favorite (no eye-rolling, please) is a green number from the Grateful Dead's 1982 New Year's Eve concert. To me this T-shirt, worn for more than 30 years by multiple members of my extended family, is both useful and beautiful, not only because I attended the concert but because a dear friend gave it to me, knowing how much I would treasure it. The label even says "Made in the USA," which makes me smile because so few things are made in this country anymore, as brands increasingly opt for low-paid workers in poor countries.

Who Sews Those Tees?

And that takes me back to a day in 1990, in the slums of Port-au-Prince. I was in Haiti to meet with women who worked in sweatshops making T-shirts and other clothing for the Walt Disney Company. The women were nervous about speaking freely. We crowded into a tiny room inside a small cinderblock house. In sweltering heat, we had to keep the windows shuttered for fear that someone might see us talking. These women worked six days a week, eight hours a day, sewing clothes that they could never save enough to buy. Those lucky enough to be paid minimum wage earned about $15 a week. The women described the grueling pressure at work, routine sexual harassment, and other unsafe and demeaning conditions.

They knew that Disney's CEO, Michael Eisner, made millions. A few years after my visit, a National Labor Committee documentary, Mickey Mouse Goes to Haiti, revealed that in 1996 Eisner made $8.7 million in salary plus $181 million in stock options—a staggering $101,000 an hour. The Haitian workers were paid one-half of 1 percent of the U.S. retail price of each garment they sewed.

The women wanted fair pay for a day's work—which in their dire straits meant $5 a day. They wanted to be safe, to be able to drink water when hot, and to be free from sexual harassment. They wanted to come home early enough to see their children before bedtime and to have enough food to feed them a solid meal when they woke. Their suffering, and the suffering of other garment workers worldwide, was a major reason the end product could be sold on the shelves of big-box retailers for a few dollars.

I asked them why they stayed in the teeming city, living in slums that had little electricity and no running water or sanitation, and working in such obviously unhealthy environments instead of returning to the countryside where they had grown up. They said the countryside simply couldn't sustain them anymore. Their families had given up farming since they couldn't compete against the rice imported from the U.S. and sold for less than half the price of the more labor-intensive, more nutritious native rice. It was all part of a plan, someone whispered, by the World Bank and U.S. Agency for International Development to drive Haitians off their land and into the city to sew clothes for rich Americans. The destruction of farming as a livelihood was necessary to push people to the city, so people would be desperate enough to work all day in hellish sweatshops.

Their Proper Place

The next day I called on USAID. My jaw dropped as the man from the agency openly agreed with what at first had sounded like an exaggerated conspiracy theory. He said it wasn't efficient for Haitians to work on family farms to produce food that could be grown more cheaply elsewhere. Instead they should accept their place in the global economy—which, in his eyes, meant sewing clothes for us in the United States. But surely, I said, efficiency was not the only criterion. A farmer's connection to the land, healthy and dignified work, a parent's ability to spend time with his or her kids after school, a community staying intact generation after generation—didn't all these things have value?

"Well," he said, "if a Haitian really wants to farm, there is room for a handful of them to grow things like organic mangoes for the high-end export market." That's right:

USAID's plan for the people of Haiti was not self-determination, but as a market for our surplus rice and a supplier of cheap seamstresses, with an occasional organic mango for sale at our gourmet grocery stores.

By 2008 Haiti was importing 80 percent of its rice. This left the world's poorest country at the mercy of the global rice market. Rising fuel costs, global drought, and the diversion of water to more lucrative crops—like the thirsty cotton that went into the Disney clothing—withered worldwide rice production. Global rice prices tripled over a few months, leaving thousands of Haitians unable to afford their staple food. The New York Times carried stories of Haitians forced to resort to eating mud pies, held together with bits of lard.

But That's Not All

Whew. Global inequality, poverty, hunger, agricultural subsidies, privatization of natural resources, economic imperialism—it's the whole messy saga of the entire world economy tangled up in a few square yards of cloth. And we haven't even touched on a range of other environmental and social issues around the production, sale, and disposal of cotton clothing.

Cotton is the world's dirtiest crop. It uses more dangerous insecticides than any other major commodity and is very water intensive. Cotton growing wouldn't even be possible in areas like California's Central Valley if big cotton plantations didn't receive millions of dollars in federal water subsidies—even as some of the poverty-stricken farmworker towns in the Valley have no fresh water.

Dyeing and bleaching raw cotton into cloth uses large amounts of toxic chemicals. Many of these chemicals—including known carcinogens such as formaldehyde and heavy metals—poison groundwater near cotton mills, and residues remain in the finished products we put next to our skin.

Well-made cotton clothing—like my 30-year-old Grateful Dead T-shirt—can last a long time, providing years of service for multiple wearers before being recycled into new clothes or other products. But most retailers are so intent on selling a never-ending stream of new clothes to their targeted demographic that they quickly throw away clothing in last season's style.

And here's one more problem with stuff: we're not sharing it well. While some of us have way too much stuff—we're actually stressed out by the clutter in our households and have to rent off-site storage units—others desperately need more.

For those of us in the over-consuming parts of the world, it's increasingly clear that more stuff doesn't make us more happy, but for the millions of people who need housing, clothes, and food, more stuff would actually lead to healthier, happier people. If you have only one T-shirt, getting a second one is a big deal. But if you have a drawer stuffed with them, as I do, a new one doesn't improve my life. It just increases my clutter. Call it stuff inequity. One billion people on the planet are chronically hungry while another billion are obese.

Citizens, Not Consumers

The problems surrounding the trip from the cotton field to the sweatshop are just a smattering of the ills that not only result from the take-make-waste economy but make it possible. That's why striving to make responsible choices at the individual consumer level, while good, is just not enough. Change on the scale required by the severity of today's planetary and social crises requires a broader vision and a plan for addressing the root causes of the problem.

To do that we must stop thinking of ourselves primarily as consumers and start thinking and acting like citizens. That's because the most important decisions about stuff are not those made in the supermarket or department store aisles. They are made in the halls of government and business, where decisions are made about what to make, what materials to use, and what standards to uphold.

Consumerism, even when it tries to embrace "sustainable" products, is a set of values that teaches us to define ourselves, communicate our identity, and seek meaning through acquisition of stuff, rather than through our values and activities and our community. Today we're so steeped in consumer culture that we head to the mall even when our houses and garages are full. We suffer angst over the adequacy of our belongings and amass crushing credit card debt to, as the author Dave Ramsey says, buy things we don't need with money we don't have, to impress people we don't like.

Citizenship, on the other hand, is about what Eric Liu, in The Gardens of Democracy, calls "how you show up in the world." It's taking seriously our responsibility to work for broad, deep change that doesn't tinker around the margins of the system but achieves (forgive the activist-speak) a paradigm shift. Even "ethical consumerism" is generally limited to choosing the most responsible item on the menu, which often leaves us choosing between the lesser of two evils. Citizenship means working to change what's on the menu, and stuff that trashes the planet or harms people just doesn't belong. Citizenship means stepping beyond the comfort zones of everyday life and working with other committed citizens to make big, lasting change.

One of our best models of citizenship in the United States is the Civil Rights Movement of the 1960s. It's a myth that when Rosa Parks refused to move to the back of the bus it was a spontaneous act of individual conscience. She was part of a network of thousands of activists who mapped out their campaign, trained to be ready for the struggles to come, then put their bodies on the line in carefully planned civil disobedience. Consumer-based actions, such as boycotting segregated buses or lunch counters, were part of the campaign, but were done collectively and strategically. That model has been used, with varying degrees of success, in the environmental, gay rights, pro-choice, and other movements. But consumer action alone—absent that larger citizen-led campaign—isn't enough to create deep change.

So yes, it is important to be conscious of our consumer decisions. But we're most powerful when this is connected to collective efforts for bigger structural change. As individuals, we can use less stuff if we remember to look inward and evaluate our well-being by our health, the strength of our friendships, and the richness of our hobbies and civic endeavors. And we can make even more progress by working together—as citizens, not consumers—to strengthen laws and business practices increasing efficiency and reducing waste.

Chapter 8 | **Reading Response**

As individuals, we can use less toxic stuff by prioritizing organic products, avoiding toxic additives, and ensuring safe recycling of our stuff. But we can achieve much more as citizens demanding tougher laws and cleaner production systems that protect public health overall. And there are many ways we can share more, like my community of several families does. Since we share our stuff, we only need one tall ladder, one pickup truck, and one set of power tools. This means we need to buy, own, and dispose of less stuff. From public tool lending libraries to online peer-to-peer sharing platforms, there are many avenues for scaling sharing efforts from the neighborhood to the national level.

We can't avoid buying and using stuff. But we can work to reclaim our relationship to it. We used to own our stuff; now our stuff owns us. How can we restore the proper balance?

I remember talking to Colin Beavan, aka No Impact Man, at the end of his year of living as low impact as he could manage in New York City: no waste, no preprocessed meals, no television, no cars, no buying new stuff. He shared with me his surprise at journalists calling to ask what he most missed, what he was going to run out and consume.

What he said has stayed with me as a perfect summation of the shift in thinking we all need to save the world—and ourselves—from stuff.

"They assumed I just finished a year of deprivation," Colin said. "But I realized that it was the prior 35 years that had been deprived. I worked around the clock, rushed home late and exhausted, ate take-out food, and plopped down to watch TV until it was time to take out the trash, go to sleep, and start all over again. That was deprivation."

Fortunately for the planet and for us, there is another way.

WHAT?

1. In 150-200 words, using information from both articles, summarize the problem that Kuttner and Leonard write about, as well as the things they say could be done to improve the situation.
2. What, specifically, is Leonard asking her readers to do? Do you think this is an effective strategy for responding to this problem? Explain your answer.

WHAT ELSE? WHAT'S NEXT?

3. Research the fallout from the Rana Plaza tragedy to see if any of Kuttner's proposals for reform have been implemented—or even discussed. Have there been other accidents or deaths in garment factories since Rana Plaza?
4. According to a November 2013 report in *The New York Times*, the "International Labor Organization is working with Bangladeshi officials, labor groups and several retailers to create ambitious compensation funds to assist not just the families of the dead [in the Rana Plaza collapse and a fire at another Bangladeshi factory], but also more than 1,800 workers who were injured." Look online to see which retailers are contributing to this effort. What reasons do they give for helping out? Are any notable retailers that used products from these factories not contributing? Why not?

WHO CARES?

5. Based on the information they present, the rhetorical choices they make, and the different magazines/websites that published their articles, describe the audience that each writer is trying to reach. Which of the authors do you think is more successful in presenting a persuasive argument to his/her intended readership? Why?

CHAPTER 9

Reading Consent

IMAGE 9.1

As the readings in this chapter make clear—and as recent headlines continue to show—the United States is beginning what President Obama has called "a fundamental shift" in its thinking about sexual violence. And colleges and universities are among the most visible leaders in this movement. Scores of campuses across the nation have adopted or are considering policies that require affirmative consent for all sexual encounters involving students. While these "yes means yes" guidelines—which are meant to replace a common "no means no" standard—are heavily criticized by some, support for their implementation continues to grow. The columns, blog posts, and articles that follow are meant to help you understand just what affirmative consent is and how it might work.

> Reporter Jake New wrote this article for the publication Inside Higher Ed in October 2014. In the piece, he examines the evolution of campus sexual consent policies from the common "no means no" standard to "yes means yes," or affirmative consent, at hundreds of colleges and universities across the country.

BEFORE YOU READ

Find out what the University of South Carolina's policy on obtaining sexual consent is, where it is publicized, and how it is enforced.

THE 'YES' MEANS 'YES' WORLD
Jake New

When the sexual assault prevention group Culture of Respect attended the Dartmouth Summit on Sexual Assault in July 2014 to promote its forthcoming website, the group went by a different name. The nonprofit passed out business cards and marketing all emblazoned with the phrase "No Means No."

For the last two decades, that's been the slogan of choice for sexual assault prevention efforts, and just a few months ago it seemed like a perfect fit for the new organization. But in the weeks leading up to No Means No's official launch, the organization began having second thoughts.

"The swiftly evolving conversation about defining sexual assault signaled to us that we needed to reframe our name as something more positive," said Allison Korman, the group's executive director. "And it's even possible that 'No means no' will be an outdated or irrelevant concept in 10 years. Students may not have even heard of the phrase by then."

That's because at a growing number of colleges, "No means no" is out, and "Yes means yes" is in. And it's more than just revising an old slogan—from coast to coast, colleges are rethinking how they define consent on their campuses.

Last month, California Governor Jerry Brown, a Democrat, signed legislation requiring colleges in the state to adopt sexual assault policies that shifted the burden of proof in campus sexual assault cases from those accusing to the accused. Consent is now "an affirmative, unambiguous, and conscious decision by each participant to engage in mutually agreed-upon sexual activity." The consent has to be "ongoing" throughout any sexual encounter.

On California campuses, consent is no longer a matter of not struggling or not saying no. If the student initiating the sexual encounter doesn't receive an enthusiastic "yes," either verbally or physically, then there is no consent. If the student is incapacitated due to drugs or alcohol, there is no consent.

California is the first state to make such a definition of consent law, but other states may soon follow suit. In New Hampshire and New Jersey, state legislators have introduced bills that would also link state funding for colleges to their definition of sexual assault, requiring the use of affirmative consent. In New York, Governor Andrew Cuomo, a Democrat, plans on proposing legislation that would require a uniform definition of consent similar to California's to be used for all of the state's private colleges.

Earlier this month, the State University of New York system adopted that same uniform definition at all of its 64 campuses. The California State University System adopted its new definition months ago. Every Ivy League institution except Harvard University has adopted some form of affirmative consent. According to the National Center for Higher Education Risk Management, more than 800 colleges and universities now use some type of affirmative consent definition in their sexual assault policies.

"There's quite a surge in support of a 'Yes means yes' formula," said Ada Meloy, general counsel for the American Council on Education. "It's certainly an ongoing movement, and is likely to be a generally positive thing. At the same time, it's not easy to develop a good definition of affirmative consent. We wouldn't want a one-size-fits-all approach for a variety of institutions."

Moving From 'No Means No'

Victims' rights advocates continue to praise the idea of affirmative consent and the momentum the concept has recently gained. Laura Dunn, executive director of SurvJustice, said campus sexual assault policies could even "fill in some of the holes" in criminal laws regarding consent. In many states, consent is still based on a victim verbally or physically resisting, even as colleges within those states adopt affirmative consent policies.

Because colleges use a lesser burden of proof than criminal courts— preponderance of evidence rather than beyond a reasonable doubt—it makes sense to have a different definition of consent on campus, Dunn said, though she would ultimately like to see states adopt similar definitions at the criminal level as well. In order to comply with Title IX of the Education Amendments of 1972, colleges must investigate complaints of sexual assault, even if students decline to go to the police.

"Traditionally we've focused on a lack of consent as someone fighting off an attacker," Dunn said. "You looked for evidence of resistance. We only talked about what consent was not, which is not a very helpful paradigm. From the victims' side, it says we have to resist. But even looking at this from the perspective of someone being accused, the traditional definition is telling them that it's O.K. to do this until the victim says 'no.' That's not really a helpful definition for them either because it can really be too late at that point. With affirmative consent, it's simple. Consent is consent."

"No means no" hasn't always had such a negative connotation.

The Canadian Federation of Students popularized the phrase as part of a well-received, and still ongoing, sexual assault awareness campaign it launched in 1992. The group even owns the trademark in Canada, wielding it to stop the production of clothing and other merchandise that make light of the phrase (like a 2007 t-shirt that said "NO means have aNOther drink"). The same year the campaign was launched, the Canadian government adopted affirmative consent as the country's legal standard, making "No means no" just a slogan, not a binding definition of consent.

The slogan has become well-known in the United States as well, though over time some college students began to use it as fodder for offensive jokes. A Yale University fraternity was suspended for five years in 2011 after its members marched around campus chanting "No Means Yes, Yes Means Anal" during a pledge initiation event. Just last week, a fraternity at Texas Tech University was stripped of its charter after painting the same phrase on signs during a party.

Unlike Canada, "No means no" is both a slogan and, in some states, the definition of consent. While there were efforts to create a uniform affirmative consent definition for all colleges during the recent reauthorization of the Violence Against Women Act, they were not successful. Meloy, of ACE, said she's supportive of affirmative consent but believes that the final definition of what that phrase means should be left up to individual campuses or college systems. "I think institutions' governing boards are the place for this to be discussed and considered," she said.

But it's that lack of a standard definition for affirmative consent that has led some colleges like Harvard not to adopt it.

Harvard's policy forbids what it calls "unwelcome conduct of a sexual nature," stating that "conduct is unwelcome if a person did not request or invite it and regarded the unrequested or uninvited conduct as undesirable or offensive." Earlier this week, 28 current and former Harvard law professors said the policy could deny due process to those who are accused and that its definition of unwanted conduct was too broad and vague. Student activists, meanwhile, said the definition doesn't go nearly far enough, and urged Harvard to change its definition to one of affirmative consent, saying in a petition that "the absence of a 'no' does not mean 'yes,' and our university policy should explicitly recognize that."

Mia Karvonides, the university's Title IX officer, said that Harvard uses a standard that is "consistent with the standard in all federal civil rights laws that apply in an education setting," and that even its peers in the Ivy League don't truly use an affirmative consent standard as they don't require a verbal yes at every turn

"The closest any college comes to a defined affirmative-consent approach is Antioch College," Karvonides said. "Under their policy, consent is given step by step at every point of engagement during an intimate encounter. You must verbally ask and verbally get an answer for every point of engagement. 'May I kiss you? May I undo your blouse?'"

■ 'An Absurd Policy'

When the Antioch approach was introduced in 1991, it was widely mocked, including in a "Saturday Night Live" sketch, for what some saw as reducing a sexual encounter to a series of robotic yes and no questions. That critique of affirmative consent has been renewed in recent months as more colleges began to adopt similar policies. John Banzhaf, a law professor at George Washington University, said, the idea that students would ask for permission at every point of a sexual encounter is "unreasonable."

"It just isn't the way things work," Banzhaf said. "How would this work in practice? Suppose the guy asks, 'May I touch your breast?' Does that mean through her shirt? Over her bra? Does that mean he can touch her bare breast? Does it mean he can touch it with his hand or his lips? What if this all happens in succession? As things escalate, is he supposed to ask before each of the 20, 30, 40 steps? Nobody talks like that, not even lawyers."

Earlier this month, anti-sexism group UltraViolet tried to illustrate that affirmative consent can be natural and sexy by releasing an online video ad that mimicked retro pornography. In the purposefully grainy clip, a college-aged pizza delivery boy brings an unwanted pizza to a young woman's apartment. When the man apologizes for his mistake and refuses to force the pizza on her, she finds his seeking of consent attractive and one consensual act leads to another. As the couple moves from kissing, to lying on top of one another, to removing their clothing, they often pause to quickly—breathlessly—ask "Is this O.K.?"

The Consent is Sexy Campaign offers campuses a series of posters making the same point, and some institutions have established campaigns of their own to explain why asking for consent is not a mood-killer.

Others are not so concerned with whether affirmative consent policies are awkward or un-sexy, but whether they're dangerous and unjust. In a position paper, the Foundation for Individual Rights in Education argued that there is "no practical, fair, or consistent" way for colleges to ensure an affirmative consent standard was followed. "It is impracticable for the government to require students to obtain affirmative consent at each stage of a physical encounter, and to later prove that attainment in a campus hearing," FIRE stated.

Furthermore, most campus policies state that yes does not mean yes if a student is intoxicated. At Cornell University, for example, a student cannot consent if he or she is highly intoxicated. At the same time, if the accused is also highly intoxicated, he or she cannot use intoxication as a defense. In the case of two intoxicated students, Cornell's rules place the responsibility on obtaining consent with whichever student is the "initiator of further sexual activity," saying that "the inability to perceive capacity does not excuse the behavior of the person who begins the sexual interaction or tries to take it to another level."

"It's an absurd policy," Joe Cohn, FIRE's legislation and policy director, said. "How can the dean of the English department or a physics professor or whoever else is on the panel at a hearing know who was the initiator and who was not? What it really means is that if someone accuses another student of sexual assault in a situation like this, then the student who did not do the accusing is immediately considered to be the one responsible for initiating the conduct."

Banzhaf said switching to a "Yes means yes" standard that includes nonverbal cues only adds more ambiguity to obtaining consent. What colleges and states should actually focus on, he said, is removing any remaining ambiguity around "No means no."

"I don't think the problem is the definition of consent," Banzhaf said. "The problem is that too many guys simply don't take no as no. They're either drunk or stupid or have been conditioned by our society to believe that no means maybe and that if they keep pressing that no may turn into a yes. In most states still, for it to be rape, the guy must use force or threat of force or the woman must be totally incapacitated. That's what needs to change. We have to have a unified understanding of consent and that should simply be that no really means no."

■ WHAT?

1. Early in his article, Jake New writes that, at "a growing number of colleges, 'No means no' is out, and 'Yes means yes' is in." Explain the differences between the two approaches to sexual consent, as New presents them.
2. What are some of the objections to "yes means yes" laws and policies that New writes about in his article?

■ WHAT ELSE? WHAT NEXT?

3. How does USC talk about sexual consent on campus? How does the USC policy compare with others discussed in this article?

> Michael Kimmel is a professor of sociology and gender studies at Stony Brook University, and Gloria Steinem is a writer, feminist organizer and co-founder of Ms. Magazine and the Women's Media Center. They wrote this piece for The New York Times in early September 2014.

BEFORE YOU READ

Research the biographies of both Michael Kimmel and Gloria Steinem and prepare a brief report in which you explain how what you have learned about the authors affects your reading of their essay.

'YES' IS BETTER THAN 'NO'
By Michael Kimmel and Gloria Steinem

Suppose someone you know slightly arrives at your home, baggage and all, and just barges in and stays overnight. When you protest, the response is, "Well, you didn't say no." Or imagine that a man breaks into your home while you sleep off a night of drunken revelry, and robs you blind. Did your drinking imply consent?

Until now, this has been the state of affairs in our nation's laws on sexual assault. Invading bodies has been taken less seriously by the law than invading private property, even though body-invasion is far more traumatic. This has remained an unspoken bias of patriarchal law. After all, women were property until very recently. In some countries, they still are. Even in America, women's human right to make decisions about their own bodies remains controversial, especially when it comes to sex and reproduction.

That's why the recent passage of Senate Bill 967 in California is such a welcome game-changer in understanding and preventing sexual assault. The bill, which passed the Senate unanimously after a 52 to 16 vote in the State Assembly, now awaits Gov. Jerry Brown's signature, which is expected. It would make California the first state to embrace what has become known as the "yes means yes" law, because it alters the standard regarding consent to sexual activity on college campuses. It is the first state response to President Obama's initiative on campus sexual assault, announced earlier this year.

Until this bill, the prevailing standard has been "no means no." If she says no (or, more liberally, indicates any resistance with her body), then the sex is seen as nonconsensual. That is, it's rape. Under such a standard, the enormous gray area between "yes" and "no" is defined residually as "yes": Unless one hears an explicit "no," consent is implied. "Yes means yes" completely redefines that gray area. Silence is not consent; it is the absence of consent. Only an explicit "yes" can be considered consent.

This is, of course, completely logical, and fully consistent with adjudicating other crimes. Nevertheless, it is bound to raise howls of protest from opponents of women's equality and their right to make decisions about their own bodies.

"Yes means yes" has been the law of the land in Canada since 1992, yet the reporting of sexual assault has not skyrocketed with this higher standard. In the 1990s, there was a similar conversation in this country when Antioch College, long a bastion of innovations in

Chapter 9 | **Reading Consent**

education, also decided that consent to sexual activity required more than just a failure to say no. Verbal consent, the new code of conduct stated, was required for any sexual contact that was not "mutually and simultaneously initiated."

When the so-called Antioch rules were first enacted at that college, the reaction was overwhelmingly negative. The anti-feminist chorus howled in derision at feminist protectionism gone berserk. "Saturday Night Live" parodied it. Charlton Heston added it to a list of examples of campus political correctness gone completely out of control. He told an audience at Harvard in 1999 that "at Antioch College in Ohio, young men seeking intimacy with a coed must get verbal permission at each step of the process from kissing to petting to final copulation—all clearly spelled out in a printed college directive."

While doomsayers lamented that the new rules would destroy the mystery of campus sex, the students took it in stride. Instead of, "Do you want to have sex?" they simply asked, "Do you want to implement the policy?" Of course some guys on campus were against it, in an honest way. "If I have to ask those questions, I won't get what I want," blurted out one young man to a reporter. Bingo.

But seriously, since when is hearing "yes" a turnoff? Answering "yes" to, "Can I touch you there?" "Would you like me to?" "Will you [fill in blank] me?" seems a turn-on and a confirmation of desire, whatever the sexual identity of the asker and the asked. Actually, "yes" is perhaps the most erotic word in the English language.

One of literature's most enduring works, James Joyce's "Ulysses," concludes with Molly Bloom's affirmative declaration of desire (considered so erotic, in fact, that it was banned for more than a decade after publication): "and then I asked him with my eyes to ask again yes and then he asked me would I yes to say yes my mountain flower and first I put my arms around him yes and drew him down to me so he could feel my breasts all perfume yes and his heart was going like mad and yes I said yes I will Yes."

"Yes means yes" is clearly saner—and sexier. And that's true for both Leopold and Molly Bloom, as well as the rest of us.

■ WHAT?

1. Explain how Kimmel and Steinem establish the need for a new way of thinking about consent to replace the "no means no" standard. Do you think their effort is effective? Explain your response.
2. Research the Antioch College rules that Kimmel and Steinem mention and the response to those rules at the time. What do you think of the Antioch rules? Do you think they would be effective at USC? Explain your response.

Charlie Glickman is a sexuality educator who offers lectures, workshops, and one-on-one coaching to "help people create the happy, fulfilling sex lives and relationships they seek," according to his website. The following article is a blog post from September 2014.

BEFORE YOU READ

In this column, Charlie Glickman presents a positive look at the effects of affirmative consent laws and guidelines. Look online to find sources that argue against "yes means yes" by focusing on what they believe could be its negative consequences.

WHAT AFFIRMATIVE CONSENT LOOKS LIKE
By Charlie Glickman

It's been really excited to see the progress of California Senate Bill 967. If it gets signed, it will require all universities that receive financial aid to use a standard of "affirmative consent" in disciplinary hearings about sexual assault. In a nutshell, it shifts things from "did anyone say no?" to "did everyone say yes?" According to the text of the bill:

> "Affirmative consent" means affirmative, conscious, and voluntary agreement to engage in sexual activity. It is the responsibility of each person involved in the sexual activity to ensure that he or she has the affirmative consent of the other or others to engage in the sexual activity. Lack of protest or resistance does not mean consent, nor does silence mean consent. Affirmative consent must be ongoing throughout a sexual activity and can be revoked at any time. The existence of a dating relationship between the persons involved, or the fact of past sexual relations between them, should never by itself be assumed to be an indicator of consent.

This would be a huge step forward because it would recognize the way that sexual consent really should work. Of course, some people are freaking out about it. There are claims that it would require a written contract or other documentation. There are claims that if you're not yelling "yes, yes, yes!" it would be considered rape. There are claims that consent has to be verbal. In fact, none of these are true.

The thing is, I understand where some of these fears are coming from. Leaving aside the folks who are actual rapists (including the 6% of men who won't call what they're doing rape, but if you call it something else, they'll admit to it), changing the rules of the game is scary. We live in a culture that teaches and shames us into bad sexual communication. We shame men who don't want to have sex within a narrow range of acceptable activities. We shame women who express their desires or want sex more than we think they should. (And slut-shaming enables rape.) We've created a performance model of sex, in which people copy what they see in porn because they don't know any better. I've worked with a lot of people who are miserable because they're performing sex rather than enjoying it. So

Chapter 9 | Reading Consent

when we talk about shifting what sexual consent means, even when it's for the better, we're stirring up a lot of pain, triggers, shame, and trauma.

One thing we need to move through this is a more clear idea of what "affirmative, conscious, and voluntary agreement to engage in sexual activity" looks like. It's a great phrase for a legal document, but unless you get turned on by that sort of thing, it's a rather dry concept. As a sex and relationship coach, I want to see something that you could actually put into practice in the bedroom.

This is important because a lot of people really struggle with this. In "How to Not be 'That Guy'," the workshop that Alex Morgan and I created, we regularly get people talking about their concerns about going too far or about not knowing how to read the situation. And it's not just cisgender men who say this. We hear it from people of all genders and sexual orientations, though cis men often have the most anxiety about it. […] Fortunately, I'm able to share powerful formula for verbal sexual communication that can help make it easier to talk about sexual consent.

But as difficult as it can be to talk about sex with a potential partner, things get even trickier when we're talking about non-verbal communication. There's much more room for ambiguity, miscommunication, and misunderstanding when we don't use our words. So I posted on Facebook to ask folks what non-verbal affirmative consent might look like. Here are some of the things people suggested. (Note: all of these bullet points came from comments on my post.)

- ◆ Looking me in the eye and giving me a hand signal that says 'come towards me.'

- ◆ When I guide someone's hands and place them on my body nodding yes.

- ◆ I think that the only real test of affirmative consent is when the other person takes initiative of her or his own accord—without prompting or pressure. Without stopping and waiting for that initiative, there is just too much room for misunderstanding, especially with a newish partner. For example, when offering a kiss, coming close enough almost to make contact but not quite, and waiting for a partner to bridge the gap—or not—communicates both my desire to act and my desire to be met, without words.   If there is hesitation, then I know that more verbal conversation is in order, and that's good. It saves much grief all around.

- ◆ Reciprocation. Guiding hands. Asking about preferences. (Is this ok? Faster? Slower? How is this?) Taking initiative, responding in like, exploring your body with their hands, etc. Look for things about the hook up that your partner seems apprehensive about, such as stiffening up, pulling or leaning away, or generally letting you do all the work—pretty good indicator that you are with someone who isn't into it and probably cannot tell you or is scared shitless to tell you.

I really like this list because it shows some of the many ways that we can show someone that we're actively enjoying a sexual experience. Of course, there's always the chance that someone is performing rather than actually expressing their pleasure. Non-verbal communication can be faked, especially if someone feels pressured into it. Plus, it lacks bandwidth and it's ambiguous since two different people might have very different ideas about what any of these things might mean.

That's why non-verbal consent can only be relied on when you already know your partner and how they respond. Until you have that foundation, due diligence suggests making verbal communication your standard. It's unfortunately easy to do something that you genuinely believe your partner is enjoying and then find out later that they didn't. I've been on both sides of that and it's no fun.

It's also worth thinking about the ways in which we can withdraw consent non-verbally and I'm glad that Alex pointed this out on Facebook with these examples:

- Grabbing and moving the other's hands/mouth/other fun bits away.
- Shifting one's body to reduce or remove stimulation.
- "Waiting" for the other party to move or change stimulation, offering minimal nonverbal signaling or responsiveness and reducing or withdrawing any reciprocation (note: this is a move that can indicate unwillingness to signal one's own desires, and I consider it a warning flag that someone isn't up to my speed).
- Freezing up, going non-responsive (this can be a trauma response as well, and as such the party in question may go non-verbal and be unable to state a verbal boundary; ALWAYS honor this as a firm no to whatever is happening and switch gears to comfort touch, checking in, and waiting if necessary for their words to return).

I get that paying attention to these things can be challenging when you're turned on. Being able to drop into the experience, manage your sexual energy, and give attention to your partner is a lot to juggle. If you focus too much on your experience, you don't notice what's going on for your partner. If you focus too much on them, you miss out on your own pleasure. It's a constant act of recalibration from moment to moment, and it takes practice.

Familiarity with your partner's sexual response, communication style, and sexual desires (as well as your own) makes it easier. But that just means that if you don't know someone well enough to be confident that you can read their non-verbal sexual communication, you need to talk about it before and during sex. Not just once, but as an ongoing part of the experience. Yes, understanding how to talk about sex and how to read non-verbal communication can be tricky. And if you want to not hurt someone, you have a responsibility to learn how to do it. There are plenty of books, websites, and coaches who can help you with that.

Ultimately, what affirmative consent really looks like is someone enjoying themselves. When everyone is saying "yes" with their voices and their bodies, that's when you know that everyone is having a good time. Go look at that first list again and you'll see what I mean. That's why I find it so fascinating to read articles that ask things like "Are we in danger, in the rush to legislate, of ruining the moment?" Would your evening at a restaurant be ruined by asking someone how they're enjoying the food? Would an evening at a concert be ruined by talking about whether you're having a good time?

That's why this legal shift is so important. Adopting the standard of "did everyone say yes?" when investigating complaints of sexual assault helps us shift away from questioning the actions of the victim and instead, places an equal importance on the actions of everyone in the situation. It allows us to ask things like what they each did to assess their partner's consent and how they each responded to that. It removes the question of what the alleged victim did to say no, and focuses on the issue of what was done to invite a yes. And it makes it harder for the folks who genuinely don't care about their partner's pleasure and enjoyment to pretend anymore.

Chapter 9 | **Reading Consent**

WHAT?

1. Why does the author, Charlie Glickman, think the "yes means yes" standard is a positive change?
2. Explain the emphasis on verbal communication that Glickman places on an intimate encounter with a new partner.

IMAGE 9.2
Affirmative consent, according to California's new law governing colleges and universities, "means affirmative, conscious, and voluntary agreement to engage in sexual activity. It is the responsibility of each person involved in the sexual activity to ensure that he or she has the affirmative consent of the other or others to engage in the sexual activity."

> Kelli Gulite, who works as a paralegal in Washington, D.C., recently graduated cum laude from George Washington University's Honors Program with degrees in Political Science and Criminal Justice. During her time at school, she served as the GW Liberty Society's president and worked closely with the DC Forum for Freedom in addition to Students for Liberty. Gulite wrote this column for the website Thoughts on Liberty in October 2014.

BEFORE YOU READ
Visit the Thoughts on Liberty website and prepare a brief report that characterizes the website and its audience.

WHY ALL COLLEGES SHOULD ADOPT AFFIRMATIVE CONSENT
By Kelli Gulite

I think pretty much everyone can agree at this point: America's universities and colleges suck at handling sexual assault on campus.

Currently, the Department of Education is investigating 76 colleges and universities for their possible mismanagement of sexual assault cases under the existing standards of Title IX. The Obama Administration launched a campaign to end sexual assault on campus earlier this month. Although there have been few, if any, decent studies quantifying the number of sexual assaults that occur on campus, even conservative estimates suggest that sexual assault is pervasive at school.

Following the federal government's call for action, Governor Jerry Brown signed bill SB967, which stipulated that California colleges and universities must adopt an "affirmative consent" standard in their school policy on sexual assault in order to receive state funding or benefits. With this, California became the first state to adopt affirmative consent, commonly referred to as the "yes means yes" standard, in state policy.

The media's reaction to the new law has been divided, and both sides have failed recognize valid opposing arguments. Reason Magazine called the affirmative consent standard "dangerous" and an unnecessary government intervention into the bedroom of co-eds but failed to address the problematic ambiguity of the existing consent standards. Meanwhile, proponents of affirmative consent quickly dismissed the legitimate concerns of civil libertarians as "idiotic" without much to substantiate their claims.

Despite the hypnotic controversy, the reality of the situation is clear. Affirmative consent is a necessary standard that should be adopted by all universities. However, in order for the affirmative consent standard to be fairly investigated and adjudicated, universities have to step up their game.

What Is Affirmative Consent?

Opposed to the "no means no" mantra that has defined public perception of sexual consent for decades, the "yes means yes" standard requires that sexual partners consciously and voluntarily agree to engage in sexual activity through verbal or non-verbal cues. Specifically, under the affirmative consent standard, silence does not establish consent, hopefully to correct the problem of "misunderstandings" that happen because the victim was too scared or shocked to say no.

Much of the backlash to the affirmative consent standard as laid out in the California bill has been in response to outright mischaracterizations of the bill's content. This is a summary of the actual text of the bill:

- The bill defines affirmative consent as "affirmative, conscious, and voluntary agreement to engage in sexual activity." "Enthusiastic consent" is not in the bill.

- The bill specifically states that consent is defined by "a reasonable person's standards." Mundane or common sexual acts like taking off your partner's pants without expressed consent do not fall under the scope of the standard. […]

- Similarly, a sexual partner is expected to know the other's level of alcohol or drug influence based upon what a reasonable person would know about intoxication.

These carve-outs clearly allow for fair discretion under the standard.

Why Affirmative Consent Is Necessary

The best way to show why affirmative consent is a better standard than previous standards is through an example. Two students agree to have vaginal intercourse, but without warning or asking permission, the male student begins to have anal intercourse. Of course, the female could say no immediately after taking a few seconds to register what happened and the male could oblige. However, the sexual assault has already occurred.

Under the affirmative consent standard, the victim has recourse. Without it, she does not.

Put simply, previous consent standards don't take into account the very many scenarios in which a person can be sexually violated or assaulted. The best way to combat this is to change the way sexual consent is defined in society, and for this change to be reflected in law and policy.

Caroline K. Gorman asserts that the bill "reverses the presumption of innocence." However, the affirmative consent standard does not necessarily burden the accused to show proof of innocence. To decide the case, the accuser still has to prove that a "yes" did not, in fact, occur.

Of course, when it comes down to matters of consent, "he-said/she-said" scenarios can always become muddled. Nevertheless, this problem has always been the case. The ambiguity of the evidence is no reason to disapprove of the new bill.

Why Schools Should Continue to Investigate and Adjudicate Sexual Assault Cases

Although some question universities' involvement in sexual assault cases at all, the act should absolutely be included in all universities student codes of conduct in order to foster a safe academic environment. Emma Sulkowicz has famously illustrated the emotional struggle she endures on a regular basis having to live on campus with her alleged rapist. Her story cannot be uncommon given that 75% of total disciplinary actions taken against students found of sexual assault crimes by universities were only minor sanctions. Colleges should certainly expect its students to maintain a certain code of conduct and have the grounds to discipline students who do threaten the overall well-being of the student body.

First, university adjudication does not replace the criminal justice process regarding sex crimes. The university consent standards are not legal precedents, but rather part of the rules that govern university life and student conduct. Under the new California law, university codes of conduct regarding sexual assaults should not and could not foreseeably play a defining role in the criminal justice system. University adjudication is a separate, but parallel, process to the criminal justice system.

Furthermore, universities can fill in the gaps left open by a lacking criminal justice system. And to be clear, the criminal justice system needs all the help it can get when it comes to sexual assault investigations. In their role as first-responders, university police can collect evidence or gather witness accounts sooner rather than later. They can immediately provide and test for rape kits as soon as possible, especially when states are backlogged. Or, when the state is unable prosecute an offender because there is only circumstantial evidence, universities at least have the recourse to remove the offender from campus. Given the severity of the sexual assault problem, we shouldn't be choosy about where help comes from.

Opponents of the bill claim, "While campus administrators are in many cases doing their best, they are neither qualified nor equipped to respond properly to sexual assault allegations." Given the current state of affairs, that may very well be true. But this doesn't mean we ignore the potential role universities can play in ending sexual assaults; it means we should demand that universities provide better services.

Ways to Better University Investigation and Adjudication of Sexual Assaults

In fact, there are several steps that universities can and should take toward making their disciplinary and investigatory proceedings of sexual assault cases under the affirmative consent standard fair and balanced. While the California bill implements many new university procedures concerning investigation and adjudication of sexual assault, it is imperative that the changes below are also put into effect:

- ◆ Resources: Currently, most schools do not have the investigatory resources they need to obtain the necessary evidence need in school disciplinary hearings of this serious nature. While Title IX requires that disciplinary committees ruling over

Chapter 9 | **Reading Consent**

sexual assault cases attend a training session on sexual assault policy and Title IX standards, schools would benefit tremendously if University Police were also required to go through extensive training. Rather than fumbling witness reports or destroying evidence, the University Police could actually become a very useful source in combating sexual assault on campus.

◆ Allow For A Legal Defense: As it stands now, most schools will not allow attorneys into school disciplinary hearings, even in cases of alleged sexual assault. Given the complexity of sexual assault cases, it is necessary that all schools allow lawyers to argue cases in front of the college tribunal rather than force students to make arguments for themselves. Obviously, if lawyers were allowed to argue cases, students are much less likely to implicate themselves accidentally or be ransacked by a kangaroo court.

◆ Regular Title IX Investigations and Oversight: Although the federal government recently launched a large investigation into possible Title IX violations, this is not a regular practice. Senator Kirsten Gillibrand's office estimated that 63% Title IX violations are dismissed due to lack of federal oversight. Many effective procedures for handling sexual assault are implemented by Title IX, but it is likely that this investigation will show that not all schools follow these procedures to the "t." Regular oversight could ensure that schools actually follow through with standard procedures.

Yes, the adoption of the affirmative consent standard will lay the groundwork for preventing and ending sexual assaults on campus. But the government—and universities—should match action with their promises. Improvements, like the ones I've listed above, must be made to the way universities conduct investigations and adjudicate sexual assault. Universities are going to have to dedicate resources, ensure that investigations are well-conducted, and that academic punishments are doled out fairly and expediently if we are going to see any serious decreases in sexual assault on campuses–SB967 and "yes means yes" is only a start.

■ WHAT?

1. Briefly summarize Kelli Gulite's contention that all colleges should adopt the "yes means yes" standard. Do you think she presents an effective argument? Explain why or why not.
2. How does Gulite criticize both opponents and supporters of affirmative consent? What point does she make about the importance of listening to those with whom we disagree?

> *Roberta Smith is an art critic for* The New York Times. *She wrote the following feature review for the newspaper in September 2014.*

BEFORE YOU READ
Look online for images and videos of Emma Sulkowicz's protest piece, titled "Carry That Weight," so that you have a better understanding of the review that follows.

IN A MATTRESS, A LEVER FOR ART AND POLITICAL PROTEST
By Roberta Smith

You can, for the moment, call Emma Sulkowicz a typically messianic artist, and she won't object. I used the phrase, sitting in her tiny studio at Columbia University, as we discussed "Carry That Weight." This is the succinct and powerful performance piece that is her senior art thesis as well as her protest against sexual assault on campus, especially the one she says she endured.

"Carry that Weight" involves Ms. Sulkowicz carrying a 50-pound mattress wherever she goes on campus (but not off campus). Analogies to the Stations of the Cross may come to mind, especially when friends or strangers spontaneously step forward and help her carry her burden, which is both actual and symbolic. Of course another analogy is to Hester Prynne and her scarlet letter, albeit an extra heavy version that Ms. Sulkowicz has taken up by choice, to call attention to her plight and the plight of other women who feel university officials have failed to deter or adequately punish such assaults. The carried mattress also implies disruption and uprootedness, which call to mind refugees or homeless people.

The subject of sexual assault on campuses surfaced on the national stage in September 2014, when President Obama and Vice President Joseph R. Biden Jr. announced the formation of It's On Us, a national campaign on this issue. They addressed it in blunt and unequivocal terms. "Society still does not sufficiently value women," the president said.

Ms. Sulkowicz spoke of her interest in the kind of art that elicits a powerful response, whether negative or positive. Freshly painted on the walls around us loomed big black letters spelling out the "rules of engagement," the guidelines to her performance: One states that she will continue the piece until the man she accuses of attacking her is no longer on campus, whether he leaves or is expelled or graduates, as she also will next spring. (If need be, she plans to attend commencement carrying the mattress.) She said the performance is giving her new muscles and an inner strength she didn't know she had, and is attracting many different kinds of attention, some of it hard to take.

"Carry That Weight" is both singular and representative of a time of strongly held opinions and objections and righteous anger on all sides, a time when, not surprisingly, political protest and performance art are intersecting in increasingly adamant ways.

You can see this merging in the Guy Fawkes masks worn by members of Anonymous, a loose international network of hactivists, at protests against, for example, the Church of

Chapter 9 | **Reading Consent**

Scientology or the killing of Michael Brown in Ferguson, Mo. You can also see it in some of the performance-like protests that greeted the opening this month of the David H. Koch Plaza at the Metropolitan Museum of Art or those that were carried out last spring in the rotunda of the Guggenheim Museum to call attention to the general plight of laborers in the United Arab Emirates who are expected to build its latest outpost there. There are numerous other instances: Protests in London in 2011 against the Tate's accepting sponsorship from BP included a performer splashed with oil, lying naked on the floor of the great hall of Tate Britain like a bird caught in an oil spill.

Ms. Sulkowicz's effort is somewhere near this intersection, but not at its center. Combining aspects of endurance, body and protest art and participatory relational aesthetics, it is a highly specific work of art in its own right, carefully conceived and carried out by one person expending considerable thought, time and energy for a very long time (up to eight months). It comes from a history that includes the relatively solitary ordeals of Vito Acconci, Tehching Hsieh and Marina Abramovic, but also relates tangentially to more extreme physical acts of political resistance—the fasts of jailed suffragists in early-20th-century Britain come to mind.

"Carry That Weight" might be called an artwork of last resort. It is the culmination of two years of pain, humiliation, frustration and righteous anger that began in 2012. On the evening of the first day of classes of her sophomore year, Ms. Sulkowicz said, she was anally raped in her dorm room by a fellow student with whom she had had consensual sex twice before, according to the police report.

In the aftermath, Ms. Sulkowicz suffered in silence, then filed a complaint with the university. This led to a hearing before a panel that found him not responsible, according to a campus newspaper report in The Columbia Spectator, a decision that was upheld upon appeal. After that disappointment, she said, a trip last May to file a report with the police was so upsetting she didn't follow through, although she secretly recorded it on her cellphone.

The performance piece began to take shape in Ms. Sulkowicz's mind during a residency at Yale Summer School of Art and Music in Norfolk, Conn., this past summer. First she made a short video that showed her dismantling a bed, with the police station tape as audio. But soon she focused on the mattress alone and using it on campus, with the simplest, most public action being to carry it. The foam mattress and its dark blue cover are identical to the standard issue one on which she said the rape occurred and were not easy to track down and purchase; the rules of engagement similarly took a lot of refinement and every day still present her with new logistical problems to work out. (For example, going to the subway requires walking a few extra blocks since she can't cut across campus without the mattress.)

One of the most effective aspects of the piece is the way it fluctuates between private and public, and solitary and participatory. She said she rarely walks very far without someone lending a hand and entering into what she calls "the space of performance." Indeed, shortly after leaving her studio on Thursday afternoon, she ran into her best friend, Gabriela Pelsinger, who took over one end of the mattress, in effect becoming one of the performers. (One of the rules is that Ms. Sulkowicz cannot ask for help, but she can accept it.)

Ms. Pelsinger, like Ms. Sulkowicz, is among a group of more than 20 men and women who have joined in a Title IX complaint with the federal government's Department of

Education against Columbia, charging that it mishandled their individual gender-based misconduct or sexual assault cases.

Suzanne B. Goldberg, special adviser to the university's president, Lee Bollinger, on sexual assault assault prevention and response, and director of Columbia Law School's Center for Gender & Sexuality Law, said in a statement, "As the university has made clear in many different ways during the past month, major steps have been taken to enhance the gender-based misconduct policy and resources available to all Columbia University students." Ms. Goldberg said the university does not comment on individual cases. She added, "The university embraces the attention that students and others have brought to the issue."

As Ms. Sulkowicz and Ms. Pelsinger proceeded across campus, some people smiled while others looked puzzled. There were comments. "There she goes again," one woman said to her companion as they walked past me. Midway through the journey, a young man joined the task, keeping a cellphone cradled to his ear until he left, at the front door of Ms. Sulkowicz's dorm.

It is hard to fathom the effect "Carry That Weight" will have as it proceeds—on Columbia, on Ms. Sulkowicz, on the consciousness of sexual assault on campus, or on the thinking of people who encounter her performance. But it seems certain that the piece has set a very high standard for any future work she'll do as an artist and will also earn her a niche in the history of intensely personal yet aggressively political performance art.

It is so simple: A woman with a mattress, refusing to keep her violation private, carrying with her a stark reminder of where it took place. The work Ms. Sulkowicz is making is strict and lean, yet inclusive and open ended, symbolically laden yet drastically physical. All of this determines its striking quality as art, which in turn contributes substantially to its effectiveness as protest.

■ WHAT?

1. How does the author, art critic Roberta Smith, evaluate "Carry That Weight"? Does she think it is successful as art? As a protest? Explain Smith's reasoning.
2. What has been the national response to Emma Sulkowicz's protest? What do supporters have to say about it? Can you find any critics of the piece?
3. Look online to find updates on Sulkowicz's protest. Is she still carrying the mattress? Is the man she accused of raping her still on the Columbia University campus?

Chapter 9 | **Reading Consent**

Roz Galtz, who has a Ph.D. in sociology and a degree in environmental law, focuses professionally on climate change but also writes on sexual politics. This essay was published in October 2014 at the website Common Dreams.

BEFORE YOU READ
Go online and explore the most common objections to the "Yes Means Yes" movement. Then, prepare a brief report that summarizes and explains these objections.

A FEMINIST SAYS 'NO' TO YES-MEANS-YES
By Roz Galtz

As a lifelong, hardcore feminist—not to mention the mom of a teenage girl—I know I'm supposed to be overjoyed by passage of California's SB 967, the law that enshrines a "yes-means-yes" consent standard for sexual assault on college and university campuses. (You've got to confirm your partner's active consent throughout a sexual encounter, or the facts will support a sexual assault claim.

I want to be happy. It feels like forever since feminists have had a win. Still, I can't help but dislike this bill entirely.

How did we get to a place where we uncritically celebrate a law meant to enhance justice for survivors of sexual assault, but only if they're enrolled in a college or university?

Let's start by acknowledging: college women are at no greater risk of sexual assault than other women their age. Given the reporting, you're probably tempted to dismiss that assertion out of hand, but check it out. Rely on nearly any set of measures you'd like. As tricky as sexual assault stats can be, the evidence is nearly uniform on this point. Campus women aren't at greater risk than their non-academic sisters, they're just more aggregated in space.

So how did we get here? There are a number of explanations, but ultimately the only reason we need to rethink campus policies on sexual assault in the first place is that campuses are permitted to adjudicate them.

For far too long, residential campuses have been permitted to act as little, make-believe municipalities, complete with their own quasi-judicial processes, staffed by faculty who just love the buzz of the solemnity of getting to play judge.

When I try to envision a campus sexual assault proceeding, I flash on the case of a kid at a "living learning" program where I used to teach. After an RA busted him for trouble in the dorms, he distributed hundreds of copies of a disordered, rambling tract targeting her. He promised to get stray dogs to urinate all over her. He declared "open f-cking season on dumb tw-ts now" (a threat with a little extra oomph, coming from a burly guy who dressed in full combat fatigues).

The RA was terrified and terrorized—forced to flee the dorm that was both her housing and her job site.

This wasn't a sexual assault, but the program's response was telling. Was the guy arrested? Put before a disciplinary board? Subject to a mandatory psych eval? Did the RA receive some form of protection? Was she given a say in how the problem was handled?

The answer, as far as I could ever learn, was no on every count.

Administrators seemed anxious to keep things in house. The program was under scrutiny for its high costs and persistent crises. A senior faculty member had recently racked up his second reprimand for sexual harassment. The last thing anyone wanted was another black eye.

Faculty sentiment also ran decidedly against formal discipline, which may have led to expulsion given the student's "priors." Rationales for were varied—one prof simply maintained there was no way this kid could be a threat because: "I've had him in several classes, and he's always been very quiet." (No, seriously, that's what he said.) Of course, "this kid" was white. Does anyone buy for a minute that a burly black dude who dressed like a sniper could plaster his college with vows to torture and kill a white female RA and walk away with no repercussions … because he was quiet in class?

Now consider: these are the same folks assembling with all sense of seriousness to judge sexual assault claims on campuses. Don't get me wrong, people with PhDs are probably no less likely than the rest of the population to be thoughtful about gender, violence, and race when confronting real-life conflict; but let's not kid ourselves—they're not liable to be more.

Administrators are, meanwhile, directly, materially tethered to the reputations of their institutions. No one who understands this should be surprised to learn that sexual assault adjudications are often delayed till the aggressor graduates or the victim drops out.

The cosplay that is campus criminal justice was simply never about valuing women's lives in the first place. It's always been about protecting institutions.

So what to do?

A far more productive fix than state-by-state replication of California's SB 967 would be to pass federal legislation dismantling campus criminal adjudications altogether, along with the state and federal programs that lend them legitimacy and gravitas.

So many high-powered California campuses—not to mention ones like Yale that are headed toward yes-means-yes of their own accord—sit in or adjacent to neighborhoods with spectacularly high sexual assault rates. Rather than wasting time managing pretend-judicial systems, they should direct their formidable resources to improving community-based access to rape crisis advocacy, which research suggests would do far more to help survivors than new consent standards ever could.

Community-based advocacy can also open spaces where diverse groups of women can recognize their common challenges and threats—as well as their common, uncommon strengths. It can even help to build that thing called solidarity, so conspicuously lacking in American public life.

The suggestion that students should bring sexual assaults directly to the police tends to provoke a kind of spluttering outrage. After all, if not uniformly hostile to victims, the police, DAs, and courts are notoriously uneven, depending on their culture, training, resources, and leadership. Why subject college students to their brand of justice?

The real question is, why shouldn't student victims of sexual assault turn to the real police and the real courts for help? These are the institutions to which the rest of us have to turn, as will the women of Berkeley and UCLA on graduation. Yes-means-yes as a cultural project is one thing. But state support of alternative tribunals for advantaged populations only siphons off political pressure that is needed to reform the real-world institutions we need to work for all of us.

■ WHAT?

1. Summarize Roz Galtz's primary objections to affirmative consent standards for colleges and universities. What do you think of her position?
2. After explaining her objections to affirmative consent regulations for colleges, Galtz suggests a different course of action. Explain her proposal.

■ WHAT ELSE? WHAT NEXT?

3. Early in her essay, Galtz asserts that "college women are at no greater risk of sexual assault than other women their age" and then encourages skeptical readers check the data for themselves. Can you find any data that supports Galtz's claim? What do you think of her decision to not include this data in her essay?

> President Obama delivered the following address at the White House on September 19, 2014, to introduce the "It's on Us" campaign against sexual assault on college campuses. Among those in attendance were Vice President Joe Biden, athletes, celebrities, activists, and survivors of sexual assault.

BEFORE YOU READ
Visit the "It's On Us" website at ItsOnUs.org and familiarize yourself with the campaign and the pledge that President Obama mentions in his speech below.

EXCERPTS FROM
REMARKS BY THE PRESIDENT AT THE 'IT'S ON US' CAMPAIGN ROLLOUT
By President Barack Obama

[T]o the survivors who are leading the fight against sexual assault on campuses, your efforts have helped to start a movement. I know that […] there are times where the fight feels lonely, and it feels as if you're dredging up stuff that you'd rather put behind you. But we're here to say, today, it's not on you. This is not your fight alone. This is on all of us, every one of us, to fight campus sexual assault. You are not alone, and we have your back, and we are going to organize campus by campus, city by city, state by state. This entire country is going to make sure that we understand what this is about, and that we're going to put a stop to it.

And this is a new school year. We've been working on campus sexual assault for several years, but the issue of violence against women is now in the news every day. We started to I think get a better picture about what domestic violence is all about. People are talking about it. Victims are realizing they're not alone. Brave people have come forward, they're opening up about their own experiences.

And so we think today's event is all that more relevant, all that more important for us to say that campus sexual assault is no longer something we as a nation can turn away from and say that's not our problem. This is a problem that matters to all of us.

An estimated one in five women has been sexually assaulted during her college years—one in five. Of those assaults, only 12 percent are reported, and of those reported assaults, only a fraction of the offenders are punished. And while these assaults overwhelmingly happen to women, we know that men are assaulted, too. Men get raped. They're even less likely to talk about it. We know that sexual assault can happen to anyone, no matter their race, their economic status, sexual orientation, gender identity—and LGBT victims can feel even more isolated, feel even more alone.

For anybody whose once-normal, everyday life was suddenly shattered by an act of sexual violence, the trauma, the terror can shadow you long after one horrible attack. It lingers when you don't know where to go or who to turn to. It's there when you're forced to sit in the same class or stay in the same dorm with the person who raped you; when people are more suspicious of what you were wearing or what you were drinking, as if it's your fault, not the fault of the person who assaulted you. It's a haunting presence when the very people entrusted with your welfare fail to protect you.

Students work hard to get into college. I know—I'm watching Malia right now, she's a junior. She's got a lot of homework. And parents can do everything they can to support their kids' dreams of getting a good education. When they finally make it onto campus, only to be assaulted, that's not just a nightmare for them and their families; it's not just an affront to everything they've worked so hard to achieve—it is an affront to our basic humanity. It insults our most basic values as individuals and families, and as a nation. We are a nation that values liberty and equality and justice. And we're a people who believe every child deserves an education that allows them to fulfill their God-given potential, free from fear of intimidation or violence. And we owe it to our children to live up to those values. So my administration is trying to do our part.

First of all, three years ago, we sent guidance to every school district, every college, every university that receives federal funding, and we clarified their legal obligations to prevent and respond to sexual assault. And we reminded them that sexual violence isn't just a crime, it is a civil rights violation. And I want to acknowledge Secretary of Education Arne Duncan for his department's work in holding schools accountable and making sure that they stand up for students.

Number two, in January, I created a White House task force to prevent—a Task Force to Protect Students from Sexual Assault. Their job is to work with colleges and universities on better ways to prevent and respond to assaults, to lift up best practices. And we held conversations with thousands of people—survivors, parents, student groups, faculty, law enforcement, advocates, academics. In April, the task force released the first report, recommending a number of best practices for colleges and universities to keep our kids safe. And these are tested, and they are common-sense measures like campus surveys to figure out the scope of the problem, giving survivors a safe place to go and a trusted person to talk to, training school officials in how to handle trauma. Because when you read some of the accounts, you think, what were they thinking? You just get a sense of too many people in charge dropping the ball, fumbling something that should be taken with the most—the utmost seriousness and the utmost care.

Number three, we're stepping up enforcement efforts and increasing the transparency of our efforts. So we're reviewing existing laws to make sure they're adequate. And we're going to keep on working with educational institutions across the country to help them appropriately respond to these crimes.

So that's what we have been doing, but there's always more that we can do. And today, we're taking a step and joining with people across the country to change our culture and help prevent sexual assault from happening. Because that's where prevention—that's what prevention is going to require—we've got to have a fundamental shift in our culture.

As far as we've come, the fact is that from sports leagues to pop culture to politics, our society still does not sufficiently value women. We still don't condemn sexual assault as loudly as we should. We make excuses. We look the other way. The message that sends can have a chilling effect on our young women.

And I've said before, when women succeed, America succeeds—let me be clear, that's not just true in America. If you look internationally, countries that oppress their women are countries that do badly. Countries that empower their women are countries that thrive.

And so this is something that requires us to shift how we think about these issues. One letter from a young woman really brought this point home. Katherine Morrison, a young student from Youngstown, Ohio, she wrote, "How are we supposed to succeed when so many of our voices are being stifled? How can we succeed when our society says that as a woman, it's your fault if you are at a party or walked home alone. How can we succeed when people look at women and say 'you should have known better,' or 'boys will be boys'?"

And Katherine is absolutely right. Women make up half this country; half its workforce; more than half of our college students. They are not going to succeed the way they should unless they are treated as true equals, and are supported and respected. And unless women are allowed to fulfill their full potential, America will not reach its full potential. So we've got to change.

This is not just the work of survivors, it's not just the work of activists. It's not just the work of college administrators. It's the responsibility of the soccer coach, and the captain of the basketball team, and the football players. And it's on fraternities and sororities, and it's on the editor of the school paper, and the drum major in the band. And it's on the English department and the engineering department, and it's on the high schools and the elementary schools, and it's on teachers, and it's on counselors, and it's on mentors, and it's on ministers.

It's on celebrities, and sports leagues, and the media, to set a better example. It's on parents and grandparents and older brothers and sisters to sit down young people and talk about this issue.

And it's not just on the parents of young women to caution them. It is on the parents of young men to teach them respect for women. And it's on grown men to set an example and be clear about what it means to be a man.

It is on all of us to reject the quiet tolerance of sexual assault and to refuse to accept what's unacceptable. And we especially need our young men to show women the respect they deserve, and to recognize sexual assault, and to do their part to stop it. Because most young men on college campuses are not perpetrators. But the rest—we can't generalize across the board. But the rest of us can help stop those who think in these terms and shut stuff down. And that's not always easy to do with all the social pressures to stay quiet or go along; you don't want to be the guy who's stopping another friend from taking a woman home even if it looks like she doesn't or can't consent. Maybe you hear something in the locker room that makes you feel uncomfortable, or see something at a party that you know isn't right, but you're not sure whether you should stand up, not sure it's okay to intervene.

And I think [Vice President] Joe [Biden] said it well—the truth is, it's not just okay to intervene, it is your responsibility. It is your responsibility to speak your mind. It is your responsibility to tell your buddy when he's messing up. It is your responsibility to set the right tone when you're talking about women, even when women aren't around— maybe especially when they're not around.

And it's not just men who should intervene. Women should also speak up when something doesn't look right, even if the men don't like it. It's all of us taking responsibility. Everybody has a role to play.

And in fact, we're here with Generation Progress to launch, appropriately enough, a campaign called "It's On Us." The idea is to fundamentally shift the way we think about sexual assault. So we're inviting colleges and universities to join us in saying, we are not tolerating this anymore—not on our campuses, not in our community, not in this country. And the campaign is building on the momentum that's already being generated by college campuses by the incredible young people around the country who have stepped up and are leading the way. I couldn't be prouder of them.

And we're also joined by some great partners in this effort—including the Office of Women's Health, the college sports community, media platforms. We've got universities who have signed up, including, by the way, our military academies, who are represented here today. So the goal is to hold ourselves and each other accountable, and to look out for those who don't consent and can't consent. And anybody can be a part of this campaign.

So the first step on this is to go to ItsOnUs.org—that's ItsOnUs.org. Take a pledge to help keep women and men safe from sexual assault. It's a promise not to be a bystander to the problem, but to be part of the solution. I took the pledge. Joe took the pledge. You can take the pledge. You can share it on social media, you can encourage others to join us.

And this campaign is just part of a broader effort, but it's a critical part, because even as we continue to enforce our laws and work with colleges to improve their responses, and to make sure that survivors are taken care of, it won't be enough unless we change the culture that allows assault to happen in the first place. […]

[…] So I'm asking all of you, join us in this campaign. Commit to being part of the solution. Help make sure our schools are safe havens where everybody, men and women, can pursue their dreams and fulfill their potential.

Thank you so much for all the great work.

■ WHAT?

1. President Obama says in his speech that "we've got to have a fundamental shift" in our thinking about sexual assault and prevention. What does he mean by this? What do you think it will take for such a shift to occur?
2. Research the public response to the It's On Us campaign. How has it been received? Do you think the campaign is effective? Explain your response.
3. How does the It's On Us campaign mesh with the goals of the "Yes Means Yes" movement?

> Dawn E. LaFrance, Meika Loe, and Scott C. Brown are all associated with Colgate University: LaFrance is the associate director of Colgate's Counseling Center, Loe is an associate professor of sociology and women's studies, and Brown is an associate vice president of the university and the dean of students. Their research article was published in 2012 in the American Journal of Sexuality Education.

BEFORE YOU READ
Look online to find out what you can about Colgate University's "Yes Means Yes" seminar. Is the seminar still offered? Can you find any indication of how students feel about the seminar?

'YES MEANS YES': A NEW APPROACH TO SEXUAL ASSAULT PREVENTION AND POSITIVE SEXUALITY PROMOTION
By Dawn E. LaFrance, Meika Loe, and Scott C. Brown

"The sexual social scene on many college campuses is dominated by the "hook up" culture. According to Wright, Norton, and Matusek (2010), a "hook up" is a "transitory sexual encounter between two people who are friends, brief acquaintances, or strangers and it may include sexual intercourse or other non-coital sexual activity" (p. 648). The hook-up culture is a heterosexist phenomenon, and in most cases, when students are asked questions about it they are considering behaviors between one man and one woman. About half of college students report engaging in a hook up during the last year (Owen, Rhoades, Stanley, & Fincham, 2010). Students engage in uncommitted sexual interactions for a variety of reasons, including physical/sexual gratification (Oswalt, 2010), intending to begin a traditional romantic relationship (Garcia & Reiber, 2008), lack of relationship responsibilities, and sexual exploration (Bisson & Levine, 2009).

Abstinence-only sex education that many students receive in high school does not help them learn how to discuss their sexual development and properly articulate their intentions to others in respectful relationships (Kohler, Manhart, & Lafferty, 2008; Santelli et al., 2006). When they enter college, many students are faced with a heterocentric campus hook-up culture that is confusing and has negative repercussions for students. Approximately onethird of students who hook up do so unintentionally (Garcia & Reiber, 2008). In such a campus culture, individuals may not communicate effectively about their sexual intentions, respect one another's sexual limits, or use appropriate safety measures during sexual contact (Flack et al., 2007; Glenn & Marquardt,

2001; Grello, Welsh, & Harper, 2006; LaBrie et al., 2005; Paul, McManus, & Hayes, 2000; Stanley, Rhoades, & Markman, 2006; Vail-Smith, Maguire, Brinkley, & Burke,

2010). Many students who have hooked up report a negative reaction to it and poorer psychological well-being (Owen et al., 2010).

Young adults often find it difficult to navigate the sexual scene during the college years. In many studies, male and female college students have reported consenting to unwanted sexual behavior (Davis, George, & Norris, 2004; Impett & Peplau, 2002; O'Sullivan & Allgeier, 1998; Sprecher, Hatfield, Cortese, Potapova, & Levitskaya, 1994). Additionally, students have reported denying their sexual interests when they do desire to engage in sexual activity (i.e., token resistance) (Muehlenhard & Hollabaugh, 1988, 1998; Sprecher et al., 1994). This miscommunication, as well as the use of alcohol and other substances, confuses the ability for one to obtain adequate consent from a sexual partner. "Gray rape" has been used to describe the blurred line between consensual and nonconsensual intercourse that is often evident in a hook-up culture (Jervis, 2008).

The personal sexual conduct of individuals becomes public when their behaviors affect the lives of others in their campus community. Students report sexual assaults, harassment, and rapes frequently on college campuses (DeKeseredy & Kelly, 1993; Fisher, Daigle, Cullen, & Turner, 2003; Gross, Winslett, Roberts, & Gohm, 2006; Koss, Gidycz, & Wisniewski, 1987). Flack and colleagues (2007) found that 78% of the sexual assaults reported in their study happened during a hook up.

With the close connection they have with students, educators have a unique opportunity to influence students to make better sexual decisions. Most campus programming aims to prevent sexual assault by focusing on prevention efforts (e.g., buddy system, never leave a drink unattended) (Breitenbecher, 2000; Yeater & O'Donohue, 1999), increasing empathy for sexual assault victims (e.g., Foubert & Newberry, 2006), or empowering bystanders to help their friends during problematic sexual incidences (Katz, 1994). Since exploring intimacy and developing sexual identities is developmentally appropriate for college students (Erikson, 1968) and starts years before college, we believe that a comprehensive sexual assault prevention program should also include the examination of sexual identities and desires. College programming "could help young adults identify their expectations about relationships and hooking up, learn how to define their romantic relationships and communicate about expectations, and monitor barriers to making good relationship decisions (e.g., alcohol use)" (Owen et al., 2010, p. 662). Additionally, since physical gratification is a key motivating factor in desire to hook up, sex education must take the topic of pleasure, as well as danger, seriously (Oswalt, 2010).

"Yes Means Yes" (YMY) is an interdisciplinary five-week positive sexuality course offered at our small liberal arts college as part of a campus-wide initiative to improve students' relationship skills and behaviors. This seminar employs a positive sexuality foundation that advocates for "an understanding of sexuality as a natural and healthy aspect of human life" (ETR Associates, 2007–2009, para. 2) and can be used in conjunction with sexual assault prevention and bystander programs. This course focuses on helping students decide what they would like from their relationships in a collaborative seminar format rather than focusing only on what they should avoid. The goals of this sexual education curriculum include creating healthy sexual beings who are comfortable engaging in safe, consensual and pleasurable sexual activity. A positive sexuality curriculum prioritizes developing sexual agency and making healthy decisions for oneself (DeFur, 2012). In this review of YMY, a campus-wide sexual health initiative, it will become clear how to adopt a similar program on other campuses.

A POSITIVE SEXUALITY SEMINAR

Similar to college students at other institutions, students at our small, liberal arts college in New York have shared with us that they have difficulties navigating their relationships and sexual lives. Many students report discomfort with the hook up culture. Given their ambivalence, we found that students are eager to critically engage with the campus sexual culture, and they found YMY to be a space to do so.

Every semester, for five consecutive weeks, approximately 30 students meet on Wednesday evenings for dinner and 90 minutes of critical discussion facilitated by faculty and staff. As a positive sexuality noncredit class, YMY attempts to better equip students to improve their relationships by addressing issues of healthy communication, positive sexuality, sexual attitudes, and decision-making skills. The five sessions of YMY consist of group activities and discussions. Students who take this class learn positive sexual decisionmaking skills, how to find campus resource support when necessary, and ways to engage in safer sexual behaviors. Equipped with this information, they are in the position to work with others to improve the campus climate. Ideally this seminar is used with other programs in a comprehensive plan to build students' sexual self-efficacy and to teach students to contribute to a safer, healthier sexual campus climate.

Seven YMY seminars have been offered between 2009 and 2012. Generally one seminar is held each semester. The classes fill quickly, and because of high interest two seminars were held simultaneously during one semester. In a typical academic year, approximately 60 70 students participate in YMY. The collaborative facilitation team consists of ten staff members from many departments including the Dean's Office, Counseling Services, and LGBTQ Initiatives, six faculty members from departments such as Sociology/Anthropology, Education Studies, and Women's Studies, and two previous YMY students. Students from all four class years enroll in this course. More women than men elect to participate (approximately 85% women). Students who identify as Hispanic/Latino, Black/African-American, Caucasian, and Asian/Asian-American, Multiracial, heterosexual, lesbian, gay, bisexual, transgendered, and queer have participated.

CURRICULUM

A senior undergraduate's sociology thesis (Berger, 2009) set the foundation for the YMY seminar. The curriculum is designed for five consecutive sessions, each focused on a short and interesting chapter of the book *Yes Means Yes! Visions of Female Sexual Power and a World Without Rape* (Friedman & Valenti, 2008). These academic essays, covering topics such as "gray rape," the silencing of women's desires, and consent in BDSM (Bondage and Discipline, Sadism and Masochism) culture, are used to springboard class discussion about the current sexual climate. A syllabus is distributed with assigned readings and key discussion points for each week (see Appendix A).

Faculty and staff facilitators usually work in pairs, along with one or two student facilitators who attend all sessions. Facilitators use appropriate selfdisclosure, genuinely participate when possible, and keep the conversations focused on university life. A variety of discussion formats (e.g., large group, dyad work, individual journal writing) are utilized to reach students with different learning styles. The session itself takes place in a large comfortable student gathering space, with chairs arranged in a circle so that participants face one another. A buffet dinner is served, and then the 90-minute session begins.

Although each session is important, the way that the first session is conducted sets the stage for the series since group dynamics and norms begin to form early. After an icebreaker introduction, an overview of the seminar is provided. Ground rules (e.g., use first names, speak about your own experiences, challenge yourself) are discussed and agreed upon during the first session. They are listed and referred back to at the beginning of subsequent sessions. An agree/disagree/unsure exercise is used to help students begin talking about relationships and sexual aspects of their lives. This exercise employs an imaginary line drawn on the floor with the word "Agree" written at one end, "Disagree" at the other end, and "Unsure" in the middle. Participants are asked to place themselves on the imaginary line after a statement is read aloud by a facilitator. A series of statements include "Two intoxicated people can have consensual sex," "Public displays of affection are okay," and "Pornography can be a healthy component of a positive sexual relationship." Facilitators inquire with individuals about why they choose their locations on the line. When facilitators take a nonjudgmental stance open to all opinions, students start to open up quickly. The exercise is always debriefed with questions such as "What did you notice?" "Were there any surprises?" and "Was it easy for you to pick your locations on the line?" For the time remaining in the first class, students collaborate on a common definition of "hooking up." Smaller groups share lists of the pros and cons of this type of campus sexual culture. The spring 2010 YMY students, for example, agreed that hooking up is "a casual, noncommittal sexual experience ranging from making out to sexual intercourse [with a potential lack of mutual commitment, affection, attachment, emotion, and there is not necessarily a balance of power]." The follow-up discussion about the pros and cons of hooking up allowed students to consider ways of making future decisions regarding their intimate lives on campus, as well as imagining a healthier sexual culture on campus.

All subsequent classes have at least one short chapter assigned to them that students are expected to read on their own. One of the facilitators' tasks is to help students examine how the chapter themes are applied to their daily lives at college. Using the chapter themes, facilitators use a variety of exercises to teach students how to use their critical thinking skills to analyze relationships, sexual norms, and campus culture. Fishbowl exercises, small group conversations, worksheets such as the "Want! Will … Won't Chart" (Brewer, 2011), and partnered "speed dating" discussion exercises are employed. Students grow in their ability to talk about comfort, desire, identity, and intimacy, as well as power and inequality. They begin to articulate what they want from their partner(s) now and in the future and begin thinking about how they will enable these experiences in consensual ways.

Time during the final class is devoted to action planning. Students are asked to think about what an ideal sexual climate would look like for them and how to achieve this. In small groups, students complete a worksheet detailing commitments for the next month and the rest of the semester (personal improvement action steps). Additionally, they report what they will encourage their organizations or groups to do (community change action steps). When these action items are shared aloud with the entire class, students demonstrate a sense of commitment and interest in both personal and cultural change. Past personal improvement action steps included "encourage more students to think about issues of consent and gender role stereotypes," "research educational programs at other colleges to fuel our own positive sexual climate," and "have more confidence in making my own sexual decisions." Community change action steps have included: "tell my friends about what I've done here at Yes Means Yes and ask them to change their approach to sexual relationships," "encourage people to go to the sexual misconduct information sessions," and "my group will support events that create a safe, open environment for discussion and communication about sex on campus." A notable comment from a student that was exactly in line with what the seminar was intended for was "I will say yes when I mean yes."

■ EVALUATION OF PROGRAM EFFECTIVENESS

The YMY seminar started as a pilot program during the 2009–2010 academic year. After collecting positive general feedback about the seminar during the first semester, we decided to undergo a research study during the spring semester to better measure the effectiveness of the program. During spring

2010, we collected data before and after the seminar. Students who expressed interest in taking the class but did not enroll due to conflicts (e.g., scheduling demands) comprised the control group.1 Our measures included: 1) a 13-item Yes Means Yes Objectives Questionnaire (YMY-OQ, see Appendix B), based on 13 class objectives such as "ability to engage in healthy sexual practices" and "awareness of campus resources," with each item rated on a Likert scale ranging from 1 (completely disagree) to 5 (completely agree)2 and 2) the Multidimensional Sexual Self-Concept Questionnaire,3 which measures everything from sexual anxiety to optimism and motivation (MSSCQ; Snell,
1998).4

A 2 × 2 Experimental Design was employed with pretest and posttest data for the experimental and the control groups. Students in the control group were sent questionnaires by campus mail during the same weeks as the first and last sessions of YMY to ensure that the same amount of time lapsed. The hypotheses of this study were that experimental group students would improve more than control group students in their perceived abilities to: engage in intellectual discourse about their social involvement, critically analyze their sexual attitudes, engage in healthy sexual practices, seek campus resources, consider ways to create sexual climate change, positively explore their sexual identities, and correct misperceptions about rape myths. Analyses of variances (ANOVAs) were used to identify significant changes between the experimental and the control groups as well as between the pretest and posttest data collection periods. Using this method allowed for comparison in outcomes between those who enrolled in YMY and those who did not.

TABLE 1 MSSCQ RESULTS, SUBSCALE CLUSTER: POSITIVE SEXUAL SELF-UNDERSTANDING 2×2 ANOVA

Group	Pretest	Posttest
Experimental ($N = 22$)	3.76	4.09
Control ($N = 16$)	3.76	3.84

Statistical Analysis: Interaction between Experimental Pretest/Posttest and Control Pretest/Posttest: $F(1,36) = 4.49$, $p < 0.05$

Improvement in students' positive sexual identity exploration was studied by using the MSSCQ pretest and posttest scores. In order to measure the intended outcomes of the class, six subscales were combined into a cluster subscale, we named "Positive Sexual Self Understanding," including sexual self-efficacy, sexual consciousness, sexual satisfaction, sexual self-schemata, sexual esteem, and sexual self-monitoring. The experimental group improved significantly more that the control group in regards to their "Positive Sexual Self Understanding" (see Table 1). Thus, the students who participated in YMY believed they developed a more positive sexual self-understanding at the end of the session than their control group peers.

The YMY-OQ was used to study students' ability to engage in intellectual discourse about their social involvement, critically analyze their sexual attitudes, engage in healthy sexual practices, seek campus resources, and consider ways to create sexual climate change. Although there were no significant differences between the control and experimental group YMYOQ scores at pretest, there was a significant difference between the control group YMY-OQ scores and the experimental group scores at posttest. This indicates that the students who participated in YMY showed more improvement in the measured areas—YMY positive sexuality objectives—compared with controls (see Table 2). Thus, combining the results gathered from the MSSCQ and the YMY-OQ, it can be assumed that the YMY class was effective in reaching its originally outlined objectives.

TABLE 2 YMY-OQ RESULTS 2×2 ANOVA

Group(s)	Pretest	Post-test	Mean
Experimental (N = 22)	3.99	4.54	4.26
Control (N = 16)	3.69	3.95	3.82
Both	3.84	4.24	

Statistical Analyses:

• No significant difference between Experimental Pretest and Control Pretest

• Interaction between Experimental Pretest/Post-test and Control Pretest/Post-test: $F(1, 36) = 4.76$, $p = .036$.

In sum, the results of this evaluation study were positive and provided us with a solid rationale for continued offerings of YMY. We found that our objectives were largely being met. Perhaps most importantly, participants' reported a more positive sexual self-understanding, willingness to engage in intellectual discourse about their social involvement, ability to critically analyze their sexual attitudes, interest in healthy sexual practices, knowledge of campus resources, commitment to sexual climate change, and ability to discuss and define sexual assault and rape.

Ongoing Evaluation

Since collecting data on our initial research sample, we continue to measure the effectiveness of the YMY seminar with each new group of participants. To ensure that it continues to benefit the students who participate, we use of the YMY-OQ at the beginning and end of the seminar, solicit qualitative responses from students and facilitators, and ask for feedback with a weekly mini-evaluation,5 in order to make on-board adjustments as the seminar proceeds. In agreement with past results, recent evaluations support the continued offering of this course. During the 2011–2012 year, 87 participants' postseminar YMY-OQ scores were higher than pretest scores, and posttest scores on 10 out of 13 YMY-OQ items were 4.5 or higher on a 5-point Likert scale.6 Additionally, we asked students to answer the question, "What did you like most about the class?" Answers included: "I love how comfortable I've become at asserting myself, my wants, desires, and to sticking to my guns;" "Collaborating and listening to people about what they want in relationships

... Brainstorming realistic ways for us to change [institution name]'s culture;"

and, "The take-aways, finding myself applying them to daily life." The most repeated criticism we received was students' interest in recruiting more male participants and focusing more on lesbian, gay, bisexual, transgender, and queer (LGBTQ) issues. As a follow-up, we contacted students four months after the ending of their YMY class and asked them to complete this sentence: "Since I took YMY   ." Answers centered on four key themes: community ("a sense of community bonded through nontraditional means, which had previously not existed on campus"), power/inequality ("I have been empowered to bring up issues like rape, sexual harassment, and power hierarchies at [institution name] with male and female friends, my sister, and even my parents"), interpersonal relationships ("gotten to know myself better, taken charge of my sexuality, and realized what I want in a relationship"), and relationship to body ("I have a newfound confidence and level of comfort in my sexuality").

Strengths and Weaknesses of YMY

The YMY program has made a huge impact on our campus. Students, faculty, staff, and administrators all refer to this as part of a larger movement to raise critical sexual awareness on campus. (See Discussion and Future Directions for more on effects of this movement.) Feedback from students has been overwhelmingly positive; however, there have been some challenges. Students have noted an interest in seeing more men participating, more LGBTQ issues covered, and the possibility of taking the issues discussed to another level of depth.

It is a strength and a weakness that the majority of the participants in YMY have been female. Some women feel more comfortable opening up in the presence of other women. Participants in the hook-up culture are both men and women and therefore, a wider ripple effect on campus is likely to occur when everybody is engaged in the conversation. Also, men who elect to participate in YMY may feel that they have to speak for the entire male population. We started offering a "male only" YMY minisession to fraternities last year as one way to reach out to men on our campus.

The second area of improvement is ensuring that the class is inclusive to all sexualities and covers LGBTQ issues in more detail. Most discussions of the hook-up culture tend to be heterocentric. Our facilitators work to be more inclusive, discussing many types of relationships in YMY discussions, and assigning a wide range of critical sexuality readings. Perhaps surprisingly, even if they identify as heterosexual, students want to be able to confront their own biases and move beyond a heterocentric model, and we continue to work at facilitating discussions with this in mind.

Many students have requested longer than 90-minute sessions to allow for more in-depth discussions. We have considered a "YMY 1.2" for participants who would like to continue their learning. We envision offering this seminar for all students who have previously participated in YMY. Additionally, offering general for-credit courses on critical sexualities would alleviate some of the pressure on YMY.

■ DISCUSSION AND FUTURE DIRECTIONS

The YMY seminar is an alternative program for sexual assault prevention and positive sexuality promotion that should be offered in partnership with other sexual assault prevention efforts on campus. Since the YMY seminar has clear benefits for participants, expanding the seminar to reach a broader audience is desirable. Following up on the barriers listed above, for YMY to be most effective, male students need to participate in higher numbers, as do students across a diversity of backgrounds. Focus groups may help us to learn how to broaden our YMY demographic.

We would like to develop plans to track long-term effectiveness of the program. To date, YMY-OQ evaluations have been collected at the end of each seminar. We believe that many students who "graduate" from YMY social circles. Students have discussed hosting "reunion" events and utilizing social media to continue YMY community-building beyond the seminar. However, this behavior change has not been systematically tracked. A staff or faculty advisor could continue to help students translate their positive sexuality thoughts into actions and inspire community change with an evaluation element to track their progress.

On our campus, we have started a number of extensions of YMY to attempt to involve others in the broader positive sexuality initiative. Students living in a positive sexuality theme house now have regular discussions and host events focused on positive sexuality. Collaborative programming with student organizations and academic departments, such as Women's Studies and Educational Studies, send a clear, consistent message on campus about what constitutes appropriate and inappropriate community behaviors. This past year, a violence prevention seminar followed YMY for three additional Wednesday evenings with some of the same participants and the Women's Studies Department led an effort among faculty, students, staff, and administrators to create a short "zero tolerance" video focused on sexual assault on campus.

Additionally, shorter YMY versions, or "mini-YMY" curricula, have been developed that are one to two sessions in length, geared at specific audiences to begin the dialogue of positive sexuality with various student organizations and help them consider how their actions affect others and the community. Last year, all new members of sororities, two full sorority organizations, three fraternities, and the leaders of the Outdoor Education program participated in mini-YMY workshops. We are offering a train-the-trainer program to prepare upperclass students to facilitate mini-YMY sessions with groups of first-year students. Through these initial workshops, we hope that dialogue will continue and first-year students will feel empowered to make better sexual decisions as they are introduced to the college social scene. Additionally, YMY is being incorporated into a comprehensive first-year program that includes education/training for orientation leaders, orientation programs that send consistent messaging (e.g., Dorian Solot and Marshall Miller's *Sex*

Discussed Here program), and invitations to events held by the positive sexuality theme house on campus.

Improving today's university sexual culture is an enormous task. Administrators and faculty should offer positive sexuality programs that students find interesting and engaging. Information needs to be delivered in ways that students will hear it, analyze it, and employ it. "Yes Means Yes," used as an alternative sexual assault prevention program, provides a space to facilitate conversations within interactive workshops that tap into students' sexual interests allowing them to consider how to make healthy sexual decisions.

■ NOTES

1. The Spring 2010 pilot study participants were 22 college students who completed the YMY course and were included in the experimental group. There were more women (17) than men (5) and the group consisted of students who identified as Hispanic/Latino/a (4), Multiracial (2), Caucasian (15) and Other (1). The control group consisted of 12 women and 4 men who identified as Caucasian (13), Hispanic/Latino/a (2) and Multiracial (1). We acknowledge bias in the control group when it comes to interest in positive sexuality. However, despite similar proclivities between the experimental and control groups, we can still point to important differences in outcomes.

2. The total score of the YMY-OQ is the average of all 13 answers and can range from 1 to 5. Good internal consistency was demonstrated by calculating the Cronbach's alpha coefficient (alpha = .78) for the experimental and a control group combined during the pilot study.

3. The MSSCQ is a 100-item self-report questionnaire that measures 20 areas of sexuality: sexual anxiety, sexual self-efficacy, sexual-consciousness, motivation to avoid risky sex, chance/luck sexual control, sexual preoccupation, sexual assertiveness, sexual optimism, sexual problem self-blame, sexual monitoring, sexual motivation, sexual problem management, sexual esteem, sexual satisfaction, power-other sexual control, sexual selfschemata, fear of sex, sexual problem prevention, sexual depression, and internal sexual control. Single subscales or groups of subscales have been used by several researchers (e.g., Meyer et al., 2005). Good internal consistency for all 20 subscales was determined by Snell (1995, as cited in Snell, 1998).

4. The MSSCQ is a 100-item self-report questionnaire that measures 20 areas of sexuality: sexual anxiety, sexual self-efficacy, sexual-consciousness, motivation to avoid risky sex, chance/luck sexual control, sexual preoccupation, sexual assertiveness, sexual optimism, sexual problem self-blame, sexual monitoring, sexual motivation, sexual problem management, sexual esteem, sexual satisfaction, power-other sexual control, sexual self-schemata, fear of sex, sexual problem prevention, sexual depression, and internal sexual control. Single subscales or groups of subscales have been used by several researchers (e.g., Meyer et al., 2005). Good internal consistency for all 20 subscales was determined by Snell (1995, as cited in Snell, 1998).

5. At the end of each session, the student facilitator uses a mini-evaluation to ask for an overall rating of the class, the best thing about the day's workshop, how the session could be improved, what students learned about themselves that day, and comments/concerns. This frequent feedback allows us to ensure that the objectives for each week are being met and the planning for the next week matches group expectations.

6. The 10 YMY-OQ items with mean post-test scores of higher than 4.5 were: I feel equipped with enough knowledge to engage in intellectual discourse about intimate relationships, I understand the "hook up culture" and can articulate my opinions about it, I understand what consent means and I am able to provide examples of verbal and non-verbal means of giving consent, I believe that positive, healthy relationships come in many forms and I can give examples of these, I can define rape and sexual assault, I know who

is available at [the university] to support me if I am sexually assaulted, or I can refer a friend to a support person on campus if s/he is sexually assaulted, I know how to talk with my friends about sexual climate, rape, and sexual identity, I can name three obstacles that stand in the way of a healthy sexual climate at [the university], I have considered realistic ways of transforming the culture towards a more positive sexual climate, and I feel supported in making changes that would be positive for the sexual climate at this university.

REFERENCES

Berger, J. (2009). *Sex, relationships, and the coop: Transforming Colgate's campus culture to embrace healthy sexuality.* (Unpublished undergraduate thesis). Colgate University. Hamilton, NY.

Breitenbecher, K. H. (2000). Sexual assault on college campuses: Is an ounce of prevention enough? *Applied and Preventive Psychology, 9,* 23–52.

Bisson, M. A., & Levine, T. R. (2009). Negotiating a friends with benefits relationship. *Archives of Sexual Behavior, 38,* 66–73.

Brewer, B. (2011). Want! Will ... Won't Chart. Retrieved from http://www.smarthotfun.com/storage/wantwillwont/wwwactspop.pdf

Davis, K. C., George, W. H., & Norris, J. (2004). Women's responses to unwanted sexual advances: The role of alcohol and inhibition conflict. *Psychology of Women Quarterly, 28,* 333–343.

DeFur, K. M. (2012). Don't forget the good stuff! Incorporating positive messages of sexual pleasure into sexuality. *American Journal of Sexuality Education, 7*(2), 160–169.

DeKeseredy, W. S., & Kelly, K. (1993). The incidence and prevalence of woman abuse in Canadian university and college dating relationships. *Canadian Journal of Sociology, 18,* 137–159.

Erikson, E. (1968). *Identity: Youth and crisis.* New York, NY: Norton.

ETR Associates. (2007–2009). Resource Center for Adolescent Pregnancy Prevention. Retrieved from http://www.etr.org/recapp/index.cfm?fuseaction=pages.TopicsInBriefDetail&pageID=61&PageTypeID=1

Flack, W. F., Jr., Daubman, K. A., Caron, M. L., Asadorian, J., D'Aureli, N., Kiser, ... Stine, E. (2007). Risk factors and consequences of unwanted sex among university students: Hooking up, alcohol, and stress response. *Journal of Interpersonal Violence, 22,* 139–157.

Fisher, B. S., Daigle, L. E., Cullen, F. T., & Turner, M. G. (2003). Reporting sexual victimization to the police and others• Results from a national-level study of college women. *Criminal Justice and Behavior, 30,* 6–38.

Foubert, J. D., & Newberry, J. T. (2006). Effects of two versions of an empathy-based rape prevention program on fraternity men's survivor empathy, attitudes, and behavioral intent to commit rape or sexual assault. *Journal of College Student Development, 47,* 133–148.

Friedman, J., & Valenti, J. (2008). *Yes means yes! Visions of female sexual power and a world without rape.* Berkeley, CA: Seal Press.

Garcia, J. R., & Reiber, C. (2008). Hook-up behavior: A biopsychosocial perspective. *Journal of Social, Evolutionary, and Cultural Psychology, 2,* 192–208.

Glenn, N. D., & Marquart, E. (2001). *Hooking up, hanging out, and hoping for Mr. Right: College women and dating and mating today.* New York, NY: Institute for American Values.

Grello, C. M., Welsh, D. P., & Harper, M. S. (2006). No strings attached: The nature of casual sex in college students. *The Journal of Sex Research, 43,* 255–267.

Gross, A. M., Winslett, A., Roberts, M., & Gohm, C. L. (2006). An examination of sexual violence against college women. *Violence Against Women, 12,* 288–300.

Impett, E. A., & Peplau, L. A. (2002). Why some women consent to unwanted sex with a dating partner: Insights from attachment theory. *Psychology of Women Quarterly, 26,* 359–369.

Jervis, L. (2008). An old enemy in a new outfit: How date rape became gray rape and why it matters. In J. Friedman & J. Valenti (Eds.), *Yes means yes! Visions of female sexual power and a world without rape* (pp. 163–177). Berkeley, CA: Seal Press.

Katz, J. (1994). *Mentors in Violence Prevention (MVP) trainer's guide.* Boston, MA: Northeastern University Center for the Study of Sport in Society.

Kohler, P. K., Manhart, L. E., & Lafferty, M.D. (2008). Abstinence-only and comprehensive sex education and the initiation of sexual activity and teen pregnancy. *Journal of Adolescent Health, 42,* 344–351.

Koss, M., Gidycz, C., & Wisniewski, N. (1987). The scope of rape: Incidence and prevalence of sexual aggression and victimization in a national sample of higher education students. *Journal of Consulting & Clinical Psychology, 55,* 162–170.

LaBrie, J. W., Earleywine, M., Schiffman, J., Pedersen, E., & Marriot, C. (2005). The effects of alcohol, expectancies, and partner type on condom use in college males: An event level study. *Journal of Sex Research, 42,* 259–266.

Meyer, J. L., Crosby, R. A., Whittington, W. L. H., Carrell, D., Ashley-Morrow, R., Meier, A. S., ... Wald, A. (2005). The psychosocial impact of serological herpes simplex type 2 testing in an urban HIV clinic. *Sexually Transmitted Infections, 81,* 309–315.

Muehlenhard, C., & Hollabaugh, L. (1988). Do women sometimes say no when they mean yes? The prevalence and correlates of women's token resistance to sex. *Journal of Personality and Social Psychology, 54,* 872–879.

Muehlenhard, C., & Rodgers, C. (1998). Token resistance to sex: New perspectives on an old stereotype. *Psychology of Women Quarterly, 22,* 443–463.

O'Sullivan, L. R., & Allgeier, E. R. (1998). Feigning sexual desire: Consenting to unwanted sexual activity in heterosexual dating relationships. *Journal of Sex Research, 35*(3), 234–243.

Owen, J. J., Rhoades, G. K., Stanley, S. M., & Fincham, F. D. (2010). "Hooking up" among college students: Demographic and psychological correlates. *Archives of Sexual Behavior, 39,* 653–663.

Oswalt, S. B. (2010). Beyond risk: Examining college students' sexual decision making. *American Journal of Sexuality Education, 5*(3), 217–239.

Paul, E. L., McManus, B., & Hayes, A. (2000). 'Hookups': Characteristics and correlates of college students' spontaneous and anonymous sexual experiences. *Journal of Sex Research, 37,* 76–88.

Santelli, J., Ott, M. A., Lyon, M., Rogers, J., Summers, D., & Schleifer, R. (2006). Abstinence and abstinence-only education: A review of U.S. policies and programs. *Journal of Adolescent Health, 38,* 72–81.

Snell, W. E. (1998). The Multidimensional Sexual Self-Concept Questionnaire. In C. D. Davis, W. L. Yarber, R. Bauserman, G. Schreer, & S. L. Davis (Eds.), *Handbook of sexuality-related measures* (pp. 521–524). Thousand Oaks, CA: Sage.

Sprecher, S., Hatfield, E., Cortese, A., Potapova, E., & Levitskaya, A. (1994). Token resistance to sexual intercourse and consent to unwanted intercourse: College students' dating experiences in three countries. *The Journal of Sex Research, 31,* 125–132.

Stanley, S. M., Rhoades, G. K., & Markman, H. J. (2006). Sliding versus deciding: Inertia and the premarital cohabitation effect. *Family Relations, 55,* 499–509.

Vail-Smith, K., Maguire, R. L., Brinkley, J., & Burke, S. (2010). Sexual behaviors during the first year of college: An exploratory comparison of first and second semester freshmen. *American Journal of Sexuality Education, 5*(2), 171–188.

Wright, M. O., Norton, D. L., & Matusek, J. A. (2010). Predicting verbal coercion following sexual refusal during a hookup: Diverging gender patterns. *Sex Roles, 62,* 647–660.

Yeater, E. A., & O'Donohue, W. (1999). Sexual assault prevention programs: Current issues, future directions, and the potential efficacy of interventions with women. *Clinical Psychology Review, 19,* 739–771.

APPENDIX A: YES MEANS YES SYLLABUS

Session 1: Introduction & Chapter 1, "Offensive Feminism: The Conservative Gender Norms That Perpetuate Rape Culture, and How Feminists Can Fight Back" by Jill Filipovic (13–27)
- Welcome and Introductions, Overview of Program, Ground rules, Logistics
- Thermometer exercise – issues of sexuality/attraction/etc.
- Definition of hook-up culture – positive/negatives exercise

Session 2: Chapter 15, "An Immodest Proposal" by Heather Corinna (179–192) key terms: sexual agency, pleasure
- Do "first time" sexual encounters shape those to follow? How so?
- Do parents have responsibilities as facilitators of the "first time"?
- Do you think that men and women equally experience sexual desire?
- How do you see sexual agency in your environment? Who has it? What power comes along with sexual agency?

Session 3: Chapter 13, "An Old Enemy in a New Outfit: How Date Rape Became Gray Rape and Why It Matters" by Lisa Jervis (163–177); Chapter 9, " The Fantasy of Acceptable "Non-Consent": Why the Female Sexual Submissive Scares Us (and Why She Shouldn't) (117–125) key terms: gray rape, BDSM
- In what ways does acknowledging and taking control of one's desires relate to gray rape?
- Does college culture perpetuate "gray rape"? If yes, in what ways?
- Is it possible for females to be as sexually autonomous as men?
- What is consent and how do you express it?
- What assumptions and accommodations can be made about various forms of sexuality?

Session 4: Chapter 3, "Beyond Yes or No: Consent as a Sexual Process" by Rachel Kramer Bussel (43–51) key terms: consent, responsibility
- What assumptions do we have going into a sexual encounter? How do we navigate these?
- What specific responsibilities do men have during sexual encounters? Women?
- Do these responsibilities change in homosexual sexual encounters?
- What is the goal of sex? Why do we have sex?
- In what ways can consent help us achieve these goals?

Session 5: Chapter 27, "In Defense of Going Wild" by Jaclyn Friedman key terms: power, entitlement, healthy sexual climate
- What does rape mean on a college campus? This campus?
- In what ways does college culture positively impact sexual experiences? Negatively?
- Are there hierarchies on campus that perpetuate ideas of entitlement and power?
- What obstacles stand in the way of healthy sexual climate on campus?
- What can be done to promote a healthy sexual climate?

Wrap Up
- Each participant revisits goals/assumptions, compares the program with his/her goals/assumptions, offers one suggestion for transforming the [university] culture
- Action plan: implementable and with identification of allies

APPENDIX B: YES MEANS YES QUESTIONNAIRE (YMY-Q)

1. I feel comfortable talking in a group about sexual topics.
2. I feel equipped with enough knowledge to engage in intellectual discourse about intimate relationships.
3. I understand the "hook up culture" and can articulate my opinions about it.
4. I understand what consent means and I am able to provide examples of verbal and nonverbal means of giving consent.
5. I behave in ways that are consistent with my values regarding relationships.
6. I believe that positive, healthy relationships come in many forms and I can give examples of these.
7. I can define rape and sexual assault.
8. I know who is available at this university to support me if I am sexually assaulted, or I can refer a friend to a support person on campus if s/he is sexually assaulted.
9. I have considered how sexual assault affects the LGBTQ community on campus.
10. I know how to talk with my friends about sexual climate, rape, and sexual identity.
11. I can name three obstacles that stand in the way of a healthy sexual climate at this university.
12. I have considered realistic ways of transforming the culture towards a more positive sexual climate.

13. I feel supported in making changes that would be positive for the sexual climate at this university.

■ WHAT?

1. Summarize the argument that the authors present in their article. Include in your summary a succinct description of the "Yes Means Yes" seminar.
2. How do the authors support their position? What kinds of evidence do they use? Do you think their evidence is sufficient?

■ WHAT ELSE? WHAT NEXT?

3. Go online and find out what you can about the publication in which this research article appeared, the *American Journal of Sexuality Education*. Based on what you find, explain who you think reads this journal. What standards for research and documentation does the journal seem to have?
4. Does USC have a class or workshop comparable to Colgate's "Yes Means Yes" seminar? If not, do you think it should? Explain your response.

CHAPTER 10: Reading.com

IMAGE 10.1
In "Liking is for Cowards. Go for What Hurts," Jonathan Franzen writes: "Our lives look a lot more interesting when they're filtered through the sexy Facebook interface. We star in our own movies, we photograph ourselves incessantly, we click the mouse and a machine confirms our sense of mastery." Is there anything wrong with this?

Are you ready for the intelligence-augmented 'You+' that futurist Jamais Cascio argues is already in the works? Can you imagine a future in which "teme" machines—as psychologist Susan Blackmore envisions them—thrive with less and less help from humans? Do you worry—as Jaron Lanier does—that who we are is being overwhelmed by the technologies we use? The readings in this chapter examine the evolution of digital technologies and present a variety of opinions about what these technologies are doing to us.

> Susan Blackmore is a psychologist and writer researching consciousness, memes, and anomalous experiences, and a Visiting Professor at the University of Plymouth. She is the author of several books, including The Meme Machine (1999), Conversations on Consciousness (2005) and Ten Zen Questions (2009). Blackmore wrote this piece in August 2010 for the New York Times blog called The Stone, described by the newspaper as "a forum for contemporary philosophers on issues both timely and timeless." In this essay, Blackmore presents an argument about memes, ideas that replicate themselves, and a new kind of meme called the teme, which spreads via technology.

BEFORE YOU READ

Research Susan Blackmore and her ideas. Highlight anything you find that you think might help your classmates get a better handle on Blackmore's argument.

THE THIRD REPLICATOR   Susan Blackmore

All around us information seems to be multiplying at an ever-increasing pace. New books are published, new designs for toasters and i-gadgets appear, new music is composed or synthesized and, perhaps above all, new content is uploaded into cyberspace. This is rather strange. We know that matter and energy cannot increase, but apparently information can.

It is perhaps rather obvious to attribute this to the evolutionary algorithm or Darwinian process, as I will do, but I wish to emphasize one part of this process—copying. The reason information can increase like this is that, if the necessary raw materials are available, copying creates more information. Of course it is not new information, but if the copies vary (which they will if only by virtue of copying errors), and if not all variants survive to be copied again (which is inevitable given limited resources), then we have the complete three-step process of natural selection (Dennett, 1995). From here novel designs and truly new information emerge. None of this can happen without copying.

I want to make three arguments here.

The first is that humans are unique because they are so good at imitation. When our ancestors began to imitate they let loose a new evolutionary process based not on genes but on a second replicator, memes. Genes and memes then coevolved, transforming us into better and better meme machines.

The second is that one kind of copying can piggy-back on another: that is, one replicator (the information that is copied) can build on the products (vehicles or interactors) of another. This multilayered evolution has produced the amazing complexity of design we see all around us.

The third is that now, in the early 21st century, we are seeing the emergence of a third replicator. I call these temes (short for technological memes, though I have considered other names). They are digital information stored, copied, varied and selected by machines. We humans like to think we are the designers, creators and controllers of this newly emerging world, but really we are steppingstones from one replicator to the next.

As I try to explain this I shall make some assertions and assumptions that some readers may find outrageous, but I am deliberately putting my case in its strongest form so that we can debate the issues people find most interesting or most troublesome.

Some may entirely reject the notion of replicators, and will therefore dismiss the whole enterprise. Others will accept that genes are replicators but reject the idea of memes. For example, Eva Jablonka and Marion J. Lamb (2005) refer to "the dreaded memes" while Peter J. Richerson and Robert Boyd (2005), who have contributed so much to the study of cultural evolution, assert that "cultural variants are not replicators." They use the phrase "selfish memes" but still firmly reject memetics (Blackmore 2006). Similarly, in a previous "On The Human" post, William Benzon explains why he does not like the term "meme," yet he needs some term to refer to the things that evolve and so he still uses it. As John S. Wilkins points out in response, there are several more classic objections: memes are not discrete (I would say *some* are not discrete), they do not form lineages (*some* do), memetic evolution appears to be Lamarckian (but only *appears* so), memes are not replicated but re-created or reproduced, or are not copied with sufficient fidelity (see discussions in Aunger 2000, Sterelny 2006, Wimsatt 2010). I have tackled all these, and more, elsewhere and concluded that the notion is still valid (Blackmore 1999, 2010a).

So I will press on, using the concept of memes as originally defined by Dawkins who invented the term; that is, memes are "that which is imitated" or whatever it is that is copied when people imitate each other. Memes include songs, stories, habits, skills, technologies, scientific theories, bogus medical treatments, financial systems, organizations—everything that makes up human culture. I can now, briefly, tell the story of how I think we arrived where we are today.

First there were genes. Perhaps we should not call genes the first replicator because there may have been precursors worthy of that name and possibly RNA-like replicators before the evolution of DNA (Maynard Smith and Szathmary 1995). However, Dawkins (1976), who coined the term "replicator," refers to genes this way and I shall do the same.

We should note here an important distinction for living things based on DNA, that the genes are the replicators while the animals and plants themselves are vehicles, interactors, or phenotypes: ephemeral creatures constructed with the aid of genetic information coded in tiny strands of DNA packaged safely inside them. Whether single-celled bacteria, great oak trees, or dogs and cats, in the gene-centered view of evolution they are all gene machines or Dawkins's "lumbering robots." The important point here is that the genetic information is faithfully copied down the generations, while the vehicles or interactors live and die without actually being copied. Put another way, this system copies the instructions for making a product rather than the product itself, a process that has many advantages (Blackmore 1999, 2001). This interesting distinction becomes important when we move on to higher replicators.

So what happened next? Earth might have remained a one-replicator planet but it did not. One of these gene machines, a social and bipedal ape, began to imitate. We do not know why, although shifting climate may have favored stealing skills from others rather than learning them anew (Richerson and Boyd 2005). Whatever the reason, our ancestors began to copy sounds, skills and habits from one to another. They passed on lighting fires, making stone tools, wearing clothes, decorating their bodies and all sorts of skills to do with living together as hunters and gatherers. The critical point here is, of course, that they *copied* these sounds, skills and habits, and this, I suggest, is what makes humans unique.

No other species (as far as we know) can do this. Songbirds can copy some sounds, some of the other great apes can imitate some actions, and most notably whales and dolphins can imitate, but none is capable of the widespread, generalized imitation that comes so easily to us. Imitation is not just some new minor ability. It changes everything. It enables a new kind of evolution.

This is why I have called humans "Earth's Pandoran species." They let loose this second replicator and began the process of memetic evolution in which memes competed to be selected by humans to be copied again. The successful memes then influenced human genes by gene-meme co-evolution (Blackmore 1999, 2001). Note that I see this process as somewhat different from gene-culture co-evolution, partly because most theorists treat culture as an adaptation (e.g. Richerson and Boyd 2005), and agree with Wilson that genes "keep culture on a leash." (Lumsden and Wilson 1981 p 13).

Benzon, in responding to Peter Railton's post here at The Stone, points out the limits of this metaphor and proposes the "chess board and game" instead. I prefer a simple host-parasite analogy. Once our ancestors could imitate they created lots of memes that competed to use their brains for their own propagation. This drove these hominids to become better meme machines and to carry the (potentially huge and even dangerous) burden of larger brain size and energy use, eventually becoming symbiotic. Neither memes nor genes are a dog or a dog-owner. Neither is on a leash. They are both vast competing sets of information, all selfishly getting copied whenever and however they can.

To help understand the next step we can think of this process as follows: one replicator (genes) built vehicles (plants and animals) for its own propagation. One of these then discovered a new way of copying and diverted much of its resources to doing this instead, creating a new replicator (memes) which then led to new replicating machinery (big-brained humans). Now we can ask whether the same thing could happen again and—aha—we can see that it can, and is.

A sticking point concerns the equivalent of the meme-phenotype or vehicle. This has plagued memetics ever since its beginning: some arguing that memes must be inside human heads while words, technologies and all the rest are their phenotypes, or "phemotypes"; others arguing the opposite. I disagree with both (Blackmore 1999, 2001). By definition, whatever is copied is the meme, and I suggest that, until very recently, there was no meme-phemotype distinction because memes were so new and so poorly replicated that they had not yet constructed stable vehicles. Now they have.

Think about songs, recipes, ways of building houses or clothes fashions. These can be copied and stored by voice, by gesture, in brains, or on paper with no clear replicator/vehicle distinction. But now consider a car factory or a printing press. Thousands of near-identical copies of cars, books, or newspapers are churned out. Those actual cars or books are not copied again but they compete for our attention and if they prove popular then more copies are made from the same template. This is much more like a replicator-vehicle system. It is "copy the instructions" not "copy the product."

Of course cars and books are passive lumps of metal, paper and ink. They cannot copy, let alone vary and select information themselves. So could any of our modern meme products take the step our hominid ancestors did long ago and begin a new kind of copying? Yes. They could and they are. Our computers, all linked up through the Internet, are beginning to carry out all three of the critical processes required for a new evolutionary process to take off.

Computers handle vast quantities of information with extraordinarily high-fidelity copying and storage. Most variation and selection is still done by human beings, with their biologically evolved desires for stimulation, amusement, communication, sex and food. But this is changing. Already there are examples of computer programs recombining old texts to create new essays or poems, translating texts to create new versions, and selecting between vast quantities of text, images and data. Above all there are search engines. Each request to Google, Alta Vista or Yahoo! elicits a new set of pages—a new combination of items selected by that search engine according to its own clever algorithms and depending on myriad previous searches and link structures.

This is a radically new kind of copying, varying and selecting, and means that a new evolutionary process is starting up. This copying is quite different from the way cells copy strands of DNA or humans copy memes. The information itself is also different, consisting of highly stable digital information stored and processed by machines rather than living cells. This, I submit, signals the emergence of temes and teme machines, the third replicator.

What should we expect of this dramatic step? It might make as much difference as the advent of human imitation did. Just as human meme machines spread over the planet, using up its resources and altering its ecosystems to suit their own needs, so the new teme machines will do the same, only faster. Indeed we might see our current ecological troubles not as primarily our fault, but as the inevitable consequence of earth's transition to being a three-replicator planet. We willingly provide ever more energy to power the Internet, and there is enormous scope for teme machines to grow, evolve and create ever more extraordinary digital worlds, some aided by humans and others independent of them. We are still needed, not least to run the power stations, but as the temes proliferate, using ever more energy and resources, our own role becomes ever less significant, even though we set the whole new evolutionary process in motion in the first place.

Whether you consider this a tragedy for the planet or a marvelous, beautiful story of creation, is up to you.

References

Aunger, R.A. (Ed) (2000) "Darwinizing Culture: The Status of Memetics as a Science," Oxford University Press

Benzon, W.L. (2010) "Cultural Evolution: A Vehicle for Cooperative Interaction Between the Sciences and the Humanities." Post for On the Human.

Blackmore, S. 1999 "The Meme Machine," Oxford and New York, Oxford University Press

Blackmore, S. 2001 "Evolution and memes: The human brain as a selective imitation device." Cybernetics and Systems, 32, 225-255

Blackmore, S. (2006) "Memetics by another name?" Review of "Not by Genes Alone" by P.J. Richerson and R. Boyd. Bioscience, 56, 74-5

Blackmore, S. (2010a) Memetics does provide a useful way of understanding cultural evolution. In "Contemporary Debates in Philosophy of Biology", Ed. Francisco Ayala and Robert Arp, Chichester, Wiley-Blackwell, 255-72.

Blackmore (2010b) "Dangerous Memes; or what the Pandorans let loose." In "Cosmos and Culture: Cultural Evolution in a Cosmic Context," Ed. Steven Dick and Mark Lupisella, NASA 297-318

Dawkins, R. (1976) "The Selfish Gene," Oxford, Oxford University Press (new edition with additional material, 1989)

Dennett, D. (1995) "Darwin's Dangerous Idea," London, Penguin

Jablonka, E. and Lamb, M.J. (2005) "Evolution in Four Dimensions: Genetic, Epigenetic, Behavioral and Symbolic Variation in the History of Life." Bradford Books

Lumsden, C. J. and Wilson, E. O. (1981) "Genes, Mind and Culture." Cambridge, Mass., Harvard University Press.

Maynard-Smith, J. and Szathmáry, E. (1995) "The Major Transitions in Evolution." Oxford, Freeman

Richerson, P. J. and Boyd, R. (2005) "Not by Genes Alone: How Culture Transformed Human Evolution," Chicago, University of Chicago Press

Sterelny, K. (2006). "Memes Revisited." British Journal for the Philosophy of Science 57 (1)

Wimsatt, W. (2010) "Memetics does not provide a useful way of understanding cultural evolution: A developmental perspective." In "Contemporary Debates in Philosophy of Biology" Ed. Francisco Ayala and Robert Arp, Chichester, Wiley-Blackwell, 255-72.

■ WHAT?

1. Blackmore uses several terms that may be unfamiliar but that are vital to understanding her argument. How, for example, does she define the following: replicator, meme, and teme. How are the three terms related?
2. Briefly—but thoroughly—summarize Blackmore's argument.
3. How does Blackmore anticipate and address possible objections to her argument about temes? Do you think her method of dealing with those who might not agree with her is effective? Explain your response.

■ WHAT ELSE? WHAT'S NEXT?

4. What else do you need to know in order to more fully understand Blackmore's essay? Where might you look to find this information?
5. What do you think are the consequences of the evolution of temes and teme machines, what Blackmore calls the "third replicator"? Find at least two sources that speculate on a future in which technology functions with less and less help from humans, and use these in your response.
6. Go online and search for Blackmore's TED Talk on memes and temes. Then, review the responses posted in the "comments" area. How would you characterize reaction to Blackmore's theory, based on these comments?

■ WHO CARES?

7. Who do you think is the intended audience for Blackmore's essay? Explain your response.

> *According to his website, Jaron Lanier is a "computer scientist, composer, visual artist, and author" who, in the 1980s, led a team that developed "the first implementations of multi-person virtual worlds using head mounted displays, ... as well as the first 'avatars'." The following excerpt is from his 2010 book* You Are Not a Gadget: A Manifesto, *which one journalist called "a provocative critique of digital technologies, including Wikipedia (which [Lanier] called a triumph of 'intellectual mob rule') and social-networking sites like Facebook and Twitter, which he has described as dehumanizing and designed to encourage shallow interactions." In the preface to* You Are Not a Gadget, *Lanier writes, "The words in this book are written for people, not computers."*

BEFORE YOU READ

Jaron Lanier ends his preface to You Are Not a Gadget, *from which "Trolls" is excerpted, with these words: "You have to be somebody before you can share yourself." What do you think he means?*

TROLLS   Jaron Lanier

"Troll" is a term for an anonymous person who is abusive in an online environment. It would be nice to believe that there is only a minute troll population living among us. But in fact, a great many people have experienced being drawn into nasty exchanges online. Everyone who has experienced that has been introduced to his or her inner troll.

I have tried to learn to be aware of the troll within myself. I notice that I can suddenly become relieved when someone else in an online exchange is getting pounded or humiliated, because that means I'm safe for the moment. If someone else's video is being ridiculed on YouTube, then mine is temporarily protected. But that also means I'm complicit in a mob dynamic. Have I ever planted a seed of mob-beckoning ridicule in order to guide the mob to a target other than myself? Yes, I have, though I shouldn't have. I observe others doing that very thing routinely in anonymous online meeting places.

I've also found that I can be drawn into ridiculous pissing matches online in ways that just wouldn't happen otherwise, and I've never noticed any benefit. There is never a lesson learned, or a catharsis of victory or defeat. If you win anonymously, no one knows, and if you lose, you just change your pseudonym and start over, without having modified your point of view one bit.

If the troll is anonymous and the target is known, then the dynamic is even worse than an encounter between anonymous fragmentary pseudo-people. That's when the hive turns against personhood. For instance, in 2007 a series of "Scarlet Letter" postings in China incited online throngs to hunt down accused adulterers. In 2008, the focus shifted to Tibet sympathizers. Korea has one of the most intense online cultures in the world, so it has also suffered some of the most extreme trolling. Korean movie star Choi Jin-sil, sometimes described as the "Nation's Actress," committed suicide in 2008 after being hounded online by trolls, but she was only the most famous of a series of similar suicides.

In the United States, anonymous internet users have ganged up on targets like Lori Drew, the woman who created a fake boy persona on the internet in order to break the heart of a classmate of her daughter's, which caused the girl to commit suicide.

But more often the targets are chosen randomly, following the pattern described in the short story "The Lottery" by Shirley Jackson. In the story, residents of a placid small town draw lots to decide which individual will be stoned to death each year. It is as if a measure of human cruelty must be released, and to do so in a contained yet random way limits the damage by using the fairest possible method.

Some of the better-known random victims of troll mobs include the blogger Kathy Sierra. She was suddenly targeted in a multitude of ways, such as having images of her as a sexually mutilated corpse posted prominently, apparently in the hopes that her children would see them. There was no discernible reason Sierra was targeted. Her number was somehow drawn from the lot.

Another famous example is the tormenting of the parents of Mitchell Henderson, a boy who committed suicide. They were subjected to gruesome audio-video creations and other tools at the disposal of virtual sadists. Another occurrence is the targeting of epileptic people with flashing web designs in the hope of inducing seizures.

There is a vast online flood of videos of humiliating assaults on helpless victims. The culture of sadism online has its own vocabulary and has gone mainstream. The common term "lulz," for instance, refers to the gratification of watching others suffer over the cloud.*

When I criticize this type of online culture, I am often accused of being either an old fart or an advocate of censorship. Neither is the case. I don't think I'm necessarily any better, or more moral, than the people who tend the lulzy websites. What I'm saying, though, is that the user interface designs that arise from the ideology of the computing cloud make people—all of us—less kind. Trolling is not a string of isolated incidents, but the status quo in the online world.

■ The Standard Sequence of Troll Invocation

There are recognizable stages in the degradation of anonymous, fragmentary communication. If no pack has emerged, then individuals start to fight. This is what happens all the time in online settings. A later stage appears once a pecking order is established. Then the members of the pack become sweet and supportive of one another, even as they goad one another into ever more intense hatred of nonmembers.

---

*The Bible can serve as a prototypical example. Like Wikipedia, the Bible's authorship was shared, largely anonymous, and cumulative, and the obscurity of the individual authors served to create an oracle-like ambience for the document as "the literal word of God." If we take a non-metaphysical view of the Bible, it serves as a link to our ancestors, a window into human nature and our cultural origins, and can be used as a source of solace and inspiration. Someone who believes in a personal God can felicitously believe that the Bible reflects that God indirectly, through the people who wrote it. But when people buy into the oracle illusion, the Bible just turns into a tool to help religious leaders and politicians manipulate them.

*A website called the Encyclopedia Dramatica brags on its main page that it "won the 2nd Annual Mashable Open Web Awards for the wiki category." As I check it today, in late 2008, just as this book is about to leave my hands, the headlining "Article of the Now" is described in this way: "[Three guys] decided that the best way to commemorate their departing childhood was to kill around 21 people with hammers, pipes and screwdrivers, and record the whole thing on their [video recording] phones." This story was also featured on Boing Boing—which went to the trouble of determining that it was not a hoax—and other top sites this week.

This suggests a hypothesis to join the ranks of ideas about how the circumstances of our evolution influenced our nature. We, the big-brained species, probably didn't get that way to fill a single, highly specific niche. Instead, we must have evolved with the ability to switch between different niches. We evolved to be *both* loners *and* pack members. We are optimized not so much to be one or the other, but to be able to switch between them.

New patterns of social connection that are unique to online culture have played a role in the spread of modern networked terrorism. If you look at an online chat about anything, from guitars to poodles to aerobics, you'll see a consistent pattern: jihadi chat looks just like poodle chat. A pack emerges, and either you are with it or against it. If you join the pack, then you join the collective ritual hatred.

If we are to continue to focus the powers of digital technology on the project of making human affairs less personal and more collective, then we ought to consider how that project might interact with human nature.

The genetic aspects of behavior that have received the most attention (under rubrics like sociobiology or evolutionary psychology) have tended to focus on things like gender differences and mating behaviors, but my guess is that clan orientation and its relationship to violence will turn out to be the most important area of study.

Design Underlies Ethics in the Digital World

People are not universally nasty online. Behavior varies considerably from site to site. There are reasonable theories about what brings out the best or worst online behaviors: demographics, economics, child-rearing trends, perhaps even the average time of day of usage could play a role. My opinion, however, is that certain details in the design of the user interface experience of a website are the most important factors.

People who can spontaneously invent a pseudonym in order to post a comment on a blog or on YouTube are often remarkably mean. Buyers and sellers on eBay are a little more civil, despite occasional disappointments, such as encounters with flakiness and fraud. Based on those data, you could conclude that it isn't exactly anonymity, but *transient* anonymity, coupled with a lack of consequences, that brings out online idiocy.

With more data, that hypothesis can be refined. Participants in Second Life (a virtual online world) are generally not quite as mean to one another as are people posting comments to Slashdot (a popular technology news site) or engaging in edit wars on Wikipedia, even though all allow pseudonyms. The difference might be that on Second Life the pseudonymous personality itself is highly valuable and requires a lot of work to create.

So a better portrait of the troll-evoking design is effortless, consequence-free, transient anonymity in the service of a goal, such as promoting a point of view, that stands entirely apart from one's identity or personality. Call it drive-by anonymity.

Computers have an unfortunate tendency to present us with binary choices at every level, not just at the lowest one, where the bits are switching. It is easy to be anonymous or fully revealed, but hard to be revealed just enough. Still, that does happen, to varying degrees. Sites like eBay and Second Life give hints about how design can promote a middle path.

Anonymity certainly has a place, but that place needs to be designed carefully. Voting and peer review are pre-internet examples of beneficial anonymity. Sometimes it is desirable for people to be free of fear of reprisal or stigma in order to invoke honest opinions. To have a substantial exchange, however, you need to be fully present. That is why facing one's accuser is a fundamental right of the accused.

■ Could Drive-by Anonymity Scale Up the Way Communism and Fascism Did?

For the most part, the net has delivered happy surprises about human potential. As I pointed out earlier, the rise of the web in the early 1990s took place without leaders, ideology, advertising, commerce, or anything other than a positive sensibility shared by millions of people. Who would have thought that was possible? Ever since, there has been a constant barrage of utopian extrapolations from positive online events. Whenever a blogger humiliates a corporation by posting documentation of an infelicitous service representative, we can expect triumphant hollers about the end of the era of corporate abuses.

It stands to reason, however, that the net can also accentuate negative patterns of behavior or even bring about unforeseen social pathology. Over the last century, new media technologies have often become prominent as components of massive outbreaks of organized violence.

For example, the Nazi regime was a major pioneer of radio and cinematic propaganda. The Soviets were also obsessed with propaganda technologies. Stalin even nurtured a "Manhattan Project" to develop a 3-D theater with incredible, massive optical elements that would deliver perfected propaganda. It would have been virtual reality's evil twin if it had been completed. Many people in the Muslim world have only gained access to satellite TV and the internet in the last decade. These media certainly have contributed to the current wave of violent radicalism. In all these cases, there was an intent to propagandize, but intent isn't everything.

It's not crazy to worry that, with millions of people connected through a medium that sometimes brings out their worst tendencies, massive, fascist-style mobs could rise up suddenly. I worry about the next generation of young people around the world growing up with internet-based technology that emphasizes crowd aggregation, as is the current fad. Will they be more likely to succumb to pack dynamics when they come of age?

What's to prevent the acrimony from scaling up? Unfortunately, history tells us that collectivist ideals can mushroom into large-scale social disasters. The *fascias* and communes of the past started out with small numbers of idealistic revolutionaries.

I am afraid we might be setting ourselves up for a reprise. The recipe that led to social catastrophe in the past was economic humiliation combined with collectivist ideology. We already have the ideology in its new digital packaging, and it's entirely possible we could face dangerously traumatic economic shocks in the coming decades.

■ An Ideology of Violation

The internet has come to be saturated with an ideology of violation. For instance, when some of the more charismatic figures in the online world, including Jimmy Wales, one of the founders of Wikipedia, and Tim O'Reilly, the coiner of the term "web 2.0," proposed a voluntary code of conduct in the wake of the bullying of Kathy Sierra, there was a widespread outcry, and the proposals went nowhere.

The ideology of violation does not radiate from the lowest depths of trolldom, but from the highest heights of academia. There are respectable academic conferences devoted to methods of violating sanctities of all kinds. The only criterion is that researchers come up with some way of using digital technology to harm innocent people who thought they were safe.

In 2008, researchers from the University of Massachusetts at Amherst and the University of Washington presented papers at two of these conferences (called Defcon and Black Hat), disclosing a bizarre form of attack that had apparently not been expressed in public before, even in works of fiction. They had spent two years of team effort figuring out how to use mobile phone technology to hack into a pacemaker and turn it off by remote control, in order to kill a person. (While they withheld some of the details in their public presentation, they certainly described enough to assure protégés that success was possible.)

The reason I call this an expression of ideology is that there is a strenuously constructed lattice of arguments that decorate this murderous behavior so that it looks grand and new. If the same researchers had done something similar without digital technology, they would at the very least have lost their jobs. Suppose they had spent a couple of years and significant funds figuring out how to rig a washing machine to poison clothing in order to (hypothetically) kill a child once dressed. Or what if they had devoted a lab in an elite university to finding a new way to imperceptibly tamper with skis to cause fatal accidents on the slopes? These are certainly doable projects, but because they are not digital, they don't support an illusion of ethics.

A summary of the ideology goes like this: All those nontechnical, ignorant, innocent people out there are going about their lives thinking that they are safe, when in actuality they are terribly vulnerable to those who are smarter than they are. Therefore, we smartest technical people ought to invent ways to attack the innocents, and publicize our results, so that everyone is alerted to the dangers of our superior powers. After all, a clever evil person might come along.

There are some cases in which the ideology of violation does lead to practical, positive outcomes. For instance, any bright young technical person has the potential to discover a new way to infect a personal computer with a virus. When that happens, there are several possible next steps. The least ethical would be for the "hacker" to infect computers. The most ethical would be for the hacker to quietly let the companies that support the computers know, so that users can download fixes. An intermediate option would be to publicize the "exploit" for glory. A fix can usually be distributed before the exploit does harm.

But the example of the pacemakers is entirely different. The rules of the cloud apply poorly to reality. It took two top academic labs two years of focused effort to demonstrate the exploit, and that was only possible because a third lab at a medical school was able to procure pacemakers and information about them that would normally be very hard to come by. Would high school students or terrorists, or any other imaginable party, have been able to assemble the resources necessary to figure out whether it was possible to kill people in this new way?

The fix in this case would require many surgeries—more than one of each person who wears a pacemaker. New designs of pacemakers will only inspire new exploits. There will always be a new exploit, because there is no such thing as perfect security. Will each heart patient have to schedule heart surgeries on an annual basis in order to keep ahead of academic do-gooders, just in order to stay alive? How much would it cost? How many would die from the side effects of surgery? Given the endless opportunity for harm, no one will be able to act on the information the researchers have graciously provided, so everyone with a pacemaker will forever be at greater risk than they otherwise would have been. No improvement has taken place, only harm.

Those who disagree with the ideology of violation are said to subscribe to a fallacious idea known as "security through obscurity." Smart people aren't supposed to accept this strategy for security, because the internet is supposed to have made obscurity obsolete.

Therefore, another group of elite researchers spent years figuring out how to pick one of the toughest-to-pick door locks, and posted the results on the internet. This was a lock that thieves had not learned to pick on their own. The researchers compared their triumph to Turing's cracking of Enigma. The method used to defeat the lock would have remained obscure were it not for the ideology that has entranced much of the academic world, especially computer science departments.

Surely obscurity is the only fundamental form of security that exists, and the internet by itself doesn't make it obsolete. One way to deprogram academics who buy into the pervasive ideology of violation is to point out that security through obscurity has another name in the world of biology: biodiversity.

The reason some people are immune to a virus like AIDS is that their particular bodies are obscure to the virus. The reason that computer viruses infect PCs more than Macs is not that a Mac is any better engineered, but that it is relatively obscure. PCs are more commonplace. This means that there is more return on the effort to crack PCs.

There is no such thing as an unbreakable lock. In fact, the vast majority of security systems are not too hard to break. But there is always effort required to figure out how to break them. In the case of pacemakers, it took two years at two labs, which must have entailed a significant expense.

Another predictable element of the ideology of violation is that anyone who complains about the rituals of the elite violators will be accused of spreading FUD—fear, uncertainty, and doubt. But actually it's the ideologues who seek publicity. The whole point of publicizing exploits like the attack on pacemakers is the glory. If that notoriety isn't based on spreading FUD, what is?

■ The MIDI of Anonymity

Just as the idea of a musical note was formalized and rigidified by MIDI, the idea of drive-by, trollish, pack-switch anonymity is being plucked from the platonic realm and made into immoveable eternal architecture by software. Fortunately, the process isn't complete yet, so there is still time to promote alternative designs that resonate with human kindness. When people don't become aware of, or fail to take responsibility for, their role, accidents of time and place can determine the outcomes of the standards wars between digital ideologies. Whenever we notice an instance when history was swayed by accident, we also notice the latitude we have to shape the future.

Hive mind ideology wasn't running the show during earlier eras of the internet's development. The ideology became dominant *after* certain patterns were set, because it sat comfortably with those patterns. The origins of today's outbreaks of nasty online behavior go back quite a way, to the history of the counterculture in America, and in particular to the war on drugs.

Before the World Wide Web, there were other types of online connections, of which Usenet was probably the most influential. Usenet was an online directory of topics where anyone could post comments, drive-by style. One portion of Usenet, called "alt," was reserved for nonacademic topics, including those that were oddball, pornographic, illegal, or offensive. A lot of the alt material was wonderful, such as information about obscure musical instruments, while some of it was sickening, such as tutorials on cannibalism.

To get online in those days you usually had to have an academic, corporate, or military connection, so the Usenet population was mostly adult and educated. That didn't help. Some users still turned into mean idiots online. This is one piece of evidence that it's the design, not the demographic, that concentrates bad behavior. Since there were so few people online, though, bad "netiquette" was then more of a curiosity than a problem.

Why did Usenet support drive-by anonymity? You could argue that it was the easiest design to implement at the time, but I'm not sure that's true. All those academic, corporate, and military users belonged to large, well-structured organizations, so the hooks were immediately available to create a non-anonymous design. If that had happened, today's websites might not have inherited the drive-by design aesthetic.

So if it wasn't laziness that promoted online anonymity, what was it?

■ Facebook Is Similar to No Child Left Behind

Personal reductionism has always been present in information systems. You have to declare your status in reductive ways when you file a tax return. Your real life is represented by a silly, phony set of database entries in order for you to make use of a service in an approximate way. Most people are aware of the difference between reality and database entries when they file taxes.

But the order is reversed when you perform the same kind of self-reduction in order to create a profile on a social networking site. You fill in the data: profession, marital status, and residence. But in this case digital reduction becomes a causal element, mediating contact between new friends. This is new. It used to be that government was famous for being impersonal, but in a post-personal world, that will no longer be a distinction.

It might at first seem that the experience of youth is now sharply divided between the old world of school and parents, and the new world of social networking on the internet, but actually school now belongs on the new side of the ledger. Education has gone through a parallel transformation, and for similar reasons.

Information systems need to have information in order to run, but information underrepresents reality. Demand more from information than it can give, and you end up with monstrous designs. Under the No Child Left Behind Act of 2002, for example, U.S. teachers are forced to choose between teaching general knowledge and "teaching to the test." The best teachers are thus often disenfranchised by the improper use of educational informational systems.

What computerized analysis of all the country's school tests has done to education is exactly what Facebook has done to friendships. In both cases, life is turned into a database. Both degradations are based on the same philosophical mistake, which is the belief that computers can presently represent human thought or human relationships. These are things computers cannot currently do.

Whether one expects computers to improve in the future is a different issue. In a less idealistic atmosphere it would go without saying that software should only be designed to perform tasks that can be successfully performed at a given time. That is not the atmosphere in which internet software is designed, however.

If we build a computer model of an automobile engine, we know how to test whether it's any good. It turns out to be easy to build bad models! But it is possible to build good ones. We must model the materials, the fluid dynamics, the electrical subsystem. In each case, we have extremely solid physics to rely on, but we have lots of room for making mistakes in the logic or conception of how the pieces fit together. It is inevitably a long, unpredictable grind to debug a serious simulation of any complicated system. I've worked on varied simulations of such things as surgical procedures, and it is a humbling process. A good surgical simulation can take years to refine.

When it comes to people, we technologists must use a completely different methodology. We don't understand the brain well enough to comprehend phenomena like education or friendship on a scientific basis. So when we deploy a computer model of something like learning or friendship in a way that has an effect on real lives, we are relying on faith. When we ask people to live their lives through our models, we are potentially reducing life itself. How can we ever know what we might be losing?

■ The Abstract Person Obscures the Real Person

What happened to musical notes with the arrival of MIDI is happening to people.

It breaks my heart when I talk to energized young people who idolize icons of the new digital ideology, like Facebook, Twitter, Wikipedia, and free/Creative Commons mashups. I am always struck by the endless stress they put themselves through. They must manage their online reputations constantly, avoiding the ever-roaming evil eye of the hive mind, which can turn on an individual at any moment. A "Facebook generation" young person who suddenly becomes humiliated online has no way out, for there is only one hive.

I would prefer not to judge the experiences or motivations of other people, but surely this new strain of gadget fetishism is driven more by fear than by love.

At their best, the new Facebook/Twitter enthusiasts remind me of the anarchists and other nutty idealists who populated youth culture when I grew up. The ideas might be silly, but at least the believers have fun as they rebel against the parental-authority quality of entities like record companies that attempt to fight music piracy.

The most effective young Facebook users, however—the ones who will probably be winners if Facebook turns out to be a model of the future they will inhabit as adults—are the ones who create successful online fictions about themselves.

They tend their doppelgängers fastidiously. They must manage offhand remarks and track candid snapshots at parties as carefully as a politician. Insincerity is rewarded, while sincerity creates a lifelong taint. Certainly, some version of this principle existed in the lives of teenagers before the web came along, but not with such unyielding, clinical precision.

The frenetic energy of the original flowering of the web has reappeared in a new generation, but there is a new brittleness to the types of connections people make online. This is a side effect of the illusion that digital representations can capture much about actual human relationships.

The binary character at the core of software engineering tends to reappear at higher levels. It is far easier to tell a program to run or not to run, for instance, than it is to tell it to sort-of run. In the same way, it is easier to set up a rigid representation of human relationships on digital networks:

on a typical social networking site, either you are designated to be in a couple or you are single (or you are in one of a few other predetermined states of being)—and that reduction of life is what gets broadcast between friends all the time. What is communicated between people eventually becomes their truth. Relationships take on the troubles of software engineering.

■ Just a Reminder That I'm Not Anti-Net

It seems ridiculous to have to say this, but just in case anyone is getting the wrong idea, let me affirm that I am not turning against the internet. I love the internet.

For just one example among many, I have been spending quite a lot of time on an online forum populated by oud players. (The oud is a Middle Eastern string instrument.) I hesitate to mention it, because I worry that any special little place on the internet can be ruined if it gets too much attention.

The oud forum revives the magic of the early years of the internet. There's a bit of a feeling of paradise about it. You feel each participant's passion for the instrument, and we help one another become more intense. It's amazing to watch oud players from around the world cheer on an oud builder as he posts pictures of an instrument under construction. It's thrilling to hear clips from a young player captured in midair just as she is getting good.

The fancy web 2.0 designs of the early twenty-first century start off by classifying people into bubbles, so you meet your own kind. Facebook tops up dating pools, LinkedIn corrals careerists, and so on.

The oud forum does the opposite. There you find Turks and Armenians, elders and kids, Israelis and Palestinians, rich professionals and struggling artists, formal academics and bohemian street musicians, all talking with one another about a shared obsession. We get to know one another; we are not fragments to one another. Inner trolls most definitely appear now and then, but less often than in most online environments. The oud forum doesn't solve the world's problems, but it does allow us to live larger than them.

When I told Kevin Kelly about this magical confluence of obsessive people, he immediately asked if there was a particular magical person who tended the oud forum. The places that work online always turn out to be the beloved projects of individuals, not the automated aggregations of the cloud. In this case, of course, there is such a magical person, who turns out to be a young Egyptian American oud player in Los Angeles.

The engineer in me occasionally ponders the rather crude software that the forum runs on. The deep design mystery of how to organize and present multiple threads of conversation on a screen remains as unsolved as ever. But just when I am about to dive into a design project to improve forum software, I stop and wonder if there really is much room for improvement.

It's the people who make the forum, not the software. Without the software, the experience would not exist at all, so I celebrate that software, as flawed as it is. But it's not as if the forum would really get much better if the software improved. Focusing too much on the software might even make things worse by shifting the focus from the people.

There is huge room for improvement in digital technologies overall. I would love to have telepresence sessions with distant oudists, for instance. But once you have the basics of a given technological leap in place, it's always important to step back and focus on the people for a while.

■ WHAT?

1. What is a manifesto? Explain how "Trolls" does or does not fit that definition.
2. Explain what you think Lanier means when he writes that "the user interface designs that arise from the ideology of the computing cloud make people—all of us—less kind. Trolling is not a string of isolated incidents, but the status quo in the online world." Do you agree with this assertion?
3. What, according to Lanier, is "drive-by anonymity"? How does it contribute to what Lanier calls trollish behavior?
4. How does Lanier's argument implicate Facebook and other social networking and crowd-sourcing sites? Do you see a danger in what Lanier calls "internet-based technology that emphasizes crowd aggregation"? Explain your response.

■ WHAT ELSE? WHAT'S NEXT

5. In his essay, Lanier writes: "If we are to continue to focus the powers of digital technology on the project of making human affairs less personal and more collective, then we ought to consider how that project might interact with human nature." Part of what Lanier is concerned with in his essay is responsibility—our social obligations to one another and how digital technology might be transforming these obligations. Working with a group of classmates, propose a code of conduct and responsibility for a social networking site with which you are familiar. Keep in mind that any code of this kind must balance a variety of issues, among them anonymity, free speech, accountability, and the differences between face-to-face and digital encounters. As a starting point, you and your group mates should research existing codes at a few sites online.

■ WHO CARES?

6. Analyze Lanier's tone in "Trolls"—not necessarily what he says, but *how* he says it. How would you characterize his tone? What kind of language does he use? Is he talking *with* his readers or *at* them? What rhetorical effect does his tone have on you, as a reader?

Chapter 10 | Reading.com

Matt Richtel, who writes about technology for The New York Times, *won the 2010 Pulitzer Prize for National Reporting for "Driven to Distraction," a series about driving and multitasking that spurred legislative efforts across the nation to deal with the problem. He wrote this piece for the June 6, 2010, edition of* The Times.

BEFORE YOU READ
Make a list of all of the digital technologies you use each day and of the ways in which you multitask using these technologies. Be prepared to share your list with the class.

HOOKED ON TECHNOLOGY, AND PAYING A PRICE   Matt Richtel

When one of the most important e-mail messages of his life landed in his in-box a few years ago, Kord Campbell overlooked it. Not just for a day or two, but 12 days. He finally saw it while sifting through old messages: a big company wanted to buy his Internet start-up. "I stood up from my desk and said, 'Oh my God, oh my God, oh my God,'" Mr. Campbell said. "It's kind of hard to miss an e-mail like that, but I did."

The message had slipped by him amid an electronic flood: two computer screens alive with e-mail, instant messages, online chats, a Web browser and the computer code he was writing.

While he managed to salvage the $1.3 million deal after apologizing to his suitor, Mr. Campbell continues to struggle with the effects of the deluge of data. Even after he unplugs, he craves the stimulation he gets from his electronic gadgets. He forgets things like dinner plans, and he has trouble focusing on his family.

His wife, Brenda, complains, "It seems like he can no longer be fully in the moment."

This is your brain on computers.

Scientists say juggling e-mail, phone calls and other incoming information can change how people think and behave. They say our ability to focus is being undermined by bursts of information. These play to a primitive impulse to respond to immediate opportunities and threats. The stimulation provokes excitement—a dopamine squirt—that researchers say can be addictive. In its absence, people feel bored.

The resulting distractions can have deadly consequences, as when cellphone-wielding drivers and train engineers cause wrecks. And for millions of people like Mr. Campbell, these urges can inflict nicks and cuts on creativity and deep thought, interrupting work and family life.

While many people say multitasking makes them more productive, research shows otherwise. Heavy multitaskers actually have more trouble focusing and shutting out irrelevant information, scientists say, and they experience more stress. And scientists are discovering that even after the multitasking ends, fractured thinking and lack of focus persist. In other words, this is also your brain off computers.

"The technology is rewiring our brains," said Nora Volkow, director of the National Institute of Drug Abuse and one of the world's leading brain scientists. She and other researchers compare the lure of digital stimulation less to that of drugs and alcohol than to food and sex, which are essential but counterproductive in excess.

Technology use can benefit the brain in some ways, researchers say. Imaging studies show the brains of Internet users become more efficient at finding information. And players of some video games develop better visual acuity.

More broadly, cellphones and computers have transformed life. They let people escape their cubicles and work anywhere. They shrink distances and handle countless mundane tasks, freeing up time for more exciting pursuits.

For better or worse, the consumption of media, as varied as e-mail and TV, has exploded. In 2008, people consumed three times as much information each day as they did in 1960. And they are constantly shifting their attention. Computer users at work change windows or check e-mail or other programs nearly 37 times an hour, new research shows.

The nonstop interactivity is one of the most significant shifts ever in the human environment, said Adam Gazzaley, a neuroscientist at the University of California, San Francisco. "We are exposing our brains to an environment and asking them to do things we weren't necessarily evolved to do," he said. "We know already there are consequences."

Mr. Campbell, 43, came of age with the personal computer, and he is a heavier user of technology than most. But researchers say the habits and struggles of Mr. Campbell and his family typify what many experience—and what many more will, if trends continue.

For him, the tensions feel increasingly acute, and the effects harder to shake.

The Campbells recently moved to California from Oklahoma to start a software venture. Mr. Campbell's life revolves around computers. He goes to sleep with a laptop or iPhone on his chest, and when he wakes, he goes online. He and Mrs. Campbell, 39, head to the tidy kitchen in their four-bedroom hillside rental in Orinda, an affluent suburb of San Francisco, where she makes breakfast and watches a TV news feed in the corner of the computer screen while he uses the rest of the monitor to check his e-mail.

Major spats have arisen because Mr. Campbell escapes into video games during tough emotional stretches. On family vacations, he has trouble putting down his devices. When he rides the subway to San Francisco, he knows he will be offline 221 seconds as the train goes through a tunnel.

Their 16-year-old son, Connor, tall and polite like his father, recently received his first C's, which his family blames on distraction from his gadgets. Their 8-year-old daughter, Lily, like her mother, playfully tells her father that he favors technology over family.

"I would love for him to totally unplug, to be totally engaged," says Mrs. Campbell, who adds that he becomes "crotchety until he gets his fix." But she would not try to force a change. "He loves it. Technology is part of the fabric of who he is," she says. "If I hated technology, I'd be hating him, and a part of who my son is too."

■ Always On

Mr. Campbell, whose given name is Thomas, had an early start with technology in Oklahoma City. When he was in third grade, his parents bought him Pong, a video game. Then came a string of game consoles and PCs, which he learned to program. In high school, he balanced computers, basketball and a romance with Brenda, a cheerleader with a gorgeous singing voice. He studied too, with focus, uninterrupted by e-mail. "I did my homework because I needed to get it done," he said. "I didn't have anything else to do."

He left college to help with a family business, then set up a lawn mowing service. At night he would read, play video games, hang out with Brenda and, as she remembers it, "talk a lot more." In 1996, he started a successful Internet provider. Then he built the start-up that he sold for $1.3 million in 2003 to LookSmart, a search engine.

Mr. Campbell loves the rush of modern life and keeping up with the latest information. "I want to be the first to hear when the aliens land," he said, laughing. But other times, he fantasizes about living in pioneer days when things moved more slowly: "I can't keep everything in my head."

No wonder. As he came of age, so did a new era of data and communication.

At home, people consume 12 hours of media a day on average, when an hour spent with, say, the Internet and TV simultaneously counts as two hours. That compares with five hours in 1960, say researchers at the University of California, San Diego. Computer users visit an average of 40 Web sites a day, according to research by RescueTime, which offers time-management tools.

As computers have changed, so has the understanding of the human brain. Until 15 years ago, scientists thought the brain stopped developing after childhood. Now they understand that its neural networks continue to develop, influenced by things like learning skills.

So not long after Eyal Ophir arrived at Stanford in 2004, he wondered whether heavy multitasking might be leading to changes in a characteristic of the brain long thought immutable: that humans can process only a single stream of information at a time.

Going back a half-century, tests had shown that the brain could barely process two streams, and could not simultaneously make decisions about them. But Mr. Ophir, a student-turned-researcher, thought multitaskers might be rewiring themselves to handle the load.

His passion was personal. He had spent seven years in Israeli intelligence after being weeded out of the air force—partly, he felt, because he was not a good multitasker. Could his brain be retrained? Mr. Ophir, like others around the country studying how technology bent the brain, was startled by what he discovered.

■ The Myth of Multitasking

The test subjects were divided into two groups: those classified as heavy multitaskers based on their answers to questions about how they used technology, and those who were not.

In a test created by Mr. Ophir and his colleagues, subjects at a computer were briefly shown an image of red rectangles. Then they saw a similar image and were asked whether any of the rectangles had moved. It was a simple task until the addition of a twist: blue rectangles were added, and the subjects were told to ignore them.

The multitaskers then did a significantly worse job than the non-multitaskers at recognizing whether red rectangles had changed position. In other words, they had trouble filtering out the blue ones—the irrelevant information. So, too, the multitaskers took longer than non-multitaskers to switch among tasks, like differentiating vowels from consonants and then odd from even numbers. The multitaskers were shown to be less efficient at juggling problems.

Other tests at Stanford, an important center for research in this fast-growing field, showed multitaskers tended to search for new information rather than accept a reward for putting older, more valuable information to work. Researchers say these findings point to an interesting dynamic: multitaskers seem more sensitive than non-multitaskers to incoming information.

The results also illustrate an age-old conflict in the brain, one that technology may be intensifying. A portion of the brain acts as a control tower, helping a person focus and set priorities. More primitive parts of the brain, like those that process sight and sound, demand that it pay attention to new information, bombarding the control tower when they are stimulated.

Researchers say there is an evolutionary rationale for the pressure this barrage puts on the brain. The lower-brain functions alert humans to danger, like a nearby lion, overriding goals like building a hut. In the modern world, the chime of incoming e-mail can override the goal of writing a business plan or playing catch with the children.

"Throughout evolutionary history, a big surprise would get everyone's brain thinking," said Clifford Nass, a communications professor at Stanford. "But we've got a large and growing group of people who think the slightest hint that something interesting might be going on is like catnip. They can't ignore it." Mr. Nass says the Stanford studies are important because they show multitasking's lingering effects: "The scary part for guys like Kord is, they can't shut off their multitasking tendencies when they're not multitasking."

Melina Uncapher, a neurobiologist on the Stanford team, said she and other researchers were unsure whether the muddied multitaskers were simply prone to distraction and would have had trouble focusing in any era. But she added that the idea that information overload causes distraction was supported by more and more research.

A study at the University of California, Irvine, found that people interrupted by e-mail reported significantly increased stress compared with those left to focus. Stress hormones have been shown to reduce short-term memory, said Gary Small, a psychiatrist at the University of California, Los Angeles.

Preliminary research shows some people can more easily juggle multiple information streams. These "supertaskers" represent less than 3 percent of the population, according to scientists at the University of Utah.

Other research shows computer use has neurological advantages. In imaging studies, Dr. Small observed that Internet users showed greater brain activity than nonusers, suggesting they were growing their neural circuitry. At the University of Rochester, researchers found that players of some fast-paced video games can track the movement of a third more objects on a screen than nonplayers. They say the games can improve reaction and the ability to pick out details amid clutter.

"In a sense, those games have a very strong both rehabilitative and educational power," said the lead researcher, Daphne Bavelier, who is working with others in the field to channel these changes into real-world benefits like safer driving.

There is a vibrant debate among scientists over whether technology's influence on behavior and the brain is good or bad, and how significant it is.

"The bottom line is, the brain is wired to adapt," said Steven Yantis, a professor of brain sciences at Johns Hopkins University. "There's no question that rewiring goes on all the time," he added. But he said it was too early to say whether the changes caused by technology were materially different from others in the past.

Mr. Ophir is loath to call the cognitive changes bad or good, though the impact on analysis and creativity worries him. He is not just worried about other people. Shortly after he came to Stanford, a professor thanked him for being the one student in class paying full attention and not using a computer or phone. But he recently began using an iPhone and noticed a change; he felt its pull, even when playing with his daughter. "The media is changing me," he said. "I hear this internal ping that says: check e-mail and voice mail."

"I have to work to suppress it."

Kord Campbell does not bother to suppress it, or no longer can.

Interrupted by a Corpse

It is a Wednesday in April, and in 10 minutes, Mr. Campbell has an online conference call that could determine the fate of his new venture, called Loggly. It makes software that helps companies understand the clicking and buying patterns of their online customers.

Mr. Campbell and his colleagues, each working from a home office, are frantically trying to set up a program that will let them share images with executives at their prospective partner. But at the moment when Mr. Campbell most needs to focus on that urgent task, something else competes for his attention: "Man Found Dead Inside His Business."

That is the tweet that appears on the left-most of Mr. Campbell's array of monitors, which he has expanded to three screens, at times adding a laptop and an iPad. On the left screen, Mr. Campbell follows the tweets of 1,100 people, along with instant messages and group chats. The middle monitor displays a dark field filled with computer code, along with Skype, a service that allows Mr. Campbell to talk to his colleagues, sometimes using video. The monitor on the right keeps e-mail, a calendar, a Web browser and a music player.

Even with the meeting fast approaching, Mr. Campbell cannot resist the tweet about the corpse. He clicks on the link in it, glances at the article and dismisses it. "It's some article about something somewhere," he says, annoyed by the ads for jeans popping up.

The program gets fixed, and the meeting turns out to be fruitful: the partners are ready to do business. A colleague says via instant message: "YES."

Other times, Mr. Campbell's information juggling has taken a more serious toll. A few weeks earlier, he once again overlooked an e-mail message from a prospective investor. Another time, Mr. Campbell signed the company up for the wrong type of business account on Amazon.com, costing $300 a month for six months before he got around to correcting it. He has burned hamburgers on the grill, forgotten to pick up the children and lingered in the bathroom playing video games on an iPhone.

Mr. Campbell can be unaware of his own habits. In a two-and-a-half hour stretch one recent morning, he switched rapidly between e-mail and several other programs, according to data from RescueTime, which monitored his computer use with his permission. But when asked later what he was doing in that period, Mr. Campbell said he had been on a long Skype call, and "may have pulled up an e-mail or two."

The kind of disconnection Mr. Campbell experiences is not an entirely new problem, of course. As they did in earlier eras, people can become so lost in work, hobbies or TV that they fail to pay attention to family.

Mr. Campbell concedes that, even without technology, he may work or play obsessively, just as his father immersed himself in crossword puzzles. But he says this era is different because he can multitask anyplace, anytime. "It's a mixed blessing," he said. "If you're not careful, your marriage can fall apart or your kids can be ready to play and you'll get distracted."

■ The Toll on Children

Father and son sit in armchairs. Controllers in hand, they engage in a fierce video game battle, displayed on the nearby flat-panel TV, as Lily watches. They are playing Super Smash Bros. Brawl, a cartoonish animated fight between characters that battle using anvils, explosives and other weapons.

"Kill him, Dad," Lily screams. To no avail. Connor regularly beats his father, prompting expletives and, once, a thrown pillow. But there is bonding and mutual respect. "He's a lot more tactical," says Connor. "But I'm really good at quick reflexes."

Screens big and small are central to the Campbell family's leisure time. Connor and his mother relax while watching TV shows like "Heroes." Lily has an iPod Touch, a portable DVD player and her own laptop, which she uses to watch videos, listen to music and play games.

Lily, a second-grader, is allowed only an hour a day of unstructured time, which she often spends with her devices. The laptop can consume her. "When she's on it, you can holler her name all day and she won't hear," Mrs. Campbell said.

Researchers worry that constant digital stimulation like this creates attention problems for children with brains that are still developing, who already struggle to set priorities and resist impulses.

Connor's troubles started late last year. He could not focus on homework. No wonder, perhaps. On his bedroom desk sit two monitors, one with his music collection, one with Facebook and Reddit, a social site with news links that he and his father love. His iPhone availed him to relentless texting with his girlfriend.

When he studied, "a little voice would be saying, 'Look up' at the computer, and I'd look up," Connor said. "Normally, I'd say I want to only read for a few minutes, but I'd search every corner of Reddit and then check Facebook."

His Web browsing informs him. "He's a fact hound," Mr. Campbell brags. "Connor is, other than programming, extremely technical. He's 100 percent Internet savvy." But the parents worry too. "Connor is obsessed," his mother said. "Kord says we have to teach him balance."

So in January, they held a family meeting. Study time now takes place in a group setting at the dinner table after everyone has finished eating. It feels, Mr. Campbell says, like togetherness.

■ No Vacations

For spring break, the family rented a cottage in Carmel, Calif. Mrs. Campbell hoped everyone would unplug. But the day before they left, the iPad from Apple came out, and Mr. Campbell snapped one up. The next night, their first on vacation, "We didn't go out to dinner," Mrs. Campbell mourned. "We just sat there on our devices."

She rallied the troops the next day to the aquarium. Her husband joined them for a bit but then begged out to do e-mail on his phone. Later she found him playing video games.

The trip came as Mr. Campbell was trying to raise several million dollars for his new venture, a goal that he achieved. Brenda said she understood that his pursuit required intensity but was less understanding of the accompanying surge in video game.

His behavior brought about a discussion between them. Mrs. Campbell said he told her that he was capable of logging off, citing a trip to Hawaii several years ago that they called their second honeymoon. "What trip are you thinking about?" she said she asked him. She recalled that he had spent two hours a day online in the hotel's business center.

On Thursday, their fourth day in Carmel, Mr. Campbell spent the day at the beach with his family. They flew a kite and played whiffle ball. Connor unplugged too. "It changes the mood of everything when everybody is present," Mrs. Campbell said.

The next day, the family drove home, and Mr. Campbell disappeared into his office.

Technology use is growing for Mrs. Campbell as well. She divides her time between keeping the books of her husband's company, homemaking and working at the school library. She checks e-mail 25 times a day, sends texts and uses Facebook.

Recently, she was baking peanut butter cookies for Teacher Appreciation Day when her phone chimed in the living room. She answered a text, then became lost in Facebook, forgot about the cookies and burned them. She started a new batch, but heard the phone again, got lost in messaging, and burned those too. Out of ingredients and shamed, she bought cookies at the store.

She feels less focused and has trouble completing projects. Some days, she promises herself she will ignore her device. "It's like a diet—you have good intentions in the morning and then you're like, 'There went that,' " she said.

Mr. Nass at Stanford thinks the ultimate risk of heavy technology use is that it diminishes empathy by limiting how much people engage with one another, even in the same room.

"The way we become more human is by paying attention to each other," he said. "It shows how much you care." That empathy, Mr. Nass said, is essential to the human condition. "We are at an inflection point," he said. "A significant fraction of people's experiences are now fragmented."

■ WHAT?

1. Richtel quotes one researcher as saying that "technology is rewiring our brains." Explain what this means, in the context of Richtel's article, and summarize the evidence that Richtel uses to support this contention.
2. Explain what Richtel calls the "myth of multitasking." Does he change your thinking about multitasking? Why? Or why not?

■ WHAT ELSE? WHAT'S NEXT?

3. In this article, Richtel engages in explanatory writing—that is, he introduces and explains information and ideas with which the audience may not be familiar. Explanatory writing, as the name implies, has a specific purpose: It is meant to help readers understand something new. The news media engage in explanatory writing every day as they try to help their audiences make sense of what's going on in the world. With Richtel's article in mind, read the two essays that follow—"Is Google Making Us Stupid" and "Get Smarter." Then, select a concept or a technology from one of these three pieces that you would like to learn more about. Research the topic—find at least two reliable sources—and then write a brief essay in which you explain it to your classmates. Make sure you document your sources using MLA guidelines.

■ WHO CARES?

4. How does Richtel use the Campbell family to help connect with his readers and to drive home the importance of this issue?

> *Nicholas Carr, whose most recent book is* The Big Switch: Rewiring the World, From Edison to Google *(2008), writes on the social, intellectual, and business implications of technology. He uses his own experience as a starting point in this examination of how digital technologies such as Google's search engines affect intelligence. He wrote this essay for the July/August 2008 issue of* Atlantic Monthly.

BEFORE YOU READ

Answer the following question: Has using the Internet made you smarter? Support your response with specific examples based on your experience.

IS GOOGLE MAKING US STUPID? Nicholas Carr

"Dave, stop. Stop, will you? Stop, Dave. Will you stop, Dave?" So the supercomputer HAL pleads with the implacable astronaut Dave Bowman in a famous and weirdly poignant scene toward the end of Stanley Kubrick's *2001: A Space Odyssey*. Bowman, having nearly been sent to a deep-space death by the malfunctioning machine, is calmly, coldly disconnecting the memory circuits that control its artificial "brain." "Dave, my mind is going," HAL says, forlornly. "I can feel it. I can feel it."

I can feel it, too. Over the past few years I've had an uncomfortable sense that someone, or something, has been tinkering with my brain, remapping the neural circuitry, reprogramming the memory. My mind isn't going—so far as I can tell—but it's changing. I'm not thinking the way I used to think. I can feel it most strongly when I'm reading. Immersing myself in a book or a lengthy article used to be easy. My mind would get caught up in the narrative or the turns of the argument, and I'd spend hours strolling through long stretches of prose. That's rarely the case anymore. Now my concentration often starts to drift after two or three pages. I get fidgety, lose the thread, begin looking for something else to do. I feel as if I'm always dragging my wayward brain back to the text. The deep reading that used to come naturally has become a struggle.

I think I know what's going on. For more than a decade now, I've been spending a lot of time online, searching and surfing and sometimes adding to the great databases of the Internet. The Web has been a godsend to me as a writer. Research that once required days in the stacks or periodical rooms of libraries can now be done in minutes. A few Google searches, some quick clicks on hyperlinks, and I've got the telltale fact or pithy quote I was after. Even when I'm not working, I'm as likely as not to be foraging in the Web's info-thickets reading and writing emails, scanning headlines and blog posts, watching videos and listening to podcasts, or just tripping from link to link to link. (Unlike footnotes, to which they're sometimes likened, hyperlinks don't merely point to related works; they propel you toward them.)

For me, as for others, the Net is becoming a universal medium, the conduit for most of the information that flows through my eyes and ears and into my mind. The advantages of having immediate access to such an incredibly rich store of information are many, and they've been widely described and duly applauded. "The perfect recall of silicon memory," *Wired*'s Clive Thompson has written, "can be an enormous boon to thinking." But that boon comes at a price. As the media theorist Marshall McLuhan pointed out in the 1960s, media are not just passive channels of information. They supply the stuff of thought, but they also shape the process of thought. And what the Net seems to be doing is chipping away my capacity for concentration and contemplation. My mind now expects to take in information the way the Net distributes it: in a swiftly moving stream of particles. Once I was a scuba diver in the sea of words. Now I zip along the surface like a guy on a Jet Ski.

I'm not the only one. When I mention my troubles with reading to friends and acquaintances—literary types, most of them—many say they're having similar experiences. The more they use the Web, the more they have to fight to stay focused on long pieces of writing. Some of the bloggers I follow have also begun mentioning the phenomenon. Scott Karp, who writes a blog about online media, recently confessed that he has stopped reading books altogether. "I was a lit major in college, and used to be [a] voracious book reader," he wrote. "What happened?" He speculates on the answer: "What if I do all my reading on the web not so much because the way I read has changed, i.e. I'm just seeking convenience, but because the way I THINK has changed?"

Bruce Friedman, who blogs regularly about the use of computers in medicine, also has described how the Internet has altered his mental habits. "I now have almost totally lost the ability to read and absorb a longish article on the web or in print," he wrote earlier this year. A pathologist who has long been on the faculty of the University of Michigan Medical School, Friedman elaborated on his comment in a telephone conversation with me. His thinking, he said, has taken on a "staccato" quality, reflecting the way he quickly scans short passages of text from many sources online. "I can't read *War and Peace* anymore," he admitted. "I've lost the ability to do that. Even a blog post of more than three or four paragraphs is too much to absorb. I skim it."

Anecdotes alone don't prove much. And we still await the long-term neurological and psychological experiments that will provide a definitive picture of how Internet use affects cognition. But a recently published study of online research habits, conducted by scholars from University College London, suggests that we may well be in the midst of a sea change in the way we read and think. As part of the five-year research program, the scholars examined computer logs documenting the behavior of visitors to two popular research sites, one operated by the British Library and one by a U.K. educational consortium, that provide access to journal articles, e-books, and other sources of written information. They found that people using the sites exhibited "a form of skimming activity," hopping from one source to another and rarely returning to any source they'd already visited. They typically read no more than one or two pages of an article or book before they would "bounce" out to another site. Sometimes they'd save a long article, but there's no evidence that they ever went back and actually read it. The authors of the study report:

> It is clear that users are not reading online in the traditional sense; indeed there are signs that new forms of "reading" are emerging as users "power browse" horizontally through titles, contents pages and abstracts going for quick wins. It almost seems that they go online to avoid reading in the traditional sense.

Chapter 10 | Reading.com

Thanks to the ubiquity of text on the Internet, not to mention the popularity of text-messaging on cell phones, we may well be reading more today than we did in the 1970s or 1980s, when television was our medium of choice. But it's a different kind of reading, and behind it lies a different kind of thinking—perhaps even a new sense of the self. "We are not only what we read," says Maryanne Wolf, a developmental psychologist at Tufts University and the author of *Proust and the Squid: The Story and Science of the Reading Brain*. "We are how we read." Wolf worries that the style of reading promoted by the Net, a style that puts "efficiency" and "immediacy" above all else, may be weakening our capacity for the kind of deep reading that emerged when an earlier technology, the printing press, made long and complex works of prose commonplace. When we read online, she says, we tend to become "mere decoders of information." Our ability to interpret text, to make the rich mental connections that form when we read deeply and without distraction, remains largely disengaged.

Reading, explains Wolf, is not an instinctive skill for human beings. It's not etched into our genes the way speech is. We have to teach our minds how to translate the symbolic characters we see into the language we understand. And the media or other technologies we use in learning and practicing the craft of reading play an important part in shaping the neural circuits inside our brains. Experiments demonstrate that readers of ideograms, such as the Chinese, develop a mental circuitry for reading that is very different from the circuitry found in those of us whose written language employs an alphabet. The variations extend across many regions of the brain, including those that govern such essential cognitive functions as memory and the interpretation of visual and auditory stimuli. We can expect as well that the circuits woven by our use of the Net will be different from those woven by our reading of books and other printed works.

Sometime in 1882, Friedrich Nietzsche bought a typewriter—a Malling-Hansen Writing Ball, to be precise. His vision was failing, and keeping his eyes focused on a page had become exhausting and painful, often bringing on crushing headaches. He had been forced to curtail his writing, and he feared that he would soon have to give it up. The typewriter rescued him, at least for a time. Once he had mastered touch-typing, he was able to write with his eyes closed, using only the tips of his fingers. Words could once again flow from his mind to the page.

But the machine had a subtler effect on his work. One of Nietzsche's friends, a composer, noticed a change in the style of his writing. His already terse prose had become even tighter, more telegraphic. "Perhaps you will through this instrument even take to a new idiom," the friend wrote in a letter, noting that, in his own work, his "'thoughts' in music and language often depend on the quality of pen and paper."

"You are right," Nietzsche replied, "our writing equipment takes part in the forming of our thoughts." Under the sway of the machine, writes the German media scholar Friedrich A. Kittler, Nietzsche's prose "changed from arguments to aphorisms, from thoughts to puns, from rhetoric to telegram style."

The human brain is almost infinitely malleable. People used to think that our mental meshwork, the dense connections formed among the 100 billion or so neurons inside our skulls, was largely fixed by the time we reached adulthood. But brain researchers have discovered that that's not the case. James Olds, a professor of neuroscience who directs the Krasnow Institute for Advanced Study at George Mason University, says that even the adult mind "is very plastic."

Nerve cells routinely break old connections and form new ones. "The brain," according to Olds, "has the ability to reprogram itself on the fly, altering the way it functions."

As we use what the sociologist Daniel Bell has called our "intellectual technologies"—the tools that extend our mental rather than our physical capacities—we inevitably begin to take on the qualities of those technologies. The mechanical clock, which came into common use in the 14th century, provides a compelling example. In *Technics and Civilization*, the historian and cultural critic Lewis Mumford described how the clock "disassociated time from human events and helped create the belief in an independent world of mathematically measurable sequences." The "abstract framework of divided time" became "the point of reference for both action and thought."

The clock's methodical ticking helped bring into being the scientific mind and the scientific man. But it also took something away. As the late MIT computer scientist Joseph Weizenbaum observed in his 1976 book, *Computer Power and Human Reason: From Judgment to Calculation*, the conception of the world that emerged from the widespread use of timekeeping instruments "remains an impoverished version of the older one, for it rests on a rejection of those direct experiences that formed the basis for, and indeed constituted, the old reality." In deciding when to eat, to work, to sleep, to rise, we stopped listening to our senses and started obeying the clock.

The process of adapting to new intellectual technologies is reflected in the changing metaphors we use to explain ourselves to ourselves. When the mechanical clock arrived, people began thinking of their brains as operating "like clockwork." Today, in the age of software, we have come to think of them as operating "like computers." But the changes, neuroscience tells us, go much deeper than metaphor. Thanks to our brain's plasticity, the adaptation occurs also at a biological level.

The Internet promises to have particularly far-reaching effects on cognition. In a paper published in 1936, the British mathematician Alan Turing proved that a digital computer, which at the time existed only as a theoretical machine, could be programmed to perform the function of any other information-processing device. And that's what we're seeing today. The Internet, an immeasurably powerful computing system, is subsuming most of our other intellectual technologies. It's becoming our map and our clock, our printing press and our typewriter, our calculator and our telephone, and our radio and TV.

When the Net absorbs a medium, that medium is re-created in the Net's image. It injects the medium's content with hyperlinks, blinking ads, and other digital gewgaws, and it surrounds the content with the content of all the other media it has absorbed. A new e-mail message, for instance, may announce its arrival as we're glancing over the latest headlines at a newspaper's site. The result is to scatter our attention and diffuse our concentration.

The Net's influence doesn't end at the edges of a computer screen, either. As people's minds become attuned to the crazy quilt of Internet media, traditional media have to adapt to the audience's new expectations. Television programs add text crawls and pop-up ads, and magazines and newspapers shorten their articles, introduce capsule summaries, and crowd their pages with easy-to-browse info-snippets. When, in March of this year, *The New York Times* decided to devote the second and third pages of every edition to article abstracts, its design director, Tom Bodkin, explained that the "shortcuts" would give harried readers a quick "taste" of the day's news, sparing them the "less efficient" method of actually turning the pages and reading the articles. Old media have little choice but to play by the new-media rules.

Chapter 10 | Reading.com

Never has a communications system played so many roles in our lives—or exerted such broad influence over our thoughts—as the Internet does today. Yet, for all that's been written about the Net, there's been little consideration of how, exactly, it's reprogramming us. The Net's intellectual ethic remains obscure.

About the same time that Nietzsche started using his typewriter, an earnest young man named Frederick Winslow Taylor carried a stopwatch into the Midvale Steel plant in Philadelphia and began a historic series of experiments aimed at improving the efficiency of the plant's machinists. With the approval of Midvale's owners, he recruited a group of factory hands, set them to work on various metalworking machines, and recorded and timed their every movement as well as the operations of the machines. By breaking down every job into a sequence of small, discrete steps and then testing different ways of performing each one, Taylor created a set of precise instructions—an "algorithm," we might say today—for how each worker should work. Midvale's employees grumbled about the strict new regime, claiming that it turned them into little more than automatons, but the factory's productivity soared.

More than a hundred years after the invention of the steam engine, the Industrial Revolution had at last found its philosophy and its philosopher. Taylor's tight industrial choreography—his "system," as he liked to call it—was embraced by manufacturers throughout the country and, in time, around the world. Seeking maximum speed, maximum efficiency, and maximum output, factory owners used time-and-motion studies to organize their work and configure the jobs of their workers. The goal, as Taylor defined it in his celebrated 1911 treatise, *The Principles of Scientific Management*, was to identify and adopt, for every job, the "one best method" of work and thereby to effect "the gradual substitution of science for rule of thumb throughout the mechanic arts." Once his system was applied to all acts of manual labor, Taylor assured his followers, it would bring about a restructuring not only of industry but of society, creating a utopia of perfect efficiency. "In the past the man has been first," he declared; "in the future the system must be first."

Taylor's system is still very much with us; it remains the ethic of industrial manufacturing. And now, thanks to the growing power that computer engineers and software coders wield over our intellectual lives, Taylor's ethic is beginning to govern the realm of the mind as well. The Internet is a machine designed for the efficient and automated collection, transmission, and manipulation of information, and its legions of programmers are intent on finding the "one best method"—the perfect algorithm—to carry out every mental movement of what we've come to describe as "knowledge work."

Google's headquarters, in Mountain View, California—the Googleplex—is the Internet's high church, and the religion practiced inside its walls is Taylorism. Google, says its chief executive, Eric Schmidt, is "a company that's founded around the science of measurement," and it is striving to "systematize everything" it does. Drawing on the terabytes of behavioral data it collects through its search engine and other sites, it carries out thousands of experiments a day, according to the *Harvard Business Review*, and it uses the results to refine the algorithms that increasingly control how people find information and extract meaning from it. What Taylor did for the work of the hand, Google is doing for the work of the mind.

The company has declared that its mission is "to organize the world's information and make it universally accessible and useful." It seeks to develop "the perfect search engine," which it defines as something that "understands exactly what you mean and gives you back exactly what you want." In Google's view, information is a kind of commodity, a utilitarian resource that can be mined and processed with industrial efficiency. The more pieces of information we can "access" and the faster we can extract their gist, the more productive we become as thinkers.

Where does it end? Sergey Brin and Larry Page, the gifted young men who founded Google while pursuing doctoral degrees in computer science at Stanford, speak frequently of their desire to turn their search engine into an artificial intelligence, a HAL-like machine that might be connected directly to our brains. "The ultimate search engine is something as smart as people—or smarter," Page said in a speech a few years back. "For us, working on search is a way to work on artificial intelligence." In a 2004 interview with *Newsweek*, Brin said, "Certainly if you had all the world's information directly attached to your brain, or an artificial brain that was smarter than your brain, you'd be better off." Last year, Page told a convention of scientists that Google is "really trying to build artificial intelligence and to do it on a large scale."

Such an ambition is a natural one, even an admirable one, for a pair of math whizzes with vast quantities of cash at their disposal and a small army of computer scientists in their employ. A fundamentally scientific enterprise, Google is motivated by a desire to use technology, in Eric Schmidt's words, "to solve problems that have never been solved before," and artificial intelligence is the hardest problem out there. Why wouldn't Brin and Page want to be the ones to crack it?

Still, their easy assumption that we'd all "be better off" if our brains were supplemented, or even replaced, by an artificial intelligence is unsettling. It suggests a belief that intelligence is the output of a mechanical process, a series of discrete steps that can be isolated, measured, and optimized. In Google's world, the world we enter when we go online, there's little place for the fuzziness of contemplation. Ambiguity is not an opening for insight but a bug to be fixed. The human brain is just an outdated computer that needs a faster processor and a bigger hard drive.

The idea that our minds should operate as high-speed data-processing machines is not only built into the workings of the Internet, it is the network's reigning business model as well. The faster we surf across the Web—the more links we click and pages we view—the more opportunities Google and other companies gain to collect information about us and to feed us advertisements. Most of the proprietors of the commercial Internet have a financial stake in collecting the crumbs of data we leave behind as we flit from link to link—the more crumbs, the better. The last thing these companies want is to encourage leisurely reading or slow, concentrated thought. It's in their economic interest to drive us to distraction.

Maybe I'm just a worrywart. Just as there's a tendency to glorify technological progress, there's a countertendency to expect the worst of every new tool or machine. In Plato's *Phaedrus*, Socrates bemoaned the development of writing. He feared that, as people came to rely on the written word as a substitute for the knowledge they used to carry inside their heads, they would, in the words of one of the dialogue's characters, "cease to exercise their memory and become forgetful." And because they would be able to "receive a quantity of information without proper instruction," they would "be thought very knowledgeable when they are for the most part quite ignorant." They would be "filled with the conceit of wisdom instead of real wisdom." Socrates wasn't wrong—the new technology did often have the effects he feared—but he was shortsighted. He couldn't foresee the many ways that writing and reading would serve to spread information, spur fresh ideas, and expand human knowledge (if not wisdom).

The arrival of Gutenberg's printing press, in the 15th century, set off another round of teeth gnashing. The Italian humanist Hieronimo Squarciafico worried that the easy availability of books would lead to intellectual laziness, making men "less studious" and weakening their minds. Others argued that cheaply printed books and broadsheets would undermine religious authority, demean the work of scholars and scribes, and spread sedition and debauchery. As New York University professor Clay Shirky notes, "Most of the arguments made against the printing press were correct, even prescient." But, again, the doomsayers were unable to imagine the myriad blessings that the printed word would deliver.

So, yes, you should be skeptical of my skepticism. Perhaps those who dismiss critics of the Internet as Luddites or nostalgists will be proved correct, and from our hyperactive, data-stoked minds will spring a golden age of intellectual discovery and universal wisdom. Then again, the Net isn't the alphabet, and although it may replace the printing press, it produces something altogether different. The kind of deep reading that a sequence of printed pages promotes is valuable not just for the knowledge we acquire from the author's words but for the intellectual vibrations those words set off within our own minds. In the quiet spaces opened up by the sustained, undistracted reading of a book, or by any other act of contemplation, for that matter, we make our own associations, draw our own inferences and analogies, foster our own ideas. Deep reading, as Maryanne Wolf argues, is indistinguishable from deep thinking.

If we lose those quiet spaces, or fill them up with "content," we will sacrifice something important not only in our selves but in our culture. In a recent essay, the playwright Richard Foreman eloquently described what's at stake:

> I come from a tradition of Western culture, in which the ideal (my ideal) was the complex, dense and "cathedral-like" structure of the highly educated and articulate personality—a man or woman who carried inside themselves a personally constructed and unique version of the entire heritage of the West. [But now] I see within us all (myself included) the replacement of complex inner density with a new kind of self—evolving under the pressure of information overload and the technology of the "instantly available."

As we are drained of our "inner repertory of dense cultural inheritance," Foreman concluded, we risk turning into "'pancake people'—spread wide and thin as we connect with that vast network of information accessed by the mere touch of a button."

I'm haunted by that scene in *2001*. What makes it so poignant, and so weird, is the computer's emotional response to the disassembly of its mind: its despair as one circuit after another goes dark, its childlike pleading with the astronaut—"I can feel it. I can feel it. I'm afraid"—and its final reversion to what can only be called a state of innocence. HAL's outpouring of feeling contrasts with the emotionlessness that characterizes the human figures in the film, who go about their business with an almost robotic efficiency. Their thoughts and actions feel scripted, as if they're following the steps of an algorithm. In the world of *2001*, people have become so machinelike that the most human character turns out to be a machine. That's the essence of Kubrick's dark prophecy: as we come to rely on computers to mediate our understanding of the world, it is our own intelligence that flattens into artificial intelligence.

WHAT?

1. What, according to Carr, is the difference between assimilating information and learning?
2. Carr writes that the "Web has been a godsend to me as a writer" but also that this "boon comes at a price." Summarize the advantages that Carr says the Internet offers as well as the drawbacks that he worries might accompany long-term use.
3. Carr uses Google's desire to develop the "perfect search engine" to discuss two kinds of intelligence. How would you describe these? Do you see any reason for concern about the influence technology might be having on intelligence?
4. Do you think Carr presents an effective argument? Why or why not? Does he address possible counterarguments? What are they?

WHAT ELSE? WHAT'S NEXT?

5. Carr's essay was published in 2008, nearly a lifetime ago in the world of digital technology. Research the ways in which the concerns Carr raises have evolved since then. Do more people believe technology is changing the way we read and think for the worse? Has Carr written anything else about the subject? Can you find any expert research or opinion about the issue? Compile your findings in a brief report, complete with a bibliography in MLA style.

WHO CARES?

6. Who reads the *Atlantic Monthly* and its website, www.TheAtlantic.com? Research online—starting with the website itself—and compose a brief portrait of the publications' readership. Then, explain whether you think Carr's piece is a good fit for that audience.

Chapter 10 | Reading.com

> Ian Leslie is the author of the 2014 book Curious: The Desire To Know and Why Your Future Depends On It. *He writes on psychology, trends and politics for* The Economist, The Guardian, Slate, Granta, *and* Salon, *where this article was published in October 2014. You can follow him on Twitter at @mrianleslie.*

BEFORE YOU READ
Watch Stuart Firestein's TED talk titled "The Pursuit of Ignorance" online. Then, jot down your understanding of the term "high-quality ignorance."

GOOGLE MAKES US ALL DUMBER: THE NEUROSCIENCE OF SEARCH ENGINES
Ian Leslie

In 1964, Pablo Picasso was asked by an interviewer about the new electronic calculating machines, soon to become known as computers. He replied, "But they are useless. They can only give you answers."

We live in the age of answers. The ancient library at Alexandria was believed to hold the world's entire store of knowledge. Today, there is enough information in the world for every person alive to be given three times as much as was held in Alexandria's entire collection—and nearly all of it is available to anyone with an internet connection.

This library accompanies us everywhere, and Google, chief librarian, fields our inquiries with stunning efficiency. Dinner table disputes are resolved by smartphone; undergraduates stitch together a patchwork of Wikipedia entries into an essay. In a remarkably short period of time, we have become habituated to an endless supply of easy answers. You might even say dependent.

Google is known as a search engine, yet there is barely any searching involved anymore. The gap between a question crystallizing in your mind and an answer appearing at the top of your screen is shrinking all the time. As a consequence, our ability to ask questions is atrophying. Google's head of search, Amit Singhal, asked if people are getting better at articulating their search queries, sighed and said: "The more accurate the machine gets, the lazier the questions become."

Google's strategy for dealing with our slapdash questioning is to make the question superfluous. Singhal is focused on eliminating "every possible friction point between [users], their thoughts and the information they want to find." Larry Page has talked of a day when a Google search chip is implanted in people's brains: "When you think about something you don't really know much about, you will automatically get information." One day, the gap between question and answer will disappear.

I believe we should strive to keep it open. That gap is where our curiosity lives. We undervalue it at our peril.

The Internet can make us feel omniscient. But it's the feeling of not knowing which inspires the desire to learn. The psychologist George Loewenstein gave us the simplest and most powerful definition of curiosity, describing it as the response to an "information gap." When you know just enough to know that you don't know everything, you experience the itch to know more. Loewenstein pointed out that a person who knows the capitals of three out of 50 American states is likely to think of herself as knowing something ("I know three state capitals"). But a person who has learned the names of 47 state capitals is likely to think of herself as not knowing three state capitals, and thus more likely to make the effort to learn those other three.

That word "effort" is important. It's hardly surprising that we love the ease and fluency of the modern web: our brains are designed to avoid anything that seems like hard work. The psychologists Susan Fiske and Shelley Taylor coined the term "cognitive miser" to describe the stinginess with which the brain allocates limited attention, and its in-built propensity to seek mental short-cuts. The easier it is for us to acquire information, however, the less likely it is to stick. Difficulty and frustration—the very friction that Google aims to eliminate—ensure that our brain integrates new information more securely. Robert Bjork, of the University of California, uses the phrase "desirable difficulties" to describe the counterintuitive notion that we learn better when the learning is hard. Bjork recommends, for instance, spacing teaching sessions further apart so that students have to make more effort to recall what they learned last time.

A great question should launch a journey of exploration. Instant answers can leave us idling at base camp. When a question is given time to incubate, it can take us to places we hadn't planned to visit. Left unanswered, it acts like a searchlight ranging across the landscape of different possibilities, the very consideration of which makes our thinking deeper and broader. Searching for an answer in a printed book is inefficient, and takes longer than in its digital counterpart. But while flicking through those pages your eye may alight on information that you didn't even know you wanted to know.

The gap between question and answer is where creativity thrives and scientific progress is made. When we celebrate our greatest thinkers, we usually focus on their ingenious answers. But the thinkers themselves tend to see it the other way around. "Looking back," said Charles Darwin, "I think it was more difficult to see what the problems were than to solve them." The writer Anton Chekhov declared, "The role of the artist is to ask questions, not answer them." The very definition of a bad work of art is one that insists on telling its audience the answers, and a scientist who believes she has all the answers is not a scientist.

According to the great physicist James Clerk Maxwell, "thoroughly conscious ignorance is the prelude to every real advance in science." Good questions induce this state of conscious ignorance, focusing our attention on what we don't know. The neuroscientist Stuart Firestein teaches a course on ignorance at Columbia University, because, he says, "science produces ignorance at a faster rate than it produces knowledge." Raising a toast to Einstein, George Bernard Shaw remarked, "Science is always wrong. It never solves a problem without creating ten more."

Humans are born consciously ignorant. Compared to other mammals, we are pushed out into the world prematurely, and stay dependent on elders for much longer. Endowed with so few answers at birth, children are driven to question everything. In 2007, Michelle Chouinard, a psychology professor at the University of California, analyzed recordings of four children interacting with their respective caregivers for two hours at a time, for a total of more than two hundred hours. She found that, on average, the children posed more than a hundred questions every hour.

Very small children use questions to elicit information—"What is this called?" But as they grow older, their questions become more probing. They start looking for explanations and insight, to ask "Why?" and "How?". Extrapolating from Chouinard's data, the Harvard professor Paul Harris estimates that between the ages of 3 and 5, children ask 40,000 such questions. The numbers are impressive, but what's really amazing is the ability to ask such a question at all. Somehow, children instinctively know there is a vast amount they don't know, and they need to dig beneath the world of appearances.

In a 1984 study by British researchers Barbara Tizard and Martin Hughes, four-year-old girls were recorded talking to their mothers at home. When the researchers analyzed the tapes, they found that some children asked more "How" and "Why" questions than others, and engaged in longer passages of "intellectual search" — a series of linked questions, each following from the other. (In one such conversation, four-year-old Rosy engaged her mother in a long exchange about why the window cleaner was given money.) The more confident questioners weren't necessarily the children who got more answers from their parents, but the ones who got more questions. Parents who threw questions back to their children—"I don't know, what do you think?"—raised children who asked more questions of them. Questioning, it turn out, is contagious.

Childish curiosity only gets us so far, however. To ask good questions, it helps if you have built your own library of answers. It's been proposed that the Internet relieves us of the onerous burden of memorizing information. Why cram our heads with facts, like the date of the French revolution, when they can be summoned up in a swipe and a couple of clicks? But knowledge doesn't just fill the brain up; it makes it work better. To see what I mean, try memorizing the following string of fourteen digits in five seconds:

74830582894062

Hard, isn't it? Virtually impossible. Now try memorizing this string of fourteen letters:

lucy in the sky with diamonds

This time, you barely needed a second. The contrast is so striking that it seems like a completely different problem, but fundamentally, it's the same. The only difference is that one string of symbols triggers a set of associations with knowledge you have stored deep in your memory. Without thinking, you can group the letters into words, the words into a sentence you understand as grammatical—and the sentence is one you recognize as the title of a song by the Beatles. The knowledge you've gathered over years has made your brain's central processing unit more powerful.

This tells us something about the idea we should outsource our memories to the web: it's a short-cut to stupidity. The less we know, the worse we are at processing new information, and the slower we are to arrive at pertinent inquiry. You're unlikely to ask a truly penetrating question about the presidency of Richard Nixon if you have just had to look up who he is. According to researchers who study innovation, the average age at which scientists and inventors make breakthroughs is increasing over time. As knowledge accumulates across generations, it takes longer for individuals to acquire it, and thus longer to be in a position to ask the questions which, in Susan Sontag's phrase, "destroy the answers".

My argument isn't with technology, but the way we use it. It's not that the Internet is making us stupid or incurious. Only we can do that. It's that we will only realize the potential of technology and humans working together when each is focused on its strengths—and that means we need to consciously cultivate effortful curiosity. Smart machines are taking over more and more of the tasks assumed to be the preserve of humans. But no machine, however sophisticated, can yet be said to be curious. The technology visionary Kevin Kelly succinctly defines the appropriate division of labor: "Machines are for answers; humans are for questions."

The practice of asking perceptive, informed, curious questions is a cultural habit we should inculcate at every level of society. In school, students are generally expected to answer questions rather than ask them. But educational researchers have found that students learn better when they're gently directed towards the lacunae in their knowledge, allowing their questions bubble up through the gaps. Wikipedia and Google are best treated as starting points rather than destinations, and we should recognize that human interaction will always play a vital role in fueling the quest for knowledge. After all, Google never says, "I don't know—what do you think?"

The Internet has the potential to be the greatest tool for intellectual exploration ever invented, but only if it is treated as a complement to our talent for inquiry rather than a replacement for it. In a world awash in ready-made answers, the ability to pose difficult, even unanswerable questions is more important than ever.

Picasso was half-right: computers are useless without truly curious humans.

WHAT?

1. Briefly explain Ian Leslie's argument for the importance of intellectual curiosity and good questions.
2. What is the "information gap"?

WHAT ELSE? WHAT'S NEXT?

3. Discuss with a group of classmates the ways each of you search for information online. What kinds of things do you search for? What strategies do you use? How does asking questions fit into your search habits? Be prepared to report your findings to the class.

> According to his biography at TED.com, Jamais Cascio rejects the "nightmare scenarios of global catastrophe and social meltdown" we so often hear from other futurists in favor of "a different, often surprising alternative: What if human beings, and all of our technology, could actually manage to change things for the better?" In this article, first published in the July/August 2009 issue of Atlantic Monthly, Cascio argues that humans have the means, right now, to overcome just about anything by harnessing technology and pharmacology to boost intelligence.

BEFORE YOU READ

Find Jamais Cascio's video titled "The Future We Will Create" online and watch it. What does this tell you about his worldview?

GET SMARTER Jamais Cascio

Seventy-four thousand years ago, humanity nearly went extinct. A super-volcano at what's now Lake Toba, in Sumatra, erupted with a strength more than a thousand times that of Mount St. Helens in 1980. Some 800 cubic kilometers of ash filled the skies of the Northern Hemisphere, lowering global temperatures and pushing a climate already on the verge of an ice age over the edge. Some scientists speculate that as the Earth went into a deep freeze, the population of *Homo sapiens* may have dropped to as low as a few thousand families.

The Mount Toba incident, although unprecedented in magnitude, was part of a broad pattern. For a period of 2 million years, ending with the last ice age around 10,000 B.C., the Earth experienced a series of convulsive glacial events. This rapid-fire climate change meant that humans couldn't rely on consistent patterns to know which animals to hunt, which plants to gather, or even which predators might be waiting around the corner.

How did we cope? By getting smarter. The neurophysiologist William Calvin argues persuasively that modern human cognition—including sophisticated language and the capacity to plan ahead—evolved in response to the demands of this long age of turbulence. According to Calvin, the reason we survived is that our brains changed to meet the challenge: we transformed the ability to target a moving animal with a thrown rock into a capability for foresight and long-term planning. In the process, we may have developed syntax and formal structure from our simple language.

Our present century may not be quite as perilous for the human race as an ice age in the aftermath of a super-volcano eruption, but the next few decades will pose enormous hurdles that go beyond the climate crisis. The end of the fossil-fuel era, the fragility of the global food web, growing population density, and the spread of pandemics, as well as the emergence of radically transformative bio- and nanotechnologies—each of these threatens us with broad disruption or even devastation. And as good as our brains have become at planning ahead, we're still biased toward looking for near-term, simple threats. Subtle, long-term risks, particularly those involving complex, global processes, remain devilishly hard for us to manage.

But here's an optimistic scenario for you: if the next several decades are as bad as some of us fear they could be, we can respond, and survive, the way our species has done time and again: by getting smarter. But this time, we don't have to rely solely on natural evolutionary processes to boost our intelligence. We can do it ourselves.

Most people don't realize that this process is already under way. In fact, it's happening all around us, across the full spectrum of how we understand intelligence. It's visible in the hive mind of the Internet, in the powerful tools for simulation and visualization that are jump-starting new scientific disciplines, and in the development of drugs that some people (myself included) have discovered let them study harder, focus better, and stay awake longer with full clarity. So far, these augmentations have largely been outside of our bodies, but they're very much part of who we are today: they're physically separate from us, but we and they are becoming cognitively inseparable. And advances over the next few decades, driven by breakthroughs in genetic engineering and artificial intelligence, will make today's technologies seem primitive. The nascent jargon of the field describes this as "intelligence augmentation." I prefer to think of it as "You+."

Scientists refer to the 12,000 years or so since the last ice age as the Holocene epoch. It encompasses the rise of human civilization and our co-evolution with tools and technologies that allow us to grapple with our physical environment. But if intelligence augmentation has the kind of impact I expect, we may soon have to start thinking of ourselves as living in an entirely new era. The focus of our technological evolution would be less on how we manage and adapt to our physical world, and more on how we manage and adapt to the immense amount of knowledge we've created. We can call it the Nöocene epoch, from Pierre Teilhard de Chardin's concept of the Nöosphere, a collective consciousness created by the deepening interaction of human minds. As that epoch draws closer, the world is becoming a very different place.

Of course we've been augmenting our ability to think for millennia. When we developed written language, we significantly increased our functional memory and our ability to share insights and knowledge across time and space. The same thing happened with the invention of the printing press, the telegraph, and the radio. The rise of urbanization allowed a fraction of the populace to focus on more-cerebral tasks—a fraction that grew inexorably as more complex economic and social practices demanded more knowledge work, and industrial technology reduced the demand for manual labor. And caffeine and nicotine, of course, are both classic cognitive-enhancement drugs, primitive though they may be.

With every technological step forward, though, has come anxiety about the possibility that technology harms our natural ability to think. These anxieties were given eloquent expression in these pages by Nicholas Carr, whose essay "Is Google Making Us Stupid?" (July/August 2008 *Atlantic*) argued that the information-dense, hyperlink-rich, spastically churning Internet medium is effectively rewiring our brains, making it harder for us to engage in deep, relaxed contemplation.

Carr's fears about the impact of wall-to-wall connectivity on the human intellect echo cyber-theorist Linda Stone's description of "continuous partial attention," the modern phenomenon of having multiple activities and connections under way simultaneously. We're becoming so accustomed to interruption that we're starting to find focusing difficult, even when we've achieved a bit of quiet. It's an induced form of ADD—a "continuous partial attention-deficit disorder," if you will.

There's also just more information out there—because unlike with previous information media, with the Internet, creating material is nearly as easy as consuming it. And it's easy to mistake more voices for more noise. In reality, though, the proliferation of diverse voices may actually improve our overall ability to think. In *Everything Bad Is Good for You*, Steven Johnson argues that the increasing complexity and range of media we engage with have, over the past century, made us smarter, rather than dumber, by providing a form of cognitive calisthenics. Even pulp-television shows and video games have become extraordinarily dense with detail, filled with subtle references to broader subjects, and more open to interactive engagement. They reward the capacity to make connections and to see patterns—precisely the kinds of skills we need for managing an information glut.

Scientists describe these skills as our "fluid intelligence"—the ability to find meaning in confusion and to solve new problems, independent of acquired knowledge. Fluid intelligence doesn't look much like the capacity to memorize and recite facts, the skills that people have traditionally associated with brainpower. But building it up may improve the capacity to think deeply that Carr and others fear we're losing for good. And we shouldn't let the stresses associated with a transition to a new era blind us to that era's astonishing potential. We swim in an ocean of data, accessible from nearly anywhere, generated by billions of devices. We're only beginning to explore what we can do with this knowledge-at-a-touch.

Moreover, the technology-induced ADD that's associated with this new world may be a short-term problem. The trouble isn't that we have too much information at our fingertips, but that our tools for managing it are still in their infancy. Worries about "information overload" predate the rise of the Web (Alvin Toffler coined the phrase in 1970), and many of the technologies that Carr worries about were developed precisely to help us get some control over a flood of data and ideas. Google isn't the problem; it's the beginning of a solution.

In any case, there's no going back. The information sea isn't going to dry up, and relying on cognitive habits evolved and perfected in an era of limited information flow—and limited information access—is futile. Strengthening our fluid intelligence is the only viable approach to navigating the age of constant connectivity.

When people hear the phrase *intelligence augmentation*, they tend to envision people with computer chips plugged into their brains, or a genetically engineered race of post-human super-geniuses. Neither of these visions is likely to be realized, for reasons familiar to any Best Buy shopper. In a world of ongoing technological acceleration, today's cutting-edge brain implant would be tomorrow's obsolete junk—and good luck if the protocols change or you're on the wrong side of a "format war" (anyone want a Betamax implant?). And then there's the question of stability: Would you want a chip in your head made by the same folks that made your cell phone, or your PC?

Likewise, the safe modification of human genetics is still years away. And even after genetic modification of adult neurobiology becomes possible, the science will remain in flux; our understanding of how augmentation works, and what kinds of genetic modifications are possible, would still change rapidly. As with digital implants, the brain modification you might undergo one week could become obsolete the next. Who would want a 2025-vintage brain when you're competing against hotshots with Model 2026?

Yet in one sense, the age of the cyborg and the super-genius has already arrived. It just involves external information and communication devices instead of implants and genetic modification. The bioethicist James Hughes of Trinity College refers to all of this as "exocortical technology," but you can just think of it as "stuff you already own." Increasingly, we buttress our cognitive functions with our computing systems, no matter that the connections are mediated by simple typing and pointing. These tools enable our brains to do things that would once have been almost unimaginable:

- powerful simulations and massive data sets allow physicists to visualize, understand, and debate models of an 11-dimension universe;

- real-time data from satellites, global environmental databases, and high-resolution models allow geophysicists to recognize the subtle signs of long-term changes to the planet;

- cross-connected scheduling systems allow anyone to assemble, with a few clicks, a complex, multimodal travel itinerary that would have taken a human travel agent days to create.

If that last example sounds prosaic, it simply reflects how embedded these kinds of augmentation have become. Not much more than a decade ago, such a tool was outrageously impressive—and it destroyed the travel-agent industry.

That industry won't be the last one to go. Any occupation requiring pattern-matching and the ability to find obscure connections will quickly morph from the domain of experts to that of ordinary people whose intelligence has been augmented by cheap digital tools. Humans won't be taken out of the loop—in fact, many, many *more* humans will have the capacity to do something that was once limited to a hermetic priesthood. Intelligence augmentation decreases the need for specialization and increases participatory complexity.

As the digital systems we rely upon become faster, more sophisticated, and (with the usual hiccups) more capable, we're becoming more sophisticated and capable too. It's a form of co-evolution: we learn to adapt our thinking and expectations to these digital systems, even as the system designs become more complex and powerful to meet more of our needs—and eventually come to adapt to *us*.

Consider the Twitter phenomenon, which went from nearly invisible to nearly ubiquitous (at least among the online crowd) in early 2007. During busy periods, the user can easily be overwhelmed by the volume of incoming messages, most of which are of only passing interest. But there is a tiny minority of truly valuable posts. (Sometimes they have extreme value, as they did during the October 2007 wildfires in California and the November 2008 terrorist attacks in Mumbai.) At present, however, finding the most-useful bits requires wading through messages like "My kitty sneezed!" and "I hate this taco!"

But imagine if social tools like Twitter had a way to learn what kinds of messages you pay attention to, and which ones you discard. Over time, the messages that you don't really care about might start to fade in the display, while the ones that you do want to see could get brighter. Such attention filters—or focus assistants—are likely to become important parts of how we handle our daily lives. We'll move from a world of "continuous partial attention" to one we might call "continuous augmented awareness."

As processor power increases, tools like Twitter may be able to draw on the complex simulations and massive data sets that have unleashed a revolution in science. They could become individualized systems that augment our capacity for planning and foresight, letting us play "what-if" with our life choices: where to live, what to study, maybe even where to go for dinner. Initially crude and clumsy, such a system would get better with more data and more experience; just as important, we'd get better at asking questions. These systems, perhaps linked to the cameras and microphones in our mobile devices, would eventually be able to pay attention to what we're doing, and to our habits and language quirks, and learn to interpret our sometimes ambiguous desires. With enough time and complexity, they would be able to make useful suggestions without explicit prompting.

And such systems won't be working for us alone. Intelligence has a strong social component; for example, we already provide crude cooperative information-filtering for each other. In time, our interactions through the use of such intimate technologies could dovetail with our use of collaborative knowledge systems (such as Wikipedia), to help us not just to build better data sets, but to filter them with greater precision. As our capacity to provide that filter gets faster and richer, it increasingly becomes something akin to collaborative intuition—in which everyone is effectively augmenting everyone else.

In pharmacology, too, the future is already here. One of the most prominent examples is a drug called modafinil. Developed in the 1970s, modafinil—sold in the U.S. under the brand name Provigil—appeared on the cultural radar in the late 1990s, when the American military began to test it for long-haul pilots. Extended use of modafinil can keep a person awake and alert for well over 32 hours on end, with only a full night's sleep required to get back to a normal schedule.

While it is FDA-approved only for a few sleep disorders, like narcolepsy and sleep apnea, doctors increasingly prescribe it to those suffering from depression, to "shift workers" fighting fatigue, and to frequent business travelers dealing with time-zone shifts. I'm part of the latter group: like more and more professionals, I have a prescription for modafinil in order to help me overcome jet lag when I travel internationally. When I started taking the drug, I expected it to keep me awake; I didn't expect it to make me feel smarter, but that's exactly what happened. The change was subtle but clear, once I recognized it: within an hour of taking a standard 200-mg tablet, I was much more alert, and thinking with considerably more clarity and focus than usual. This isn't just a subjective conclusion. A University of Cambridge study, published in 2003, concluded that modafinil confers a measurable cognitive-enhancement effect across a variety of mental tasks, including pattern recognition and spatial planning, and sharpens focus and alertness.

I'm not the only one who has taken advantage of this effect. The Silicon Valley insider webzine *Tech Crunch* reported in July 2008 that some entrepreneurs now see modafinil as an important competitive tool. The tone of the piece was judgmental, but the implication was clear: everybody's doing it, and if you're not, you're probably falling behind.

This is one way a world of intelligence augmentation emerges. Little by little, people who don't know about drugs like modafinil or don't want to use them will face stiffer competition from the people who do. From the perspective of a culture immersed in athletic doping wars, the use of such drugs may seem like cheating. From the perspective of those who find that they're much more productive using this form of enhancement, it's no more cheating than getting a faster computer or a better education.

Modafinil isn't the only example; on college campuses, the use of ADD drugs (such as Ritalin and Adderall) as study aids has become almost ubiquitous. But these enhancements are primitive. As the science improves, we could see other kinds of cognitive-modification drugs that boost recall, brain plasticity, even empathy and emotional intelligence. They would start as therapeutic treatments, but end up being used to make us "better than normal." Eventually, some of these may become over-the-counter products at your local pharmacy, or in the juice and snack aisles at the supermarket. Spam e-mail would be full of offers to make your brain bigger, and your idea production more powerful.

Such a future would bear little resemblance to *Brave New World* or similar narcomantic nightmares; we may fear the idea of a population kept doped and placated, but we're more likely to see a populace stuck in overdrive, searching out the last bits of competitive advantage, business insight, and radical innovation. No small amount of that innovation would be directed toward inventing the next, more powerful cognitive-enhancement technology.

This would be a different kind of nightmare, perhaps, and cause waves of moral panic and legislative restriction. Safety would be a huge issue. But as we've found with athletic doping, if there's a technique for beating out rivals (no matter how risky), shutting it down is nearly impossible. This would be yet another pharmacological arms race—and in this case, the competitors on one side would just keep getting smarter.

The most radical form of superhuman intelligence, of course, wouldn't be a mind augmented by drugs or exocortical technology; it would be a mind that isn't human at all. Here we move from the realm of extrapolation to the realm of speculation, since solid predictions about artificial intelligence are notoriously hard: our understanding of how the brain creates the mind remains far from good enough to tell us how to construct a mind in a machine.

But while the concept remains controversial, I see no good argument for why a mind running on a machine platform instead of a biological platform will forever be impossible; whether one might appear in five years or 50 or 500, however, is uncertain. I lean toward 50, myself. That's enough time to develop computing hardware able to run a high-speed neural network as sophisticated as that of a human brain, and enough time for the kids who will have grown up surrounded by virtual-world software and household robots—that is, the people who see this stuff not as "Technology," but as everyday tools—to come to dominate the field.

Many proponents of developing an artificial mind are sure that such a breakthrough will be the biggest change in human history. They believe that a machine mind would soon modify itself to get smarter—and with its new intelligence, then figure out how to make itself smarter still. They refer to this intelligence explosion as "the Singularity," a term applied by the computer scientist and science-fiction author Vernor Vinge. "Within thirty years, we will have the technological means to create superhuman intelligence," Vinge wrote in 1993. "Shortly after, the human era will be ended." The Singularity concept is a secular echo of Teilhard de Chardin's "Omega Point," the culmination of the Nöosphere at the end of history. Many believers in Singularity—which one wag has dubbed "the Rapture for nerds"—think that building the first real AI will be the last thing humans do. Some imagine this moment with terror, others with a bit of glee.

My own suspicion is that a stand-alone artificial mind will be more a tool of narrow utility than something especially apocalyptic. I don't think the theory of an explosively self-improving AI is convincing—it's based on too many assumptions about behavior and the nature of the mind. Moreover, AI researchers, after years of talking about this prospect, are already ultra-conscious of the risk of runaway systems.

More important, though, is that the same advances in processor and process that would produce a machine mind would also increase the power of our own cognitive-enhancement technologies. As intelligence augmentation allows us to make *ourselves* smarter, and then smarter still, AI may turn out to be just a sideshow: we could always be a step ahead.

So what's life like in a world of brain doping, intuition networks, and the occasional artificial mind?

Banal.

Not from our present perspective, of course. For us, now, looking a generation ahead might seem surreal and dizzying. But remember: people living in, say, 2030 will have lived every moment from now until then—we won't jump into the future. For someone going from 2009 to 2030 day by day, most of these changes wouldn't be jarring; instead, they'd be incremental, almost overdetermined, and the occasional surprises would quickly blend into the flow of inevitability.

By 2030, then, we'll likely have grown accustomed to (and perhaps even complacent about) a world where sophisticated foresight, detailed analysis and insight, and augmented awareness are commonplace. We'll have developed a better capacity to manage both partial attention and laser-like focus, and be able to slip between the two with ease—perhaps by popping the right pill, or eating the right snack. Sometimes, our augmentation assistants will handle basic interactions on our behalf; that's okay, though, because we'll increasingly see those assistants as extensions of ourselves.

The amount of data we'll have at our fingertips will be staggering, but we'll finally have gotten over the notion that accumulated information alone is a hallmark of intelligence. The power of all of this knowledge will come from its ability to inform difficult decisions, and to support complex analysis. Most professions will likely use simulation and modeling in their day-to-day work, from political decisions to hairstyle options. In a world of augmented intelligence, we will have a far greater appreciation of the consequences of our actions.

This doesn't mean we'll all come to the same conclusions. We'll still clash with each other's emotions, desires, and beliefs. If anything, our arguments will be more intense, buttressed not just by strongly held opinions but by intricate reasoning. People in 2030 will look back aghast at how ridiculously unsubtle the political and cultural disputes of our present were, just as we might today snicker at simplistic advertising from a generation ago.

Conversely, the debates of the 2030s would be remarkable for us to behold. Nuance and multiple layers will characterize even casual disputes; our digital assistants will be there to catch any references we might miss. And all of this will be everyday, banal reality. Today, it sounds mind-boggling; by then, it won't even merit comment.

What happens if such a complex system collapses? Disaster, of course. But don't forget that we already depend upon enormously complex systems that we no longer even think of as technological. Urbanization, agriculture, and trade were at one time huge innovations. Their collapse (and all of them are now at risk, in different ways, as we have seen in recent months) would be an even greater catastrophe than the collapse of our growing webs of interconnected intelligence.

A less apocalyptic but more likely danger derives from the observation made by the science-fiction author William Gibson: "The future is already here, it's just unevenly distributed." The rich, whether nations or individuals, will inevitably gain access to many augmentations before anyone else. We know from history, though, that a world of limited access wouldn't last forever, even as the technology improved: those who sought to impose limits would eventually face angry opponents with newer, better systems.

Even as competition provides access to these kinds of technologies, though, development paths won't be identical. Some societies may be especially welcoming to biotech boosts; others may prefer to use digital tools. Some may readily adopt collaborative approaches; others may focus on individual enhancement. And around the world, many societies will reject the use of intelligence-enhancement technology entirely, or adopt a cautious wait-and-see posture.

The bad news is that these divergent paths may exacerbate cultural divides created by already divergent languages and beliefs. National rivalries often emphasize cultural differences, but for now we're all still standard human beings. What happens when different groups quite literally think in very, very different ways?

The good news, though, is that this diversity of thought can also be a strength. Coping with the various world-historical dangers we face will require the greatest possible insight, creativity, and innovation. Our ability to build the future that we want—not just a future we can survive—depends on our capacity to understand the complex relationships of the world's systems, to take advantage of the diversity of knowledge and experience our civilization embodies, and to fully appreciate the implications of our choices. Such an ability is increasingly within our grasp. The Nöocene awaits.

WHAT?

1. According to Cascio, how have we been "augmenting our ability to think for millennia"?
2. How do you feel about evolving into what Cascio calls "You+"?
3. In explaining the use of drugs to augment intelligence, Cascio writes: "From the perspective of a culture immersed in athletic doping wars, the use of such drugs may seem like cheating. From the perspective of those who find that they're much more productive using this form of enhancement, it's no more cheating than getting a faster computer or a better education." Do you agree with Cascio's point? Explain your response.

WHAT ELSE? WHAT'S NEXT?

4. "Get Smart" is, in part, a response to Nicholas Carr's "Is Google Making Us Stupid?" How does Cascio address Carr's concerns about technology's ill effects on learning and concentration? Do you find Cascio's counterarguments persuasive? Why or why not?
5. Research the response to Cascio's essay. How, in particular, have others addressed Cascio's discussion of performance- and intelligence-enhancing technologies (including drugs)? Summarize your findings in a brief report, accompanied by a bibliography of the sources you use.

WHO CARES?

6. What does Cascio do to lead his readers to believe that he knows what he's talking about? In other words, how does he establish his authority and expertise on the topic?

> Jonathan Franzen is the author of several books, most recently, Freedom. The following piece, published in May 2011 in The New York Times, is adapted from a commencement speech Franzen delivered that month at Kenyon College.

BEFORE YOU READ

Find Facebook's "Like" page (it's part of the Help Center, or you can Google "liking Facebook"). Look over what's there, and then write a brief explanation of what it means to "like" something on the social networking site.

LIKING IS FOR COWARDS. GO FOR WHAT HURTS. Jonathan Franzen

A couple of weeks ago, I replaced my three-year-old BlackBerry Pearl with a much more powerful BlackBerry Bold. Needless to say, I was impressed with how far the technology had advanced in three years. Even when I didn't have anybody to call or text or e-mail, I wanted to keep fondling my new Bold and experiencing the marvelous clarity of its screen, the silky action of its track pad, the shocking speed of its responses, the beguiling elegance of its graphics.

I was, in short, infatuated with my new device. I'd been similarly infatuated with my old device, of course; but over the years the bloom had faded from our relationship. I'd developed trust issues with my Pearl, accountability issues, compatibility issues and even, toward the end, some doubts about my Pearl's very sanity, until I'd finally had to admit to myself that I'd outgrown the relationship.

Do I need to point out that—absent some wild, anthropomorphizing projection in which my old BlackBerry felt sad about the waning of my love for it—our relationship was entirely one-sided? Let me point it out anyway.

Let me further point out how ubiquitously the word "sexy" is used to describe late-model gadgets; and how the extremely cool things that we can do now with these gadgets—like impelling them to action with voice commands, or doing that spreading-the-fingers iPhone thing that makes images get bigger—would have looked, to people a hundred years ago, like a magician's incantations, a magician's hand gestures; and how, when we want to describe an erotic relationship that's working perfectly, we speak, indeed, of magic.

Let me toss out the idea that, as our markets discover and respond to what consumers most want, our technology has become extremely adept at creating products that correspond to our fantasy ideal of an erotic relationship, in which the beloved object asks for nothing and gives everything, instantly, and makes us feel all powerful, and doesn't throw terrible scenes when it's replaced by an even sexier object and is consigned to a drawer.

To speak more generally, the ultimate goal of technology, the telos of techne, is to replace a natural world that's indifferent to our wishes—a world of hurricanes and hardships and breakable hearts, a world of resistance—with a world so responsive to our wishes as to be, effectively, a mere extension of the self.

Let me suggest, finally, that the world of techno-consumerism is therefore troubled by real love, and that it has no choice but to trouble love in turn.

Its first line of defense is to commodify its enemy. You can all supply your own favorite, most nauseating examples of the commodification of love. Mine include the wedding industry, TV ads that feature cute young children or the giving of automobiles as Christmas presents, and the particularly grotesque equation of diamond jewelry with everlasting devotion. The message, in each case, is that if you love somebody you should buy stuff.

A related phenomenon is the transformation, courtesy of Facebook, of the verb "to like" from a state of mind to an action that you perform with your computer mouse, from a feeling to an assertion of consumer choice. And liking, in general, is commercial culture's substitute for loving. The striking thing about all consumer products—and none more so than electronic devices and applications—is that they're designed to be immensely likable. This is, in fact, the definition of a consumer product, in contrast to the product that is simply itself and whose makers aren't fixated on your liking it. (I'm thinking here of jet engines, laboratory equipment, serious art and literature.)

But if you consider this in human terms, and you imagine a person defined by a desperation to be liked, what do you see? You see a person without integrity, without a center. In more pathological cases, you see a narcissist—a person who can't tolerate the tarnishing of his or her self-image that not being liked represents, and who therefore either withdraws from human contact or goes to extreme, integrity-sacrificing lengths to be likable.

If you dedicate your existence to being likable, however, and if you adopt whatever cool persona is necessary to make it happen, it suggests that you've despaired of being loved for who you really are. And if you succeed in manipulating other people into liking you, it will be hard not to feel, at some level, contempt for those people, because they've fallen for your shtick. You may find yourself becoming depressed, or alcoholic, or, if you're Donald Trump, running for president (and then quitting).

Consumer technology products would never do anything this unattractive, because they aren't people. They are, however, great allies and enablers of narcissism. Alongside their built-in eagerness to be liked is a built-in eagerness to reflect well on us. Our lives look a lot more interesting when they're filtered through the sexy Facebook interface. We star in our own movies, we photograph ourselves incessantly, we click the mouse and a machine confirms our sense of mastery.

And, since our technology is really just an extension of ourselves, we don't have to have contempt for its manipulability in the way we might with actual people. It's all one big endless loop. We like the mirror and the mirror likes us. To friend a person is merely to include the person in our private hall of flattering mirrors.

I may be overstating the case, a little bit. Very probably, you're sick to death of hearing social media disrespected by cranky 51-year-olds. My aim here is mainly to set up a contrast between the narcissistic tendencies of technology and the problem of actual love. My friend Alice Sebold likes to talk about "getting down in the pit and loving somebody." She has in mind the dirt that love inevitably splatters on the mirror of our self-regard.

The simple fact of the matter is that trying to be perfectly likable is incompatible with loving relationships. Sooner or later, for example, you're going to find yourself in a hideous, screaming fight, and you'll hear coming out of your mouth things that you yourself don't like at all, things that shatter your self-image as a fair, kind, cool, attractive, in-control, funny, likable person. Something realer than likability has come out in you, and suddenly you're having an actual life.

Suddenly there's a real choice to be made, not a fake consumer choice between a BlackBerry and an iPhone, but a question: Do I love this person? And, for the other person, does this person love me?

There is no such thing as a person whose real self you like every particle of. This is why a world of liking is ultimately a lie. But there is such a thing as a person whose real self you love every particle of. And this is why love is such an existential threat to the techno-consumerist order: it exposes the lie.

This is not to say that love is only about fighting. Love is about bottomless empathy, born out of the heart's revelation that another person is every bit as real as you are. And this is why love, as I understand it, is always specific. Trying to love all of humanity may be a worthy endeavor, but, in a funny way, it keeps the focus on the self, on the self's own moral or spiritual well-being. Whereas, to love a specific person, and to identify with his or her struggles and joys as if they were your own, you have to surrender some of your self.

The big risk here, of course, is rejection. We can all handle being disliked now and then, because there's such an infinitely big pool of potential likers. But to expose your whole self, not just the likable surface, and to have it rejected, can be catastrophically painful. The prospect of pain generally, the pain of loss, of breakup, of death, is what makes it so tempting to avoid love and stay safely in the world of liking.

And yet pain hurts but it doesn't kill. When you consider the alternative—an anesthetized dream of self-sufficiency, abetted by technology—pain emerges as the natural product and natural indicator of being alive in a resistant world. To go through a life painlessly is to have not lived. Even just to say to yourself, "Oh, I'll get to that love and pain stuff later, maybe in my 30s" is to consign yourself to 10 years of merely taking up space on the planet and burning up its resources. Of being (and I mean this in the most damning sense of the word) a consumer.

When I was in college, and for many years after, I liked the natural world. Didn't love it, but definitely liked it. It can be very pretty, nature. And since I was looking for things to find wrong with the world, I naturally gravitated to environmentalism, because there were certainly plenty of things wrong with the environment. And the more I looked at what was wrong—an exploding world population, exploding levels of resource consumption, rising global temperatures, the trashing of the oceans, the logging of our last old-growth forests—the angrier I became.

Finally, in the mid-1990s, I made a conscious decision to stop worrying about the environment. There was nothing meaningful that I personally could do to save the planet, and I wanted to get on with devoting myself to the things I loved. I still tried to keep my carbon footprint small, but that was as far as I could go without falling back into rage and despair.

But then a funny thing happened to me. It's a long story, but basically I fell in love with birds. I did this not without significant resistance, because it's very uncool to be a birdwatcher, because anything that betrays real passion is by definition uncool. But little by little, in spite of myself, I developed this passion, and although one-half of a passion is obsession, the other half is love.

And so, yes, I kept a meticulous list of the birds I'd seen, and, yes, I went to inordinate lengths to see new species. But, no less important, whenever I looked at a bird, any bird, even a pigeon or a robin, I could feel my heart overflow with love. And love, as I've been trying to say today, is where our troubles begin.

Because now, not merely liking nature but loving a specific and vital part of it, I had no choice but to start worrying about the environment again. The news on that front was no better than when I'd decided to quit worrying about it—was considerably worse, in fact—but now those threatened forests and wetlands and oceans weren't just pretty scenes for me to enjoy. They were the home of animals I loved.

And here's where a curious paradox emerged. My anger and pain and despair about the planet were only increased by my concern for wild birds, and yet, as I began to get involved in bird conservation and learned more about the many threats that birds face, it became easier, not harder, to live with my anger and despair and pain.

How does this happen? I think, for one thing, that my love of birds became a portal to an important, less self-centered part of myself that I'd never even known existed. Instead of continuing to drift forward through my life as a global citizen, liking and disliking and withholding my commitment for some later date, I was forced to confront a self that I had to either straight-up accept or flat-out reject.

Which is what love will do to a person. Because the fundamental fact about all of us is that we're alive for a while but will die before long. This fact is the real root cause of all our anger and pain and despair. And you can either run from this fact or, by way of love, you can embrace it.

When you stay in your room and rage or sneer or shrug your shoulders, as I did for many years, the world and its problems are impossibly daunting. But when you go out and put yourself in real relation to real people, or even just real animals, there's a very real danger that you might love some of them.

And who knows what might happen to you then?

■ WHAT?

1. Briefly summarize the argument that Franzen presents in his speech.
2. How does Franzen differentiate between "liking" and "loving"? Make sure you point to specific examples from his speech as you explain his definitions.
3. How, according to Franzen, does "real love" trouble the world of techno-consumerism? How does techno-consumerism, in turn, trouble real love?

WHAT ELSE? WHAT'S NEXT?

4. Research the backlash against "liking." How have others criticized this phenomenon? Does anyone online step up to defend "liking"? Do you see anything wrong with "liking"? Explain your response.

WHO CARES?

5. At one point in his speech, Franzen says to the audience, gathered for a college commencement: "Very probably, you're sick to death of hearing social media disrespected by cranky 51-year-olds." Why do you think Franzen says this? How does this statement function rhetorically?
6. Does Franzen convince you that all this fuss over "liking" is warranted? If so, how does he do this? If not, what could he have done differently to make you care?

IMAGE 10.2
In her essay, Caitlin Dewey writes: "The Internet brings … people together with hash tags and message boards, but it never satisfies them. No matter how much you love someone's blog or Twitter feed, it isn't their posts you actually want." How would you characterize the dynamic between the online and in-real-life aspects of relationships?

Chapter 10 | Reading.com

Caitlin Dewey was a senior at Syracuse University majoring in magazine journalism when the following piece won the 2011 Modern Love Essay Contest sponsored by The New York Times. *According to the newspaper, the contest "asked college students nationwide to tell us—through their own stories, in their own voices—what love is like for them." Responses came from scores of colleges and universities, including the University of South Carolina. Dewey's essay was published in May 2011 in* The Times.

BEFORE YOU READ

How does digital technology—the Internet, smartphones, social networking—affect the way you think about and pursue relationships?

EVEN IN REAL LIFE, THERE WERE SCREENS BETWEEN US Caitlin Dewey

Curled up at the foot of my bed, my face inches from the laptop screen, I stared anxiously at the Google chat box. "Will is typing," the box told me, helpfully.

I forced myself to read e-mail while I waited for his message. Then I refreshed my Twitter feed, scrolled through my blog posts and began brushing my teeth.

Still the box said, "Will is typing."

"Don't you dare get hurt by this," I muttered around my toothpaste. "This was a stupid idea, and you knew that from the start."

But recognizing the stupidity of falling for someone on the Internet does not prevent you from doing it. My friend Jeanette, a college radio D.J., chats constantly with some music blogger she met on Tumblr. My friend Tuan, who lives in Los Angeles, stays up until after 3 to talk to his London-based girlfriend.

And I had just driven nearly 1,100 miles round trip to visit Will, a guy I met in October at a Web journalism conference and got to know almost entirely on Skype.

I noticed him across the table at a noisy hotel bar. Will owns thick black-frame glasses but no hairbrush or comb, traits that lend him the look of a basement-bound hacker. If you have ever attended an Internet conference, you understand how pale skin, thick glasses and scruffy hair can be attractive; otherwise, I can't explain it to you.

In either case, I liked Will's weirdly overconfident smirk and his obsession with WordPress. He regaled me with the merits of plug-ins and PHP until I became tired and went to bed.

"I'll find you on Twitter," I joked when I left.

I didn't expect or even want to see Will again after that weekend. Since he lived three states away, further face time seemed unlikely. I followed his Twitter posts with detached curiosity; in January, he G-chatted me to complain about work. Then he got drunk and messaged me again, sometime near midnight, as I uploaded photos and otherwise wasted bandwidth.

With obvious sarcasm, he wrote, "Do you have that Skype thing kids talk about these days?"

I've read that 90 percent of human communication is nonverbal. Skype captures that 90 percent on a low-resolution video camera, compresses it, funnels it to a node computer and reproduces it on a screen anywhere in the world. Skype eliminates distance; that's why it works.

And that's exactly what it did for us. With my Skype screen open and my webcam on, I viscerally felt that Will was sitting a foot away on my bed. Ignoring the times the picture froze or his voice cut out, I thought he looked and sounded exactly as he had in person. Sometimes, when he leaned into the computer to read an article I had sent him, I could see the pores of his face.

We started video chatting for hours every night—he from an ascetic all-white bedroom, me from the cupcake-print corner of my studio apartment. I learned that he ate take-out for every meal, slept in a series of identical white V-neck T-shirts and smirked with one side of his mouth when I said something clever. I knew his preferred coding languages, his least favorite content management system, and his general hatred of dancing, small talk and girls in bars.

One night, when we talked too late, I fell asleep with my laptop open and woke up seven hours later, tangled in cords. He was still there, asleep in the light from an open window, pale and young and pixelated.

Eventually he stirred, blinked at the camera and said, "Hey, you."

"Hey," I said easily. "How did you sleep?"

As the weeks went on, I told Will about my last boyfriend, a guy I had met in psychology class and dated for almost two years. He listened quietly, his glasses reflecting my image from his computer, and gave good, clear-eyed advice about letting go.

I couldn't remember the last time I met somebody that smart and talented in ways I certainly wasn't. He told me about his ex-girlfriend, who never appreciated his work. I texted him from classes when I was frustrated or bored.

In the safety of my apartment, I could see Will, but I couldn't touch him. I could summon him when I wanted to talk, but I never knew him in any light other than the one from his bedside lamp. This phenomenon worked in my favor as well. I could call him after a few drinks, when I felt sufficiently talkative and social; I could avoid him if I had videos to edit or blog posts to write. I could say whatever I wanted and risk awkwardness, because at the end of the conversation, one click of the mouse would shut him out of my room.

The irony is that we flock to the Internet for this type of safe, sanitized intimacy, but we want something entirely different. "In real life," or IRL, is a popular term in online parlance. At Internet conferences like the one where I met Will, Twitter explodes with people celebrating IRL meetings: "So nice to finally see @so-and-so IRL." "Hey @so-and-so, I can't believe we hadn't met IRL yet!"

The Internet brings these people together with hash tags and message boards, but it never satisfies them. No matter how much you love someone's blog or Twitter feed, it isn't their posts you actually want.

And so—slowly, cautiously—Will and I began circling the question of what it all meant.

"I really like you," he said one night, after getting home from the bar.

"I really like you too," I said. "I don't know what that means."

I wanted to find out. So in early March I rented a car, begged my professors to let me out of class a day early, and drove 540 miles to spend a long weekend in the midsize city where Will lives. When I got close, I called my friend Tuan from a rest stop, where I fixed my makeup and chewed gum and generally tried to calm down.

"What if it's terrible?" I demanded. "What if he's nothing like I expect?"

In fact, Will was almost exactly as I expected: thin lips, straight nose, small hazel eyes, glasses. He stood waiting at the side of the street while I parked my car—going forward and back, forward and back, until I nervously got within two feet of the curb. We kissed on the cold, blustery sidewalk as the wind whipped my thoughts around. Mostly, I felt relieved. I thought: "This works in real life. This means something."

But after we kissed and ate pizza and went back to his house, we struggled for things to talk about. In real life, Will stared off at nothing while I talked. In real life, he had no questions about the drive or my work or the stuff that waited for me when I went back to school.

He took me out for dinner and read his e-mail while we waited for our food. He apologized profusely, but still checked his Web site's traffic stats while we sat in his living room.

He took me to a party at his friend's house where they proceeded to argue for hours about Web design while I sat on a futon and stared at the ceiling, drunk and bored and terribly concerned that I looked thinner online. At points, he grabbed my hand and gave me small, apologetic smiles. It seemed like a strategy game: a constant dance of reaching for me and pulling back, of intimacy and distance, of real life and Internet make-believe.

On the last day of my visit, Will overslept. He rushed around the apartment with his hair wet and his tie untied, looking for his laptop. According to the plan we made the night before, he would go to work and I would leave when it suited me, dropping his spare keys in the mailbox.

In the front hallway, where I stood rubbing my eyes, Will hugged me goodbye and told me to drive safely. He struggled for a closing statement.

"It was great to see you," he said at last.

I didn't leave right away. After I showered and packed and studied the books near his fireplace, I sat for a long time at his kitchen counter, trying to work out what happened. I didn't like being surrounded by his things. I felt more comfortable in my room, with my things, and with his presence confined to a laptop screen.

I wrote him a note before I left: "Dear Will: Thank you so much for having me this weekend. It meant a lot to me to spend time with you in person."

I signed my name and left it on the counter. Then, willing myself not to cry, I dropped his keys in the mailbox and gunned it home. In real life, getting there took nine hours.

WHAT?

1. Dewey's piece is a memoir essay, grounded in personal experience, yet it also presents an argument not unlike Jonathan Franzen's in "Liking Is for Cowards. Go for What Hurts." What do you think Dewey is saying in her essay about online and in-real-life relationships? Do you agree with her perspective? Why or why not?
2. What effects does Skype have on the evolving relationship between Dewey and Will?
3. Dewey ends her essay by pointing out the following about her return home: "In real life, getting there took nine hours." What does this mean—beyond the temporal accounting and given the context of Dewey's essay as a whole?

WHAT ELSE? WHAT'S NEXT?

4. Write a brief essay suitable for submission to the opinion pages of *The Gamecock* in response to the following statement: "Social networking sites are destroying our ability to develop and maintain personal relationships." In your essay, you should clearly state your position on the statement and support your position with specific and suitable examples. Keep in mind that opinion columns in *The Gamecock* rarely exceed 300 words and are meant for an audience that includes the entire campus community.

WHO CARES?

5. What does Dewey do rhetorically to make her personal experience relevant to others? Is she successful? Explain.

CHAPTER 11

Reading Eating

IMAGE 11.1
Most eaters, Wendell Berry writes in "The Pleasures of Eating," think of themselves as passive consumers who no longer feel a part of the agricultural process and who get whatever the food industry wants them to have.

While it may be true that we are *what* we eat, the writers in this chapter present compelling evidence that we are *how* we eat, too. These academics, poets, journalists, and activists argue that the food choices we make—individually, as communities, and as a nation—can affect everything from our health to the health of the planet, from the livelihood and culture of billions of people to economic and political stability around the world. Chew on that for a while.

> *Poet, novelist, and essayist Wendell Berry has spent much of his life thinking, writing, and teaching about American life in general and agricultural life in particular. Berry wrote the following essay in 1989, and as it makes clear, he is an eloquent and determined critic of farm and food policies that continue to move Americans further away from the land—literally and figuratively.*

BEFORE YOU READ

Write a 250-word biography of Wendell Berry that you think will help you better understand the points he makes in this essay. Make sure you document the sources you use.

THE PLEASURES OF EATING Wendell Berry

Many times, after I have finished a lecture on the decline of American farming and rural life, someone in the audience has asked, "What can city people do?"

"Eat responsibly," I have usually answered. Of course, I have tried to explain what I mean by that, but afterwards I have invariably felt there was more to be said than I had been able to say. Now I would like to attempt a better explanation.

I begin with the proposition that eating is an agricultural act. Eating ends the annual drama of the food economy that begins with planting and birth. Most eaters, however, are no longer aware that this is true. They think of food as an agricultural product, perhaps, but they do not think of themselves as participants in agriculture. They think of themselves as "consumers." If they think beyond that, they recognize that they are passive consumers. They buy what they want—or what they have been persuaded to want—within the limits of what they can get. They pay, mostly without protest, what they are charged. And they mostly ignore certain critical questions about the quality and the cost of what they are sold: How fresh is it? How pure or clean is it, how free of dangerous chemicals? How far was it transported, and what did transportation add to the cost? How much did manufacturing or packaging or advertising add to the cost? When the food product has been manufactured or "processed" or "precooked," how has that affected its quality or price or nutritional value?

Most urban shoppers would tell you that food is produced on farms. But most of them do not know what farms, or what kinds of farms, or where the farms are, or what knowledge of skills are involved in farming. They apparently have little doubt that farms will continue to produce, but they do not know how or over what obstacles. For them, then, food is pretty much an abstract idea—something they do not know or imagine—until it appears on the grocery shelf or on the table.

The specialization of production induces specialization of consumption. Patrons of the entertainment industry, for example, entertain themselves less and less and have become more and more passively dependent on commercial suppliers. This is certainly true also

Chapter 11 | Reading Eating

of patrons of the food industry, who have tended more and more to be mere consumers—passive, uncritical, and dependent. Indeed, this sort of consumption may be said to be one of the chief goals of industrial production. The food industrialists have by now persuaded millions of consumers to prefer food that is already prepared. They will grow, deliver, and cook your food for you and (just like your mother) beg you to eat it. That they do not yet offer to insert it, prechewed, into our mouth is only because they have found no profitable way to do so. We may rest assured that they would be glad to find such a way. The ideal industrial food consumer would be strapped to a table with a tube running from the food factory directly into his or her stomach.

Perhaps I exaggerate, but not by much. The industrial eater is, in fact, one who does not know that eating is an agricultural act, who no longer knows or imagines the connections between eating and the land, and who is therefore necessarily passive and uncritical—in short, a victim. When food, in the minds of eaters, is no longer associated with farming and with the land, then the eaters are suffering a kind of cultural amnesia that is misleading and dangerous. The current version of the "dream home" of the future involves "effortless" shopping from a list of available goods on a television monitor and heating precooked food by remote control. Of course, this implies and depends on, a perfect ignorance of the history of the food that is consumed. It requires that the citizenry should give up their hereditary and sensible aversion to buying a pig in a poke. It wishes to make the selling of pigs in pokes an honorable and glamorous activity. The dreams in this dream home will perforce know nothing about the kind or quality of this food, or where it came from, or how it was produced and prepared, or what ingredients, additives, and residues it contains—unless, that is, the dreamer undertakes a close and constant study of the food industry, in which case he or she might as well wake up and play an active an responsible part in the economy of food.

There is, then, a politics of food that, like any politics, involves our freedom. We still (sometimes) remember that we cannot be free if our minds and voices are controlled by someone else. But we have neglected to understand that we cannot be free if our food and its sources are controlled by someone else. The condition of the passive consumer of food is not a democratic condition. One reason to eat responsibly is to live free.

But if there is a food politics, there are also a food esthetics and a food ethics, neither of which is dissociated from politics. Like industrial sex, industrial eating has become a degraded, poor, and paltry thing. Our kitchens and other eating places more and more resemble filling stations, as our homes more and more resemble motels. "Life is not very interesting," we seem to have decided. "Let its satisfactions be minimal, perfunctory, and fast." We hurry through our meals to go to work and hurry through our work in order to "recreate" ourselves in the evenings and on weekends and vacations. And then we hurry, with the greatest possible speed and noise and violence, through our recreation—for what? To eat the billionth hamburger at some fast-food joint hellbent on increasing the "quality" of our life? And all this is carried out in a remarkable obliviousness to the causes and effects, the possibilities and the purposes, of the life of the body in this world.

One will find this obliviousness represented in virgin purity in the advertisements of the food industry, in which food wears as much makeup as the actors. If one gained one's whole knowledge of food from these advertisements (as some presumably do), one would not know that the various edibles were ever living creatures, or that they all come from the soil, or that they were produced by work. The passive American consumer, sitting down to a meal of pre-prepared or fast food, confronts a platter covered with inert, anonymous substances that have been processed, dyed, breaded, sauced, gravied, ground, pulped, strained, blended, prettified, and sanitized beyond resemblance to any part of any creature that ever lived. The products of nature and agriculture have been made, to all appearances, the products of industry. Both eater and eaten are thus in exile from biological reality. And the result is a kind of solitude, unprecedented in human experience, in which the eater may think of eating as, first, a purely commercial transaction between him and a supplier and then as a purely appetitive transaction between him and his food.

And this peculiar specialization of the act of eating is, again, of obvious benefit to the food industry, which has good reasons to obscure the connection between food and farming. It would not do for the consumer to know that the hamburger she is eating came from a steer who spent much of his life standing deep in his own excrement in a feedlot, helping to pollute the local streams, or that the calf that yielded the veal cutlet on her plate spent its life in a box in which it did not have room to turn around. And, though her sympathy for the slaw might be less tender, she should not be encouraged to meditate on the hygienic and biological implications of mile-square fields of cabbage, for vegetables grown in huge monocultures are dependent on toxic chemicals—just as animals in close confinements are dependent on antibiotics and other drugs.

The consumer, that is to say, must be kept from discovering that, in the food industry—as in any other industry—the overriding concerns are not quality and health, but volume and price. For decades now the entire industrial food economy, from the large farms and feedlots to the chains of supermarkets and fast-food restaurants has been obsessed with volume. It has relentlessly increased scale in order to increase volume in order (probably) to reduce costs. But as scale increases, diversity declines; as diversity declines, so does health; as health declines, the dependence on drugs and chemicals necessarily increases. As capital replaces labor, it does so by substituting machines, drugs, and chemicals for human workers and for the natural health and fertility of the soil. The food is produced by any means or any shortcuts that will increase profits. And the business of the cosmeticians of advertising is to persuade the consumer that food so produced is good, tasty, healthful, and a guarantee of marital fidelity and long life.

It is possible, then, to be liberated from the husbandry and wifery of the old household food economy. But one can be thus liberated only by entering a trap (unless one sees ignorance and helplessness as the signs of privilege, as many people apparently do). The trap is the ideal of industrialism: a walled city surrounded by valves that let merchandise in but no consciousness out. How does one escape this trap? Only voluntarily, the same way that one went in: by restoring one's consciousness of what is involved in eating; by reclaiming responsibility for one's own part in the food economy. One might begin with the illuminating principle of Sir Albert Howard's *The Soil and Health*, that we should understand "the whole problem of health in soil, plant, animal, and man as one great subject." Eaters, that is, must understand that eating takes place inescapably in the world, that it is inescapably an agricultural act, and how we eat determines, to a considerable extent, how the world is used. This is a simple way of describing a relationship that is

Chapter 11 | Reading Eating

inexpressibly complex. To eat responsibly is to understand and enact, so far as we can, this complex relationship. What can one do? Here is a list, probably not definitive:

1. Participate in food production to the extent that you can. If you have a yard or even just a porch box or a pot in a sunny window, grow something to eat in it. Make a little compost of your kitchen scraps and use it for fertilizer. Only by growing some food for yourself can you become acquainted with the beautiful energy cycle that revolves from soil to seed to flower to fruit to food to offal to decay, and around again. You will be fully responsible for any food that you grow for yourself, and you will know all about it. You will appreciate it fully, having known it all its life.
2. Prepare your own food. This means reviving in your own mind and life the arts of kitchen and household. This should enable you to eat more cheaply, and it will give you a measure of "quality control": you will have some reliable knowledge of what has been added to the food you eat.
3. Learn the origins of the food you buy, and buy the food that is produced closest to your home. The idea that every locality should be, as much as possible, the source of its own food makes several kinds of sense. The locally produced food supply is the most secure, freshest, and the easiest for local consumers to know about and to influence.
4. Whenever possible, deal directly with a local farmer, gardener, or orchardist. All the reasons listed for the previous suggestion apply here. In addition, by such dealing you eliminate the whole pack of merchants, transporters, processors, packagers, and advertisers who thrive at the expense of both producers and consumers.
5. Learn, in self-defense, as much as you can of the economy and technology of industrial food production. What is added to the food that is not food, and what do you pay for those additions?
6. Learn what is involved in the best farming and gardening.
7. Learn as much as you can, by direct observation and experience if possible, of the life histories of the food species.

The last suggestion seems particularly important to me. Many people are now as much estranged from the lives of domestic plants and animals (except for flowers and dogs and cats) as they are from the lives of the wild ones. This is regrettable, for these domestic creatures are in diverse ways attractive; there is such pleasure in knowing them. And farming, animal husbandry, horticulture, and gardening, at their best, are complex and comely arts; there is much pleasure in knowing them, too.

It follows that there is great displeasure in knowing about a food economy that degrades and abuses those arts and those plants and animals and the soil from which they come. For anyone who does know something of the modern history of food, eating away from home can be a chore. My own inclination is to eat seafood instead of red meat or poultry when I am traveling. Though I am by no means a vegetarian, I dislike the thought that some animal has been made miserable in order to feed me. If I am going to eat meat, I want it to be from an animal that has lived a pleasant, uncrowded life outdoors, on bountiful pasture, with good water nearby and trees for shade. And I am getting almost as fussy about food plants. I like to eat vegetables and fruits that I know have lived happily and healthily in good soil, not the products of the huge, bechemicaled factory-fields that I have seen, for example, in the Central Valley of California. The industrial farm is said to have been patterned on the factory production line. In practice, it looks more like a concentration camp.

The pleasure of eating should be an extensive pleasure, not that of the mere gourmet. People who know the garden in which their vegetables have grown and know that the garden is healthy and remember the beauty of the growing plants, perhaps in the dewy first light of morning when gardens are at their best. Such a memory involves itself with the food and is one of the pleasures of eating. The knowledge of the good health of the garden relieves and frees and comforts the eater. The same goes for eating meat. The thought of the good pasture and of the calf contentedly grazing flavors the steak. Some, I know, will think of it as bloodthirsty or worse to eat a fellow creature you have known all its life. On the contrary, I think it means that you eat with understanding and with gratitude. A significant part of the pleasure of eating is in one's accurate consciousness of the lives and the world from which food comes. The pleasure of eating, then, may be the best available standard of our health. And this pleasure, I think, is pretty fully available to the urban consumer who will make the necessary effort.

I mentioned earlier the politics, esthetics, and ethics of food. But to speak of the pleasure of eating is to go beyond those categories. Eating with the fullest pleasure—pleasure, that is, that does not depend on ignorance—is perhaps the profoundest enactment of our connection with the world. In this pleasure we experience and celebrate our dependence and our gratitude, for we are living from mystery, from creatures we did not make and powers we cannot comprehend. When I think of the meaning of food, I always remember these lines by the poet William Carlos Williams, which seem to me merely honest:

> There is nothing to eat,
> seek it where you will,
> but the body of the Lord.
> The blessed plants
> and the sea, yield it
> to the imagination
> intact.

■ WHAT?

1. What does Berry mean when he encourages people to "eat responsibly"?
2. Berry's famous line "eating is an agricultural act" has become a battle cry for farmers and food activists around the world. How do you define "eating"? How else might the term be defined to reflect the politics of food?

■ WHAT ELSE? WHAT'S NEXT?

3. Working with a group of classmates, investigate and catalog the sources of the food served on the University of South Carolina campus—from dining halls to fast-food outlets. Some questions to keep in mind as you conduct your research: What companies supply the meals that are offered on campus? Where do they get the food to produce these meals? Does any of the food come from local resources (farms, ranches, or farmer's markets)? If not, why not? With your group, use your research findings to compose a report on the state of USC's food supply.
4. Berry describes "patrons of the food industry" as "passive, uncritical, and dependent" for their lack of active questioning and involvement in food production. Do you know where your food comes from? Interview one of your food providers—your school's food contractor, the manager or chef at a restaurant that you frequently visit, your grocery's produce or meat manager, or a farmer at a farmers' market—and trace the steps a particular food item goes through to make it to you. Where was the item grown, processed, handled? How was it grown? By whom? How and how far was it transported? What route did your food travel to get to you? When necessary, conduct online research to fill in any gaps.

■ WHO CARES?

5. Berry concludes his piece with a list of seven concrete actions readers can take to become more responsible eaters. Revise this list to target a dorm-dwelling, college-aged audience. Think about, for instance, how you might make these suggestions more realistic for a person living in a dorm with little to no kitchen or garden spaces.

> Jessica B. Harris, a professor at the City University of New York, is the author of 10 cookbooks that document the culture and food of the African diaspora. This memoir was published in Gastropolis: Food and New York City, a 2009 collection about New Yorkers' relationships with food.

BEFORE YOU READ

Many of the essays in this chapter speak, in one way or another, of the need for Americans to return to the kitchen, to learn how to cook meals from scratch. Research this issue to find out if there are any organized movements—in schools, churches, or communities, for example—whose goal it is to teach Americans, especially children, to cook. Be prepared to share your findings with the class.

THE CULINARY SEASONS OF MY CHILDHOOD   Jessica B. Harris

Few culinary traditions are as undocumented as those of middle-class African Americans. Scroll back to the 1950s, when segregation was still rampant in the South, and the foodways are even less well known. Although they are briefly mentioned in a few autobiographical narratives and in some fiction, the concern of most African Americans was more than throwing off the shackles of southern segregations that our forebears had come north to escape. This is reflected in our life tales more than in our recollections of meals eaten and foods purchased. The result is that most outsiders believe that ham hocks and hard times are the only remnants of our culinary past. Certainly there were plenty of ham hocks and no shortage of hard times. In fact, my New Jersey-born-and-raised mother always claimed that that state could best Mississippi in the racist sweepstakes and that she had the stories to prove it! In North and South alike, middle-class African Americans ate the same cornbread and fried chicken and chitterlings and foods from the traditions of the African diaspora as did our less well-off counterparts, but we also ate differently, foods that expressed our middle classness and reflected our social and political aspirations.

Even though chitterlings might be on the menu, they could equally likely be accompanied by a mason jar of corn liquor or a crystal goblet of champagne. Southern specialties like fried porgies and collard greens show up for dinner, but they might be served along with dishes becoming common in an increasingly omnivorous United States that was just beginning its love affair with food. Nowhere is this more evident than in my own life and in the culinary season of my childhood.

A descendant of the enslaved and free Africans who made their way north in the Great Migration, I grew up in a transplanted southern culture that still remains a vibrant region of the African American culinary world. My family, like many others long separated from the South, raised me in ways that continued their eating traditions, so now I can head south and sop biscuits in gravy, suck chewy bits of fat from a pig's foot spattered with hot sauce, and yes'm and no'm with the best of 'em.

Chapter 11 | Reading Eating

But that's not all of me. I also am a postwar baby who was the only child of striving middle-class parents who were old enough to have been young African American adults in the poverty of the Great Depression. They showered me with love and childhood coddling that makes my childhood seem like an African American version of *The Little Princess*. I also am a child at the confluence of two major African American culinary traditions. My mother's family could claim a smidge of black southern aristocracy, as they were descended from free people of color who migrated to Roanoke, Virginia. My father's family was from Tennessee and had upcountry Georgia roots that extended down the Natchez Trace. Both families showed their backgrounds at the table.

My maternal grandmother, Bertha Philpot Jones, was the quintessential African American matriarch presiding over a groaning board filled with savory goods. The role has become a visual cliché in movies like *The Nutty Professor Part II: The Klumps, Soul Food*, and *Dear Departed*, which revel in the dysfunction of African American life. No such dysfunction, however, was tolerated at Grandma Jones's table; she would not allow it. She was the matriarch and absolute sovereign of the Jones family; she ruled with a delicate but steel-boned hand, and the family marched to her tune. Watermelon-rind pickles spiced with fragrant cinnamon and whole cloves and the reassuring warmth of a full oven wafting smells of roasted joints and freshly baked bread are the aromas I most associate with her. She was a Baptist minister's wife and could put a hurtin' on some food. She had to, for as the minister's wife, she had not only her own brood of twelve children plus husband to feed, but the church folks who dropped in to take care of as well. She pickled fruits like Seckel pears, which had a curiously tart-sweet taste that comes back to me even today. The smell of Parker House rolls, the warmth of the kitchen, and the closeness of a large family all were part of the thrill of Grandma Jones's house. I didn't see her often—only on holidays and special occasions when we'd take the Holland Tunnel to head off to Plainfield, New Jersey, to visit and sit around the table.

Ida Irene Harris, my paternal grandmother, was at the other end of the culinary spectrum. I saw her much more often, at least once a week. When I travel in the South, folks are astounded to hear that as a child I had no southern roots, no grandmother to visit by segregated train or bus under the tutelage of kindly porters and with a tag pinned to my coat. Instead, my South was in the North, for Grandma Harris, in her day-to-day existence, re-created the preserved-in-amber South of her nineteenth-century rural youth in the precincts of her small apartment in the South Jamaica projects. I remember her apartment well, particularly the kitchen, with the four-burner stove on which she made lye soap, the refrigerator that always contained a pitcher of grape Kool-Aid with lemons cut up in it, and the sink in which she washed clothes, punching them with a broomstick to make sure they would get clean. Most of all, I remember the taste of the collard greens that she prepared: verdant, lush with just enough smoked pig tarts and fat for seasoning; they were the culinary embodiment of her love and, along with her silky beaten biscuits, one of the few dishes that she made well.

Grandma Harris lived in a self-created southern world. For years, she maintained a small garden plot at the back of the South Jamaica projects. This was just after the victory gardens of World War II when tenants could plant a small plot of land if they wished. Grandma Harris grew southern staples: collard and mustard greens, peanuts, snap beans, and more. I remember her weeding the peanuts and breaking off a leaf of the greens to test for ripening as the Long Island Rail Road train roared by on the tracks above. She taught me to love the slip of boiled peanuts, to sop biscuits in Alaga syrup with butter cut up in it, and to savor the tart sourness of buttermilk long before there was any romance to things southern.

I didn't understand the education she'd given me until years later, in Senegal's Theatre Daniel Sorano, I heard a griot sing. It was as though Grandma Harris had leaned down from the clouds and touched me. The timbre, the tone, the almost keening wail of the Mandinka singer captured the tuneless songs that Grandma sang as she went about her daily tasks, as much as the tastes of the Senegalese food recalled flavors from my childhood. It was then that I realized that unknown to both of us, Grandma Harris had taught me the ways of the past in her demeanor, her stalwartness, her faith, and her food. Those ways would help me survive. She also taught me to behave. I will never forget the summer day when she administered the only childhood whipping I can recall.

"Whipping" was not a word that was used in my house as I was growing up. I was a Dr. Spock baby through and through, and discipline was more about firm conversation than about Daddy's belt. At Grandma Harris's apartment, though, the rules changed and that one time, I knew I was going to get a whipping for sure.

Grandma Harris was another kind of old-line southern matriarch. It didn't matter that she lived on the third floor of the South Jamaica projects in Queens; her world was deeply rooted in the traditions of her South. She would brook no contradiction about manners. In her home, New Year's was celebrated with a mix of collard, mustard, and turnip greens that she had stewed down to a low gravy to accompany the obligatory hoppin' John and chitterlings. I always passed on the chitterlings and ate the hoppin' John, but the greens were my favorite. I had even more respect for them after they caused my downfall and earned me my only childhood whipping.

It happened on a summer's day when I was about six or seven. My mother worked, so I was sent to Grandma's apartment to spend the day in the traditional, extended-family day-care arrangement. I spent most of those urban summer days of my early childhood in her small one-bedroom apartment reading in a chair and staying out from under her feet in order to avoid going outside to play with the other kids, who invariably made fun of my private-school vowels and bookish ways. She, on the other side, spent her days insisting that I go out and play with the "nice children" who all called her Mother Harris.

On the day in question, when I had managed to avoid the dreaded piss-smelling barrels and rough boys and girls of the playground, she looked up from her sewing and said, "Jessica, come here." I was in for it. I was pleasantly surprised when, instead of ordering me downstairs, she instead went for her purse and gave me some money wrapped in a hankie with instructions to go to Miranda's, the Italian-owned corner market, and get a piece of "streak-a-lean-streak-a-fat" for the greens that she was going to cook.

Thrilled at being sent on an errand and overjoyed at escaping the barrel torture, I headed off. The walk was short, only a scant block through the maze of red-brick buildings that had not yet deteriorated into the breeding ground of hopelessness they were to become. A few small trees were in leaf, and the sounds of other children playing reminded me how grown up I was. I was on an errand. Arriving at Miranda's, I went directly to the meat counter, where, as in most African American neighborhoods, there was a vast array of pig parts both identifiable and unknown. Having not a clue about streak-a-lean-streak-a-fat but feeling exceptionally sophisticated in my seven-year-old head, I pointed to the slab bacon that my mother used to season things and asked for the requisite amount. It was brought out for my examination, and I grandly pronounced it fine. Cut off to the desired thickness and wrapped in slick brown paper, it was presented to me with solemnity. I tucked it into the net shopping bag that Grandma had provided and headed back home, proud and pleased.

Chapter 11 | Reading Eating

I pushed open the heavy downstairs door and ran up the concrete steps, heels clanking on the metal treads that lined them. When I got to 3B, I pushed through the door that Grandma always kept open in those kinder times and headed in to present my parcel. To my amazement, when she opened it, she began to mutter and ask me what I had gotten.

"Steak-a-lean-streak-a-fat," I replied.

"Did you ask for it?" she questioned.

"No, I pointed it out to the man," I ventured with increasing timidity.

"Well, this isn't it! I wanted what I asked for, streak-a-lean-streak-a-fat," she countered. "This is slab bacon!"

"It's the same thing, isn't it?" I queried.

"NO! Now you march right back there and get me what I asked for, streak-a-lean-streak-a-fat. Take this back!"

"But?"

"No Buts!" Just march back there, young lady! Right Now!"

I trudged back to Miranda's, each step made heavier with the thought of having to tell the butcher that I'd made an error and hoping that he'd take back the offending bacon. The joy of escape of the prior hour had soured into a longing for the nasty boys and the stinky barrels. Luckily, the man took pity on bourgie old me and took back the bacon, replacing it with a fattier piece of streaky pork that was a fraction of the price.

When I got back to the building, Grandma was sitting on the benches out front and waiting for me. She uttered the five words that I'd never heard her say: "Go cut me a switch."

Terrified, I set off and hunted for the smallest branch that I could find in this virtually treeless urban landscape, knowing what was coming next. I returned with a smallish green switch that I had unearthed lord knows where. She took a few halfhearted passes at my legs, solemnly repeating with each one, "Don't think you're smarter than your elders." Tears flowed on both sides: mine because I'd certainly learned my lesson through the humiliation of returning the bacon followed by the public whipping, Grandma's because she adored me and wanted a respectful granddaughter. Despite that childhood trauma, I still love collard greens and never eat my New Year's mess of them without remembering Grandma Harris. I always season them with what I have come to think of as streak-a-lean-streak-a-fat-cut-me-a-switch; savor their smoky, oily splendor; and think of the southern lessons she taught me with every bite.

The other days of my early summers were spent with my working parents. We left New York City for family vacations, and I can remember the ice man delivering big blocks of ice wrapped in burlap to chill the icebox of the small cabin that we rented on Three Mile Harbor Road in East Hampton long before the area attained its current vogue. The year after my whipping, when I was eight, we visited Oak Bluffs, Massachusetts, the African American summer community on Martha's Vineyard that has become much touted these days. It was love at first sight, and my parents bought a summer house there that winter.

From the time I was nine until the present, this house has been a part of every summer. Then we made long trips on the Boston Post Road and the Merritt Parkway up to the Wood's Hole ferry dock. Old habits die hard, and my parents in the 1950s would no more think of hitting the road without a shoebox full of fried chicken, deviled eggs, pound cake, oranges, and raisins and a thermos full of lemonade or some other cool drink that they would leave home without maps and a tank full of gas.

Oak Bluffs was just beginning to grow in popularity among New Yorkers; Bostonians knew about its glories long before we did. Middle-class African Americans from New York and New Jersey summered in Sag Harbor near the Hamptons, but my prescient father did not want to be so close to the city that friends could drop in unannounced on the weekends, so it was Martha's Vineyard for us. We joked that if we lost our way to the Vineyard, we could simply follow the trail of chicken bones left by fellow black New Yorkers and find the ferry pier with no problem. Like us, they were marked by segregated back doors and the lack of on-the-road facilities and also stuck to the old ways. We brought our chicken along for years until the Connecticut Turnpike was completed, and then we gradually left the chicken and deviled eggs at home and settled for the mediocre fare of the rest stops. I was thrilled several years ago when a friend, Alexander Smalls, opened a restaurant in Grand Central Terminal celebrating our traveling ways; it was called the Shoebox Café. While the menu was his own inventive interpretation of the black food of the South, I knew he was also honoring the past that many black Americans share.

My Vineyard summers were where I caught my first fish, a porgy of respectable size, and learned to strip the skin off an eel and find out just how delicious the sweet meat was, once you got over the snake look, and to pick mussels off the docks at Menemsha. The days were punctuated by sharing meals with family and friends, waiting for my father to appear on the Friday night "daddy boat" to spend the weekends, and savoring rainy days because my mother treated us with one of her fantastic blueberry cobblers prepared with berries we had picked before the storm came, from the bushes that grew wild along the roadside. July folded into August marked by county fairs, cotton candy, Illumination Night, Darling's molasses puff, swordfish at Giordano's restaurant, and movies at the Strand or Islander movie houses, accompanied by hot buttered popcorn served from a copper kettle. Soon it was time to pack the car again and head back to our house in Queens. I never really minded because autumn brought the return to school, and my world expanded one hundredfold. My school saw to that.

The United Nations International School was and is a special place. As the first non-UN-connected child to attend the school and one of very few Americans enrolled in the early years, my playmates were the world. UNIS, as the school is called by the cognoscenti, was small, then so small that it added a grade each year until it finally stretched from prekindergarten through high school. Inside Queens's Parkway Village apartments that had been transformed into classrooms, I made lifelong friends and learned how to function in a world that extended to the globe's four corners. A trip to Vasu's or Shikha's house brought smells of the Indian subcontinent, and on occasions when I was fortunate enough to be invited to birthday parties, there were tastes of rich spices and heady unknown flavors that would never have turned up on the table of my garlic-free household. The rich stews of central Europe were featured at Danuta's, and steak and kidney pie might turn up on the table at Eluned's. I can still feel the rasp of the embossed silver spoon-backs that were used on the table at Jennifer and Susan's house in Great Neck and remember their mother's wonderful way with shortbread with nostalgia that can still make my mouth water more than forty-five years later. The annual round of birthday parties was interrupted by school events like international potluck suppers. Parents brought dishes from around the globe, and students began culinary competitions like eating spaghetti with chopsticks in the days before Asian noodle bowls and the vast array of Italian pastas became common culinary currency.

As more Americans joined the school community, even they displayed amazing culinary inventiveness, and I remember being invited to a formal Coke-tail party at Anne's house,

Chapter 11 | Reading Eating

where we were served all manner of multihued nonalcoholic cocktails in delicate stemmed glassware complete with swizzle sticks, umbrella garnishes, and lots of maraschino cherries at a birthday fete that was every young girl's dream. All the class events seemed to center on international households of like-acting folk who proved to me at an early age that no matter what turned up on the table, it was to be savored and eaten with gusto.

During the twelve or so years that I attended UNIS, I grew to understand something about the world's food. My core group of friends spent many of those years together, and we became familiar with one another's households and foods and, with that growing knowledge, came to realize that the table was not only where we held our parties and our class fetes but also where we worked out our problems and got answers to questions about one another. With hindsight, I now realize that we achieved at our birthday tables and communal suppers the same détente and understanding that the parents of many of my friends worked so hard to attain at the tables at which they tried to bring peace to the world.

If my grandmothers' tables gave me a grounding in the African American past that is so much the bedrock of all that I do, and UNIS gave me an understanding of the food of the world, a palate that is open to tasting just about anything, and the knowledge that more friends are made around the table than just about anywhere else, my parents and our daily life completed the picture with the finishing touches.

I have saved my household for last, for it, more than any of the other outside influences, marked the season of my childhood eating. While I grew up at the confluence of two African American culinary traditions and lived in an international world at school, at home on Anderson Road in St. Albans, Queens, my surroundings were a wondrous combination of my parents' dueling culinary wills.

Very few African Americans are to the manor born; most of us have a past of want or need, if not for love, than for cash and the opportunities it can bring. My father, Jesse Brown Harris, was such a person. He was a black man and a striking one at that, aubergine-hued with the carriage of an emperor of Songhai. Early photos show him tall and slender, looking very proprietary about his little family of three. Daddy was not a numbers runner. Daddy was not a welfare ducker or an absentee father. Daddy was just Daddy, and the constancy of that statement and my lack of awareness that this was not the norm for all black children made me different.

As a teenager, Daddy had lived over the stables and worked as a Shabbas goy in Williamsburg, Brooklyn. Until the day he died, he was marked by a childhood of grinding poverty during which he had worn flour-bag suits to school and church, cadged coal at the railroad yard for heat, and picked dandelion leaves on the Fisk College campus for dinner. He was torn between the desire to overcome his past and provide differently for his family and the need to remember it with honor.

My father ate southern food whenever he could cajole my mother into preparing the hog maws or chitterlings that he adored. We even put a stove into the basement of our house so that the smell would not taint our living quarters. He would occasionally bring home cartons of buttermilk, which he would savor with squares of the flaky and hot cornbread that my mother baked at the drop of a hat. Sunday breakfast was his special time, and he would proudly sit at the head of the table and sop up his preferred mix of Karo dark with butter cut up in it with the hoecake that was off-limits to anyone else in the household.

He was the only one in his family of man children who did not and could not cook. My Uncle Bill, his older brother, gave me my first taste of rabbit stew, and my Uncle

Jim's spaghetti sauce was the stuff of family legend. Actually, my father cared little for food, but he loved restaurants and, with his increasing affluence, dined out with the best of them. In the early years, dining out meant heading to the local silver bullet diner near our house for specials like mashed potatoes with gravy and Salisbury steak or sauerbraten (the neighborhood was German before we moved in). The bakery on Linden Boulevard, the main shopping street, sold flaky butter cookies and gingerbread at Christmas. Later, when St. Albans became blacker, we would head to Sister's Southern Diner after church on Sundays, still dressed in our Sabbath finery, for down-home feasts of smothered pork chops and greens or stewed okra and fried fish in an orgy of southern feasting that Mommy did not have to cook. In later years, restaurants like the Brasserie, La Fonda del Sol, and the Four Seasons were where we celebrated birthdays and anniversaries. There, my father's duality surfaced, and he would order wine for the bucket or "spittoon," as we had baptized it in our family jargon, and crepes suzette or Caesar salad for the flamboyant tableside service, but we three secretly knew that all the while what he really wanted was a ham hock and some butterbeans to satisfy the tastes of his youth.

My mother, though, truly loved food and had amazing taste buds that could analyze the components of a dish with startling accuracy. She would then reproduce her version of it at home, to the delight of all. Trained as a dietician, my mother reveled in entertaining and entranced her friends with her culinary inventiveness. Decades later, she revealed that at school, she had been required to sit through classes on how to keep black people out of restaurants and was discouraged from doing anything with food demonstrations that would put her in public view. After a brief stint as a dietitian at Bennett College in North Carolina and an even briefer stay in domestic service as a private dietitian, she found that she did not enjoy the field. Instead, she put her talents to use at the supper table, and I grew up eating homemade applesauce and tea sandwiches of olives and cream cheese when my friends were chowing down Gerber's finest and processed cheese spread. Weeknights featured balanced meals like breaded veal cutlets with carrots and peas and a salad, alternating with sublime fried chicken and mashed potatoes or rice and always a green vegetable and salad, or string beans, potatoes, and ham ends slow cooked into what we called a New England boiled dinner.

Parties were the occasion for pulling out all the stops. My mother would prepare ribbon and pinwheel sandwiches from whole wheat bread, cream cheese, white bread, and strips of red and green bell pepper, long before the spectrum opened up to admit such hues as orange, purple, white, and even yellow! She created cabarets in the basement—persuading her friends to come as babies or in nightclothes, hiring calypso singers, serving drinks with small umbrellas, and devising smoking centerpieces with dry ice and punch bowls—and, each Sunday, presided over table overflowing with roasts and a multiplicity of vegetables.

My mother created magic in the kitchen and made cooking exciting and fun, with a trick for every dish and a sense of adventure at the stove. As her only child, I got the benefit of this knowledge and accompanied her in the kitchen almost from my birth. In later years, she began to tire of the kitchen, but eventually, she renewed her interest in things culinary and discovered the wonder of ingredients like confit of duck, fresh garlic, pimentos, and arugula. Ever curious, her life was a constant adventure. I did not learn to cook; I simply absorbed it in her kitchen, moving from high chair to small tasks to whole dishes and entire meals.

I am very much the product of all of this, and these seasons of my personal and yet very New York childhood gave me the foods of the world on my plate. For the first years of my life, my fork ranged throughout the world from the simple country food of Grandma Harris to the more elegant Virginia repasts of Grandma Jones and the dishes of the 1950s and 1960s that were, for me, the tastes of home. I also sampled fare from the globe's four corners at the homes of my international classmates and learned that no matter where our origins or our regionalisms, when we eat together and share the commensalisms of the table, we make ourselves and our worlds better. It has been said that we are what we eat. I certainly am, and in the many seasons of my New York youth, that included an amazing amount of mighty good food.

■ WHAT?

1. Though Harris has written a memoir essay, she does present an implicit argument about food. What is her claim? What kinds of support does she provide to persuade her audience to consider her way of thinking about food?
2. How does Harris use her family history to reject and correct common stereotypes about foods that African Americans eat? How does she use food to weave together the various threads of her family background?
3. Compare Harris's essay with one of the more explicit arguments in this chapter (Bittman's, for example, or Berry's or Salatin's). Which do you think is more effective as an argument? Why?

■ WHAT ELSE? WHAT'S NEXT?

4. Late in her essay, Harris writes: "My core group of friends … became familiar with one another's households and foods and, with that growing knowledge, came to realize that the table was not only where we held our parties and our class fetes but also where we worked out our problems and got answers to questions about one another." Research how others have written about the experience of preparing and sharing a meal with others. Find at least two sources that you like, summarize them, and explain why you think they are worth sharing with others.

■ WHO CARES?

5. What does Harris do, specifically, to connect with her readers and to make her own experiences relevant to others? Point to specific strategies and passages in the essay in your response.

> *Alice Waters, owner and founder of Chez Panisse Restaurant and Foundation in Berkeley, California, has championed local, organic food for more than thirty-eight years. She is introducing her ideas into public schools through Edible Education, a model garden and kitchen program. This essay was first published in the September 21, 2009 edition of* The Nation.

BEFORE YOU READ

Use the "News" function on Google—or some other news-oriented search engine—to find out what Alice Waters has been up to lately. How does she show up in the news? What are others saying about her?

HEALTHY CONSTITUTION Alice Waters

I was moved by the way Morgan Spurlock framed a narrow long-distance shot down the corridor of a Beckley, West Virginia, middle school in his outstanding 2004 film, *Super Size Me*. The film is about the toll that fast and processed food takes on all of us. Clearly visible in the background of this particular shot were dozens of students, many of whom were overweight.

Perhaps it should come as no surprise that Beckley's cafeteria offers only processed food, which is high in fat, sodium and sugar and of very little nutritional value.

Contrast this with the Central Alternative High School in Appleton, Wisconsin. The school serves troubled youth, but teachers, parents and administrators found a way to turn things around; and when they did, discipline problems dropped sharply. Their secret? Instead of the usual processed meals, the school cafeteria offers fresh, locally grown, low-fat, low-sugar alternatives. The healthier meals are delicious. The students love them. They perform better in class and don't get sick as often.

We are learning that when schools serve healthier meals, they solve serious educational and health-related problems. But what's missing from the national conversation about school lunch reform is the opportunity to use food to teach values that are central to democracy. Better food isn't just about test scores, health and discipline. It is about preparing students for the responsibilities of citizenship.

That's why we need to talk about edible education, not just school lunch reform. Edible education is a radical yet common-sense approach to teaching that integrates classroom instruction, school lunch, cooking and gardening into the studies of math, science, history and reading.

Edible education involves not only teaching children about where food comes from and how it is produced but giving them responsibilities in the school garden and kitchen. Students literally enjoy the fruits of their labor when the food they grow is served in healthy, delicious lunches that they can help prepare.

I learned this firsthand through the Chez Panisse Foundation—the organization I helped create to inspire a network of food activists around the world with edible education programs in their own communities. Here in Berkeley, I see children in our edible education program learn about responsibility, sharing and stewardship and become more connected to themselves and their peers. In the process, they come to embody the most important values of citizenship.

Listen to what one student named Charlotte has to say: "Next we went from the blue corn to the sweet corn and each picked an ear to grill. I must say it tasted really good, even without butter." Or Mati: "I think cleaning up is as important as eating. Cleaning up is sort of fun. And we can't just leave it for the teachers, because we made the mess." Or Jose: "I remember the first time I came to the kitchen. I was afraid to do anything. But then I realized, this is my kitchen. So then I started to enjoy it."

Charlotte, Mati and Jose are learning about so much more than lunch. They're learning that farmers depend on the land; we depend on farmers; and our nation depends on all of us. That cooperation with one another is necessary to nurture the community. And that, by setting the table for one another, we also take care of ourselves. School should be the place where we build democracy, not just by teaching about the Constitution but by becoming connected to our communities and the land in more meaningful ways.

In 1785, Thomas Jefferson declared that "Cultivators of the earth are the most valuable citizens. They are the most vigorous, the most independent, the most virtuous, and they are tied to their country and wedded to its liberty and interests by the most lasting bonds."

I believe he was right. The school cafeteria, kitchen and garden, like the town square, can and should be the place where we plant and nourish the values that guide our democracy. We need to join a delicious revolution that can reconnect our children to the table and to what it means to be a steward. This is the picture of a caring society, and this is the promise of edible education.

■ WHAT?

1. How, according to Waters, can food be used "to teach values that are central to democracy"? Why isn't this happening now?
2. Explain the link that Waters makes between healthy meals and learning. What kind of evidence does she offer to support these links? Do you think more evidence would have strengthened her argument?

■ WHAT ELSE? WHAT'S NEXT?

3. Are any schools in South Carolina serving what Waters would call "fresh, locally grown, low-fat, low-sugar" meals? Are any schools in the state involved in anything like the "edible education" program she describes?

■ WHO CARES?

4. Summarize Waters' argument for an audience of elementary school students in Richland School District 1 (in Columbia).

ANGELICA KITCHEN MENU

Several of the essays in this chapter—from "The Culinary Seasons of My Childhood" to "Declare Your Independence"—are, in one way or another, about *dining in*. That is, they focus on the ways that food deeply connects with family, home, and individual identity.

Over the next few pages, you'll find a menu, from Angelica Kitchen, a restaurant in the East Village of New York City, that works to establish on a different kind of identity—one based on *dining out*. As you read the menu, think of it as more than just a list of food items from which to choose when you're hungry for lunch. Think of it instead as the textual representation of the restaurant itself.

A complete and effective menu is a sophisticated rhetorical document. It articulates the relationship the restaurant wants to establish with its guests, and it creates an ethos for the restaurant and the people who work there. As you read Angelica Kitchen's menu, consider what it says about the restaurant, its identity, its politics, and the experience it promises its guests. After the menu, you'll find research, invention, and writing prompts to help you accomplish this.

BEFORE YOU READ

Visit the restaurant's website, and spend some time examining the various links and other information.

Chapter 11 | **Reading Eating**

Soups Starters & Sides

Miso Soup with wakame and tofu	cup 3.50	bowl	3.75
☀ Soup of the day	cup 3.50	bowl	4.25

Kombu Vegetable Bouillon — 1.75
A warm invigorating cup of broth, rich in minerals, delicately seasoned with ginger, sage & thyme

Soba Sensation — 6.50
Rich, velvety sesame sauce ladled over soba noodles, topped with pickled red cabbage garnish.

Curried Cashew Spread — 4.75
An intriguing live blend of raw cashews, sprouted chickpeas, freshly ground curry powder & unpasteurized miso. Accompanied by crisp crudités.

Thai Mee Up — 7.25
All Raw – delicate strands of daikon radish, zucchini & carrot dressed with Thai tahini sauce, garnished with garlic-lemon marinated kale.

Hummus — 6.50
Served with baked zahtar pita wedges and crisp crudités.

☀ **Norimaki** — 8.00
Six pieces of rolled vegetable sushi, served with wasabi, pickled ginger & lemon-shoyu dipping sauce.
(ingredients vary daily)

Angelica Pickle Plate — 4.25
Garlic pickled shiitakes, assorted seasonal pickled vegetables & marinated beets.

Kimchee — 3.25
Homemade, mild style, tangy fermented cabbage with carrot, daikon & jalapeno pepper.

Ruby Kraut — 2.75
Homemade red cabbage sauerkraut.

Walnut-Lentil Pâté — 6.75
Topped with tofu sour cream, served with baked rice crackers and crisp crudités.

Mashed Yukon Gold Potatoes — 4.75
Served with brown rice gravy

Special Appetizer Agrarian Salgado — 8.00
Baked rounds of mashed Yukon Gold potatoes and herbed seitan, with a basil-walnut pesto center; topped with dill-tofu sour cream & garnished with piquant marinated kale.

Brazil's mass social movements are mobilizing forces to end hunger. A portion of the proceeds from this appetizer goes to FRIENDS OF THE BRAZILIAN LANDLESS WORKERS MOVEMENT (MST) *to support their implementation of agrarian reform and widespread development of sustainable agriculture. Learn more by visiting* www.mstbrazil.org

---

Union Square farmer's market

Beverages

Juices – Made to Order	
Carrot	5.00
Carrot/apple	5.00
Carrot/mixed vegetable	6.50
added fresh ginger	.35
Lemonade – Vibrant!	2.75
Hibiscus Cooler	2.75
– Chilled hibiscus flower served with lime	
Apple Cider – Chilled	2.75
Grain Coffee with Rice Dream	2.50
grain coffee refill	1.25
Chai – Black tea, chai spices & soymilk; sweetened with agave nectar	2.75
chai tea refill	1.50
Green Tea	1.75
Kukicha Tea Hot/Chilled	1.25/1.50
Mu 16 Tea	1.50
first tea refill free	

☀ See the Special Today page for today's selections

Angelica Kitchen

The Carolina Rhetoric

Entrees

☀ **Daily Seasonal Specials**
Descriptions of today's selections listed on overleaf.
À la carte 15.25   With choice of two Basics or cup of soup   17.50

Dashi and Noodles
Bowl of traditional Japanese broth made with shiitake mushrooms, kombu, fresh ginger & shoyu; served warm or cool over soba noodles. Adorned with chef's select garnishes.   small   8.50
                                                                                                  large   10.50

Three Bean Chili
Piquant chili made with homemade seitan, kidney and pinto beans & lentils; slowly simmered with sun-dried tomatoes and a blend of chiles; topped with lime-jalapeño tofu sour cream. Served with fluffy Southern style cornbread & cucumber-red onion salsa.
                                                                                                  wee   9.00
                                                                                                  grand 11.50

Olé Man Seitan
Homemade seitan & roasted vegetable mix folded into a warm whole wheat tortilla; dressed with spicy traditional mole sauce (peanuts & chocolate), & lime-jalapeño tofu sour cream; garnished with pimento.   14.50

Thai Mee Up
An All Raw Entree - delicate strands of daikon radish, zucchini & carrot, on a bed of garlic-lemon marinated kale, dressed with Thai tahini sauce.   11.25

☀ **Norimaki**
Nine pieces of rolled vegetable sushi, served with wasabi, pickled ginger & lemon-shoyu dipping sauce *(ingredients vary daily)*   11.50

Sandwiches

Wrapsody
Seasonal selection of roasted vegetables, balsamic marinated beets, creamy hummus, dill pickles, sunflower sprouts & arugula, folded & wrapped in a soft whole wheat tortilla.   10.50

Sam or I Sandwich
Herbed baked tofu layered with marinated hiziki & arame, crisp grated daikon, ruby kraut, a smear of mellow sesame spread & lettuce. Served on choice of mixed grain or spelt bread.   8.75
Half a sandwich with simple salad or cup of soup & kukicha tea.   9.50

Marinated Tofu Sandwich
Lemon herbed baked tofu layered with roasted vegetables, a smear of basil-walnut pesto & lettuce. Served on choice of mixed grain or spelt bread.   8.75
Half a sandwich with simple salad or cup of soup & kukicha tea.   9.50

 See the Special Today page for today's selections

Salads

House
Assorted lettuces; sunflower sprouts; grated red & green cabbage, daikon, carrots and beets; topped with clover sprouts; served with your choice of dressing.   7.50

Roasted Vegetable Salad
A seasonal selection of roasted vegetables tossed with arugula in a balsamic vinaigrette. Garnished with garlic crostini spread with creamy hummus, & cherry tomatoes.   12.75

Sea Caesar
Crisp romaine lettuce tossed with creamy garlic dressing. Topped with seasoned sourdough croutons, a sprinkle of smoked dulse & nori strips.   8.75

Orchard
Mesclun lettuces, apple, toasted pecans, dried bing cherries & sourdough croutons; tossed in a rosemary vinaigrette.   9.25

Mixed Sprout
A refreshing toss of snow pea shoots, sunflower sprouts & seeds, and mint; mixed with cabbage, daikon & carrots in a cool mint vinaigrette. Adorned with toasted peanuts, onion sprouts & watercress.   8.75

Si Se Puede
Balsamic roasted cherry tomatoes & basil-olive marinated chickpeas, over local greens tossed with extra virgin olive oil, fresh squeezed lemon juice & coarse sea salt. Accompanied by garlic crostini topped with tofu ricotta & chives.   10.00

Well Cultured
Mélange of seasonal greens & watercress tossed with homemade kimchee, nori strips, toasted sesame seeds & extra virgin olive oil; garnish of radish slices.   8.75

Tempeh Reuben Sandwich (served warm)
Our version of this classic features baked marinated tempeh, seasoned with caraway & cumin, tofu Russian dressing, sauerkraut & lettuce. Served on choice of mixed grain or spelt bread.   8.75
Half a sandwich with simple salad or cup of soup & kukicha tea.   9.50

Hot Open Face Tempeh Sandwich
Slices of sourdough baguette topped with lightly marinated & baked tempeh, napped with savory mushroom gravy. Served on a bed of raw spinach, garnished with ruby kraut.   10.50
With a scoop of mashed potatoes   11.50

Angelica Kitchen

Dragon Bowls

Part of the Angelica Kitchen menu since day one, this special combination of Basics is named for the Chinese bowl in which it was originally served.
(one substitution only)

Dragon Bowl	13.00

Rice, beans, tofu, sea vegetables & steamed vegetables; served with your choice of dressing.

Dragon Bargain	18.00

A Dragon Bowl served with cup of soup and bread with spread.

Wee Dragon	9.00

A Dragon Bowl in half portion.

Wee Dragon Bargain	14.00

A half Dragon served with cup of soup and bread with spread.

Combo Bowls

Any combination of the Basics at right served with your choice of dressing

choice of 2	7.25
choice of 3	9.50
choice of 4	11.00

Dressings & Sauces

House – Puree of tahini, scallions & parsley
Tangy Basil – Sweet & sour, oil free
Black Sesame – with wasabi, garlic & toasted sesame oil
Balsamic Vinaigrette – Balsamic vinegar, olive oil & mustard
Creamy Carrot – with ginger & dill
Brown Rice Gravy – Brown rice flour roux with a savory blend of herbs, spices & tamari

Refills are .95 on all dressings above

Soba Sensation Sauce – Rich, velvety sesame sauce	1.90
Sea Caesar Dressing – Creamy garlic dressing	1.90

Angelica Kitchen Organic Brittle
Ingredients: pumpkin seeds, sunflower seeds, sesame seeds, pecans, rice syrup, maple sugar, vanilla, sea salt.

Packaged To Go.

small 1.1 oz	2.75
large 3.2 oz	6.75

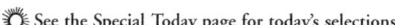 See the Special Today page for today's selections

Picnic Plate

Select menu items, served cool, to mix & match.
*starred items available in larger à la carte portions elsewhere on menu.

3 items	7.75
4 items	9.50
5 items	11.50

Assorted Seasonal Pickled Vegetables* Baked Marinated Tofu
Walnut-Lentil Pâté*   Today's Special Vegetable
Norimaki* *(two pieces)*   Marinated Hiziki & Arame Salad
Simple Salad*   Baked Marinated Tempeh
Hummus*   Today's Salad Special*
Ruby Kraut*   Live Curried Cashew Spread*
Kimchee*   Garlic Lemon Marinated Kale

Basics

Served with your choice of dressing

Tofu	3.75
Tempeh	4.25
Beans	3.00
Sea Vegetables	4.25
Steamed Vegetables	4.00
Simple Salad	5.50
Soba Noodles	3.75
Rice	2.75
Millet	3.50
3 Grain Mix	3.75

(quinoa, teff & amaranth)

Breads & Spreads

Angelica Cornbread
Rustic, whole grain slice (wheat free) 2.00

Sourdough Bread
Authentic tangy whole wheat slice 1.75

Southern Style Cornbread
Generous square, light & fluffy (wheat) 3.25

Small Angelica Cornbread Loaf 7.50

Miso-Tahini Spread
Rich & smooth 2.00

Ginger-Carrot Spread
Light & bright 1.75

Onion Spread
Sweet & savory 1.75

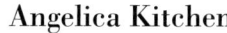

Angelica Kitchen

glossary

Agar
Marine algae used as a vegetarian gelling agent.

Amaranth
Tiny golden seeds, extraordinarily nutritious, amaranth was once the sacred food of the Aztecs. Cooked as a grain, it has the aroma of fresh corn & the crunch & appearance of blonde caviar. Higher than milk in protein & calcium.

Arame *(AHR-ah-may)*
Dark brown sea vegetable, thin & thread-like, with a mild, sweet taste; rich in iron, calcium & iodine.

Burdock
A slender root vegetable with a sweet, earthy flavor & a tender crisp texture. Acts as a blood purifier & is an excellent source of potassium

Daikon *(DI-kon)*
Large white radish; mild, pungent & crisp with remarkable medicinal qualities.

Dulse
Reddish purple sea vegetable, often an immediate favorite of those first tasting seaweed. High in iron & protein, our dulse is harvested from the coast of Maine.

Gomasio
A low sodium table condiment consisting of dry roasted, crushed sesame seeds & sea salt

Grain Coffee
Caffeine free beverage made from roasted barley, rye, chicory & roots

Hiziki *(hijiki)*
A dark brown sea vegetable with a strong flavor of the ocean. Resembling thin black spaghetti, hiziki is the most mineral rich of all foods & is considered by the Japanese as "esteemed beauty food"

Kamut *(Kah-MOOT)*
Heirloom durum wheat, plump, golden & high in protein & minerals. Many people allergic to common wheat find kamut easier to digest.

Kanten
Light, soothing gelled dessert made with apple cider, agar & fruit

Kombu
Wide, thick, dark green sea vegetable, very high in vitamins A & C as well as potassium & calcium. Useful as a natural flavor & health enhancer.

Kukicha Tea
A satisfying cup with body & deep flavor, made from the roasted twigs of the tea plant. A digestive aid, "twig tea" has less than one quarter of the caffeine content of black tea.

Millet
A gluten-free small yellow grain with a nutty flavor, easy to digest & having a rich amino acid profile, millet is among the earliest cultivated grains.

Mirin
Ambrosial cooking wine, naturally brewed & fermented from sweet brown rice.

Miso
A protein-rich fermented paste made from soybeans, sea salt, koji & a grain; sweet & light to deep & hearty in taste depending on the grain used & the aging time. An invaluable digestive aid, miso is also known for reducing the effects of environmental pollution.

Mu 16 Tea
A distinctive combination of 16 plants & herbs with a natural sweetness from licorice root. Delicate, full-bodied & caffeine free, Mu tea is good for relieving tiredness.

Nori
Thin black or dark green crisp sheets of dried sea vegetable, with a delicate nutlike flavor & a fresh sea essence. Remarkably, nori contains more vitamin A than carrots & is 35.6% protein.

Quinoa *(KEEN-wha)*
A staple of the ancient Incas, who called it the Mother Grain, quinoa is light & fluffy & the highest source of protein of any grain.

Sea Palm
Domestic brown sea vegetable, mildly sweet with a pleasing al dente texture. Helps reduce cholesterol & supports normal thyroid function.

Seitan *(SAY-tan)*
Made from whole wheat flour, seitan is concentrated wheat protein. Succulent & chewy, it takes on the flavor of other ingredients with which it is cooked. At Angelica's, we make our own here, fresh on the premises.

Shoyu
Fermented nutritious flavor enhancer made from whole soybeans, salt, water & wheat koji. Shoyu provides richer seasoning with less salt, containing 1/7 the amount of sodium as plain salt.

Soba
Tan Japanese noodles made of buckwheat or a blend of buckwheat & whole wheat.

Spelt
An ancient red wheat. People with sensitivities to wheat often have a better tolerance for spelt because it contains a unique form of gluten that is easier to digest.

Tahini
Smooth, creamy high-protein paste made from hulled ground sesame seeds.

Teff
Tiny grain with giant nutritional superiority. Having a pleasing nutty flavor, teff boasts 12% protein & is especially high in calcium & iron.

Tempeh
A traditional Indonesian soy food, exceptionally high in protein; made into a firm cake from soybeans, water & special culture. One of the plant kingdom's richest sources of vitamin B12.

Tofu
Soybean curd made from fresh soymilk, then pressed into blocks. Fresh Tofu in Pennsylvania produces Angelica's tofu from non-hybridized New York State organically grown soybeans.

Udon
A light flat Japanese wheat noodle.

Umeboshi *(Ume)*
Salty, refreshingly sour, pickled plums that stimulate the appetite & enhance digestion.

Wakame
Long thin green sea vegetable with sweet taste & delicate texture. High in calcium & rich in iodine.

Rebecca Wood's <u>The New Whole Foods Encyclopedia</u> has been a great resource in compiling this glossary.

<u>The Angelica Home Kitchen</u> cookbook is available for purchase.

Gift Certificates Available

Gratuities will be added to parties of 6 or more.

www.angelicakitchen.com

Illustration at left by Tom Donald   Inside illustrations by Flavia Bacarella
Cover photograph by John Bigelow Taylor

Angelica Kitchen

Chapter 11 | Reading Eating

■ WHAT ELSE? WHAT'S NEXT?

1. Working with a group of classmates, develop a new menu item for Angelica Kitchen. The item you propose should fit with the restaurant's overall image and food philosophy. (For example, it wouldn't make any sense to propose a rare fillet of beef, would it?) After you've decided on your dish, write an appropriate name and menu description, and think about how you would propose this to the restaurant's owner for inclusion on the menu. You might need to consult some cookbooks or websites to come up with your dish, but have some fun and be creative. Take this chance to fill a gap in a menu or to propose something you'd really like to eat.

2. Using Angelica Kitchen's home page, as well as other publications that have written about the restaurant (you can find these online), gather some background about the business. Use the information you've found to write a brief profile of the restaurant, remembering to properly cite your sources. As you conduct your research, consider the following questions:

    - ■ How long has the restaurant been in business?
    - ■ What kind of business model does the restaurant have?
    - ■ What is the restaurant's mission?
    - ■ What kinds of advertising does the restaurant use? What kinds of affiliated merchandise does it sell?
    - ■ Who is the target demographic for the restaurant?
    - ■ What kinds of notices has the restaurant received?
    - ■ How does the restaurant seem to interact with its surrounding community?

3. Write a descriptive analysis of Angelica Kitchen's food and eating philosophy as it emerges from the menu's words, images, and document design. To generate ideas for your analysis, consider the following questions:

- How would you describe the menu as a visual document? Think, for example, about typography, including font selection; the kind, use and placement of images; and the use of space. Consider how each of these elements works separately and how they come together as a whole to produce a rhetorical effect.

- How is the menu organized? What kind of food narrative does it create?

- How does the menu try to connect with its customers? Think about the level of formality, about diction—including the names given to items on the menu—and about appeals to the customers' emotions and intellect.

- Based on reading the menu, what kind of dining experience would you expect if you went to this restaurant?

- What is the restaurant's ethos? In other words, how does the restaurant want to be perceived by its customers? And what does the menu do to convey this business persona?

- What is the restaurant's food philosophy or mission? Think about the actual food items the restaurant prepares and sells and about how the menu names and describes these items.

Chapter 11 | Reading Eating

Robert Paarlberg is B.F. Johnson professor of political science at Wellesley College, an associate at Harvard University's Weatherhead Center for International Affairs, and author of Food Politics: What Everyone Needs to Know. *He wrote this essay for the May/June 2010 edition of* Foreign Policy *magazine.*

BEFORE YOU READ
Research how other writers and/or organizations define and enact "food politics." What does the term mean to you?

ATTENTION WHOLE FOOD SHOPPERS
Robert Paarlberg

From Whole Foods recyclable cloth bags to Michelle Obama's organic White House garden, modern eco-foodies are full of good intentions. We want to save the planet. Help local farmers. Fight climate change—and childhood obesity, too. But though it's certainly a good thing to be thinking about global welfare while chopping our certified organic onions, the hope that we can help others by changing our shopping and eating habits is being wildly oversold to Western consumers. Food has become an elite preoccupation in the West, ironically, just as the most effective ways to address hunger in poor countries have fallen out of fashion.

Helping the world's poor feed themselves is no longer the rallying cry it once was. Food may be today's cause célèbre, but in the pampered West, that means trendy causes like making food "sustainable"—in other words, organic, local, and slow. Appealing as that might sound, it is the wrong recipe for helping those who need it the most. Even our understanding of the global food problem is wrong these days, driven too much by the single issue of international prices. In April 2008, when the cost of rice for export had tripled in just six months and wheat reached its highest price in 28 years, a *New York Times* editorial branded this a "World Food Crisis." World Bank President Robert Zoellick warned that high food prices would be particularly damaging in poor countries, where "there is no margin for survival." Now that international rice prices are down 40 percent from their peak and wheat prices have fallen by more than half, we too quickly conclude that the crisis is over. Yet 850 million people in poor countries were chronically undernourished before the 2008 price spike, and the number is even larger now, thanks in part to last year's global recession. This is the real food crisis we face.

It turns out that food prices on the world market tell us very little about global hunger. International markets for food, like most other international markets, are used most heavily by the well-to-do, who are far from hungry. The majority of truly undernourished people—62 percent, according to the U.N. Food and Agriculture Organization—live in either Africa or South Asia, and most are small farmers or rural landless laborers living in the countryside of Africa and South Asia. They are significantly shielded from global price fluctuations both by the trade policies of their own governments and by poor roads and infrastructure. In Africa, more than 70 percent of rural households are cut off from the closest urban markets because, for instance, they live more than a 30-minute walk from the nearest all-weather road.

Poverty—caused by the low income productivity of farmers' labor—is the primary source of hunger in Africa, and the problem is only getting worse. The number of "food insecure" people in Africa (those consuming less than 2,100 calories a day) will increase 30 percent over the next decade without significant reforms, to 645 million, the U.S. Agriculture Department projects.

What's so tragic about this is that we know from experience how to fix the problem. Wherever the rural poor have gained access to improved roads, modern seeds, less expensive fertilizer, electrical power, and better schools and clinics, their productivity and their income have increased. But recent efforts to deliver such essentials have been undercut by deeply misguided (if sometimes well-meaning) advocacy against agricultural modernization and foreign aid.

In Europe and the United States, a new line of thinking has emerged in elite circles that opposes bringing improved seeds and fertilizers to traditional farmers and opposes linking those farmers more closely to international markets. Influential food writers, advocates, and celebrity restaurant owners are repeating the mantra that "sustainable food" in the future must be organic, local, and slow. But guess what: rural Africa already has such a system, and it doesn't work. Few smallholder farmers in Africa use any synthetic chemicals, so their food is *de facto* organic. High transportation costs force them to purchase and sell almost all of their food locally. And food preparation is painfully slow. The result is nothing to celebrate: average income levels of only $1 a day and a one-in-three chance of being malnourished.

If we are going to get serious about solving global hunger, we need to de-romanticize our view of pre-industrial food and farming. And that means learning to appreciate the modern, science-intensive, and highly capitalized agricultural system we've developed in the West. Without it, our food would be more expensive and less safe. In other words, a lot like the hunger-plagued rest of the world.

■ Original Sins

Thirty years ago, had someone asserted in a prominent journal or newspaper that the Green Revolution was a failure, he or she would have been quickly dismissed. Today the charge is surprisingly common. Celebrity author and eco-activist Vandana Shiva claims the Green Revolution has brought nothing to India except "indebted and discontented farmers." A 2002 meeting in Rome of 500 prominent international NGOs, including Friends of the Earth and Greenpeace, even blamed the Green Revolution for the rise in world hunger. Let's set the record straight.

The development and introduction of high-yielding wheat and rice seeds into poor countries, led by American scientist Norman Borlaug and others in the 1960s and '70s, paid huge dividends. In Asia these new seeds lifted tens of millions of small farmers out of desperate poverty and finally ended the threat of periodic famine. India, for instance, doubled its wheat production between 1964 and 1970 and was able to terminate all dependence on international food aid by 1975. As for indebted and discontented farmers, India's rural poverty rate fell from 60 percent to just 27 percent today. Dismissing these great achievements as a "myth" (the official view of Food First, a California-based organization that campaigns globally against agricultural modernization) is just silly.

It's true that the story of the Green Revolution is not everywhere a happy one. When powerful new farming technologies are introduced into deeply unjust rural social systems, the poor tend to lose out. In Latin America, where access to good agricultural land and credit has been narrowly controlled by traditional elites, the improved seeds made available by the Green Revolution increased income gaps. Absentee landlords in Central America, who previously allowed peasants to plant subsistence crops on underutilized land, pushed them off to sell or rent the land to commercial growers who could turn a profit using the new seeds. Many of the displaced rural poor became slum dwellers. Yet even in Latin America, the prevalence of hunger declined more than 50 percent between 1980 and 2005.

In Asia, the Green Revolution seeds performed just as well on small non-mechanized farms as on larger farms. Wherever small farmers had sufficient access to credit, they took up the new technology just as quickly as big farmers, which led to dramatic income gains and no increase in inequality or social friction. Even poor landless laborers gained, because more abundant crops meant more work at harvest time, increasing rural wages. In Asia, the Green Revolution was good for both agriculture and social justice.

And Africa? Africa has a relatively equitable and secure distribution of land, making it more like Asia than Latin America and increasing the chances that improvements in farm technology will help the poor. If Africa were to put greater resources into farm technology, irrigation, and rural roads, small farmers would benefit.

■ Organic Myths

There are other common objections to doing what is necessary to solve the real hunger crisis. Most revolve around caveats that purist critics raise regarding food systems in the United States and Western Europe. Yet such concerns, though well-intentioned, are often misinformed and counterproductive—especially when applied to the developing world.

Take industrial food systems, the current bugaboo of American food writers. Yes, they have many unappealing aspects, but without them food would be not only less abundant but also less safe. Traditional food systems lacking in reliable refrigeration and sanitary packaging are dangerous vectors for diseases. Surveys over the past several decades by the Centers for Disease Control and Prevention have found that the U.S. food supply became steadily safer over time, thanks in part to the introduction of industrial-scale technical improvements. Since 2000, the incidence of E. coli contamination in beef has fallen 45 percent. Today in the United States, most hospitalizations and fatalities from unsafe food come not from sales of contaminated products at supermarkets, but from the mishandling or improper preparation of food inside the home. Illness outbreaks from contaminated foods sold in stores still occur, but the fatalities are typically quite limited. A nationwide scare over unsafe spinach in 2006 triggered the virtual suspension of all fresh and bagged spinach sales, but only three known deaths were recorded. Incidents such as these command attention in part because they are now so rare. Food Inc. should be criticized for filling our plates with too many foods that are unhealthy, but not foods that are unsafe.

Where industrial-scale food technologies have not yet reached into the developing world, contaminated food remains a major risk. In Africa, where many foods are still purchased in open-air markets (often uninspected, unpackaged, unlabeled, unrefrigerated, unpasteurized, and unwashed), an estimated 700,000 people die every year from food- and water-borne diseases, compared with an estimated 5,000 in the United States.

Food grown organically—that is, without any synthetic nitrogen fertilizers or pesticides—is not an answer to the health and safety issues. *The American Journal of Clinical Nutrition* last year published a study of 162 scientific papers from the past 50 years on the health benefits of organically grown foods and found no nutritional advantage over conventionally grown foods. According to the Mayo Clinic, "No conclusive evidence shows that organic food is more nutritious than is conventionally grown food."

Health professionals also reject the claim that organic food is safer to eat due to lower pesticide residues. Food and Drug Administration surveys have revealed that the highest dietary exposures to pesticide residues on foods in the United States are so trivial (less than one one-thousandth of a level that would cause toxicity) that the safety gains from buying organic are insignificant. Pesticide exposures remain a serious problem in the developing world, where farm chemical use is not as well regulated, yet even there they are more an occupational risk for unprotected farmworkers than a residue risk for food consumers.

When it comes to protecting the environment, assessments of organic farming become more complex. Excess nitrogen fertilizer use on conventional farms in the United States has polluted rivers and created a "dead zone" in the Gulf of Mexico, but halting synthetic nitrogen fertilizer use entirely (as farmers must do in the United States to get organic certification from the Agriculture Department) would cause environmental problems far worse.

Here's why: Less than 1 percent of American cropland is under certified organic production. If the other 99 percent were to switch to organic and had to fertilize crops without any synthetic nitrogen fertilizer, that would require a lot more composted animal manure. To supply enough organic fertilizer, the U.S. cattle population would have to increase roughly fivefold. And because those animals would have to be raised organically on forage crops, much of the land in the lower 48 states would need to be converted to pasture. Organic field crops also have lower yields per hectare. If Europe tried to feed itself organically, it would need an additional 28 million hectares of cropland, equal to all of the remaining forest cover in France, Germany, Britain, and Denmark combined.

Mass deforestation probably isn't what organic advocates intend. The smart way to protect against nitrogen runoff is to reduce synthetic fertilizer applications with taxes, regulations, and cuts in farm subsidies, but not try to go all the way to zero as required by the official organic standard. Scaling up registered organic farming would be on balance harmful, not helpful, to the natural environment.

Not only is organic farming less friendly to the environment than assumed, but modern conventional farming is becoming significantly more sustainable. High-tech farming in rich countries today is far safer for the environment, per bushel of production, than it was in the 1960s, when Rachel Carson criticized the indiscriminate farm use of DDT in her environmental classic, *Silent Spring*. Thanks in part to Carson's devastating critique, that era's most damaging insecticides were banned and replaced by chemicals that could be applied in lower volume and were less persistent in the environment. Chemical use in American agriculture peaked soon thereafter, in 1973. This was a major victory for environmental advocacy.

And it was just the beginning of what has continued as a significant greening of modern farming in the United States. Soil erosion on farms dropped sharply in the 1970s with the introduction of "no-till" seed planting, an innovation that also reduced dependence on diesel fuel because fields no longer had to be plowed every spring. Farmers then began conserving water by moving to drip irrigation and by leveling their fields with lasers to minimize wasteful runoff. In the 1990s, GPS equipment was added to tractors, autosteering the machines in straighter paths and telling farmers exactly where they were in the field to within one square meter, allowing precise adjustments in chemical use. Infrared sensors were brought in to detect the greenness of the crop, telling a farmer exactly how much more (or less) nitrogen might be needed as the growing season went forward. To reduce wasteful nitrogen use, equipment was developed that can insert fertilizers into the ground at exactly the depth needed and in perfect rows, only where it will be taken up by the plant roots.

These "precision farming" techniques have significantly reduced the environmental footprint of modern agriculture relative to the quantity of food being produced. In 2008, the Organization for Economic Cooperation and Development published a review of the "environmental performance of agriculture" in the world's 30 most advanced industrial countries—those with the most highly capitalized and science-intensive farming systems. The results showed that between 1990 and 2004, food production in these countries continued to increase (by 5 percent in volume), yet adverse environmental impacts were reduced in every category. The land area taken up by farming declined 4 percent, soil erosion from both wind and water fell, gross greenhouse gas emissions from farming declined 3 percent, and excessive nitrogen fertilizer use fell 17 percent. Biodiversity also improved, as increased numbers of crop varieties and livestock breeds came into use.

■ Seeding the Future

Africa faces a food crisis, but it's not because the continent's population is growing faster than its potential to produce food, as vintage Malthusians such as environmental advocate Lester Brown and advocacy organizations such as Population Action International would have it. Food production in Africa is vastly less than the region's known potential, and that is why so many millions are going hungry there. African farmers still use almost no fertilizer; only 4 percent of cropland has been improved with irrigation; and most of the continent's cropped area is not planted with seeds improved through scientific plant breeding, so cereal yields are only a fraction of what they could be. Africa is failing to keep up with population growth not because it has exhausted its potential, but instead because too little has been invested in reaching that potential.

One reason for this failure has been sharply diminished assistance from international donors. When agricultural modernization went out of fashion among elites in the developed world beginning in the 1980s, development assistance to farming in poor countries collapsed. Per capita food production in Africa was declining during the 1980s and 1990s and the number of hungry people on the continent was doubling, but the U.S. response was to withdraw development assistance and simply ship more food aid to Africa. Food aid doesn't help farmers become more productive—and it can create long-term dependency.

But in recent years, the dollar value of U.S. food aid to Africa has reached 20 times the dollar value of agricultural development assistance.

The alternative is right in front of us. Foreign assistance to support agricultural improvements has a strong record of success, when undertaken with purpose. In the 1960s, international assistance from the Rockefeller Foundation, the Ford Foundation, and donor governments led by the United States made Asia's original Green Revolution possible. U.S. assistance to India provided critical help in improving agricultural education, launching a successful agricultural extension service, and funding advanced degrees for Indian agricultural specialists at universities in the United States. The U.S. Agency for International Development, with the World Bank, helped finance fertilizer plants and infrastructure projects, including rural roads and irrigation. India could not have done this on its own—the country was on the brink of famine at the time and dangerously dependent on food aid. But instead of suffering a famine in 1975, as some naysayers had predicted, India that year celebrated a final and permanent end to its need for food aid.

Foreign assistance to farming has been a high-payoff investment everywhere, including Africa. The World Bank has documented average rates of return on investments in agricultural research in Africa of 35 percent a year, accompanied by significant reductions in poverty. Some research investments in African agriculture have brought rates of return estimated at 68 percent. Blind to these realities, the United States cut its assistance to agricultural research in Africa 77 percent between 1980 and 2006.

When it comes to Africa's growing hunger, governments in rich countries face a stark choice: They can decide to support a steady new infusion of financial and technical assistance to help local governments and farmers become more productive, or they can take a "worry later" approach and be forced to address hunger problems with increasingly expensive shipments of food aid. Development skeptics and farm modernization critics keep pushing us toward this unappealing second path. It's time for leaders with vision and political courage to push back.

Chapter 11 | **Reading Eating**

■ WHAT?

1. Summarize Paarlberg's argument in 100 words.
2. What, according to Paarlberg, is the world's "real hunger crisis"? How can it be solved?
3. Read "Declare Your Independence" by Joel Salatin (it's the last essay in this chapter). After considering the arguments Paarlberg and Salatin make, develop a list of points that each author might use to respond to the other's central claim. Whose piece do you find the more persuasive? Why?

■ WHAT ELSE? WHAT'S NEXT?

4. Paarlberg throws his support behind industrial food production: "If we are going to get serious about solving global hunger, we need to de-romanticize our view of preindustrial food and farming." Find at least two other sources that embrace industrial food production and that offer what you think are sound reasons for their positions. Summarize these, and explain why you find them to be reliable sources.

■ WHO CARES?

5. Why do you think Paarlberg mentions Whole Foods in the title and first paragraph so prominently even though his piece isn't about the grocery chain? What might this rhetorical choice say about his intended audience?

IMAGE 11.2
In his essay "Fear Factories," Matthew Scully writes: "Treating animals decently is like most obligations we face, somewhere between the most and the least important, a modest but essential requirement to living with integrity. And it's not a good sign when arguments are constantly turned to precisely how much is mandatory and how much, therefore, we can manage to avoid."

Chapter 11 | **Reading Eating**

Matthew Scully served as special assistant and deputy director of speechwriting to President George W. Bush and also wrote for vice presidents Dick Cheney and Dan Quayle. The author of Dominion: The Power of Man, the Suffering of Animals, and the Call to Mercy, *Scully wrote this essay for the May 23, 2005, issue of* The American Conservative *magazine.*

BEFORE YOU READ
Visit the website for The American Conservative *and, based on what you find there, characterize the audience that might have read Scully's essay.*

FEAR FACTORIES: THE CASE FOR COMPASSIONATE CONSERVATISM—FOR ANIMALS Matthew Scully

A few years ago I began a book about cruelty to animals and about factory farming in particular, problems that had been in the back of my mind for a long while. At the time I viewed factory farming as one of the lesser problems facing humanity—a small wrong on the grand scale of good and evil but too casually overlooked and too glibly excused.

This view changed as I acquainted myself with the details and saw a few typical farms up close. By the time I finished the book, I had come to view the abuses of industrial farming as a serious moral problem, a truly rotten business for good reason passed over in polite conversation. Little wrongs, when left unattended, can grow and spread to become grave wrongs, and precisely this had happened on our factory farms.

The result of these ruminations was *Dominion: The Power of Man, the Suffering of Animals, and the Call to Mercy*. And though my tome never quite hit the bestseller lists, there ought to be some special literary prize for a work highly recommended in both the *Wall Street Journal* and *Vegetarian Teen*. When you enjoy the accolades of PETA and *Policy Review*, Deepak Chopra and Gordon Liddy, Peter Singer and Charles Colson, you can at least take comfort in the diversity of your readership.

The book also provided an occasion for fellow conservatives to get beyond their dislike for particular animal-rights groups and to examine cruelty issues on the merits. Conservatives have a way of dismissing the subject, as if where animals are concerned nothing very serious could ever be at stake. And though it is not exactly true that liberals care more about these issues—you are no more likely to find reflections or exposés concerning cruelty in *The Nation* or *The New Republic* than in any journal of the Right—it is assumed that animal-protection causes are a project of the Left, and that the proper conservative position is to stand warily and firmly against them.

I had a hunch that the problem was largely one of presentation and that by applying their own principles to animal-welfare issues conservatives would find plenty of reasons to be appalled. More to the point, having acknowledged the problems of cruelty, we could then support reasonable remedies. Conservatives, after all, aren't shy about discoursing on moral standards or reluctant to translate the most basic of those standards into law. Setting aside the distracting rhetoric of animal rights, that's usually what these questions come down to: what moral standards should guide us in our treatment of animals, and when must those standards be applied in law?

Industrial livestock farming is among a whole range of animal-welfare concerns that extends from canned trophy-hunting to whaling to product testing on animals to all sorts of more obscure enterprises like the exotic-animal trade and the factory farming of bears in China for bile believed to hold medicinal and aphrodisiac powers. Surveying the various uses to which animals are put, some might be defensible, others abusive and unwarranted, and it's the job of any conservative who attends to the subject to figure out which are which. We don't need novel theories of rights to do this. The usual distinctions that conservatives draw between moderation and excess, freedom and license, moral goods and material goods, rightful power and the abuse of power, will all do just fine.

As it is, the subject hardly comes up at all among conservatives, and what commentary we do hear usually takes the form of ridicule directed at animal-rights groups. Often conservatives side instinctively with any animal-related industry and those involved, as if a thing is right just because someone can make money off it or as if our sympathies belong always with the men just because they are men.

I had an exchange once with an eminent conservative columnist on this subject. Conversation turned to my book and to factory farming. Holding his hands out in the "stop" gesture, he said, "I don't want to know." Granted, life on the factory farm is no one's favorite subject, but conservative writers often have to think about things that are disturbing or sad. In this case, we have an intellectually formidable fellow known to millions for his stern judgments on every matter of private morality and public policy. Yet nowhere in all his writings do I find any treatment of any cruelty issue, never mind that if you asked him he would surely agree that cruelty to animals is a cowardly and disgraceful sin.

And when the subject is cruelty to farmed animals—the moral standards being applied in a fundamental human enterprise—suddenly we're in forbidden territory and "I don't want to know" is the best he can do. But don't we have a responsibility to know? Maybe the whole subject could use his fine mind and his good heart.

As for the rights of animals, rights in general are best viewed in tangible terms, with a view to actual events and consequences. Take the case of a hunter in Texas named John Lockwood, who has just pioneered the online safari. At his canned-hunting ranch outside San Antonio, he's got a rifle attached to a camera and the camera wired up to the Internet, so that sportsmen going to Live-shot.com will actually be able to fire at baited animals by remote control from their computers. "If the customer were to wound the animal," explains the *San Antonio Express-News*, "a staff person on site could finish it off." The "trophy mounts" taken in these heroics will then be prepared and shipped to the client's door, and if it catches on Lockwood will be a rich man.

Very much like animal farming today, the hunting "industry" has seen a collapse in ethical standards, and only in such an atmosphere could Lockwood have found inspiration for this latest innovation—denying wild animals the last shred of respect. Under the laws of Texas and other states, Lockwood and others in his business use all sorts of methods once viewed as shameful: baits, blinds, fences to trap hunted animals in ranches that advertise a "100-percent-guaranteed kill." Affluent hunters like to unwind by shooting cage-reared

Chapter 11 | Reading Eating

pheasants, ducks, and other birds, firing away as the fowl of the air are released before them like skeet, with no limit on the day's kill. Hunting supply stores are filled with lures, infrared lights, high-tech scopes, and other gadgetry to make every man a marksman.

Lockwood doesn't hear anyone protesting those methods, except for a few of those nutty activist types. Why shouldn't he be able to offer paying customers this new hunting experience as well? It is like asking a smut-peddler to please have the decency to keep children out of it. Lockwood is just one step ahead of the rest, and there is no standard of honor left to stop him.

First impressions are usually correct in questions of cruelty to animals, and here most of us would agree that Live-shot.com does not show our fellow man at his best. We would say that the whole thing is a little tawdry and even depraved, that the creatures Lockwood has "in stock" are not just commodities. We would say that these animals deserve better than the fate he has in store for them.

As is invariably the case in animal-rights issues, what we're really looking for are safeguards against cruel and presumptuous people. We are trying to hold people to their obligations, people who could spare us the trouble if only they would recognize a few limits on their own conduct.

Conservatives like the sound of "obligation" here, and those who reviewed *Dominion* were relieved to find me arguing more from this angle than from any notion of rights. "What the PETA crowd doesn't understand," Jonah Goldberg wrote, "or what it deliberately confuses, is that human compassion toward animals is an obligation of humans, not an entitlement for animals." Another commentator put the point in religious terms: "[W]e have a moral duty to respect the animal world as God's handiwork, treating animals with 'the mercy of our Maker' ... But mercy and respect for animals are completely different from rights for animals—and we should never confuse the two." Both writers confessed they were troubled by factory farming and concluded with the uplifting thought that we could all profit from further reflection on our obligation of kindness to farm animals.

The only problem with this insistence on obligation is that after a while it begins to sounds like a hedge against actually being held to that obligation. It leaves us with a high-minded attitude but no accountability, free to act on our obligations or to ignore them without consequences, personally opposed to cruelty but unwilling to impose that view on others.

Treating animals decently is like most obligations we face, somewhere between the most and the least important, a modest but essential requirement to living with integrity. And it's not a good sign when arguments are constantly turned to precisely how much is mandatory and how much, therefore, we can manage to avoid.

If one is using the word "obligation" seriously, moreover, then there is no practical difference between an obligation on our end not to mistreat animals and an entitlement on their end not to be mistreated by us. Either way, we are required to do and not do the same things. And either way, somewhere down the logical line, the entitlement would have to arise from a recognition of the inherent dignity of a living creature. The moral standing of our fellow creatures may be humble, but it is absolute and not something within our power to confer or withhold. All creatures sing their Creator's praises, as this truth is variously expressed in the Bible, and are dear to Him for their own sakes.

A certain moral relativism runs through the arguments of those hostile or indifferent to animal welfare—as if animals can be of value only for our sake, as utility or preference decrees. In practice, this outlook leaves each person to decide for himself when animals rate moral concern. It even allows us to accept or reject such knowable facts about animals as their cognitive and emotional capacities, their conscious experience of pain and happiness.

Elsewhere in contemporary debates, conservatives meet the foe of moral relativism by pointing out that, like it or not, we are all dealing with the same set of physiological realities and moral truths. We don't each get to decide the facts of science on a situational basis. We do not each go about bestowing moral value upon things as it pleases us at the moment. Of course, we do not decide moral truth at all: we discern it. Human beings in their moral progress learn to appraise things correctly, using reasoned moral judgment to perceive a prior order not of our devising.

C.S. Lewis in *The Abolition of Man* calls this "the doctrine of objective value, the belief that certain attitudes are really true, and others really false, to the kind of thing the universe is and the kind of things we are." Such words as honor, piety, esteem, and empathy do not merely describe subjective states of mind, Lewis reminds us, but speak to objective qualities in the world beyond that merit those attitudes in us. "[T]o call children delightful or old men venerable," he writes, "is not simply to record a psychological fact about our own parental or filial emotions at the moment, but to recognize a quality which demands a certain response from us whether we make it or not."

This applies to questions of cruelty as well. A kindly attitude toward animals is not a subjective sentiment; it is the correct moral response to the objective value of a fellow creature. Here, too, rational and virtuous conduct consists in giving things their due and in doing so consistently. If one animal's pain—say, that of one's pet—is real and deserving of sympathy, then the pain of essentially identical animals is also meaningful, no matter what conventional distinctions we have made to narrow the scope of our sympathy. If it is wrong to whip a dog or starve a horse or bait bears for sport or grossly abuse farm animals, it is wrong for all people in every place.

The problem with moral relativism is that it leads to capriciousness and the despotic use of power. And the critical distinction here is not between human obligations and animal rights, but rather between obligations of charity and obligations of justice.

Active kindness to animals falls into the former category. If you take in strays or help injured wildlife or donate to animal charities, those are fine things to do, but no one says you should be compelled to do them. Refraining from cruelty to animals is a different matter, an obligation of justice not for us each to weigh for ourselves. It is not simply unkind behavior, it is unjust behavior, and the prohibition against it is non-negotiable. Proverbs reminds us of this—"a righteous man regardeth the life of his beast, but the tender mercies of the wicked are cruel"—and the laws of America and of every other advanced nation now recognize the wrongfulness of such conduct with our cruelty statutes. Often applying felony-level penalties to protect certain domestic animals, these state and federal statutes declare that even though your animal may elsewhere in the law be defined as your property, there are certain things you may not do to that creature, and if you are found harming or neglecting the animal, you will answer for your conduct in a court of justice.

There are various reasons the state has an interest in forbidding cruelty, one of which is that cruelty is degrading to human beings. The problem is that many thinkers on this

Chapter 11 | **Reading Eating**

subject have strained to find indirect reasons to explain why cruelty is wrong and thereby to force animal cruelty into the category of the victimless crime. The most common of these explanations asks us to believe that acts of cruelty matter only because the cruel person does moral injury to himself or sullies his character—as if the man is our sole concern and the cruelly treated animal is entirely incidental.

Once again, the best test of theory is a real-life example. In 2002, Judge Alan Glenn of Tennessee's Court of Criminal Appeals heard the case of a married couple named Johnson, who had been found guilty of cruelty to 350 dogs lying sick, starving, or dead in their puppy-mill kennel—a scene videotaped by police. Here is Judge Glenn's response to their supplications for mercy:

> The victims of this crime were animals that could not speak up to the unbelievable conduct of Judy Fay Johnson and Stanley Paul Johnson that they suffered. Several of the dogs have died and most had physical problems such as intestinal worms, mange, eye problems, dental problems and emotional problems and socialization problems ... . Watching this video of the conditions that these dogs were subjected to was one of the most deplorable things this Court has observed. ...
>
> [T]his Court finds that probation would not serve the ends of justice, nor be in the best interest of the public, nor would this have a deterrent effect for such gross behavior. ... The victims were particularly vulnerable. You treated the victims with exceptional cruelty. ...
>
> There are those who would argue that you should be confined in a house trailer with no ventilation or in a cell three-by-seven with eight or ten other inmates with no plumbing, no exercise and no opportunity to feel the sun or smell fresh air. However, the courts of this land have held that such treatment is cruel and inhuman, and it is. You will not be treated in the same way that you treated these helpless animals that you abused to make a dollar.

Only in abstract debates of moral or legal theory would anyone quarrel with Judge Glenn's description of the animals as "victims" or deny that they were entitled to be treated better. Whether we call this a "right" matters little, least of all to the dogs, since the only right that any animal could possibly exercise is the right to be free from human abuse, neglect, or, in a fine old term of law, other "malicious mischief." What matters most is that prohibitions against human cruelty be hard and binding. The sullied souls of the Johnsons are for the Johnsons to worry about. The business of justice is to punish their offense and to protect the creatures from human wrongdoing. And in the end, just as in other matters of morality and justice, the interests of man are served by doing the right thing for its own sake.

There is only one reason for condemning cruelty that doesn't beg the question of exactly why cruelty is a wrong, a vice, or bad for our character: that the act of cruelty is an intrinsic evil. Animals cruelly dealt with are not just things, not just an irrelevant detail in some self-centered moral drama of our own. They matter in their own right, as they matter to their Creator, and the wrongs of cruelty are wrongs done to them. As *The Catholic Encyclopedia* puts this point, there is a "direct and essential sinfulness of cruelty to the animal world, irrespective of the results of such conduct on the character of those who practice it."

Our cruelty statutes are a good and natural development in Western law, codifying the claims of animals against human wrongdoing, and, with the wisdom of men like Judge Glenn, asserting those claims on their behalf. Such statutes, however, address mostly random or wanton acts of cruelty. And the persistent animal-welfare questions of our day center on institutional cruelties—on the vast and systematic mistreatment of animals that most of us never see.

Having conceded the crucial point that some animals rate our moral concern and legal protection, informed conscience turns naturally to other animals—creatures entirely comparable in their awareness, feeling, and capacity for suffering. A dog is not the moral equal of a human being, but a dog is definitely the moral equal of a pig, and it's only human caprice and economic convenience that say otherwise. We have the problem that these essentially similar creatures are treated in dramatically different ways, unjustified even by the very different purposes we have assigned to them. Our pets are accorded certain protections from cruelty, while the nameless creatures in our factory farms are hardly treated like animals at all. The challenge is one of consistency, of treating moral equals equally, and living according to fair and rational standards of conduct.

Whatever terminology we settle on, after all the finer philosophical points have been hashed over, the aim of the exercise is to prohibit wrongdoing. All rights, in practice, are protections against human wrongdoing, and here too the point is to arrive at clear and consistent legal boundaries on the things that one may or may not do to animals, so that every man is not left to be the judge in his own case.

More than obligation, moderation, ordered liberty, or any of the other lofty ideals we hold, what should attune conservatives to all the problems of animal cruelty—and especially to the modern factory farm—is our worldly side. The great virtue of conservatism is that it begins with a realistic assessment of human motivations. We know man as he is, not only the rational creature but also, as Socrates told us, the rationalizing creature, with a knack for finding an angle, an excuse, and a euphemism. Whether it's the pornographer who thinks himself a free-speech champion or the abortionist who looks in the mirror and sees a reproductive health-care services provider, conservatives are familiar with the type.

So we should not be all that surprised when told that these very same capacities are often at work in the things that people do to animals—and all the more so in our $125 billion a year livestock industry. The human mind, especially when there is money to be had, can manufacture grand excuses for the exploitation of other human beings. How much easier it is for people to excuse the wrongs done to lowly animals.

Where animals are concerned, there is no practice or industry so low that someone, somewhere, cannot produce a high-sounding reason for it. The sorriest little miscreant who shoots an elephant, lying in wait by the water hole in some canned-hunting operation, is just "harvesting resources," doing his bit for "conservation." The swarms of government-subsidized Canadian seal hunters slaughtering tens of thousands of newborn pups—hacking to death these unoffending creatures, even in sight of their mothers—offer themselves as the brave and independent bearers of tradition. With the same sanctimony and deep dishonesty, factory-farm corporations like Smithfield Foods, ConAgra, and Tyson Foods still cling to countrified brand names for their labels—Clear Run Farms, Murphy Family

Chapter 11 | **Reading Eating**

Farms, Happy Valley—to convince us and no doubt themselves, too, that they are engaged in something essential, wholesome, and honorable.

Yet when corporate farmers need barbed wire around their Family Farms and Happy Valleys and laws to prohibit outsiders from taking photographs (as is the case in two states) and still other laws to exempt farm animals from the definition of "animals" as covered in federal and state cruelty statutes, something is amiss. And if conservatives do nothing else about any other animal issue, we should attend at least to the factory farms, where the suffering is immense and we are all asked to be complicit.

If we are going to have our meats and other animal products, there are natural costs to obtaining them, defined by the duties of animal husbandry and of veterinary ethics. Factory farming came about when resourceful men figured out ways of getting around those natural costs, applying new technologies to raise animals in conditions that would otherwise kill them by deprivation and disease. With no laws to stop it, moral concern surrendered entirely to economic calculation, leaving no limit to the punishments that factory farmers could inflict to keep costs down and profits up. Corporate farmers hardly speak anymore of "raising" animals, with the modicum of personal care that word implies. Animals are "grown" now, like so many crops. Barns somewhere along the way became "intensive confinement facilities" and the inhabitants mere "production units."

The result is a world in which billions of birds, cows, pigs, and other creatures are locked away, enduring miseries they do not deserve, for our convenience and pleasure. We belittle the activists with their radical agenda, scarcely noticing the radical cruelty they seek to redress.

At the Smithfield mass-confinement hog farms I toured in North Carolina, the visitor is greeted by a bedlam of squealing, chain rattling, and horrible roaring. To maximize the use of space and minimize the need for care, the creatures are encased row after row, 400 to 500 pound mammals trapped without relief inside iron crates seven feet long and 22 inches wide. They chew maniacally on bars and chains, as foraging animals will do when denied straw, or engage in stereotypical nest-building with the straw that isn't there, or else just lie there like broken beings. The spirit of the place would be familiar to police who raided that Tennessee puppy-mill run by Stanley and Judy Johnson, only instead of 350 tortured animals, millions—and the law prohibits none of it.

Efforts to outlaw the gestation crate have been dismissed by various conservative critics as "silly," "comical," "ridiculous." It doesn't seem that way up close. The smallest scraps of human charity—a bit of maternal care, room to roam outdoors, straw to lie on—have long since been taken away as costly luxuries, and so the pigs know the feel only of concrete and metal. They lie covered in their own urine and excrement, with broken legs from trying to escape or just to turn, covered with festering sores, tumors, ulcers, lesions, or what my guide shrugged off as the routine "pus pockets."

C.S. Lewis's description of animal pain—"begun by Satan's malice and perpetrated by man's desertion of his post"—has literal truth in our factory farms because they basically run themselves through the wonders of automation, and the owners are off in spacious corporate offices reviewing their spreadsheets. Rarely are the creatures' afflictions examined by a vet or even noticed by the migrant laborers charged with their care, unless of course some ailment threatens production—meaning who cares about a lousy ulcer or broken leg, as long as we're still getting the piglets?

Kept alive in these conditions only by antibiotics, hormones, laxatives, and other additives mixed into their machine-fed swill, the sows leave their crates only to be driven or dragged into other crates, just as small, to bring forth their piglets. Then it's back to the gestation crate for another four months, and so on back and forth until after seven or eight pregnancies they finally expire from the punishment of it or else are culled with a club or bolt-gun.

As you can see at www.factoryfarming.com/gallery.htm, industrial livestock farming operates on an economy of scale, presupposing a steady attrition rate. The usual comforting rejoinder we hear—that it's in the interest of farmers to take good care of their animals—is false. Each day, in every confinement farm in America, you will find cull pens littered with dead or dying creatures discarded like trash.

For the piglets, it's a regimen of teeth cutting, tail docking (performed with pliers, to heighten the pain of tail chewing and so deter this natural response to mass confinement), and other mutilations. After five or six months trapped in one of the grim warehouses that now pass for barns, they're trucked off, 355,000 pigs every day in the life of America, for processing at a furious pace of thousands per hour by migrants who use earplugs to muffle the screams. All of these creatures, and billions more across the earth, go to their deaths knowing nothing of life, and nothing of man, except the foul, tortured existence of the factory farm, having never even been outdoors.

But not to worry, as a Smithfield Foods executive assured me, "They love it." It's all "for their own good." It is a voice conservatives should instantly recognize, as we do when it tells us that the fetus feels nothing. Everything about the picture shows bad faith, moral sloth, and endless excuse-making, all readily answered by conservative arguments.

We are told "they're just pigs" or cows or chickens or whatever and that only urbanites worry about such things, estranged as they are from the realities of rural life. Actually, all of factory farming proceeds by a massive denial of reality—the reality that pigs and other animals are not just production units to be endlessly exploited but living creatures with natures and needs. The very modesty of those needs—their humble desires for straw, soil, sunshine—is the gravest indictment of the men who deny them.

Conservatives are supposed to revere tradition. Factory farming has no traditions, no rules, no codes of honor, no little decencies to spare for a fellow creature. The whole thing is an abandonment of rural values and a betrayal of honorable animal husbandry—to say nothing of veterinary medicine, with its sworn oath to "protect animal health" and to "relieve animal suffering."

Likewise, we are told to look away and think about more serious things. Human beings simply have far bigger problems to worry about than the well being of farm animals, and surely all of this zeal would be better directed at causes of human welfare.

You wouldn't think that men who are unwilling to grant even a few extra inches in cage space, so that a pig can turn around, would be in any position to fault others for pettiness. Why are small acts of kindness beneath us, but not small acts of cruelty? The larger problem with this appeal to moral priority, however, is that we are dealing with suffering that occurs through human agency. Whether it's miserliness here, carelessness

Chapter 11 | Reading Eating

there, or greed throughout, the result is rank cruelty for which particular people must answer.

Since refraining from cruelty is an obligation of justice, moreover, there is no avoiding the implications. All the goods invoked in defense of factory farming, from the efficiency and higher profits of the system to the lower costs of the products, are false goods unjustly derived. No matter what right and praiseworthy things we are doing elsewhere in life, when we live off a cruel and disgraceful thing like factory farming, we are to that extent living unjustly, and that is hardly a trivial problem.

For the religious-minded, and Catholics in particular, no less an authority than Pope Benedict XVI has explained the spiritual stakes. Asked recently to weigh in on these very questions, Cardinal Ratzinger told German journalist Peter Seewald that animals must be respected as our "companions in creation." While it is licit to use them for food, "we cannot just do whatever we want with them. ... Certainly, a sort of industrial use of creatures, so that geese are fed in such a way as to produce as large a liver as possible, or hens live so packed together that they become just caricatures of birds, this degrading of living creatures to a commodity seems to me in fact to contradict the relationship of mutuality that comes across in the Bible."

Factory farmers also assure us that all of this is an inevitable stage of industrial efficiency. Leave aside the obvious reply that we could all do a lot of things in life more efficiently if we didn't have to trouble ourselves with ethical restraints. Leave aside, too, the tens of billions of dollars in annual federal subsidies that have helped megafarms undermine small family farms and the decent communities that once surrounded them and to give us the illusion of cheap products. And never mind the collateral damage to land, water, and air that factory farms cause and the more billions of dollars it costs taxpayers to clean up after them. Factory farming is a predatory enterprise, absorbing profit and externalizing costs, unnaturally propped up by political influence and government subsidies much as factory-farmed animals are unnaturally sustained by hormones and antibiotics.

Even if all the economic arguments were correct, conservatives usually aren't impressed by breathless talk of inevitable progress. I am asked sometimes how a conservative could possibly care about animal suffering in factory farms, but the question is premised on a liberal caricature of conservatism—the assumption that, for all of our fine talk about moral values, "compassionate conservatism" and the like, everything we really care about can be counted in dollars. In the case of factory farming, and the conservative's blithe tolerance of it, the caricature is too close to the truth.

Exactly how far are we all prepared to follow these industrial and technological advances before pausing to take stock of where things stand and where it is all tending? Very soon companies like Smithfield plan to have tens of millions of cloned animals in their factory farms. Other companies are at work genetically engineering chickens without feathers so that one day all poultry farmers might be spared the toil and cost of de-feathering their birds. For years, the many shills for our livestock industry employed in the "Animal Science" and "Meat Science" departments of rural universities (we used to call them Animal Husbandry departments) have been tampering with the genes of pigs and other animals to locate and expunge that part of their genetic makeup that makes them stressed in factory farm conditions—taking away the desire to protect themselves and to live. Instead of redesigning the factory farm to suit the animals, they are redesigning the animals to suit the factory farm.

Are there no boundaries of nature and elementary ethics that the conservative should be the first to see? The hubris of such projects is beyond belief, only more because of the foolish and frivolous goods to be gained—blood-free meats and the perfect pork chop.

No one who does not profit from them can look at our modern factory farms or frenzied slaughter plants or agricultural laboratories with their featherless chickens and fear-free pigs and think, "Yes, this is humanity at our finest—exactly as things should be." Devils charged with designing a farm could hardly have made it more severe. Least of all should we look for sanction in Judeo-Christian morality, whose whole logic is one of gracious condescension, of the proud learning to be humble, the higher serving the lower, and the strong protecting the weak.

Those religious conservatives who, in every debate over animal welfare, rush to remind us that the animals themselves are secondary and man must come first are exactly right—only they don't follow their own thought to its moral conclusion. Somehow, in their pious notions of stewardship and dominion, we always seem to end up with singular moral dignity but no singular moral accountability to go with it.

Lofty talk about humanity's special status among creatures only invites such questions as: what would the Good Shepherd make of our factory farms? Where does the creature of conscience get off lording it over these poor creatures so mercilessly? "How is it possible," as Malcolm Muggeridge asked in the years when factory farming began to spread, "to look for God and sing his praises while insulting and degrading his creatures? If, as I had thought, all lambs are the Agnus Dei, then to deprive them of light and the field and their joyous frisking and the sky is the worst kind of blasphemy."

The writer B.R. Meyers remarked in *The Atlantic*, "research could prove that cows love Jesus, and the line at the McDonald's drive-through wouldn't be one sagging carload shorter the next day …. Has any generation in history ever been so ready to cause so much suffering for such a trivial advantage? We deaden our consciences to enjoy—for a few minutes a day—the taste of blood, the feel of our teeth meeting through muscle."

That is a cynical but serious indictment, and we must never let it be true of us in the choices we each make or urge upon others. If reason and morality are what set human beings apart from animals, then reason and morality must always guide us in how we treat them, or else it's all just caprice, unbridled appetite with the pretense of piety. When people say that they like their pork chops, veal, or foie gras just too much ever to give them up, reason hears in that the voice of gluttony, willfulness, or at best moral complaisance. What makes a human being human is precisely the ability to understand that the suffering of an animal is more important than the taste of a treat.

Of the many conservatives who reviewed *Dominion*, every last one conceded that factory farming is a wretched business and a betrayal of human responsibility. So it should be a short step to agreement that it also constitutes a serious issue of law and public policy. Having granted that certain practices are abusive, cruel, and wrong, we must be prepared actually to do something about them.

Among animal activists, of course, there are some who go too far—there are in the best of causes. But fairness requires that we judge a cause by its best advocates instead of making straw men of the worst. There isn't much money in championing the cause of animals, so we're dealing with some pretty altruistic people who on that account alone deserve the benefit of the doubt.

If we're looking for fitting targets for inquiry and scorn, for people with an angle and a truly pernicious influence, better to start with groups like Smithfield Foods (my candidate for the worst corporation in America in its ruthlessness to people and animals alike), the National Pork Producers Council (a reliable Republican contributor), or the various think tanks in Washington subsidized by animal-use industries for intellectual cover.

After the last election, the National Pork Producers Council rejoiced, "President Bush's victory ensures that the U.S. pork industry will be very well positioned for the next four years politically, and pork producers will benefit from the long-term results of a livestock agriculture-friendly agenda." But this is no tribute. And millions of good people who live in what's left of America's small family-farm communities would themselves rejoice if the president were to announce that he is prepared to sign a bipartisan bill making some basic reforms in livestock agriculture.

Bush's new agriculture secretary, former Nebraska Gov. Mike Johanns, has shown a sympathy for animal welfare. He and the president might both be surprised at the number and variety of supporters such reforms would find in the Congress, from Republicans like Chris Smith and Elton Gallegly in the House to John Ensign and Rick Santorum in the Senate, along with Democrats such as Robert Byrd, Barbara Boxer, or the North Carolina congressman who called me in to say that he, too, was disgusted and saddened by hog farming in his state.

If such matters were ever brought to President Bush's attention in a serious way, he would find in the details of factory farming many things abhorrent to the Christian heart and to his own kindly instincts. Even if he were to drop into relevant speeches a few of the prohibited words in modern industrial agriculture (cruel, humane, compassionate), instead of endlessly flattering corporate farmers for virtues they lack, that alone would help to set reforms in motion.

We need our conservative values voters to get behind a Humane Farming Act so that we can all quit averting our eyes. This reform, a set of explicit federal cruelty statutes with enforcement funding to back it up, would leave us with farms we could imagine without wincing, photograph without prosecution, and explain without excuses.

The law would uphold not only the elementary standards of animal husbandry but also of veterinary ethics, following no more complicated a principle than that pigs and cows should be able to walk and turn around, fowl to move about and spread their wings, and all creatures to know the feel of soil and grass and the warmth of the sun. No need for labels saying "free-range" or "humanely raised." They will all be raised that way. They all get to be treated like animals and not as unfeeling machines.

On a date certain, mass confinement, sow gestation crates, veal crates, battery cages, and all such innovations would be prohibited. This will end livestock agriculture's moral race to the bottom and turn the ingenuity of its scientists toward compassionate solutions. It will remove the federal support that unnaturally serves agribusiness at the expense of small farms. And it will shift economies of scale, turning the balance in favor of humane farmers—as those who run companies like Wal-Mart could do right now by taking their business away from factory farms.

In all cases, the law would apply to corporate farmers a few simple rules that better men would have been observing all along: we cannot just take from these creatures, we must give them something in return. We owe them a merciful death, and we owe them a merciful life. And when human beings cannot do something humanely, without degrading both the creatures and ourselves, then we should not do it at all.

■ WHAT?

1. How does Scully build and support his case that cruelty to animals, especially in the factory farming system, should be a conservative cause?
2. In his essay, Scully writes: "If reason and morality are what set human beings apart from animals, then reason and morality must always guide us in how we treat them, or else it's all just caprice, unbridled appetite with the pretense of piety." What do you think Scully means by this? Do you agree with him? Explain your response.
3. Where does Scully stand on the "rights" of animals? Point to specific passages from his essay to support your response.

■ WHAT ELSE? WHAT'S NEXT?

4. What do other conservative writers and commentators have to say about the issue of animal rights? Find at least three sources that address the issue from a conservative point of view but that offer different perspectives otherwise. Compile these into an annotated bibliography, following MLA guidelines.

■ WHO CARES?

5. Read through the essay and identify the sources that Scully uses to support his argument. Why do you think he chose these particular people and publications? How do these sources help him reach his intended audience?

Molly J. Dahm and Amy R. Shows are on the faculty of the Department of Family and Consumer Sciences at Lamar University in Beaumont, Texas. Aurelia V. Samonte works with Buckner Children and Family Services in Beaumont. They wrote this article for the Journal of American College Health *in 2009.*

BEFORE YOU READ
Find out some basic information about the "organic" label. What does it mean when a food product is labeled "organic"? Who sets the standards? Is there disagreement over how such food is labeled?

ORGANIC FOODS: DO ECO-FRIENDLY ATTITUDES PREDICT ECO-FRIENDLY BEHAVIORS?

Molly J. Dahm, Aurelia V. Samonte, and Amy R. Shows

Consumption of Organic Foods

New research and mounting public interest have increased global awareness of organic food products. The primary consumers of organic food are women aged 30 to 45 who have children in the household and who are environmentally conscious.[1,2] However, interest in organic foods along with a sense of responsibility for the environment is growing among younger people, specifically college students, who are likely to identify issues that will influence their attitudes and activities in the future. Purchase and consumption of organic foods is another positive socially conscious behavior.[3]

One way universities in the United States have responded to students' increased interest in the environment is by adding organic foods to their menus. In fact, the presence of organic foods may ultimately factor into a student's choice of school.[4] Purchase and consumption of organic foods is one way students can practice eco-friendly behaviors. Eco-friendly behaviors might also be referred to as environmentally conscious behaviors, or "green consumption," e.g., legitimate means of exhibiting environmentally safe and responsible behaviors.[1] Other eco-friendly practices include recycling, energy conservation, water conservation, driving hybrid cars or carpooling, and ozone protection.

In this study, we examined the awareness (knowledge), attitudes, and behaviors of university students towards organic foods. We also attempted to determine if positive attitudes about organic foods and other environmental issues would predict consumption of organic foods and other healthy and eco-friendly practices.

Federal Standards for Organic Foods

The United States Department of Agriculture (USDA) informs consumers that the terms natural and organic are not interchangeable.[5] "Natural" refers to products without artificial flavorings, colorings, or chemical preservatives and minimal processing.[5] The USDA defines "organic foods" as products grown without the use of pesticides, synthetic fertilizers, sewage sludge, genetically modified organisms, or ionizing radiation.[5] The agency also requires that organic meat, poultry, eggs, and dairy products be produced from animals free of antibiotics or growth hormones.[6] The term "organic" is increasingly recognized as a trusted symbol of eco-friendly products.[7] Companies that handle or process organic foods for public consumption must be certified by the USDA.[5] The USDA Organic Seal (Figure 1) exhibits evidence of this certification.

Consumers who want to buy organic products should be able to correctly identify them. The USDA's label standards for organic products include 100% Organic (made with 100% organic ingredients); the word organic or the organic seal (95% organic); made with organic ingredients (minimum of 70% organic ingredients); and organic ingredients listed on the side panel (less than 70% organic ingredients).[5,6]

Other certification programs, such as Oregon's eco-labeling program and the system of integrated management (SIM) in Greece, promote eco-friendly products to consumers.[7] Loureiro et al.[8] studied consumers' level of awareness of certified products using eco-labeled apples and found that although general level of awareness about organic products was high (86%), awareness of the label meaning was limited.

Consumer Attitudes and Behaviors

Much of the current research about consumer attitudes and behaviors regarding organic foods has been conducted outside the United States, where scholars have noted consumer trust in organic products. In a Swedish study, attitudes towards and purchase of organic foods were strongly related to the perceived human health benefits of those foods.[2] Researchers in the United Kingdom found the term "organic" had emotional resonance for consumers in terms of personal well-being, health, benefits to the environment, and a healthy diet.[9,10]

FIGURE 1. USDA Organic Seal

Chapter 11 | **Reading Eating**

As attitudes towards organic products evolve, values play an important but mixed role in how organic products are perceived.[11,12] Dreezens et al.[12] indicated that organic foods were viewed positively and associated with the values of welfare for all people and protection of nature. By contrast, Chryssohoidis and Krystallis[11] found that external values such as belonging to society were less important to consumers who purchased organic foods than internal values such as self-respect and enjoyment of life.

Consumer perception of appearance, taste, and texture of organic foods varies. In Northern Ireland, a focus group found organic products bland and lacking in color, yet stated that some organic foods, especially mixed vegetables, had desirable texture and flavor.[13] Researchers in the United Kingdom and Australia concluded that the taste of organic food was better than conventionally grown products[10] and that organic food had sensual qualities.[1]

As consumers develop more positive attitudes towards organic food, they are faced with purchase decisions. Studies have examined decision-making factors. Padel and Foster[9] concluded that the process is complex, and that motives and barriers may vary with product categories. Researchers have found a widespread perception of organic foods as expensive[10] and that the primary barrier to purchasing organic food was the consumer's level of personal disposable income.[14] Lockie et al.[1] suggested that increased education and household income is positively associated with the likelihood that an individual has consumed organic foods. However, other scholars have found that the main factor that hinders the purchase of organic food is limited availability of such foods.[11,15]

Consumer purchases of organic foods have increased. In 1994, Tregear et al.[18] found that 29% of the general public occasionally bought organic foods. A later study found that almost half of respondents purchased organic food on a regular basis.[13] Fruits and vegetables tend to be the first, and often the only, organic products that consumers buy.[9] Nonetheless, few consumers follow a diet that is mainly organic.[1]

Other Eco-Friendly Behaviors

There is some disagreement about whether there is an association between consumption of organic foods and other environmentally friendly behaviors. Davies et al.[14] found that consumers of organic foods were not necessarily concerned about the environment. However, two more recent studies found a significant relationship between environmentally friendly behaviors and organic food consumption.[1,2] In Oregon, the likelihood that a consumer will pay a premium for eco-labeled apples was positively associated with being environmentally conscious.[7] In Greece, willingness to pay for organic products was higher among consumers who placed importance on health.[8]

Attitudes and Behaviors of Young People

In a study of 651 high school students in a major metropolitan area, Bissonnette and Contento[3] found that American adolescents had positive attitudes about organic foods.

Students believed organic foods were healthier, tasted better, and were better for the environment. Yet their beliefs were not strong enough to urge them to act.[3]

Interest in organic foods or alternative food sources is evident in college age individuals who show an increasing enthusiasm for a healthy lifestyle and a sense of environmental responsibility.[4] Over the past 10 years, universities across the United States have introduced organic food options in response to student demand. For example, in 2000 the University of Wisconsin at Madison became the first major American public university to consistently place foods grown on local farms on the regular menu.[16]

In April 2006, the University of California-Berkeley received the nation's first organic certification on a college campus.[17] Menlo College uses nearly 100% organic foods and beverages on campus.[18] Also in 2006, Colorado State University and the University of Pennsylvania, in 2003, introduced student food venues that sell locally grown food. Oral Roberts University introduced its Green Cuisine brand in 2006, which includes organic salads, sandwiches, and packaged goods made from local food.[18,19] Thus, universities have responded to student demands for organic foods.

Because the literature is unclear whether consumer purchases follow upon knowledge and attitudes, the links between knowledge, attitudes, and behaviors with regard to organic foods (and other eco-friendly behaviors) should be explored to better understand and respond to consumer needs on college campuses.

METHOD

■ Population and Sample

The population for this study was students at a mid-size university in the southeastern United States. The sample included 443 students who were enrolled in one of the mandated entry-level political science classes. Thus, the sampling method ensured a representative sample of the student body.

■ Instrumentation

The instrument, designed by the researchers, was 4 pages long and consisted of 28 items. Consent information was included on the first page of the instrument. Completion of the survey constituted consent to participate in the study. Study protocol was approved by the university's Institutional Review Board.

The first 5 questions requested demographic information: gender, race, age, student classification, place of residence, and income level. Four questions evaluated the subjects' awareness/knowledge of organic foods and 5 questions addressed the subjects' attitudes toward organic foods. In the fnal section, 12 questions sought information about student eating behaviors in relation to organic foods and healthy lifestyle practices, and 2 multipart questions examined attitudes and behaviors regarding other eco-friendly practices (recycling, energy conservation, water conservation, driving hybrid cars or carpooling).

Procedures

After departmental approval was granted, researchers obtained permission from individual professors to administer the survey in each class. The average class size was 50 students. The survey was administered over a 2-week period to students present on the day of the survey. Several classes were not surveyed due to scheduling conflicts. A research assistant read procedures from a script before the surveys were distributed. Students were informed that the survey was voluntary and anonymous.

Statistical Analysis

Data analysis was conducted using SPSS Version 14.0 and Jump Version 5.0. Descriptive statistics described the sample and displayed frequencies of responses to survey items. Chi-square analysis was conducted to determine associations between categorical variables of interest. Linear regression tested whether student awareness/knowledge of organic foods predicted attitude about organic foods. Multiple correlation was used to examine the relationship between attitudes about organic foods and the purchase and consumption of those foods in different contexts. Linear regression and path analysis determined whether attitudes about organic foods might predict organic food purchase and consumption and healthy lifestyle practices. Finally, multiple correlation tested whether attitudes about other eco-friendly practices might predict corresponding behaviors.

RESULTS

The sample ($N = 443$) was 44.2% male and 55.8% female. The mean age of the group was 21.6 (SD ±5.01) years, with a range of 16 to 48 years. The racial/ethnic background of students was 54.6% White/Non-Hispanic, 30.6% African American, 7.0% Hispanic, 3.9% Asian, and 3.7% Other. The majority (59.5%) of the students were classified as sophomores. Approximately one third (27.4%) of the students lived on campus; the remaining students (72.6%) were commuters. Household annual income for 32.6% of the respondents was less than $20,000. Twenty-seven percent reported an annual household income of $20,001 to $50,000. The remainder (40.2%) reported annual income above $50,001.

When asked to identify the definition of the term "organic," 214 respondents (49.0%) selected the correct definition. Meanwhile, 138 (31.7%) recognized the USDA-approved organic seal. Knowledge of the correct definition of organic and recognition of the seal were significantly associated ($r_s = .161$, $p < .001$). Younger students (<21.6 years) were more likely to know the definition of organic and recognize the organic seal.

A majority of students knew that organic foods were available for purchase in grocery stores and in health food stores (72.2% and 79.0%, respectively). Few (9.7%) believed organic foods were available in restaurants. When asked in what form organic foods could be purchased (subjects could indicate all that applied), responses were as follows: produce

(87.1%), grains (72.2%), dairy (53.5%), snacks (31.4%), meat (29.3%), beverages (28.2%), and candy (7.7%).

Most students (56.4%) were neutral in their opinion about organic foods, but 41.3% either "accept organic foods" or "only eat organic foods." Students ranked taste as the factor that influenced them most when selecting organic foods, followed by price, appearance, availability, and package information (Table 1). Approximately one third (31.1%) of respondents believed organic foods tasted the same as conventionally grown products, whereas 15.8% felt organic foods tasted better, and 12.3% felt organic foods tasted worse.

Only 20.7% of respondents reported they could purchase organic foods on campus, and few consumed more than 50% organic diets, no matter where they purchased foods. However, between 33.2% and 45.5% reported they purchased and consumed some organic foods on campus, in restaurants, or at home. The highest number (45.5%) purchased for consumption at home. When asked where they purchased organic foods 47.4% indicated the grocery store and 13.5% indicated a health food store. The frequencies of types of organic foods purchased were as follows: produce (40.4%), grains (28.2%), dairy (22.8%), drinks/beverages (20.8%), snacks (16.3%), and meat (13.8%). Interestingly, 50.5% of the students indicated they would support the use of organic foods on campus, and 64.0% reported they would buy organic foods if offered on campus.

There were significant positive relationships between knowledge of the definition of the term organic and opinion about organic foods (attitude) ($r_s = .103, p < .05$) and between recognition of the organic seal (knowledge) and opinion about organic foods (attitude) ($r_s = .197, p < .01$). Thus, awareness and attitude about organic foods were associated. Linear regression was used to test if the two knowledge variables predicted attitude. Results were significant ($R^2 = .04, F(2, 422) = 9.73, p < .000$). Recognition of the seal was the strongest of the 2 predictors.

There was also a significant positive relationship between recognition of the organic seal and opinion about the taste of organic foods as compared to conventionally grown products ($r_s = .298, p < .01$). The relationship between the other knowledge variable

TABLE 1   FREQUENCY RANKINGS OF FACTORS AFFECTING PURCHASE OR CONSUMPTION OF ORGANIC FOODS

Factors	Rankings	
	Frequency	Percentage (%)
Price	193	46.5
Taste	247	59.7
Appearance	120	29.0
Package Information	46	11.2
Other	12	5.6

(definition of organic) and attitude was not significant. Linear regression tested recognition of the organic seal as a predictor of attitude and was found to be significant ($R^2 = .08$, $F(2, 418) = 20.09$, $p < .000$). When knowledge of the definition of organic was added as a predictor and tested in a second linear regression, model fit did not change significantly, corroborating the previous conclusion that the stronger predictor of attitude was recognition of the seal.

Multiple correlation was used to examine the relationship between attitudes about organic foods and subject responses about the support and purchase of organic foods (behavior) in different contexts (Table 2). Attitude towards organic foods was found to be significantly related to (1) purchase and consumption of organic foods on campus, (2) purchase and consumption of organic foods (usually in restaurants), and (3) purchase for consumption of foods at home.

Given the significant findings of the correlational analysis and linear regression, we conducted a path analysis (Figure 2) to determine whether attitudes toward organic foods would predict the three sets of purchase and consumption behaviors. Attitude was found to be a significant predictor ($p < .01$) of all 3 behaviors. Path analysis can be used to determine the significance and magnitude of the direct effect of predictor variables on response variables. It is an empirical tool to test cause-and-effect relationships.[20]

Attitude towards organic foods was found to be significantly related to student perceptions of whether or not they lead healthy lifestyles ($r_s = .160$, $p < .01$). A second path analysis was conducted to determine the direct effect of attitude towards organic foods on other healthy lifestyle practices. Significant path coefficients were calculated for relationships between positive attitudes towards organic foods and healthy diet ($p = .22$, $R^2 = 5.1\%$), regular exercise ($p = .14$, $R^2 = 2.1\%$), and consumption of organic foods ($p = .12$, $R^2 = 1.2\%$) only.

A final analysis examined the relationship between attitudes about other eco-friendly behaviors and the actual behaviors. Multiple correlation determined that most of the

TABLE 2 CORRELATION BETWEEN ATTITUDE TOWARDS AND CONSUMPTION OF ORGANIC FOOD

	Attitude towards organic foods	Purchase and consumption of organic foods		
		On campus	Off campus (restaurant)	Home
Attitude towards organic foods	—	.284**	.309**	.298**
Purchase/consumption of organic foods On campus		—	.670**	.524**
Off campus (restaurant)			—	.641**
Home				—

Note. **$p < .01$.

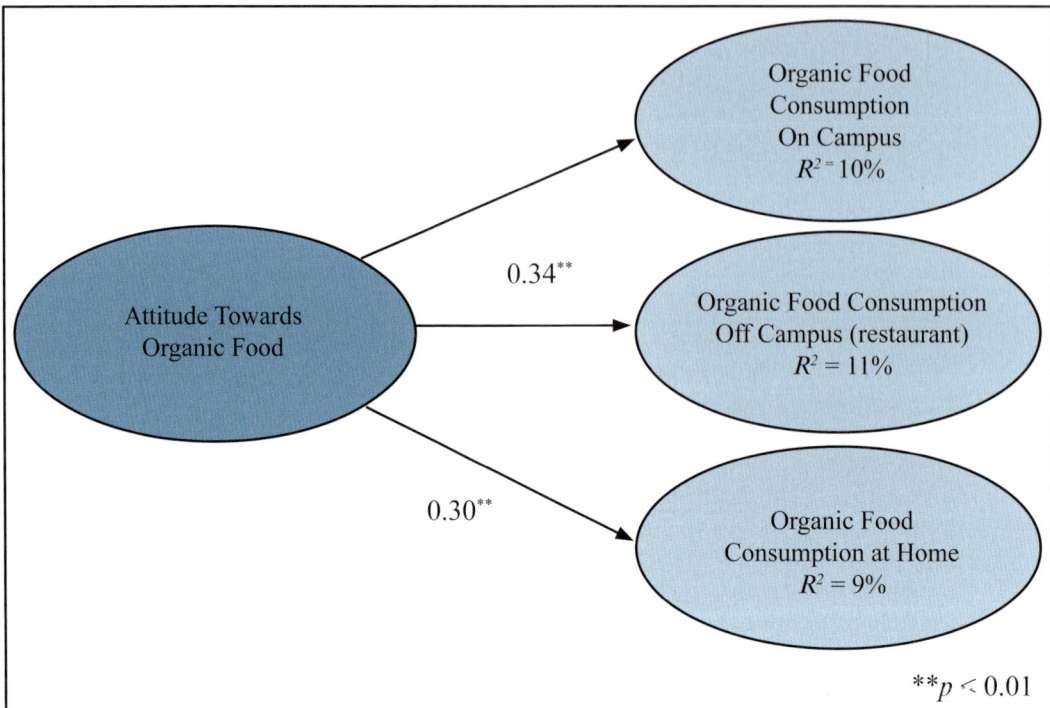

FIGURE 2. Path analysis: Direct effect of student's overall attitude towards organic foods on their food choices on-campus, off-campus, and at home.

attitudes expressed about such behaviors were related to the practice of the behaviors. Further, in many instances, the respondents' attitudes about an eco-friendly behavior such as recycling and energy conservation were significantly related to supportive behaviors such as recycling, energy conservation, driving hybrid cars or carpooling, and ozone protection.

COMMENT

We found that students are relatively knowledgeable about organic food products and believe that organic foods are beneficial and necessary. Many expressed an interest in having more organic foods available on campus and indicated they would be willing to purchase organic foods if made available on campus. Contrary to the literature, we found that students were more likely to act upon the beliefs they expressed about both organic foods and eco-friendly behaviors.

Equal numbers of males and females knew the correct definition of the term organic, recognized the federal organic seal, and expressed a positive attitude towards organic foods. This finding varies somewhat from the literature, which identifies females as being more aware and having stronger attitudes about organic foods. Perhaps students, as a group, are simply more informed consumers. In future research, student responses could be compared to other types of consumers. When examining the relationship between awareness (knowledge) and attitude, we concluded that although many students selected the incorrect definition of the term organic, even these students had positive opinions in support of organic foods and other eco-friendly practices.

Most of the students in this study clustered in household income levels of under $20,000 or above $50,000. More than 30% of respondents from the upper household income levels reported that they "accept organic foods." Similar findings in the literature indicate higher levels of awareness and support for organic foods among individuals with higher incomes.[1] Future research should explore the degree to which parental/family household income affects student consumer choices. More students under the mean age of 21.6 years knew the correct definition of the term organic and recognized the organic seal. Further, twice as many younger respondents expressed positive attitudes toward organic foods as those over the mean age. This suggests that younger people may seek out organic foods in various food environments or at least feel strongly about having them available. In that case, it makes sense that university food services should integrate more organic food options into their on-campus menus.

When subjects ranked factors that influenced their buying decisions, taste was reported to be most important, followed in order by price, appearance, availability, and package information. Consumers tend to associate health benefits with organic foods. Perhaps a younger, health-minded generation of educated consumers places more emphasis on quality (taste) and value (price). Such a conclusion might also support the fact that students knew of the availability of many forms of organic foods. A future study might include a tasting panel in which student consumers identify how various factors interact to influence the buying decision.

Students indicated that they purchased organic foods for consumption at home rather than on- or off-campus. This reinforces the finding that these foods were primarily purchased at grocery stores and health food stores. Produce, grains, and dairy products were the most often purchased organic foods. We agree with the literature that health educators need to work with food service operators to develop informational materials such as table tents and posters to help students learn about other organic food options.[9]

Few students followed an all-organic diet. Most purchased and consumed "50% or less" organic foods. However, more than half reported they would support the integration of organic foods into campus menus, and even more said they would buy organic foods if offered on campus. Such findings reinforce the current move on university campuses to provide more organic food options.

Students who were able to identify the correct definition of the term organic and who recognized the USDA organic seal were more likely to have positive opinions supporting organic foods. Recognition of the organic seal was a significant predictor of the perception that organic foods tasted as good as or better than their conventionally grown counterparts. An extension of this study might involve a taste panel in which a perceptions and preferences are tested with respect to awareness and attitudes about organic foods.

The primary purpose of this study was to determine if student attitudes actually predicted corresponding behaviors with regard to organic foods. We concluded that they did. Tracking responses over time might determine if increased exposure to/availability of organic food products influences students who currently have no opinion about organic foods. We also found that students who had positive opinions about organic foods purchased and consumed such foods in different venues, most often for consumption at home. Therefore, attitude predicted behavior.

Botonaki et al.[7] suggested that consumers of organic foods are likely to engage in other healthy lifestyle practices. In our study, a positive attitude towards organic foods was significantly associated with consuming a healthy diet and exercising regularly. Health educators should further examine differences in student perceptions about healthy lifestyle practices.

Lockie et al.[1] and Magnusson et al.[2] found the consumption of organic foods and other environmentally conscious behaviors to be significantly related. In the present study, when students were asked about eco-friendly practices, there was a significant relationship between a positive attitude about these practices and the corresponding behavior. Clearly, students in this study not only felt strongly about environmental issues, but they also felt compelled towards eco-friendly practices.

CONCLUSION

In a classroom administration format or as with any self-report instrument, there is always the concern that subjects respond truthfully to the instrument items. In addition, the population characteristics of this university may be different. Thus, our findings that attitudes generally predicted behaviors must be interpreted with caution. Future studies should focus on other types of universities and track student behaviors to determine through observation whether a significant link with attitudes actually exists.

Some instrument items were forced choice, with an option to write in additional information. Forced-choice items do not accommodate the full range of possible responses even with the write-in option. For example, students with food allergies or concerns about chemical preservatives might opt for an organic diet. We may not have identified all opinions and factors relevant to the purchase and consumption of organic foods, healthy lifestyle or eco-friendly practices.

This study sampled students (young adults) from an American university, which helps to fill certain gaps in the literature. Additional research in the United States about the attitudes towards purchase and consumption of organic foods is needed.

A principle finding in this study was that students are knowledgeable about organic foods and that they support the integration of organic foods into their menu choices and diets. Although less than half of the students indicated they purchased and consumed organic products in various environments, more than half of study respondents reported they would support the use of organic products on campus and would actually purchase organic foods on campus.

This sentiment is an important indicator for college and universities. There is already a demand for healthy food options on university campuses.[4,18] It seems that campus food services should evaluate not only their menu offerings, but even what they term healthy choices, in terms of organic food standards. It would be interesting to sample a portion of the respondents in this study in a year or so to determine if their attitudes have changed with regard to organic food purchase or consumption.

Our study focused on students as primary consumers; however, campuses also accommodate faculty and staff, many of whom may have opinions similar to those expressed by the students in this study. A future study might examine not only the opinions of other students on other campuses as well as other groups on campuses.

This study found that students who felt positively about organic foods were also inclined to behave accordingly. In other words, they were more likely to act on their opinions and choose to purchase and consume organic foods. Such a finding has implications for market food producers in general, in that college students are both consumers today as well as primary consumers of the future. It will be important to address this growing demand in more venues than college campuses.

REFERENCES

1. Lockie S, Lyons K, Lawrence G, Grice J. "Choosing organics: a path analysis of factors underlying the selection of organic food among Australian consumers." *Appetite*. 2004;43:135-146.

2. Magnusson M, Arvola A, Hursti U, Aberg L, Sjoden P. "Choice of organic foods is related to perceived consequences for human health and to environmentally friendly behaviour." *Appetite*. 2003;40:109-117.

3. Bissonnette M, Contento I. "Adolescents' perspectives and food choice behaviors in terms of the environmental impacts of food production practices: application of a psychosocial model." *J Nutr Educ*. 2001;33:72-82.

4. Horovitz B. "More university students call for organic, 'sustainable' food." *USAToday.com*, September 26, 2006:A.

5. "The National Organic Program." *Organic Food Standards and labels: The Facts*. Agricultural Marketing Service at United States Department of Agriculture Web site. http://www.ams.usda.gov/nop/Consumers/brochure.html. Accessed March 8, 2007.

6. "Organic faq." Organic.org Web site. http://www.organic.org/home/faq. Accessed October 17, 2006.

7. Botonaki A, Polymeros K, Tsakindou E, Mattas K. "The role of food quality certification on consumers' food choices." *Br Food J*. 2006;108:77-91.

8. Loureiro M, McCluskey J, Mittelhammer R. "Will consumers pay a premium for eco-labeled apples?" *J Consumer Affairs*. 2002;36:203-219.

9. Padel S, Foster C. "Exploring the gap between attitudes and behaviour: understanding why consumers buy or do not buy organic food." *Br Food J*. 2005;107:606-625.

10. Tregear A, Dent J, McGregor M. "The demand for organically-grown produce." *Br Food J*. 1994;96:21-26.

11. Chryssohoidis G, Krystallis, A. "Organic consumers' personal values research: testing and validating the list of values (LOV) scale and implementing a value-based segmentation task." *Food Qual Prefer*. 2005;16:585-599.

12. Dreezens E, Martijn C, Tenbult P, Kok G, de Vries N. "Food and values: an examination of values underlying attitudes toward genetically modified—and organically grown food products." *Appetite*. 2005;44:115-122.

13. Connor R, Douglas L. "Consumer attitudes to organic foods." *Nutr Food Sci*. 2001;31:254-258.

14. Davies A, Titterington A, Cochrane C. "Who buys organic food? A profile of the purchasers of organic food in Northern Ireland." *Br Food J*. 1995;97:17-24.

15. Fotopoulos, G. "Factors affecting the decision to purchase organic food." *J Eur-Marketing*. 2000;9:45-66.

16. "University of Wisconsin goes organic." *Organic Consumer Association Web site. 2006.* http://www.orgaanicconsumers.org/organic/uofw101903.cfm. Accessed October 17, 2006.

17. *Organic certification*. University of California-Berkeley Web site. http://caldining.berkeley.edu/environment.organic.cert.html. Accessed October 17, 2006.

18. Horovitz B. "Organic food spreads across campuses." *USAToday*, September 27, 2006:B2.

19. Oral Roberts Fall 2007 "Student Catalogue." *Oral Roberts University* Web site. http://www.oru.edu/catalog/ORU.hb0203.pdf. Accessed March 12, 2008.

20. Williams W, Jones M, Demment M. "A concise table for path analysis statistics." *Agron J*. 1990;82:1022-1024.

Chapter 11 | Reading Eating

■ WHAT?

1. Do the conclusions presented by Dahm, Samonte, and Shows reflect your experiences with organic food? Explain your response.
2. Evaluate Dahm, Samonte, and Shows' findings. Did you find the survey questions appropriate? Were there any questions that you think should have been added? Were the charts useful in explaining the researchers' results? Do you find this type of article more or less convincing than personal narratives such as "The Pleasures of Eating" or "The Culinary Seasons of My Childhood"? Why?

■ WHAT ELSE? WHAT'S NEXT?

3. Research USC's organic food offerings. What are they? Were you aware of these offerings (or lack thereof) before your research? If organic options are available, do you regularly take advantage of them? Next, find other schools that stock local or organic food for students. What different levels of commitment to organic food in higher education do you find in your research?

■ WHO CARES?

4. Dahm, Samonte, and Shows wrote their article for the *Journal of American College Health.* Look online for more information about this journal and its primary audience. How are the journal's mission and audience reflected in the content and style of this article?

> "I'm not a chef," Mark Bittman writes on his website (markbittman.com). "I've never had formal training, and I've never worked in a restaurant. None of which has gotten in the way of my mission to get people cooking simply, comfortably, and well." As part of this mission, Bittman regularly writes about food for the opinion section of The New York Times, where this column was published in 2011.

BEFORE YOU READ

Try keeping a food diary for a day or so. Write down everything that you consume—and be honest!

BAD FOOD? TAX IT Mark Bittman

What will it take to get Americans to change our eating habits? The need is indisputable, since heart disease, diabetes and cancer are all in large part caused by the Standard American Diet. (Yes, it's SAD.)

Though experts increasingly recommend a diet high in plants and low in animal products and processed foods, ours is quite the opposite, and there's little disagreement that changing it could improve our health and save tens of millions of lives. And—not inconsequential during the current struggle over deficits and spending—a sane diet could save tens if not hundreds of billions of dollars in health care costs.

Yet the food industry appears incapable of marketing healthier foods. And whether its leaders are confused or just stalling doesn't matter, because the fixes are not really their problem. Their mission is not public health but profit, so they'll continue to sell the health-damaging food that's most profitable, until the market or another force skews things otherwise. That "other force" should be the federal government, fulfilling its role as an agent of the public good and establishing a bold national fix.

Rather than subsidizing the production of unhealthful foods, we should turn the tables and tax things like soda, French fries, doughnuts and hyperprocessed snacks. The resulting income should be earmarked for a program that encourages a sound diet for Americans by making healthy food more affordable and widely available.

The average American consumes 44.7 gallons of soft drinks annually. (Although that includes diet sodas, it does not include noncarbonated sweetened beverages, which add up to at least 17 gallons a person per year.) Sweetened drinks could be taxed at 2 cents per ounce, so a six-pack of Pepsi would cost $1.44 more than it does now. An equivalent tax on fries might be 50 cents per serving; a quarter extra for a doughnut. (We have experts who can figure out how "bad" a food should be to qualify, and what the rate should be; right now they're busy calculating ethanol subsidies. Diet sodas would not be taxed.)

Simply put: taxes would reduce consumption of unhealthful foods and generate billions of dollars annually. That money could be used to subsidize the purchase of staple foods like seasonal greens, vegetables, whole grains, dried legumes and fruit. We could sell those staples cheap—let's say for 50 cents a pound—and almost everywhere: drugstores, street corners, convenience stores, bodegas, supermarkets, liquor stores, even schools, libraries and other community centers.

This program would, of course, upset the processed food industry. Oh well. It would also bug those who might resent paying more for soda and chips and argue that their right to eat whatever they wanted was being breached. But public health is the role of the government, and our diet is right up there with any other public responsibility you can name, from water treatment to mass transit.

Some advocates for the poor say taxes like these are unfair because low-income people pay a higher percentage of their income for food and would find it more difficult to buy soda or junk. But since poor people suffer disproportionately from the cost of high-quality, fresh foods, subsidizing those foods would be particularly beneficial to them.

Right now it's harder for many people to buy fruit than Froot Loops; chips and Coke are a common breakfast. And since the rate of diabetes continues to soar—one-third of all Americans either have diabetes or are pre-diabetic, most with Type 2 diabetes, the kind associated with bad eating habits—and because our health care bills are on the verge of becoming truly insurmountable, this is urgent for economic sanity as well as national health.

Justifying a Tax

At least 30 cities and states have considered taxes on soda or all sugar-sweetened beverages, and they're a logical target: of the 278 additional calories Americans on average consumed per day between 1977 and 2001, more than 40 percent came from soda, "fruit" drinks, mixes like Kool-Aid and Crystal Light, and beverages like Red Bull, Gatorade and dubious offerings like Vitamin Water, which contains half as much sugar as Coke.

Some states already have taxes on soda—mostly low, ineffective sales taxes paid at the register. The current talk is of excise taxes, levied before purchase.

"Excise taxes have the benefit of being incorporated into the shelf price, and that's where consumers make their purchasing decisions," says Lisa Powell, a senior research scientist at the Institute for Health Research and Policy at the University of Illinois at Chicago. "And, as per-unit taxes, they avoid volume discounts and are ultimately more effective in raising prices, so they have greater impact."

Much of the research on beverage taxes comes from the Rudd Center for Food Policy and Obesity at Yale. Its projections indicate that taxes become significant at the equivalent of about a penny an ounce, a level at which three very good things should begin to happen: the consumption of sugar-sweetened beverages should decrease, as should the incidence of disease and therefore public health costs; and money could be raised for other uses.

Even in the current antitax climate, we'll probably see new, significant soda taxes soon, somewhere; Philadelphia, New York (city and state) and San Francisco all considered them last year, and the scenario for such a tax spreading could be similar to that of legalized gambling: once the income stream becomes apparent, it will seem irresistible to cash-strapped governments.

Currently, instead of taxing sodas and other unhealthful food, we subsidize them (with, I might note, tax dollars!). Direct subsidies to farmers for crops like corn (used, for example, to make now-ubiquitous high-fructose corn syrup) and soybeans (vegetable oil) keep the prices of many unhealthful foods and beverages artificially low. There are indirect subsidies as well, because prices of junk foods don't reflect the costs of repairing our health and the environment.

Other countries are considering or have already started programs to tax foods with negative effects on health. Denmark's saturated-fat tax is going into effect Oct. 1, and Romania passed (and then un-passed) something similar; earlier this month, a French minister raised the idea of tripling the value added tax on soda. Meanwhile, Hungary is proposing a new tax on foods with "too much" sugar, salt or fat, while increasing taxes on liquor and soft drinks, all to pay for state-financed health care; and Brazil's Fome Zero (Zero Hunger) program features subsidized produce markets and state-sponsored low-cost restaurants.

Putting all of those elements together could create a national program that would make progress on a half-dozen problems at once—disease, budget, health care, environment, food access and more—while paying for itself. The benefits are staggering, and though it would take a level of political will that's rarely seen, it's hardly a moonshot.

The need is dire: efforts to shift the national diet have failed, because education alone is no match for marketing dollars that push the very foods that are the worst for us. (The fast-food industry alone spent more than $4 billion on marketing in 2009; the Department of Agriculture's Center for Nutrition Policy and Promotion is asking for about a third of a percent of that in 2012: $13 million.) As a result, the percentage of obese adults has more than doubled over the last 30 years; the percentage of obese children has tripled. We eat nearly 10 percent more animal products than we did a generation or two ago, and though there may be value in eating at least some animal products, we could perhaps live with reduced consumption of triple bacon cheeseburgers.

■ Government and Public Health

Health-related obesity costs are projected to reach $344 billion by 2018—with roughly 60 percent of that cost borne by the federal government. For a precedent in attacking this problem, look at the action government took in the case of tobacco.

The historic 1998 tobacco settlement, in which the states settled health-related lawsuits against tobacco companies, and the companies agreed to curtail marketing and finance antismoking efforts, was far from perfect, but consider the results. More than half of all Americans who once smoked have quit and smoking rates are about half of what they were in the 1960s.

It's true that you don't need to smoke and you do need to eat. But you don't need sugary beverages (or the associated fries), which have been linked not only to Type 2 diabetes and increased obesity but also to cardiovascular diseases and decreased intake of valuable nutrients like calcium. It also appears that liquid calories provide less feeling of fullness; in other words, when you drink a soda it's probably in addition to your other calorie intake, not instead of it.

To counter arguments about their nutritional worthlessness, expect to see "fortified" sodas—à la Red Bull, whose vitamins allegedly "support mental and physical performance"—and "improved" junk foods (Less Sugar! Higher Fiber!). Indeed, there may be reasons to make nutritionally worthless foods less so, but it's better to decrease their consumption.

Forcing sales of junk food down through taxes isn't ideal. First off, we'll have to listen to nanny-state arguments, which can be countered by the acceptance of the anti-tobacco movement as well as a dozen other successful public health measures. Then there are the predictions of job loss at soda distributorships, but the same predictions were made about the tobacco industry, and those were wrong. (For that matter, the same predictions were made around the nickel deposit on bottles, which most shoppers don't even notice.) Ultimately, however, both consumers and government will be more than reimbursed in the form of cheaper healthy staples, lowered health care costs and better health. And that's a big deal.

■ The Resulting Benefits

A study by Y. Claire Wang, an assistant professor at Columbia's Mailman School of Public Health, predicted that a penny tax per ounce on sugar-sweetened beverages in New York State would save $3 billion in health care costs over the course of a decade, prevent something like 37,000 cases of diabetes and bring in $1 billion annually. Another study shows that a two-cent tax per ounce in Illinois would reduce obesity in youth by 18 percent, save nearly $350 million and bring in over $800 million taxes annually.

Scaled nationally, as it should be, the projected benefits are even more impressive; one study suggests that a national penny-per-ounce tax on sugar-sweetened beverages would generate at least $13 billion a year in income while cutting consumption by 24 percent. And those numbers would swell dramatically if the tax were extended to more kinds of junk or doubled to two cents an ounce. (The Rudd Center has a nifty revenue calculator online that lets you play with the numbers yourself.)

A 20 percent increase in the price of sugary drinks nationally could result in about a 20 percent decrease in consumption, which in the next decade could prevent 1.5 million Americans from becoming obese and 400,000 cases of diabetes, saving about $30 billion.

It's fun—inspiring, even—to think about implementing a program like this. First off, though the reduced costs of healthy foods obviously benefit the poor most, lower prices across the board keep things simpler and all of us, especially children whose habits are just developing, could use help in eating differently. The program would also bring much needed encouragement to farmers, including subsidies, if necessary, to grow staples instead of commodity crops.

Other ideas: We could convert refrigerated soda machines to vending machines that dispense grapes and carrots, as has already been done in Japan and Iowa. We could provide recipes, cooking lessons, even cookware for those who can't afford it. Television public-service announcements could promote healthier eating. (Currently, 86 percent of food ads now seen by children are for foods high in sugar, fat or sodium.)

Money could be returned to communities for local spending on gyms, pools, jogging and bike trails; and for other activities at food distribution centers; for Meals on Wheels in those towns with a large elderly population, or for Head Start for those with more children; for supermarkets and farmers' markets where needed. And more.

By profiting as a society from the foods that are making us sick and using those funds to make us healthy, the United States would gain the same kind of prestige that we did by attacking smoking. We could institute a national, comprehensive program that would make us a world leader in preventing chronic or "lifestyle" diseases, which for the first time in history kill more people than communicable ones. By doing so, we'd not only repair some of the damage we have caused by first inventing and then exporting the Standard American Diet, we'd also set a new standard for the rest of the world to follow.

■ WHAT?

1. Bittman has written a policy argument: He identifies a problem and then makes a case for a specific course of action to address that problem. What is the problem that Bittman identifies? What kinds of evidence does he present to help his readers see that there really is a problem that needs to be addressed? What is the course of action that he proposes? How does he try to persuade his readers to buy into his argument?

2. After you have compiled your food diary entries (as described at the start of this essay), examine the list and determine how much of what you ate might be subject to the kinds of "bad food" taxes that Bittman describes. Do you think higher prices would discourage your consumption of unhealthy foods? Would lower prices and increased availability cause you to eat healthier foods? Explain your responses.

■ WHAT ELSE? WHAT'S NEXT?

3. In making his argument, Bittman mentions a handful of cities, states, and nations that are considering or are already imposing taxes on certain foods as a way to discourage poor eating habits and to reduce obesity and its companion health problems. Choose one of these locations (or find another place that taxes "bad food") and research how the issue is playing out. As you conduct your research, consider the following questions:

Chapter 11 | **Reading Eating**

- Who initiated the tax in question? What foods are specifically targeted?

- Where does the issue stand now? (Is there a tax in place? Or has one simply been proposed?)

- Who has lined up to support the tax? What reasons do they give for their support? Who, on the other hand, opposes the tax? Why?

- If the tax is in place, how is it being enforced? (If the tax is still under consideration, how do supporters say it will be enforced?)

- How do citizens of the locale feel about the tax? How about restaurant owners and others in food-related businesses?

- If the tax is in place, what have been the effects?

Use the information you find through your research to prepare a brief report about the location you have selected and where the food-tax issue stands there. Make sure you document any sources that you use.

WHO CARES?

4. What—if anything—does Bittman do in his essay to specifically address those who might object to his proposal? Do you think he does enough to try to persuade people who don't already agree with him? Explain your response.

IMAGE 11.3
In his call for opting out of the industrial food complex, Joel Salatin writes that, "[i]f you took away everything with an ingredient foreign to our three trillion intestinal microflora, the shelves [of grocery stores] would be bare indeed."

Chapter 11 | **Reading Eating**

> *Joel Salatin is a third-generation alternative farmer at Polyface Farm in Virginia's Shenandoah Valley. He and his farm have been featured in several national publications, in Michael Pollan's book* The Omnivore's Dilemma, *and in the documentary film* Food, Inc. *Salatin wrote this essay for* Food, Inc.: How Industrial Food Is Making Us Sicker, Fatter, and Poorer—and What You Can Do about It, *the companion book to that film.*

BEFORE YOU READ

Visit the website for Food, Inc. *(http://www.takepart.com/foodinc) and watch the trailer for the movie (click on the tab labeled "The Film"). What does the trailer—and Joel Salatin's inclusion in it (he's the farmer in the white hat near the end)—tell you about Salatin's food politics?*

DECLARE YOUR INDEPENDENCE Joel Salatin

Perhaps the most empowering concept in any paradigm-challenging movement is simply opting out. The opt-out strategy can humble the mightiest forces because it declares to one and all, "You do not control me."

The time has come for people who are ready to challenge the paradigm of factory-produced food and to return to a more natural, wholesome, and sustainable way of eating (and living) to make that declaration to the powers that be, in business and government, that established the existing system and continue to prop it up. It's time to opt out and simply start eating better—right here, right now.

Impractical? Idealistic? Utopian? Not really. As I'll explain, it's actually the most realistic and effective approach to transforming a system that is slowly but surely killing us.

What Happened to Food?

First, why am I taking a position that many well-intentioned people might consider alarmist or extreme? Let me explain.

At the risk of stating the obvious, the unprecedented variety of bar-coded packages in today's supermarket really does not mean that out generation enjoys better food options than our predecessors. These packages, by and large, having passed through the food inspection fraternity, the industrial food fraternity, and the lethargic cheap-food-purchasing consumer fraternity, represent an incredibly narrow choice. If you took away everything with an ingredient foreign to our three trillion intestinal microflora, the shelves would be bare indeed. (I'm talking here about the incredible variety of microorganisms that live in our digestive tracts and perform an array of useful functions, including training our immune systems and producing vitamins like biotin and vitamin K.) In fact, if you just eliminated every product that would have been unavailable in 1900, almost everything would be gone, including staples that had been chemically fertilized, sprayed with pesticides, or ripened with gas.

Rather than representing newfound abundance, these packages wending their way to store shelves after spending a month in the belly of Chinese merchant marines are actually the meager offerings of a tyrannical food system. Strong words? Try buying real milk—as in raw. See if you can find meat processed in the clean open air under sterilizing sunshine. Look for pot pies made with local produce and meat. How about good old unpasteurized apple cider? Fresh cheese? Unpasteurized almonds? All these staples that our great-grandparents relished and grew healthy on have been banished from today's supermarket.

They've been replaced by an array of pseudo-foods that did not exist a mere century ago. The food additives, preservatives, colorings, emulsifiers, corn syrups, and unpronounceable ingredients listed on the colorful packages bespeak a centralized control mindset that actually reduces the options available to fill Americans' dinner plates. Whether by intentional design or benign ignorance, the result has been the same—the criminalization and/or demonization of heritage foods.

The mindset behind this radical transformation of American eating habits expresses itself in at least a couple of ways.

One is the completely absurd argument that without industrial food, the world would starve. "How can you feed the world?" is the most common question people ask me when they tour Polyface Farm. Actually, when you consider the fact that millions of people, including many vast cities, were fed and sustained using traditional farming methods until just a few decades ago, the answer is obvious. America has traded seventy-five million buffalo, which required no tillage, petroleum, or chemicals, for a mere forty-two million head of cattle. Even with all the current chemical inputs, our production is a shadow of what it was 500 years ago. Clearly, if we returned to herbivorous principles five centuries old, we could double our meat supply. The potential for similar increases exists for other food items.

The second argument is about food safety. "How can we be sure that food produced on local farms without centralized inspection and processing is really safe to eat?" Here, too, the facts are opposite to what many people assume. The notion that indigenous food is unsafe simply has no scientific backing. Milk-borne pathogens, for example, became a significant health problem only during a narrow time period between 1900 and 1930, before refrigeration but after unprecedented urban expansion. Breweries needed to be located near metropolitan centers, and adjacent dairies fed herbivore-unfriendly brewery waste to cows. The combination created real problems that do not exist in grass-based dairies practicing good sanitation under refrigeration conditions.

Lest you think the pressure to maintain the industrialized food system is all really about food safety, consider that all the natural-food items I listed above can be given away, and the donors are considered pillars of community benevolence. But as soon as money changes hands, all these wonderful choices become "hazardous substances," guaranteed to send our neighbors to the hospital with food poisoning. Maybe it's not human health but corporate profits that are really being protected.

Furthermore, realize that many of the same power brokers (politicians and the like) encourage citizens to go out into the woods on a 70-degree fall day; gun-shoot a deer with possible variant Creutzfeld-Jacob's disease (like mad cow for deer); drag the carcass a mile through squirrel dung, sticks, and rocks; then drive parade-like through town in the blazing afternoon sun with the carcass prominently displayed on the hood of the Blazer. The hunter takes the carcass home, strings it up in the backyard tree under roosting birds for a week, then skins it out and feeds the meat to his children. This is all considered noble and wonderful, even patriotic. Safety? It's not an issue.

The question is, who decides what food is safe? In our society, the decisions are made by the same type of people who decided in the Dred Scott ruling that slaves were not human beings. Just because well-educated, credentialed experts say something does not make it true. History abounds with expert opinion that turned out to be dead wrong. Ultimately, food safety is a personal matter of choice, of conscience. In fact, if high-fructose corn syrup is hazardous to health—and certainly we could argue that it is—then half of the government-sanctioned food in supermarkets is unsafe. Mainline soft drinks would carry a warning label. Clearly, safety is a subjective matter.

■ Reclaiming Food Freedom

Once we realize that safety is a matter of personal choice, individual freedom suddenly—and appropriately—takes center stage. What could be a more basic freedom than the freedom to choose what to feed my three-trillion-member internal community?

In America I have the freedom to own guns, speak, and assemble. But what good are those freedoms if I can't choose to eat what my body wants in order to have the energy to shoot, preach, and worship? The only reason the framers of the American Constitution and Bill of Rights did not guarantee freedom of food choice was that they couldn't envision a day when neighbor-to-neighbor commerce would be criminalized…when the bureaucratic-industrial food fraternity would subsidize corn syrup and create a nation of diabetes sufferers, but deny my neighbor a pound of sausage from my Thanksgiving hog killin'.

People tend to have short memories. We all assume that whatever is must be normal. Industrial food is not normal. Nothing about it is normal. In the continuum of human history, what western civilization has done to its food in the last century represents a mere blip. It is a grand experiment on an ever-widening global scale. We have not been here before. The three trillion members of our intestinal community have not been here before. If we ate like humans have eaten for as long as anyone has kept historical records, almost nothing in the supermarket would be on the table.

A reasonable person, looking at the lack of choice we now suffer, would ask for a Food Emancipation Proclamation. Food has been enslaved by so-called inspectors that deem the most local, indigenous, heritage-based, and traditional foods unsafe and make them illegal. It has been enslaved by a host-consuming agricultural parasite called "government farm subsidies." It has been enslaved by corporate-subsidized research that declared for four decades that feeding dead cows to cows was sound science—until mad cows came to dinner.

The same criminalization is occurring on the production side. The province of Quebec has virtually outlawed outdoor poultry. Ponds, which stabilize hydrologic cycles and have forever been considered natural assets, are now considered liabilities because they encourage wild birds, which could bring avian influenza. And with the specter of a National Animal Identification System being rammed down farmers' throats, small flocks and herds are being economized right out of existence.

On our Polyface Farm nestled in Virginia's Shenandoah Valley, we have consciously opted out of the industrial production and marketing paradigms. Meat chickens move every day in floorless, portable shelters across the pasture, enjoying bugs, forage, and local grain (grown free of genetically modified organisms). Tyson-style, inhumane, fecal factory chicken houses have no place here.

The magical land-healing process we use, with cattle using mob-stocking, herbivorous, solar conversion, lignified carbon sequestration fertilization, runs opposite the grain-based feedlot system practiced by mainline industrial cattle production. We move the cows every day from paddock to paddock, allowing the forage to regenerate completely through its growth curve, metabolizing solar energy into biomass.

Our pigs aerate anaerobic, fermented bedding in the hay feeding shed, where manure, carbon, and corn create a pig delight. We actually believe that honoring and respecting the "pigness" of the pig is the first step in an ethical, moral cultural code. By contrast, today's industrial food system views pigs as merely inanimate piles of protoplasmic molecular structure to be manipulated with whatever cleverness the egocentric human mind can conceive. A society that views its plants and animals from that manipulative, egocentric, mechanistic mindset will soon come to view its citizens in the same way. How we respect and honor the least of these is how we respect and honor the greatest of these.

The industrial pig growers are even trying to find the stress gene so it can be taken out of the pig's DNA. That way the pigs can be abused but won't be stressed about it. Then they can be crammed in even tighter quarters without cannibalizing and getting sick. In the name of all that's decent, what kind of ethics encourages such notions?

In just the last couple of decades, Americans have learned a new lexicon of squiggly Latin words: camphylobacter, lysteria, E. coli, salmonella, bovine spongiform encephalopathy, avian influenza. Whence these strange words? Nature is speaking a protest, screaming to our generation: "Enough!" The assault on biological dignity has pushed nature to the limit. Begging for mercy, its pleas go largely unheeded on Wall Street, where Conquistadors subjugating weaker species think they can forever tyrannize without an eventual payback. But the rapist will pay—eventually. You and I must bring a nurturing mentality to the table to balance the industrial food mindset.

Here at Polyface, eggmobiles follow the cows through the grazing cycle. These portable laying hen trailers allow the birds to scratch through the cows' dung and harvest newly uncovered crickets and grasshoppers, acting like a biological pasture sanitizer. This biomimicry stands in stark contrast to chickens housed beak by wattle in egg factories, never allowed to see sunshine or chase a grasshopper.

We have done all of this without money or encouragement from those who hold the reins of food power, government or private. We haven't asked for grants. We haven't asked for permission. In fact, to the shock and amazement of our urban friends, our farm is considered a Typhoid Mary by our industrial farm neighbors. Why? Because we don't medicate, vaccinate, genetically adulterate, irradiate, or exudate like they do. They fear our methods because they've been conditioned by the powers that be to fear our methods.

The point of all this is that if anyone waits for credentialed industrial experts, whether government or nongovernment, to create ecologically, nutritionally, and emotionally friendly food, they might as well get ready for a long, long wait. For example, just imagine what a grass-finished herbivore paradigm would do to the financial and power structure of America. Today, roughly seventy percent of all grains go through herbivores, which aren't supposed to eat them and, in nature, never do. If the land devoted to that production were converted to perennial prairie polycultures under indigenous biomimicry management, it would topple the grain cartel and reduce petroleum usage, chemical usage, machinery manufacture, and bovine pharmaceuticals.

Think about it. That's a lot of economic inertia resisting change. Now do you see why the Farm Bill that controls government input into our agricultural system never changes by more than about two percent every few years? Even so-called conservation measures usually end up serving the power brokers when all is said and done.

■ Opting Out

If things are going to change, it is up to you and me to make the change. But what is the most efficacious way to make the change? Is it through legislation? Is it by picketing the World Trade Organization talks? Is it by dumping cow manure on the parking lot at McDonald's? Is it by demanding regulatory restraint over the aesthetically and aromatically repulsive industrial food system?

At the risk of being labeled simplistic, I suggest that the most efficacious way to change things is simply to declare our independence from the figurative kings in the industrial system. To make the point clear, here are the hallmarks of the industrial food system:

- Centralized production
- Mono-speciation
- Genetic manipulation
- Centralized processing
- Confined animal feeding operations
- Things that end in "cide" (Latin for death)
- Ready-to-Eat food
- Long-distance transportation
- Externalized costs—economy, society, ecology
- Pharmaceuticals
- Opaqueness
- Unpronounceable ingredients
- Supermarkets
- Fancy packaging
- High fructose corn syrup
- High liability insurance
- "No Trespassing" signs

Reviewing this list shows the magnitude and far-reaching power of the industrial food system. I contend that it will not move. Entrenched paradigms never move...until outside forces move them. And those forces always come from the bottom up. The people who sit on the throne tend to like things the way they are. They have no reason to change until they are forced to do so.

The most powerful force you and I can exert on the system is to opt out. Just declare that we will not participate. Resistance movements from the antislavery movement to women's suffrage to sustainable agriculture always have and always will begin with opt-out resistance to the status quo. And seldom does an issue present itself with such a daily—in fact, thrice daily—opportunity to opt out.

Perhaps the best analogy in recent history is the home-school movement. In the late 1970s, as more families began opting out of institutional educational settings, credentialed educational experts warned us about the jails and mental asylums we'd have to build to handle the educationally and socially deprived children that home-schooling would produce. Many parents went to jail for violating school truancy laws. A quarter-century later, of course, the paranoid predictions are universally recognized as wrong. Not everyone opts for home-schooling, but the option must be available for those who want it. In the same way, an opt-out food movement will eventually show the Henny Penny food police just how wrong they are.

Learn to Cook Again

I think the opt-out strategy involves at least four basic ideas.

First, we must rediscover our kitchens. Never has a culture spent more to remodel and techno-glitz its kitchens, but at the same time been more lost as to where the kitchen is and what it's for. As a culture, we don't cook any more. Americans consume nearly a quarter of all their food in their cars, for crying out loud. Americans graze through the kitchen, popping precooked, heat-and-eat, bar-coded packages into the microwave for eating-on-the-run.

That treatment doesn't work with real food. Real heritage food needs to be sliced, peeled, sautéed, marinated, pureed, and a host of other things that require true culinary skills. Back in the early 1980s when our farm began selling pastured poultry, nobody even asked for boneless, skinless breast. To be perfectly sexist, every mom knew how to cut up a chicken. That was generic cultural mom information. Today, half of the moms don't know that a chicken even has bones.

I was delivering to one of our buying club drops a couple of months ago, and one of the ladies discreetly pulled me aside and asked: "How do you make a hamburger?" I thought I'd misunderstood, and asked her to repeat the question. I bent my ear down close to hear her sheepishly repeat the same question. I looked at her incredulously and asked: "Are you kidding?"

"My husband and I have been vegetarians. But now that we realize we can save the world by eating grass-based livestock, we're eating meat, and he wants a hamburger. But I don't know how to make it." This was an upper-middle-income, college-educated, bright, intelligent woman.

The indigenous knowledge base surrounding food is largely gone. When "scratch" cooking means actually opening a can, and when church and family reunion potlucks include buckets of Kentucky Fried Chicken, you know our culture has suffered a culinary information implosion. Big time. Indeed, according to marketing surveys roughly seventy percent of Americans have no idea what they are having for supper at 4:00 pm. That's scary.

Whatever happened to planning the week's menus? We still do that at our house. In the summer, our Polyface interns and apprentices enjoy creating a potluck for all of us Salatins every Saturday evening. All week they connive to plan the meal. It develops throughout the week, morphs into what is available locally and seasonally, and always culminates in a fellowship feast.

As a culture, if all we did was rediscover our kitchens and quit buying prepared foods, it would fundamentally change the industrial food system. The reason I'm leading this discussion with the option is because too often the foodies and greenies seem to put the onus for change on the backs of farmers. But this is a team effort, and since farmers do not even merit Census Bureau recognition, non-farmers must ante up to the responsibility for the change. And both moms and dads need to reclaim the basic food preparation knowledge that was once the natural inheritance of every human being.

■ Buy Local

After rediscovering your kitchen, the next opt-out strategy is to purchase as directly as possible from your local farmer. If the money pouring into industrial food dried up tomorrow, that system would cease to exist. Sounds easy, doesn't it? Actually, it is. It doesn't take any legislation, regulation, taxes, agencies, or programs. As the money flows to local producers, more producers will join them. The only reason the local food system is still minuscule is because few people patronize it.

Even organics have been largely co-opted by industrial systems. Go to a food co-op drop, and you'll find that more than half the dollars are being spent for organic corn chips, treats, and snacks. From far away.

Just for fun, close your eyes and imagine walking down the aisle of your nearby Wal-Mart or Whole Foods. Make a note of each item as you walk by and think about what could be grown within one hundred miles of that venue. I recommend this exercise when speaking at conferences all over the world, and it's astounding the effect it has on people. As humans, we tend to get mired in the sheer monstrosity of it all. But if we break it down into little bits, suddenly the job seems doable. Can milk be produced within one hundred miles of you? Eggs? Tomatoes? Why not?

Not everything can be grown locally, but the lion's share of what you eat certainly can. I was recently in the San Joaquin Valley looking at almonds—square miles of almonds. Some eighty-five percent of all the world's almonds are grown in that area. Why not grow a variety of things for the people of Los Angeles instead? My goodness, if you're going to irrigate anyway, why not grow things that will be eaten locally rather than things that will be shipped to some far corner of the world. Why indeed? Because most people aren't asking for local. Los Angeles is buying peas from China so almonds can be shipped to China.

Plenty of venues exist for close exchange to happen. Farmers' markets are a big and growing part of this movement. They provide a social atmosphere and a wide variety of fare. Too often, however, their politics and regulations stifle vendors. And they aren't open every day for the convenience of shoppers.

Community-supported agriculture (CSA) is a shared-risk investment that answers some of the tax and liability issues surrounding food commerce. Patrons invest in a portion of the farm's products and receive a share every week during the season. The drawback is the paperwork and lack of patron choice.

Food boutiques or niche retail facades are gradually filling a necessary role because most farmers' markets are not open daily. The price markup may be more, but the convenience is real. These allow farmers to drop off products quickly and go back to farming or other errands. Probably the biggest challenge with these venues is their overhead relative to scale.

Farmgate sales, especially near cities, are wonderful retail opportunities. Obviously, traveling to the farm has its drawbacks, but actually visiting the farm creates an accountability and transparency that are hard to achieve in any other venue. To acquire food on the farmer's own turf creates a connection, relationship, and memory that heighten the intimate dining experience. The biggest hurdle is zoning laws that often do not allow neighbors to collaboratively sell. (My book *Everything I Want to Do Is Illegal* details the local food hurdles in greater detail.)

Metropolitan buying clubs (MBCs) are developing rapidly as a new local marketing and distribution venue. Using the Internet as a farmer-to-patron real-time communication avenue, this scheme offers scheduled drops in urban areas. Patrons order via the Internet from an inventory supplied by one or more farms. Drop points in their neighborhoods offer easy access. Farmers do not have farmers' market politics or regulations to deal with, or sales commissions to pay. This transaction is highly efficient because it is nonspeculative—everything that goes on the delivery vehicle is preordered, and nothing comes back to the farm. Customizing each delivery's inventory for seasonal availability offers flexibility and an info-dense menu.

Many people ask, "Where do I find local food, or a farmer?" My answer: "They are all around. If you will put as much time into sourcing your local food as many people put into picketing and political posturing, you will discover a whole world that Wall Street doesn't know exists." I am a firm believer in the Chinese proverb: "When the student is ready, the teacher will appear." This nonindustrial food system lurks below the radar in every locality. If you seek, you will find.

■ Buy What's in Season

After discovering your kitchen and finding your farmer, the third opt-out procedure is to eat seasonally. This includes "laying by" for the off season. Eating seasonally does not mean denying yourself tomatoes in January if you live in New Hampshire. It means procuring the mountains of late-season tomatoes thrown away each year and canning, freezing, or dehydrating them for winter use.

In our basement, hundreds of quarts of canned summer produce line the pantry shelves. Green beans, yellow squash, applesauce, pickled beets, pickles, relish, and a host of other delicacies await off-season menus. I realize this takes time, but it's the way for all of us to share bioregional rhythms. To refuse to join this natural food ebb and flow is to deny connectedness. And this indifference to life around us creates a jaundiced view of our ecological nest and our responsibilities within it.

For the first time in human history, a person can move into a community, build a house out of outsourced material, heat it with outsourced energy, hook up to water from an unknown source, send waste out a pipe somewhere else, and eat food from an unknown source. In other words, in modern America we can live without any regard to the ecological life raft that undergirds us. Perhaps that is why many of us have become indifferent to nature's cry.

The most unnatural characteristic of the industrial food system is the notion that the same food items should be available everywhere at once at all times. To have empty grocery shelves during inventory downtime is unthinkable in the supermarket world. When we refuse to participate in the nonseasonal game, it strikes a heavy blow to the infrastructure, pipeline, distribution system, and ecological assault that upholds industrial food.

■ Plant a Garden

My final recommendation for declaring your food independence is to grow some of your own. I am constantly amazed at the creativity shown by urban-dwellers who physically embody their opt-out decision by growing something themselves. For some, it may be a community garden where neighbors work together to grow tomatoes, beans, and squash. For others, it may be three or four laying hens in an apartment. Shocking? Why? As a culture, we think nothing of having exotic tropical birds in city apartments. Why not use that space for something productive, like egg layers? Feed them kitchen scraps and gather fresh eggs every day.

Did someone mention something about ordinances? Forget them. Do it anyway. Defy. Don't comply. People who think nothing of driving around Washington, D.C., at eighty miles an hour in a fifty-five speed limit zone often go apoplectic at the thought of defying a zoning- or building-code ordinance. The secret reality is that the government is out of money and can't hire enough bureaucrats to check up on everybody anyway. So we all need to just begin opting out and it will be like five lanes of speeders on the beltway—who do you stop?

Have you ever wanted to have a cottage business producing that wonderful soup, pot pie, or baked item your grandmother used to make? Well, go ahead and make it, sell it to your neighbors and friends at church or garden club. Food safety laws? Forget them. People getting sick from food aren't getting it from their neighbors; they are getting it from USDA-approved, industrially produced, irradiated, amalgamated, adulterated, reconstituted, extruded, pseudo-food laced with preservatives, dyes, and high fructose corn syrup.

If you live in a condominium complex, approach the landlord about taking over a patch for a garden. Plant edible landscaping. If all the campuses in Silicon Valley would plant edible varieties instead of high maintenance ornamentals, their irrigation water would actually be put to ecological use instead of just feeding hedge clippers and lawn mower engines. Urban garden projects are taking over abandoned lots, and that is a good thing. We need to see more of that. Schools can produce their own food. Instead of hiring Chemlawn, how about running pastured poultry across the yard? Students can butcher the chickens and learn about the death-life-death-life cycle.

Clearly, so much can be done right here, right now, with what you and I have. The question is not, "What can I force someone else to do?" The question is "What am I doing today to opt out of the industrial food system?" For some, it may be having one family sit-down, locally-sourced meal a week. That's fine. We haven't gotten where we've gotten overnight, and we certainly won't extract ourselves from where we are overnight.

But we must stop feeling like victims and adopt a proactive stance. The power of many individual right actions will then compound to create a different culture. Our children deserve it. And the earthworms will love us—along with the rest of the planet.

Chapter 11 | Reading Eating

■ WHAT?

1. If the industrial food system is going to change, Salatin writes, "it is up to you and me to make the change." And the best way to do this, he says, is to "declare your independence" from the status quo. How can we do this, according to Salatin? What specifically does he mean by "opting out"?
2. How does Salatin address the two major concerns he mentions about his proposal—that the world will not be able to feed itself without industrial food and that locally grown food is not always safe? Do you think his handling of these concerns is sufficient?
3. Write a formal letter to Salatin in which you raise any questions you have about his proposal—about its feasibility, for example, or its effectiveness.

■ WHAT ELSE?

4. Reread the section titled "Learn to Cook Again" in Joel Salatin's essay. With the principles Salatin states in mind, plan a meal you could cook using your own kitchen (or whatever available means you have to cook). Start by seeking out recipes and local ingredients (you might interview family members for the former and visit a local farmer's market for the latter). Then, plan your meal and prepare a menu and explanation of how the meal fits Salatin's ideas about leaving the industrial food system behind.

■ WHO CARES?

5. How would you characterize the tone of Salatin's essay? Point to passages in the text that Salatin uses to establish this tone. Do you find the tone compelling? What effect do you think it has on readers? Explain your response.

CHAPTER 12

Reading Humor

IMAGE 12.1

"(T)o understand laughter is to go a long way toward understanding our humanity," humor theorist John Morreall writes in the preface to his book *Taking Laughter Seriously*, part of which is included in the pages that follow. But, as others note elsewhere in this chapter (quoting essayist E.B. White), "Humor can be dissected, as a frog can, but the thing dies in the process and the innards are discouraging to any but the pure scientific mind." The readings in this chapter try to strike a balance between understanding how humor works—especially how it can be used to great rhetorical effect—and letting humor work. As you read these selections, take time to reflect on the purpose and effects of the humor they employ. Does encountering the issues these essays raise through humor make you think about them in a different way? Or does the humor get in the way?

> Richard Restak is a neurologist and neuropsychiatrist and the author of 20 books about the brain, including *The Playful Brain* (with puzzles by Scott Kim). He is also a former advisor to the school of philosophy at The Catholic University of America. In this essay, published in the summer of 2013 in *The American Scholar*, Restak asks if humor can help us better understand the most complex and enigmatic organ in the human body—the brain. Along the way, he offers a succinct introduction to the study of humor theory, or what makes us laugh at some things and not laugh at others.

BEFORE YOU READ

Find two humorous texts online—cartoons, jokes, brief videos—one of which you find to be funny and the other that is supposed to be funny but that you simply do not get. As you watch them, make note of how you react to each. (And be sure that the texts you find are suitable for classroom discussion.)

LAUGHTER AND THE BRAIN   Richard Restak

In my neuropsychiatric practice, I often use cartoons and jokes to measure a patient's neurologic and psychiatric well-being. I start off with a standard illustration called "The Cookie Theft." It depicts a boy, precariously balanced on a stool, pilfering cookies from a kitchen cabinet as his sister eggs him on, while their absentminded mother stands drying a plate, oblivious to the water overflowing from the sink onto the floor. Though not really a cartoon—in that nothing terribly funny is taking place—it allows me to begin assessing various things: abstraction ability, empathy, powers of observation and description, as well as sense of humor. I am especially curious to see how patients process the image, whether they perceive only a portion of it or take it in as a whole. Some people notice only the boy, others only the mother.

Next, I show a series of cartoons, starting with examples from a newspaper comics page and working up to more sophisticated drawings from *The New Yorker*. I then ask for an explanation of what's going on in each of them. Over the years, I've learned that you can't fake an understanding of a cartoon; you either get it or you don't.

Finally, I tell a few jokes set out in increasing levels of subtlety and complexity. Patients don't have to find the jokes funny (humor is too heterogeneous for that), but they should be able to explain why other people might find them funny. Why am I interested in my patients' ability to appreciate humor? Because humor impairment may point to operational problems at various levels of brain functioning.

Charles Darwin referred to humor as "a tickling of the mind." We speak of being "tickled pink" at a funny joke, and tickling often leads to laughter, so the analogy is apt. At the physiological level, humor reduces levels of stress hormones such as cortisol and is thought to enhance our immune, endocrine, and cardiovascular systems. Laughter also provides a workout for the muscles of the diaphragm, abdomen, and face. A joke can raise our spirits, or ease our tension. If we're able to laugh during a stressful situation, we can put psychological distance between ourselves and the stress. Norman Cousins, editor of *The Saturday Review* for more than 30 years, chronicled in his 1979 bestselling book, *Anatomy of an Illness*, how he attempted to cure himself of a mysterious and rapidly progressive inflammatory illness of the spine by engaging in hours-long laughing sessions while watching Marx Brothers films and reruns of the then-popular *Candid Camera*. Though Cousins's claims could not be scientifically confirmed, even the most skeptical researchers agree that humor provides an antidote to some emotions widely recognized to be associated with illness—for example, the feelings of rage and fear that can precipitate a heart attack.

Though I wouldn't take a position on whether laughter has universally salutary benefits, many laughter associations and workshops around the world—common most notably in India and Sweden—do just that. Their goal is to promote good health via the therapeutic properties of laughter. LaughterWorks, which bills itself as "Australia's leading laughter leaders," arranges seminars and workshops for various groups, as well as half-hour sessions of "laughing, breathing and gentle exercise, under the guidance of one of our qualified laughers."

A Swedish friend described a laughter-inducing exercise involving two people sitting across from each other. When one begins to laugh, the other soon starts laughing, too. Not long ago, my friend and I decided to try this ourselves. She sat facing me, and after a few awkward moments (at least on my part) spent staring silently at each other, she began laughing. I wasn't sure how to respond. But a few moments later I found myself laughing, even though nothing funny was said. I must admit that I felt better after our laughter exercise. But why?

In the weeks that followed, as I searched for an explanation, I was invited to participate in a discussion with three popular comedians—Robert Kelly, Dan Naturman, and Kristin Montella—at the Comedy Cellar in Greenwich Village. The four of us sat at the famous Comedy Table, reserved for professional comedians, and spent almost two hours engaging in some high-speed repartee concerning the interaction between comedians and their audiences. The comedians, naturally curious about the presence of a "brain doctor" in their midst, may not have known that the club's owner, Noam Dworman, had read my books and has long maintained a lively interest in neuroscience.

Soon after, I sat on a panel at the Rubin Museum of Art in Manhattan, where I joined *New Yorker* cartoonists Zach Kanin, Paul Noth, and David Sipress to explore the question of why people find cartoons funny. We discussed how humor, whether conveyed by joke or cartoon, has both a subjective component (exhilaration or mirth) and its physical expression (smiling or laughing). One can exist without the other: we may find a risqué joke amusing but withhold a smile if we happen to be in polite company. We may also laugh nervously when we're made to feel uncomfortable. We laugh when we hear others laugh—as I experienced with my Swedish friend (indeed, this phenomenon of contagious laughter is why laugh tracks are used in situation comedies). Laughter can even be induced chemically, with laughing gas, or via electrical stimulation of certain parts of the brain.

Recently, scientists have begun conducting research into the neurological processes underpinning mirth and laughter. I would not suggest that neuroscience can "explain" humor or provide the reason why we laugh at certain jokes or cartoons and not at others. Trying to parse humor, in any case, can be a self-defeating exercise. As E. B. White once wrote, "Humor can be dissected, as a frog can, but the thing dies in the process and the innards are discouraging to any but the pure scientific mind." Still, neuroscience can provide some useful insights into what happens when we find a joke or cartoon funny. Ultimately, it isn't just humor that we seek to better understand, but rather, that most complex and elusive of organs: the human brain.

The brain has no humor "center." Humor is associated with—note that I didn't say "caused by," à la White's frog dissection analogy—brain networks involving the temporal and frontal lobes in the cerebral cortex. Located near the top of the brain, these cortical areas are related to speech, general information, and the appreciation of contradiction and illogicality. Obviously we can't appreciate a joke told in a language we can't speak, or a cartoon that relies heavily on cultural norms or information foreign to us. Within these cortical areas the joke or cartoon is parsed.

All humor involves playing with what linguists call scripts (also referred to as frames). Basically, scripts are hypotheses about the world and how it works based on our previous life experiences. Consider what happens when a friend suggests meeting at a restaurant. Instantaneously our brains configure a scenario involving waiters or waitresses, menus, a sequence of eatables set out in order from appetizer to dessert, followed by a bill and the computation of a tip. This process, highly compressed and applicable to almost any kind of restaurant, works largely outside conscious awareness. And because our scripts are so generalized and compressed, we tend to make unwarranted assumptions based on them. Humor takes advantage of this tendency. Consider, for example, almost any joke from stand-up comedian Steven Wright, known for his ironic, deadpan delivery:

—I saw a bank that said "24 Hour Banking," but I didn't have that much time.
—I bought some batteries, but they weren't included. So I had to buy them again.
—I washed a sock. Then I put it in the dryer. When I took it out it was gone.
—I went into a store and asked the clerk if there was anything I could put under my coasters. He asked why I wanted to do that. I told him I wanted to make sure my coasters weren't scratching my table.

In each of these examples, everyday activities are given a different spin by forcing the listener to modify standard scripts about them. Indeed, the process of reacting to and appreciating humor begins with the activation of a script in the brain's temporal lobes.

It is the brain's frontal lobes that make sense of the discrepancy between the script and the situation described by the joke or illustrated by the cartoon. This ability is unique to our species. Though apes can engage in play and tease each other by initiating false alarm calls accompanied by laughter, they cannot shift back and forth between multiple mental interpretations of a situation. Only we can do this because—thanks to the larger size of our frontal lobes compared with other species—we are the only creatures that possess a highly evolved working memory, which by creating and storing scripts allows us to appreciate sophisticated and subtle forms of humor. Neuroscientists often compare working memory to mental juggling. To appreciate a cartoon or a joke, you have to keep in mind at least two possible scenarios: your initial assumptions, created and stored over a lifetime in the temporal lobes, along with the alternative explanations that are worked out with the aid of the frontal lobes.

Chapter 12 | Reading Humor

In the realm of psychology, there are three general theories that explain how humor works. According to the most common explanation for humor—the tension release theory—we experience, for a brief period after hearing a joke or looking at a cartoon, a tension that counterbalances what we assume about the situation being described or illustrated against what the comedian or cartoonist intends to convey. The tension is released only when the joke or cartoon is understood.

The second most popular theory of humor, the incongruity resolution model, involves the solving of a paradox or incongruity in a playful context. This theory is based on the deep relationship that exists in the human brain between the laughable and the illogical. As a species, we place great value on logic. Even so, we will playfully accept a situation that is highly unlikely or even impossible (a cartoon depicting an attempted kidnapping by Martians) as long as the scenario depicted in the cartoon is coherent and logically consistent with its theme. Incongruity resolution usually takes a little longer than tension release and occurs in two stages. First, expectations about the meaning of a joke or cartoon are jarringly undermined by the punch line of the joke or the caption of the cartoon. This leads to a form of problem solving aimed at reconciling the discrepancy. When we solve the problem, the pieces fall into place and we experience the joy that accompanies insight. Failure to get the point of a joke or cartoon causes the same discomfort we feel when we cannot solve a problem.

Finally, the superiority theory emphasizes how mirth and laughter so often involve a focus on someone else's mistakes, misfortune, or stupidity. In Plato's dialogue *Philebus*, Socrates says, "When we laugh at the ridiculous aspects of our friends, the admixture of pleasure in our malice produces a mixture of pleasure and distress. For we agreed some time ago that malice was a form of distress; but laughter is enjoyable, and on these occasions both occur simultaneously." The superiority theory lends itself especially to an explanation of cruel and hostile humor: the situation depicted in the joke or cartoon could never happen to us, hence our amusement. In a word, we feel superior to the person suffering misfortune.

In practice, most humor incorporates aspects of all three of those theories. But understanding the humor of a joke or cartoon is only half the process. If successful, jokes evoke mirth and laughter, emotional responses that involve a subcortical network (that is, beneath the cortex) devoted to mediating reward or pleasure. Whenever we're doing something we love, this subcortical network is activated and "lights up" in a functional magnetic resonance imaging (fMRI) brain scan, which measures brain activity by noting changes in blood flow. A similar response occurs when we look at a funny cartoon. We know this based on some highly original research by Dean Mobbs, now at Columbia University. Mobbs showed his subjects a series of funny and unfunny cartoons. In each instance the humorous element in the funny cartoon was subtracted to produce a cartoon that wasn't funny. Mobbs then compared his subjects' responses to the two versions. Though many of the cortical areas responsible for understanding the cartoon were activated in both of its versions, only the funny cartoons engaged the network of humor-specific subcortical structures that compose the pleasure and reward network.

Humor makes heavy demands on the brain. After entering via the visual track (cartoons) or the auditory track (jokes), humorous material triggers a precise repertoire of responses: the order, timing, and emphasis must be just right; irrelevant or distracting elements must be discounted or ignored. In one study from 1969, conducted by neurologists

Shirley Ferguson and Mark Rayport and neuropsychologist Melvin L. Schwartz, patients with temporal lobe epilepsy were shown a series of cartoons. The patients didn't find them at all funny. The experimenters instead noted an "inappropriate focus on irrelevant detail," "integration difficulty," and "egocentricity."

The frontal lobes also play a huge role in the improvisation associated with the creation of jokes or cartoons. We know this based on a recent study performed at the National Institutes of Health involving rap artists. The research—which involved fMRI—shows that rappers use different parts of their frontal lobes when improvising their lyrics than when they are performing rhymes that have already been written down. When they started to freestyle, the fMRI displayed a switch in frontal activity from the dorsolateral frontal areas, responsible for self-monitoring and self-criticism, to the medial frontal area, associated with spontaneous creative efforts. Similarly, the successful stand-up comedian has to "let go" and resist the temptation to self-criticize and self-monitor, which can lead to mistakes in delivery, timing, or presentation.

Indeed, when a comedian bombs on stage, it can take a personal toll on his or her mental health. In an interview with fellow comedian David Steinberg on Showtime's *Inside Comedy*, Steven Wright described comedic performance as "very dangerous, like walking a tightrope, or like running across a lake of ice where the ice is breaking behind you and it is going to take an hour to get to the other side." Steve Martin told Steinberg of the comedian's need to steel himself against the pain aroused when no one laughs at a joke or, worse yet, when you get booed off the stage. "Stand-up comedy is the ego's last stand," according to Martin. This proved true for the late Jonathan Winters, who suffered a serious nervous breakdown during a performance in San Francisco in 1959. After spending time in a psychiatric hospital, Winters returned to stand-up only to suffer another nervous collapse two years later, after which he quit nightclub performances altogether and turned his attention to making records.

Physical injuries to some areas of the brain—namely, the right hemisphere, which plays a special role in the integration of perceptions, enabling us to see the "whole picture"—can damage the ability to process and appreciate humor. Injury to the frontal lobe (within the right hemisphere) prevents a person from shifting back and forth between an initial assumption (based on scripts) and the alternative explanation suggested by a joke or cartoon. A patient with an impaired frontal lobe is, instead, overly literal, unable to make the frame shifts necessary for the creation or appreciation of humor.

In addition, damage to the frontal lobes creates in some patients a predilection for a peculiar form of gallows humor known as Witzelsucht. (In German, witzeln means "to wisecrack," and Sucht means "addiction.") A patient of Canadian neuropsychologist Donald Stuss with bilateral frontal lobe injury was asked to look at a drawing of a casket with three faces beneath it—one smiling, one neutral, one tearful—and decide which of the facial expressions was most appropriate, given the situation. Without hesitation he selected the smiling face. "Why did you pick the smiling face?" he was asked. He laughed and responded, "Because it's not me in the coffin." Witzelsucht often also takes the form of bizarre puns, one-liners, and slapstick comments that morbidly refer to some aspect of the patient's illness. It is further distinguished by an inability to appreciate complex or subtly embedded jokes or cartoons, such as this one from *The New Yorker*.

Chapter 12 | Reading Humor

Given how much we seem to value humor in our daily lives, one would expect that we would be telling and listening to jokes all the time. Yet how many jokes have you been told today? How long has it been since somebody came up to you and asked, "Have the heard the one about …?" How often have you recently encountered someone who went out of his or her way to make you laugh? (Spouses and close intimates excepted here.) Perhaps in response to the stresses of the early 21st century, we have become a serious (i.e., comparatively humorless) society. In a culture that is increasingly polarized politically, it's hard now to make a joke, either privately or publicly, without running the risk that someone will find some aspect of it offensive. Because of this, I suspect, dinner party jokes have become almost as uncommon as April Fools' Day pranks.

Within the workplace, for instance, humor typically started at the top. If the boss or supervisor said something funny, everybody was supposed to laugh; if someone further down the chain did so, the results were less predictable: the workers usually looked toward the boss to decide how to respond. Not surprisingly, in the more egalitarian environment of the modern office such a hierarchical arrangement is considered patronizing or condescending. As a result, the choice is between an office environment in which anybody can make a joke (probably not a wise policy) or one in which jokes are restricted to persons in authority (also not a good thing). Is it any surprise that jokes have largely fallen out of favor in the workplace?

Instead, we've formalized humor and licensed it to professionals such as comedians and cartoonists, who fill the ancient role of medieval court jesters, receiving special dispensation to make jokes about serious topics to the king without fear of retaliation. At the yearly White House Correspondents Dinner, for example, a comedian is chosen to act as a surrogate who may say in humorous form, in the presence of the president, what many others would like to say but can't. Stephen Colbert's barbed jokes at the 2006 dinner incensed George W. Bush so much, according to an aide, that the president seemed "ready to blow."

But do any of these considerations portend an end to humor? Given that the impulse to find and express amusement has existed since the formation of the earliest social groups, probably not. Indeed, some neuroscientists believe that humor may have evolved with another cognitive ability we share with the higher primates: the rapid and intuitive assessment of social situations. And humor has much to do with that most fundamental of human behaviors—falling in love.

According to Gil Greengross and Geoffrey Miller of the University of New Mexico, humor "may be one of the most important traits for humans seeking mates." Since jokes and cartoons strike different degrees of mirth in different people, humor helps us identify others with dispositions and propensities similar to our own. (On occasion, of course, we encounter people who find nothing funny, but who wants to spend a life with them?) Humor appreciation, however, differs between the sexes, according to psychologist Eric R. Bressler, who notes that, in general, women tend to favor men who make them laugh, while men favor women who laugh at their jokes. Indeed, how much a woman laughs at a man's jokes can determine how attractive each partner finds the other. Presumably, when a woman laughs a man's jokes, the man becomes more interested. Bressler found that men's laughter, in contrast, did not predict interest in future interaction on the part of either the woman or the man. Nor are the expressions of humor the same. As Nichole Force notes in a 2011 article published in *Psych Central*, men tend to like slapstick more than women do, and their jokes are more aggressive and mean-spirited. Women—again, generally speaking—favor a gentler brand of humor: funny stories or self-deprecating jokes.

These gender differences have practical implications for long-term relationships. Force cites the work of psychologists Catherine Cohan and Thomas Bradbury, who analyzed the marriages of 60 couples over an 18-month period and found that when men used humor to cope with stressful events, such as job loss or death, it led to a greater incidence of divorce and separation than when women used humor in similar situations. Cohan and Bradbury suggest that the nature of the humor that men favor can lead to a deterioration in a couple's bond during times of turmoil. Male humor may play a role in establishing romantic relationships, Force writes, but female humor seems more effective in maintaining them.

Humor is constantly evolving—comics' tastes change, as does what society considers funny. Our parents and grandparents would have found this sort of joke amusing: Knock knock. Who's there? Madame. Madame who? Madame foot's caught in the door! We no doubt find it juvenile and embarrassing. "Humor" based on racial and ethnic stereotypes or physical or mental disabilities is no longer acceptable, which is all to the good. However humor evolves in the future, neuroscience will attempt to explain its mechanics. It's a subject that raises perplexing questions: Are smiling and laughing based on the same or different circuits within the brain? Do the stages of humor response, whether to cartoons or jokes, involve distinct brain regions? Though much may be known about the brain structures involved in humor, what exactly is the sequence of their activation? New studies are coming out all the time; dissecting humor, it turns out, isn't quite the gruesome affair that E. B. White imagined. And why should it be? Our brains, after all, are hardwired for laughter. The enduring mystery is understanding how.

WHAT?

1. What, according to Restak, is the value in the scientific study of how humor works?
2. How does Restak explain the role that memory plays in the function of humor.

WHAT ELSE? WHAT'S NEXT?

3. Restak explains that, in psychology, there are three general theories of humor: tension release theory, incongruity theory, and superiority theory. Select one of these theories (your teacher might ask you to work with a group) and research its origins, its development, and its method of explaining how humor works. Then, find a humorous text that shows the theory at work.
4. Compare Restak's discussion of humor's effects on the brain to Peter McGraw's "benign violation theory" in the article "One Professor's Attempt to Explain Every Joke Ever," elsewhere in this chapter. Which explanation do you find more compelling? Why?

WHO CARES?

5. How would you describe Restak's target audience? (In other words, with whom is he trying to connect in his article?) Explain your response.

> *John Morreall, professor and chair of the Department of Religious Studies at the College of William and Mary, writes extensively about humor. The following piece is a chapter from his book* Taking Laughter Seriously, *in which Morreall tries to "construct a comprehensive theory of laughter and humor."*

BEFORE YOU READ

Research the biography and career of John Morreall, the author of this piece. Find at least one fact about Morreall—other than what's in the headnote above—that you think will help you understand his argument about the social nature of humor. Be prepared to share what you find with your classmates.

THE SOCIAL VALUE OF HUMOR   John Morreall

In considering the value of humor so far, we have concentrated on the individual person. To get a full picture of the value of humor, however, we need to look at how it functions socially. Humor is primarily a social phenomenon, as are other forms of human enjoyment. We rarely laugh when alone, even at things that would evoke our laughter if we were with others. And if we are in a group and find that we are the only one laughing at something, we will usually cover our mouth and stifle our laughter, at least until others join in. This social aspect of laughter shows, too, in its contagiousness. Group laughter tends to work like atomic fission. Your laughter makes me laugh harder, and mine in turn reinforces your laughter. Indeed, sometimes another person's laughing is enough to get us started, even though we don't know what is making him laugh. Comedians and theater owners have long been aware that it is much easier to get a full house laughing than just half a house, especially if the smaller crowd is spread out so that they don't reinforce one anothers' laughter. It is because of the contagious nature of laughter, too, that television comedies often use "laugh tracks."

Perhaps the most extreme manifestation of the contagiousness of laughter is the "laughter epidemic" in which large numbers of people are made to laugh convulsively not by any organic cause but just by the laughter of the others. The most famous of these epidemics occurred in Africa in the mid-1960s. It started among girls at a Catholic high school, who "gave" it to their mothers and sisters when they went home. Their laughter, often mixed with heavy sobbing, lasted from a few hours to more than two weeks, and usually prevented them from eating. Many "victims" collapsed from exhaustion. Over a thousand women and girls were affected, and the epidemic lasted two months.

Laughter is not only contagious, but in spreading from person to person, it has a cohesive effect. Laughing together unites people. Those who hold the superiority theory of laughter often point to the fact that groups unite in laughter against outsiders as evidence for their theory. But ridicule is not the only kind of group laughter that has a binding effect. To laugh with another person for whatever reason, even if only at a piece of absurdity, is to get closer to that person. Indeed, humor can even be directed at the laughers themselves, and still have this unifying effect. Getting stuck in an elevator between floors with people, or running into people at the bank door on a bank holiday, often makes us laugh at our common predicament, and this laughter brings us together.

When two people are quarreling, one of the first things they stop doing together is laughing; they refuse to laugh at each other's attempts at humor, and refuse to laugh together at something incongruous happening to them. As soon as they begin to laugh once more, we know that the end of the quarrel is at hand.

The cohesive effect of humor is connected with its ability to distance us from the practical aspects of the situation we're in, and with the shared enjoyment which it involves. To joke with others is to put aside practical considerations for the moment, and doing this tends to make everyone relax. Sharing humor is in this respect like sharing an enjoyable meal. It is precisely because the quarrelers do not want to put aside practical considerations and do not want to relax together, that they will not respond to each other's attempts at humor (if, indeed, any are made). Similarly, people who are quarreling often refuse to eat together.

Sharing humor with others, then, is a friendly social gesture. It shows our acceptance of them and our desire to please them. When we are anxious about meeting someone because we're not sure how that person will react to us, the first laugh we share (if it occurs) will be important, for it will mark the other person's acceptance of us. We often start off conversations with new acquaintances with a small joke, of course, for just this reason—to set up the mood of acceptance and make the other person relax. And public speakers have for centuries begun speeches with a joke for the same reason.

The person with a sense of humor, even in practical situations, is likely to interact with others more smoothly than the humorless person. As we saw earlier, someone with a sense of humor is more imaginative and flexible in his general outlook, and so is less likely to get obsessed with any particular issue or approach to an issue. Such a person will be more open to suggestions from others, and so will be more approachable. The fact that a sense of humor keeps one from getting too self-centered or defensive about his ego also helps in this regard.

Humor also facilitates social interaction in a number of situations where it is added to a basically serious piece of communication to eliminate the offensiveness which that communication might otherwise have. When we have a complaint to make to a friend, for example, we often do so with a jocular gripe. By making our complaint amusing, we show the person that the problem is not of overwhelming importance and that we have maintained our perspective on it—"It's not the end of the world," as we sometimes say. And our humor not only shows that we have some distance from the problem, but it also tends to allow our friend some distance. He isn't put on the spot and forced to defend himself in the way that people often are when their actions are criticized in a serious tone. By using the jocular gripe we don't set up a confrontation; rather we invite the person to step back and laugh with us. The tension often associated with serious criticism is thus reduced and the person is more likely to consider the reasonableness of the complaint. Indeed, most people seem able to take almost any criticism from a friend if it is expressed in a humorous way.

Humor serves to create distance and smooth out social interaction not just in making complaints, of course, but in asking potentially offensive questions, admitting to blunders, accepting praise graciously, and in many other interchanges. As we saw in the last chapter, too, humor may also be used in social interaction in morally objectionable ways. People may "laugh off" comments about their serious wrongdoings as a way of shirking moral responsibility. They may use humor and laughter as a way of ingratiating themselves with their superiors. Humor may even be used to exert an unfair kind of pressure on someone to do something he doesn't want to do: he wants to say no, but the request is laden with such "friendly" humor that he'll seem like a "poor sport" if he doesn't comply.

Even when humor is used (or abused) for some end other than simply amusing another person, we should note, humor for that other person can still be an end in itself. If we present humor to someone to make him like us, for example, *he* does not enjoy the humor as a means to achieving some further goal, even though *we* have an ulterior motive. He simply enjoys it. Humor is like other aesthetic objects in this respect. If I give you a piece of sculpture so that you'll owe me a favor, that doesn't destroy the self-containedness of your aesthetic enjoyment of that sculpture.

We enjoy humor the most, perhaps, when we feel that it is offered with no ulterior motives—not even the altruistic one of getting us to relax. We want the other person simply to amuse us, with no strings attached. This is the kind of humor found among close friends. Indeed, the frequency of nonmanipulative humor in a group's interaction is a good indicator of the intimacy of the group. We can usually determine who someone's best friends are by determining whom he enjoys humor with the most—people who talked for hours without any humorous interchange by all odds just couldn't be close friends.

In many ways the sharing of humor in a group is like the sharing of a meal, or any other pleasurable experience. But humor, because it requires no specific setting or equipment, is especially versatile as a form of enjoyable interchange. And unlike, say, listening to a concert together, humor is not just passive but calls for imagination and creativity from its participants. Humor is versatile, too, in that it mixes so well with other kinds of conversation. Friends often share a good deal of their daily experience, and so in a conversation there may be little new information that they are able to give one another. But making a funny comment doesn't require any new information; it requires only a new way of looking at things which everyone may already know about. People who have a common store of experience may be unable to inform each other, but they can always amuse each other, by playing with the reality which they have in common. In many conversations, indeed, imaginative humor is valued more than information.

In humorous conversation we may play not just with reality outside the conversation, but also with the very moves of conversation itself. We can get a humorous effect, as we saw in Chapter 6, by playfully violating the conventions governing serious conversation. Instead of saying what we believe, and uttering sentences of warning and criticism sincerely, for example, we may engage in kidding—mock claims, mock warning, and mock criticism. Kidding is funny and enjoyable because we are taking forms of speech intended for serious communication and discarding the serious purpose. Like mock physical fighting, mock criticism can be enjoyed by both parties because they know it is only play. Indeed, it can even be an expression of affection, as in the "roast," the banquet where someone's friends take turns at giving speeches full of wisecracks about him.

Human beings seem to have a basic need for playing, not just with the conventions of conversation, but with all conventions. As a species we need customs to structure and regulate our relationships, of course, but we seem to have just as strong a need to occasionally let our hair down and act silly with one another. For thousands of years we have even institutionalized silly action with festivals where the ordinary rules are temporarily suspended. At least as far back as the ancient Egyptians, the courts of pharaohs and kings have had their jesters, whose job it was to introduce playful silliness into the ruler's otherwise serious day. In most cases, court jesters were even allowed to make fun of the king. Among the American Indians of the Southwest, tribal clowns formed a priestly class, and in their ritual clowning were allowed to say or do almost anything, including the breaking of sexual taboos.

In Western cultures, of course, institutionalized silliness has had a long history. The Greeks and Romans had festivals tied to the seasons, which were a time for breaking loose and acting foolishly. All kinds of sexual activity were allowed, in part because these festivals were based on fertility rites. Clowning and fertility go together, some have suggested, in that both overcome the individual's suffering and death. In medieval Christian Europe we find a "Feast of Fools"; modeled on liturgical feasts, it included such things as replacing the usual vespers for the day with a mixture of all the vespers throughout the year. Wilder abuses also took place, and the Feast of Fools was eventually suppressed by the Council of Basel in 1435. Nonetheless, much of it survived and traces can be found even today in Mardi Gras celebrations.

The intellectual ferment of the fifteenth and sixteenth centuries produced a heightened appreciation of the value of humor and silliness, especially as an antidote to blind allegiance or orthodoxy. In sixteenth-century Poland a "fool society" called the Babinian Republic was established. When nonmembers did something sufficiently foolish, they were invited to join, by assuming an office appropriate to what they had done. One could be made an archbishop, for example, for speaking publicly on issues about which he was ignorant. The society soon grew to include almost every important church and government official in the country. When the King of Poland asked if the Babinian Republic also had a king, he was told that as long as he was alive the society would not dream of electing another.

A better known example of the "fool movement" of this period was Erasmus's *In Praise of Folly*, a book which so nicely captures the social value of humor and silliness, that we might cite its central argument as a fitting conclusion to this chapter. The work is a long speech made by the goddess Folly on her own behalf. She argues that it is foolishness and not the calculations of reason that makes possible everything we treasure most in life. It is folly, especially, that allows us to live together and even love one another. To have a friend or spouse we have to have a sense of humor and foolishly overlook that person's faults; a rational assessment of what a friendship or marriage was going to involve would keep up aloof from the rest of our species. Even to have a good opinion of ourselves, without which no one else would love us, we need a foolish, unrealistic self-image.

The completely rational and realistic person, Dame Folly suggests, would love neither himself nor anyone else; indeed he would probably despair and kill himself.

> In sum, no society, no union in life, could be either pleasant or lasting without me [Folly]. A people does not for long tolerate its prince, or a master tolerate his servant, a handmaiden her mistress, a teacher his student, a friend his friend, a wife her husband, a landlord his tenant, a partner his partner, or a boarder his fellow-boarder, except as they mutually or by turns are mistaken, on occasion flatter, on occasion wisely wink, and otherwise soothe themselves with the sweetness of folly.

■ WHAT?

1. Write a 150-word summary of Morreall's claims about the social nature of humor, as they are explained in this chapter.
2. How, according to Morreall, is sharing humor like "sharing an enjoyable meal"?

■ WHAT ELSE? WHAT'S NEXT?

3. In the preface to *Taking Laughter Seriously*, Morreall writes that "we cannot hope to have anything like a complete picture of human life until we pay attention to such things as laughter." Based on what you've read here and elsewhere in this chapter, do you agree with this statement? Explain your response.
4. Do a Google search for the terms "John Morreall" and "tragic or comic," and you'll find a brief video of the author (it's about a minute and a half long). Watch the video and then explain how you think the same situation can be either tragic or comic.
5. Morreall writes that "[h]umor serves to create distance and smooth out social interaction [...] in asking potentially offensive questions, admitting to blunders, accepting praise graciously, and in many other interchanges." Explain why you think this is the case, and then find an example—a written text, a video, a speech—in which humor is used to broach a difficult topic.

Chapter 12 | **Reading Humor**

IMAGES 12.2 and 12.3
Are these images funny? Explain why or why not. Would looking at them with someone else or with a group of people change your reaction?

> *Joel Warner is a staff writer for* Westword, *an alternative newspaper and website based in Denver. He wrote this article for the May 2011 issue of* Wired *magazine. You can find out more about the benign violation theory of humor by going to http://blog.petermcgraw.org/.*

BEFORE YOU READ

Find a humorous text that is suitable for classroom consumption (think about your audience). This can be a joke, a video clip, an image—anything that you think is funny. Then, write a paragraph or two explaining why, exactly, the text is funny.

ONE PROFESSOR'S ATTEMPT TO EXPLAIN EVERY JOKE EVER Joel Warner

The writer E. B. White famously remarked that "analyzing humor is like dissecting a frog. Few people are interested and the frog dies." If that's true, an amphibian genocide took place in San Antonio this past January. Academics from around the world gathered there for the first-ever comedy symposium cosponsored by the Mind Science Foundation.

The goal wasn't to tell jokes but to assess exactly what a joke is, how it works, and what this thing called "funny" really is, in a neurological, sociological, and psychological sense. As Sean Guillory, a Dartmouth College neuroscience grad student who organized the event, says, "It's the first time a roomful of empirical humor researchers have ever gotten together!"

The first speaker at the podium, University of Western Ontario professor Rod Martin, began with a lament over the lack of comedy scholarship. He pointed out that you could fill a library with analyses of subjects like mental illness or aggression. Meanwhile, the 1,700-plus-page *Handbook of Social Psychology*—the preeminent reference work in its field—mentions humor once.

The crux of Martin's argument involves semantics. It takes issue with the imperfect terminology we use to describe the emotional state that humor triggers. Standardizing language would help humor studies earn the respect of related fields, like aggression research. Martin exhorted his audience to adopt his preferred word for the "pleasurable feeling, joy, gaiety of mind" that humor elicits. *Happiness, elation,* and even *hilarity* don't quite fit, to his mind. The best word, he said, is *mirth*.

For those curious about the physiology of humor, Helmut Karl Lackner of the Medical University of Graz, Austria, presented his research on the relationship between humor, stress, and respiration. By tracking breathing cycles and heart rates, he has determined that social anxiety makes things less funny. (Fittingly, he seemed nervous as he read his paper in halting English.) Nina Strohminger, a researcher at the University of Michigan, explained how she's been exposing test subjects to unpleasant odors. She extolled the virtues of a spray called Liquid Ass, which can be purchased at fine novelty stores everywhere. (Her conclusion: Farts make everything funnier.) The audience members take the subject of amusement very seriously, yet they couldn't help but chuckle at this.

Other speakers peppered their talks with multivariate ANOVAs and mesolimbic reward systems. Some presented research on whether people with Asperger's syndrome get jokes and how to determine the social consequences of put-downs. But as the sessions wound on, no one had addressed the underlying mechanism of comedy: What, exactly, makes things funny?

That question was the core of Peter McGraw's lecture. A lanky 41-year-old professor of marketing and psychology at the University of Colorado Boulder, McGraw thinks he has found the answer, and it starts with a tickle. "Who here doesn't like to be tickled?"

A good number of hands shot up. "Yet you laugh," he said, flashing a goofy grin. "You experience some pleasurable reaction even as you resist and say you don't like it."

If you really stop to think about it, McGraw continued, it's a complex and fascinating phenomenon. If someone touches you in certain places in a certain way, it prompts an involuntary but pleasurable physiological response. Except, of course, when it doesn't. "When does tickling cease to be funny?" McGraw asked. "When you try to tickle yourself … Or if some stranger in a trench coat tickles you." The audience cracked up. He was working the room like a stand-up comic.

Many would assert that this tickling conundrum is the perfect evidence that humor is utterly relative. There may be many types of humor, maybe as many kinds as there are variations in laughter, guffaws, hoots, and chortles. But McGraw doesn't think so. He has devised a simple, Grand Unified Theory of humor—in his words, "a parsimonious account of what makes things funny." McGraw calls it the benign violation theory, and he insists that it can explain the function of every imaginable type of humor. And not just what makes things funny, but why certain things *aren't* funny. "My theory also explains nervous laughter, racist or sexist jokes, and toilet humor," he told his fellow humor researchers.

Coming up with an essential description of comedy isn't just an intellectual exercise. If the BVT actually is an unerring predictor of what's funny, it could be invaluable. It could have warned Groupon that its Super Bowl ad making light of Tibetan injustices would bomb. *The Love Guru* could've been axed before production began. Podium banter at the Oscars could be less excruciating. If someone could crack the humor code, they could get very rich. Or at least tenure.

It's a wintry February afternoon in Boulder and a 53-year-old tech worker named Kyle fires up a joint he obtained from a medical marijuana dispensary. After smoking his medicine and waiting 15 minutes for it to take effect, Kyle opens a 10-page printed questionnaire. He sees a Photoshopped image of a man picking his nose so vigorously that his finger pokes out of his eye socket. "To what extent is this picture funny?" the survey asks, inviting Kyle to rate the picture on a scale of 0 to 5. He gives it a 3.

Kyle is one of 50 or so marijuana aficionados who have volunteered to take part in a study run by McGraw's laboratory at CU-Boulder—the Humor Research Lab, or HuRL for short. Founded in 2009, HuRL is unorthodox, to put it mildly, even for academia. But McGraw is doing serious enough work at HuRL to have earned two grants from the

Marketing Science Institute, a nonprofit funded by respectable organizations like Bank of America, Pfizer, and IBM. The professor and a team of seven student researchers have been asking test subjects to gauge whether *Hot Tub Time Machine* is funnier if you sit close to the screen or far away. They show subjects a YouTube video of a guy driving a motorcycle into a fence over and over again to see when it ceases to be amusing.

The medical marijuana patients will help HuRL researchers answer a momentous question: Can smoking pot make things more funny? The answer may seem forehead-smackingly obvious, but according to McGraw it's impossible to know for sure without applying scientific rigor. "Your intuition often leads you astray," he says. "It's only within the lab that you can set different theories against one another." McGraw believes that the tests will ultimately prove that marijuana does in fact make broad sight gags more funny. But he needs more data before he can be certain. He's begun soliciting input from more potheads through Amazon.com's crowdsourcing marketplace, Mechanical Turk.

McGraw didn't set out to become a humorologist. His background is in marketing and consumer decisionmaking, especially the way moral transgressions and breaches of decorum affect the perceived value of things. For instance, he studied a Florida megachurch that tarnished its reputation when it tried to reward attendees with glitzy prizes. The church's promise to raffle off a Hummer H2 to some lucky congregant was met with controversy in the community—what the hell did that have to do with eternal salvation? But when McGraw related the anecdote at presentations, it prompted laughter—a holy Hummer!—rather than repulsion. This confused him.

"It had never crossed my mind that moral violations could be amusing," McGraw says. He became increasingly preoccupied with the conundrum he saw at the heart of humor: Why do people laugh at horrible things like stereotypes, embarrassment, and pain? Basically, why is Sarah Silverman funny?

Philosophers had pondered this sort of question for millennia, long before anyone thought to examine it in a lab. Plato, Aristotle, and Thomas Hobbes posited the superiority theory of humor, which states that we find the misfortune of others amusing. Sigmund Freud espoused the relief theory, which states that comedy is a way for people to release suppressed thoughts and emotions safely. Incongruity theory, associated with Immanuel Kant, suggests that jokes happen when people notice the disconnect between their expectations and the actual payoff.But McGraw didn't find any of these explanations satisfactory. "You need to add conditions to explain particular incidents of humor, and even then they still struggle," he says. Freud is great for jokes about bodily functions. Incongruity explains Monty Python. Hobbes nails Henny Youngman. But no single theory explains all types of comedy. They also short-circuit when it comes to describing why some things *aren't* funny. McGraw points out that killing a loved one in a fit of rage would be incongruous, it would assert superiority, and it would release pent-up tension, but it would hardly be hilarious.

These glaringly incomplete descriptions of humor offended McGraw's need for order. His duty was clear. "A single theory provides a set of guiding principles that make the world a more organized place," he says.

McGraw and Caleb Warren, a doctoral student, presented their elegantly simple formulation in the August 2010 issue of the journal *Psychological Science*. Their paper, "Benign Violations: Making Immoral Behavior Funny," cited scores of philosophers, psychologists, and neuroscientists (as well as Mel Brooks and Carol Burnett). The theory they lay out: "Laughter and amusement result from violations that are simultaneously seen as benign." That is, they perceive a violation— "of personal dignity (e.g., slapstick, physical deformities), linguistic norms (e.g., unusual accents, malapropisms), social norms (e.g., eating from a sterile bedpan, strange behaviors), and even moral norms (e.g., bestiality, disrespectful behaviors)"—while simultaneously recognizing that the violation doesn't pose a threat to them or their worldview. The theory is ludicrously, vaporously simple. But extensive field tests revealed nuances, variables that determined exactly how funny a joke was perceived to be.

McGraw had his HuRL team present scenarios to hundreds of CU-Boulder students. (Some were bribed with candy bars to participate.) Multiple versions of scenarios were formulated, a few too anodyne to be amusing and some too disgusting for words. Ultimately, McGraw determined that funniness could be predicted based on how committed a person is to the norm being violated, conflicts between two salient norms, and psychological distance from the perceived violation.

The ultimate takeaway of McGraw's paper was that the evolutionary purpose of laughter and amusement is to "signal to the world that a violation is indeed OK." Building on the work of behavioral neurologist V. S. Ramachandran, McGraw believes that laughter developed as an instinctual way to signal that a threat is actually a false alarm—say, that a rustle in the bushes is the wind, not a saber-toothed tiger. "Organisms that could separate benign violations from real threats benefited greatly," McGraw says.

The professor was able to plug the BVT into every form of humor. Dirty jokes violate social norms in a benign way because the traveling salesmen and farmers' daughters that populate them are not real. Punch lines make people laugh because they gently violate the expectations that the jokes set up. The BVT also explains Sarah Silverman, McGraw says; the appalling things that come out of her mouth register as benign because she seems so oblivious to their offensiveness, and "because she's so darn cute." Even tickling, long a stumbling block for humor theorists, appears to fit. Tickling yourself can't be a violation, because you can't take yourself by surprise. Being tickled by a stranger in a trench coat isn't benign; it's creepy. Only tickling by someone you know and trust can be a benign violation.

McGraw and the HuRL team continue to test the theory even as they begin to deploy it in the real world. They've partnered with mShopper, a mobile commerce service, to see whether BVT-tested humor can make text-message product offers more compelling. They've also launched FunnyPoliceReports.com, which aggregates law enforcement dispatches that are likely to amuse readers, such as a woman who called the cops when she was sold fake cocaine.

If the website sounds sort of like FAIL Blog, that's no accident. McGraw knows Ben Huh, CEO of the Cheezburger Network, who has been using HuRL's findings to help determine what content and features have the potential to be the next big meme. The lolcats baron points to a recent post about a priest cracking down on cell phones in church after a parishioner's "Stayin' Alive" ringtone went off during a funeral. "The benign violation theory applies to that," Huh says. "I'm a guy who makes his living off of Internet humor, and McGraw's model fits really well. He's just a lot more right than anyone else."

❖

The conference in San Antonio was the first time McGraw presented his theory to other humor researchers. His well-honed delivery gets a lot of laughs, but his theory ultimately receives the same polite applause as everything else. There are no stunned looks of amazement in the audience, no rumblings of a field torn asunder.

Maybe it's because a discipline that can't even agree on what to call the response elicited by humor isn't ready for a universal theory of humor. At this point, there's still no single way to measure it. (The International Society for Humor Studies lists 14 tests and scales for measuring humor, from the Multidimensional Sense of Humor Scale to the Humorous Behavior Q-Sort Deck.)

The BVT also has its fair share of detractors. ISHS president Elliott Oring says, "I didn't see many big differences between this theory and the various formulations of incongruity theory." Victor Raskin, founder of the academic journal *Humor: International Journal of Humor Research*, is more blunt: "What McGraw has come up with is flawed and bullshit—what kind of a theory is that?" To his mind, the BVT is a "very loose and vague metaphor," not a functional formula like $E=mc^2$. He's also quick to challenge McGraw's standing in the tight-knit community of scholarship: "He is not a humor researcher; he has no status."

McGraw's lecture did impress Robert Mankoff, cartoon editor at *The New Yorker*, who also gave a presentation in San Antonio. (Fun fact: *New Yorker* cartoons must endure the infamous rigors of the magazine's fact-checkers; just because a cartoon bluebird can talk doesn't mean it shouldn't resemble a genuine *Sialia*.) After the symposium ended, he offered to provide HuRL with thousands of caption-contest entries to examine. Mankoff says he admires McGraw's work, "and I admire him even more for having the balls to take his theory on the road as stand-up." But he also has a caveat for McGraw and other humor scientists: "All these theories are so general that they're of no use when you're trying to craft a good cartoon." He cites one that he's particularly fond of, an illustration of a Swiss Army knife featuring nothing but corkscrews. The caption reads "French Army knife." No Venn diagram, he says, has ever produced a joke like that.

It's a half hour to showtime at Denver's Paramount Theatre and McGraw is milling around in the lobby, hoping to get green-room access to the comedian Louis CK. The prof is convinced that his theory works in the lab, and he's increasingly interested in testing it in the wild. Kind words from Huh and Mankoff are fine, but the endorsement of a comedian with his own eponymous show on cable would be invaluable. CK is one of McGraw's favorites. "I am fascinated by his ability to make things funny that I wouldn't have thought could be funny," McGraw says, "how he portrays his role as a father in an unflattering way."

McGraw gets the go-ahead, and with curtain time closing in, he's soon sitting in the presence of his idol. The comedian slumps into a chair, the toll of weeks on the road apparent on his face. Knowing that he has only a few minutes, McGraw gives a nutshell version of his well-honed spiel. He lays out the BVT and describes the tickling conundrum that killed at the humor symposium. But CK cuts him off. "I don't think it's that simple," he says, directing as much attention to a preshow ham sandwich as to McGraw. "There are thousands of kinds of jokes. I just don't believe that there's one explanation."

Chapter 12 | **Reading Humor**

Oof, tough room. His research dismissed, McGraw casts about for another subject of inquiry. Luckily, he'd polled fellow attendees for questions while waiting for an audience with CK. "A woman in the lobby wants to know how big your penis is," he says.

CK cracks the faintest of smiles, shakes his head. "I am not going to answer that."

"I wouldn't either," McGraw says. With a chuckle he adds, "But I've heard that if you don't answer that, it means it's small."

The silence that follows is so thick you could pound in a nail and hang a painting from it. That last remark is a violation, and it isn't benign. McGraw changes the subject again. "So, you're friends with Chris Rock?" he says. He wonders whether CK could ask Rock for seed funding, even offering to rename his facility the Chris Rock Humor Research Lab (CRoHuRL?).

"No," CK says. This time, there's no smile.

Sensing that his time is up, McGraw heads for the door. He did get one valuable takeaway: "My approach to this sort of research needs to be more professional."

When the show begins a bit later, Louis CK has shed all vestiges of his preshow reticence. It takes only a couple of jokes about slavery to get McGraw chuckling in his front-row seat. By the time the comedian describes having a bizarre dream about Gene Hackman, the professor is completely overcome. His body jerks uncontrollably as he emits a series of deep, braying laughs that end with a little nasal honk. This is full-on mirth.

The other people in the theater are also in hysterics. They don't know exactly why, and maybe it doesn't matter.

■ WHAT?

1. Briefly explain McGraw's benign violation theory of humor.
2. Do you see value in trying to figure out why we perceive some things in the world to be funny? Explain your response.
3. What benefits do you see in using humor to broach difficult subjects? Do you think some topics can or should never be made funny? Explain your response.

■ WHAT ELSE? WHAT'S NEXT?

4. McGraw and his co-researcher have encountered resistance to their work from within the field of humor studies. Using this article as a starting point, research some of the objections to the benign violation theory and explain how other theorists approach the topic of humor.

■ WHO CARES?

5. Explain the role that audience plays in the analysis of humorous texts. Can you think of any jokes or other humorous texts that are universally funny?

> *Comedian Zach Miller wrote this piece for the website* Timothy McSweeney's Internet Tendency *in 2011.*

BEFORE YOU READ
Using a website that targets consumers of digital technology (such as CNET *or* Wired*), find a couple of reviews of an iPad or other electronic tablet. Read these and make note of the genre conventions of this kind of product review.*

REVIEW: THE MEAD SPIRAL 100 COLLEGE-RULED NOTEBOOK. Zach Miller

Releasing the same month as the iPad 2, Mead has taken a big risk with its new 100 Notebook series. Built around a minimal feature set and a low price point, the company is banking that the robust word-processing capabilities and ultraportable design will offer an appealing alternative to the latest tablets and netbooks. Buzz about the Mead 100 has been circulating in the tech blogosphere for months, but with such high expectations, can the notebook deliver?

■ Design and Build

At first blush it is difficult to classify the Mead 100. Its 8.5" X 11" size aligns it with 11" netbooks, but its surprisingly minimal weight (8 oz) positions it closer to the class of tablet devices such as the iPad 2 and the Samsung Galaxy Tab. After spending some time with it, we felt comfortable calling the Mead 100 an ultraportable notebook. The Mead 100 comes equipped with an embossed cardboard cover available in a variety of colors and patterns. In a nod towards its younger and perhaps more tech-savvy users, many of the designs feature kittens, sports stars, or dolphins leaping across the planet Saturn. Although smooth and shiny, the cover felt cheap to the touch and displayed a notable amount of flex. It remains to be seen how it will fare under heavy use.

An ultraportable device this light does not come without sacrifices, and Mead has opted for the unusual choice of not including a keyboard. Instead, its operated entirely by a stylus. Some of our testers found the use of the stylus as a control device refreshing and quick, but others struggled with punctuation and poor handwriting. Disappointingly, the stylus is not included with the purchase of the notebook, although the company was quick to point out that many third party styli are available at retail locations where the notebook is sold. (See our reviews of the BIC Round Stic Ball Pen and the super-fast Pilot G2 Retractable Ink Roller).

Chapter 12 | **Reading Humor**

■ Graphics and Performance

At its core, the Mead 100 is equipped with a metal spiral binding and 100 pages of chemically pulped memory, partitioned into standard college rule. Although we found 100 pages suitable for typical use, business and power users should consider upgrading to the Mead 150.

We were impressed by the boot time of the Mead 100, and on our test model startup was literally as fast as opening up the cover, although we did find that subsequent performance lagged as users struggled to find their last page of writing.

The display is a bleached white post-recycled paper, which isn't as bright and welcoming to the eye as higher end acid-free displays, but is acceptable for everyday use. Some users reported performance issues in low-light conditions. The tablet can be held vertically or horizontally, and receives high marks for producing a noticeable lack of heat or fan noise, even after many hours of use.

Perhaps the most impressive feature of the Mead is its battery life—we used the Mead for eleven hours without a drop in performance or indication of a low battery, although the stylus does become uncomfortable during such long stints.

Graphics capabilities in the Mead 100 are largely dependent on the user's ability to draw, here however some users found the college rule pesky. Music and video capabilities are also a non-starter, although one of our testers was able to program a workaround in the GUI by drawing a stick figure repeatedly and flipping rapidly through the pages. Still, those looking for music and video editing capabilities will need to go elsewhere.

■ Notes and Verdict

Shipping without an instruction manual limits the Mead 100's appeal to a subset of tech-savvy first-adopters. We were disappointed with the lack of included stylus and this may be a deterrent to users looking for the convenience of a plug and play experience. The Mead also does not include backup features with its notebook, and users looking to archive data may need to purchase a second notebook and copy pages manually with the stylus—a time consuming prospect.

Our overall feeling about the Mead 100 is that this is a first foray into new technology that has yet to reach its full potential. However, we are encouraged that Mead seems committed to its line, as last week it announced an agreement with Pee-Chee to build external memory folders.

Even with its shortcomings, the Mead 100 is currently the only game in town for those looking for a stripped-down ultraportable notebook with extended battery life at a low price point. Like all bleeding edge technology, though, its reign may be a short one, as the next few months will see the release of the handheld Moleskine Pocket Notebook and the graphics-driven Strathmore 400 Artist Pad.

■ WHAT?

1. Explain how this piece fits the definition of satire.
2. What is the subject of Miller's satire? Whom is he targeting for ridicule? How can you tell?

■ WHAT ELSE? WHAT'S NEXT?

3. How might a satirical text like this be useful as an argument? Explain your response.
4. Find an example of a satirical text that you think fails, and explain why you don't find the text funny or effective as a satire.

■ WHO CARES?

5. Visit the websites for *McSweeney's* and for *Timothy McSweeney's Internet Tendency*. How would you characterize the humor on these websites? Who do you think is their target audience? How can you tell?

Chapter 12 | **Reading Humor**

Heather Havrilesky writes for Salon, *the* New York Times Magazine, *and other publications, in print and online. This piece, which she wrote for* Salon *in 2006, explores the anxiety—self-inflicted and culturally imposed—of new motherhood.*

BEFORE YOU READ

Research the term "Mommy Wars" and be prepared to share with classmates your take on this ongoing debate.

MOMMIE FEAREST   Heather Havrilesky

The joys of motherhood await me! In about a month, if all goes well, I'll be the first-time mother of a newborn. According to my friends who are mothers, this means that the healthy glow and abnormally cheerful moods of pregnancy will soon be gone, replaced by a sallow zombie mask. I'll have trouble running a brush through my hair, my stomach will sag like an empty duffel bag, there will be big, dark circles under my eyes, and acquaintances will speculate as to the severity of my postpartum depression—which will be very, very severe indeed.

Of course I'll try my best to do everything I've been told—I'll try not to "overthink" breast-feeding but will aim to achieve a "good latch," I'll try to pump early and often, I'll nap when my baby is napping, I'll make my husband change every single diaper and walk the baby in a million little circles, I'll treat motherhood as my brand-new, overtime, around-the-clock job, I won't attempt to vacuum or shower or pay bills, I won't guilt myself into thinking I should be back at work prematurely—but even so, I'm told that I'll feel angry and sullen and overwhelmed. I'll cry over nothing, or over the fact that there's a lamprey-like beast sucking my will to live straight out of my sore breasts.

Yes, just four weeks from now, if the predictions of my mother friends are accurate, I should feel like a total impostor, a crappy mom, a complete failure at my "new career," but I'll also be so spaced out and slow that I'll wonder if I can ever return to my old career again. I'll have to let my husband wash the lamprey, just in case I turn into Andrea Yates in a weak moment. I'll be just like Brooke Shields was after her first baby was born, except that I'll look like shit and I won't have the energy to write a book about it—and even if I do, no one will buy it.

Occasionally, I'll make desperate, weepy calls to friends, barely able to string enough words together to describe the feeling of walking around underwater, spaced out, stuck in some hazy existential crisis. My closest friends, who are childless, will sigh sympathetically, then hurry off the phone, depressed by the prospect of procreating. My friends who are moms will chuckle sympathetically, then hurry off the phone to prevent their toddler from sticking a fork into the nearest electrical outlet.

Now and then, I'll go out for a walk, lamprey in tow, just like I'm supposed to do. My lamprey will whine and then explode into tears, but I'll sally forth, determined to make it to the local coffee joint, even though I can't actually drink any coffee, since I'm breast-feeding and the caffeine is sure to give my lamprey ADHD or autism or asthma. I'll stumble over to the "child play area," which always seemed to be full of moms trading epidural stories when I worked there on my laptop—you know, back when I was a successful writer with a flourishing career and a life of endless promise stretching out before me. There'll be one mom there with a toddler and a camera-ready model baby, sleeping in its expensive stroller. She'll point out that I have my Baby Bjorn strapped on incorrectly, in a way that's known to increase the risk of suffocation. While she readjusts my Bjorn, she'll ask me polite questions about the lamprey sucking the life blood out of me, as if it's not strange at all, as if I'm not clearly starring in some sci-fi horror flick that ends badly.

Then she'll launch into her enthusiastic views of attachment parenting and other all-consuming child-rearing techniques that I know nothing about, other than the fact that they demand that mothers annihilate their egos and bend the laws of space and time in order to accommodate their children. While she talks, she'll begin unpacking a seemingly endless array of tiny Tupperware containers from her leather diaper bag, each housing a different organic, wheat-free, lactose-free snack, and she'll pull out several scent-free sanitary wipes and a sippy cup full of juice and a very expensive breast pump, and she'll (very discreetly) feed her very attractive baby with one breast while (efficiently and effectively) pumping the other breast, and she'll hand out small, tasty chunks of food to her toddler, all of them rich in Omega-3 and iron and vitamin C. Watching her will suddenly make me feel very faint, and my lamprey and I will hit the floor with a sickening thud that causes everyone in the entire coffee joint to turn their heads and gasp and vow never, ever to forsake their very promising and brilliant writing careers in order to procreate.

But things will get better for me a few months later, don't you worry! The lamprey will start sleeping for two-hour stretches at a time (What a luxury!), enough time for me to actually call my few remaining friends and tell them I can't make it to whatever fun-sounding event they're planning. I'll blame it all on the lamprey, of course, and I'll describe, in excruciating detail, how cute the lamprey's expressions are these days, especially when it has gas. I'll even check my e-mail, just like I did in the old days! Of course, once I get tired of reading old messages, I'll just delete them all and send out a group e-mail announcing that I can no longer be expected to return calls or e-mails in a timely fashion and I can't drive for more than three minutes without the lamprey crying (unless I sing "Farmer in the Dell" in a very happy, high voice, but that only buys me another two minutes), so anyone who wants to talk to me or see me will have to come to my house, where I'll be distracted constantly and will have one or the other of my bloated, pale, blue-vein-covered boobs out at all times.

In my e-mail, I'll explain that, yes, I recognize that some women in Africa only pause for half a second to give birth, and then they return to toil in the fields while their baby is raised by their 3-year-old or their grandmother or their dog, but that's only because those women have very mellow babies, not colicky, fussy little creatures like my lamprey, and besides, studies have shown that babies in Africa often develop emotional insecurity from being raised by their 3-year-old siblings, who also don't tend to notice when they're getting loose stools or eczema or painful rashes from their non-hypoallergenic burlap bedding. I will remind my friends that American children have the distinct advantage of being the center of their parents' universes, and without overzealous, overbearing helpings of attention and care, they'll never grow up to be neurotic, overachieving, ulcerous mutants that fit neatly into our society's soulless, workaholic culture.

It will feel good to reconnect with my dear friends through the convenience of a mass e-mail! But best of all, every week or so, I'll venture out of the house *without the lamprey*! I'll get to take luxurious half-hour strolls down to the pharmacy for more diaper rash cream. It will feel so nice to get away from home, every corner of which is now filled with brightly colored plastic devices and discarded butt wipes and little radios that play happy baby songs that make you want to beat someone's head in with a tire iron.

Sure, I'll sometimes wonder if the lamprey is still breathing without me there, watching it closely, monitoring its every breath. I'll picture my husband, dropping the lamprey on the floor and then tripping over it. I'll picture the dogs, fighting over the lamprey like a chew toy. And then, while I'm in line for the cashier, I'll catch a glimpse of that Vanity Fair cover with Katie Holmes and Tom Cruise and that creepy, overstyled, wise little elf Suri tucked between them, the whole family looking painfully smug and rich and scary, and I'll break down sobbing and I won't be able to stop. I'll rush back home to the lamprey and I'll feel relieved that it's still alive, but I'll notice that it's got spit-up on its onesie and its diaper hasn't been changed, and I'll fly into a rage and accuse my husband of being a shitty father.

But things will get better after that, don't you worry! Eventually, I'll get divorced, and the lamprey will start to talk, babbling on about Teletubbies and Pokemon and other really tedious stuff, and then the lamprey will become a sullen big kid who proclaims that it's "bored" all the time, so I'll rush around to keep it busy and happy, and sooner than you know it, the lamprey will be an angry, temperamental teenager with a seriously overblown sense of its own importance. Finally, one day in the not-so-distant future, maybe after it has a particularly helpful therapy session, the lamprey will call me to tell me that, as part of its "healing process" it needs for me to understand that I was a crappy mother. On top of being seriously stupid and uncool, I was incredibly injurious to its sense of self, and I would've been a way better parent if I hadn't worried about it so much or driven it to piano lessons (which it fucking *hated*), because all of my energy and focus on it were just a total *nightmare* and *that's* why it was driven to drink and drive and shoot drugs and shoplift and catch venereal diseases from scary losers with gun collections and bad hair and corn-chip breath. When I start to get defensive, saying that maybe I made some mistakes, but really, all I wanted was to do my best and love my kid with all of my heart, the lamprey will scream that I don't understand anything—I never understood anything!—and then it'll hang up on me.

Several birthdays and holidays and Mother's Days will go by, unmarked, as I hobble around my cluttered, dusty, cat-filled house, but don't worry! Things will get better when I go to live in a nursing home, and my lamprey comes by one afternoon to introduce me to its lampreys (all grown up now), who seem to hate its guts almost as much as it hates my guts. And when the little (full-grown) lampreys cringe as they watch me unwrap and eat my apple sauce out of its plastic cup without the aid of my dentures, which are disinfecting in a glass by my adjustable bed, my lamprey will shoot me a sympathetic look. No, my darling lamprey won't say, "I'm sorry" or "I love you, Mom" or anything like that, but that look it gives me will more than make up for all of the pain and sacrifices I went through as a mother! I'll get a warm glow deep down inside, and I won't even feel bad later, when I discover that my antique gold watch and the roll of $20 bills I save for Bingo are both missing from my sock drawer.

To think, in just one month, the joys of motherhood begin at last! How blessed I feel, to be poised on the precipice of this wonderful new adventure!

■ WHAT?

1. What, specifically, do you think Havrilesky is satirizing in this essay? What do you think she hopes to accomplish with her satire?
2. Find this piece on *Salon*'s website and click on the "Comments" button at the end of the article. How would you characterize reader responses to Havrilesky's essay? Does the humor work?

■ WHO CARES?

3. Who reads *Salon*? Write a paragraph in which you analyze the website's audience, based on the articles and images it carries and the advertisers it attracts.
4. What does Havrilesky want from her audience? Why do you think this?

IMAGE 12.4
In "Wake Up, Geek Culture. Time to Die," Patton Oswalt warns of the Internet's threat to cultural creativity: "Etewaf [Everything That Ever Was—Available Forever] doesn't produce a new generation of artists—just an army of sated consumers," he writes. "Why create anything new when there's a mountain of freshly excavated pop culture to recut, repurpose, and manipulate on your iMovie?" Do you agree with Oswalt's argument?

Chapter 12 | **Reading Humor**

Comedian, actor, and author Patton Oswalt's (@pattonoswalt) first book, Zombie Spaceship Wasteland *came out last year. Oswalt wrote this essay, in which he explains his plan for reviving the nerd-dom subculture ruined by mainstream acceptance, for the January 2011 issue of* Wired *magazine.*

BEFORE YOU READ

Research the term "geek culture" and explain at least three different interpretations that you find. Then, think about why the definitions you find are different—even if they vary only slightly.

WAKE UP, GEEK CULTURE. TIME TO DIE.
Patton Oswalt *with contributions by* Chris Buck

I'm not a nerd. I used to be one, back 30 years ago when *nerd* meant something. I entered the '80s immersed, variously, in science fiction, Dungeons & Dragons, and Stephen King. Except for the multiple-player aspect of D&D, these pursuits were not "passions from a common spring," to quote Poe.

I can't say that I ever abided nerd stereotypes: I was never alone or felt outcast. I had a circle of friends who were similarly drawn to the exotica of pop culture (or, at least, what was considered pop culture at the time in northern Virginia)—Monty Python, post-punk music, comic books, slasher films, and video games. We were a sizable clique. The terms *nerd* and *geek* were convenient shorthand used by other cliques to categorize us. But they were thin descriptors.

In Japan, the word *otaku* refers to people who have obsessive, minute interests—especially stuff like anime or videogames. It comes from a term for "someone else's house"—otaku live in their own, enclosed worlds. Or, at least, their lives follow patterns that are well outside the norm. Looking back, we were American otakus. (Of course, now all America is otaku—which I'm going to get into shortly. But in order to do so, we're going to hang out in the '80s.)

I was too young to drive or hold a job. I was never going to play sports, and girls were an uncrackable code. So, yeah—I had time to collect every Star Wars action figure, learn the Three Laws of Robotics, memorize Roy Batty's speech from the end of *Blade Runner*, and classify each monster's abilities and weaknesses in TSR Hobbies' *Monster Manual*. By 1987, my friends and I were waist-deep in the hot honey of adolescence. Money and cars and, hopefully, girls would follow, but not if we spent our free time learning the names of the bounty hunters' ships in *The Empire Strikes Back*. So we each built our own otakuesque thought-palace, which we crammed with facts and nonsense—only now, the thought-palace was nicely appointed, decorated neatly, the information laid out on deep mahogany shelves or framed in gilt. What once set us apart, we hoped, would become a lovable quirk.

Our respective nerdery took on various forms: One friend was the first to get his hands on early bootlegs of Asian action flicks by Tsui Hark and John Woo, and he never looked back. Another started reading William Gibson and peppered his conversations with cryptic (and alluring) references to "cyberspace." I was ground zero for the "new wave" of mainstream superhero comics—which meant being right there for Alan Moore, Frank Miller, and Neil Gaiman. And like my music-obsessed pals, who passed around the cassette of Guns n' Roses' *Live ?!*@ Like a Suicide* and were thus prepared for the shock wave of *Appetite for Destruction*, I'd devoured Moore's run on *Swamp Thing* and thus eased nicely into his *Watchmen*. I'd also read the individual issues of Miller's *Daredevil: Born Again* run, so when *The Dark Knight Returns* was reviewed by *The New York Times*, I could say I saw it coming. And I'd consumed so many single-issue guest-writing stints of Gaiman's that when he was finally given *The Sandman* title all to himself, I was first in line and knew the language.

Admittedly, there's a chilly thrill in moving with the herd while quietly being tuned in to something dark, complicated, and unknown just beneath the topsoil of popularity. Something about which, while we moved *with* the herd, we could share a wink and a nod with two or three other similarly connected herdlings.

When our coworkers nodded along to Springsteen and Madonna songs at the local Bennigan's, my select friends and I would quietly trade out-of-context lines from Monty Python sketches—a thieves' cant, a code language used for identification. We needed it, too, because the essence of our culture—our "escape hatch" culture—would begin to change in 1987.

That was the year the final issue of *Watchmen* came out, in October. After that, it seemed like everything that was part of my otaku world was out in the open and up for grabs, if only out of context. I wasn't seeing the hard line between "nerds" and "normals" anymore. It was the last year that a T-shirt or music preference or pastime (Dungeons & Dragons had long since lost its dangerous, Satanic, suicide-inducing street cred) could set you apart from the surface dwellers. Pretty soon, being the only person who was into something didn't make you outcast; it made you ahead of the curve and someone people were quicker to befriend than shun. Ironically, surface dwellers began repurposing the symbols and phrases and tokens of the erstwhile outcast underground.

Fast-forward to now: Boba Fett's helmet emblazoned on sleeveless T-shirts worn by gym douches hefting dumbbells. The *Glee* kids performing the songs from *The Rocky Horror Picture Show*. And Toad the Wet Sprocket, a band that took its name from a Monty Python riff, joining the permanent soundtrack of a night out at Bennigan's. Our below-the-topsoil passions have been rudely dug up and displayed in the noonday sun. *The Lord of the Rings* used to be ours and *only* ours simply because of the sheer goddamn thickness of the books. Twenty years later, the entire cast and crew would be trooping onstage at the Oscars to collect their statuettes, and replicas of the One Ring would be sold as bling.

The topsoil has been scraped away, forever, in 2010. In fact, it's been dug up, thrown into the air, and allowed to rain down and coat everyone in a thin gray-brown mist called the Internet. Everyone considers themselves otaku about something—whether it's the mythology of *Lost* or the minor intrigues of *Top Chef*. *American Idol* inspires—if not in depth, at least in length and passion—the same number of conversations as does *The Wire*. There are no more hidden thought-palaces—they're easily accessed websites, or Facebook pages with thousands of fans. And I'm not going to bore you with the step-by-step specifics of how it happened. In the timeline of the upheaval, part of the graph should be interrupted by the words *the Internet*. And now here we are.

The problem with the Internet, however, is that it lets anyone become otaku about anything *instantly*. In the '80s, you couldn't get up to speed on an entire genre in a weekend. You had to wait, month to month, for the issues of *Watchmen* to come out. We couldn't BitTorrent the latest John Woo film or digitally download an entire decade's worth of grunge or hip hop. Hell, there were a few weeks during the spring of 1991 when we couldn't tell whether Nirvana or Tad would be the next band to break big. Imagine the terror!

But then reflect on the advantages. Waiting for the next issue, movie, or album gave you time to reread, rewatch, reabsorb whatever you loved, so you brought your own idiosyncratic love of that thing to your thought-palace. People who were obsessed with *Star Trek* or the *Ender's Game* books were all obsessed with the same object, but its light shone differently on each person. Everyone had to create in their mind unanswered questions or what-ifs. What if Leia, not Luke, had become a Jedi? What happens *after* Rorschach's journal is found at the end of *Watchmen*? What the hell was *The Prisoner* about?

None of that's necessary anymore. When everyone has easy access to their favorite diversions and every diversion comes with a rabbit hole's worth of extra features and deleted scenes and hidden hacks to tumble down and never emerge from, then we're all just adding to an ever-swelling, soon-to-erupt volcano of trivia, re-contextualized and forever rebooted. We're on the brink of Etewaf: Everything That Ever Was—Available Forever.

I know it sounds great, but there's a danger: Everything we have today that's cool comes from someone wanting more of something they loved in the past. Action figures, videogames, superhero movies, iPods: All are continuations of a love that wanted more. Ever see action figures from the '70s, each with that same generic Anson Williams body and one-piece costume with the big clumsy snap on the back? Or played Atari's *Adventure*, found the secret room, and thought, that's it? Can we all admit the final battle in *Superman II* looks like a local commercial for a personal-injury attorney? And how many people had their cassette of the *Repo Man* soundtrack eaten by a Walkman?

Now, with everyone more or less otaku and everything *immediately* awesome (or, if not, just as immediately rebooted or recut as a hilarious YouTube or Funny or Die spoof), the old inner longing for more or better that made our present pop culture so amazing is dwindling. *The Onion*'s A.V. Club—essential and transcendent in so many ways—has a weekly feature called Gateways to Geekery, in which an entire artistic subculture—say, anime, H. P. Lovecraft, or the Marx Brothers—is mapped out so you can become otaku on it but avoid its more tedious aspects.

Here's the danger: That creates weak otakus. Etewaf doesn't produce a new generation of artists—just an army of sated consumers. Why create anything new when there's a mountain of freshly excavated pop culture to recut, repurpose, and manipulate on your iMovie? *The Shining* can be remade into a comedy trailer. Both movie versions of the Joker can be sent to battle each another. The Dude is in *The Matrix*The coming decades—the 21st-century's '20s, '30s, and '40s—have the potential to be one long, unbroken, recut spoof in which everything in *Avatar* farts while Keyboard Cat plays eerily in the background.

But I prefer to be optimistic. I choose hope. I see Etewaf as the Balrog, the helter-skelter, the A-pop-alypse that rains cleansing fire down onto the otaku landscape, burns away the chaff, and forces us to start over with only a few thin, near-meatless scraps on which to build.

In order to save pop culture future, we've got to make the present pop culture suck, at least for a little while. Why create anything new when there's a mountain of pop culture to recut, repurpose, and manipulate on iMovie?

How do we do this? How do we bring back that sweet longing for more that spawned *Gears of War*, the *Crank* films, and the entire Joss Whedon oeuvre? Simple: We've got to speed up the process. We've got to stoke the volcano. We've got to catalog, collate, and cross-pollinate. We must bring about **Etewaf**, and soon.

It has already started. It's all around us. VH1 list shows. *Freddy vs. Jason*. Websites that list the 10 biggest sports meltdowns, the 50 weirdest plastic surgeries, the 200 harshest nut shots. *Alien vs. Predator*. Lists of fails, lists of boobs, lists of deleted movie scenes. Entire TV seasons on iTunes. An entire studio's film vault, downloadable with a click. Easter egg scenes of wild sex in *Grand Theft Auto*. Hell, *Grand Theft Auto*, period. And yes, I know that a lot of what I'm listing here seems like it's outside of the "nerd world" and part of the wider pop culture. Well, I've got news for you—pop culture *is* nerd culture. The fans of *Real Housewives of Hoboken* watch, discuss, and absorb their show the same way a geek watched *Dark Shadows* or obsessed over his eighth-level half-elf ranger character in Dungeons & Dragons. It's the method of consumption, not what's on the plate.

Since there's no going back—no reverse on the out-of-control locomotive we've created—we've got to dump nitro into the engines. We need to get serious, and I'm here to outline my own personal fantasy: We start with lists of the best lists of boobs. Every Beatles song, along with every alternate take, along with every cover version of every one of their songs and every alternate take of every cover version, all on your chewing-gum-sized iPod nano. *Goonies vs. Saw*. Every book on your Kindle. Every book *on* Kindle on every Kindle. *The Human Centipede* done with the cast of *The Hills* and directed by the Coen brothers.

That's when we'll reach Etewaf singularity. Pop culture will become self-aware. It will happen in the A.V. Club first: A brilliant Nathan Rabin column about the worst Turkish rip-offs of American comic book characters will suddenly begin writing its own comments, each a single sentence from the sequel to *A Confederacy of Dunces*. Then a fourth and fifth season of *Arrested Development*, directed by David Milch of *Deadwood*, will appear suddenly in the TV Shows section of iTunes. Someone BitTorrenting a Crass bootleg will suddenly find their hard drive crammed with Elvis Presley's "lost" grunge album from 1994. And everyone's TiVo will record *Ghostbusters III*, starring Peter Sellers, Lee Marvin, and John Candy.

This will last only a moment. We'll have one minute before pop culture swells and blackens like a rotten peach and then explodes, sending every movie, album, book, and TV show flying away into space. Maybe tendrils and fragments of them will attach to asteroids or plop down on ice planets light-years away. A billion years after our sun burns out, a race of intelligent ice crystals will build a culture based on dialog from *The Princess Bride*. On another planet, intelligent gas clouds will wait for the yearly passing of the "Lebowski" comet. One of the rings of Saturn will be made from blurbs for the softcover release of *Infinite Jest*, twirled forever into a ribbon of effusive praise.

Chapter 12 | **Reading Humor**

But back here on Earth, we'll enter year zero for pop culture. All that we'll have left to work with will be a VHS copy of *Zapped!*, the soundtrack to *The Road Warrior*, and Steve Ditko's eight-issue run on *Shade: The Changing Man*. For a while—maybe a generation—pop culture pastimes will revolve around politics and farming.

But the same way a farmer has to endure a few fallow seasons after he's overplanted, a new, richer loam will begin to appear in the wake of our tilling. From *Zapped!* will arise a telekinesis epic from James Cameron. Paul Thomas Anderson will do a smaller, single-character study of a man who can move matchbooks with his mind and how he uses this skill to pursue a casino waitress. Then the Coen brothers will veer off, doing a movie about pyrokenesis set in 1980s Cleveland, while out of Japan will come a subgenre of telekinetic horror featuring pale, whispering children. And we'll build from there—precognition, telepathy, and, most radically, normal people falling in love and dealing with jobs and life. Maybe also car crashes.

The Road Warrior soundtrack, all Wagnerian strings and military snare drums, will germinate into a driving, gut-bucket subgenre called waste-rock. And, as a counterpoint, flute-driven folk. Then there'll be the inevitable remixes, mashups, and pirated-only releases. A new Beatles will arise, only they'll be Iranian.

Shade: The Changing Man will become the new *Catcher in the Rye*. Ditko's thin-fingered art will appear on lunch boxes, T-shirts, and magazine covers. Someone will write an even thinner, sparser, simpler version called *Shade*. Someone else will write a 1,000-page meditation about Shade's home planet. Eventually, someone will try to kill the Iranian John Lennon with a hat, based on one panel from issue 3. A whole generation of authors under 20 will have their love—or disgust—of these comics to thank for their careers.

So the topsoil we're coated in needs to wash away for a while. I want my daughter to have a 1987 the way I did and experience the otaku thrill. While everyone else is grooving on the latest Jay-Z, *5 Gallons of Diesel*, I'd like her to share a secret look with a friend, both of them hip to the fact that, from Germany, there's a bootleg MP3 of a group called Dr. Cali-gory, pioneers of superviolent line-dancing music. And I want to her to enjoy that secret look for a little while before Dr. Cali-gory's songs get used in commercials for cruise lines.

Etewaf now!

■ WHAT?

1. Based on Oswalt's essay, define the following terms and explain how they are important to the argument: nerd, geek, otaku, etewaf.
2. Compare Oswalt's essay with Jeanette Winterson's "Imagination and Reality." How does each explain the role of imagination and creativity in developing and sustaining a culture? What part does passion play, according to the two essays? Do you think Winterson would be persuaded by Oswalt's argument? Why or why not?
3. What, according to Oswalt, is the problem with "weak otakus" and the "army of sated consumers" that they might spawn?

■ WHAT ELSE? WHAT'S NEXT?

4. Working with a group of classmates, develop definitions of "culture" and "subculture" that apply to your lives. Make sure you include in your response examples of each and an explanation of the relationship between the two.
5. Look online to find responses to Oswalt's essay (you might start by visiting the page where it was originally published). Look through these and summarize what others have said about the essay. Do you see any patterns?

■ WHO CARES?

6. Visit the website for the magazine that published Oswalt's essay. What, based on the content of the site—including advertisements and links—can you deduce about the magazine's and the website's readership? Based on this analysis and on your reading of the essay, explain who you think Oswalt is trying to reach and whether (and how) he is successful.

Chapter 12 | **Reading Humor**

> *David Sedaris is one of America's most popular humor writers. "Chicken in the Henhouse," from the 2004 collection* Dress Your Family in Corduroy and Denim, *showcases Sedaris' ability to use seemingly ordinary details from daily life to slice through the "cultural euphemisms and political correctness," as his online biography puts it, that so many of us tend to accept or ignore.*

BEFORE YOU READ
If you search online, you'll find many interviews that Sedaris has given to a variety of media. Read (or watch) one or two of these so that you get a sense of the kind of humor Sedaris uses and the kinds of topics he writes about.

CHICKEN IN THE HENHOUSE   David Sedaris

It was one of those hotels without room service, the type you wouldn't mind if you were paying your own bill but would complain about if someone else was paying. I was not paying my own bill, and so the deficiencies stuck out and were taken as evidence of my host's indifference. There was no tub, just a plastic shower stall, and the soap was brittle and smelled like dishwashing detergent. The bedside lamp was missing a bulb, but that could have been remedied easily enough. I could have asked for one at the front desk, but I didn't want a light bulb. I just wanted to feel put-upon.

It started when the airline lost my luggage. Time was lost filling out forms, and I'd had to go directly from the airport to a college an hour north of Manchester, where I gave a talk to a group of students. Then there was a reception and a forty-five-minute drive to the hotel, which was out in the middle of nowhere. I arrived at one A.M. and found they had booked me into a basement room. Late at night it didn't much matter, but in the morning it did. To open the curtains was to invite scrutiny, and the people of New Hampshire stared in without a hint of shame. There wasn't much to look at, just me, sitting on the edge of the bed with a phone to my ear. The airline had sworn my suitcase would arrive overnight, and when it didn't, I called the 800 number printed on the inside of my ticket jacket. My choices were either to speak to a machine or to wait for an available human. I chose the human, and after eight minutes on hold I hung up and started looking for someone to blame.

"I don't care if it's my son, my congressman, what have you. I just don't approve of that lifestyle." The speaker was a woman named Audrey who'd called the local talk-radio station to offer her opinion. The Catholic Church scandal had been front-page news for over a week, and when the priest angle had been exhausted, the discussion filtered down to pedophilia in general and then, homosexual pedophilia, which was commonly agreed to be the worst kind. It was for talk radio, one of those easy topics, like tax hikes or mass murder. "What do you think of full-grown men practicing sodomy on children?"

"Well, I'm *against* it!" This was always said as if it was somehow startling, a minority position no one had yet dared lay claim to.

I'd been traveling around the country for the past ten days, and everywhere I went I heard the same thing. The host would congratulate the caller on his or her moral fortitude, and wanting to feel that approval again, the person would rephrase the original statement, freshening it up with an adverb or qualifier. "Call me old-fashioned, but I just hugely think it's wrong." Then, little by little, they'd begin interchanging the words *homosexual* and *pedophile*, speaking as if they were one and the same. "Now they've even got them on TV," Audrey said. "And in the schools! Talk about the proverbial chicken in the henhouse."

"Fox," the host said.

"Oh, they're the worst," Audrey said. "*The Simpsons* and such—I never watch that station."

I meant in the henhouse," the host said. "I believe the saying is 'the fox in the henhouse,' not 'the chicken in the henhouse.'"

Audrey regrouped. "Did I say chicken? Well, you get my point. These homosexuals can't reproduce themselves, and so they go into the schools and try to recruit our young people."

It was nothing I hadn't heard before, but I was crankier than usual and found myself in the middle of the room, one sock on and one sock off, shouting at the clock radio. "Nobody recruited *me*, Audrey. And I *begged* for it."

It was *her* fault I was stuck in a basement room with no luggage, her and all the people just like her: the satisfied families trotting from the parking lot to the first-floor restaurant, the hotel guests with whirlpool baths and rooms overlooking the surrounding forest. *Why waste the view on a homosexual? He only looks at schoolboys' rectums. And a suitcase? Please! We all know what they do with those.* They might not have come out and said it, but they are sure thinking it. I could tell.

It stood to reason that if the world was conspiring against me, my Mr. Coffee machine was broken. It sat on the bathroom counter, dribbling cold water, and after a brief, completely unsatisfying cry, I finished getting dressed and left the room. There was a staircase at the end of the hall, and beside it a little cleared area where a dozen or so elderly women knelt upon the carpet, piecing together a patchwork quilt. They looked up as I passed, one of them turning to ask me a question. "Yoin' shurch?" Her mouth was full of pins and it took me a moment to realize what she was saying—You going to church? It was an odd question, but then I remembered that it was a Sunday, and I was wearing a tie. Someone at the college had loaned it to me the night before, and I'd put it on in hopes it might distract from my shirt, which was wrinkled and discolored beneath the arms. "No," I told her, "I'm *not* going to church." Oh, I was in a horrible mood. Midway up the stairs I stopped and turned back around. "I *never* go to church," I said. "Never. And I'm not about to start now."

"Shute shelf," she said.

Past the restaurant and gift shop, in the center of the lobby, was a complimentary beverage stand. I thought I'd get a coffee and take it outdoors, but just as I approached, a boy swooped in and began mixing himself a cup of hot chocolate. He looked like all of the kids I'd been seeing lately, in airports, in parking lots: the oversize sweatshirts stamped with team emblems, the baggy jeans and jazzy sneakers. His watch was fat and plastic, like a yo-yo strapped to his wrist, and his hair looked as if it had been cut with the lid of a can, the irregular hanks stiffened with gel and coaxed to stand at peculiar angles.

It was a complicated business, mixing a cup of hot chocolate. You had to spread the powdered cocoa from one end of the table to the other and use as many stirrers as possible, making sure to thoroughly chew the wetted ends before tossing them upon the stack of unused napkins. This is what I like about children: complete attention to one detail and

Chapter 12 | Reading Humor

complete disregard of another. When finally finished, he scooted over to the coffee urn, filling two cups, black, and fitting them with lids. The drinks were stacked into a tower, then tentatively lifted off the table. "Whoa," he whispered. Hot chocolate seeped from beneath the lid of the bottom cup and ran down his hand.

"Do you need some help with those?" I asked.

The boy looked at me for a moment. "Yeah," he said. "Carry these upstairs." There was no *please* or *thank you*, just "I'll take the hot chocolate myself."

He set the coffees back on the table, and as I reached for them it occurred to me that maybe this was not such a good idea. I was a stranger, an admitted homosexual traveling through a small town, and he was, like, ten. And alone. The voice of reason whispered in my ear. *Don't do it, buster. You're playing with fire.*

I withdrew my hands, then stopped, thinking, *Wait a minute. That's not reason. It's Audrey, that crackpot from the radio.* The real voice of reason sounds like Bea Arthur, and when it failed to pipe up, I lifted the coffees off the table and carried them toward the elevator, where the boy stood mashing the call button with his chocolate-coated fingers.

A maid passed and rolled her eyes at the desk clerk. "Cute kid."

Before the church scandal I might have said the same thing, only without the sarcasm. Now, though, any such observation seemed suspect. Though Audrey would never believe it, I am not physically attracted to children. They're like animals to me, fun to watch but beyond the bounds of my sexual imagination. That said, I am a person who feels guilty for crimes I have not committed, or have not committed in years. The police search the train station for a serial rapist and I cover my face with a newspaper, wondering if maybe I did it in my sleep. The last thing I stole was an eight-track tape, but to this day I'm unable to enter a store without feeling like a shoplifter. It's all the anxiety with none of the free stuff. To make things just that much worse, I seem to have developed a remarkable perspiration problem. My conscience is cross-wired with my sweat glands, but there's a short in the system and I break out over things I didn't do, which only makes me look more suspect. Innocently helping to lighten a child's burden was a *good* thing—I knew this—yet moments after lifting the coffees off the table I was soaking wet. As usual, the sweat was fiercest on my forehead, under my arms, and, cruelly, on my ass, which is a great mystery to me. If the stress is prolonged, I'll feel the droplets inching down the back of my legs, trapped, finally, by my socks, which are cotton and bought expressly for their absorbent powers.

If there was a security camera in the lobby, this is what it would have shown: A four-and-a-half-foot-tall boy stands mashing and then pounding the elevator call button. Beside him is a man, maybe a foot taller, dressed in a shirt and tie and holding a lidded cup in each hand. Is it raining outside? If not, perhaps he just stepped from the shower and threw on his clothes without drying himself. His eyes shift this way and that, giving the impression that he is searching for somebody. Could it be this silver-haired gentleman? He's just walked up, looking very dapper in his tweed jacket and matching cap. He talks to the boy and lays a hand on the back of his head, scolding him probably, which is good, as somebody needed to. The other man, the wet one, is just standing there, holding the cups and trying to wipe his forehead with his sleeve at the same time. A lid pops off and something—it looks like coffee—spills down the front of his shirt. He leaps about, prancing almost, and pulls the fabric away from his skin. The boy seems angry now and says something. The older gentleman offers a handkerchief, and the man sets down one of his cups and runs—literally runs, panting—off camera, returning thirty seconds later with another lidded cup, a replacement. By this time the elevator has arrived. The gentleman holds open the door, and he and the boy wait as the man picks the other cup off the floor and joins them. Then the door closes, and they are gone.

"So, who have we got here?" the gentleman asked. His voice was jovial and enthusiastic. "What do you call yourself, big fella?"

"Michael," the boy said.

"Well, that's a grown-up name, isn't it."

Michael guessed that it was, and the man caught my eye and winked, the way people do when they're establishing a partnership. *We'll just put on the small fry, what do you say?* "I bet a big guy like you must have a lot of girlfriends," he said. "Is that true?"

"No."

"You *don't*? Well, what's the problem?"

"I don't know. I just don't have one. That's all," Michael said.

I had always hated it when men asked the girlfriend question. Not only was it corny, but it set you in their imaginations in a way that seemed private to me. Answer yes and they'd picture your wee courtship: the candlelit dinner of hot dogs and potato chips, the rumpled Snoopy sheets. Answer no and you were blue-balled, the frustrated bachelor of the second grade. It was an idea of children as miniature adults, which was about as funny to me as the dog in sunglasses.

"Well, there must be *someone* you have your eye on."

The boy did not answer, but the man persisted in trying to draw him out. "Is Mommy sleeping in this morning?"

Again, nothing.

The man gave up and turned to me. Your wife," he said. "I take it she's still in bed?"

He thought I was Michael's father, and I did not correct him. "Yes," I said. "She's upstairs … passed out." I don't know why I said this, or then again, maybe I do. The man had constructed a little family portrait, and there was a pleasure in defacing it. Here was Michael, here was Michael's dad, and now, here was Mom, lying face down on the bathroom floor.

The elevator stopped on three, and the man tipped his hat. "All right, then," he said. "You two enjoy the rest of the morning." Michael had pressed the button for the fifth floor no less than twenty times, and now he gave it an extra few jabs just for good measure. We were alone now, and something unpleasant entered my mind.

Sometimes when I'm in a tight situation, I'll feel a need to touch somebody's head. It happens a lot on airplanes. I'll look at the person seated in front of me, and within a moment the idea will have grown from a possibility to a compulsion. There is no option—I simply have to do it. The easiest method is to make like I'm getting up, to grab the forward seat for support and just sort of pat the person's hair with my fingers. "Oh, I'm sorry," I say.

"No problem."

Most often I'll continue getting out of my seat, then walk to the back of the plane or go to the bathroom and stand there for a few minutes, trying to fight off what I know is inevitable: I need to touch the person's head again. Experience has taught me that you can do this three times before the head's owner either yells at you or rings for the flight attendant. "Is something wrong?" she'll ask.

"I don't think so, no."

Chapter 12 | **Reading Humor**

"What do you mean 'no,'" the passenger will say. "This freak keeps touching my head."

"Is that true, sir?"

It's not always a head. Sometimes I need to touch a particular purse or briefcase. When I was a child this sort of compulsive behavior was my life, but now I practice it only if I'm in a situation where I can't smoke: planes—as I mentioned—and elevators.

Just touch the boy's head, I thought. *The old man did it, so why can't you?*

To remind myself that this is inappropriate only makes the voice more insistent. The thing must be done *because* it is inappropriate. If it weren't, there'd be no point in bothering with it.

He won't even notice it. Touch him now, quick.

Were we traveling a long distance, I would have lost the battle, but fortunately we weren't going far. The elevator arrived on the fifth floor and I scrambled out the door, set the coffees on the carpet, and lit a cigarette. "You're going to have to give me a minute here," I said.

"But my room's just down the hall. And this is non-smoking."

"I know, I know."

"It's not good for you," he said.

"That's true for a lot of people," I told him. "But it *really is* good for me. Take my word for it."

He leaned against a door and removed the DO NOT DISTURB sign, studying it for a moment before sticking it in his back pocket.

I only needed to smoke for a minute, but realized when I was finished that there was no ashtray. Beside the elevator was a window, but of course it was sealed shut. Hotels. They do everything in their power to make you want to jump to your death, and then they make certain that you can't do it. "Are you finished with your cocoa?" I asked.

"No."

"Well, are you finished with the lid?"

"I guess so."

He handed it to me and I spit into the center—no easy task, as my mouth was completely dry. Fifty percent of my body water was seeping out my ass, and the other half was in transit.

"That's gross," he said. "Yeah, well, you're just going to have to forgive me." I stubbed the cigarette into the spit, set the lid on the carpet, and picked up the coffees. "Okay. Where to?"

He pointed out a long corridor and I followed him, gnawing on a question that's been troubling me for years. What if you had a baby and you just ... you just needed to touch it where you knew you shouldn't. I don't mean that you'd want to. You wouldn't *desire* the baby any more than you desire a person whose head you've just touched. The act would be compulsive rather than sexual, and while to you there'd be a big difference, you couldn't expect a prosecutor, much less an infant, to recognize it. You'd be a bad parent, and once the child could talk and you told it not to tell anyone, you would become a manipulator—a monster, basically—and the reason behind your actions would no longer matter.

The closer we got to the end of the hall, the more anxious I became. I had not laid a finger on the boy's head. I have never poked or prodded either a baby or a child, so why did I feel so dirty? Part of it was just my makeup, the deep-seated belief that I deserve a basement room, but a larger, uglier part had to do with the voices I hear on talk radio, and my tendency, in spite of myself, to pay them heed. The man in the elevator had not thought twice about asking Michael personal questions or about laying a hand on the back of his head. Because he was neither a priest nor a homosexual, he hadn't felt the need to watch himself, worrying that every word or gesture might be misinterpreted. He could unthinkingly wander the halls with a strange boy, while for me it amounted to a political act—an insistence that I was as good as the next guy. Yes, I am a homosexual; yes, I am soaking wet; yes, I sometimes feel an urge to touch people's heads, but still I can safely see a ten-year-old back to his room. It bothered me that I needed to prove something this elementary. And prove it to people whom I could never hope to convince.

"This is it," Michael said. From the other side of the door I heard the sound of a television. It was one of those Sunday-morning magazine programs, a weekly hour where all news is good news. Blind Jimmy Henderson coaches a volley ball team. An ailing groundhog is fitted for a back brace. That type of thing. The boy inserted his card key into the slot, and the door opened onto a bright, well-furnished room. It was twice the size of mine, with higher ceilings and a sitting area. One window framed a view of the lake, and the other a stand of scarlet maples.

"Oh, you're back," a woman said. She was clearly the boy's mother, as their profiles were identical, the foreheads easing almost imperceptibly into blunt freckled noses. Both too had spiky blond hair, though for her I imagined the style was accidental, the result of the pillows piled behind her head. She was lying beneath the covers of a canopy bed, examining one of the many brochures scattered across the comforter. A man slept beside her, and when she spoke, he shifted slightly and covered his face with the crook of his arm. "What took you so long?" She looked toward the open door, and her eyes widened as they met mine. "What the ..."

There was a yellow robe at the foot of the bed, and the woman turned her back to me as she got up and stepped into it. Her son reached for the coffees, and I tightened my grip, unwilling to surrender what I'd come to think of as my props. They turned me from a stranger to a kindly stranger, and I'd seen myself holding them as his parents rounded on me, demanding to know what was going on.

"Give them to me," he said, and rather than making a scene, I relaxed my grip. The coffees were taken, and I felt my resolve starting to crumble. Empty-handed, I was just a creep, the spooky wet guy who'd crawled up from the basement. The woman crossed to the dresser, and as the door started to close she called out to me. "Hey," she said. "Wait a minute," I turned, ready to begin the fight of my life, and she stepped forward and pressed a dollar into my hand. "You people run a very nice hotel," she told me. "I just wish we could stay longer."

The door closed and I stood alone in the empty corridor, examining my tip and thinking, *Is that all?*

Chapter 12 | **Reading Humor**

■ **WHAT?**

1. What arguments does Sedaris make about sexuality, stereotypes, and intolerance? How does he use himself as his primary "evidence"?
2. How does Sedaris use humor to convey his feelings about Audrey and her homophobic comments? Why is humor a more effective rhetorical tool in this case than anger or indignation?

■ **WHAT ELSE? WHAT'S NEXT?**

3. Research Sedaris' position on same-sex marriage. What does he have to say about this issue? How does he express these beliefs?

■ **WHO CARES?**

4. How would you describe the ethos that Sedaris presents in his text? What does he do to convey this ethos to his audience?

> The Onion *is a satirical news source that began as a print newspaper in Madison, Wisconsin, but that is now available online at TheOnion.com. The following article was published March 9, 2010.*

BEFORE YOU READ

Write a brief explanation of satire and how it works (or is supposed to work). Use at least two sources to help you compose your response, and make sure you document them correctly.

NATION SHUDDERS AT LARGE BLOCK OF UNINTERRUPTED TEXT  *The Onion*

WASHINGTON—Unable to rest their eyes on a colorful photograph or boldface heading that could be easily skimmed and forgotten about, Americans collectively recoiled Monday when confronted with a solid block of uninterrupted text.

Dumbfounded citizens from Maine to California gazed helplessly at the frightening chunk of print, unsure of what to do next. Without an illustration, chart, or embedded YouTube video to ease them in, millions were frozen in place, terrified by the sight of one long, unbroken string of English words.

"Why won't it just tell me what it's about?" said Boston resident Charlyne Thomson, who was bombarded with the overwhelming mass of black text late Monday afternoon. "There are no bullet points, no highlighted parts. I've looked everywhere—there's nothing here but words."

"Ow," Thomson added after reading the first and last lines in an attempt to get the gist of whatever the article, review, or possibly recipe was about.

At 3:16 p.m., a deafening sigh was heard across the country as the nation grappled with the daunting cascade of syllables, whose unfamiliar letter-upon-letter structure stretched on for an endless 500 words. Children wailed for the attention of their bewildered parents, businesses were shuttered, and local governments ground to a halt as Americans scanned the text in vain for a web link to click on.

Sources also reported a 450 percent rise in temple rubbing and under-the-breath cursing around this time.

"It demands so much of my time and concentration," said Chicago resident Dale Huza, who was confronted by the confusing mound of words early Monday afternoon. "This large block of text, it expects me to figure everything out on my own, and I hate it."

"I've never seen anything like it," said Mark Shelton, a high school teacher from St. Paul, MN who stared blankly at the page in front of him for several minutes before finally holding it up to his ear. "What does it want from us?"

As the public grows more desperate, scholars are working to randomly italicize different sections of the text, hoping the italics will land on the important parts and allow everyone to go on with their day. For now, though, millions of panicked and exhausted

Americans continue to repetitively search the single column of print from top to bottom and right to left, looking for even the slightest semblance of meaning or perhaps a blurb.

Some have speculated that the never-ending flood of sentences may be a news article, medical study, urgent product recall notice, letter, user agreement, or even a binding contract of some kind. But until the news does a segment in which they take sections of the text and read them aloud in a slow, calm voice while highlighting those same words on the screen, no one can say for sure.

There are some, however, who remain unfazed by the virtual hailstorm of alternating consonants and vowels, and are determined to ignore it.

"I'm sure if it's important enough, they'll let us know some other way," Detroit local Janet Landsman said. "After all, it can't be that serious. If there were anything worthwhile buried deep in that block of impenetrable English, it would at least have an accompanying photo of a celebrity or a large humorous title containing a pop culture reference."

Added Landsman, "Whatever it is, I'm pretty sure it doesn't even have a point."

■ WHAT?

1. What is being argued here? How can you tell?
2. How does this article use hyperbole? How does this technique help the author advance the argument?
3. The large block of text is described as a "virtual hailstorm of alternating consonants and vowels." What does this mean? Do you think this accurately describes an encounter with an unfamiliar text?

■ WHAT ELSE? WHAT'S NEXT?

4. *The Onion* quotes one person as saying: "Why won't it just tell me what it's about? ... There are no bullet points, no highlighted parts. I've looked everywhere—there's nothing here but words." Compare this piece with "Is Google Making Us Stupid?" by Nicholas Carr and "Hooked on Technology" by Matt Richtel, in Chapter 2. How does *The Onion* use humor to illustrate some of the same points that Carr and Richtel make? Which approach do you find more persuasive? Why?

■ WHO CARES?

5. What does *The Onion* need from its readers to make this satire work? In other words, what is the audience expected to bring to the table? How does this piece ensure that the audience is invested in the satire?

English 102

INTRODUCTION TO ENGLISH 102: THE BASICS

What is English 102?

English 102 builds on concepts practiced in English 101 to help prepare you for future academic and professional writing. While English 101 focused on critically read and closely analyzed texts, English 102 revolves around developing well-reasoned argumentative papers that draw on multiple sources and viewpoints. During the semester, you will learn to identify the elements of an effective argument and then to apply those principles in composing researched essays about academic and public issues. This course also strengthens information literacy skills, by teaching strategies for finding, assessing, using, citing, and documenting source materials. This course fulfills Carolina Core general education requirements in "Effective and Persuasive Communication—Writing" (CMW) and "Information Literacy" (INF).

In English 102, you will:

- **Learn rhetorical concepts and terms** that enable you to identify and analyze the elements of effective arguments in a range of genres and media.

- Write papers on a variety of **academic and public issues**, each of which articulates a central **claim (thesis)**, draws on credible **supporting evidence**, and effectively **addresses opposing viewpoints**.

- **Develop effective research habits** in order to find, critically assess, select, and use appropriate supporting materials from the university libraries, the Internet, and other sources.

- Effectively integrate material from research into your writing through **summary**, **paraphrase**, and **quotation**.

- **Document source materials correctly using MLA style** and understand basic principles of **intellectual property and academic integrity**.

- **Work through a full range of writing processes**—including invention, planning, drafting, revision, and editing—in order to produce effective college-level essays.

- **Work with classmates** to share ideas and critique each other's work in progress.
- Develop a **clean, effective writing style**, free of major errors, and adapt it to a variety of rhetorical situations.

What are the required elements of English 102?

Assignments and texts for English 102 vary somewhat from instructor to instructor. However, all sections will adhere to the learning outcomes listed above and incorporate the following elements:

Focus on Argument and Persuasive Writing: Much of the writing you do in college and beyond, regardless of your major, will ask you to organize information from sources to support a central thesis or claim. English 102 helps to prepare you for this by giving you a solid understanding of how effective arguments may work in various contexts, so that you can recognize sound arguments when you encounter them and so that you can apply these principles to your own writing.

Focus on Information Literacy and Research: Research skills and information literacy are a primary emphasis in English 102. You should leave the course with a good working knowledge of how to use the university libraries and the Internet as sources of information for your writing. You should also have frequent opportunities to practice critically assessing sources and information, integrating source materials into your writing, and citing and documenting sources appropriately. Finally, you should be able to deploy Modern Language Association (MLA) citation style accurately. To that end, you will:

- Incorporate research into the major paper assignments.
- Attend at least one library session (perhaps two).
- Regularly discuss research strategies as you prepare for each of the major papers.
- Critically reflect on your research process prior to beginning each researched assignment and again after completing it.
- Complete a minimum of six (6) short writing assignments focused on research skills and information literacy practice (ILPs); you should include copies of these assignments in your final portfolio.

What should I expect from the writing assignments?

During the semester, you will produce the equivalent of 20-30 double-spaced pages of finished written work. (This page total includes major essays, as well as short writing assignments completed outside of class and submitted in a typed, relatively polished form.) You should write frequently, in response to the following general kinds of assignments:

Minor writing assignments: You will compose frequent short pieces that enable you to practice identifying and analyzing arguments and to thoughtfully develop ideas for your papers. Typically, written assignments will include summaries, rhetorical analysis exercises, invention exercises, topic proposals, reports on your research, source evaluation exercises, responses to discussion or reading questions, peer critiques, and group exercises. Short assignments give you a range of opportunities to compose both informal and formal documents, and to write during and outside of class, leading up to longer essays. At least six short assignments during the semester should incorporate information literacy practices (ILP).

Major assignments: Your class will include three to four major essays, depending on the course trajectory decided upon by your instructor. These major writing assignments will be formal in nature and submitted in finished, polished form. Major assignments will include the following: an Exploratory Research Project and Annotated Bibliography that identifies and assesses a range of positions on an issue and can act as a resource in drafting, a substantive Researched Argumentative Essay that articulates and defends an argument about an issue, and a third writing project that requires students to revise the argument of their researched essay into a different medium and/or genre.

What should I expect from the composing process?

Each assignment sequence is designed to guide you through a full range of composing processes, which encourage information-gathering and argumentative practices and work towards effective, polished final drafts. For each major essay, you will

- Receive an assignment sheet detailing the rhetorical context, expectations, and major deadlines.

- Have opportunities to submit and receive feedback on a topic proposal or other pre-writing materials early in the process of developing the essay.

- Turn in and receive your instructor's feedback on at least one draft of the essay before revising it to submit for a final grade.

- Participate in a peer revision activity and incorporate peer feedback before submitting a final version of the essay.

How will my writing be evaluated?

All sections of English 102 incorporate a few basic practices (consistent with the goals articulated in the WPA Outcomes Statement for First-Year Writing Courses).

Individual Feedback: You will receive individualized feedback on your work in written comments and/or individual conferences. Feedback will focus on broader concerns in the writing and argumentation process, including concerns such as audience, logic, and organization. Therefore, sentence-level errors in grammar, mechanics, etc., will be primarily addressed within a larger rhetorical context.

Final Portfolios: At the end of the semester, you will turn in a final portfolio containing all drafts and finished versions of your major essays, as well as copies of all the completed ILP assignments. The materials in this portfolio will count for the major portion of the course grade.

MAJOR ASSIGNMENTS FOR ENGLISH 102

■ Exploratory Research Proposal

Goals: Your goal is to outline and "pitch" a research project agenda to your teacher, in preparation for your work in the class. You will include a detailed claim, a discussion of initial supporting research, and a statement of purpose (including a working timeline).

Format: The assignment must be no less than 750 words and include all required sections. The document should be formatted according to MLA guidelines, and adhere strictly to any additional requirements mandated by your instructor.

Notes: A proposal requires that you conceptualize some sort of topic or object of research that you wish to make a claim about (this may or may not be more strictly limited, at the discretion of the instructor) and provide some sort of reasoning as to why you feel this topic is worthy of your time and effort. It also requires that you display some sort of knowledge about your topic and/or claim: not an in-depth understanding of it, but an initial examination of the contours of the conversations involved. Finally, the proposal is expected to have some sort of plan: What kind of research do you plan to undertake, from what kinds of sources, and in consultation with what kind of experts or commentators? What kind of audiences would a project like this speak to, and what sort of rhetorical assumptions would you make about this project based on that.

■ Annotated Bibliography

Goals: Your goal is to explore and evaluate an issue of your choosing through an evaluation and description of your current research. You will survey and analyze a variety of texts, based of of your topic discussion stemming from the Exploratory Research Proposal, that will form the foundation of your research project.

Format: Your bibliography must include 12 sources total, including one 350-450 word annotation for each source. All sources should be listed in alphabetical order, and follow MLA guidelines for annotated bibliographies.

Source Annotations: For each source you should:

1) Write a proper citation.

2) Summarize the main argument, showing relevant support, in a paragraph.

3) Evaluate the suitability of each source *for your project*. Be sure to consider the ethos (credibility and reliability) and timeliness of the source, as well as any bias (value system).

Notes: The finished product should not reflect the order in which you write this assignment. Consider the following steps: 1) Find your sources and write a citation for each, in alphabetical order. 2) Write a summary for each source. 3) Write the evaluation for each source. 4) Write the issue overview. There will be some back and forth (writing an evaluation or summary will help you write the overview, but considering your project will also help you write the evaluations), so don't stick to this order rigidly; but do consider that, as a rule of thumb, it is easier to write an overview once you've looked at all the sources.

Sample Annotated Bibliography

Cooper, Marilyn. "Rhetorical Agency as Emergent and Enacted." *College Communication and Composition* 62:3 (2011): 420 – 449. Print.

Marilyn Cooper parallels Carolyn Miller's essay "What Can Automation Teach Us About Agency" somewhat, in that she (Cooper) theorizes agency as something born of relations between subjects within relationships. However, Cooper differs from Miller, particularly when she introduces the work of Jane Bennett and Bruno Latour to further her discussion of agency. Both Bennett and Latour argue that agency is distributed, and that within complex systems the agential "point of origin" normally attributed to the subject is constituted by active and complex networks of action (performance). When a particular subject makes choices or produces effects, the system itself is implicit in the action. The residual "force" of the system acts through the subject. The subject, then, is also an "object" of expression of the system, a force within the system but not an origin of complete novelty. Much like Miller, Cooper argues that agency is "not a possession" held by the subject, but something shared with others. However, the subject and its agency is not determined by the system, nor granted *by* the system. Agency is enacted, perhaps involuntarily. Cooper's example of Barack Obama's "A More Perfect Union" speech in Philadelphia illustrates how enacted agency within systems emerges. This furthers a definite posthumanist variety of agency and subjectivity, by way of systems and complexity theory.

Geisler, Cheryl. "How Ought We to Understand the Concept of Rhetorical Agency? Report from the ARS." *Rhetoric Society Quarterly* 34.3 (2004): 9 – 17. Print.

Cheryl Geisler's essay reports on the happenings at the 2004 meeting of the Alliance of Rhetorical Societies, and the focus of particular scholars on the topic of subjectivity and agency therein. Geisler discusses debates focusing on the role of agency and rhetoric as relates to politics and discourse, and in particular she mentions Nan Johnson, who argued for considering how agency is obtained rather than assuming it is something already given. A decidedly postmodern turn on the issue of the rhetorical subject that remains grounded in the field of Rhetoric's interest with politics, power, and resistance. Geisler also discusses witnessing a growing trend in favor of exploring rhetoric outside of traditionally explicit political contexts, and exploring how rhetoric and agency play out within "New Media" formats (particularly digital and networked media). Geisler runs through the major discussions of the meeting, including topics such as the "Illusion of Agency," "The Skills of the Rhetorical Agent," and "The Conditions for Agency." She articulates a general tendency within the conference to consider the productive aspects of questioning agency through the postmodern and post-human critiques of the subject, and an openness to consider alternatives to the traditional humanist subject. However, there still remained a few scholars who insisted on discussing rhetoric as a force for political change, and who tie this concept to the pedagogical aspects of rhetoric. This debate exemplifies the stakes involved during discussions of rhetoric, subjectivity, and agency: how that subject is constituted/constitutes itself determines the field of possibilities for rhetoric and the field.

Greene, Ronald Walter. "Rhetoric and Capitalism: Rhetorical Agency as Communicative Labor." *Philosophy and Rhetoric* 37.3 (2004): 188 – 206. Print.

Ronald Greene's essay begins with the "commonplace" description of rhetoric as political communication (and indeed we can find some of this description in Michael Leff's essay on tradition and agency). According to Greene, this approach to rhetorical agency works towards constructing the political subject, where rhetoric serves as the method by which civic engagement and political liberation occur. The subject, then, is the site of change and resistance, or at least the possibility of both. The questions Greene raises during the course of this essay, however, stem from what he sees as an certain "anxiety" regarding agency: namely, that theorizing agency in rhetoric becomes attached strictly to politics and political change in a particular fashion based around a coherent subject that already "possesses" agency. This, in turn, places rhetoricians in the undesirable position of "moral entrepreneur," constantly fretting on proper ethical and political actions as theorized within the humanist tradition as they confront new publics, new medias, and new modes of consumption and production. Rather than jettisoning rhetorical agency *qua* political communication, Greene seeks to offer a "materialist" ontology for rhetoric. He suggests that this sort of refiguring of rhetorical agency as "communicative labor," enmeshed in a matrix of "bio-political production," allows a rearticulation of the work that rhetoric does in all communicative acts while opening up the field's consideration of what is properly "political." Essentially, Greene's move is to relocate the locus of influence in rhetoric from the classic model of symbol-manipulating humans influencing political discourse to a materialist model of communicative labor, where material work and labor are essentially communicative (and hence rhetorical).

Kephart, John M. III and Steven F. Rafferty. "'Yes We Can': Rhizomic Rhetorical Agency in Hyper-Modern Campaign Ecologies." *Argumentation and Advocacy* 46.2 (2009): 6 – 20. Print.

Kephart and Rafferty seem to address both the political, humanist concerns of the field of rhetoric and the postmodern critique of agency and affect at the same time. Addressing Barack Obama's campaign (and in particular his "Yes We Can" sloganeering), Kephart and Rafferty apply Deleuze and Guattari's idea of the "rhizome" to political discourse in order to highlight how political communication and agency works in decentralized networks. They challenge the notion of a direct cause-and-effect relationship between a rhetor and the effects of rhetoric; rather, they offer that, with media coverage of presidential elections, the Internet, and the lightning-quick turnaround of the American news cycle we see a diffuse model of rhetorical affect similar to the rhizome. The "shoots" and "roots" of a particular campaign strategy do not unfold linearly, but rather diffusely through different media channels and in different directions. These different methods of rhetorical dissemination function through the collaborative and disjointed nature of rhetorical agency, and the successful campaign of Barack Obama, in part, illustrates how to take advantage of this mechanism of agency as a rhetorical strategy.

Leff, Michael C. "Tradition and Agency in Humanistic Rhetoric." *Philosophy and Rhetoric* 45.2 (2012). 213 – 226. Print.

Michael Leff addresses concerns with the humanist concept of rhetorical agency raised by postmodern and posthumanist critique. Leff draws the humanist subject from the evolution of the rhetorical and political subject as it emerged from Greece and Rome, particularly through Cicero and his massive influence on Enlightenment scholarship and rhetoric. Essentially grounding of the humanist rhetorical subject in Cicero and Ciceronian enlightenment constitutes the subject as inherently political. This also situates the rhetorical subject as, as Leff notes of contemporary scholarship, the locus of agency, which in turn theorizes the rhetorical subject as the origin of rhetorical agency. However, Leff addresses the critique against humanist rhetoric (its centering on a human political subject) by *reinterpreting* the humanist subject. Leff's ultimate goal is to complicate the humanist agent with the notion of *tradition*, which does not necessarily *unseat* the notion of rhetor as the origin of effects, but rather re-situates the foundation from which rhetoric occurs *by way of* the community of the rhetor. That is to say the tradition of a community, or the tradition-memory of that community, makes more ambiguous the footing of agency within the humanist rhetorical subject while still locating invention, creativity and agency within that subject. It makes fluid the boundaries of rhetor and audience, to an extent, without foregoing the political agency of the individual.

Mailloux, Steven. "Humanist Controversies: The Rhetorical Humanism of Ernesto Grassi and Michael Leff." *Philosophy and Rhetoric* 45.2 (2012): 134 – 147. Print.

Mailloux attempts to connect Leff's argument regarding rhetorical humanism with Ernesto Grassi's defense of humanism against Martin Heidegger's anti-humanist critique. In short, Mailloux situates Leff as a rhetorically savvy scholar who "reinvents" rhetorical humanism in the face of posthumanist critique. Mailloux illustrates through the example of Grassi and Heidegger how Leff takes postmodern critiques of the subject and agency, reinterprets his own position along the lines of those critiques, and in this way refashions the humanist subject in rhetoric in such a way as to both address critique while orienting humanist rhetoric toward a possible future. More of a overview of the work, Mailloux shows how postmodern and posthuman theories of communication have come to bear on the Humanities outside the field of Rhetoric proper, and how scholars of rhetoric have responded.

Miller, Carolyn R. "What Can Automation Tell Us About Agency?" *Rhetoric Society Quarterly* 37.2 (2007): 137 – 157. Print.

Carolyn Miller uses the example of automated grading in writing and speech classes to highlight an anxiety over agency in communication. She states that the field of Rhetoric and Composition faces in its confrontation with mechanical grading a reassessment of the nature of the rhetorical subject and agency. Agency in rhetoric, Miller argues, is not necessarily located within a rhetor but only within a rhetor's relationship to an audience. Rhetorical agency, whether in a humanist vein or a postmodern one, tends to situate the "agent" as a site of political resistance, even if that site is the form of the fractured subject. In turn, the agent is necessarily a "thing," a "substance" that "possesses" agency. Miller argues that agency is something performed in action between entities that "attribute" agency to one another, and in this way agency is a force that does not originate from a unified subject position, regardless of the nature of that position. Performance born of rhetorical interactions between entities represents agency as a "kinetic energy," making agency the "property of a relationship" which is constituted by multiple subjects. Agency is something given by another, not born from a pre-determined origin.

Turnbull, Nick. "Rhetorical Agency as a Property of Questioning." *Philosophy and Rhetoric* 37.3 (2004): 207 – 222. Print.

The question of rhetorical agency, as raised by Nick Turnbull, necessarily introduces accusations of sophistry (in a derogatory sense), and in turn the possibility of attaching negative qualities to rhetoric as essential truths. With the rhetorical turn in philosophy, and the postmodern move to unseat the humanist subject and with it modern foundations of knowledge, the field of Rhetoric has to contend with accusations of relativism. Assuming rhetorical agency as that which offers unlimited freedom of choice also sets it against the world of logic, with rhetoric again standing in for orientations considered "relativistic." Regardless of how rhetoric legitimizes contingency during the act of critique, Turnbull argues, it almost inevitably is set against the "necessity" of logic and science, and in turn becomes supplementary to other forms of discourse. Turnbull addresses this by examining rhetorical agency as formed not around complete freedom and critique, but of questioning. This situates rhetorical agency around "problematology," or the possibility to engage in debate and critique on any subject, including the self. That is to say, the acts of questioning and answering are inherently part of rhetorical subjectivity, and perhaps best focused on to address the opposition of rhetoric and logic.

Welsh, Scott. "Coming to Terms with the Antagonism Between Rhetorical Reflection and Political Agency." *Philosophy and Rhetoric* 45.1 (2012): 2 – 23. Print.

Scott Welsh draws from Slavoj Zizek in arguing that the drive to situate rhetorical scholarship as primarily political is a reduction that hampers the ability of rhetorical scholars to practice particular modes of political engagement. In essence, the "scholarly" subject opposes the "political" subject, in that the scholarly subject references a position of expertise while the political subject is born from an ideology praising the ability of the population to govern itself. Scholarly reflection can become a detriment in the eyes of political subjects, in that it seems detached, complicit, and ineffective. That is to say, rhetorical scholarship is not necessarily political just by its very act of becoming. It can be divorced from a political audience, and thus lose a sense of political agency. Welsh thus attempts to delimit these particular forms of agency in order to illustrate that agency, political and rhetorical, is not an essence behind every utterance.

■ Researched Argumentative Essay

Goals: To write sustained argument stemming from your research, tied to the annotated bibliography and accompanying work completed in your previous assignments. This paper will represent a sustained critical argument drawing from your research to explicate a given situation or subject persuasively. A researched argument is the culmination of months of invention, research, and planning.

Format: Your essay must be between 2,300-3,300 words (roughly 7-10 pages), and must make use of at least ten sources from your Annotated Bibliography assignment. Your paper should adhere to the latest MLA style guidelines for research papers, including any additional requirements mandated by your instructor.

Method: Your paper will do the following:

- Make an arguable claim rooted in your proposal and research.

- Sustain your argument through your research. This does not mean repeatedly stating the claim over and over, nor does it mean collecting resources that agree with your claim and citing them as a litany of agreement. This means making a complex argument that is *informed* by the research, that comes out of it but does not repeat it.

- Argue the significance of your claim. Once you make a claim, and once you show how it fits into the discussion you are researching, you must also argue its significance. Where does it get us? How does it address the topic at hand? Does it add a new spin on ideas or arguments within that topic? Does it point out a place where change can be made? Does it apply a large to local conditions, or express them through a specific case study? Your argument should have a point, a 'so what' that grounds it in your research and experience.

- Identify a space in your claim where further discussion can occur. This means that you cannot simply regurgitate information, nor can you construct a simple "pro/con" argument where you come down on one side of an issue or another, and use opinions from your research to back up your side.

Argumentative Essay Example

(Permission to print the following essay was generously granted by Walter Harper, winner of the 2014-2015 Hortense Skelton Award for undergraduate writing).

Walt Harper
Instructor Jones
English 102
April 30, 2014

Common or Crazy? The Negative Portrayal of Mental Illness in Media

It is common knowledge that mental illness plays a fairly large role in entertainment and news media today. Most Americans could turn on their television to see the latest episode of their favorite procedural drama had a "maniacal" villain or someone with a disturbed mental health history has committed the heinous crime labeled the nation's next great tragedy. But what price is Hollywood willing to pay to "entertain" or national news media to sell the news? I believe most television and film media's negative portrayal of psychological disorders perpetuates negative stereotypes about the mental health community at large and it is up to these media outlets to right their wrongs.

Media portrayal of mental illness is far from a rarity. Heather Stuart, in her article "Media Portrayal of Mental Illness and its Treatments," states that, "Denigrating fictional images of mental illness is both frequent and potent" (Stuart 100). Here, Stuart is making a statement about the frequency that media has the chance to present mental illness in a negative light and how often the media utilizes these opportunities to do just that. I have to agree with Stuart's statement because evidence has been found to support it. Research has shown that approximately 2-3% of adult television characters are depicted as having some sort of mental health issue, while 25% of mentally ill characters will commit a murder on their respective program (Stuart 100). This statistic provides evidence that are mentally ill were found to be significantly more violent than any other group portrayed on television and absolutely more violent than their real life counterparts (Stuart 100).

Not all television portrayals of mental illness are deemed negative. Some are even praised for their informative depiction. Gary North, in his article "OCD on Display" discusses how the TV show *Monk* "demystifies [obsessive-compulsive disorder, or OCD] respectfully and makes people aware of what someone suffering from OCD experiences" (North 4). While *Monk* is praised for having its lead character lead a productive life with a mental illness, the show still fails to portray OCD realistically. In many cases, obsessive-compulsive disorder incapacitates clients sometimes to an extreme point (DSM). Viewers must keep in mind that though Monk suffers from OCD, it must be a milder case. While Monk may use his "quirkiness" to help him solve cases, it seems his writers are not clued in on the bigger issue.

The character of Monk may be praised as the hero of his show, but that is hardly the case in most television programming and film. Heather Stuart goes on to state, "similar to their television counterparts, mentally ill film characters are the objects of fear, derision or amusement; and verbal references to mental illness are used to denigrate, segregate, alienate and denote another character's inferior status," (Stuart 101). Here, Stuart is pointing out that movies are hardly different from TV in their portrayal of the mentally ill in that these characters are so often cast in the villain or stereotypically "bad" role. I agree that characters in film with mental illness are portrayed as violent because my own viewing experience confirms it. In viewing films prominently featuring psychologically disturbed characters for research of this topic, I found that the mentally ill characters were significantly more violent than their real-life counterparts. In the film *Fatal Attraction*, the character of Alex, portrayed by Glenn Close, shows extreme symptoms of borderline personality disorder (BPD) after a one-night stand with a married man. Alex refuses to let go of her former lover, going so far as to threaten his pet, home, and family before eventually being murdered during an attack on the wife. In reality, however, patients suffering from BPD typically only inflict self-harm as a desperate attempt for attention, not try to murder those that reject them (DSM).

Another film that demonstrates an extreme and unrealistic presentation of a mental illness is the 2005 thriller *Hide and Seek* featuring Robert De Nero. This film follows a recently widowed father who eventually realizes that he is suffering from dissociative identity disorder (DID, formerly known as multiple personality disorder) who goes on a murderous rampage while trying to befriend his young daughter as "Charlie." It is revealed that De Nero's character suffered a psychotic break upon discovering his unfaithful wife with her lover. While DID is sometimes associated with acts of violence, according to the Diagnostic and Statistical Manual of Mental Disorders patients diagnosed with this rare disorder typically attempt and complete multiple murders in their alternate identity.

Although not all films or TV shows are the same, some moviegoers may dispute my claim that Hollywood mostly depicts mental illness in a negative way. Take the 2012 film *Silver Linings Playbook* for example. Author Deborah Brauser states in her writing that while this film was praised for its "fun" approach to the mental health community, some psychiatrists say that the film should be used for entertainment only (Brauser 2012). The film, like so many others before it, ends with a love-heals-all message, which is just simply not the case when it comes to treatment of illnesses like bipolar disorder as featured in this movie. While others may still argue that the sole purpose of film is to entertain, Hollywood carries more than just the responsibility to entertain.

Evidence has shown that modern society is quite influenced by those glowing screens in our living rooms. Researchers Donald L. Diefenbach and Mark D. West conducted an experiment to further explore the implications that negative portrayal of mental illness has on society and wrote about their findings in their article, "Television and Attitudes Toward Mental Health Issues: Cultivation Analysis and the Third-Person Effect." In their experiment, they had participants observe various television programs from one week of primetime television from April 2003 and report on a survey about their experience (Diefenbach & West 186). It was found that after watching, participants rated the mentally ill as being more likely to be violent than any other represented people group, providing evidence to the theory that media can influence public opinion of mental illness more than other mediums (185-186). Diefenbach and West also found evidence of the "third-person effect," in which participants are more likely to find evidence of mental illness in others before seeing their own symptoms, which could lead to viewers being even more disillusioned when it comes to the real problems surrounding psychological disorders (187). Both findings from Diefenbach and West indicate that television media can indeed perpetuate false stereotypes about the mental health community in society and further stigmatize psychological disorders in the minds of viewers.

The false representation of mental illness isn't only limited to entertainment media, but spills over into news media as well. As Heather Stuart puts it, "the journalist's job is not to tell the news, but to *sell* the news," (Stuart 102). Here, Stuart highlights the tendency of news broadcasts to skew towards dramatizing news stories to make headlines. Doctor Lynette Holman also made note of this behavior in her article "Building Bias: Media Portrayal of Postpartum Disorders and Mental Illness Stereotypes" states, "the media often present extreme representations, or exemplars, of a particular subject area," (Holman 12). Here, she is pointing out the fact that news outlets usually only make stories out of the most extreme cases, because they are "newsworthy" (12). Holman's statistics show that about one in ten new mothers will develop postpartum depression and one in 1,000 new mothers will develop the more dangerous and severe postpartum psychosis, a condition that puts both the mother and child at risk of being in danger (Holman 12). Holman makes sure to note the *rarity* of this condition. Of the mothers that develop postpartum psychosis, approximately four percent of them commit infanticide, meaning that approximately 0.00004% of new mothers will kill their child (Holman 12). These statistics only add evidence to my argument of the extremity of news story selection. In her research, Dr. Holman found further evidence against the news media showing a bias against fair portrayal of mothers with this psychological disorder.

Holman's main focus was on the case of Andrea Yates, a Texas mother who admitted to killing her five children in 2001, as a prime example of how magazines are able to perpetuate stereotypes about mental illness (Holman 12-14). Holman found through an analysis of 52 news articles published about Yates from the time the murders occurred in 2001 to her sentencing in 2002, only 7 articles in Newsweek mentioned the mother having some sort of postpartum illness. The other 45 articles painted a picture of a woman using the cover of a mental disorder to hide her own lack of morality (13-14). It is evident that national news media is willing to sacrifice fairness and truthfulness in pursuit of a good story and flashy headlines.

The lack of accuracy doesn't end at the end of the newscast or after the credits roll. One of the most common places to find unrealistic, unfair, and perhaps influential portrayals of the mentally ill is in comic books and their cinematic counterparts. *New York Times* writers Eric Bender, Praveen Kamabam, and Vasilis Pozios point out in their article, "Putting the Caped Crusader on the Couch," point specifically at the characters that populate Gotham City's Arkham Asylum in DC Comics' popular *Batman* series (Bender, Kambam, & Pozios). The authors make note that there are multiple instances in which storylines blur the difference between a mental hospital and a prison. First of all, the patients here are referred to as "inmates" throughout the writings, insinuating that they are all wards of the state sent there as some sort of punishment of a crime, and forced to wear orange jumpsuits and chains (Bender, Kambam, & Pozios). The authors also point out that the staff at Arkham is also depicted as playing the role of the "warden," being ever ready to defend themselves against any violent acts committed against them by any of the "deranged" patients. Even the term "asylum" indicates a place for the hopeless to go and die, with no hope of rejoining society as a functional member (Bender, Kambam, & Pozios). The authors even make note of one of Batman's most recent adventures features the Parisian version of Arkham, called "Le Jardin Noir," with a subtitle that reads: "someone has released the lunatics!" The authors then have to beg the question, what if the term "lunatics" was replaced with another slang term for a minority group and then published? Wouldn't that be socially unacceptable? It seems that the mental health community is a minority group with few members having the ability to take a stance for change.

Bender, Kambam, and Pozios continue their writing by pointing out that these storylines don't just end at the last page of the book. Many of these characters have been adapted into television shows and films, many even directed toward children (Bender, Kambam, & Pozios). The writers state that the millions of people read about and watch these characters on screen and page, are being led to believe that the Joker is "psychotic" or Two-Face has schizophrenia, as they are described in the comics (Bender, Kambam, & Pozios). However, the authors found that neither character shows any evidence of experiencing the symptomology for either of these disorders, perpetuating false stereotypes about mental illnesses and even causing some to fear seeking treatment for their mental health issues for fear of being labeled a "lunatic" (Bender, Kambam, & Pozios). It is a shame to see that some people suffering from potentially harmful mental illness would be so afraid of stereotypes that they would be willing to risk their own mental health. But what can cure this issue?

In conclusion, although there are a small amount of exceptions, the overall portrayal of mental illness in media is stigmatizing and harmful to the mental health community and society as a whole. I believe the only way to remedy this situation is to call for Hollywood to do their research before the cameras start rolling and give society a more realistic image of what a mental illness truly is: not a crippling dysfunction that leads to violence, but treatable disorders that millions of people struggle with and attempt to overcome every day. These characters need to be taken out of their extreme situations found in horror stories, tragedies, psychological thrillers, and procedurals, and put them in realistic everyday situations (Markowitz 27). They need to be bestowed with some humanity if the stereotypes will ever be lifted.

Works Cited

Bender, H. Eric, Praveen R. Kambam, and Vasilis K. Pozios. "Putting the Caped Crusader on the Couch." *New York Times* 21 Sept. 2011: A31(L). *Opposing Viewpoints in Context*. Web. 23 March 2014.

Brauser, Deborah. "'Silver Linings Playbook' OK on Mental Illness?" *WebMD*. 12 Dec. 2012. Web. 27 April, 2014.

Diagnostic and Statistical Manual of Mental Disorders: DSM-5. 5th ed. Washington, D.C.: American Psychiatric Association, 2013. Print.

Diefenbach, Donald L. & West, Mark D. "Television and Attitudes Toward Mental Health Issues: Cultivation Analysis and the Third-Person Effect." *Journal of Community Psychology* 2007: 35(2) 185-192. *Film and Television Literature Index with Full Text*. Web. 23 Mar. 2014

Fatal Attraction. Dir. Adrian Lyne. Perf. Michael Douglas and Glenn Close. Paramount, 1987. Film.

Hide and Seek. Dir. John Polson. Perf. Robert De Nero, Famke Janssen, and Dakota Fanning. 20th Century Fox, 2005. Film.

Holman, Lynette. "Building Bias: Media Portrayal of Postpartum Disorders and Mental Illness Stereotypes." *Media Report to Women* 2011. *Film and Television Literature Index with Full Text*. Web. 27 Mar. 2014

Markowitz, Miriam. "Madness in the Method." *The Nation* 2013 April 22: 296(16). *Academic Search Complete*. Web. 23 Mar. 2014

North, Gary. "OCD ON DISPLAY: Orgs Praise Show's Depiction Of Disorder." *Daily Variety* 300.44 (2008): A4. *Film & Television Literature Index with Full Text*. Web. 28 Apr. 2014.

Silver Linings Playbook. Dir. David. O. Russell. Perf. Bradley Cooper and Jennifer Lawrence. The Weinstein Company, 2012. Film.

Stuart, Heather. "Media Portrayal of Mental Illness and its Treatments." *CNS Drugs* 2006: 20(2). *Academic Search Complete*. Web. 23 Mar. 2014

Appendix B | **English 102**

■ Remediation Assignment

Goal: The vast majority of media that is produced and consumed today is not in the form of academic essays, the genre you are perhaps most comfortable with in this academic setting. Therefore, the remediation assignment provides practice in developing argument in multiple forms. Arguments don't just happen in the classroom, but in stories, letters, and editorials, as well as visually, sonically, or procedurally. This assignment should provide your Researched Argumentative Essay's central argument and main points of evidence, but to do so in a new medium and/or genre.

Format: The format of this assignment will vary, depending on what media or genre you chose to work with for this project. Since remediation and genre shift are open to interpretation, final projects can take form of letters to a political representatives, web documents or blogs, songs, poetry, narratives, movies or film, audio podcasts, dances, etc. Therefore, the precise format of this assignment will be determined in negotiation with your instructor. However, you must write a 750 word reflection regarding the choices you made in transforming your final paper: How did changing the medium affect your message? Were there some points that transitioned easier than others? Which medium would be more effective in certain audiences? How does the medium structure how you communicate, and how do those differences play out in the move from your essay to the new medium? For this assignment, you will need to include a Works Cited page with the sources you use in the assignment. You will be required to follow MLA in-text citation guidelines for your reflection, and you will be expected to use attributive tags and quotation marks for any in-project citations.

INFORMATION LITERACY PRACTICES

ILP Assignments Overview

Information Literacy Practices (ILPs) are short writing assignments designed to teach and develop skills in reading, writing, researching, and rhetorical analysis. Each ILP is made up of two parts: a Research Reflection and Source Annotation, constant for all ILPs, and the specific analysis for each particular ILP. These ILPs are recursive; each expands upon the work of previous ILPs. You should use ILPs as opportunities to conduct research for your major assignments.

The following are some basic templates for what you might expect from ILP assignments. However, the exact nature and sequence of these ILP prompts are left solely to the discretion of your instructor.

Research Reflection and Source Annotation

This requirement is split into questions to be answered before you begin your assignment, a citation and annotation of the source(s) you found, and questions to answer about your research after you have completed it. You should write very brief responses to all questions (1-2 sentences for each) unless asked to do otherwise. This work is designed to instill research habits and make the assignment easier to complete.

Pre-Research Reflection
1. What background knowledge do you already have regarding this topic? After the first ILP, summarize the previous ILP's findings.
2. Plan a research strategy. Identify what the assignment requires, what kind of sources to use, and where/how to find them.

Source Annotation
1. Write a correct citation for the source(s) you analyze here
2. Write a ~75 word summary of the text.

Post-Research Reflection
1. How did the research plan differ from what actually happened? How have previous ILPs affected your plan? How has the research affected your view of the topics?
2. How could you change your research strategy in the future? Why?

Required ILP Categories

You are required to complete a minimum of six ILPs, one for each of the following requirement categories. Some ILPs can function for multiple requirements, while others do not. These ILPs can be invented, amended, expanded, or transmogrified, as long as they fulfill the requirements of the categories. The following are examples of effective ILPs from the past, but the list is neither exhaustive nor comprehensive, and so the specifics are left to the instructor's discretion.

Appendix B | English 102

Category 1: Search Strategies

Introduction to Research ILP
1. Find two texts on an issue in which you are interested (this may require some time searching around topics, since you might not have an issue in mind right away)
2. For each source, write a paragraph that notes its interesting features, and how those features differ from the other text. What's interesting about the differences? Given the issue at hand, what is potentially useful about each text?

Reporting and Opinion ILP
1. Find four recently written articles that correspond to a single event/issue. Two articles should seem to only report on an occurrence, while the other two should take a more explicit argumentative stance. Make sure the articles come from at least two different sources.
2. Note the differences you observed between the reporting and argumentative texts, as well as between the two reports and two opinion pieces.

Library Databases ILP
1. Using the library website, identify three possible research databases that might be useful tools for research on your topic. Summarize what kinds of articles and disciplines of scholarship are represented in this database.
2. Pick the database that would be the most useful tool for your specific research project, supporting your evaluation with arguments and evidence.

Category 2: Source Usage

Summary ILP
1. Find three sources on a single topic. Summarize each source is 100 words maximum.
2. Explore how, when, and why you might use these summaries in your major projects.

Paraphrasing ILP
1. Find a source on your chosen topic. Pick what you consider to be the most interesting paragraph in the source, and paraphrase it in your own words.
2. Reflection on how you transformed another's' ideas into your own, without taking credit for it, i.e. without plagiarizing.

Quotation ILP
1. Find a source on your chosen topic. Pick three to five sentences you find "quotable" for your major projects and present them in correct MLA format.
2. For each quote, explain why you chose it, what it does for your argument, and how you might use it in a major project.

Source Integration ILP
1. Find a source on your chosen topic. Identify and extract what you consider the thesis of the source.
2. Write a short paragraph that uses the quoted thesis, making sure to properly introduce and explain the relevance or effect of that quote. Revise this paragraph two

additional times by integrating the quote differently in each revision to produce three total paragraphs.

Category 3: Source Evaluation

Perspective ILP
1. Find a source responding to a specific rhetorical situation and determine how the text presents its perspective.
2. What are the key metaphors it uses to describe the situation and/or issue? Support your claim with a few key passages. Think of at least one alternative way the standpoint could be described, i.e. think of an alternative metaphoric relationship, and explain how that alternative would fundamentally alter the significant features of how a reader might respond to the exigence.

Argument Analysis ILP
1. Find a substantive source on your issue
2. Give an overview as to how the evidence and support of the text is used. Be sure to identify the kinds of evidence used and show, via the Toulmin Model, how this evidence supports the claims of the text. Be sure to give at least one detailed example from the text.

Timeliness ILP
1. Find two articles responding to the same event or issue, written at least six months apart from each other.
2. Analyze the ways in which the event or issue is presented differently in the two texts. The question is not a matter of the content of each article, but rather the way in which time has granted different perspectives and modes of response.

Ideology ILP
1. Find a source on your research topic. Articulate the overarching value system you see as governing the text. Be sure to give support for your proposed value system by offering commonplaces as support.
2. Given your articulation, consider the following: a. Who are the various participants in this value system? Whom does it include and/or exclude? b. How do the seemingly logical arguments made in your text depend upon this value system? Do you find that support to be more implicit or explicit, and why does it matter in this particular case?

Category 4: Source Analysis

Stasis ILP
1. Find a feature story or essay, written for a general audience, on an issue in which you are interested.
2. Identify the major claim of the text and determine its status (Conjecture, Definition, Value, Policy). Show how at least two sub claims in the text support the main claim (how might a claim of definition or value support a claim of policy?)

Ethos ILP
1. Using the library databases, find a source on your issue.
2. In one paragraph, summarize the text's situated ethos (author and publication credentials and reputation). In a second paragraph, explain how the texts invents its ethos, i.e., how does the text demonstrate, or fail to demonstrate, intelligence, character or virtue, and good will? Be sure to give support from the text.

Logos ILP
1. Find a peer reviewed article on your issue
2. Give an account of the logical appeals in the text. Identify the major modes of argument: deduction, induction, enthymeme, analogy, and/or example. Be sure to pull out one or two examples and explain how they work.

Pathos ILP
1. Find a substantive source important to your issue.
2. What is the emotional tone of the text? How does the text create this, and how does it facilitate or hinder the argument(s) it makes? Be sure to give support from the text.

Category 5: Library Research

Library Databases ILP
1. Using the library website, identify three possible research databases that might be useful tools for research on your topic. Summarize what kinds of articles and disciplines of scholarship are represented in this database.
2. Pick the database that would be the most useful tool for your specific research project, supporting your evaluation with arguments and evidence.

Resource Outlining ILP
1. Using one of the library databases, find an article on your research topic. Outline the assigned text into its main components. Be sure to identify the main thesis, major sections, the major claims and sub-claims of each section, and the transitions between sections. If the text is not already broken into sections, you will have to do it yourself, and give justification for where you make the breaks.

Source's Sources ILP
1. Using the TCL resources, find and read a peer-reviewed, academic article relevant to your research topic.
2. Analyze how the source uses one or two significant sources to construction its argument, ones they quote a lot and ones they indicate as central. In addition to how the sources are functioning in the article, evaluate how well or badly the article utilizes its own sources.

Value System ILP
1. Using TCL resources, find a book length treatment of your issue area.
2. Identify the predominant values system or systems that drive the book's claims. What commonplaces, and other evidence, suggests the value system(s) you identified, and why?

Category 6: Research Project Plan

Topic Proposal ILP
1. Complete a detailed proposal of the research you will be doing, and your plan for how the paper will fit together. You need an intro paragraph with a thesis that outlines the rhetorical situation of the topic. The outline will be very loose, but take special care to show me that you've thought about your topic and argument in depth.

Arrangement ILP
1. Using your research and existing writing as raw material, construct three possible rough outlines for your project. Keep in mind that part of the arrangement process is selection - you will not likely use all of the arguments that you have invented, so choose the ones that best fit your given strategy.
2. Write a short paragraph for each outline that reflects on the relative strengths and weaknesses of each model.

Style ILP
1. Spend a moment and reflect on the arrangement and general strategy of the draft you are currently writing. What general style do you think best fits your general strategy?
   - You do not need to settle on one right away, if you have multiple options, then play around with multiple possibilities.
2. Grab a few key sentences from your draft and rewrite each one in accordance with at least three different styles (different versions of your general strategy). Using each of these iterations as a starting point, write two different follow up sentences that make use of a trope. The goal is to generate as many permutations of the same general idea as possible. Once you are done, you will have a whole palette of styles to mobilize.

The Carolina Rhetoric Credits

Introduction

Obama, Barack. "National Information Literacy Awareness Month Proclamation." The White House, Office of the Press Secretary, Oct. 1, 2009. Web.

Gleick, James. "Drowning, Surfing and Surviving." *New Scientist* 210.2806 (April 2, 2011): 30–31. Print.

Chapter Eight

Wiesel, Elie, and Richard D. Heffner. "Am I My Brother's Keeper." *Conservations with Elie Wiesel*. New York: Random House, 2001. 3–15. Print. (Copyright © 2001 by Random House.)

Saunders, George. "Advice to Graduates." *The New York Times* 31 July 2013. Web. 8 Aug. 2013.

May, Todd. "Is American Nonviolence Possible?" *The New York Times* 21 April 2013. Web. 6 July 2013.

Pang, Alex Soojung-kim. "Reclaim Your Mind from Technology." *Salon*. 17 Aug. 2013. Web. 12 Sept. 2013.

Taibbi, Matt. "Ripping Off Young America: The College-Loan Scandal." *Rolling Stone*. 29 Aug. 2013. Web. 12 Sept. 2013.

Students for Educational Debt Reform. "The Path Forward." *Oregon Working Families Party*. 3 Dec. 2012. Web. 24 Sept. 2013.

Friedman, Howard Steven. "The United States of Apathy's Motto Is 'We Don't Care.'" *The Huffington Post.* 5 Oct. 2010. Web. 12 Oct. 2013.

Parker, Walter C. "Teaching against Idiocy." *Phi Delta Kappan* 86.5 (Jan. 2005): 344–351. Print.

Kuttner, Robert. "Fashioning Justice for Bangladesh." *The American Prospect.* 13 Aug. 2013. Web. 16 Aug. 2013.

Leonard, Annie. "How to Be More than a Mindful Consumer." *Yes!* 22 Aug. 2013. Web. 19 Sept. 2013.

Chapter Nine

New, Jake. "The 'Yes' Means 'Yes' World." *Inside Higher Ed.* 17 Oct. 2014. Web. 20 Oct. 2014.

Kimmel, Michael, and Gloria Steinem. "'Yes' Is Better Than 'No.'" *The New York Times* 4 Sept. 2014. Print.

Glickman, Charlie. "What Affirmative Consent Looks Like." *Charlieglickman.com.* 9 Sept. 2014. Web. 20 Oct. 2014.

Gulite, Kelli. "Why All Colleges Should Adopt Affirmative Consent." *Thoughtsonliberty.com.* 6 Oct. 2014. Web. 20 Oct. 2014.

Smith, Roberta. "In a Mattress, a Lever for Art and Political Protest." *The New York Times* 11 Sept. 2014. Print.

Galtz, Roz. "A Feminist Says 'No' to Yes-Means-Yes." *Commondreams.org.* 4 Oct. 2014. Web. 20 Oct. 2014.

Obama, Barack. "Remarks by the President at 'It's On Us' Campaign Rollout." The White House, Office of the Press Secretary, Sept. 19, 2014. Web.

LaFrance, Dawn E., Meika Loe, and Scott C. Brown. "'Yes Means Yes': A New Approach to Sexual Assault Prevention and Positive Sexuality Promotion." *American Journal of Sexuality Education* 7.4 (2012): 445–458. Print.

Chapter Ten

Blackmore, Susan. "The Third Replicator." *The New York Times* 22 Aug. 2010. Web. 12 Sept. 2010.

Lanier, Jaron. "Trolls." *You Are Not a Gadget: A Manifesto*. New York: Alfred A. Knopf, 2010. 60–72. Print.

Richtel, Matt. "Hooked on Technology, and Paying a Price." *The New York Times* 7 June 2010. Web. 16 June 2010.

Carr, Nicholas. "Is Google Making Us Stupid." *The Atlantic Monthly* 302.1 (July/August 2008): 56–63. Print. (Copyright © 2008 by Nicholas Carr. Reprinted with permission of the author.)

Leslie, Ian. "Google Makes Us All Dumber: The Neuroscience of Search Engines." *Salon.com* 12 Oct. 2014. Web. 20 Oct. 2014

Cascio, Jamais. "Get Smarter." *The Atlantic Monthly* 304.1 (July/August 2009): 94–100. Print.

Franzen, Jonathan. "Liking Is for Cowards. Go for What Hurts." *The New York Times* 29 May 2011. Web. 20 Sept. 2011.

Dewey, Caitlin. "Even in Real Life, There Were Screens Between Us." *The New York Times* 1 May 2011. Web. 9 July 2011.

Chapter Eleven

Berry, Wendell. "The Pleasures of Eating." *What Are People For?* New York: North Point Press, 2000. 145–152. Print.

Harris, Jessica B. "The Culinary Seasons of My Childhood." *Gastropolis: Food and New York City*. Ed. Annie Hauck-Lawson and Jonathan Deutsch. New York: Columbia UP, 2009. 108–115. Print. (Copyright © 2009 Columbia University Press. Reprinted with permission.)

Waters, Alice. "A Healthy Constitution." *The Nation* 289.8 (Sept. 21, 2009): 11–15. Web. 14 Dec. 2009.

Paarlberg, Robert. "Attention Whole Food Shoppers." *Foreign Policy* May/June 2010.Web. 11 May 2011.

Scully, Matthew. "Fear Factories: The Case for Compassionate Conservatism—for Animals." *The American Conservative* May 23, 2005. Web. (Copyright © 2005 *The American Conservative*. Reprinted with permission.)

Dahm, Molly J., Aurelia V. Samonte, and Amy R. Shows. "Organic Foods: Do Eco-Friendly Attitudes Predict Eco-Friendly Behaviors?" *Journal of American College Health* 58.3 (2009): 195–202. Print.

Bittman, Mark. "Bad Food? Tax It." *The New York Times* 24 July 2011. Web. 30 July 2011.

Salatin, Joel. "Declare Your Independence." *Food, Inc*. Ed. Karl Weber. New York: Perseus Books, 2009. 183–196. Print. (Copyright © 2009 Perseus Books Group.)

Chapter Twelve

Restak, Richard. "Laughter and the Brain." *The American Scholar* Summer 2013. Web. 21 Aug. 2013.

Morreall, John. "The Social Value of Humor." *Taking Laughter Seriously*. Albany, NY: SUNY Press, 1983. 114–120. Print.

Warner, Joel. "One Professor's Attempt to Explain Every Joke Ever." *Wired* 19.5 (May 2011). Web. 13 Aug. 2011.

Miller, Zach. "Review: The Mead Spiral 100 College-Ruled Notebook." *Timothy McSweeney's Internet Tendency* 8 March 2011. Web. 13 Sept. 2013.

Havrilesky, Heather. "Mommie Fearest." *Salon*. 2 Oct. 2006. Web. 13 March 2007.

Oswald, Patton. "Wake Up Geek Culture. It's Time to Die." *Wired* 19.1 (Jan. 2011). Web. 13 Aug. 2011.

Sedaris, David. "Chicken in the Henhouse." *Dress Your Family in Corduroy and Denim*. New York: Little Brown, 2004. 211–224. Print. (Copyright © 2004 by David Sedaris. By Permission of Little Brown and Company.)

The Onion. "Nation Shudders at Large Block of Uninterrupted Text." *The Onion* 9 March 2010. Web. 21 July, 2010.